END USER DEVELOPMENT

HUMAN-COMPUTER INTERACTION SERIES

VOLUME 9

End User Development

Edited by

Henry Lieberman

Fabio Paternò

and

Volker Wulf

 Springer

A C.I.P. Catalogue record for this book is available from the Library of Congress.

ISBN   978-1-4020-5309-2   ISBN 978-1-4020-5386-3 (eBook)
DOI 10.1007/978-1-4020-5386-3

Published by Springer,
P.O. Box 17, 3300 AA Dordrecht, The Netherlands.

www.springer.com

Printed on acid-free paper

First edition 2006. Secont Printing

Contents

Preface

Imagine, for a moment, that you hired a new assistant to work for you. He came highly recommended, and had a long and extensive resume of experience in the general area of what you wanted him to work on. The first day on the job, however, you find out that he is really set in his ways. If you want him to do something, you have to explain it precisely in terms of what he did on his previous jobs. He does every task exactly the same way he did in all his former positions. He doesn't have any interest in learning anything new. If he hadn't performed exactly the same task before, he is simply unable to do it. He can't accept any criticism or feedback on his performance. How useful would such an assistant be? I don't know about you, but I certainly wouldn't be happy about his job performance.

It's that way with almost all of today's software. So-called "applications" software for end-users comes with an impressive array of capabilities and features. But it is up to you, the user, to figure out how to use each operation of the software to meet your actual needs. You have to figure out how to cast what you want to do into the capabilities that the software provides. You have to translate what you want to do into a sequence of steps that the software already knows how to perform, if indeed that is at all possible. Then, you have to perform these steps, one by one.

And what's worse is, even if you succeed in doing this for a particular problem, it doesn't help you very much the next time you have a similar problem. You'll have to go through a similar sequence of steps again. Even if the system could combine or modify capabilities it already has to perform a new task, you can't do it. The best you can hope for is that enough other people will have the same problem so that the software company will include something to solve that problem in the next release. Why can't you extend the computer's repertoire of capabilities yourself?

What is sad about the whole thing is that we could do much better. While end-users often feel powerless in the face of inflexible and unforgiving software, that small minority of people who learn software development techniques perceive the capabilities of computers quite differently. To them, a computer is like the kind of helpful and eager assistant who is always willing to take on new challenges. If you teach the computer carefully, you can get it to put together things it already knows to be able to solve new problems. If you don't like what it does, you can always change it. If you want it to do something slightly differently, a few changes to the program—its "job description"—can get it done. For people who are knowledgeable enough, the process of software development gives them the empowering feeling that they can do practically anything. That's what's so seductive about computers to programmers. Problem is, the price of entry—knowing the complex and arcane world of programming languages and tools—is, today, very high. But we can bring that price down. That's what this book is about.

Even if you don't believe in the dream of Artificial Intelligence enough to think that a computer could ever provide as much helpful assistance as a human assistant would, the argument still stands. No prepackaged commercial software can ever fully meet everyone's needs. Even when computers help humans with very simple and boring tasks, flexibility is still needed to deal with changing contexts. Details change from one job to the next, managers or customers are always asking for small changes in specifications, unforeseen situations occur. What we would like to achieve is the ability for end-users to construct or modify existing software themselves without "waiting for the next release".

AI holds out the promise of the ability to do some learning, adaptation and advice-taking at run time. Those capabilities would certainly be useful in enabling end-users to develop software, if indeed they are possible. But even if the end-users have to specify everything themselves without explicit help from the system, we hope to convince you that even the most simple capability for application programs to modify and extend their own behaviour from interaction with end-users could have an enormous impact on the usefulness of computers.

The vanguard target audience for End-User Development consists of two distinct communities of users. Interestingly, they fall at opposite ends of the spectrum of so-phistication of computer use.

The first are beginning users. Today, beginning users start by learning how to use application software such as text editors, spreadsheets, browsers, etc. But if they want to do something even slightly different than what the software provides, they're stuck. Because their needs are casual, and they can't spend much money, companies are not motivated to provide specialized application software to do particular things that a beginning user might want to do. So they would well appreciate easy-to-use systems that allowed them to make or modify there own software. Some ideas that would make it possible for beginning users to write software without learning conventional programming languages, including visual programming languages, scripting languages and Programming by Example.

Some of these are discussed in this book. Some beginners will also eventually want to learn how to program as professional programmers do. But it is generally too difficult to begin to learn a conventional programming language such as C++ or Java, directly. So, ideas like visual programming languages or Programming by Example can be used as teaching tools. The beginner can first come to understand the fundamental concepts of programming, such as variables, functions, loops and conditionals and only later (if ever) deal with the messy details of programming languages and compilers.

The second group that is a major constituency for End-User development is profes-sionals in diverse areas outside of computer science, such as engineering, medicine, graphic design, business and more, who are not professional programmers. These people need to get specific jobs done in their fields that might benefit by computer automation, but that are not common enough to warrant commercial development of applications just for that purpose. An accountant needs to specialize a bookkeeping program to the idiosyncracies of a particular business. A physicist needs to make a specialized data collection program for a particular experiment. These users are very sophisticated in the fields of their expertise, but have little time or interest in learning a programming language or software engineering methodology.

The papers in this book span a wide variety of conceptual issues, technical topics, applications areas and experience. First, we begin with some introductory papers that survey the area, provide background and a taste of what is to come. Next, there are some contributions which draw on inspiration from the field of Software Engineering, which has long studied issues relating to the software life-cycle. These chapters try to present novel methods for EUD exploiting and enriching some concepts from Software Engineering. The following section shows some systems where End-User Development has been specialized to particular application areas or reports on some industrial case studies. The diverse application areas give an indication of the broad usefulness of End-User Development, and show the importance of user context.

To start off the introductory section, Alan Blackwell gives us the cognitive science, psychological and philosophical perspective in his "Psychological Issues in End-User Programming". His paper gives us insight into what is known about how people approach the cognitive skill of programming. He reviews the psychological impact of several popular End-User Development systems. And he provides us with a window onto the rich interdisciplinary literature relevant to this topic.

John Pane and Brad Myers, in "More Natural Programming Languages and Environments", continue on the theme of using studies of people to inspire End-User Development systems. Their approach of Natural Programming begins by studying how non-programming users describe a programming task, and analysing the results for what kinds of conceptual constructs are used. Only then do they design an End-User Development environment, HANDS, that embodies some of the principles discovered in the user studies.

Alexander Repenning and Andri Ioannidou, in "What Makes End-User Development Tick", deliver a set of guidelines for End-User Development environments born out of their vast experience with the AgentSheets environment. The article balances conceptual guidelines with concrete illustrations of applications built by users with this system, illustrating the principles. This report from the trenches of End-User Development gives a candid look at the promise and pitfalls of the field.

The next set of articles describes Software Engineering-based approaches and methods for EUD. Margaret Burnett, Gregg Rothermel and Curtis Cook's "An Integrated Software Engineering Approach for End-User Programmers" show us why End-User Development is about more than just programming. Their work takes place in that most common of End-User Development environments, the spreadsheet. Spreadsheets' success in giving end-users the ability to do programming with cell formulas shows that they must be doing something right, and Burnett's group gives us a full-blown End-User Programming environment based on the spreadsheet paradigm. They focus on providing testing and debugging facilities that draw users' attention to likely problems.

Their innovative "Help Me Test" feature provides mixed-initiative heuristic help from the system in an unobtrusive way.

In "Component-based Approaches to Tailorable Systems" by Markus Won, Oliver Stiemerling and Volker Wulf, they use the idea of plug-and-play "component" software modules to achieve End-User Development. The FreEvolve platform allows to (re-)assemble components at runtime. A graphical component diagram editor lets end-users visually connect components, allowing users to customize and develop new applications without going directly to code. The paper gives an account on a long term research effort presenting experiences with different types of graphical editors as well as features which support users in connecting components appropriately.

Silvia Berti, Fabio Paterno and Carmen Santoro, in "Using Conceptual Descriptions to Achieve Natural Development of Nomadic Applications" show an End-User Development environment oriented to the currently hot topic of "nomadic" applications, those that are accessible through a variety of devices, including wireless devices, that are distributed geographically. Often, the problem in developing such applications is to make it so that they will work under a wide variety of user contexts. Applications may run on different platforms, with different interfaces, possibly restricted by small screens and different input methods.

In "End User Development of Web Applications", Jochen Rode, Mary Beth Rosson and Manuel A. Pérez Quiñones provide us with a reality check on the activities and needs of present-day Web developers. Since the Web is such an important platform, it is instructive to see such a careful survey of what today's Webmasters actually do and how End-User Development might fit into today's Web engineering environments. Beyond particular Web technologies, there is focus here on the mental models adopted by both professional developers and non-professional users for Web applications, and understanding how End-User Development might support and extend those models.

Costabile, Fogli, Mussio and Piccinno present an environment that allows domain-experts to modify their applications for their needs in "End-User Development: The Software Shaping Workshop Approach", by analogy to the workshops used by artisans and craftsmen. They illustrate their approach by an analysis of problem solving in a medical domain, looking at the communication between a radiologist and a pneumologist (lung specialist) cooperating in a diagnostic task.

While there are a number of projects that aim at general-purpose End-User Development, sometimes one way to make a more effective development tool is to specialize the environment to a particular application area or category of users. In the next section, we explore some End-User Development environments that have been constructed with specific application users in mind, and provide facilities that have been thoughtfully customized to the needs of that class of users. We also report on some interesting industrial case studies.

Catherine Letondal, in "Participatory Programming: Developing Programmable Bioinformatics Tools for End-Users", uses a participatory design philosophy to understand the needs of biologists. She presents a discussion of the issue of when programmability is needed and what kind of programmability is best for professional scientists in fields other than computer science. She then proposes the Biok environment, which provides some End-User Programming in a gene sequencing application. This application is basically a pattern-matching task that requires programmability for semi-repetitive tasks. Her biologist users can be considered typical of a wide range of scientific users in areas other than computer science. She shows how providing a vocabulary and operations well-suited to the users' tasks facilitates their problem-solving ability.

The computer revolution is now filtering down from personal computers to consumer electronics and appliances, and Boris de Ruyter and Richard van de Sluis give us, in "Challenges for End-User Development in Intelligent Environments", some preliminary thoughts on how End-User Development might impact the world of consumer electronics. It holds the promise of liberating us from an unruly tangle of buttons, switches, modes, flashing lights and complex remote controls as consumer electronics increases in sophistication.

Yasunori Harada and Richard Potter offer us a particularly innovative EUD approach to interactive graphic applications such as games, based on "Fuzzy Rewriting". Systems like Alex Repenning's Agentsheets and Allen Cypher and David C. Smith's Stagecast Creator have showed that even young children can effectively use a Programming by Example system based on rewriting rules. But insisting on exact matching of rule conditions puts a damper on the generality of such systems. Harada and Potter show how relaxed matching conditions can get these kinds of systems "out of the box" and dramatically extend the scope of applications possible with them.

Stevens, Quaisser and Klann apply the component-based approach in an industrial case study. While realizing a highly tailorable access control module by means of the FreEvolve platform, the authors had to break the application down into components which could be understood and manipulated by end-users. The paper demonstrates, how such a modularization can be obtained by using ethnographic methods and design metaphors. The ethnographic study helps to capture tailoring needs within the application context while the selection of the design metaphor helps to define components which are meaningful for ordinary users.

Yvonne Dittrich, Lars Lundberg and Olle Lindeberg's article, "End-User Development as Adaptive Maintenance", reflects the reality that what seems to be small, routine maintenance changes sometimes escalate to the point that they really become development of a new application. Rather than bemoan the lack of clear separation between maintenance and tailoring of applications, they look for new ways to take advantage of it, including an innovative use of the meta-object protocol in object-oriented languages.

End-User Development at the workplace has its particular organizational and social aspects. The activity to "tailor" an application to fit the diverse and changing use situations has been addressed in its effects on software architecture as well as application interfaces. Volkmar Pipek and Helge Kahler turn toward the collaborative aspects that can be encountered in practice, and give an overview on different approaches for "Supporting Collaborative Tailoring". Two studies with prototypes supporting collaboration in End-User Development activities at the workplace are described in more detail, and open-up a perspective on "appropriation support" as a category of functionality that aims at visualizing and sharing use cultures among end-users.

Stefania Bandini and Carla Simone deal with collaborative EUD from the angle of component-based software development. In an empirical case study the authors explore the cooperation in a company which develops software by means of component technology. Different types of artifacts are used as boundary objects to represent organizational knowledge about software components. These artifacts help actors who do not have experience in programming to understand the qualities of given sets of components. Based on the findings of the case study, Bandini and Simone discuss how similar artifacts could help cooperative EUD which is understood here as a creative discovery and integration of off-the-shelf components.

The perception of End-User Development in organizations today is also the subject of Darren Lee, Nikolay Mehandijev and Alistair Sutcliffe's article, "Organisational View of End-User Development". They present a detailed survey of management viewpoints on the issue. Though as End-User Development systems are evolving, these perceptions are likely to change rapidly, their paper gives a here-and-now look at what private and public organizations are thinking. They treat the issues of motivation to adopt it, control, and risk issues. The article is likely to be useful for managers considering adopting End-User Development, as well as for innovators seeking to understand the adoption path for new technology.

The final section takes us to a set of more reflective and speculative articles, pointing the way to future directions in the field. Sometimes, interdisciplinary progress can come from synergy with another academic field that, at first, is seemingly unrelated. Clarisse Sieckenius de Souza and Simone Barbosa, in "A Semiotic Framing of End-User Development", take us on a journey to the field of semiotics, the study of the meaning of symbols.

Gerhard Fischer and Elisa Giaccardi present their manifesto, "Meta-Design: A Framework for the Future of End User Development". They see End-User Development as another species of design, where the artifacts being designed are themselves interfaces for designing—hence, meta-design. They urge us to apply many known principles of good design, both in the human and machine ends of the equation.

Henry Lieberman and Hugo Liu, in "Feasibility Studies for Programming in Natural Language", chase the Holy Grail of using natural language itself as a programming interface, reducing dependence on error-prone formal programming languages as a medium for human–machine interaction. While they don't claim to have reached the point where we can simply talk to a computer, they do present some feasibility studies based on John Pane and Brad Myers' Natural Programming experiments, where they asked non-programming users to describe programming tasks. Lieberman and Liu aim to show that, perhaps, this dream might not be so crazy, after all.

And to conclude, Markus Klann, Fabio Paterno and Volker Wulf in "Future Perspectives in End-User Development", outline some of the most promising areas for future research. They develop a roadmap on how to proceed.

By presenting overviews, specific applications areas, implemented systems, industrial experience, conceptual frameworks and exciting new directions, we hope to convince you, the reader, that End-User Development is an idea whose time has come. We hope to see the day where a computer isn't just a set of pre-packaged applications, but a set of capabilities, to be shaped according to the users' own needs and desires.

One of the major contributions of this book is bringing together people interested in End-User Development from Artificial Intelligence, Software Engineering and other perspectives. The field of Software Engineering has traditionally been hostile to working on systems that make programming easy to use for beginners and non-programming professionals. The focus of traditional software engineering is industrial software projects involving large teams of programmers and analysts where the primary concerns are reliability and efficiency. In those systems, you don't want make it too easy for individuals to introduce risky changes, so they mandate precise software development processes involving many reviews and verifications. But this is beginning to change, as the need for more flexibility in software debugging and software evolution is felt, even in traditional industrial settings. Conversely, even beginners can benefit by using some more structured software design, modification and testing approaches that are inspired by software engineering.

The word "developer" is a strange word to use for someone who writes software. Dividing people arbitrarily into "users" and "developers" is an artificial distinction that should be eliminated. We all develop, mentally and spiritually, each in our own way, every day. Let's get our computers to help us do it.

Acknowledgments

This book is the result of a discussion process among leading international research groups over a period of meanwhile more than three years. In 2002 the Commission of the European Union funded a Network of Excellence on End-User Development (EUD-NET). While strengthening the European research community and linking academia with industries, EUD-NET attracted leading US research groups to share their results and visions. Results of this discourse were presented at the International Symposium on End-User Development which took place in October 2003 in Schloss Birlinghoven.

The book documents results of the international discourse initiated by EUD-NET. It started from the presentation given at the International Symposium on End-User Development. Further contributions were solicited from leading research groups who did not participate in the event. The papers in this book underwent a thorough review process organized by the editors and the publisher. As a result of this process a considerable amount of submissions were finally rejected. So, the book presents a high quality collection of papers framing the emergent research field of End-User Development.

The book is the result of a collective effort. While we organized parts of the reviewing among the authors, we are particularly grateful to the external reviewers Sascha Alda, Gregor Engels, Andreas Lorenz, Anders Morch, Reinhard Oppermann, Philippe Palanque, Stefan Sauer and Andreas Zimmermann. Moreover, we would like to thank two anonymous reviewers who were commissioned by the publisher to review the manuscript additionally. Their input helped us to select and focus the contributions.

As already mentioned the Commission of the EU took a considerable stake in funding EUD-NET and stimulating research activities. We are indebted to Franco Accordino, Michel Lacroix and Jesus Villasante. Further support came from major European industries. We would like to mention particularly Jörg Beringer, SAP, Waldorf and Roman Englert, Deutsche Telekom, Berlin. Henry Lieberman acknowledges support from the more than 70 corporate and government sponsors of the MIT Media Laboratory.

An editorial process which takes such a long period of time needs support from the side of the publisher. F. Robbert van Berckelaer provided this support generously. He immediately grasped the importance of this emergent research field and encouraged us when doubts were on the rise. Finally, we would like to acknowledge those who worked at times even harder than us to bring this manuscript into its final shape. Andrea Bernards and Marion Kielmann did a thorough language check on most of the contributions. Daniel Breitscheidel spent a lot of time and effort on aligning the format of the different contributions. Thanks to Mary Heckbert for helping in editing. We would also like to thank Walter Lieberman for the cover artwork.

Cambridge, Pisa and Siegen
February 2005

Chapter 1

End-User Development: An Emerging Paradigm

HENRY LIEBERMAN[1], FABIO PATERNÓ[2], MARKUS KLANN[3]
and VOLKER WULF[4]

[1]*MIT, 20 Armes Street 305, Cambridge, Massachussets, 02139 USA, lieber@media.mit.edu*
[2]*ISTI—CNR, Via G. Moruzzi 1, 56124 Pisa, Italy, fabio.paterno@isti.cnr.it*
[3]*Fraunhofer FIT, Schloß Birlinghoven, 53754 Sankt Augustin, Germany,*
markus.klann@fit.fraunhofer.de
[4]*University of Siegen, Hölderlinstr. 3, 57068 Siegen and Fraunhofer FIT, Schloß*
Birlinghoven, 53754 Sankt Augustin, Germany, volker.wulf@uni-siegen.de

Abstract. We think that over the next few years, the goal of interactive systems and services will evolve from just making systems easy to use (even though that goal has not yet been completely achieved) to making systems that are easy to develop by end users. By now, most people have become familiar with the basic functionality and interfaces of computers, but they are not able to manage any programming language. Therefore, they cannot develop new applications or modify current ones according to their needs.

In order to address such challenges it is necessary a new paradigm, based on a multidisciplinary approach involving several types of expertise, such as software engineering, human-computer interaction, CSCW, which are now rather fragmented and with little interaction. The resulting methods and tools can provide results useful across many application domains, such as ERP, multi-device services (accessible through both mobile and stationary devices), and professional applications.

Key words. tailorability, end user programming, flexibility, usability

We think that over the next few years, the goal of human–computer interaction (HCI) will evolve from just making systems *easy to use* (even though that goal has not yet been completely achieved) to making systems that are *easy to develop*. By now, most people have become familiar with the basic functionality and interfaces of computers. However, developing new or modified applications that effectively support users' goals still requires considerable expertise in programming that cannot be expected from most people. Thus, one fundamental challenge for the coming years is to develop environments that allow users who do not have background in programming to develop or modify their own applications, with the ultimate aim of empowering people to flexibly employ advanced information and communication technologies.

Current trends in professional life, education, and also in leisure time are characterized by increasing change and diversity: changing work and business practices, individual qualifications and preferences, or changes in the dynamic environments in which organizations and individuals act. The diversity concerns people with different skills, knowledge, cultural background, and cognitive or physiological abilities, as well

Henry Lieberman et al. (eds.), End User Development, 1–8.

as diversity related to different tasks, contexts, and areas of work. Enhancing user participation in the initial design of systems is part of the solution. However, given that user requirements are diversified, changing, and at times hard to identify precisely, going through conventional development cycles with software professionals to keep up with evolving contexts would be too slow, time consuming, and expensive. Thus, flexibility really means that the users themselves should be able to continuously adapt the systems to their needs. End-users are generally neither skilled nor interested in adapting their systems at the same level as software professionals. However, it is very desirable to empower users to adapt systems at a level of complexity that is appropriate to their individual skills and situations. This is the main goal of EUD: empowering end-users to develop and adapt systems themselves. Some existing research partially addresses this issue, advocating casting users as the initiators of a fast, inexpensive, and tight co-evolution with the systems they are using (Arondi et al., 2002; Mørch, 2002; Wulf, 1999; see also the "Agile Programming" techniques of Beck, 1999 and Cockburn, 2002).

This insight, which developed in various fields of software engineering (SE) and HCI, has now become focused in the new research topic of end-user development (EUD). To enable systems for EUD, they must be made considerably more flexible and they must support the demanding task of EUD: they must be easy to understand, to learn, to use, and to teach. Also, users should find it easy to test and assess their EUD activities.

Though there are diverse views on what constitutes EUD, we attempt below to give a working definition of it:

EUD can be defined as a set of methods, techniques, and tools that allow users of software systems, who are acting as non-professional software developers, at some point to create, modify, or extend a software artifact.

Today, some forms of EUD have found widespread use in commercial software with some success: recording macros in word processors, setting up spreadsheets for calculations, and defining e-mail filters. While these applications only realize a fraction of EUD's potential and still suffer from many flaws, they illustrate why empowering end-users to develop the systems they are using is an important contribution to letting them become active citizens of the Information Society.

Boehm et al. (2000) predicted exponential growth of the number of end-user developers compared to the number of software professionals, underscoring the importance of research in EUD. The potential to provide EUD services over the Internet may create a shift from the conventional few-to-many distribution model of software to a many-to-many distribution model. EUD could lead to a considerable competitive advantage in adapting to dynamically changing (economic) environments by empowering end-users—in particular domain experts (Costabile et al., 2003)—to perform EUD. The increasing amount of software embedded within consumer and professional products also points to a need to promote EUD to enable effective use of these products.

On the political level EUD is important for full participation of citizens in the emerging Information Society. The Information Society is characterized by computer networks, which will becoming the leading media, integrating other traditional media within digital networks and enabling access through a variety of interaction devices ranging from small mobile phones to large flat screens. However, the creation of content and the modification of the functionality of this network infrastructure are difficult for non-professional programmers, resulting for many sectors of society in a division of labor between those who produce and those who consume. EUD has the potential to counterbalance these effects.

The emerging research field of EUD integrates different threads of discussion from HCI, SE, computer supported cooperative work (CSCW), and artificial intelligence (AI). Concepts such as tailorability, configurability, end-user programming, usability, visual programming, natural programming, and programming by example already form a fruitful base, but they need to be better integrated, and the synergy between them more fully exploited.

We can identify two types of end-user activities from a user-centered design perspective:

1. *Parameterization or customization.* Activities that allow users to choose among alternative behaviors (or presentations or interaction mechanisms) already available in the application. Adaptive systems are those where the customization happens automatically by the system in reaction to observation the user's behavior.
2. *Program creation and modification.* Activities that imply some modification, aiming at creating from scratch or modifying an existing software artifact. Examples of these approaches are: programming by example (also called programming by demonstration), visual programming, macros, and scripting languages.

EUD more properly involves the second set of activities since with the first set the modification of software is restricted to strictly predefined options or formats. However, we often want to design for a "gentle slope" of increasing complexity to allow users to easily move up from the first to the second set of activities. Examples of activities belonging to the first type are:

Parameterization. In this commonly occurring case, the user wishes to guide a computer program by indicating how to handle several parts of the data in a different way; the difference may simply lie in associating specific computation parameters to specific parts of the data, or in applying different program functionalities to the data.

Annotation. The users write comments next to data and results in order to remember what they did, how they obtained their results, and how they could reproduce them.

Examples of activities belonging to the second type are:

Programming by example. Users provide example interactions and the system infers a routine from them (Lieberman, 2001).

Incremental programming. This is close to traditional programming, but limited to changing a small part of a program, such as a method in a class. It is easier than programming from scratch.

Model-based development. The user just provides a conceptual description of the intended activity to be supported and the system generates the corresponding interactive application (Paternò, 2001).

Extended annotation or parameterization. A new functionality is associated with the annotated data or in a cooperative environment users identify a new functionality by selecting from a set of modifications other people have carried out and stored in shared repositories.

To start looking at EUD research, let us distinguish between research on end-user participation *during the initial design phase* and research on end-user modification *during usage.* As EUD implies that design can extend beyond an initial, dedicated design phase, this is not really a sharp distinction.

Providing support during a dedicated design phase aims at better capturing and satisfying user requirements. Research in this area seeks to develop domain-specific, possibly graphical modeling languages that enable users to easily express the desired functionality (cf. Mehandjiev and Bottaci, 1996; Paternò et al., 1994; Repenning et al., 2000). Such modeling languages are considered an important means of bridging the "communication gap" between the technical view of software professionals and the domain expert view of end-users (Majhew, 1992; Paternò, 2001). In particular, work is being done on using the extension mechanisms of the unified modeling language (UML), a set of graphical representations for modeling all aspects of software systems, to create a representational format for end-users. Another complementary approach to bringing these two views closer together is the use of scenarios in development as a communicative aid.

As noted above, an initial design tends to become outdated or insufficient fairly quickly because of changing requirements. Challenging the conventional view of "design-before-use," new approaches try to establish "design-during-use" (Dittrich et al., 2002; Mehandjiev and Bottaci, 1996), leading to a process that can be termed "evolutionary application development." System changes during use might be brought about by either explicit end-user requests or automatically initiated state transitions of the system. In the first case, the system is called *adaptable*, whereas in the second, *adaptive* (Oppermann and Simm, 1994).

Such a scenario raises the need for system flexibility that allows for modifications that go well beyond simple parameterizations, while being substantially easier than (re)programming. More precisely, a system should offer a range of different modification levels with increasing complexity and power of expression. This is to ensure that users can make small changes simply, while more complicated ones will only involve a proportional increase in complexity. This property of avoiding big jumps in complexity to attain a reasonable trade-off is what is called the "gentle slope" (Dertouzos, 1997; MacLean et al., 1990; Wulf and Golombek, 2001). As an example, a system might offer three levels of complexity: First, the user can set parameters and make selections. Second, the user might compose existing components. Third, the user can extend the system by programming new components (Henderson and Kyng, 1991; Mørch, 1997; Stiemerling, 2000). Modular approaches can generally provide a gentle slope for a range of complexity by allowing successive decomposition and reconfiguration of software entities that are themselves build up from smaller components (e.g., Won et al., in this volume). The precondition for this is that a system's component structure has been designed to be meaningful for its users, and that these users are able to easily translate changes in the application domain into corresponding changes in the component structure.

While adaptivity alone does not constitute EUD because the initiative of modifications is with the system, it is interesting to combine it with end-user driven activities. Users may want to stay in control of how systems adapt themselves and might have to supply additional information or take certain decisions to support system adaptivity. Conversely, the system might try to preselect the pertinent EUD options for a given context or choose an appropriate level of EUD for the current user and task at hand, thus enhancing EUD through adaptivity. Mixed forms of interactions where adaptive systems can support interaction but users can still take the initiative in the development process may provide interesting results, as well.

How do we make functionality for adaptation available at the user interface? First, adaptation should be unobtrusive, so as not to distract user attention from the primary task. At the same time, the cognitive load of switching from using to adapting should be as low as possible. There seems to be a consensus that adaptation should be made available as an extension to the existing user interface. A related issue is how to make users aware of existing EUD functions and how to make these functions easily accessible (e.g., Wulf and Golombek, 2001).

Another key research area deals with cooperative EUD activities, having its roots in research on CSCW. It investigates topics such as collaborative development by groups of end-users (Letondal, 2001; Mørch and Mehandjiev, 2000), privacy issues, and repositories for sharing artifacts among end-users (Kahler 2001; Wulf 1999). This research also includes recommending and awareness mechanisms for finding suitable EUD expertise as well as reusable artifacts. We should foster the building of communities where end-users can effectively share their EUD-related knowledge and artifacts with their peers (Costabile et al., 2002; Pipek and Kahler, in this volume).

Flexible software architectures are a prerequisite for enabling adaptivity. Approaches range from simple parameters, rules, and constraints to changeable descriptions of system behavior (meta-data) and component-based architectures (Won et al., in this volume). A key property of an EUD-friendly architecture is to allow for substantive changes during run-time, without having to stop and restart or rebuild the system.

Enabling end-users to substantially alter systems creates a number of obvious issues concerning correctness and consistency, security, and privacy. One approach to handling these issues is to let the system monitor and maintain a set of desired system properties during EUD activities. For example, properties like integrity and consistency can be maintained by only allowing safe operations. Nonetheless, user errors and incompleteness of information cannot be ruled out altogether (Lieberman, 2001). Users may often be able to supply missing information or correct errors if properly notified. For this reason, it may be best to adopt a mixed-initiative approach to dealing with errors (Horvitz, 1999).

Finally, another approach to improving EUD is to create languages that are more suited to non-programmers and to specifying requirements than are conventional programming languages. In particular, domain-specific and graphical languages are being investigated (e.g., Paternò et al., 1994).

At the center of EUD are the users and their requirements (Stiemerling et al., 1997). The increasing change and diversity engendered by networked mobile and embedded devices will enable access to interactive services anywhere and anytime in diverse contexts of use. Therefore, EUD environments should support easy generation of interfaces able to adapt the device's features (e.g., Berti et al., in this volume). Also, systems are used by diverse groups of people, with varying levels of expertise, current tasks, and other factors. Systems should be able to adapt to the changing contexts and requirements under the user's control and understanding.

EUD is a socio-cultural activity, depending on place, time, and people involved. Differences in EUD practice are likely to develop for different cultures and languages. Obviously, this is of particular importance for cross-cultural collaboration. Another area where such differences are likely to show up is EUD of groupware systems, whether this EUD is done cooperatively or not. These differences may relate to who is in control of EUD activities, to the relation between individual and collaborative EUD, and to how communities of end-user developers are organized.

Embedding systems into heterogeneous environments cannot be completely achieved before use, by determining the requirements once and deriving an appropriate design. Rather, adaptation must continue as an iterative process by the hands of the users, blurring the border between use and design. A given system design embodies a certain semiotic model (Lehman, 1980) of the context of use, and that EUD allows users to adapt this model to reflect their natural evolution. Furthermore, using a system changes the users themselves, and as they change they will use the system in new ways (Carroll and Rosson, 1992; Pipek and Wulf, 1999). Systems must be designed so that they can accommodate user needs that cannot be anticipated in the requirement phase, especially those that arise because of user evolution (Costabile et al., 2003).

Being a relatively young field, EUD is yet rather diversified in terms of terminology, approaches, and subject areas. Networking within the EUD-community has started only relatively recently (Sutcliffe and Mehandjiev, 2004). One such effort was the EU-funded Network of Excellence EUD-Net,[1] bringing together leading EUD researchers and industry players from Europe. Later on, the US National Science Foundation funded end-user software engineering systems (EUSES), investigating whether it is possible to bring the benefits of rigorous SE methodologies to end-users. It is generally felt that there is a strong need for thorough empirical investigations of new EUD-approaches in real-world projects, both to solidify the theoretical groundings of EUD, and to develop more appropriate methods and tools for deploying and using EUD-systems. Further research initiatives are on the way in the 7th Framework Program of the EU as well as by single European states such as Germany.

The present book is an effort to make many important aspects of the international EUD discussion available to a broader audience. A first set of papers resulted from

---

[1] For more information on EUD-Net see http://giove.isti.cnr.it/eud-net.htm.

two EUD-Net events: a research workshop held in September 2002 at ISTI-CNR in Pisa, Italy, and the International Symposium on EUD held in October 2003 in Schloss Birlinghoven, Germany. Beyond these contributions, we invited some papers from other leading researchers in the field. We hope that this broad look at the emerging paradigm of EUD leads you to appreciate its diversity and potential for the future. And we look forward to having you, the reader, the "end-user" of this book, contribute what you can to the field, whether it is working on a system for EUD, or simply achieving a better understanding of how EUD might fit into your work and your life.

References

Arondi, S., Baroni, P., Fogli, D. and Mussio, P. (2002). *Supporting Co-evolution of Users and Systems by the Recognition of Interaction Patterns*. Trento, Italy: AVI.

Beck, B. (1999). *Extreme Programming Explained: Embrace Change*. Reading, MA: Addison-Wesley.

Berti, S., Paternò, F. and Santoro, C. Natural Development of Nomadic Interfaces Based on Conceptual Descriptions, in this volume.

Boehm, B.W., Abts, C., Brown, A., Chulani, S., Clark, B., Horowitz, E., Modochy, R., Reifer, D. and Steece, B. (2000). *Software Cost Estimation with COCOMO II*. Upper Saddle River, NJ: Prentice Hall PTR.

Carroll, J.M. and Rosson M.B. (1992). Getting around the task-artifact cycle: How to make claims and design by Scenario. *ACM Transactions on Information Systems* 10(2), 181–212.

Cockburn, A. (2002). *Agile Software Development*. Reading, MA: Addison Wesley.

Costabile, M.F., Fogli, D., Fresta, G., Mussio, P. and Piccinno, A. (2002). *Computer Environments for Improving End-User Accessibility*. ERCIM Workshop "User Interfaces For All", Paris.

Costabile, M.F., Fogli, D., Fresta, G., Mussio, P. and Piccinno, A. (2003). Building environments for end-user development and tailoring. In: *IEEE Symposia on Human Centric Computing Languages and Environments*, Aukland.

Dertouzos, M. (1997). *What Will Be: How the New World of Information Will Change Our Lives*. New York: Harper-Collins.

Dittrich, Y., Eriksén, S. and Hansson, C. (2002). *PD in the Wild: Evolving Practices of Design in Use*. Malmö, Sweden: PDC.

Henderson, A. and Kyng M. (1991). *There's No Place Like Home. Continuing Design in Use*. Design at Work, Hillsdale, NJ: Lawrence Erlbaum Assoc. pp. 219–240.

Horvitz, E. (1999). Principles of mixed-initiative user interfaces. In *Proceedings ACM CHI 1999*, ACM Press, pp.159–166.

Kahler, H. (2001). *Supporting Collaborative Tailoring*. Ph.D.-Thesis. Roskilde University, Denmark, Roskilde.

Lehman, M. (1980). Programs, life cycles, and laws of software evolution. *IEEE 68*.

Letondal, C. (2001). *Programmation et interaction*. Orsay: Université de Paris XI.

Lieberman, H. (2001). *Your Wish is My Command: Programming by Example*. San Francisco: Morgan Kaufmann.

MacLean, A., Carter, K., Lövstrand, L. and Moran, T. (1990). User-tailorable systems: Pressing the issue with buttons. In: *Proceedings of the Conference on Computer Human Interaction (CHI '90), April 1–5, 1990. Seattle, Washington*. New York: ACM-Press, pp. 175–182.

Majhew, D.J. (1992). *Principles and Guideline in Software User Interface Design*. New York: Prentice Hall.

Mehandjiev, N. and Bottaci, L. (1996). User-enhanceability for organizational information systems through visual programming. In: *Advanced Information Systems Engineering: 8th International Conference*, CAiSE'96, Springer-Verlag.

Mørch, A.I. (1997). Three levels of end-user tailoring: Customization, integration, and extension. In: M. Kyng and L. Mathiassen (eds.), *Computers and Design in Context*. Cambridge, MA: The MIT Press, pp. 51–76.

Mørch, A.I. (2002). Evolutionary growth and control in user tailorable systems. In: N. Patel (ed.), *Adaptive Evolutionary Information Systems*. Hershey, PA: Idea Group Publishing, pp. 30–58.

Mørch, A.I. and Mehandjiev, N.D. (2000). Tailoring as collaboration: The mediating role of multiple representations and application units. *Computer Supported Cooperative Work* **9**(1), 75–100.

Oppermann, R. and Simm, H. (1994). Adaptability: User-initiated individualization. In: R. Oppermann (ed.), *Adaptive User Support—Ergonomic Design of Manually and Automatically Adaptable Software*. Hillsdale, New Jersey: Lawrence Erlbaum Ass.

Paternò, F. (2001). *Model-based Design and Evaluation of Interactive Applications*. London, UK: Springer Verlag.

Paternò, F., Campari, I. and Scopigno, R. (1994). The design and specification of a visual language: An example for customising geographic information systems functionalities. *Computer Graphics Forum* **13**(4), 199–210.

Pipek, V. and Kahler, H. Supporting Collaborative Tailoring, in this volume.

Pipek, V. and Wulf, V. (1999). A groupware's life. In: *Proceedings of the Sixth European Conference on Computer Supported Cooperative Work (ECSCW '99)*, Dordrecht, Kluwer, pp. 199–219.

Repenning, A., Ioannidou, A. and Zola, J. (2000). AgentSheets: End-user programmable simulations. *Journal of Artificial Societies and Social Simulation* **3**(3).

Stiemerling, O. (2000). *Component-Based Tailorability*. Ph.D. Thesis. Department of Computer Science, University of Bonn, Bonn.

Stiemerling, O., Kahler, H. and Wulf, V. (1997). How to make software softer—designing tailorable applications. In: *Proceedings of the ACM Symposium on Designing Interactive Systems (DIS 97), 18.–20.8.1997, Amsterdam (NL)*. New York: ACM-Press, pp. 365–376.

Sutcliffe, A. and Mehandjiev N. (2004). End User Development. *Special Issue of the Communications of the ACM* **47**(9), 31–66.

Won, M., Stiemerling, O. and Wulf, V. Component-based Approaches to Tailorable Systems, in this volume.

Wulf, V. (1999). "Let's see your Search-Tool!"—Collaborative use of tailored artifacts in groupware. In: *Proceedings of GROUP '99*, New York: ACM-Press, pp. 50–60.

Wulf, V. and Golombek, B. (2001). Direct activation: A concept to encourage tailoring activities. *Behaviour and Information Technology* **20**(4), 249–263.

Chapter 2

Psychological Issues in End-User Programming

ALAN F. BLACKWELL
University of Cambridge, alan.blackwell@cl.cam.ac.uk

Abstract. Psychological research into the usability of programming languages and environments, and the cognitive processes that must be supported to improve their usability, has been conducted for over 30 years [dating at least to Weinberg's (1971) book "The Psychology of Computer Programming"]. For the past 15 years, there have been two permanent research communities devoted to this topic: the Psychology of Programming Interest Group in Europe (www.ppig.org) and the Empirical Studies of Programmers Foundation in America. This chapter presents a survey of the research that has been conducted in those communities, the relationship between that research and end-user development, case studies of shared research themes, and design approaches that have arisen from these themes. In this chapter, I will refer to the work of both communities under the generic term "psychology of programming," although as will become clear later, this term is not completely adequate.

Key words. psychology, programming, end-users, education, spreadsheets, scripting, design models

1. Introduction

Psychology of programming research has two major objectives. The first, of slightly less relevance to end-user development (EUD), is a theoretical goal—to increase our understanding of human cognition by studying a rather extreme domain of reasoning. Programming is a highly complex problem solving task in which the problems are so large that they extend not only beyond the capacity of short term memory, but of any individual, so that they include complex issues of distributed representation use and shared understanding. The second objective of psychology of programming research is to apply this understanding: improving the usability of programming languages and environments by better anticipating human needs, and evaluating the effectiveness of design solutions for programmers. In this respect, psychology of programming can be considered a specialized field within human–computer interaction (HCI). HCI research considers the general problems of usability evaluation and design for purpose in software systems. Psychology of programming becomes relevant whenever those systems are programmable, whether by professional programmers or end-user developers.

The distinctive theoretical and applied challenges in psychology of programming have driven its research methods beyond the borders of experimental cognitive psychology, even though it finds its origins in that field. Empirical Studies of Programmers (ESP) workshops have reported a wide range of approaches to evaluating programming tools and studying the context of their use. The research presented at Psychology of Programming Interest Group (PPIG) meetings extends to educational theories,

Henry Lieberman et al. (eds.), End User Development, 9–30.
© 2006 *Springer.*

philosophical perspectives, anecdotal speculation, and relatively uncritical description of novel programming tools, in addition to traditional psychological experiments. In contrast, the mainstream of contemporary experimental psychology has become more focused on cognitive neuroscience, with greatly increased attention to brain anatomy and functional imaging studies that can localize functionality in the brain. It seems unlikely at present that neuroscience methods will be applied to the study of programming activity. Programming employs extremely diverse cognitive resources, and psychology of programming researchers do not expect any neurological findings to be very relevant in the near future.

Readers should note that cognitive psychology is by no means the only approach to studying how people use computers. Other research traditions derived from the social sciences, including ethnomethodology and activity theory, are not within the scope either of cognitive psychology or of this chapter. For researchers from those traditions, purely cognitive accounts of context (for example, analyses of "distributed cognition") may be seen as completely inadequate. It would be impossible to attempt a defense of cognitive psychology against these other approaches, so no further apology is made in this chapter for the fact that findings and design outcomes from psychology of programming research are somewhat constrained by this disciplinary perspective.

2. End-User Developers as Natural Programmers

End-user programming has always been a topic of great interest in psychology of programming. There are two reasons for this, motivated by both the theoretical and applied concerns of psychology of programming research. From a theoretical perspective, end-user developers offer the prospect to study programming behavior in its "natural" state. Many debates in computer science appeal to the notion that some programming paradigm is more "natural" than another, and hence more appropriate for inexperienced programmers (Blackwell, 1996). The intention is that, if people naturally describe computational concepts in a certain way, even before they have ever seen a programming language, then that form of description will be the most appropriate for an end-user programming language.

This idea has been most fully carried through in the impressive "natural programming" project of Pane and Myers (Pane et al., 2001). In a less sophisticated manner, such ideas have influenced computer science education, when educators claim on the grounds of their own intuition that the first language taught to students ought to be structured, or object oriented, or functional, or a declarative logic language, rather than spoil students' natural abilities by learning the bad habits of another paradigm, as in Dijkstra's famous claim:

"It is practically impossible to teach good programming to students that have had a prior exposure to BASIC: as potential programmers they are mentally mutilated beyond hope of regeneration."

Edsger Dijkstra 1975, republished as (Dijkstra, 1982).

These claims are seldom based on any research evidence, but they do come close to the research agendas of some psychology of programming research. One methodological problem in psychological studies of expert performance is that experts perform best with the tools they are know well, however, bad the mental habits that might have been acquired from those tools. This makes it very hard to assess proposed improvements to tools for expert programmers, because the "improvement" seldom results in any observable increase in performance over the "bad," but familiar tool. A common research strategy is therefore to test new tools on novice programmers—typically first year computer science students or school children who have not been mentally "mutilated" (in Dijkstra's terminology) by exposure to existing tools.

This pragmatic research strategy is often indistinguishable in practice from the theoretical research agenda that aims to discover natural thought processes of programming. Some research on end-user tools has similar motivation, as can be seen in occasional references to end-users as "naïve" or "novice" programmers. This creates problems in generalizing from research results obtained by studying children or university students (chosen precisely because of their lack of knowledge), to end-user developers, who are generally adults, skilled at their own work (which may not necessarily be programming), and who have completed their formal education. Typical experimental participants are especially unlikely to have any other professional skills, because professional people are least likely to spare the time to volunteer as participants. When we look at research into end-user programming, we find that much of the evaluation work has been conducted with children, students, or non-professionals, even though the original project aims may have been to achieve a useful product for use by end-user developers.

Whether or not end-user developers are useful objects of study as "natural" programmers, it is certainly likely that they will benefit more than professional programmers do from research into the usability of programming languages. This is because programming languages are universally designed by people who are themselves professional programmers. When making design decisions, the vast majority appeal to their own aesthetic or theoretical judgments as the best criteria for usability (e.g., Blackwell and Hague, 2001a). As a result, they eventually create new programming languages that they themselves would like to use. The design of a language for use by end-user developers cannot rely on such intuitions, because no language designers are themselves end-users. The design of languages and tools for end-users must instead be guided either by empirical studies and the participation of the users themselves, or by psychology of programming research.

This second aspect of psychology of programming research, rather than aiming to develop comprehensive theories of programming, can be better regarded as a specialized branch of HCI, addressing the specific set of challenges in cognitive ergonomics that are characteristic of programming activities. Over the last 10 years, a major research goal has therefore been the creation of design methods and guidelines that will help the designers of programming environments apply research results, especially where their own design work extends beyond the boundaries of their intuitions or

personal experience. These design methods are the most relevant outcome of psychology of programming research for EUD, and are the main emphasis in the rest of this
chapter.

3. User Perspectives on EUD Technologies

Previously published reviews of psychology of programming research have been organized either as an introduction to the methodological and theoretical foundations of the
field (Hoc et al., 1990), or in order to collect and summarize design recommendations
for language designers (Pane and Myers, 1996). Rather than duplicate those previous
reviews, this section is organized to emphasize the concerns of EUD, by considering
the major technical approaches to EUD, and reviewing the application of psychology
of programming research to each of these. The main technical approaches considered
are scripting languages, visual programming languages, graphical re-write systems,
spreadsheets and programming by demonstration or example. Each of these techniques
has turned out to be most successful with a particular class of users, and this class of user
is referred to as a "case" in the section title. However, it should be recognized that the
broader needs of these classes of user extend far beyond the specific technical approach,
and the chapter should not be considered a complete analysis of their requirements (or
even of previous research progress toward satisfying those requirements).

3.1. SCRIPTING (AND THE CASE OF APPLICATION USERS)

Many end-users already have access to programming facilities that are built-in to complex applications. These range from relatively specialized single-purpose scripting languages such as e-mail filters and keyboard macros to the full inclusion of a conventional
programming language, such as LISP in AutoCAD and EMACS. More recently, there
have been attempts to create general purpose scripting languages that are designed
specifically for inclusion within applications, as in the case of Visual Basic for Applications. The contrast between these alternative approaches has been the subject of
debate, with a well-known online dispute (Stallman, 1994) arguing that all users should
have the benefits of an established language, rather than developing new languages
for this purpose. Ironically the target of that critique, TCL, has itself become popular
as a language for general purpose application development rather than simply a Tool
Control Language as originally named.

The usual purpose of scripting languages is to automate some sequence of user actions that could otherwise have been carried out manually. This is more true of keyboard
macros than of full programming languages such as either TCL or LISP. The real benefit
of full-featured languages may not be so much for end-users, as for professional programmers, who use them for purposes such as integrating applications with corporate
systems, or as a means of imposing corporate policy programmatically on application users. (The latter has been done in the preparation of this book, where editorial
policy is imposed on authors through the use of Word macros—the contributing

authors are very definitely not encouraged to behave like end-user developers by trying to modifying those macros).

Scripting languages are also familiar in the context of command shell scripts, and the text processing tools (sed, awk, perl) used to transform text automatically. In their most basic form, these languages are also used to automate operations that can be performed by users directly from the command line or with simple text editors. More highly developed alternatives (awk, and especially perl) include sufficient generic programming functions that, like TCL, they can also be used as full programming languages in their own right. In this case, it is arguable whether they should still be described as scripting languages, where they are being used to implement sophisticated program behavior that would never be attempted as a manual sequence of user actions. There is some resulting confusion over the status of languages that might have many technical characteristics that are common in scripting languages (interpreted, simple syntax, maintained, and distributed freely), yet also have the technical capacity for serious application development. Python, for example, although not having any origin in scripting, has been proposed both as a more usable alternative to perl and TCL for end-users, and also as a good general purpose language for novices (Stajano, 2000).

A further distinct class of programmable application is that of multimedia application software whose main purpose is sophisticated visual displays for other human viewers, rather than data processing or any other system action. Some multimedia applications require substantial programming effort, and authoring tools are often innovative in the way that programming facilities are integrated with the presentation capabilities of the product. These include Hypercard on the Apple Macintosh, JavaScript for the creation of interactive web pages, and the Lingo language used to script Macromedia Director and Flash. Two multimedia systems developed specifically for novice programmers are Alice (www.alice.org), claimed to be targeted at 11-year-old girls creating virtual reality narratives, and Lego MindStorms for robot programming (mindstorms.lego.com).

Scripting facilities in the commercial and technical domains have been very little influenced by psychology of programming research, and surprisingly few studies have been made of their usability. Many companies segment their market by defining some facilities that are only intended for "power users." This is often shorthand for features that are not considered usable by most users in the target market, but have been included out of technical enthusiasm of the product developers rather than market demand. Unix scripting tools such as awk and perl are clearly designed by programmers for programmers, to an extent that has motivated more usable alternatives such as Python. However, even the innovations in improved languages have tended to be driven by good practice in programming language design and by intuition, rather than any empirical studies or psychological evidence. Critical discussion of usability has often been characterized by flame wars between their programmer advocates (e.g., Stallman, 1994) rather than applying research evidence regarding user needs. Some widely used scripting languages gain features by accretion in ways that do not even meet the standards of good programming language design (e.g., the class definition mechanism in object oriented versions of Lingo), to an extent that it is unlikely end-users would ever be able to apply them.

Despite such usability obstacles, some end-users do manage to employ scripting functions to customize their applications and operating systems. However, Mackay's seminal study of the context in which this activity takes place (Mackay, 1990) observed the way in which the actual programming is done by technically skilled users, whose work is then disseminated across organizations by others who want to customize their applications but are not able to do the work themselves. Any shortcoming in design for usability is therefore mitigated by social adaptation. As noted earlier, these social processes, although clearly essential features of EUD, are not widely studied with psychology of programming.

Of all the systems described above, the only ones for which explicit usability studies have been conducted are those that were designed with specific attention to the needs of end-users. Apple Hypercard, Lego MindStorms, and the Alice system have all been designed and validated with empirical studies of users, although few of these have extended to general theoretical contributions. One advantage of providing a well designed and usable base platform is that it enables further research into the effect of the support environment, for example, the documentation and tutorial facilities in MindStorms and other languages (DiGiano et al., 2001).

3.2. VISUAL LANGUAGES (AND THE CASE OF TECHNICAL USERS)

Many technical experts find diagrammatic representations compelling and intuitive, and propose that end-users would also benefit from the use of visual languages rather than textual ones. This intuition far predates the development of computers, for example:

> "These circles, or rather these spaces, for it is of no importance what figure they are of, are extremely commodious for facilitating our reflections on this subject, and for unfolding all the boasted mysteries of logic, which that art finds it so difficult to explain; whereas by means of these signs, the whole is rendered sensible to the eye."
>
> *Letters of Euler to a German Princess, tr. H. Hunter 1795, p. 454.*

Diagrams such as flowcharts, CASE tools, and UML have always been a feature of professional software design, and it is natural to ask, where these diagrams are sufficiently detailed to specify execution, why they should not be compiled directly rather than requiring the programmer to manually create some intermediary textual source code. There have been many proposals for such systems, including whole research venues completely dedicated to the topic such as the series of IEEE symposia on Visual Languages, and the Journal of Visual Languages and Computing.

Visual language researchers often claim that diagrammatic representations will be beneficial not only to technical specialists, but also to end-user developers, on the basis that they are more natural (Blackwell, 1996). This intuition has inspired a variety of commercial products, including National Instruments LabVIEW, Pictorius ProGraph, Sun JavaStudio, and HP VEE. Of these products, only LabVIEW has achieved long-term success, and it is notable that LabVIEW is intended for use by scientists and engineers (it is marketed as a laboratory automation product) rather than end-users from a non-technical background. Baroth and Hartsough have demonstrated in a large-scale experiment that languages such as LabVIEW and HP VEE (also a laboratory automation language) do provide quantifiable advantages to technical development teams (Baroth and Hartsough, 1995). Whitley and Blackwell (2001) have confirmed this experimental result with a survey of professional LabVIEW users, finding that many of them attribute productivity gains to their use of LabVIEW.

Despite the success of some products for a specific technical market, the claim that visual languages may provide some kind of panacea, greatly increasing the range of people who are able to undertake EUD, has been criticized both from an engineering and psychological perspective. Brooks' famous software engineering polemic "No Silver Bullet" argues that software development is always difficult, for reasons that are not addressed by visual languages (Brooks, 1987). The psychological experiments of Green and his many collaborators, first studying flowcharts (Fitter and Green, 1979) and textual programming languages (Green et al., 1987), then visual languages such as ProGraph and LabVIEW (Green and Petre, 1992) demonstrate that there is no cognitive evidence to justify "superlativism." Experiments show that some representations are better for some tasks, but none are universally superior (Green et al., 1991). Whitley (1997) has compiled an extensive review of the empirical evidence for and against the benefits of visual languages. Her review generally confirms Green's findings—visual languages are beneficial for some purposes (such as tracing data flow through a programme), but it would seem unlikely that they will be a panacea for EUD.

3.3. GRAPHICAL REWRITE SYSTEMS (AND THE CASE OF EDUCATIONAL USERS)

An influential family of development environments for end-users has been graphical rewrite systems, in which users specify a set of pattern-action rules for direct transformations of the display. Each rule consists of a left hand side showing a pattern of pixels (often superimposition of a moving sprite over a static background), and a right-hand side (often motion of that sprite to the left, right, up, or down). The first such system was Furnas' BitPict (Furnas, 1991), which although theoretically more interesting in its exploration of the computational potential of pixel-level transformations, has never been especially associated with studies of usability or any particular emphasis on EUD.

Two other systems that have been deployed with end-users are "Agentsheets" developed by Repenning at the University of Colorado in Boulder (Repenning, 1993), and a system originally developed under the name "KidSim" by Cypher and Smith at Apple Research (Smith et al., 1994), then renamed "Cocoa," and finally marketed by a spin-off company under the name "Stagecast." Both of these systems are made easier than the BitPict approach by providing users with a default organization of the screen into a grid, so that standard size elements in the rules assist users to specify the motions of characters around that grid without deriving more abstract transformations. A variety of other usability features have been added to one or both of these systems, including variables (BitPict can only store state data in local arrangements of pixels), super-rules that make it easier to define generalized motions rather than creating separate rules for up/down/left/right langevery time a moving character is introduced, more sophisticated approaches to ordering the rule set, and so on.

The great majority of end-user applications for rewrite systems are in the educational domain, especially creation of graphical simulations in which students build a model of some ecological or social science phenomenon that they can then watch being played out by moving characters on the screen. A typical simulation is an ocean scene in which a variety of fish swim around, eating each other or reproducing according to predefined rules, and implementing a population model. Children are also engaged by the potential for creating grid-based computer games.

The obvious advantage of these systems for end-users is that, if the required behavior of the application is purely graphical, it can be specified graphically. Repenning and Cypher have talked about the two systems at PPIG, but mainly in a comparison of the technical features added to support users as they struggle with more sophisticated applications. Empirical evaluations of these systems have been reported at general HCI conferences (Gilmore et al., 1995; Rader et al., 1997). These systems have also been used as the basis for a range of interesting studies around the social environment of simulation building, both in community design (Perrone et al., 1996) and in more local school scenarios (Seals et al., 2002). Rosson's work has also used StageCast as a platform to investigate software engineering issues such as code reuse and design patterns in the end-user context (Lewis et al., 2002).

Although graphical rewrite systems are a distinctive technical approach to supporting end-users that has turned out to be applied most often in schools, there is of course a very long tradition of languages designed specifically for educational use, and with specific pedagogical objectives. A full discussion of this field would require another chapter, but it is important to note some of the major streams of work. Papert's Logo has been widespread in schools, supported both by his own clear pedagogical motivations (Papert, 1980) and also a large body of ongoing educational research (Hoyles and Noss, 1992). There have been many highly innovative languages proposed for educational use, some with extensive bases of psychological theory [for example diSessa's (1986) Boxer], or empirical evaluation [Kahn's (1996) ToonTalk], but to treat these as end-user languages would be to repeat the fallacy critiqued earlier in this chapter, by assuming that end-users should be considered as being like novice programmers.

Nevertheless Pane's HANDS system (Pane et al., 2002), although designed for use by children, is interesting as an unusual example of a programming system that was developed by conducting both empirical and theoretical research to construct psychological models of user requirements before the language design even started. Empirical studies were made of relevant thought habits among prospective users (in this case school children), a thorough survey of prior research in psychology of programming was conducted, and these phases were followed by an innovative implementation and evaluation. Unfortunately, HANDS has not been widely deployed.

The only widely deployed system with a comparable design origin in empirical research is Hank, developed for use by psychology students learning about computational models of cognition (Mulholland and Watt, 1999). Students at the Open University had previously used Prolog (and prior to that a system named SOLO) for this purpose. Hank is interesting with respect to EUD because, in contrast to the problematic assumption that end users are like student or novice programmers, these students really are end-users. Their objective is not to learn about programming, but about cognitive models. As psychology students, they learn about models of cognition by writing exploratory programs in a language that is constructed to express a cognitive model.

Psychology of programming research has of course made regular contributions to more conventional computer science education, both in exploration of educational languages such as McIver's (2000) minimal-syntax "GRAIL" system and more general contributions to debates in computer science education (Soloway and Spohrer, 1988). As discussed in the opening to this chapter, novice professional programmers are often seen as interesting targets for research, but they share few of the real design imperatives of end-user developers, and are therefore not discussed further here.

3.4. SPREADSHEETS (AND THE CASE OF BUSINESS USERS)

The tool most widely used for end-user development is the spreadsheet. Although originally invented as a domain-specific tool, it has become a popular paradigm for creating a wide range of data processing, analysis and even interactive applications. A great deal of effort has been invested in usability engineering of leading spreadsheets, probably more than has ever been invested in a conventional programming environment, and this is no doubt responsible for their great popularity. Nardi (1993) has made an extensive study of the role that spreadsheets play in an organization, the way that spreadsheets are developed and shared both formally and informally, and the essential properties of the spreadsheet that have led to its success.

A few experimental studies have investigated the possibility that spreadsheets might draw on different cognitive faculties than other programmable systems, exploiting the user's ability to form mental images as a representation complementary to the more common linguistic representations of programs (Navarro-Prieto and Cañas, 1999; Saariluoma and Sajaniemi, 1994). However, the widespread commercial impact of spreadsheets means that more empirical studies have focused on applications than on users (e.g., Panko, 1998). Specialist spreadsheet user communities, such as spreadsheet risks meetings, are aware of user issues that lead to spreadsheet errors, but tend to concentrate on engineering work-arounds rather than potential design changes to the spreadsheet paradigm itself. A notable exception is the work on Forms/3 by Burnett and her colleagues over many years (Burnett and Gottfried, 1998). Forms/3 is an experimental (grid-less) spreadsheet system that is used as a testbed for a wide variety of innovative approaches to EUD. These innovations are typically integrated into the Forms/3 system, then evaluated in controlled experiments to determine the degree of benefit they bring to users. Burnett's work on end-user software engineering (discussed later in this chapter) has been a particularly significant outcome of this work.

There are signs that this research is starting to have some impact on EUD features in leading spreadsheets. Burnett, working with the author of this chapter and a leading researcher in functional programming languages, has developed a series of novel features based on psychology of programming research, that bring user-definable functions to the Excel spreadsheet in a natural way (Peyton Jones et al., 2003). This research takes EUD seriously, providing users with the means of scaling up their development projects without requiring the involvement of professional C programmers.

3.5. PROGRAMMING BY DEMONSTRATION OR EXAMPLE

The intention of programming by demonstration is the same as that of direct manipulation (Shneiderman, 1983)—the user is not required to interact in the interface domain of computational abstraction, but works directly with the data that interests him or her. In fact, the very earliest direct manipulation systems, predating the desktop metaphor, were also end-user programming systems. Ivan Sutherland's Sketchpad, in addition to being the first computer drawing software, established the principles of object oriented programming (Sutherland, 2003), while David Canfield Smith's Pygmalion, in addition to being a direct predecessor of the first desktop in the Xerox Star (Johnson et al., 1989), is also considered to be the first visual programming language (Smith, 1975).

Unfortunately, the idea of *programming* by direct manipulation introduces a significant cognitive challenge that is not present in systems such as word processors, drawing tools, and desktops. In those domains, direct manipulation means that the user demonstrates the required operation that is to be carried out on a specific object (or set of objects), and the system immediately makes that change, providing visual feedback that it has occurred. In a programming by demonstration system, the user demonstrates the required operation on some set of objects, but it will later be applied to other objects, possibly in other contexts, when the program runs. The user cannot see direct feedback of the execution results at the time of writing the program, because these things will happen in the future. This deferral of user feedback to the future is in fact the very essence of programming, when considered from the user's perspective (Blackwell, 2002).

There are two system design strategies to deal with this concern, one of which tends to be described as programming by demonstration, and the other as programming by example. In programming by demonstration, some abstract notational conventions are displayed alongside the data of interest, and the user directly manipulates that notation in addition to manipulating the data. A popular example is ToonTalk (Kahn, 1996), where data operations are specified by showing a robot what to do with the data, but functional abstraction includes notational conventions such as manipulating parameter lists. Many of the notations introduced in such systems are highly unconventional. ToonTalk resembles a videogame world containing animated characters who execute the program, Kurlander (1993) has created a comic strip notation to illustrate transformations to a drawing, and Blackwell created a system for demonstrating the behavior of domestic appliances using small wooden blocks located by induction loops (Blackwell and Hague, 2001b). In the extreme case of programming by demonstration, we can imagine that the abstract notation could become so complex and powerful as to be a fairly conventional programming language—even in a Java program, the user can "directly manipulate" letters and words on the screen to "demonstrate" the program structure.

In programming by example, the user provides several examples of the required program behavior, and the system applies an inference algorithm in order to infer a generalized program that will operate in accordance with the user's intentions in other situations not yet seen. One of the earliest examples, applied to the domain of robot programming, was Andreae's (1977) instructible machine. This approach potentially escapes the problem that the user must learn to use an abstract notation, but introduces challenges resulting from the limitations of machine learning algorithms. Many techniques for machine learning require a large number of training examples, and users would quickly lose patience with repeatedly demonstrating them. It can therefore be more effective to find a domain in which the system simply observes the user all the time, intervening when a possible generalization has been found (Cypher, 1993). If users did have to generate teaching examples, they might prefer just to write the program rather than demonstrating many cases of required behavior. Furthermore, most inference algorithms can only avoid over-generalization if they have negative examples as well as positive ones. In the programming by example domain, this might require the user to demonstrate examples of things that the program should not do. Where valuable data is being directly manipulated, users may be reluctant to, for example, demonstrate that the deletion of valuable files should not be done. The selection of the best negative examples also requires some skill, depending on the kind of inference algorithm applied (Blackwell, 2001b). A better solution may be for the system to generate plausible generalizations, and ask the user whether these should be treated as positive or negative examples.

The domains in which programming by example can be applied are constrained by these limitations, to such an extent that very few EUD tools employ this technique. Systematic transformations to text are a relatively easy target for inference (Nix, 1985; Mo and Witten, 1992), and several plausible approaches for user interaction have been proposed (Blackwell, 2001a; Masui and Nakayama, 1994). Few of these approaches have been validated empirically in user studies, although one study has used the "Wizard of Oz" technique with an experimenter manually creating the inferred behavior that users must apply (Maulsby, 1993), and both Blackwell (2001a) and Lieberman (Lieberman et al., 1999) have evaluated the ways that inference results might be presented visually to the user.

4. Theoretical Perspectives

This section describes some of the main theoretical approaches that are relevant to psychological issues in EUD. These are compared to relevant approaches in mainstream HCI, in order to clarify the way in which, for an end-user, programming activity develops out of more general computer usage.

4.1. COGNITIVE MODELS

Cognitive theories of programming behavior are substantially more complex than those used in other areas of HCI. One of the major traditions in HCI has been the creation of computational models of human performance that can be used to simulate and predict problems in human usage of a new interface. The GOMS (Goals, Operators, Methods, Selection) model is developed from a model human processor with quantitative descriptions of human perception and action when using an interface (John, 2003). GOMS provides a performance estimate of simple reasoning and memory retrieval as users formulate appropriate sub-goals and select action strategies to achieve some desired state of the interface. Programming activity is extremely challenging from this perspective, because the actions of the programmer are directed only at creating an intermediate representation (the source code), and very different programs may have source code with quite similar surface characteristics. GOMS models rely on a relatively close coupling between problem-solving and action, whereas it is quite feasible that an end-user developer might spend 24 hours in thought before making a single keystroke to fix a bug. GOMS cannot account for long-term details of cognition, where that has no corresponding observable actions.

Some attempts have been made to describe the abstract problem solving that is involved in larger programming tasks, but these have not been applied to EUD. As described in the opening to this chapter, a great deal of psychology of programming research has contrasted professional programming performance with "novice" programming as exemplified by students, children, or (by extension) end-users. There are a variety of theoretical models of the reasoning processes and mental models that might be involved in programming, but these describe expert programmers who are knowledgeable about underlying computational concepts (Gray and Anderson, 1987; Rist, 1989). When novice programmers are described, the deficiencies in their knowledge can be characterized as incomplete or incorrect components of an expert's mental model. Theoretical frameworks derived from this research tradition are likely to view end-user developers as immature or deficient programmers, rather than as having perfectly appropriate expertise that should be accommodated rather than "fixed."

4.2. MODELS OF SIMPLE DEVICES AND ACTIVITIES

A strand of research that may have more relevance to end-user developers is the study of less complex (single-purpose) microprocessor controlled devices. Where these devices have some internal state, the way that the user understands the device state involves a degree of complexity that extends beyond simple reactive interfaces, and can be described as programming-like activity (Blackwell et al., 2002). If the device state is relatively simple, then the user's model of the device state can in principle be completely describable. It therefore provides some basis for a theoretical account of cognitive processes in EUD, avoiding the inherent complexity of full programming environments and the system design context for problem solving.

Young's (1981) research into mental models of pocket calculators was an early study of user modeling of devices. More recently, sophisticated cognitive modeling architectures such as ACT-R and SOAR have allowed researchers to construct relatively complete descriptions of these cognitive models. Young and colleagues have continued to investigate other small programmable devices, including central heating controls (Cox and Young, 2000). Related work has considered user models of wristwatches (Beynon et al., 2001), and models of user errors when using VCRs (Gray, 2000). A variety of general-purpose approaches have been proposed for describing the relationship between user models of devices and the devices themselves, including Payne's Yoked State Spaces (Payne et al., 1990) and Blandford and Green's Ontological Sketch Models (Connell et al., 2003).

Although these various user models may be sufficient to describe the less complex kinds of programming that end-user developers engage in, they do not make any special attempt to describe the ways in which end-users might face different challenges to professional programmers. Blackwell's Attention Investment model of abstraction creation (Blackwell, 2002) is based on the observation that end-users are not obliged to write programs, and instead have the option (unlike professional programmers) of simply completing their task manually rather than writing a program to do it. This model quantifies the attentional costs of programming activity, along with the risks that are involved in departing from direct manipulation. The investment cost is some number of "attention units" (an integral of concentration over time) to get the work done, whether by direct manipulation or by programming. There is some pay-off, in the form of reduced future manipulation cost, and a risk that no pay-off will result (specification failure), or that additional costs will be incurred (bugs). The process of strategic decision making, using these variables, can be simulated as an alternative control structure for cognitive models.

These ideas have often been described in the past, although in ways that are less amenable to quantification. The intuitive idea that end-user developers need a "gentle slope" of cognitive challenge (Dertouzos, 1997), and that this may be interrupted by an "annoying" programming interface is one of these. The "paradox of the active user" (Carroll and Rosson, 1987) and the "irony of abstraction" (Green and Blackwell, 1996) describe the ways in which users fail to achieve their goals efficiently, or act inefficiently in pursuit of efficiency. Potter expressed the action of programmers responding to these decision criteria of cost and risk as "just-in-time programming" (Potter, 1993). The aim of the attention investment model is to express these conflicting user strategies sufficiently precisely that they can be applied as a design technique for EUD technologies (Blackwell and Burnett, 2002).

4.3. NOTATIONAL ANALYSIS

Green's research, as described earlier in this chapter, demonstrated that the benefits of visual programming languages cannot be justified simply by arguments from superlativism—claims that some kind of notation will be universally superior because more intuitive or natural. On the contrary, some representations are better for some tasks, and some for others (Green et al., 1991). This empirical observation has led to the development of the Cognitive Dimensions of Notations (CDs) framework, which provides a structured approach to assessing which properties of a programming language will be beneficial for what user activities. The CDs framework is discussed in more detail later in this chapter.

Other approaches to describing the notational properties of user interface have included Green and Benyon's (1996) Entity-Relationship Models of Information Artifacts, which describe the structural characteristics of the notation itself, and Blandford and Green's Ontological Sketch Models (2003), which describe the relationship between the visible structure and the structure of the user's mental model. Much of this research will become relevant to EUD research, as novel representations are proposed to assist end-users with a variety of development activities. Research into the cognitive implications of various notational systems also continues in the series of international conferences on theory and application of diagrams (Anderson et al., 2000; Hegarty et al., 2002), which is unique in combining cognitive modeling accounts with formal mathematical descriptions suitable for automated analysis of notations, empirical studies of users, and professional users themselves. However, these approaches are still under development, and have not yet been proven as practically applicable to the design of EUD systems.

5. Practical Usability Approaches to EUD

In commercial HCI work, it is often not feasible either to develop detailed user models or to conduct controlled experimental observations of user behavior during the product design cycle. This has led to the popularity of "discount" usability methods that provide rapid input into the product design cycle. Similar constraints exist in the design of end-user or professional programming tools. Just as few product designers have the resources to construct detailed GOMS models of a new interface design, very few programming language designers would refer directly to psychology of programming research results, let alone attempt to build comprehensive cognitive models of the developer.

Some usability methods, although motivated by cognitive models, can still be tractable for manual usability analysis of typical user interfaces. The Cognitive Walkthrough method (Wharton et al., 1994) is one such example. The disadvantage of using this method for programming products is that it relies on a description, at design time, of some optimum sequence of user actions that will provide a design target. In the case of EUD tools, it would be very hard to define an optimum sequence of actions—there are many alternative strategies that end-users might choose to take, and anticipating or enumerating them would make the application of Cognitive Walkthrough far more laborious. An early version of the technique was applied to programming (Bell et al., 1991), but the developers found that it failed to account for the "metacognitive strategies" that are central to programming (and which are the central concern of the Attention Investment model). In fact, even for non-programmable products, the possible range of user strategies renders Cognitive Walkthrough quite expensive for typical product development budgets, and "discount" versions of this method too have been proposed (Spencer, 2000).

This kind of concern for providing practical design tools rather than complete theoretical descriptions was the main motivation for the development of Green's Cognitive Dimensions of Notations (CDs) framework (Green, 1989, Green and Petre, 1996, Blackwell and Green, 2003). CDs were explicitly developed to avoid "death by detail," instead providing a discussion tool—a vocabulary that can be employed by designers to anticipate common usability problems without detailed cognitive analysis. Examples of the CDs vocabulary include the dimensions of viscosity (the amount of work required to make small changes to the program), hidden dependencies (the extent to which the relationships between separate parts of the design are obscured by the programming language), and about a dozen others.

It often happens that quite familiar phenomena are not recognized if we have no names for them. The CDs framework is a sophisticated strategy to improving design practice by improving the vocabulary that designers use. The result is a "broad brush" description of the cognitively relevant usability characteristics of programming languages, allowing designers to be informed by appropriate perspectives from relevant research, without demanding that they engage in that research themselves. However, the framework has also been highly influential in usability research, as the only well-established approach that deals directly with the usability of programmable systems. It is most familiar to researchers in EUD, visual programming, and psychology of programming, and more than 50 publications on the framework are listed on a CD archive site, including application to the design of commercially leading tools such as the Microsoft Visual Studio range (Clarke, 2001, Clarke and Becker, 2003). Most EUD researchers should be aware of this framework, and apply it as an everyday design tool.

A recent development in mainstream HCI has been the introduction of theoretically founded descriptions that are applicable both as a basis for empirical research, and as a source of simple design heuristics based on outcomes from that research. The information foraging theory of Pirolli and Card (1999) is an example of one of these theories (it describes web-browsing behavior based on an analogy to ecological models of animal behavior). Information foraging theory provides a sound mathematical basis for studies of browsing behavior, but it also provides a new way for web designers to think about the usability characteristics of their work in terms of model parameters such as "information scent" (feedback that informs users when they are in the neighborhood of the information they are looking for). Designers can incorporate such considerations into their work without necessarily understanding the mathematical models that underlie them.

In the EUD domain, attention investment theory fills a similar role to that of information foraging theory in the web design domain. It provides a mathematical model for research into the cognitive prerequisites of end-user programming, but the descriptive elements of the theory also provide a means for designers to analyze the perceived risks and payoffs that are central to end-user activities. These design guides have been applied both to the development of research prototypes for EUD (Beckwith et al., 2002) and also for EUD enhancements to Microsoft Excel (Peyton Jones et al., 2003).

6. End-User Software Engineering

A great deal of psychological research into EUD has to date concentrated on the usability of novel programming languages, rather than other software development tools (editors, change control systems, documentation repositories, etc.). That research emphasis is motivated partly by convenience for psychology researchers: programming languages offer a relatively constrained human problem-solving task, well suited to experiments, and illuminating with respect to expert-novice differences. However, far more research into novel languages is simply motivated by the fact that computer scientists like to develop new languages. The intellectual appeal of undergraduate compiler design courses far outweighs the number of new languages that computer users will ever need, and the Edinburgh AI department "Researcher's Bible" notes:

> A terminal case of 'computer bum' is to get involved in writing yet another programming language. [...] No one will use the language you write—not even you! You will have spent all your time on the language and none on the project you started with.
>
> *(Bundy et al., 1985)*

Whatever the cause of this bias—whether the research agenda of psychologists, the constraints of experimental studies, or the systems that computer scientists prefer to create, it is clear that psychology of programming research has paid far too much attention to single users engaged in short-term programming tasks, and very little indeed to the problems of maintenance, documentation, system integration and team coordination. Empirical studies in software engineering demonstrate that programming is a relatively small part of the cost of system development. The continued design and study of new programming languages, when programming is not the main problem, can be compared to the proverbial drunk who looks for his keys under the street light because that is the place where he can see best.

A paradoxical additional factor is that, even though EUD may not involve a conventional programming language at all (keyboard macros, for example), it does require most of the other skills of software engineering. Professional end-users, unlike the student-novices that are often assumed to represent their cognitive needs in experimental studies, do need to maintain their work, perform revision control, achieve correct specifications, debug, and test—concerns that are described as "end-user software engineering."

End-user software engineering is a critical priority for future research in EUD. For systems implementers and computer scientists, it will mean turning attention away from novel programming languages, toward facilities that support these other development activities. For psychology of programming researchers, it will require new research methods that allow the observation of long-term behavior, understanding of work done away from the computer screen, and interaction within informal social networks (rather than the structured teams that are more typical of professional developers). Of course, as noted in the introduction to this chapter, cognitive psychology may not be the best discipline in which to find such research methods.

However, end-user software engineering research will also require cognitive characterization of aspects of the software task that are related to debugging and maintenance, not just those involved in writing new pieces of code. The international leader in this area is Margaret Burnett, whose work with the facilities of the Forms/3 environment has extended to maintenance features such as assertion systems that are usable by end-users. Her theoretical framework for characterizing the software engineering activities of end-users includes the attention investment model described earlier (Beckwith et al., 2002), but also novel descriptions of user attitudes such as curiosity and surprise that are expected to influence the behavior of end-user developers more than they do professional software developers (Wilson et al., 2003).

7. Conclusion

Psychological research in EUD draws on a wide range of research skills and literature. It results both in novel programming systems and new theoretical characterizations of human problem solving. Unfortunately, only a few of these results—whether technical or theoretical—have achieved widespread influence. Nevertheless, they provide a better basis for future research than those who proceed in ignorance of past work, which is unfortunately still a common situation in this field. One successful approach has been the development of analytic frameworks that are specifically oriented toward helping system designers apply research results. Another that is urgently required is to broaden the field of enquiry further, investigating the facilities that will make EUD a practical long term activity, rather than simply a toy for technical enthusiasts to create relatively trivial programs that are used a few times and discarded.

Ultimately, it is the commercial availability of programming environments suitable for end-users that will empower EUD. Most users carry out complex activities within specific applications, rather than at the operating system level, and their first encounter with programming is likely to be a scripting facility built-in to such a product. Until now, these facilities have been targeted toward technical or power users, and are less likely to be subjected to extensive usability evaluation or informed by relevant empirical research. It is perhaps as a result of this commercial emphasis that psychology of programming has been something of a research ghetto within mainstream HCI. An increased emphasis on EUD as a research priority will hopefully lead to new concern for usability considerations both in that research, and in the programmable commercial applications available to end-users.

References

Anderson, M., Cheng, P. and Haarslev, V. (eds.) (2000). Theory and Applications of Diagrams. Lecture Notes in Artificial Intelligence 1889. Berlin: Springer Verlag.

Andreae, J.H. (1977). *Thinking with the Teachable Machine*. London: Academic Press.

Baroth, E. and Hartsough, C. (1995). Visual programming in the real world. In: M. Burnett, A. Goldberg and T. Lewis (eds.), *Visual Object-Oriented Programming Concepts and Environments*. Greenwich, CT: Manning, pp. 21–42.

Beckwith, L., Burnett, M. and Cook, C. (2002). Reasoning about many-to-many requirement relationships in spreadsheets. In: *Proceedings of IEEE Symposia on Human-Centric Computing Languages and Environments*, Arlington, VA, Sept. 2002.

Bell, B., Rieman, J. and Lewis, C.H. (1991). Usability testing of a graphical programming system: Things we missed in a programming walkthrough. In: *Proceedings of the SIGCHI Conference on Human Factors in Computing Systems (CHI'91)*, New Orleans, pp. 7–12.

Beynon, M., Roe, C., Ward, A. and Wong, A. (2001). Interactive situation models for cognitive aspects of user–artefact interaction. In: *Proceedings of Cognitive Technology 2001 (Lecture Notes in Artificial Intelligence 2117)*, pp. 356–372.

Blackwell, A.F. (1996). Metacognitive theories of visual programming: What do we think we are doing? In: *Proceedings IEEE Symposium on Visual Languages*. Los Alamitos, CA: IEEE Computer Society Press, pp. 240–246.

Blackwell, A.F. (2001a). See what you need: Helping end-users to build abstractions. *Journal of Visual Languages and Computing* 12(5), 475–499.

Blackwell, A.F. (2001b). SWYN: A visual representation for regular expressions. In: H. Lieberman (ed.), *Your Wish is My Command: Giving Users the Power to Instruct Their Software*. Morgan Kauffman, pp. 245–270.

Blackwell, A.F. (2002). First steps in programming: A rationale for attention investment models. In: *Proceedings of the IEEE Symposia on Human-Centric Computing Languages and Environments*, pp. 2–10.

Blackwell, A.F. and Burnett, M. (2002). Applying attention investment to end-user programming. In: *Proceedings of the IEEE Symposia on Human-Centric Computing Languages and Environments*, pp. 28–30.

Blackwell, A.F. and Green, T.R.G. (2003). Notational systems—the cognitive dimensions of notations framework. In: J.M. Carroll (ed.), *HCI Models, Theories and Frameworks: Toward a Multidisciplinary Science*. San Francisco: Morgan Kaufmann, pp. 103–134.

Blackwell, A.F. and Hague, R. (2001a). Designing a programming language for home automation. In: G. Kadoda (ed.), *Proceedings of the 13th Annual Workshop of the Psychology of Programming Interest Group (PPIG 2001)*. pp. 85–103.

Blackwell, A.F. and Hague, R. (2001b). AutoHAN: An architecture for programming the home. In: *Proceedings of the IEEE Symposia on Human-Centric Computing Languages and Environments*, pp. 150–157.

Blackwell, A.F., Robinson, P., Roast, C. and Green, T.R.G. (2002). Cognitive models of programming-like activity. In: *Proceedings of CHI'02*, pp. 910–911.

Brooks, F.P. (1987). No silver bullet—essence and accidents of software engineering. *Computer* 20(4), 10–19. Reprinted from Proc. IFIP Congress, Dublin, Ireland, 1986.

Bundy, A., du Boulay, B., Howe, J. and Plotkin, G. (1985). The Researcher's Bible. Department of AI Teaching Paper no. 4, Edinburgh University (available online at http://www.dai.ed.ac.uk/dai/teaching/modules/airm/old/lectures/resbible.html).

Burnett, M. and Gottfried, H. (1998). Graphical definitions: Expanding spreadsheet languages through direct manipulation and gestures. *ACM Transactions on Computer–Human Interaction* 5, 1–33.

Carroll, J.M. and Rosson, M.B. (1987). Paradox of the active user. In: J.M. Carroll (ed.), *Interfacing Thought: Cognitive Aspects of Human–Computer Interaction*. MIT Press, pp. 80–111.

Clarke, S. (2001). Evaluating a new programming language. In: G. Kadoda (ed.), *Proceedings of the 13th Annual Meeting of the Psychology of Programming Interest Group*. pp. 275–289.

Clarke, S. and Becker, C. (2003). Using the cognitive dimensions framework to measure the usability of a class library. In: *Proceedings Joint Conference of EASE and PPIG*, pp. 359–366.

Collins, T. and Fung, P. (1999). Evaluating Hank, a cognitive modelling language for psychologists. Collected papers of PPIG-11 Annual Workshop.

Connell, I., Green, T.R.G. and Blandford, A. (2003). Ontological sketch models: Highlighting user–system misfits. In: *Proceedings of HCI'03*, pp. 163–178.

Cox, A.L. and Young, R.M. (2000). Device-oriented and task-oriented exploratory learning of interactive devices. In: N. Taatgen and J. Aasman (eds.), *Proceedings of the 3rd International Conference on Cognitive Modeling*. Veenendaal, The Netherlands: Universal Press, pp. 70–77.

Cypher, A. (1993). Eager: Programming repetitive tasks by demonstration. In: A. Cypher (ed.), *Watch What I Do: Programming by Demonstration*. Cambridge, MA: MIT Press, pp. 205–217.

Dertouzos, M. (1997). Creating the people's computer. MIT Technology Review, pp. 20–28, Apr. 1997.

DiGiano, C., Kahn, K., Cypher, A. and Smith, D.C. (2001). Integrating learning supports into the design of visual programming systems. *Journal of Visual Languages and Computing* 12, 501–524.

Dijkstra, E.W. (1982). How do we tell truths that might hurt? Republished in E.W. Dijkstra (ed.), *Selected Writings on Computing: A Personal Perspective*. Springer-Verlag, pp. 129–131.

diSessa, A.A. (1986). Notes on the future of programming: Breaking the utility barrier. In: D.A. Norman and S.W. Draper (eds.), *User Centered System Design: New Perspectives on Human–Computer Interaction*. Hillsdale, NJ: Lawrence Erlbaum.

Fitter, M. and Green, T.R.G. (1979). When do diagrams make good computer languages? *International Journal of Man-Machine Studies*, 11(2), 235–261.

Furnas, G.W. (1991). New graphical reasoning models for understanding graphical interfaces understanding graphical interfaces. In: *Proceedings of ACM CHI'91 Conference on Human Factors in Computing Systems*, pp. 71–78.

Gilmore, D.J., Pheasey, K., Underwood, J. and Underwood, G. (1995). Learning graphical programming: An evaluation of KidSimTM. In: *Proceedings of IFIP INTERACT'95: Human–Computer Interaction*, pp. 145–150.

Gray, W.D. (2000). The nature and processing of errors in interactive behavior. *Cognitive Science* 24(2), 205–248.

Gray, W.D. and Anderson, J.R. (1987). Change-episodes in coding: When and how do programmers change their code? Empirical Studies of Programmers: Second Workshop (Ablex).

Green, T.R.G. (1989). Cognitive dimensions of notations. In: A. Sutcliffe and L. Macaulay (eds.), *People and Computers V*. Cambridge University Press.

Green, T.R.G., Bellamy, R.K.E. and Parker, J.M. (1987). Parsing and Gnisrap: A model of device use. In: G.M. Olson, S. Sheppard and E. Soloway (eds.), *Empirical Studies of Programmers*: Second Workshop, Ablex.

Green, T.R.G. and Benyon, D. (1996). The skull beneath the skin: Entity-relationship models of information artifacts. *International Journal of Human Computer Studies* 44(6), 801–828.

Green, T.R.G. and Blackwell, A.F. (1996). Ironies of abstraction. Paper presented at the Third International Conference on Thinking. British Psychological Society, London.

Green, T.R.G. and Petre, M. (1992). When visual programs are harder to read than textual programs. In: G.C. van der Veer and S. Bagnarola (eds.), *Proceedings of ECCE-6* (European Conference on Cognitive Ergonomics).

Green, T.R.G. and Petre, M. (1996). Usability analysis of visual programming environments: A 'cognitive dimensions' approach. *Journal of Visual Languages and Computing* 7, 131–174.

Green, T.R.G., Petre, M. and Bellamy, R.K.E. (1991). Comprehensibility of visual and textual programs: A test of superlativism against the 'match–mismatch' conjecture. In: J. Koenemann-Belliveau, T.G. Moher and S.P. Robertson (eds.), *Empirical Studies of Programmers*, Fourth Workshop Norwood, NJ: Ablex, pp. 121–146.

Hegarty, M., Meyer B. and Narayanan, N.H. (eds.) (2002). Diagrammatic Representation and Inference, Lecture Notes in Artificial Intelligence vol. 2317. Springer-Verlag.

Hoc, J.-M., Green, T.R.G., Samurçay, R. and Gilmore, D.J. (eds.) (1990). *Psychology of Programming*. London: Academic Press.

Hoyles C. and Noss R. (eds.) (1992). *Learning Mathematics and Logo*. Cambridge, MA: MIT Press.

John, B.E. (2003). Information processing and skilled behavior. In: J.M. Carroll (ed.), *HCI Models, Theories and Frameworks: Toward a Multidisciplinary Science*. San Francisco: Morgan Kaufmann, pp. 55–101.

Johnson, J., Roberts, T.L., Verplank, W., Smith, D.C., Irby, C.H., Beard, M. and Mackey, K. (1989). The Xerox Star: A retrospective. *IEEE Computer* **22**(9), 11–26.

Kahn, K.M. (1996). ToonTalk—an animated programming environment for children. *Journal of Visual Languages and Computing* **7**(2): 197–217.

Kurlander, D. (1993). Chimera: Example-based graphical editing. In: A. Cypher (ed.), *Watch What I Do: Programming by Demonstration*. Cambridge, MA: MIT Press, pp. 271–290.

Lewis, T., Rosson, M.B., Carroll, J.M. and Seals, C. (2002). A community learns design: Towards a pattern language for novice visual programmers. In: IEEE Symposium on Human-Centric Computing.

Lieberman, H., Nardi, B.A. and Wright, D. (1999). Training agents to recognize text by example. In: *Proc. Third ACM Conference on Autonomous Agents*, Seattle, May 1999, pp. 116–122.

Masui, T. and Nakayama, K. (1994). Repeat and predict—Two keys to efficient text editing. In: *Proc. Human Factors in Computing Systems, CHI '94*, pp. 118–123.

McIver, L. (2000). The effect of programming language on error rates of novice programmers. In: *Proceedings of the 12th Annual Workshop of the Psychology of Programming Interest Group*, pp. 181–192.

Mackay, W.E. (1990). Users and Customizable Software: A Co-Adaptive Phenomenon. Unpublished PhD Thesis at Sloan School of Management, Massachusetts Institute of Technology.

Maulsby, D. (1993). The Turvy experience: Simulating an instructible interface. In: A. Cypher (ed.), *Watch What I Do: Programming by Demonstration*. Cambridge, MA: MIT Press, pp. 238–269.

Mo, D.H. and Witten, I.H. (1992). Learning text editing tasks from examples: A procedural approach. *Behaviour and Information Technology* **11**(1), 32–45.

Mulholland, P. and Watt, S. (1999). Programming with a purpose: Hank, gardening and schema theory. In: *Proceedings 11th Annual Workshop of the Psychology of Programming Interest Group*.

Nardi, B.A. (1993). *A Small Matter of Programming: Perspectives on End User Computing*. Cambridge, MA: MIT Press.

Navarro-Prieto, R. and Cañas, J.J. (1999). Mental representation and imagery in program comprehension. In: *Proceedings 11th Annual Workshop of the Psychology of Programming Interest Group*.

Nix, R.P. (1985). Editing by example. *ACM Transactions on Programming Languages and Systems* **7**(4), 600–621.

Pane, J.F., Chotirat, A.R. and Myers, B.A. (2001). Studying the language and structure in non-programmers' solutions to programming problems. *International Journal of Human Computer Studies* **54**(2), 237–264.

Pane, J.F. and Myers, B.A. (1996). Usability Issues in the Design of Novice Programming Systems. (School of Computer Science Technical Report CMU-CS-96-132). Pittsburgh, PA: Carnegie Mellon University.

Pane, J.F., Myers, B.A. and Miller, L.B. (2002). Using HCI techniques to design a more usable programming system. In: *Proceedings of IEEE Symposia on Human Centric Computing Languages and Environments*, pp. 198–206.

Panko, R.R. (1998). What we know about spreadsheet errors. *Journal of End User Computing* **10**, 15–21.

Papert, S. (1980). *Mindstorms: Children, Computers, and Powerful Ideas*. New York: Basic Books.

Payne, S.J., Squibb, H.R. and Howes, A. (1990). The nature of device models: The yoked state space hypothesis and some experiments with text editors. *Human–Computer Interaction* 5(4), 415–444.

Perrone, C., Repenning, A., Spencer S. and Ambach, J. (1996). Computers in the classroom: Moving from tool to medium. *Journal of Computer-Mediated Communication* 2(3).

Peyton Jones, S., Blackwell, A. and Burnett, M. (2003). A user-centred approach to functions in Excel. In: *Proceedings International Conference on Functional Programming*, pp. 165–176.

Pirolli, P. and Card, S.K. (1999). Information foraging. *Psychological Review* 106, 643–675.

Potter, R. (1993). Just-in-time programming. In: A. Cypher (ed.), *Watch What I Do: Programming by Demonstration*. MIT Press, pp. 513–526.

Rader, C., Brand, C. and Lewis, C. (1997). Degrees of comprehension: Children's understanding of a visual programming environment. In: *Proceedings of ACM CHI 97 Conference on Human Factors in Computing Systems vo. 1*, pp. 351–358.

Repenning, A. (1993). Agentsheets, A tool for building domain-oriented visual programming environments. In: *INTERCHI '93, Conference on Human Factors in Computing Systems*. Amsterdam: ACM Press, pp. 142–143.

Rist, R.S. (1989). Schema creation in programming. *Cognitive Science* 13, 389–414.

Saariluoma, P. and Sajaniemi, J. (1994). Transforming verbal descriptions into mathematical formulas in spreadsheet calculation. *International Journal of Human Computer Studies* 41(6), 915–948.

Seals, C., Rosson, M.B., Carroll, J.M. and Lewis, T. 2002. Fun learning stagecast creator: An exercise in minimalism and collaboration. In: *IEEE 2002 Symposium on Human-Centric Computing: Empirical Studies of Programmers*.

Shneiderman, B. (1983). Direct manipulation: A step beyond programming languages. *IEEE Computer*, 57–69.

Smith, D.C. (1975). Pygmalion: A creative programming environment. Technical Report STAN-CS-75-499, Stanford University.

Smith, D.C., Cypher, A. and Spohrer, J. (1994). KidSim: Programming agents without a programming language." *Communications of the ACM* 37(7), 54–67.

Soloway, E. and Spohrer, J.C. (1988). *Studying the Novice Programmer*. Mahwah, NJ: Lawrence Erlbaum Associates.

Spencer, R. (2000). The streamlined cognitive walkthrough method, working around social constraints encountered in a software development company. In: *Proceedings ACM Conference on Human Factors in Computing Systems, CHI 2000*, pp. 353–359.

Stajano, F. (2000). Python in education: Raising a generation of native speakers. In: *Proceedings of the 8th International Python Conference*, Washington, DC, 24–27 Jan. 2000.

Stallman, R.M. (1994). Why you should not use TCL. Widely distributed online. In: Glenn Vanderburg (ed.), *The TCL War*. http://www.vanderburg.org/Tcl/war/

Sutherland, I.E. (1963/2003). Sketchpad, A Man-Machine Graphical Communication System. PhD Thesis at Massachusetts Institute of Technology, online version and editors' introduction by A.F. Blackwell and K. Rodden. Technical Report 574. Cambridge University Computer Laboratory: http://www.cl.cam.ac.uk/TechReports/.

Weinberg, G.M. (1971). *The Psychology of Computer Programming*. New York: Van Nostrand Reinhold.

Wharton, C., Rieman, J., Lewis, C. and Polson, P. (1994). The cognitive walkthrough method: A practitioner's guide. In: J. Nielsen and R. Mack (eds.), *Usability Inspection Methods*. New York, NY: John Wiley & Sons, Inc.

Whitley, K.N. (1997). Visual programming languages and the empirical evidence for and against. *Journal of Visual Languages and Computing* 8(1), 9–142.

Whitley, K.N. and Blackwell, A.F. (2001). Visual programming in the wild: A survey of LabVIEW programmers. *Journal of Visual Languages and Computing* **12**(4), 435–472.

Wilson, A., Burnett, M., Beckwith, L., Granatir, O., Casburn, L., Cook, C., Durham, M. and Rothermel, G. (2003). Harnessing curiosity to increase correctness in end-user programming. In: *Proc. CHI '03*, Ft. Lauderdale, FL, 5–10 Apr. 2003.

Young, R.M. (1981). The machine inside the machine: Users' models of pocket calculators. *International Journal of Man-Machine Studies* **15**(1), 51–85.

Chapter 3

More Natural Programming Languages and Environments

JOHN F. PANE[1] and BRAD A. MYERS[2]
[1]*RAND Corporation, jpane@rand.org*
[2]*Carnegie Mellon University, bam+@cs.cmu.edu*

Abstract. Over the last six years, we have been working to create programming languages and environments that are more *natural*, by which we mean closer to the way people think about their tasks. The goal is to make it possible for people to express their ideas in the same way they think about them. To achieve this, we performed various studies about how people think about programming tasks, and then used this knowledge to develop a new programming language and environment called HANDS. This chapter provides an overview of the goals and background for the Natural Programming research, the results of some of our user studies, and the highlights of the language design.

1. Introduction

The Natural Programming Project is studying ways to make learning to program significantly easier, so that more people will be able to create useful, interesting, and sophisticated programs. The goals of this project are to define and use a new programming language design process; where we study how non-programmers reason about programming concepts, create new programming languages and environments that take advantage of these findings, and evaluate them. It is somewhat surprising that in spite of over 30 years of research in the areas of empirical studies of programmers (ESP) and human–computer interaction (HCI), the designs of new programming languages have generally not taken advantage of what has been discovered. For example, the new C#, Java, and JavaScript languages use the same mechanisms for looping, conditionals, and assignments that have been shown to cause many errors for both beginning and expert programmers in the C language. Our thorough investigation of the ESP and HCI literature has revealed many results which can be used to guide the design of a new programming system, many of which have not been utilized in previous designs. However, there are many significant "holes" in the knowledge about how people reason about programs and programming. For example, research about which fundamental paradigms of computing are the most natural has not been conclusive. We are performing user studies to investigate this question. Another issue is that most of the prior research has studied people using existing languages, and so there is little information about how people might express various concepts if not restricted by these language designs.

Henry Lieberman et al. (eds.), End User Development, 31–50.

In the context of this prior work, as well as best practices in user-centered design, we adopted a *Natural Programming* design process, which treats usability as a first-class objective in programming system design by following these steps:

- *Identify the target audience and the domain*, that is, the group of people who will be using the system and the kinds of problems they will be working on.
- *Understand the target audience*, both the problems they encounter and the existing recommendations on how to support their work. This includes an awareness of general HCI principles as well as prior work in the psychology of programming and empirical studies. When issues or questions arise that are not answered by the prior work, conduct new studies to examine them.
- *Design the new system* based on this information.
- *Evaluate the system* to measure its success, and understand any new problems that the users have. If necessary, redesign the system based on this evaluation, and then re-evaluate it.

In this design process, the prior knowledge about the human aspects of programming is considered, and the strategy for addressing any unanswered questions is to conduct user studies to obtain design guidance and to assess prototypes.

This chapter summarizes the results to date for the Natural Programming project. More details were reported by Pane (2002), as well as in many other papers that are available from our web site: (http://www.cs.cmu.edu/~NatProg). First, we discuss why naturalness might be better for developers, and then discuss a survey of prior work as it relates to the design of more natural programming languages and environments. Then we discuss three studies we performed to evaluate what might be more natural in programs for graphics and data processing. The results were used in the design of a new language and environment called HANDS (Human-centered Advances for the Novice Development of Software). A user study showed that the novel aspects of HANDS were helpful to novice fifth graders writing their first programs. Finally, we discuss the current work of the Natural Programming project on making the debugging process more natural.

2. Why Natural Might be Better for End-User Developers

In Natural Programming we aim for the programming system to work in the way that people expect, especially end-user developers who may have little or no formal training or experience in programming. The premise of this approach is that the developers will have an easier job if their programming tasks are made more natural. We define *natural* as "faithfully representing nature or life."

Why would this make end-user programming easier? One way to define programming is the process of transforming a mental plan in familiar terms into one that is compatible with the computer (Hoc and Nguyen-Xuan, 1990). The closer the language is to the programmer's original plan, the easier this refinement process will be. This is closely related to the concept of *directness* that, as part of "direct manipulation," is a key principle in making user interfaces easier to use. Hutchins et al. (1986) describe directness as the distance between one's goals and the actions required by the system to achieve those goals. Reducing this distance makes systems more direct, and therefore easier to learn. User interface designers and researchers have been promoting direct- ness at least since Shneiderman (1983) identified the concept, but it has not even been a consideration in most programming language designs. Green and Petre (1996, p. 146) also argue in favor of directness, which they call *closeness of mapping:* "The closer the programming world is to the problem world, the easier the problem-solving ought to be ... Conventional textual languages are a long way from that goal."

User interfaces in general are also recommended to be natural so they are easier to learn and use, and will result in fewer errors. For example, Nielsen (1993, p. 126) recommends that user interfaces should "speak the user's language," which includes having good mappings between the user's conceptual model of the information and the computer's interface for it. One of Hix and Hartson's usability guidelines is to "use cognitive directness," which means to "minimize the mental transformations that a user must make. Even small cognitive transformations by a user take effort away from the intended task." Conventional programming languages do not provide the high-level operators that would provide this directness, instead requiring the programmer to make transformations from the intended task to a code design that assembles lower-level primitives.

Norman also discusses the conceptual gap between the representations that people use in their minds and the representations that are required to enter these into a computer. He calls these the "gulfs of execution and evaluation." He says; "there are only two ways to ... bridge the gap between goals and system: move the system closer to the user; [or] move the user closer to the system" (Norman, 1986, p. 43). We argue that if the computer language expressed algorithms and data in a way that was closer to people's natural expressions, the gaps would be smaller. As Smith et al. (1996, p. 60) have said, "regardless of the approach, with respect to programming, trying to move most people closer to the system has not worked."

The proposed research is closely aligned with the concept of "Gentle Slope Systems" (MacLean et al., 1990; Myers et al., 1992), which are systems where for each incremen- tal increase in the level of customizability, the user only needs to learn an incremental amount. This is contrasted with most systems, which have "walls" where the user must stop and learn many new concepts and techniques to make further progress (see Figure 3.1). We believe that systems can use direct manipulation and demonstrational tech- niques, where users give examples of the desired outcome (Myers, 1992), to lower the initial starting point and enable users to get useful work done immediately. Systems and languages can also be self-disclosing and easy to learn, so the number and height of the walls is minimized, if they cannot be eliminated entirely.

We note that a programming system that is designed to be natural for a particular target audience may not be universally optimal. People of different ages, from different backgrounds and cultures, or from different points in history, are likely to bring different expectations and methods to the programming task. This is why identifying the target

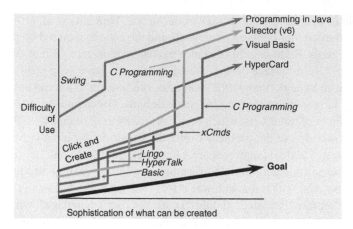

Figure 3.1. The ideal of a gentle slope system. The intent of this graph is to portray how difficult it is to use various tools to create customizations of different levels of sophistication. For example, with Java, it is quite hard to get started, so the Y intercept is high up. The vertical walls are where the designer needs to stop and learn something entirely new. For Java, the wall is where the user needs to learn Swing to do graphics. With Visual Basic, it is easier to get started, so the Y intercept is lower, but Visual Basic has two walls—one when you have to learn the Basic programming language, and another when you have to learn C programming because Visual Basic is no longer adequate. Click and Create was a menu based tool from Corel, and its line stops because it does not have an extension language, and you can only do what is available from the menus and dialog boxes.

audience is an intrinsic part of the design process, and why the process itself is important. It will have to be applied over and over again, in order to best support the particular characteristics of the people who will use each new programming system.

3. Survey of Earlier Work

Programmers are often required to think about algorithms and data in ways that are very different than the ways they already think about them in other contexts. For example, a typical C program to compute the sum of a list of numbers includes three kinds of parentheses and three kinds of assignment operators in five lines of code:

```
sum = 0;
for (i=0; i<numItems; i++) {
    sum += items[i];
}
return sum;
```

In contrast, this can be done in a spreadsheet with a single line of code using the sum operator (Green and Petre, 1996). The mismatch between the way a programmer thinks about a solution and the way it must be expressed in the programming language makes it more difficult not only for beginners to learn how to program, but also for people to carry out their programming tasks even after they become more experienced. One of the most common bugs among professional programmers using C and C++ is the accidental use of "=" (assignment) instead of "==" (equality test). This mistake is easy to make and difficult to find, not only because of typographic similarity, but also because the "=" operator does indeed mean equality in other contexts such as mathematics.

Soloway et al. (1989) found that the looping control structures provided by modern languages do not match the natural strategies that most people bring to the programming task. Furthermore, when novices are stumped they try to transfer their knowledge of natural language to the programming task. This often results in errors because the programming language defines these constructs in an incompatible way (Bonar and Soloway, 1989). For example, "then" is interpreted as meaning "afterwards" instead of "in these conditions."

One of the biggest challenges for new programmers is to gain an accurate understanding of how computation takes place. Traditionally, programming is described to beginners in completely unfamiliar terms, often based on the von Neumann model, which has no real-world counterpart (du Boulay, 1989; du Boulay et al., 1989). Beginners must learn, for example, that the program follows special rules of control flow for procedure calls and returns. There are complex rules that govern the lifetimes of variables and their scopes. Variables may not exist at all when the program is not running, and during execution they are usually invisible, forcing the programmer to use print statements or debuggers to inspect them. This violates the principle of visibility, and contributes to a general problem of memory overload (Anderson and Jeffries, 1985; Davies, 1993).

Usability could be enhanced by providing a different model of computation that uses concrete and familiar terms (Mayer, 1989; Smith et al., 1994). Using a different model of computation can have broad implications beyond beginners, because the model influences, and perhaps limits, how experienced programmers think about and describe computation (Stein, 1999).

In the 1970s, Miller (1974; 1981) examined natural language procedural instructions generated by non-programmers and made a rich set of observations about how the participants naturally expressed their solutions. This work resulted in a set of recommended features for computer languages. For example, Miller suggested that contextual referencing would be a useful alternative to the usual methods of locating data objects by using variables and traversing data structures. In contextual referencing, the programmer identifies data objects by using pronouns, ordinal position, salient or unique features, relative referencing, or collective referencing (Miller, 1981, p 213).

Although Miller's approach provided many insights into the natural tendencies of non-programmers, there have only been a few studies that have replicated or extended that work. Biermann et al. (1983) confirmed that there are many regularities in the way people express step-by-step natural language procedures, suggesting that these regularities could be exploited in programming languages. Galotti and Ganong (1985) found that they were able to improve the precision in users' natural language specifications by ensuring that the users understood the limited intelligence of the recipient of the instructions. Bonar and Cunningham (1988) found that when users translated their natural-language specifications into a programming language, they tended to use the natural-language semantics even when they were incorrect for the programming language. It is surprising that the findings from these studies have apparently had little impact on the designs of new programming languages that have been invented since then.

4. Initial User Studies

We conducted two studies that were loosely based on Miller's work, to examine the language and structure that children and adults naturally use before they have been exposed to programming. A risk in designing these studies is that the experimenter could bias the participants with the language used in asking the questions. For example, the experimenter cannot just ask: "How would you tell the monsters to turn blue when the PacMan eats a power pill?" because this may lead the participants to simply parrot parts of the question back in their answers. This would defeat the prime objective of these studies, which is to examine users' unbiased responses. Therefore our materials were constructed with great care to minimize this kind of bias, with terse descriptions and graphical depictions of the problem scenarios.

In our studies, participants were presented with programming tasks and asked to solve them on paper using whatever diagrams and text they wanted to use. Before designing the tasks, a list of essential programming techniques and concepts was enumerated, covering various kinds of applications. These include: use of variables, assignment of values, initialization, comparison of values, Boolean logic, incrementing and decrementing of counters, arithmetic, iteration and looping, conditionals and other flow control, searching and sorting, animation, multiple things happening simultaneously (parallelism), collisions and interactions among objects, and response to user input.

Because children often express interest in creating games and animated stories, the first study focused on the skills that are necessary to build such programs. In this study, the PacMan video game was chosen as a fertile source of interesting problems that require these skills. Instead of asking the participants to implement an entire PacMan game, various situations were selected from the game because they touch upon one or more of the above concepts. This allowed a relatively small set of exercises to broadly cover as many of the concepts as possible in the limited amount of time available. Many of the skills that were not covered in the first study were covered in a second study, which used a set of spreadsheet-like tasks involving database manipulation and numeric computation.

A set of nine scenarios from the PacMan game were chosen, and graphical depictions of these scenarios were developed, containing still images or animations and a minimal amount of text. The topics of the scenarios were: an overall summary of the game, how the user controls PacMan's actions, PacMan's behavior in the presence and absence of other objects such as walls, what should happen when PacMan encounters a monster under various conditions, what happens when PacMan eats a power pill,

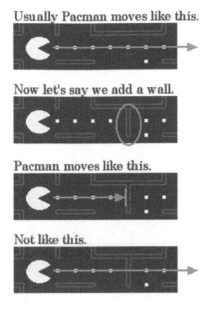

Usually Pacman moves like this.

Now let's say we add a wall.

Pacman moves like this.

Not like this.

Do this: Write a statement that summarizes how I (as the computer) should move Pacman in relation to the presence or absence of other things.

Figure 3.2. Depiction of a problem scenario in study one.

scorekeeping, the appearance and disappearance of fruit in the game, the completion of one level and the start of the next, and maintenance of the high score list. Figure 3.2 shows one of the scenario depictions. Figure 3.3 shows excerpts from participants' solutions.

We developed a rating form to be used by independent analysts to classify each participant's responses (Figure 3.4). Each question on the form addressed some facet of the participant's problem solution, such as the way a particular word or phrase was used, or some other characteristic of the language or strategy that was employed.

Each question was followed by several categories into which the participant's responses could be classified. The analyst was instructed to look for relevant sentences in the participant's solution, and classify each one by placing a tick mark in the appropriate category, also noting which problem the participant was answering when the sentence was generated. Each question also had an "other" category, which the rater marked when the participant's utterance did not fall into any of the supplied categories. When they did this, they added a brief comment.

To see whether the observations from the first study would generalize to other domains and other age groups, a second study was conducted. This study used database access scenarios that are more typical of business programming tasks, and was administered to a group of adults as well as a group of children.

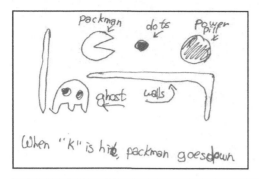

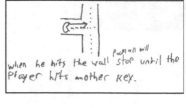

packman   dots   power pill

ghost   walls

When "k" is hit, packman goes down

when he hits the wall pacman will stop until the player hits another key.

[If score is larger than any previous score] put all scores in numeric order, then display scores 1-10.

When the left arrow key is pressed pac man moves left.
When the up arrow key is pressed pacman moves up.
  "   " down " "   "   "   "   "   " down
  "   " right " "   "   "   "   "   " right
When he goes into a wall he backs up and goes a different way.
When Pacman hits the ghost or the monster, he lose a live and start again.
When Pac man goes into a ghost he will lose a life. When pacman eats a special dot he is able to eat the ghost or monster. There is about 30 seconds when they can be eaten.
When the dot is eaten, the ghost and monsters turn a blue color and the player gets more points. Usually it will go up 50 points.
The fruit will appear every minute and disappear in 30 seconds.
After Pacman eats the last dot, a new level starts. The next level is harder, and the dots appear as the last dot is eaten.
When a person has a high score, everybody moves a place down except for the people above it. The last person then doesn't have a place. Example: The new person got in 5th place, the people from 5th - 10th move down a place. the people from 1-4 stay in their place.

Figure 3.3. Excerpts from participants' solutions to problems from Study 1.

Some observations from these studies were:

- An event-based or rule-based structure was often used, where actions were taken in response to events. For example, "when pacman loses all his lives, its game over."

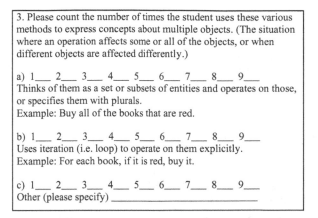

3. Please count the number of times the student uses these various methods to express concepts about multiple objects. (The situation where an operation affects some or all of the objects, or when different objects are affected differently.)

a) 1___ 2___ 3___ 4___ 5___ 6___ 7___ 8___ 9___
Thinks of them as a set or subsets of entities and operates on those, or specifies them with plurals.
Example: Buy all of the books that are red.

b) 1___ 2___ 3___ 4___ 5___ 6___ 7___ 8___ 9___
Uses iteration (i.e. loop) to operate on them explicitly.
Example: For each book, if it is red, buy it.

c) 1___ 2___ 3___ 4___ 5___ 6___ 7___ 8___ 9___
Other (please specify) _____

Figure 3.4. A question from the rating form for study one. The nine blanks on each line correspond to the nine tasks that the participants solved.

- Aggregate operations, where a set of objects is acted upon all at once, were used much more often than iteration through the set to act on the objects individually. For example, "Move everyone below the 5th place down by one."
- Participants did not construct complex data structures and traverse them, but instead performed content-based queries to obtain the necessary data when needed. For example, instead of maintaining a list of monsters and iterating through the list checking the color of each item, they would say "all of the blue monsters."
- A natural language style was used for arithmetic expressions. For example, "add 100 to score."
- Objects were expected to automatically remember their state (such as motion), and the participants only mentioned changes in this state. For example, "if pacman hits a wall, he stops."
- Operations were more consistent with list data structures than arrays. For example, the participants did not create space before inserting a new object into the middle of a list.
- Participants rarely used Boolean expressions, but when they did they were likely to make errors. That is, their expressions were not correct if interpreted according to the rules of Boolean logic used in most programming languages.
- Participants often drew pictures to sketch out the layout of the program, but resorted to text to describe actions and behaviors.

Additional details about these studies were reported by Pane et al. (2001).

5. Studying the Construction of Sets

Because operations on groups of objects and content-based queries were prevalent in non-programmers' problem solutions, we began to explore how this might be supported

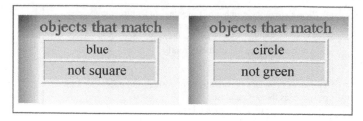

Figure 3.5. Match forms expressing the query: (blue and not square) or (circle and not green).

in a programming language. Queries are usually specified with Boolean expressions, and the accurate formulation of Boolean expressions has been a notorious problem in programming languages, as well as other areas such as database query tools (Hildreth, 1988; Hoc, 1989). In reviewing prior research we found that there are few prescriptions for how to solve this problem effectively. For example, prior work suggests avoiding the use of the Boolean keywords AND, OR, and NOT (Greene et al., 1990; McQuire and Eastman, 1995; Michard, 1982), but does not recommend a suitable replacement query language.

Therefore we conducted a new study to examine the ways untrained children and adults naturally express and interpret queries, and to test a new tabular query form that we designed.

Although some graphical query methods had been shown to be more effective than Boolean expressions, many of them were limited to expressing very simple queries. We wanted a solution that is fully expressive. Also, many of the graphical systems would not integrate well into a programming language, where the entire computer screen cannot be devoted to this one subtask of the programming process. We required a format that is compact and readable in the context of a larger program. With these points in mind, we designed a tabular form that is fully expressive and compatible with the programming language we were developing.

Since we were planning to represent data on cards containing attribute-value pairs in the HANDS programming language, we designed the query form to also use a card metaphor. For the purposes of this study, we simplified the forms by leaving out the attribute names, and limiting the number of terms to three. We called these *match forms* (see Figure 3.5). Each match form contains a vertical list of slots. Conjunction is specified by placing terms into these slots, one term per slot. Negation is performed by prefacing a term with the NOT operator, and disjunction is specified by placing additional match forms adjacent to the first one. This design avoids the need to name the AND and OR operators, provides a clear distinction between conjunction and disjunction, and makes grouping explicit. Match forms are compact enough to be suitable for incorporation into programming systems.

The study used a grid of nine colored shapes, where a subset of the shapes could be marked (see Figure 3.6). Children and adults who participated in this study were given two kinds of problems: code generation problems, where some shapes were already

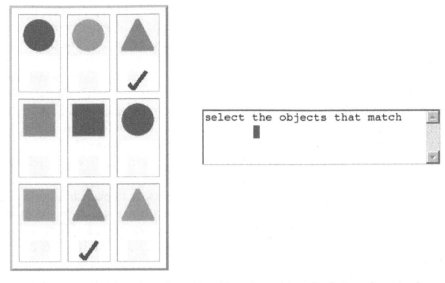

Figure 3.6. Sample problem from the study. In this problem, the participant is asked to write a textual query to select the objects that are marked. The color of each object is red, green, or blue on the computer screen.

marked and they had to formulate a query to select them; and code interpretation problems, where they were shown a query and had to mark the shapes selected by the query. They solved all of these problems twice, once using purely textual queries, and once using match forms.

The results suggest that a tabular language for specifying Boolean expressions can improve the usability of a programming or query language. On code generation tasks, the participants performed significantly better using the tabular form, while on code interpretation tasks they performed about equally in the textual and tabular conditions. The study also uncovered systematic patterns in the ways participants interpreted Boolean expressions, which contradict the typical rules of evaluation used by programming languages. These observations help to explain some of the underlying reasons why Boolean expressions are so difficult for people to use accurately, and suggest that refining the vocabulary and rules of evaluation might improve the learnability and usability of textual query languages. A general awareness of these contradictions can help designers of future query systems adhere to the HCI principle to *speak the user's language* (Nielsen, 1994). Additional details about this study were reported by Pane and Myers (2000).

6. Hands Environment and Language

The next step was to design and implement HANDS, our new programming language and environment. The various components of this system were designed in response to the observations in our studies as well as prior work:

- Beginners have difficulty learning and understanding the highly-detailed, abstract, and unfamiliar concepts that are introduced to explain how most programming languages work. HANDS provides a simple concrete model based on the familiar idea of a character sitting at a table, manipulating cards.
- Beginners have trouble remembering the names and types of variables, understanding their lifetimes and scope, and correctly managing their creation, initialization, destruction, and size, all of which are governed by abstract rules in most programming languages. In HANDS, all data are stored on cards, which are familiar, concrete, persistent, and visible. Cards can expand to accommodate any size of data, storage is always initialized, and types are enforced only when necessary, such as when performing arithmetic.
- Most programming languages require the programmer to plan ahead to create, maintain, and traverse data structures that will give them access to the program's data. Beginners do not anticipate the need for these structures, and instead prefer to access their data through content-based retrieval as needed. HANDS directly supports queries for content-based data retrieval.
- Most programming languages require the programmer to use iteration when performing operations on a group of objects. However, the details of iteration are difficult for beginners to implement correctly, and furthermore, beginners prefer to operate on groups of objects in aggregate instead of using iteration. HANDS uniformly permits all operations that can be performed on single objects to also be performed on lists of objects, including the lists returned by queries.
- Despite a widespread expectation that visual languages should be easier to use than textual languages, the prior work finds many situations where the opposite is true (Blackwell, 1996; Green and Petre, 1992; Whitley, 1997). In our studies, pictures were often used to describe setup information, but then text was used to describe dynamic behaviors. HANDS supports this hybrid approach, by permitting objects to be created and set up by direct manipulation but requiring most behaviors to be specified with a textual language. This design assumes that the environment will provide syntax coloring and other assistance with syntax. These features are commonly available in programming environments, but re-implementing them in HANDS was beyond the scope of our work.
- Programming language syntax is often unnatural, laden with unusual punctuation, and in conflict with expectations people bring from their knowledge in other domains such as mathematics. The HANDS language minimizes punctuation and has a more natural syntax that is modeled after the language used by non-programmers in our studies.
- The prior research offers few recommendations about which programming paradigm might be most effective for beginners (imperative, declarative, functional, event-based, object-oriented, etc.). In our studies of the natural ways beginners expressed problem solutions, an event-based paradigm was observed most often, and program entities were often treated with some object oriented features. HANDS therefore uses an event-based paradigm. Cards are the primary data

structure, and they have some object-like properties: they are global, named, encapsulated, persistent, and have some autonomous behaviors.

- The prior work recommends that programming systems should provide high-level support for the kinds of programs people will build, so they do not have to assemble more primitive features to accomplish their goals. In our interviews with children, they said they wanted to create interactive graphical programs like the games and simulations they use every day. HANDS provides domain-specific support for this kind of program.

All of these observations have influenced the design of HANDS. HANDS uses an event-based language that features a new concrete model for computation, provides queries and aggregate operators that match the way non-programmers express problem solutions, has high-visibility of program data, and includes domain-specific features for the creation of interactive animations and simulations.

6.1. COMPUTATIONAL MODEL

In HANDS, the computation is represented as an agent named Handy, sitting at a table manipulating a set of cards (see Figure 3.7). All of the data in the system is stored on

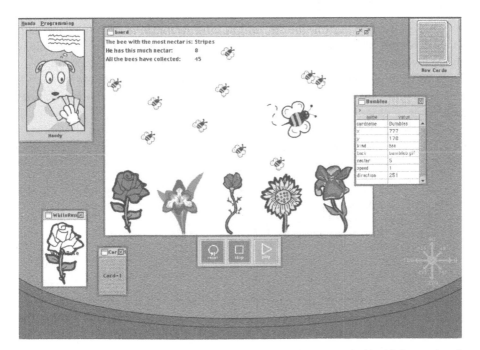

Figure 3.7. The HANDS system portrays the components of a program on a round table. All data are stored on cards, and the programmer inserts code into Handy's thought bubble at the upper left corner. When the play button is pressed, Handy begins responding to events by manipulating cards according to the instructions in the thought bubble.

these cards, which are global, persistent and visible on the table. Each card has a unique name, and an unlimited set of name-value pairs, called properties. The program itself is stored in Handy's thought bubble. To emphasize the limited intelligence of the system, Handy is portrayed as an animal—like a dog that knows a few commands—instead of a person or a robot that could be interpreted as being very intelligent.[1]

6.2. PROGRAMMING STYLE AND MODEL OF EXECUTION

HANDS is event-based, the programming style that most closely matches the problem solutions in our studies. A program is a collection of event handlers that are automatically called by the system when a matching event occurs. Inside an event handler, the programmer inserts the code that Handy should execute in response to the event. For example, this event handler would be run if the system detects a collision between a bee and flower, changing the *speed* value on the bee's card:

```
when any bee collides into any flower
      set the bee's speed to 0
end when
```

6.3. AGGREGATE OPERATIONS

In our studies, we observed that the participants used aggregate operators, manipulating whole sets of objects in one statement rather than iterating and acting on them individually. Many languages force users to perform iteration in situations where aggregate operations could accomplish the task more easily (Miller, 1981). Requiring users to translate a high-level aggregate operation into a lower-level iterative process violates the principle of closeness of mapping.

HANDS has full support for aggregate operations. All operators can accept lists as well as singletons as operands. For example, all of the following are legal operations in HANDS:

```
1 + 1  evaluates to  2
1 + (1,2,3)  evaluates to  2,3,4
(1,2,3) + 1  evaluates to  2,3,4
(1,2,3) + (2,3,4)  evaluates to  3,5,7
```

6.4. QUERIES

In our studies, we observed that users do not maintain and traverse data structures. Instead, they perform queries to assemble lists of objects on demand. For example, they say "all of the blue monsters." HANDS provides a query mechanism to support this.

---

[1] HANK (Mulholland & Watt, 2000) is another end-user programming system where the program is represented as a set of cards and an agent was represented by a cartoon dog in early prototypes. The resemblance of HANDS to HANK is coincidental.

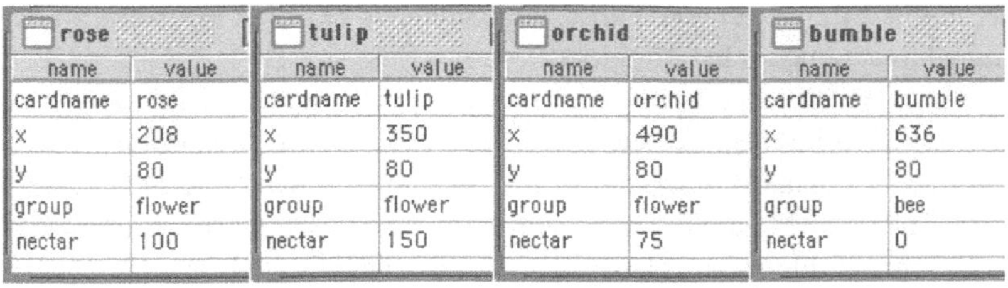

rose		tulip		orchid		bumble	
name	value	name	value	name	value	name	value
cardname	rose	cardname	tulip	cardname	orchid	cardname	bumble
x	208	x	350	x	490	x	636
y	80	y	80	y	80	y	80
group	flower	group	flower	group	flower	group	bee
nectar	100	nectar	150	nectar	75	nectar	0

Figure 3.8. When the system evaluates the query `all flowers` it returns `orchid, rose, tulip`.

The query mechanism searches all of the cards for the ones matching the programmer's criteria.

Queries begin with the word "all." If a query contains a single value, it returns all of the cards that have that value in any property. Figure 3.8 contains cards representing three flowers and a bee to help illustrate the following queries.

```
all flowers evaluates to orchid, rose, tulip
all bees evaluates to bumble
all snakes evaluates to the empty list
```

HANDS permits more complex queries to be specified with traditional Boolean expressions, however the intention is to eventually incorporate match forms into the system as an option for specifying and displaying queries.

Queries and aggregate operations work in tandem to permit the programmer to concisely express actions that would require iteration in most languages. For example,

```
set the nectar of all flowers to 0
```

6.5. DOMAIN-SPECIFIC SUPPORT

HANDS has domain-specific features that enable programmers to easily create highly-interactive graphical programs. For example, the system's suite of events directly supports this class of programs. The system automatically detects collisions among objects and generates events to report them to the programmer. It also generates events in response to input from the user via the keyboard and mouse. It is easy to create graphical objects and text on the screen, and animation can be accomplished without any programming.

7. Evaluation of the Hands Environment and Language

7.1. USER STUDY

To examine the effectiveness of three key features of HANDS—queries, aggregate operations, and data visibility—we conducted a study comparing the system with a limited version that lacks these features. In the limited version, programmers could achieve the same results but had to use more traditional programming techniques. For example, in this limited version aggregate operations were not available, so iteration was required to act upon a list of objects.

Volunteers were recruited from a fifth-grade class at a public school to participate in the study. The 23 volunteers ranged in age from 9 to 11 years old. There were 12 girls and 11 boys. All were native speakers of English, and none had computer programming experience. They came to a university campus on a Saturday morning for a three-hour session. 12 of the children used HANDS and 11 used the limited version of the system.

The HANDS users learned the system by working through a 13-page tutorial. A tutorial for the limited-feature version was identical except where it described a feature that was missing in the limited system. In those places, the tutorial taught the easiest way to accomplish the same effect using features that remained. These changes increased the length of the tutorial slightly, to 14 pages. After working through the tutorial, the children attempted to solve five programming tasks.

In this three-hour session, the children using HANDS were able to learn the system, and then use it to solve programming problems. Children using the full-featured HANDS system performed significantly better than their peers who used the reduced-feature version. The HANDS users solved an average of 2.1 programming problems, while the children using the limited version were able to solve an average of 0.1 problems ($p < .05$). This provides evidence that the three key features improve usability over the typical set of features in programming systems. Additional details about this study were reported by Pane and Myers (2002).

7.2. DISCUSSION

The ease with which these children were able to learn the system and use it to solve tasks suggests that HANDS is a gentle slope system; or, at least its curve has a gentle slope near the origin of the sophistication-difficulty chart (Figure 3.1). The system has a broad range of capabilities. Adults have used it to create interactive games and scientific simulations, as well as solutions to classical computer science problems such as *Towers of Hanoi* and the computation of prime numbers. However, additional testing is necessary to see how far the gentle slope persists, and, if there are any walls, where and how high they are.

Although HANDS was designed for children, we expect that many of its features are generally useful for end-user developers of all ages. This is because most of the factors that drove the design of HANDS (see section 6) were general to beginners and not specific to children. Anecdotally, several of the features of HANDS are attractive to highly experienced programmers; however we have not gathered any empirical evidence on whether this design is generally suitable for programmers across all levels of experience.

HANDS was designed to support the domain of highly interactive graphical programs. HANDS is not well suited to problems outside this domain, such as word processing, technical drawing, or web browsing. It is lacking domain-specific features such as text layout support; and features of HANDS such as collision detection may have little use in these other domains. However, the natural programming design process could be used to design other systems to support any of these domains. Since most of the underlying computational features, such as queries and aggregate operations, are not domain-specific, they are likely to be important features of these other systems as well.

8. Current Work

Understanding of code and debugging are significant areas of difficulty for novices (du Boulay, 1989), but somewhat surprisingly, there has been little advancement in the tools to help with these problems. Even environments aimed at novices have few facilities to help with debugging. For example, systems such as MacroMedia's Director and Flash, Microsoft's Visual Basic, and general-purpose programming environments like MetroWerks' CodeWarrior and Microsoft's Visual C++, all provide basically the same debugging techniques that have been available for 60 years: breakpoints, print statements and showing the values of variables. In contrast, the questions that programmers need to answer are at a much higher level. Our current work is investigating what questions are the most *natural* for users to ask when they are trying to understand and debug their code. Our initial user studies (Ko and Myers, 2003) have shown that often, users are trying to find the answers to "why" and "why not" questions such as:

- Why did the object become invisible?
- Why does nothing happen when I click on this button?
- What happened to my graphical object?
- Where did this value get set?

We are now developing new tools that will allow users to ask such questions directly in the programming environment while debugging. We are conducting user studies to evaluate to what extent the tools enable users to ask questions in a natural way, and to determine what kinds of code and data visualizations will provide the most helpful answers (Ko and Myers, 2004).

9. Conclusions

While making programming languages and environments more natural may be controversial when aimed at professional programmers, it has significant importance for end-user development. In addition to supplying new knowledge and tools directly, the human-centered approach followed by the Natural Programming project provides a methodology that can be followed by other developers and researchers when designing their own languages and environments. We believe this will result in more usable and effective tools that allow both end-users and professionals to write more useful and correct programs.

Acknowledgments

This research has been funded in part by the National Science Foundation under grants IRI-9900452 and IIS-0329090, and as part of the EUSES Consortium under grant ITR-0325273. Any opinions, findings and conclusions or recommendations expressed in this material are those of the authors and do not necessarily reflect those of the National Science Foundation.

References

Anderson, J.R. and Jeffries, R. (1985). Novice LISP errors: Undetected losses of information from working memory. *Human–Computer Interaction*, **1**, 107–131.

Biermann, A.W., Ballard, B.W. and Sigmon, A.H. (1983). An experimental study of natural language programming. *International Journal of Man–Machine Studies*, **18**(1), 71–87.

Blackwell, A.F. (1996). Metacognitive theories of visual programming: What do we think we are doing? In: *Proceedings of the VL'96 IEEE Symposium on Visual Languages*. Boulder, CO: IEEE Computer Society Press, pp. 240–246.

Bonar, J. and Cunningham, R. (1988). Bridge: Tutoring the programming process. In: J. Psotka, L.D. Massey and S.A. Mutter (eds.), *Intelligent Tutoring Systems: Lessons Learned*. Hillsdale, NJ: Lawrence Erlbaum Associates, pp. 409–434.

Bonar, J. and Soloway, E. (1989). Preprogramming knowledge: A major source of misconceptions in novice programmers. In E. Soloway and J.C. Spohrer (eds.), *Studying the Novice Programmer*. Hillsdale, NJ: Lawrence Erlbaum Associates, pp. 325–353.

Davies, S.P. (1993). Externalising information during coding activities: Effects of expertise, environment and task. In: C.R. Cook, J.C. Scholtz and J.C. Spohrer (eds.), *Empirical Studies of Programmers: Fifth Workshop*. Palo Alto, CA: Ablex Publishing Corporation, pp. 42–61.

du Boulay, B. (1989). Some difficulties of learning to program. In E. Soloway and J.C. Spohrer (eds.), *Studying the Novice Programmer*. Hillsdale, NJ: Lawrence Erlbaum Associates, pp. 283–299.

du Boulay, B., O'Shea, T. and Monk, J. (1989). The black box inside the glass box: Presenting computing concepts to novices. In E. Soloway and J.C. Spohrer (eds.), *Studying the Novice Programmer*. Hillsdale, NJ: Lawrence Erlbaum Associates, pp. 431–446.

Galotti, K.M. and Ganong, W.F. III. (1985). What non-programmers know about programming: Natural language procedure specification. *International Journal of Man-Machine Studies*, **22**, 1–10.

Green, T.R.G. and Petre, M. (1992). When visual programs are harder to read than textual programs. In: G.C. van der Veer, M.J. Tauber, S. Bagnarola and M. Antavolits (eds.), *Human–Computer Interaction: Tasks and Organisation, Proceedings of ECCE-6 (6th European Conference on Cognitive Ergonomics)*. Rome: CUD.

Green, T.R.G. and Petre, M. (1996). Usability analysis of visual programming environments: A 'Cognitive Dimensions' framework. *Journal of Visual Languages and Computing*, **7**(2), 131–174.

Greene, S.L., Devlin, S.J., Cannata, P.E. and Gomez, L.M. (1990). No IFs, ANDs, or ORs: A study of database querying. *International Journal of Man–Machine Studies*, **32**(3), 303–326.

Hildreth, C. (1988). Intelligent interfaces and retrieval methods for subject search in bibliographic retrieval systems. In *Research, Education, Analysis and Design*. Springfield, IL.

Hix, D. and Hartson, H.R. (1993). *Developing User Interfaces: Ensuring Usability Through Product and Process*. New York, New York: John Wiley & Sons, Inc.

Hoc, J.-M. (1989). Do we really have conditional statements in our brains? In: E. Soloway and J.C. Spohrer (eds.), *Studying the Novice Programmer*. Hillsdale, NJ: Lawrence Erlbaum Associates, pp. 179–190.

Hoc, J.-M. and Nguyen-Xuan, A. (1990). Language semantics, mental models and analogy. In J.-M. Hoc, T.R.G. Green, R. Samurçay and D.J. Gilmore (eds.), *Psychology of Programming*. London: Academic Press, pp. 139–156.

Hutchins, E.L., Hollan, J.D. and Norman, D.A. (1986). Direct manipulation interfaces. In D.A. Norman and S.W. Draper (eds.), *User Centered System Design: New Perspectives on Human–Computer Interaction*. Hillsdale, NJ: Lawrence Erlbaum Associates.

Ko, A.J. and Myers, B.A. (2003). Development and evaluation of a model of programming errors. In: *Proceedings of IEEE Symposia on Human-Centric Computing Languages and Environments*. Auckland, New Zealand. pp. 7–14.

Ko, A.J. and Myers, B.A. (2004). Designing the Whyline: A debugging interface for asking questions about program behavior. In Proceedings of CHI 2004 Conference on Human Factors in Computing Systems. Vienna, Austria: ACM Press, pp. 151–158.

MacLean, A., Carter, K., Lövstrand, L. and Moran, T.P. (1990). User-tailorable systems: Pressing the issues with buttons. In J.C. Chew and J. Whiteside (eds.), *Proceedings of CHI'90 Conference on Human Factors in Computing Systems*. Seattle, WA: ACM Press, pp. 175–182.

Mayer, R.E. (1989). The psychology of how novices learn computer programming. In E. Soloway and J.C. Spohrer (eds.), *Studying the Novice Programmer*. Hillsdale, NJ: Lawrence Erlbaum Associates, pp. 129–159.

McQuire, A. and Eastman, C.M. (1995). Ambiguity of negation in natural language queries. In *Proceedings of the 18th Annual International ACM SIGIR Conference on Research and Development in Information Retrieval*. Seattle, WA: ACM Press, p. 373.

Michard, A. (1982). Graphical presentation of Boolean expressions in a database query language: Design notes and an ergonomic evaluation. *Behaviour and Information Technology* 1(3), 279–288.

Miller, L.A. (1974). Programming by non-programmers. *International Journal of Man—Machine Studies* 6(2), 237–260.

Miller, L.A. (1981). Natural language programming: styles, strategies, and contrasts. *IBM Systems Journal* 20(2), 184–215.

Mulholland, P. and Watt, S.N.K. (2000). Learning by building: A visual modelling language for psychology students. *Journal of Visual Languages and Computing* 11(5), 481–504.

Myers, B.A. (1992). Demonstrational interfaces: A step beyond direct manipulation. *IEEE Computer* 25(8), 61–73.

Myers, B.A., Smith, D.C. and Horn, B. (1992). Report of the 'End User Programming' working group. In *Languages for Developing User Interfaces*. Boston, MA: Jones and Bartlett.

Nielsen, J. (1993). *Usability Engineering*. Chestnut Hill, MA: AP Professional.

Nielsen, J. (1994). Heuristic evaluation. In J. Nielsen and R.L. Mack (eds.), *Usability Inspection Methods*. New York: John Wiley & Sons, pp. 25–62.

Norman, D.A. (1986). Cognitive engineering. In D.A. Norman and S.W. Draper (eds.), *User Centered System Design: New Perspectives on Human–Computer Interaction*. Hillsdale, NJ: Lawrence Erlbaum Associates.

Pane, J.F. (2002). *A Programming System for Children that is Designed for Usability*. Ph.D. Thesis, Carnegie Mellon University, Pittsburgh, PA.

Pane, J.F. and Myers, B.A. (2000). Tabular and textual methods for selecting objects from a group. In *Proceedings of VL 2000: IEEE International Symposium on Visual Languages*. Seattle, WA: IEEE Computer Society, pp. 157–164.

Pane, J.F. and Myers, B.A. (2002). The impact of human-centered features on the usability of a programming system for children. In *CHI 2002 Extended Abstracts: Conference on Human Factors in Computing Systems*. Minneapolis, MN: ACM Press, pp. 684–685.

Pane, J.F., Ratanamahatana, C.A. and Myers, B.A. (2001). Studying the language and structure in non-programmers' solutions to programming problems. *International Journal of Human–Computer Studies* 54(2), 237–264.

Shneiderman, B. (1983). Direct manipulation: A step beyond programming languages. *IEEE Computer*, **16**(8), 57–69.

Smith, D.C., Cypher, A. and Schmucker, K. (1996). Making programming easier for children. *Interactions* **3**(5), 59–67.

Smith, D.C., Cypher, A. and Spohrer, J. (1994). KidSim: Programming agents without a programming language. *Communications of the ACM* **37**(7), 54–67.

Soloway, E., Bonar, J. and Ehrlich, K. (1989). Cognitive strategies and looping constructs: An empirical study. In: E. Soloway and J.C. Spohrer (eds.), *Studying the Novice Programmer*. Hillsdale, NJ: Lawrence Erlbaum Associates, pp. 191–207.

Stein, L.A. (1999). Challenging the computational metaphor: Implications for how we think. *Cybernetics and Systems* **30**(6), 473–507.

Whitley, K.N. (1997). Visual programming languages and the empirical evidence for and against. *Journal of Visual Languages and Computing*, **8**(1), 109–142.

Chapter 4

What Makes End-User Development Tick?
13 Design Guidelines

ALEXANDER REPENNING[1] AND ANDRI IOANNIDOU[2]
[1] *University of Colorado at Boulder and AgentSheets Inc., alexander@agentsheets.com*
[2] *AgentSheets Inc., andri@agentsheets.com*

Abstract. End-user development (EUD) has enormous potential to make computers more useful in a large variety of contexts by providing people without any formal programming training increased control over information processing tasks. This variety of contexts poses a challenge to EUD system designers. No individual system can hope to address all of these challenges. The field of EUD is likely to produce a plethora of systems fitting specific needs of computer end-users. The goal of this chapter is not to advocate a kind of universal EUD system, but to cut across a variety of application domains based on our experience with the AgentSheets end-user simulation-authoring tool. We have pioneered a number of programming paradigms, experienced a slew of challenges originating in different user communities, and evolved EUD mechanisms over several years. In this chapter we present design guidelines that cut across this vast design space by conceptualizing the process of EUD as a learning experience. Fundamentally, we claim that every EUD system should attempt to keep the learning challenges in proportion to the skills end-users have. By adopting this perspective, EUD can actively scaffold a process during which end-users pick up new EUD tools and gradually learn about new functionality. We structure these design guidelines in accordance to their syntactic, semantic, and pragmatic nature of support offered to end-users.

Key words. agents, end-user programming, graphical rewrite rules, programming by example, visual programming.

1. Introduction

The fundamental aim of end-user development (EUD) (Klann, 2003; Paternò, 2003) is to empower users to gain more control over their computers by engaging in a development process. The users we have in mind, called end-users, are typically not professional software developers. End-users employ pre-existing computer applications to achieve a variety of goals. They may be using email and browser applications to communicate with other users, word processors to write books, graphics applications to create computer art. Often, to make these applications truly useful, end-users may have to adapt these applications to their specific needs. Adaptation may assume many forms ranging from simple forms such as changing preference settings of applications, to more complex forms such as writing filtering rules for email applications or defining formulas for spreadsheets. The need to enable these more complex forms of adaptation is quickly increasing for various reasons. For instance, browsers are used to access quickly growing information spaces. Only the end-users of an application, not the developers of that

Henry Lieberman et al. (eds.), End User Development, 51–85.
© 2006 *Springer.*

application, can decide on how to deal with all this information. Application developers can no longer anticipate all the needs of end-users. This discrepancy between what application developers can build and what individual end-users really need can be addressed with EUD.

The term EUD is relatively new, but it stems from the field of End-User Programming: (EUP) (Bell and Lewis, 1993; Cypher, 1993; Eisenberg and Fischer, 1994; Fischer and Girgenson, 1990; Ioannidou and Repenning, 1999; Jones, 1995; Lieberman, 2001; Nardi, 1993; Pane and Myers, 1996; Rader et al., 1998; Repenning and Sumner, 1995). The shift from "programming" to "development" reflects the emerging awareness that, while the process of adapting a computer to the needs of a user may include some form of programming, it certainly is not limited to it. In that sense, most of the research questions from EUP carry over to EUD but because of the widened scope of EUD new issues need to be explored. EUD is of relevance to potentially large segments of the population including most end-users of traditional computer applications but also of information technology associated with ubiquitous computing. How, then, can the emerging field of EUD provide answers to adaptation challenges including this wide range of applications, devices, contexts, and user needs? How can we conceptualize this end-user and how can we help to make the process of EUD as simple as possible?

Focusing initially on the programming aspect of EUD we can benefit from research areas exploring strategies to make programming simpler. Visual Programming, for instance, has explored the consequences of replacing traditional, text-based, representations of programs with more visually oriented forms of representations. An early period of superlativism ascribing near magical powers to visual programming tried to polarize visual and textual programming approaches into good and bad. Many instances were found when textual programming worked just as well as, if not better than, visual programming (Blackwell, 1996). Gradually, it was recognized that the question of visual versus textual programming approaches cannot be decided on an class level but needs to be explored at the level of instances and closely investigated in the context of actual users and real problems. A number of frameworks have been postulated to evaluate programming approaches at a much finer level of granularity. The Cognitive Dimensions framework by Green (Green, 1989; Green and Petre, 1996) introduced 14 cognitive dimensions to compare programming environments. Over time this useful framework has been extended with additional dimensions and a number of case studies evaluating and comparing exiting programming environments.

A framework in support of evaluation does not necessarily support the design and implementation of systems. For this article we like to assume a more prescriptive position by providing a collection of design guidelines that we collected over a period of 12 years of developing, using and improving the AgentSheets simulation authoring tool. The majority of these guidelines emerged from user feedback initially from the AgentSheets research prototype and later the commercial product. Design intuition may initially be the only clue on building a system, but it will have to be replaced with real user experiences to be useful.

The process of EUD is about learning. Many different users ranging from elementary school kids to NASA scientists have used AgentSheets over the years. Trying to reflect and generalizing over user populations and problem domains we found one perspective of experience that all of these users had in common. EUP and EUD can be conceptualized as a learning experience. The process of EUD is not a trivial one. EUD environments cannot turn the intrinsically complex process of design into a simple one by employing clever interfaces no matter how intuitive they claim to be. Design cannot be addressed with walk-up-and-use interfaces (Lewis et al., 1990; Lewis and Rieman, 1993). We found the learning perspective useful because it allowed us to characterize the end-user as a learner and to create EUD tools in support of learning.

The essence of EUD is, we claim, to scaffold a programming or development tasks as a learning experience. We can neither make any assumptions on what the problem that a user tries to solve is nor the usage context. However, we can make some assumptions about the motivation and background of an end-user. Similar to the person trying to program a VCR, an end-user developer is not intrinsically motivated to learn about programming or development processes. Programming is simply a means to an end. The goal is to record a TV show, not to create a program. The VCR programming task is not likely to be enjoyed. At the same time an end-user programmer is not likely to have a computer science background and also not typically be paid to do end-user programming.

The appearance of an EUD system is largely irrelevant: this is not a question of visual versus textual programming. What is extremely important is that the EUD system carefully

1. balances the user's skill and the challenges posed by a development process; and
2. enables an end-user developer to gradually acquire necessary skills for tackling development challenges.

In short, it is necessary is to conceptualize the process of EUD as a learning experience.

1.1. FLOW

A framework that has allowed us to explore design options comes from psychology. The notion of flow has been introduced by Csikszentmihalyi to analyze motivational factors in learning (Csikszentmihalyi, 1990). In a nutshell, the idea of flow is that optimal learning can take place when there is a proportional relationship between the challenges a task poses and the skills the learner has. Anxiety results if the challenges outweigh the skills, while boredom results if skills outweigh the challenges (see flow diagram in Figure 4.1). Assume a really experienced tennis player is matched up against a beginner. The experienced player exhibits a large amount of skills. Playing against the beginner will pose little challenge. The beginner, in contrast, has almost no skills but will certainly perceive playing against the experienced player to be a high challenge. Putting these values into the diagram we see that the

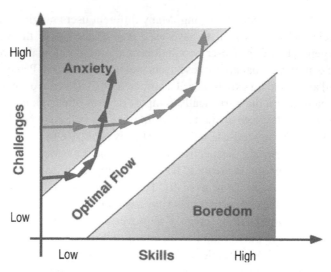

Figure 4.1. Flow: The zone of optimal flow provides good learning conditions by balancing challenges posed to users with their skills. End-user programming requires low thresholds but may not necessarily scale well. Professional programming is less concerned with initial learning.

experienced player is likely to get bored whereas the beginner is likely to enter a state of anxiety.

We have used the notion of flow during several workshops on end-user programming to discuss how users gradually learn different end-user programming tools. In the computer context we look at the programming/development skills a user is likely to have and compare that to the perceived challenge of using an EUD system. According to Csikszentmihalyi's theory the ideal learning situation is established by keeping the ratio of challenge to skill in the diagonal band of the diagram called optimal flow.

In the Syntactic, Semantic, and Pragmatic Guidelines sections of this article, we will discuss design guidelines with respect to flow. A specific EUD activity can be conceptualized as a single point reflecting development experience and problem complexity in the flow diagram. More importantly, repeated or long-term use of an EUD system is captured as arrows indicating a transition in skills and challenge. This transition may be due to using the same EUD system over time or could also be the result of transfer from using other systems.

The shape of the skill/challenge transition chains reveals the usability profile of a system. A programming environment for professional programmers is significantly different from an EUD system. The complexity of a professional programming environment such as Visual Studio is overwhelming even to new professional programmers. Because they are paid, however, they are likely to be willing to make a transition through a non-optimal territory including anxiety. EUD systems typically cannot afford this without frustrating users. A simple development task for end-users needs to be sufficiently supported that even low skills will be sufficient to solve simple challenges without the overhead of a complete computer science education first. In most cases anxiety translates into giving up. Ideally, EUD tools would strive for the goal of a "low-threshold, no ceiling" tool (Papert, 1980). Realistically, a low threshold will probably need to be traded for scalability. This may be acceptable, since nobody expects end-user programming environments such as a VCR programming interface to be scalable to the point where an operating system could be implemented with it.

The majority of our discussion relating design guidelines to flow will be focused on AgentSheets, since it is the system we have the most experience with. The following section will provide a brief introduction to AgentSheets sufficient to understand the design guidelines.

2. Agentsheets

AgentSheets (Ioannidou and Repenning, 1999; Repenning and Ioannidou, 1997; Repenning and Sumner, 1995; Repenning et al., 1998) initially grew out of the idea of building a new kind of computational media that allows casual computer users to build highly parallel and interactive simulations, replacing simple numbers and strings of spreadsheets with autonomous agents. Adding a spreadsheet paradigm to agents enabled the manipulation of large numbers of agents and, at the same time, organize them spatially through a grid. The simulations are used to communicate complex ideas or to simply serve as games. An early prototype of AgentSheets was built in 1988 to run on the Connection Machine (a highly parallel computer with 64000 CPUs).

Partially influenced by the spreadsheet paradigm, the AgentSheets agents were designed to feature a rich repertoire of multimodal communication capabilities. Users should be able to see agents and to interact with them. As more communication channels became available in mainstream computers, they got added to the repertoire of agent perceptions and actions. For instance, text-to-speech allowed agents to talk and speech recognition allowed users to talk to their agents. When the Web started to gain momentum agents got extended to be able to read and interpret data in Web pages (Figure 4.2).

An agentsheet (also called a worksheet) is a grid-structured container of agents. In contrast to a spreadsheet each cell in an agentsheet may contain any number of interacting agents stacked on top of each other. The grid allows agents to employ implicit spatial relations, e.g., adjacency, to communicate with other agents. Table 4.1 shows examples of AgentSheets used for a variety of applications.

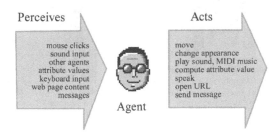

Figure 4.2. AgentSheets' includes multimodal Agents that can perceive and act.

Table 4.1. AgentSheets examples

K-12 Education: Elementary School	K-12 Education: High School

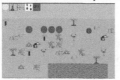

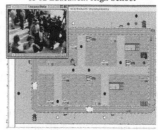

Collaborative Learning: Students learn about life science topics such as food webs and ecosystems by designing their own animals. The AgentSheets Behavior Exchange is used to facilitate collaborative animal design. Groups of students put their animals into shared worlds to study the fragility of their ecosystems.

Interactive Story Telling: History students create interactive stories of historical events such as the Montgomery bus boycott.

Training	Scientific Modeling

Distance Learning: With SimProzac patients can explore the relationships among Prozac, the neurotransmitter serotonin, and neurons. By playing with this simulation in their browsers, patients get a better sense of what Prozac does than by reading the cryptic description included with the drug.

Learning by visualization and modeling: The effects of microgravity onto E.coli bacteria are modeled by NASA. This is a simulation of an experiment that was aboard the Space Shuttle with John Glenn. This simulation requires several thousand agents.

Educational Games	Non-Educational Games

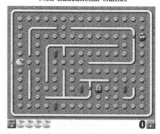

Learning through simulation use: This simple voting simulation explains concepts such as clustering, migration, and stability of two party systems. Can it predict the outcome of the next election?

Learning through design: Even if the finished simulation/game is not directly related to educational goals, the process of building the simulation may be very educational. The Ultimate Pacman is a complete game based on complex Artificial Intelligence algorithms and the non-trivial math of diffusion processes.

Interactive Illustrations	Deconstruction Kits

How does a TV work? This simulation illustrates how a picture is scanned in by a camera (left), transmitted to a TV set and converted back in to a picture (right). Users can paint their own pictures and play with TV signal processing parameters.

Learning by taking apart: What makes a bridge stable? The goal presented to the users of this simulation is to remove as many elements of the bridge as possible without making the bridge collapse. A number of connected issues are revealed including forces, architecture, and geometric perspective. This simulation was featured on the PBS Mathline.

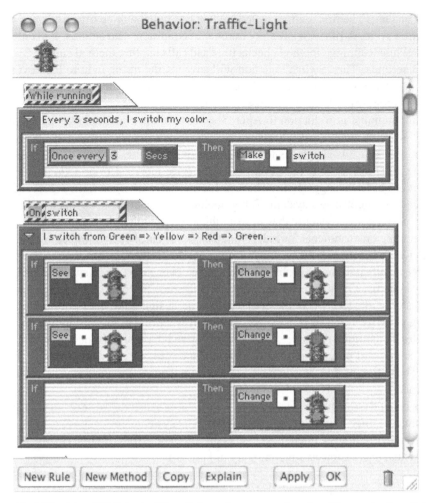

Figure 4.3. A Visual AgenTalk Behavior Editor: Rules can have any number of conditions and actions. Rules are grouped into methods including triggers defining when and how methods will be invoked.

EUD in AgentSheets consists of creating these applications by defining agent classes including the definitions of the agent looks, i.e., iconic representations, as well as the behavior of agents.

The programming part of EUD lies in the specification of agent behavior. Agent behaviors are rule-based using a language called Visual AgenTalk (VAT) (Repenning and Ambach, 1996a, 1996b; Repenning and Ioannidou, 1997). VAT is an end-user programming language that has emerged from several iterations of design, implementation, and evaluation of previous AgentSheets programming paradigms including Programming by Example using Graphical Rewrite Rules (GRR), and programming by analogous examples.

VAT rules are organized as methods including a trigger defining when and how a method will be executed. Figure 4.3 shows a traffic light agent cycling between green, yellow, and red. The first method called "While Running" will be triggered once every simulation cycle. A rule can have any number of conditions and actions. The only rule of the "While Running" method checks time and calls another method called "Switch" every 3 seconds. The "Switch" method will advance the traffic light to the next state. The next color is selected based on the current state of the traffic light. Details on how end-users program in VAT are discussed in the design guidelines.

This minimalist introduction to AgentSheets is only provided to give the reader on a quick sense on what AgentSheets is and what type of applications it has been used for. The focus of this chapter is to provide design guidelines that may help designers building EUD systems. These design guidelines are intended to provide prescriptive descriptions of EUD suggestions. These guidelines have emerged from observing people using the AgentSheets system. The guidelines are generalized as much as possible to help designers of systems that have nothing to do with simulation authoring and programming environments for kids. Nonetheless, AgentSheets examples are included to provide sufficient substance illustrating concrete problems. Our hope is that while concrete manifestations of problems may change over time (e.g., new versions of operating systems, GUIs) the guidelines will still hold. In contrast to design patterns (Alexander et al., 1977; Gamma et al., 1995), the design guidelines not only observe existing patterns, but also provide descriptive instructions in form of implementation examples. For simpler reference, we have categorized the design guidelines into syntactic, semantic, and pragmatic. Finally, all guidelines are presented with optimal flow in mind. The notion of flow can help us—to a certain degree—to design systems that can be learned.

This list of design guidelines is not by no means exhaustive. No set of design guidelines can guarantee the design of a successful EUD system. However, we want to share these design principles gathered over years of experience from reactions to breakdowns where actual users showed either anxiety or boredom.

3. Syntactic Guidelines

Syntactic problems of traditional languages, e.g., the frequently mentioned missing semicolon in programming language such as Pascal or C, pose a challenge to most beginning programmers for no good reason. This quickly leads to anxiety without contributing much towards the conceptual understanding of a programming language. A number of end-user but also professional programming environments have started to address this problem.

Visual programming (Burnett, 1999; Burnett and Baker, 1994; Glinert, 1987; Smith, 1975) is one such paradigm that attempts to pictorially represent language components that can be manipulated to create new programs or to modify existing ones. Visual programming languages are "a concerted attempt to facilitate the mental processes involved in programming by exploiting advanced user interface technology" (Blackwell, 1996). For instance, the visual representation of the language components and constructs often eliminates the need to remember syntax. Professional programming, not geared towards

Figure 4.4. Syntax Coloring in Apple's Xcode programming tools.

end-users, is following by using approaches that range from making syntactic errors hard to impossible.

3.1. MAKE SYNTACTIC ERRORS HARD

Syntax coloring of reserved words and symbols in traditional programming language environments helps the programmer's perception, which in turn helps in creating syntactically correct programs. Symbol completion in languages such as Lisp, and more recently C, helps programmers to produce complete and correct symbols already defined in the programming language, minimizing the possibility of making a typographical error and therefore a syntax error. Finally, wizards utilizing templates for defining program attributes and then generate syntactically correct code, such as the wizard in the CodeWarrior programming environment, syntactically support programmers.

3.1.1. *Example: Apple Xcode Development Environment*

Apple's Xcode developer tool set includes highly customizable syntax coloring (Figure 4.4) combined with code completion that can be manually or automatically invoked by a user. Project templates will generate boilerplate code for the user when creating certain types of projects.

Even with this type of support these tools are only marginally useful to end-users since they still pose a high challenge and require sophisticated skills such as the ability to create programs in C.

3.2. MAKE SYNTACTIC ERRORS IMPOSSIBLE

Other programming approaches employ mechanisms that help with the syntactic aspects of programming in such a way that syntactic errors are essentially impossible.

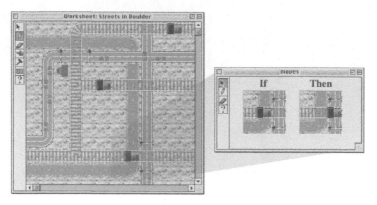

Figure 4.5. Programming by Example through Graphical Rewrite Rules.

3.2.1. *Example: Programming by Example*

In Programming by Example (PBE) (Cypher, 1993; Lieberman, 2001) syntactic problems are avoided by having the computer, not the user, generate programs. A computer observes what the user is doing and, for repetitive tasks, learns them and ultimately does them automatically.

An instantiation of the PBE approach is found in AgentSheets' GRR (Bell and Lewis, 1993). In GRR the program is the result of manipulating the world. As the user interacts with the computer world, the PBE system observes users and writes the program for them. The only skill users need to have is the skill to modify a scene. For instance, to program a train, the user creates examples of how trains interact with their environment (Figure 4.5). The fact that trains follow train tracks is demonstrated by putting a train onto a train track, telling the computer to record a rule, and moving the train along the train track to a new position. The computer records this user action as a pair of Before/After scenes. To generalize the rule, users will narrow the scope of the rule to the required minimum and, if necessary, remove irrelevant objects. A tree next to the train track is likely to be irrelevant and consequently should be removed from the rule, whereas, a traffic light could be essential to avoid accidents.

PBE works well for EUD from a flow perspective, especially at the beginning. Skills and challenges are well balanced because programming is achieved by merely manipulate scenes (moving, deleting, and creating objects). However, many PBE systems do not scale well with problem complexity. Two scenarios are possible.

1. Getting bored: Assume the user wants to create Conway's "Game of Life." A first concrete rule is built quickly but then, in order to implement the entire condition of n out of m cells alive the user is forced to create all f(n, m) rules since the system cannot generalize. Using only a medium amount of skill for basically no challenge (as all rules are simple variants of the first existing one), the user becomes bored.
2. Getting anxious: Assume the user wants to create a situation where numerical diffusion is necessary—for example to illustrate how heat diffuses in a room. The pure iconic nature of GRR makes them ill suited for implementing such numerical

problems. The mismatch of the language and the problem makes the task of implementing diffusion complex. If the complexity of the task increases in a way that the main programming paradigm gets exhausted, the user is expected to learn something new that cannot easily be connected or does not fit to the current paradigm. As a consequence, the challenges soar up disproportionally. The learning curve is no longer a gentle slope and the end-user programmer leaves the optimal flow area of the graph and ends up in a state of anxiety (Figure 4.1).

In either of these two cases, the programming paradigm worked well for a short learning distance, keeping challenges in proportion to skills. But the paradigm reaches a critical threshold at which either the challenges go way up or the existing skills are no longer well used. We called this effect "trapped by affordances" (Schneider and Repenning, 1995).

3.3. USE OBJECTS AS LANGUAGE ELEMENTS

Instead of just representing programming language elements as character strings—the way it is done in most professional programming language such as C or Java—they can be represented as complete objects with user interfaces. Visual representations of these objects (shapes, colors, and animation) may be selected in ways to strongly suggest how they should be combined into a complete working program. Drag and drop composition mechanisms including feedback functions can be employed to guide users. Additionally, language elements may embody user interfaces helping users to define and comprehend parameters of language elements.

3.3.1. *Example: Puzzle Shape Interfaces*

One approach to achieve easy program composition was languages that use a compositional interfaces for assembling programs from language components with visual representations. BLOX Pascal uses flat jigsaw-like pieces that can be snapped together (Glinert, 1987). The BLOX method was one of the first proposals on using the third dimension for visual programming. While this approach alleviates some syntactic issues such as correct sequencing of language statements and parameter setting, the BLOX Pascal language is still, in essence, a professional programming language. End-user programming languages have been developed with the same philosophy. LEGO Mindstorms includes an end-user programming environment for kids to program the LEGO RCX Brick, which can be used to control robotic LEGO creations. The language used to program the Brick is LEGO RCX Code, which uses a jigsaw puzzle user interface similar to BLOX Pascal.

3.3.2. *Example: AgentSheets VAT*

The AgentSheets simulation environment features the Visual AgenTalk (VAT) language (Repenning and Ambach, 1996a, 1996b; Repenning and Ioannidou, 1997). All language

Figure 4.6. The Visual AgenTalk action palette.

elements (conditions, actions, and triggers) in VAT are predefined and reside in palettes (Figure 4.6). Using drag and drop, users essentially copy these language elements and assemble them into complete programs, in if–then forms in an agent's behavior editor, such as the one shown in Figure 4.3.

Command parameters, called "type interactors" in AgentSheets, are set by the user via direct manipulation. For instance, the SEE condition tests for the presence of an agent with a certain depiction in a specific direction (Figure 4.7). Direction and depiction are parameters to the command and are both set via direct manipulation. This is important because, as pointed out by Nardi (1993), the way parameters are specified can affect the extent to which the programmer must learn language syntax. The integration of parameters that are directly manipulatable, such as the 2D pop-up dialogs for direction and depiction, elevate the program onto the level of a user interface combining ideas of form-based interfaces (Nardi, 1993) with end-user programming.

In terms of flow, an initial price needs to be paid because the end-user is forced to explicitly deal with programming language constructs. However, direct manipulation interfaces help to avoid syntactic problems. Aform-based interface includes iconic representations of object created by the end-user (e.g., drawings of agents). Depending on the repertoire of the end-user programming language this approach is likely to be more expressive compared to PBE approaches by allowing the end-user to combine language constructs in way that could not have been anticipated by a PBE approach.

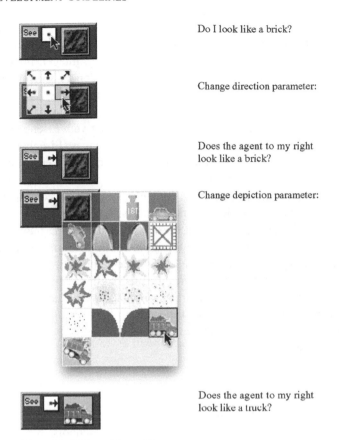

Do I look like a brick?

Change direction parameter:

Does the agent to my right look like a brick?

Change depiction parameter:

Does the agent to my right look like a truck?

Figure 4.7. SEE condition and its parameters.

4. Semantic Guidelines

The reduction of syntactic problems is a necessary but not sufficient goal of EUD. The frustration over missing or misplaced semicolons in professional programming has probably put an early end to many programming careers. However, a program that is syntactically correct not necessarily an working, meaningful, or efficient program. Support at the semantic level helps end-users with bridging the conceptual gap between problems and solutions.

4.1. MAKE DOMAIN-ORIENTED LANGUAGES FOR SPECIFIC EUD

The elements of a programming language are often close to the elements of a natural language. Using some form of syntax, programming language elements representing words such as nouns, verbs, and adjectives are aggregated into complete statements. In early, low level, programming languages these words were typically heavily inspired by the domain of computers. In assembly programming nouns refers to elements found on the CPU such as registers and verbs refer to instructions at the CPU level such as "load." Modern high-level languages have replaced references to low-level technological details with more general concepts such as data structures (e.g., integer, floats, structures, objects). But even this level is difficult for end-user developers. Correlating concepts relevant to a certain application with elements of a generic language can be a large challenge. Nardi suggest the use of task-specific programming languages (Nardi, 1993) as means to reduce this correlation effort. Along a similar vein Eisenberg and Fischer postulate the use of domain-oriented programming languages (Eisenberg and Fischer, 1994). A good example of such a domain-oriented programming environment was the pinball construction kit that allowed people not only to play a simulated pinball game but also to build their own. The pinball construction kit language consisted of a palette of pinball components such as flippers and bouncers.

With an extensible architecture, AgentSheets was used to build a number of domain-oriented languages such as the Voice Dialog Design Environment (Repenning and Sumner, 1992), the AgentSheets Genetic Evolutionary Simulations (Craig, 1997) and the EcoWorlds environment by the Science Theater team (Brand et al., 1998; Cherry et al., 1999; Ioannidou et al., 2003). Domain-orientation can dramatically reduce the challenge of using a tool but at the same time reduces the generality of a tool. In terms of flow, this translates into highly specific environments that require little training, but have a limited range of applications.

4.1.1. *Example: EcoWorlds*

The EcoWorlds system, a domain-oriented version of AgentSheets for ecosystems, was used as a life sciences learning tool in elementary schools. A learning activity consisted of students working in teams to create artificial creatures participating in an ecosystem. Large predators can eat small animals that may eat even smaller animals or plants. The goal of this activity was for students to understand the fragile nature of ecosystems. They had to tweak their designs very carefully to create stable environments. A first attempt of the project tried to use AgentSheets and KidSim (Smith et al., 1994) (later called Creator). The challenge of mapping domain concepts relevant to the curriculum such as reproduction rates and food dependencies was simply too much of a challenge for kids to achieve. The research team working on this created a domain-oriented version of AgentSheets (called EcoWorlds) to capture the domain of ecosystems. A trivial example of this process was the replacement of the Erase action with the Eat action. More complex language elements included complete templates referring to reproduction rates, food categories and other ecosystem-specific concepts.

With EcoWorlds, kids were able to create complex, and most importantly, working ecosystem simulations. There are trade offs, of course. The design of a well-working domain-oriented language is by no means trivial. Many domains tend to change over time requiring maintenance of the domain-oriented programming language. The conceptualization of a domain by the language designers may not match the conceptualizations of the same domain by the users. User-centered design (Lewis and Rieman, 1993; Norman, 1986) can help to some degree. Finally, the specificity of a language to one domain may render it useless to other, non-related domains.

4.2. INTRODUCE META-DOMAIN ORIENTATION TO DEAL WITH GENERAL EUD

A more general-purpose EUD language can make few, if any, assumptions about the application domain. Consequently, the usefulness of a domain-oriented language is severely limited. Meta-domain oriented languages are languages that are somewhat in between the application domain and the computer domain. Spreadsheets are examples of meta-domain orientation. The spreadsheet metaphor, while inspired originally by bookkeeping forms, is a neutral form of representation that is neither directly representing the application domain nor is a low-level computer domain representation. People have used spreadsheets for all kinds of applications never anticipated by the designers of spreadsheet tools. More specific applications that initially were solved with spreadsheets, such as tax forms, have meanwhile been replaced with complete, domain-oriented tools such as tax-form tools. Where domain-orientation is possible and effective (from the economic point of view, e.g., if there are enough people with the exact same problem) domain-oriented tools are likely to supersede more generic tools in the long run.

AgentSheets uses its grid-based spatial structure as a meta-domain allowing people to map general problems onto a spatial representation. A grid is an extremely general spatial structure that can be employed to represent all kinds of relationships. In some

Table 4.2. Visual AgenTalk actions, conditions, and type interactors

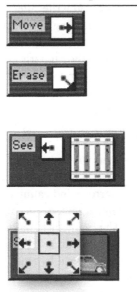

Actions: Some VAT actions are intrinsically spatial. For instance, the Move action is used to make an agent move in space from one grid location to another adjacent position. Others actions are spatial in conjunction with their parameters. The parameter of the Erase action defines where to erase an agent.

Conditions: A large number of VAT conditions are used to evaluate spatial relationships. The See condition allows an agent to check if an adjacent cell in a certain direction contains an agent with a certain depiction.

Type Interactors: Type Interactors are parameters of VAT condition/action commands that include a user interface. Some type interactors such as Direction-Type allow users to select a direction to an adjacent grid location.

cases, the grid is employed to spatially represent objects that also have a natural spatial representation. In other cases, the grid is used to capture conceptual relationships that have no equivalence in the physical world.

Meta-domain orientation manifests itself in the EUD language. In AgentSheets the VAT language includes a variety of spatial references embedded at the level of commands and type interactors (as shown in Table 4.2).

4.3. USE SEMANTIC ANNOTATIONS TO SIMPLIFY THE DEFINITION OF BEHAVIOR

EUD is not limited to programming. It includes the creation and management of resources such as icons, images, and models. The program defining the behavior of an application needs to be connected with resources defining the look of an application. EUD tools should support the creation as well as the maintenance of these connections. At a simple, syntactic level, this connection should become visible to a user. VAT, for instance, includes the Depiction-Type interactor, which essentially is a palette of all the user-defined icons. Things get more complex at the semantic level because development systems cannot automatically derive semantic information from artwork. However, with a little bit of semantic annotation or meta-data provided by users an EUD system can greatly simplify the development process.

4.3.1. *Example: Semantic Rewrite Rules*

GRR, as a form of end-user programming, suffer from their implicit underlying model. Interpretation of rewrite rules limited to syntactic properties makes it laborious for end-users to define non-trivial behavior. Semantically-enriched GRR can increase expressiveness, resulting in a significantly reduced number of rewrite rules. This reduction is essential in order to keep rewrite rule-based programming approaches feasible for end-user programming. The extension of the rewrite rule model with semantics not only benefits the definition of behavior, but additionally supports the entire visual programming process. Specifically the benefits include support for defining object look, laying out scenes consisting of dependent objects, defining behavior with a reduced number of rewrite rules, and reusing existing behaviors via rewrite rule analogies. These benefits are described in the context of the AgentSheets programming substrate.

Semantic Rewrite Rules (Repenning, 1995) allow users to annotate their icons with semantic information such as connectivity. For instance, an icon representing a horizontal strip of road can be annotated with connectivity arrows indicating that this road connects the right with the left and the left with the right. AgentSheets can then transform these icons syntactically as well as semantically. The syntactic transformation will bend, rotate, split, and intersect icons by applying bitmap operations to the original road icon (Figure 4.8). The semantic information will be transformed by automatically deriving the connectivity information of the transformed icons. Finally, the single rewrite rule describing how a train follows a train track (Figure 4.5) is now interpreted on a

Figure 4.8. Connectivity Editor. Users add semantic annotations to define the meaning of an icon. A horizontal road connects the right side with left side and the right side with the left side.

semantic level. This one rule is powerful enough that the train can follow any variant of train tracks without the need to create the large set of all the permutations of trains driving in different directions and train tracks. In terms of flow, the user can now, with the same degree of skill, tackle substantially larger challenges.

4.3.2. *Example: Programming by Analogous Examples*

Analogies are powerful cognitive mechanisms for constructing new knowledge from knowledge already acquired and understood. When analogies are combined with PBE, the result is a new end-user programming paradigm, called Programming by Analogous Examples (Repenning and Perrone, 2000; Repenning and Perrone-Smith, 2001), combining the elegance of PBE to create programs with the power of analogies to reuse programs.

This combination of programming approaches substantially increases the reusability of programs created by example. This merger preserves the advantages of PBE and at the same time enables reuse without the need to formulate difficult generalizations. For instance, if PBE is used to define the behavior of a car following roads in a traffic simulation, then by analogy this behavior can be reused for such related objects as trains and tracks by expressing that "trains follow tracks like cars follow roads" (Figure 4.10).

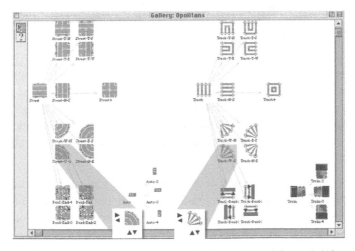

Figure 4.9. Icons and their semantic annotations are geometrically transformed. Semantic information is used to establish isomorphic structures for generalized rules and analogies.

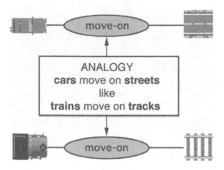

Figure 4.10. An analogous example defines the interactions between cars and roads by establishing an analogous connection to trains and train tracks.

The analogy between cars and trains can be established because of the semantic information. At the syntactic level the system could not have recognized the relationships between cars and trains but the semantic information is sufficient to allow the system to find the corresponding match based on the connectivity of icons. In terms of flow, Programming by Analogous Examples simultaneously reduces the challenge of programming and requires few skills to establish an analogy. However, sometimes analogies can be hard to see and even when they can be applied analogies may break down requiring some kind of exception handling.

5. Pragmatic Guidelines

In addition to the syntactic and semantic support described above, a programming language has to provide pragmatic support to be effective as an end-user development tool kit. That is, an EUD language should make programs personally relevant to the end-user and the programming process more practical.

5.1. SUPPORT INCREMENTAL DEVELOPMENT

When a programming language allows and supports incremental development of programs, end-user programmers do not feel that what they are asked to do with the computer is too difficult, but instead that they are building up the necessary skills in an incremental fashion, thus staying in the optimal flow of the learning experience. Incremental development provides instant gratification, avoids leaps in challenge and allows skills to grow gradually.

1. Getting instant gratification: end-user programmers have the opportunity to execute and test partially complete programs or even individual language components, getting feedback and gratification early on in the programming process without requiring a complete program first.
2. Avoiding leaps in challenge: the step-by-step creation of a program enables end-user programmers to incrementally add complexity to their program, avoiding huge leaps

in challenge and tasks that would otherwise be infeasible and would undoubtedly lead to anxiety (Figure 4.1). Traditional languages that force the programmer to have a complete program-compile-run cycle before each test of the program are typically more time-consuming and drive programmers into a style of programming where they write big chunks of code before trying it out. This often makes debugging challenging.
3. Allowing skills to grow gradually: when end-users incrementally develop, test, and debug programs, their skills grow in proportion to the challenge they face. Incremental development provides the end-user programmers with mechanisms to first tackle small parts of the challenge before incorporating them to the bigger picture.

The form of exploratory and experimental programming that is afforded by small increments of code is well suited to end-user programmers that are not experienced programmers and have not received formal education in software design methods and processes.

5.1.1. *Example: Tactile Programming*

AgentSheets' VAT is an end-user programming language that elevates the program representation from a textual or visual representation to the status of a user interface. In its elevated form, the program is the user interface. By providing language objects (conditions and actions) packaged up with user interfaces, VAT is rendered into a tactile programming language.

Tactility is used here not in the sense of complex force feedback devices that are hooked up to computers, but more in the sense used by Papert to explain the closeness of bricoleur programmers to their computational objects (Papert, 1993). One departure from Papert's framework is that the notion of computational objects in VAT is not limited to the objects that are programmed, such as the Logo turtle, but also applies to the programming components themselves, which are elevated to the level of highly manipulatable objects (Repenning and Ioannidou, 1997).

Visual Programming employs visual perception to simplify programming by increasing the readability of programs. Tactile Programming does not question this goal, but hopes to make programming more accessible to end-users by adding the perception of manipulation to visual perception. In Tactile Programming, programs are no longer static representations nor is the notion of manipulation reserved only for editing programs. Instead, tactile programs and their representations are dynamic and include manipulation, such as setting parameters by manipulating parameter spaces (Figure 4.11) or composing programs by dragging and dropping languages pieces in behavior editors.

Tactile Programming primitives and programs not only have enhanced visual representations to help program readability, but also have interactive interfaces to assist with program writability. With Tactile Programming programs can be composed incrementally along clearly defined boundaries, making program composition easy.

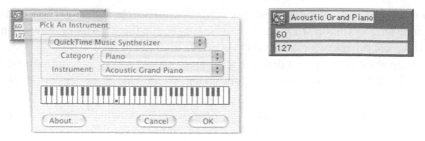

Figure 4.11. The function of a tactile programming object can be perceived through interaction.

5.2. FACILITATE DECOMPOSABLE TEST UNITS

Traditional programming languages do not allow out-of-context testing of individual statements, because for instance there may be undefined variables in that small fragment of code to be tested. In contrast, the kind of interface tactile programming provides, supports an exploratory style of programming, where users are allowed to "play" with the language and explore its functionality. Perception by manipulation afforded by tactile programming allows end-users to efficiently examine functionality in a direct exploration fashion. Any VAT language component at any time can be dragged and dropped onto any agent. The component will execute with visual feedback revealing conditions that are true or false and showing the consequences of executed actions.

Program fragments can be tested at all levels: conditions/actions, rules, and methods. For instance, dragging the move command from the action palette onto the Ball agent in the worksheet will make the ball move to the right (Figure 4.12).

Condition commands, when dragged and dropped onto agents, will reveal whether the condition holds for the agent in its current context. If the See condition is dragged onto the soccer player in the worksheet, visual and acoustic feedback will immediately indicate that this condition would not hold. In the case of Figure 4.13, it will indicate that the condition is "true."

Dragging and dropping an entire rule onto an agent will test the entire rule. Step-by-step with visual feedback, all the conditions are checked. In our example rule (Figure 4.14), only one condition exists. If the soccer player agent sees to his right a ball agent, the condition is successfully matched and, as consequence, all the actions are executed—in this case, changing the depiction of the player (Change action), colorizing him red to show who is in control of the ball (Set color to action) and keep that for a while (wait action); then tell the ball (which happens to be to his right) to run its

Figure 4.12. What does move right do? Drag program fragment onto agent to see consequences. Dragging move-right action onto the ball will make it move to the right one position.

Figure 4.13. Testing conditions: dragging See-right-ball condition onto soccer player agent will test if there currently is a ball immediately to the right. The condition is true.

"kick-right" method and reset the colorization back to its original colors. The results of the executed rule are graphically shown on the right (Figure 4.14). Had the condition of that rule failed, acoustic feedback would have been provided and the condition that failed would have blinked to indicate the problem.

Tactile programming with decomposable test units at different levels of granularity of the programming language (individual commands, rules, methods) enables easy debugging even for end-user programmers that do not possess the skills of professional programmers in debugging.

On the down side, drag and drop may not necessarily be the best mechanism for testing these language components. While drag and drop is an excellent mechanism for program composition, for this type of testing it may not be as intuitive or obvious as one may think. User testing has shown that when using the Macintosh version of the AgentSheets simulation-authoring tool, users have to be told this drag and drop testing feature exists. This was remedied in the Windows version of the software by adding a Test button in the behavior editor window. Instead of dragging and dropping commands or rules onto agents in the worksheet, a user simply selects the language component to be tested and the agent on which to test it on and presses

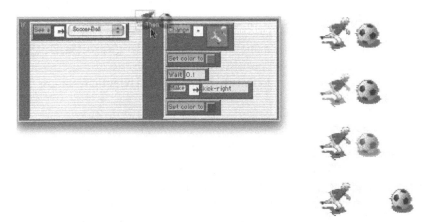

Figure 4.14. Testing Rules. If all the conditions of the rule are true then the actions will be excuted. One action after anoter get highlighted, and the consequence of running it visualized in the simulation.The agent changes to look like the kicking player, it turns red, after some time it sends the kick-right message to the ball, and turn its color back to normal.

the Test button. Not only this makes this debugging feature more apparent, but it also affords multiple tests of the same language component without the mundane effort of dragging and dropping the same piece over and over again.

Whatever the mechanism, the point remains that end-user programming languages need to allow their users to test any piece of the program at multiple granularities (command, rule, method) in the context of an agent in the worksheet at any time during the development process. This supports understandability of the language and therefore enhances program writability.

5.3. PROVIDE MULTIPLE VIEWS WITH INCREMENTAL DISCLOSURE

One of the criticisms of visual programming languages is that they use a lot of screen real estate (Green and Petre, 1996). To improve program readability and consequently program comprehension, multiple views of the same program should be available to end-user programmers. Using disclosure triangles is one technique to collapse and expand program components.

5.3.1. *Example: Disclosure Buttons and Disclosure Triangles*

In AgentSheets, disclosure triangles are used to show or hide methods in an agent's behavior editor. Figure 4.15 shows the collapsed "Advance" method of the Car agent with only its name, documentation, and number of rules contained visible in the editor.

Figure 4.16 shows the expanded version of the same method with all the rules exposed.

In terms of flow, the ability to switch between views helps to manage information clutter and consequently simplifies the location of relevant information.

5.4. INTEGRATE DEVELOPMENT TOOL WITH WEB SERVICES

The Web is a rich resource of information that can help the design process. Development tools in general and EUD tools specifically should make use of these resources by providing seamless connection mechanisms helping to find relevant resources based on the current design state.

5.4.1. *Example: Design-Based Google Image Search*

AgentSheets can locate relevant artwork based on the design state of an agent using the Google image search. Say a user creates an agent called "red car" and designs an icon quickly using a bitmap editor. Instead of creating their own artwork users may use AgentSheet's "Search Depictions on Web" function. This function will use information from the design environment, the name of the agent class "red car," compute a Google query and open a Web browser. There is no guarantee that a suitable image is found but if users do find a good match they can import images into AgentSheets (see Figure 4.17).

Red-Car

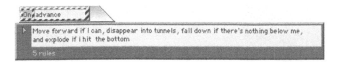

Figure 4.15. A collapsed method shows only the documentation information and, as indicator for method complexity, the number of rules contained.

Integration with Web services are relevant to flow, in the sense that integration not only extends design spaces with external resources but also reduces rough transitions between otherwise non-connected tools.

5.5. ENCOURAGE SYNTONICITY

Papert used the term syntonicity to describe how children's physical identification with the Logo turtles helped them more easily learn turtle geometry (Papert, 1980, 1993; Papert and Harel, 1993). Syntonicity helps people by allowing them to put themselves into the "shoes" of the objects they create and program. As a mindset syntonicity encourages the development of mini scenarios helping to disentangle potentially complex interaction between multiple objects: "If I where the car driving on the bridge doing ..." As an extension to Papert's stance toward syntonicity, we found that syntonicity can be actively cultivated by a system through a number of mechanisms. Moreover, we find

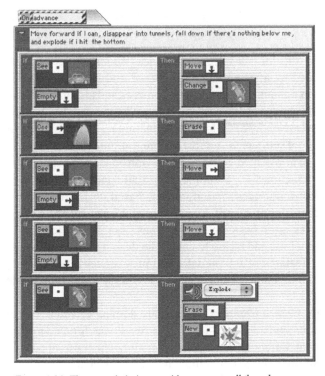

Figure 4.16. The expanded view provides access to all the rules.

Figure 4.17. A Google Image search triggered by the Design of a "red car" agent. Suitable images can be imported into AgentSheets.

syntonicity relevant to EUD in general because it helps to overcome some essential misconceptions of programming often found in non-programmers.

5.5.1. *Example: First-Person Domain-Oriented Language Components*

Students often find it difficult to map their ideas about science phenomena onto the operations provided by a visual language (Brand and Rader, 1996). Commands that match the problem domain can simplify this process and also focus the students' attention on important aspects of the content. The VAT language has been customized by researchers at the University of Colorado conducting research on modeling ecosystems in elementary school settings to support the programming of concepts in that domain. A number of domain-oriented commands was introduced to support the definition of predator–prey interactions. For example, rules that enable a predator to eat are stated as, "If I can select food <description of prey, based on features> then try to eat it, because I am <description of self, specifying why I can eat this prey>." This set of commands replaces more basic actions, such as "see" and "erase," with the specific actions of selecting food and trying to eat it. The design of the commands also requires students to enter features of the predator and prey, thereby reinforcing science ideas about structure and function (Brand et al., 1998; Cherry et al., 1999; Rader et al., 1997; Rader et al., 1998).

Not only were these customized commands domain-oriented, but they were also presented in the first person, e.g., "I eat." The result was for students to identify with the agents they were building (namely, the animals), which was apparent in their lively discussions about their ecosystem simulation. The students typically referred to their

Figure 4.18. An Animated Speech/Tooltip will explain command through a complete English sentence. Speech/Animation is synchronized with the selection of command parameters to establish the correspondence.

animals in the first person, saying for example "I can eat you" rather than "my Ozzie can eat your Purple Whippy Frog" or "I am dead" rather than "My animal is dead," Perhaps because of this identification, students were very motivated to ensure that their animals survived. Although students initially had a tendency to want their animals to survive at the expense of other populations, this tendency was often mitigated once they realized that the other species were necessary for their animal's long-term well-being (Ioannidou et al., 2003).

Whereas the benefits from domain-oriented language pieces are evident from the example above, such a method is not always the most appropriate. The language can quickly get verbose and more importantly its customized components become incompatible with the language of the standard system.

5.5.2. *Example: Explanations via Animated Speech and Animated Tool Tips*

Syntonicity can manifest itself not only as customized language pieces, but also in the form of explanations of the language components. In AgentSheets for example, individual commands and entire rules are syntonically explained via a unique combination of animation and speech (in the Mac version) or animation and textual tool tips (in the Windows version). When the "Explain" button is pressed and single command is selected, the system steps through each component of the command annotating with blinking animation and verbally explains (either with speech synthesis or animated text in tool tips) what the command does. For instance, for the WWW read condition, the system explains that the condition is true in the context of an agent, if that agent finds the string specified when reading a specified Web page (Figure 4.18). First person is used to stress the fact that language pieces only make sense in the context of an agent, as pieces of that agent's behavior.

Explanations are not static; they will interpret the current values of parameters. In some cases this will result in simple variations of sentences whereas in other cases the explanatory sentence will be considerably more restructured in order to clarity the meaning to the user (Figure 4.19).

Explanations reduce challenges based on the comprehension of programs. At the same time they eliminate the need for languages to be more verbose which is often considered a good property for beginning programmers but gets in the way for more experienced programmers.

Explanation: Remove me from the worksheet

Explanation: Erase the agent to my right.

Figure 4.19. Explanation variations depending on parameters.

5.6. ALLOW IMMERSION

Immersing end-user programmers into the task and helping them experience the results of their programming activity by directly manipulating and interacting with their artifacts is an important factor for keeping them in the optimal flow part of the learning experience.

5.6.1. *Example: LEGOsheets and Direct Control of Motors*

LEGOsheets (Gindling et al., 1995) is a programming, simulation, and manipulation environment created in AgentSheets for controlling the MIT Programmable Brick (see Figure 4.20). The brick, developed at the MIT Media Lab as the research prototype of what is now known as LEGO Mindstorms, receives input from sensors, such as light and touch sensors and controls effectors, such as motors, lights, and beepers. The combination of LEGOsheets and the Brick gives children the ability to create physical artifacts (vehicles and robots) and program them with interesting behaviors (Resnick, 1994; Resnick, Martin, Sargent and Silverman, 1996).

A lot of the children's excitement and engagement with LEGOsheets arose from the physical aspect that the Brick provided. It is interesting to create a simulation of a car running around on a computer screen, but it is richer and more interesting when the car is programmed to do so in the real world. The richness of the resulting artifact

 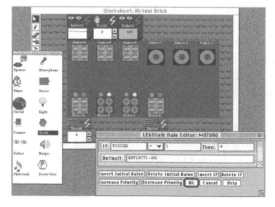

Figure 4.20. LEGOsheets a programming environment to program and directly control the MIT programmable brick. LEGOsheets programs are highly parallel putting rule-based behaviors into sensor effector agents.

Figure 4.21. "Programming" the Vehicle in the real world.

behavior does not have to stem from the complexity of the program itself, but from its interactions with the real world (Simon, 1981) (Figure 4.21).

Giving the opportunity to children to engage in interesting explorations in the world as part of social activities not only provided an engaging but also a highly motivating atmosphere that enabled even 3rd grade elementary school kids to take the step towards programming.

5.6.2. Example: Mr. Vetro, the Simulated Human Being

Mr. Vetro is an application we have developed using a unique architecture for compact, connected, continuous, customizable, and collective simulations (C5). This architecture can be generally geared towards helping students to experience and understand all kinds of complex distributed systems such as the human body, economies, ecologies, or political systems.

Mr. Vetro[1] (Figure 4.22a) is a simulated human being with a collection of simulated organs (such as heart and lungs) each of which are distributed as client simulations running on handhelds (Figure 4.22b, top).

Using these client simulations users can control Mr. Vetro's organs. For instance, a group of students can control his lungs by varying parameters such as the breathing rate and tidal volume as a response to changing conditions such as exercise or smoking. Another group can control Mr. Vetro's heart by varying heart parameters such as heart rate and stroke volume. A third group can act as the decision-making part of Mr. Vetro's brain to control decisions such as engaging in exercise and the intensity of the exercise.

With a wireless network, the client simulations send data to the server running the central simulation (the complete Mr. Vetro) each time the parameters get the updated. A life signs monitor keeps track of Mr. Vetro's vital signs and displays them in the form of graphs or numerical values. O_2 saturation in the blood, partial pressure of CO_2, and O_2 delivered to tissue are some of the values calculated and displayed (Figure 4.22b).

Activities with Mr. Vetro are compelling and engaging as they promote interesting inter-group as well as intra-group discussions and collaborations to solve the tasks

---

[1] Translated from Italian, "vetro" means "glass." The name is derived from Mr. Vetro's glass skeleton.

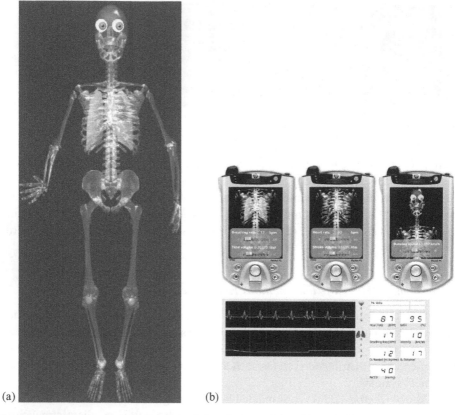

(a)   (b)

Figure 4.22. (a) Mr. Vetro is a distributed simulation of a human being. (b) Handheld controllers (top) and life signs monitor (bottom).

presented to students. Moreover they provide new ways to learn, not previously available by simply reading about human organs and systems in books.

Direct manipulation interfaces of changing the organ parameters allow users to change the simulation without having to engage in anything that can be perceived as traditional programming. As skills increase—mainly domain skills, but also skills related to interacting with the system—students can be exposed to more complex EUD activities.

EUD related to Mr. Vetro can take place at two levels. At the highest level the handheld devices representing Mr. Vetro's organs become the building blocks of a collaborative design activity. At the lower level users employ end-user programming to script organs or to analyze physiological variables. Teachers, for instance, may want students to express rules to determine different states of Mr. Vetro that need to be identified and addressed. Students could use an end-user language such as VAT to express a rule relating the level of partial pressure of CO_2 to hyperventilation and hypoventilation (Figure 4.23).

[...] when ventilation is normal the partial pressure is about 40 mm Hg. Hyperventilation: means that Alveolar Ventilation is excessive for metabolic needs. The [partial pressure] PaCO2 is less than 35 mm Hg. Hyperventilation may occur in response to hypoxia or anxiety. Hypoventilation means that the Alveolar Ventilation is too low for metabolic needs and that the PaCO2 is more than 45 mm Hg. The most common cause of hypoventilation is respiratory failure (Berne & Levy, 2000).

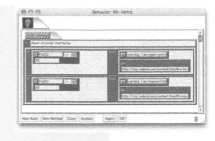

Figure 4.23. The physiological rules can be directly turned into Visual AgenTalk. Rules are used to recognize physiological conditions and link them to existing Web information such as WebMD explaining condition and treatment.

5.7. SCAFFOLD TYPICAL DESIGNS

Whereas modeling is a desired computational literacy (diSessa, 2000) for a wide spectrum of computer end-users, programming is typically not. Therefore engaging in modeling activities should not necessarily have as a prerequisite the need to learn programming, especially in classroom settings. On the one hand, given the pragmatic concerns of heavy time limitations, using existing simulations is much easier and much more attainable in current educational settings than building simulations from scratch, even with EUD approaches. On the other hand, building simulations is an educationally effective activity (Ioannidou et al., 2003; Ioannidou et al., 1998; President's Committee of Advisors on Science and Technology 1997; Wenglinsky, 1998; Zola and Ioannidou, 2000). Therefore, finding a middle ground would be essential for making simulations viable educational tools for mainstream classrooms. One such way would be to provide scaffolding mechanisms for the model-creation process. Scaffolding is the degree of structure provided by a system (Guzdial, 1994). High-level behavior specification paradigms provide a lower threshold to programming and therefore can be considered scaffolding mechanisms.

5.7.1. *Example: Programmorphosis—Multi-Layered Programming with the Behavior Wizard*

The Programmorphosis approach (Ioannidou, 2002, 2003) was developed as a multi-layered approach to end-user programming, which, at the highest level, enables novice end-user programmers to define behaviors of interacting agents in an abstract language. In Programmorphosis, behavior genres are used to group and structure domain concepts in a template. Therefore, the task of programming is elevated from a task of synthesis to one of modification and customization of existing behavior templates.

The Behavior Wizard was added to AgentSheets to instantiate Programmorphosis. Specifying behaviors is achieved by altering behavioral parameters in templates in a wizard environment that subsequently generates lower-level executable code. For instance, the behavior of an Octopus animal agent for an ecosystem simulation would

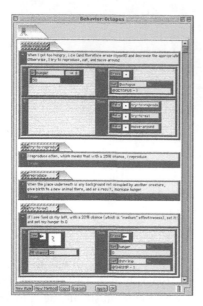

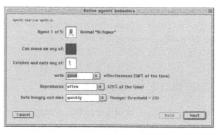

Figure 4.24. Behavior of an Octopus animal agent expressed in AgentSheets Visual AgenTalk (left). The same behavior expressed in the Behavior Wizard using the animal template (right).

be represented in VAT as shown in Figure 4.24 (left), with if–then rules defining eating, mating, and moving behaviors. In the Behavior Wizard, the user would specify the same behavior by manipulating parameters such as prey, hunting effectiveness, reproduction rate, as shown in Figure 4.24 (right).

The high-level behavior specification language featured in the Behavior Wizard essentially adds a layer in the programming process. As a result, this multi-layered programming approach enables a wide range of end-users to do the programming. Multiple levels of abstraction address the different needs or levels of ability. At the highest level, a novice end-user may be "programming" declaratively through wizards, revealing meaningful customizations of existing behaviors. At the lower level, a user may be programming procedurally in a programming language such as a rule-based language.

A general trade-off exists between the expressiveness of a programming language and its ease of use. Instead of selecting a fixed point in this space, Programmorphosis adds a high-level behavior specification layer and introduces a multi-layered approach to programming. Ideally, these programming layers should be connected to allow end-users to gradually advance, if they want to, from very casual end-user programming, which may be as simple as changing a preference, to sophisticated end-user programming.

5.8. BUILD COMMUNITY TOOLS

For end-users to harness the power of the Web and be encouraged for more active and productive participation, the image of the Web as a broadcast medium should be

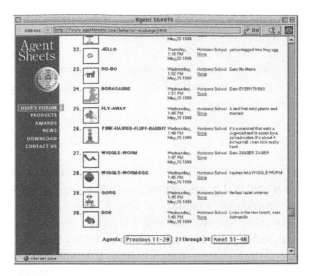

Figure 4.25. The AgentSheets Behavior Exchange. Uses can give and take agent including descriptions what these agents do and who they look like.

expanded to include end-user mechanisms that support collaborative design, construction and learning. This can be done by supporting:

1. Bi-directional use of the Web: Enable and motivate consumers of information to become producers of resources on the Web.
2. Richness of content. Make rich and expressive computational artifacts, such as simulation components and behaving agents, utilizing the Web as a forum of exchange.

The Behavior Exchange is one such forum that achieves that.

5.8.1. *Example: The Behavior Exchange*

The Behavior Exchange (Repenning and Ambach, 1997; Repenning et al., 1999; Repenning et al., 1998), a Web-based repository that enables the sharing of simulation components, namely agents. The Behavior Exchange enables white-box reuse of agents by allowing inspection of agents acquired from the exchange as well as modification of their behavior because the full specification of agents' behaviors comes along with them when they are downloaded (Figure 4.25).

The Behavior Exchange contains two kinds of information: informal and formal. Informal information is not interpreted by the computer. The look of an agent, textual descriptions concerning what the agent does, who created it, why and how it is used belong into the informal information category. Formal information is interpreted by the computer. All the rules that determine the behavior of an agent are considered formal information. The combination of informal and formal information turns these agents into a social currency of exchange. Users produce agents and share them. Other users pick them up and modify them to better fit into their own environment. This reuse mechanism allows a community of users to build and incrementally improve simulation content. The ability to build simulations by combining and modifying agents makes the agent level ideal for supporting collaboration among users, whether they reside in the same physical location or not, and for supporting the scaffolding (Guzdial, 1994) of the simulation creation process.

6. Conclusions

There cannot be one universal EUD tool useful for all possible application contexts. Whether an EUD is useful and gets accepted by an end-user community for a certain type of application depends on a number of factors. The presentation formats used are of secondary relevance. A useful and usable (Fischer, 1987, 1993) EUD tool does not need to be iconic, visual, or textural for that matter. However, one perspective that we do think is universal is the viewpoint of EUD as a learning experience balancing challenges and skills. A variety of scaffolding mechanisms presented in this article can help in making this learning experience more manageable. We have outlined a number of scaffolding mechanisms and extrapolated thirteen design guidelines from our experience with the AgentSheets simulation-authoring environment:

1. Make syntactic errors hard
2. Make syntactic errors impossible
3. Use objects as language elements
4. Make domain-oriented languages for specific EUD
5. Introduce Meta-Domain orientation to deal with general EUD
6. Support incremental development
7. Facilitate decomposable test units
8. Provide multiple views with incremental disclosure
9. Integrate development tool with web services
10. Encourage syntonicity
11. Allow Immersion
12. Scaffold typical designs
13. Build community tools

Acknowledgment

This work has been supported by the National Science Foundation (ITR 0205625, DMI 0233028).

References

Alexander, C., Ishikawa, S., Silverstein, M., Jacobson, M., Fiksdahl-King, I. and Angel, S. (1977). *A Pattern Language: Towns, Buildings, Construction.* New York, NY: Oxford University Press.

Bell, B. and Lewis, C. (1993). ChemTrains: A Language for Creating Behaving Pictures. 1993 IEEE Workshop on Visual Languages, Bergen, Norway, pp. 188–195.

Berne, R.M. and Levy, M.N. (2000). *Principles of Physiology (3rd ed.)*. St. Louis: Mosby.

Blackwell, A. (1996). Metacognitive theories of visual programming: what do we think we are doing? In: *Proceedings of the 1996 IEEE Symposium on Visual Languages*, Boulder, CO, pp. 240–245.

Brand, C. and Rader, C. (1996). How does a visual simulation program support students creating science models? In: *Proceedings of the 1996 IEEE Symposium of Visual Languages*, Boulder, CO, pp. 102–109.

Brand, C., Rader, C., Carlone, H. and Lewis, C. (1998). *Prospects and Challenges for Children Creating Science Models*. Paper presented at the annual meeting of the National Association for Research in Science Teaching, San Diego, CA.

Burnett, M. (1999). Visual Programming. In: J.G. Webster (ed.), *Encyclopedia of Electrical and Electronics Engineering*. New York: John Wiley and Sons Inc.

Burnett, M. and Baker, M. (1994). A classification system for visual programming languages. *Journal of Visual Languages and Computing*, 5(3), 287–300.

Cherry, G., Ioannidou, A., Rader, C., Brand, C. and Repenning, A. (1999). *Simulations for Lifelong Learning*. Atlantic City, NJ: NECC.

Craig, B. (1997). AGES: Agentsheets Genetic Evolutionary Simulations. Unpublished Masters Thesis, University of Colorado, Boulder, CO.

Csikszentmihalyi, M. (1990). Flow: The Psychology of Optimal Experience. New York: Harper Collins Publishers.

Cypher, A. (1993). *Watch What I Do: Programming by Demonstration*. Cambridge, MA: The MIT Press.

diSessa, A. (2000). *Changing Minds: Computers, Learning, and Literacy*. Cambridge, MA: The MIT Press.

Eisenberg, M. and Fischer, G. (1994). Programmable design environments: Integrating end-user programming with domain-oriented assistance. In: *Proceedings of the 1994 ACM CHI Conference*, Boston, MA, pp. 431–437.

Fischer, G. (1987). Making Computers more Useful and more Usable. 2nd International Conference on Human–Computer Interaction, Honolulu, Hawaii.

Fischer, G. (1993). Beyond Human Computer Interaction: Designing Useful and Usable Computational Environments. People and Computers VIII: Proceedings of the HCI'93 Conference, 17–31.

Fischer, G. and Girgenson, A. (1990). End-User Modifiability in Design Environments. CHI '90, Conference on Human Factors in Computing Systems, Seattle, WA, 183–191.

Gamma, E., Helm, R., Johnson, R. and Vlissides, J. (1995). *Design Patterns: Elements of Reusable Object-Oriented Software*. Reading, MA: Addison-Wesley.

Gindling, J., Ioannidou, A., Loh, J., Lokkebo, O. and Repenning, A. (1995). LEGOsheets: A rule-based programming, simulation and manipulation environment for the LEGO programmable brick. In: *Proceeding of Visual Languages*, Darmstadt, Germany, 172–179.

Glinert, E.P. (1987). Out of flatland: Towards 3-d visual programming. IEEE 2nd Fall Joint Computer Conference, 292–299.

Green, T.R.G. (1989). Cognitive Dimensions of Notations. In: *Proceedings of the 5th Conference of the British Computer Society*, Nottingham, pp. 443–460.

Green, T.R.G. and Petre, M. (1996). Usability analysis of visual programming environments: a 'cognitive dimensions' framework. *Journal of Visual Languages and Computing*, 7(2), 131–174.

Guzdial, M. (1994). Software-realized scaffolding to facilitate programming for science learning. *Interactive Learning Environments*, 4(1), 1–44.

Ioannidou, A. (2002). Programmorphosis: Sustained Wizard Support for End-User Programming. Unpublished Ph.D. Thesis, University of Colorado, Boulder.

Ioannidou, A. (2003). Programmorphosis: a Knowledge-Based Approach to End-User Programming. Interact 2003: Bringing the Bits together, Ninth IFIP TC13 International Conference on Human-Computer Interaction, Zürich, Switzerland.

Ioannidou, A., Rader, C., Repenning, A., Lewis, C. and Cherry, G. (2003). Making Constructionism Work in the Classroom. *International Journal of Computers for Mathematical Learning*, **8**, 63–108.

Ioannidou, A. and Repenning, A. (1999). End-User Programmable Simulations. Dr. Dobb's (302 August), 40–48.

Ioannidou, A., Repenning, A. and Zola, J. (1998). Posterboards or Java Applets? International Conference of the Learning Sciences 1998, Atlanta, GA, 152–159.

Jones, C. (1995). End-user programming. *IEEE Computer*, **28**(9), 68–70.

Klann, M. (2003). D1.1 Roadmap: End-User Development: Empowering people to flexibly employ advanced information and communication technology: EUD-Net: End-User Development Network of Excellence.

Lewis, C., Polson, P.G., Wharton, C. and Rieman, J. (1990). Testing a walkthrough methodology for theory-based design of walk-up-and-use interfaces. SIGCHI conference on Human Factors in Computing Systems: Empowering people, Seattle, Washington, USA, 235–242.

Lewis, C. and Rieman, J. (1993). Task-centered User Interface Design—A Practical Introduction. Boulder, CO: A shareware book that can be downloaded from ftp.cs.colorado.edu/pub/cs/distribs/clewis/HCI-Design-Book/.

Lieberman, H. (2001). *Your Wish Is My Command: Programming by Example*. San Francisco, CA: Morgan Kaufmann Publishers.

Nardi, B. (1993). *A Small Matter of Programming*. Cambridge, MA: MIT Press.

Norman, D.A. (1986). *Cognitive Engineering. In User Centered System Design*. Hillsdale, NJ: Lawrence Erlbaum Associates, Publishers, pp. 31–61.

Pane, J.F. and Myers, B.A. (1996). Usability Issues in the Design of Novice Programming Systems (Technical Report No. CMU-CS-96-132). Pittsburg, Pennsylvania: School of Computer Science, Carnegie Mellon University.

Papert, S. (1980). *Mindstorms: Children, Computers and Powerful Ideas*. New York: Basic Books.

Papert, S. (1993). *The Children's Machine*. New York: Basic Books.

Papert, S. and Harel, I. (Eds.). (1993). *Constructionism*. Norwood, NJ: Ablex Publishing Corporation.

Paternò, F. (2003). D1.2 Research Agenda: End-User Development: Empowering people to flexibly employ advanced information and communication technology: EUD-Net: End-User Development Network of Excellence.

"President's Committee of Advisors on Science and Technology" (1997). Report to the President on the Use of Technology to Strengthen K-12 Education in the United States.

Rader, C., Brand, C. and Lewis, C. (1997). Degrees of comprehension: children's understanding of a visual programming environment. In: *Proceedings of the 1997 Conference of Human Factors in Computing Systems*, Atlanta, GA, New York, NY: ACM Press, pp. 351–358.

Rader, C., Cherry, G., Brand, C., Repenning, A. and Lewis, C. (1998). Principles to scaffold mixed textual and iconic end-user programming languages. In: *Proceedings of the 1998 IEEE Symposium of Visual Languages*, Nova Scotia, Canada, Washington, DC: IEEE Computer Society, pp. 187–194.

Repenning, A. (1995). Bending the rules: steps toward semantically enriched graphical rewrite rules. In: *Proceedings of Visual Languages*, Darmstadt, Germany, Washington, DC: IEEE Computer Society, pp. 226–233.

Repenning, A. and Ambach, J. (1996a). Tactile programming: a unified manipulation paradigm supporting program comprehension, composition and sharing. In: *Proceedings of the 1996 IEEE Symposium of Visual Languages*, Boulder, CO, Washington, DC: IEEE Computer Society, pp. 102–109.

Repenning, A. and Ambach, J. (1996b). Visual AgenTalk: Anatomy of a Low Threshold, High Ceiling End User Programming Environment. submitted to Proceedings of UIST.

Repenning, A. and Ambach, J. (1997). The Agentsheets Behavior Exchange: Supporting Social Behavior Processing. CHI 97, Conference on Human Factors in Computing Systems, Extended Abstracts, Atlanta, Georgia, 26–27.

Repenning, A. and Ioannidou, A. (1997). Behavior processors: layers between end-uers and Java Virtual Machines. In: *Proceedings of the 1997 IEEE Symposium of Visual Languages*, Capri, Italy, New York, NY: ACM Press, pp. 402–409.

Repenning, A., Ioannidou, A. and Ambach, J. (1998). Learn to Communicate and Communicate to Learn. *Journal of Interactive Media in Education (JIME)*, **98**(7).

Repenning, A., Ioannidou, A. and Phillips, J. (1999). Collaborative use and design of interactive simulations. In: *Proceedings of Computer Supported Collaborative Learning Conference at Stanford (CSCL'99)*, Mahwah, NJ: Lawrence Erlbaum Associates, pp. 475–487.

Repenning, A., Ioannidou, A., Rausch, M. and Phillips, J. (1998). Using agents as a currency of exchange between end-users. In: *Proceedings of the WebNET 98 World Conference of the WW, Internet, and Intranet,* Orlando, FL, Chesapeake, VA: The WebNET paper was published by the Association of COmputing in Education (AACE), 762–767.

Repenning, A. and Perrone, C. (2000). Programming by Analogous Examples. *Communications of the ACM*, **43**(3), 90–97.

Repenning, A. and Perrone-Smith, C. (2001). Programming by analogous examples. In H. Lieberman (ed.), *Your Wish Is My Command: Programming by Example*, San Francisco, CA: Morgan Kaufmann Publishers, Vol. 43, pp. 90–97.

Repenning, A. and Sumner, T. (1992). Using agentsheets to create a voice dialog design environment. In: *Proceedings of the 1992 ACM/SIGAPP Symposium on Applied Computing*, Kansas City, MO, New York, NY: ACM Press, pp. 1199–1207.

Repenning, A. and Sumner, T. (1995). Agentsheets: A Medium for Creating Domain-Oriented Visual Languages. *IEEE Computer*, **28**(3), 17–25.

Schneider, K. and Repenning, A. (1995). Deceived by ease of use: using paradigmatic applications to build visual design. In: *Proceedings of the 1995 Symposium on Designing Interactive Systems*, Ann Arbor, MI, New York, NY: ACM Press, pp. 177–188.

Simon, H.A. (1981). *The Sciences of the Artificial (2nd ed.)*. Cambridge, MA: MIT Press.

Smith, D.C. (1975). PYGMALION: A Creative Programming Environment (Technical Report No. STAN-CS-75–499): Computer Science Department, Stanford University.

Smith, D.C., Cypher, A. and Spohrer, J. (1994). KidSim: Programming Agents Without a Programming Language. *Communications of the ACM*, **37**(7), 54–68.

Wenglinsky, H. (1998). *Does it Compute? The Relationship Between Educational Technology and Student Achievement in Mathematics*. Princeton, NJ: Educational Testing Service.

Zola, J. and Ioannidou, A. (2000). Learning and Teaching with Interactive Simulations. *Social Education: the Official Journal of National Council for the Social Studies*, **64**(3), 142–145.

Chapter 5

An Integrated Software Engineering Approach
for End-User Programmers

MARGARET BURNETT[1], GREGG ROTHERMEL[2] and CURTIS COOK[1]
[1] *School of Electrical Engineering and Computer Science, Oregon State University, Corvallis, Oregon, USA, burnett@cs.orst.edu, cook@cs.orst.edu*
[2] *Department of Computer Science and Engineering, University of Nebraska, Lincoln, Nebraska, USA, grother@cse.unl.edu*

Abstract. End-user programming has become the most common form of programming in use today. Despite this growth, there has been little investigation into the correctness of the programs end-users create. We have been investigating ways to address this problem via a holistic approach we call *end-user software engineering*. The concept is to bring support for aspects of software development that happen beyond the "coding" stage—such as testing and debugging—together into the support that already exists for incremental, interactive programming by end-users. In this chapter, we present our progress on three aspects of end-user software engineering: systematic "white box" testing assisted by automatic test generation, assertions in a form of postconditions that also serve as preconditions, and fault localization. We also present our strategy for motivating end-user programmers to make use of the end-user software engineering devices.

1. Introduction

There has been considerable work in empowering end-users to be able to write their own programs, and as a result, end-users are indeed doing so. In fact, the number of end-user programmers—creating programs using such devices as special-purpose scripting languages, multimedia and web authoring languages, and spreadsheets—is expected to reach 55 million by 2005 in the U.S. alone (Boehm et al., 2000). Unfortunately, evidence from the spreadsheet paradigm, the most widely used of the end-user programming languages, abounds that end-user programmers are extremely prone to introducing faults[1] into their programs (Panko, 1998). This problem is serious, because although some end-users' programs are simply explorations and scratch pad calculations, others can be quite important to their personal or business livelihood, such as programs for calculating income taxes, e-commerce web pages, and financial forecasting.

We would like to reduce the fault rate in the end-user programs that are important to the user. Although classical software engineering methodologies are not a panacea, there are several that are known to help reduce programming faults, and it would be useful to incorporate some of those successes in end-user programming. Toward

---

[1] Following standard terminology, in this chapter we use the term "failure" to mean an incorrect output value given the inputs, and the term "fault" to mean the incorrect part of the program (formula) that caused the failure.

Henry Lieberman et al. (eds.), End User Development, 87–113.
© 2006 *Springer.*

this end, we have been working on a vision we call *end-user software engineering*, a holistic approach to end-user software development tasks beyond program entry. Its goal is to bring some of the gains from the software engineering community to end-user programming environments, *without* requiring training or even interest in traditional software engineering techniques.

Our approach to end-user software engineering draws from the traditional software engineering methodologies and programming language literature to devise ways for the system to take on much of the software engineering reasoning, and draws from HCI to find ways to effectively collaborate with the user about the results of this reasoning. End-user software engineering is a highly integrated and incremental concept of software engineering support for end-users. Hence, its components are not individual tools, each with a button that can be separately invoked, but rather a blend of knowledge sources that come together seamlessly. At present there are three components that have been blended in, but the overall vision is not restricted to any particular set of components. A continually evolving prototype of the end-user software engineering concept exists for Forms/3 (Burnett et al., 2001a), a research language that follows the spreadsheet paradigm. The components we have so far blended into Forms/3 involve (1) systematic testing, (2) assertions, and (3) fault localization. Portions of the concept have also been extended to the dataflow paradigm (Karam and Smedley, 2001) and to the screen transition paradigm (Brown et al., 2003).

2. Related Work

The software engineering research community's work regarding testing, assertions, and fault localization lies at the heart of our approach, but the prerequisite knowledge required to use traditional software engineering approaches is not a good match for end-users' skills. Further, the algorithms behind traditional approaches do not usually allow the immediate semantic feedback end-user environments generally provide. These two factors are the reasons it would not be viable to simply import traditional software engineering techniques into an end-user programming environment.

Programming is a collection of problem-solving activities, and our goal is to help end-users in these activities. Hence, we draw heavily on HCI research about human problem-solving needs. The HCI research with the greatest influence on our work so far has been Blackwell's theory of Attention Investment (Blackwell, 2002), Green et al.'s work on Cognitive Dimensions (Green and Petre, 1996), Pane et al.'s empirical work (Pane et al., 2002), and psychologists' findings about how curiosity relates to problem-solving behavior (Lowenstein, 1994). Other strong influences have come from the extensive work on end-user and visual programming languages (e.g., Heger et al., 1998; Igarashi et al., 1998; Lieberman, 2001; McDaniel and Myers, 1999; Nardi, 1993; Repenning and Ioannidou, 1997).

Since end-user software engineering is tightly intertwined with the programming process, it feeds into and draws from the design of languages themselves. For example, immediate visual feedback about semantics is expected in end-user programming, and any software engineering methods that we introduce must be able to reason about the source code efficiently enough to maintain this characteristic. Classic programming language research has contributed to our design of algorithms that provide feedback efficiently, so as to satisfy this constraint. For example, in the language in which we prototype our work, we rely extensively on lazy evaluation (Henderson and Morris, 1976) and lazy memorization (Hughes, 1985) to keep the incremental costs of each user action small.

In the arena of research into end-user software development, most work to date has concentrated primarily on the "programming" phase (i.e., assisting the user in the process of creating a program). However, work has begun to emerge with the goal of assisting end-users in assessing or improving the correctness of their programs. For example, there are several interactive visual approaches related to program comprehension for debugging purposes for both professional and end-user programmers that have made important contributions in this direction. ZStep (Lieberman and Fry, 1998) provides visualizations of the correspondences between static program code and dynamic program execution. ZStep also offers a navigable visualization execution history that is similar to features found in some visual programming languages such as KidSim/Cocoa/Stagecast (Heger et al., 1998) and Forms/3 (Burnett et al., 2001a). S2 (Sajanieme, 2000) provides a visual auditing feature in Excel 7.0: similar groups of cells are recognized and shaded based upon formula similarity, and are then connected with arrows to show dataflow. This technique builds upon the Arrow Tool, a dataflow visualization device proposed earlier (Davis, 1996).

More recently, work aimed particularly at aiding end-user programmers in some software engineering tasks is beginning to emerge. Myers and Ko (2003) recently proposed research in assisting users in the debugging of code for event based languages. Woodstein, an early prototype of an e-commerce debugging tool, is an emerging approach aimed at end-user debugging of actions that go awry in e-commerce transactions (Wagner and Lieberman, 2003). Outlier finding (Miller and Myers, 2001) is a method of using statistical analysis and interactive techniques to direct end-user programmers' attention to potentially problematic areas during automation tasks. In this work, outlier finding is combined with visual cues to indicate abnormal situations while performing search and replace or simultaneous editing tasks. Raz et al. (2002) also use outlier finding, but in the setting of a particular type of end-user programs, namely web programs that incorporate on-line data feeds. Tools have also been devised to aid spreadsheet users in dataflow visualization and editing tasks (e.g., Igarashi et al., 1998). reMIND+ (Carr, 2003) is a visual end-user programming language with support for reusable code and type checking. reMIND+ also provides a hierarchical flow diagram for increased program understanding. There is also some investigation into requirements specification by end-users; early work in this direction is described in (Nardi, 1993), and there is more recent work on deriving models from informal scenarios (Paterno and Mancini, 1999).

3. Wysiwyt Testing

One of the components of end-user software engineering is the *What You See Is What You Test (WYSIWYT)* methodology for testing (Burnett et al., 2002; Rothermel et al.,

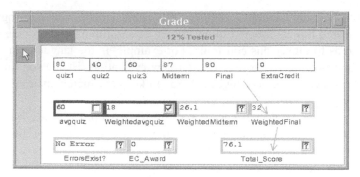

Figure 5.1. An example of WYSIWYT in the Forms/3 spreadsheet language.

1998, 2001). WYSIWYT incrementally tracks test adequacy as users incrementally edit, test, and debug their formulas as their programs evolve. All testing-related information is kept up-to-date at all times, and is communicated via the spreadsheet itself through integrated visualization devices.

For example, Figure 5.1 presents an example of WYSIWYT in Forms/3.[2] In WYSIWYT, untested spreadsheet output (i.e., non-constant) cells are given a red border (light gray in this chapter), indicating that the cell is untested. For example, the EC_Award cell has never been tested; hence, its border is red (light gray). The borders of such cells remain red until they become more "tested."

Whenever a user notices that her real or experimental input values are resulting in correct outputs, she can place a checkmark ($\sqrt{}$) in the decision box at the corner of the cells she observes to be correct: this constitutes a successful *test*. These checkmarks increase the "testedness" of a cell, which is reflected by adding more blue to the cell's border (more black in this chapter). For example, the user has checked off the Weighte-davgquiz cell in Figure 5.1, which is enough to fully test this cell, thereby changing its border from red to blue (light gray to black). Further, because a correct value in a cell C depends on the correctness of the cells contributing to C, these contributing cells participate in C's test. Consequently, in this example the border of cell avgquiz has also turned blue (black).

Although users may not realize it, the testedness colors that result from placing checkmarks reflect the use of a dataflow test adequacy criterion that measures the interrelationships in the source code that have been covered by the users' tests. Testing a program "perfectly" (i.e., well enough to detect all possible faults) is not possible without an infinite number of test cases for most programs, so a way is needed to decide when to stop testing. Serving this need, a *test adequacy criterion* is a quantitative measure used to define when a program has been tested "enough." In the spreadsheet

---

[2] In the figures, cells are not locked into a grid. One difference between Forms/3 and commercial spreadsheet systems is that Forms/3 allows "free-floating" cells rather than requiring all cells to reside in grids. (This difference also exists in some other research spreadsheet systems, including Forms/2 (Ambler and Burnett, 1990) and NoPumpG (Lewis, 1990).)

paradigm, we say that a cell is fully tested if all its interrelationships (as defined below) have been covered by tests, and those cells are the ones whose borders are painted blue (black). If only some have been covered, the cell is partially tested, and these partially tested cells would have borders in varying shades of purple (shades of gray). Also, to provide some guidance about how to make additional testing progress, if checking off a particular value will increase coverage, that cell's decision box contains a "?".

3.1. BEHIND THE SCENES: THE BASIS FOR WYSIWYT'S REASONING

In order to precisely define a test adequacy criterion for use in spreadsheets, we defined an abstract model for spreadsheets, called a *cell relation graph* (CRG). We use CRGs to model those spreadsheets and to define and support testing. A CRG is a pair (V, E), where V is a set of *formula graphs*, and E is a set of directed edges called *cell dependence edges* connecting pairs of elements in V. Each formula graph in V represents the formula for a cell, and each edge in E models the data dependencies between a pair of cells. In the basic form of WYSIWYT, there is one formula graph for each cell in the spreadsheet.[3] Each formula graph models flow of control within a cell's formula, and is comparable to a control flow graph representing a procedure in an imperative program (Aho et al., 1986; Rapps and Weyuker, 1985). Thus, a formula graph is a set of nodes and edges. The nodes in a formula graph consist of an *entry node* modeling initiation of the associated formula's execution, an *exit node* modeling termination of that formula's execution, and one or more *predicate nodes* or *computation nodes*, modeling execution of if-expressions' predicate tests and all other computational expressions, respectively. The edges in a formula graph model control flow between pairs of formula graph nodes. The two out-edges from each predicate node are labeled with the values (one true, one false) to which the conditional expression in the associated predicate must evaluate for that particular edge to be taken.

Using the CRG model, we defined a test adequacy criterion for spreadsheets, which we refer to as the *du-adequacy criterion*.We summarize it briefly here; a full formal treatment has been provided elsewhere (Rothermel et al., 2001). The du-adequacy criterion is a type of dataflow adequacy criterion (Duesterwald et al., 1992; Frankl and Weyuker, 1988; Laski and Korel, 1993; Rapps and Weyuker, 1985). Such criteria relate test adequacy to interrelationships between definitions and uses of variables in source code. In spreadsheets, cells play the role of variables; a *definition* of cell C is a node in the formula graph for C representing an expression that defines C, and a *use* of cell C is either a *computational use* (a non-predicate node that refers to C) or a *predicate use* (an out-edge from a predicate node that refers to C). The interrelationships between these definitions and uses are termed *definition-use associations*, abbreviated *du-associations*. Under the du-adequacy criterion, cell C is said to have been *adequately tested* (*covered*) when all of the du-associations whose uses occur in C have been *exercised* by at least one test: that is, where inputs have been found that cause the

---

[3] WYSIWYT has also been extended to reason about multiple cells sharing a single formula (Burnett et al., 2001b, 2002), but we will not discuss these extensions in this chapter.

expressions associated with both the definitions and uses to be executed, and where this execution produces a value in some cell that is pronounced "correct" by a user validation. [The closest analogue to this criterion in the literature on testing imperative programs is the *output-influencing-All-du* dataflow adequacy criterion (Duesterwald et al., 1992), a variant of the *all-uses* criterion (Rapps and Weyuker, 1985).] In this model, a *test* is a user decision as to whether a particular cell contains the correct value, given the input cells' values upon which it depends.

To facilitate understanding the structure of a spreadsheet, Forms/3 allows the user to pop up dataflow arrows between cells—in Figure 5.1 the user has triggered the dataflow arrows for the WeightedFinal cell—and even between subexpressions within cell formulas (not shown). The system refers to these as interrelationships in its pop-up tool tips, but the tie to the CRG model is that dataflow arrows between two cells depict the presence of du-associations between those cells. Further, if formulas have been opened on the display (not shown in this figure), the dataflow arrows operate at the granularity of relationships among subexpressions, thus making the du-associations explicit. Dataflow arrows use the same testedness colorization as the cell borders do, so that the users can see exactly which relationships (du-associations) have been tested and which have not. Dataflow arrows for any cell can be displayed and hidden at will by the user.

3.2. "HELP ME TEST"

Empirical work has shown that the WYSIWYT methodology is helpful to end-users[4] (Krishna et al., 2001) but, as presented so far, the WYSIWYT methodology relies on the intuitions of spreadsheet users to devise test cases for their spreadsheets. Even with additional visual devices such as colored arrows between formula subexpressions to indicate the relationships remaining to be covered, after doing a certain amount of testing, users sometimes find it difficult to think of suitable test values that will cover the as-yet-untested relationships. At this point, they can invoke the *Help Me Test (HMT)* feature (Fisher et al., 2002a), to automate the task of input selection.

To see how the approach works, suppose a user creating the spreadsheet in Figure 1 desires help conjuring up test cases that can increase the testedness of that spreadsheet. With HMT, the user selects any combination of cells or dataflow arrows on the visible display (or, selecting none, signals interest in the entire spreadsheet), and then pushes the "Help Me Test" button on the environment's toolbar.

At this point, the underlying system responds, attempting to generate a test case that will help increase coverage in the user's area of interest. To do this, the system first calculates the set of du-associations that have not yet been tested, that have endpoints within the user's specified area of interest. These du-associations are potential targets for

---

[4] The particular study referenced involved business students experienced with spreadsheets. Their task was to add new features to a given spreadsheet. We have conducted more than a dozen empirical studies related to the end-user software engineering devices described in this chapter. The participants were usually business students, and the tasks were usually testing, debugging, or maintenance. Details can be found at http://www.engr.oregonstate.edu/~burnett/ITR2000/empirical.html.

test generation. Next, the system calculates the set of input cells (cells whose formulas are simply constant values, thus serving as the sources of values) that can potentially cause one or more of the target du-associations to be exercised, that is, cause the defining and using subexpressions associated with those du-associations to both be evaluated. Given these two sets of entities (relevant du-associations and relevant input cells) the system can attempt to generate a test case, by manipulating input cells until one or more relevant du-associations can be covered. To perform the manipulations that find the actual test values, our system uses an algorithm adapted from Ferguson and Korel's "Chaining Technique" (Ferguson and Korel, 1996).

At any point during these manipulations, if the target du-association is exercised, the system leaves the newly generated values in the cells, and the user can now validate cell values in their area of interest. Alternatively, if they do not like these values (perhaps because the correctness of the particular values is difficult to judge), they can run HMT again to generate different ones. If the process exhausts all possibilities, or reaches an internal time limit, the system informs the user that it has not succeeded. (There is also a "Stop" button available, if the user decides HMT is taking too long.)

Our empirical studies of HMT show that it succeeds in generating test values a high percentage of the time; in one study its success rate always exceeded 94%, and in most cases exceeded 99%. Surprisingly, providing estimates of the ranges in which input values are expected to fall does not improve HMT's success rate. Also, comparison of HMT to an alternative technique that randomly generates values shows that in all cases HMT was significantly more effective. Response times for HMT were also typically reasonable: in 81% of the trials considered, HMT succeeded in less than 4 seconds, and in 88% of the trials it succeeded in less than 10 seconds. Here, providing range values for input cells can help: with such values available, 91% of responses occurred within 4 seconds, and 96% within 10 seconds.

HMT's efforts to find suitable test values are somewhat transparent to the user—that is, they can see the values it is considering spinning by. The transparency of its behavior turns out to contribute to the understandability of both HMT and assertions. We will return to the tie between HMT and assertions after the next section, which introduces assertions.

4. Assertions

When creating a spreadsheet, the user has a mental model of how it should operate. One approximation of this model is the formulas they enter. These formulas, however, are only one representation of the user's model of the problem and its solution: they contain information on how to generate the desired result, but do not provide ways for the user to cross-check the computations or to communicate other properties. Traditionally, assertions (preconditions, postconditions, and invariants) have fulfilled this need for professional programmers: they provide a method for making explicit the properties the programmers expect of their program logic, to reason about the integrity of their logic, and to catch exceptions. We have devised an approach to assertions (Burnett et al.,

2003; Wilson et al., 2003) that attempts to provide these same advantages to end-user programmers.

Our assertions are composed of Boolean expressions, and reason about program variables' values (spreadsheet cell values, in the spreadsheet paradigm). Assertions are "owned" by a spreadsheet cell. Cell X's assertion is the postcondition of X's formula. X's postconditions are also preconditions to the formulas of all other cells that reference X in their formulas, either directly or transitively through a network of references.

To illustrate the amount of power we have chosen to support with our assertions, we present them first via an abstract syntax. An *assertion* on cell N is of the form:

(N, {*and-assertions*}), where:
each *and-assertion* is a set of *or-assertions*,
each *or-assertion* is a set of (*unary-relation*, *value-expression*) and (*binary-relation*,
    value-expression-pair) tuples,
each *unary-relation* $\in \{=, <, \leq, >, \geq\}$,
each *binary-relation* $\in \{$to-closed, to-open, to-openleft, to-openright$\}$,
each *value-expression* is a valid formula expression in the spreadsheet language,
each *value-expression-pair* is two *value-expressions*.

For example, an assertion denoted using this syntax as $(N, \{\{$(to-closed, 10, 20), $(=3)\}, \{= X2\}\})$ means that N must either be between 10 and 20 or equal to 3; and must also equal the value of cell $X2$.

This abstract syntax is powerful enough to support a large subset of traditional assertions that reason about values of program variables. This abstract syntax follows Conjunctive Normal Form (CNF): each cell's collection of and-assertions, which in turn is composed of or-assertions, is intended to evaluate to true, and hence a spreadsheet's assertion is simply an "and" composition of all cells' assertions.

The abstract syntax just presented is not likely to be useful to end-users. Thus, we have developed two concrete syntaxes corresponding to it: one primarily graphical and one textual. The user can work in either or both as desired.

The graphical concrete syntax, depicted in Figure 5.2, supports all of the abstract syntax (but in the current prototype implementation, value-expressions have been

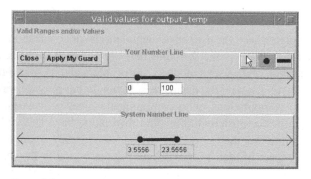

Figure 5.2. Two (conflicting) assertions "and" ed on the same cell.

U_EffMidterm

Figure 5.3. Two assertions in the textual syntax.

implemented for only constants). The example is a representation of (output_temp, {{(to-closed, 0, 100)}, {(to-closed, 3.5556, 23.5556)}}). A thick dot is a data point in an ordinal domain; it implements "=". The thick horizontal lines are ranges in the domain, implementing "to-closed" when connected to dots. A range with no lower (upper) bound implements "$\leq$" ("$\geq$"). It is also possible to halve a dot, which changes from closed ranges to open ranges, "$\leq$" to "<", and so on. Disconnected points and ranges represent the or-assertions. Multiple assertions vertically in the same window represent the and-assertions. (We will expand upon how assertions get in and what it means to be "conflicting" shortly.)

The textual concrete syntax, depicted in Figure 5.3, is more compact, and supports the same operators as the graphical syntax. Or-assertions are represented with comma separators on the same line (not shown), while and-assertions are represented as assertions stacked up on the same cell, as in Figure 5.3. There is also an "except" modifier that supports the "open" versions of "to" (e.g., "0 to 10 except 10").

Our system does not use the term "assertion" in communicating with users. Instead, assertions are termed *guards*, so named because they guard the correctness of the cells. The user opens a "guard tab" above a cell to display the assertion using the textual syntax, or double-clicks the tab t open the graphical window. Although both syntaxes represent assertions as points and ranges, note that points and ranges, with the composition mechanisms just described, are enough to express the entire abstract syntax.

Note that although "and" and "or" are represented, they are not explicit operators in the syntaxes. This is a deliberate choice, and is due to Pane et al.'s research, which showed that end-users are not successful at using "and" and "or" explicitly as logical operators (Pane et al., 2002).

Assertions protect cells from "bad" values, i.e., from values that disagree with the assertion(s). Whenever a user enters an assertion (a *user-entered assertion*) it is propagated as far as possible through formulas, creating *system-generated assertions* on downstream cells. The user can use tabs (not shown) to pop up the assertions, as has been done on all cells in Figure 5.4. The stick figure icons on cells Monday, Tuesday, . . . identify the user-entered assertions. The computer icon on cell WDay_Hrs identifies a system-generated assertion, which the system generated by propagating the assertions from Monday, Tuesday, . . . , through WDay_Hrs's formula. A cell with both a system-generated and user-entered assertion is in a conflict state (has an *assertion conflict*) if the two assertions do not match exactly. The system communicates an assertion conflict by circling the conflicting assertions in red. In Figure 5.4 the conflict on WDay_Hrs is due to a fault in the formula (there is an extra Tuesday). Since the cell's

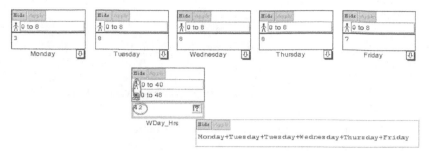

Figure 5.4. In the Forms/3 environment, cell formulas can be displayed via the tab at the lower right hand side of the cell, as has been done in WDay_Hrs. The assertions on each cell have been popped up at the top of the cells.

value in WDay_Hrs is inconsistent with the assertions on that cell (termed a *value violation*), the value is also circled. When conflicts or violations occur, there may be either a fault in the program (spreadsheet formulas) or an error in the assertions. In Burnett et al. (2003), we report the results of an empirical study that measured whether assertions contributed to end-user programmers' debugging effectiveness; the results were that the participants using assertions were significantly more effective at debugging than were participants without access to assertions.

4.1. ASSERTIONS: DETAILED EXAMPLE

We close this section by presenting a detailed example of our prototype assertion mechanism. Figure 5.5 (top left) shows a portion of a Forms/3 spreadsheet that converts temperatures in degrees Fahrenheit to degrees Celsius. The input_temp cell has a constant value of 200 in its formula and is displaying the same value. There is a user assertion on this cell that limits the value of the cell to between 32 and 212. The formulas of the a, b, and output_temp cells each perform one step in the conversion, first subtracting 32 from the original value, then multiplying by five and finally dividing by nine. The a and b cells have assertions generated by the system (as indicated by the computer icon) which reflect the propagation of the user assertion on the input_temp cell through their formulas. The spreadsheet's creator has told the system that the output_temp cell should range from 0 to 100, and the system has agreed with this range. This agreement was determined by propagating the user assertion on the input_temp cell through the formulas and comparing it with the user assertion on the output_temp cell.

Suppose a user has decided to change the direction of the conversion and make the spreadsheet convert from degrees Celsius to degrees Fahrenheit. A summary follows of the behavior shown by an end-user in this situation in a think-aloud study we conducted early in our design of the approach (Wallace et al., 2002). The quotes are from a recording of that user's commentary.

First, the user changed the assertion on input_temp to range from 0 to 100. This caused several red violation ovals to appear, as in Figure 5.5 (top right), because the

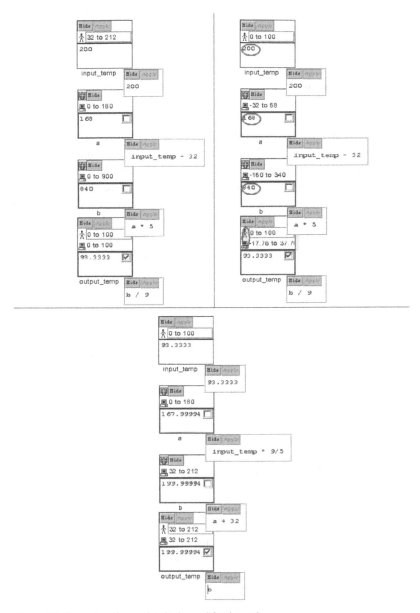

Figure 5.5. Example at three points in the modification task.

values in input_temp, a, b, and output_temp were now out of range and the assertion
on output_temp was now in conflict with the previously specified assertion for that
cell. The user decided "that's OK for now," and changed the value in input_temp from
200 to 75 ("something between zero and 100"), and then set the formula in cell a to
"input_temp* 9/5" and the formula in cell b to "a + 32".

At this point, the assertion on cell b had a range from 32 to 212. Because the user combined two computation steps in cell a's formula (multiplication and division), the correct value appeared in cell b, but not in output_temp (which still had the formula "b/9"). The user now chose to deal with the assertion conflict on output_temp, and clicked on the guard icon to view the details in the graphical syntax (refer back to Figure 5.2).

Seeing that the Forms/3 assertion specified 3.5556 to 23.556, the user stated "There's got to be something wrong with the formula" and edited output_temp's formula, making it a reference to cell b. This resulted in the value of output_temp being correct, although a conflict still existed because the previous user assertion remained at 0 to 100. Turning to the graphical syntax window, upon seeing that Forms/3's assertion was the expected 32 to 212, the user changed the user assertion to agree, which removed the final conflict. Finally, the user tested by trying 93.3333, the original output value, to see if it resulted in approximately 200, the original input value. The results were as desired, and the user checked off the cell to notify the system of the decision that the value was correct, as in Figure 5.5 (bottom).

5. If we Build it, will they Come?

Of course, the benefits of assertions can be realized only if users can be enticed into entering their own assertions and acting on them. In the studies on assertions alluded to above, we introduced assertions to our experiment participants via short tutorial sessions. But, without such introductions, will users choose to enter assertions?

Blackwell's model of attention investment (Blackwell, 2002) is one model of user problem-solving behavior that suggests users will not want to enter assertions. The model considers the costs, benefits, and risks users weigh in deciding how to complete a task. For example, if the ultimate goal is to forecast a budget using a spreadsheet, then exploring an unknown feature such as assertions has cost, benefit, and risk. The cost is figuring out what assertions do and how to succeed at them. The benefit of finding faults may not be clear until long *after* the user proceeds in this direction. The risk is that going down this path will be a waste of time or, worse, will leave the spreadsheet in a state from which it is hard to recover. What the model of attention investment implies is that it is necessary not only for our strategy to make the users curious about assertions, but also to make the benefits of using assertions clear from the outset.

In this section, we describe a strategy for doing so. We describe the strategy in the context of assertions, but we intend to eventually generalize it as a way to motivate users toward *any* appropriate software engineering devices in the environment. We term our strategy the *Surprise-Explain-Reward* strategy (Wilson et al., 2003). The strategy draws on the model of attention investment and on findings about the psychology of curiosity. As the name suggests, the strategy consists of three components: a collection of surprises, a collection of rewards, and an explanation component pointing out the links from the surprises to the rewards.

Research about curiosity [surveyed in (Lowenstein, 1994)], points out that if an information gap is illustrated to the user, the user's curiosity about the subject of the illustrated gap may increase, potentially causing them to search for an explanation. Without challenging their assumptions and arousing their curiosity, as the information-gap perspective explains and much empirical programming literature bears out (e.g., Krishna et al., 2001; Panko, 1998; Wilcox et al., 1997), users are likely to assume that their programs are more correct than is warranted. This is the motivation for the first component of our Surprise-Explain-Reward strategy: to arouse users' curiosity, through surprise, enough that they search for explanations. Thus, the first component of our strategy might be characterized as following a "principle of *most* astonishment."

The strategy is used in two situations: first to entice users to use the features, and later to help them benefit from the features. In the first situation, the strategy attempts to surprise the user into entering assertions. If the user becomes curious about the assertions, she can find out more via an explanation system. If the strategy causes the user to act by entering an assertion, the second situation becomes possible. This time, the surprise comes when an assertion identifies a potentially faulty cell formula. (Actually, the assertion identifies a failure rather than a fault, but since even intermediate cells in the dataflow chain can be monitored by assertions, the probability of the fault and failure being in the same cell is greater than would be the case if only final outputs were monitored.) The users can again look to explanations to explain the surprise and suggest possible actions. If the user successfully fixes the fault called to their attention by the assertion, they see that the program's behavior is more correct, a clear reward for using assertions. In the remainder of this section we expand upon the approach we have just summarized.

5.1. SURPRISES

The first step of our strategy is to generate a meaningful surprise for the user. That is, the system needs to violate the user's assumptions about their program. We have devised a pseudo-assertion for this purpose, termed an *HMT assertion* because it is produced by the "Help Me Test" (HMT) device described earlier. An HMT assertion is a guess at a possible assertion for a particular cell.

The guesses are actually reflections of HMT's behavior. That is, they report the range of HMT's attempts to find suitable test cases. For example, in Figure 5.6 (which is part of the weekly payroll program of Figure 5.4), the HMT assertion for cell Monday is "-1 to 0." This indicates that HMT has considered values for Monday between -1 and 0 before it settled upon its current value of -1. If HMT is invoked again it might consider a different selection of values for Monday such as 1 and 2, which would widen the HMT assertion to "-1 to 2." (Note that this tie between HMT's test case generation behavior and the assertions it guesses creates a reward opportunity for manipulating the assertions.) The primary job of the HMT assertions is to surprise the user, and thereby to generate user interest in "real" assertions (i.e., user-entered and system-generated

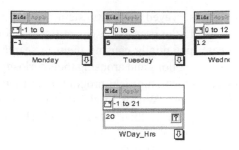

Figure 5.6. HMT has guessed assertions for the input cells (top row). (Since HMT changed the values of the input cells, they are highlighted with a thicker border.) The guesses then propagated through WDay_Hrs's formula to create an HMT assertion for that cell as well.

assertions). Thus, HMT assertions are—by design—usually bad guesses. The worse the guess, the bigger the surprise.

HMT assertions exist to surprise and thereby to create curiosity. For example, in Figure 5.4, the user may expect values for Monday to range from 0 to 8, and rightly so, because employees cannot be credited with fewer than 0 or more than 8 hours per day. Since HMT was not aware of this, it attempted inputs less than zero. Thus, the HMT assertion for Monday probably violates the user's assumptions about the correct values for Monday. This is precisely what triggers curiosity according to the information-gap perspective.

Once an HMT assertion has been generated, it behaves as any assertion does. Not only does it propagate, but if a value arrives that violates it, the value is circled in red. This happens even as HMT is working to generate values. Thus, red circles sometimes appear as HMT is doing its transparent search for suitable test cases. These red circles are another use of surprise.

It is important to note that, although our strategy rests on surprise, it does not attempt to rearrange the user's work priorities by requiring users to do anything about the surprises. No dialog boxes are presented and there are no modes. HMT assertions are a passive feedback system; they try to win user attention but do not require it. If users choose to follow up, they can mouse over the assertions to receive an explanation, which explicitly mentions the rewards for pursuing assertions. In a behavior study we performed (Wilson et al., 2003), users did not always attend to HMT assertions for the first several minutes of their task; thus it appears that the amount of visual activity is reasonable for requesting but not demanding attention. However, almost all of them did eventually turn their attention to assertions, and when they did, they used assertions effectively.

5.2. EXPLANATIONS

As the above paragraph implies, our strategy's explanation component rests upon self-directed exploration, following in the direction advocated by several researchers who have empirically studied this direction and have found it to result in superior learning

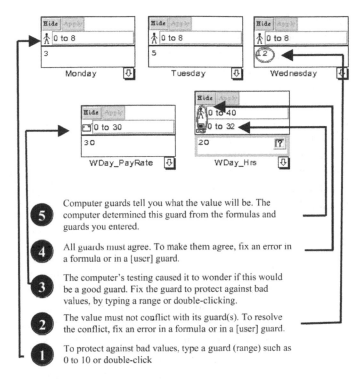

Figure 5.7. Five explanation examples.

and performance of computer tasks (e.g., Carroll and Mack, 1984; Wulf and Golombek, 2001). To support self-directed exploration, in our strategy a feature that surprises a user must inform the user. As the second component of our Surprise-Explain-Reward strategy, we devised an on-demand explanation system structured around each object that might arouse curiosity. Users can begin exploring the object by viewing its explanation, on demand, in a low-cost way via tool tips.

For example, when a user mouses over an HMT assertion they receive explanation 3 in Figure 5.7. The explanation describes the semantics: the computer was responsible for creating this assertion, and the assertion was a product of the computer's testing. The end of the explanation suggests a possible action for the user to try (fixing the assertion) and specifies a potential reward (protecting against bad values).

Note that the computer "wonders" about this assertion. This makes explicit that the HMT assertion may not be correct and that the computer would like the user's advice. Previous empirical work has revealed that some users think the computer is always correct (e.g., Beckwith et al., 2002). Thus it is important to emphasize the tentative nature of the HMT assertions.

The explanation system spans all the objects in the environment. In general, the three main components of explanations include: the semantics of the object, suggested action(s) if any, and the reward. Including the semantics, action, and reward as part of the explanation are not arbitrary choices. Regarding semantics, although many help systems for end-users focus mostly on syntax, a study assessing how end-users learn to use spreadsheets found that the successful users focused more on the semantics of the spreadsheet than on syntax (Reimann and Neubert, 2000). Regarding actions, Reimann and Neubert are among those who have examined learning by exploration. They point out that users (novices or experts) often form sub-goals using clues in the environment. The actions in the explanations suggest such sub-goals. Getting the user to take action in order to learn is, in fact, a principle of the minimalist model of instruction (Carroll and Mack, 1984; Rosson and Seals, 2001; Seals et al., 2002). Regarding reward, the attention investment model emphasizes the fact that the suggested action will cost the user effort and that, unless the potential rewards are made clear, users may not be able to make an informed decision about whether or not to expend the effort.

5.3. REWARDS

When the user edits an HMT assertion to create a user-entered assertion, there are three types of short-term rewards that can follow. There is also a fourth, longer term reward, namely the bridge to "real" assertions and their long-term rewards.

The first reward, which visibly occurs in some situations, is input value validation. This reward can occur immediately when the user edits an HMT assertion. Consider again cell Monday in Figure 5.5. Suppose the user notices the HMT assertion, reads explanation 3 from Figure 5.7 and, deciding to take the explanation's advice to fix the assertion, changes it to "0 to 8." (The HMT assertion helps show how to succeed by acting as a template, exemplifying assertion syntax.) Despite the assertion entry, the cell's *value* is still −1, and the system circles the value, since it is now in violation with its assertion. Thus, by taking the advice of the system the user has been immediately rewarded: the system is indeed "protect(ing) against bad values."

The second reward always occurs. Once a user places an assertion on an input cell, the behavior of HMT changes to honor the assertion. Continuing the previous example, once cell Monday has the assertion "0 to 8" and the user runs HMT again, HMT will always choose values satisfying the assertion. Since HMT's "thought process" is displayed as it mulls over values to choose, this behavior change is noticeable to some users. Since HMT's selected values can seem odd from the user's perspective, given their knowledge of the program's purpose, getting HMT to choose sensible input values is rewarding if noticed. In our empirical work, a few of the participants' comments showed that they not only noticed this tie but that the tie was what motivated them to use assertions.

The third reward also pertains to changes in HMT's behavior. HMT becomes an aggressive seeker of test values that will expose faults. As other test generators in the software engineering community have done (e.g., Korel and Al-Yami, 1996), HMT attempts to violate user-entered or system-generated assertions. This behavior is focused on non-input cells (i.e., cells that have formulas instead of constant values), and potentially creates a value violation. A value violation on a non-constant cell indicates one of three things: an erroneous assertion, a situation in which the program could fail given inappropriate values in upstream input cells not protected by assertions, or the presence of a faulty formula. For example, for cell WDay_Hrs, HMT will attempt to violate the assertion "0 to 40" by looking for values in the inputs contributing to WDay_Hrs that produce a value violation. When HMT's pursuit of faults succeeds, the user is not only rewarded, but also is probably surprised at the presence of the heretofore unnoticed fault, leading to a longer term use of the Surprise-Explain-Reward strategy.

HMT assertions are intended to help users learn and appreciate assertions, but after that goal has been accomplished, some users will not need HMT's guessed assertions. They will have learned how to enter assertions, regardless of whether HMT guesses assertions on the cells they wish to protect. The Surprise-Explain-Reward strategy carries over to a longer term, to help maintain correctness.

Assertions can lead to three kinds of surprises, and these surprises are themselves rewards, since they mean a fault has been semi-automatically identified. First, the value violations are surprises. As already discussed, they identify faults or assertion errors, and are circled in red. Second, assertion conflicts are surprises. As explained earlier, assertion conflicts arise when the system's propagating the user-entered assertions through formulas produce system-generated assertions that disagree with user-entered assertions. Like value violations, they are circled in red (as in WDay_Hrs in Figure 5.4 and Figure 5.7) and indicate faults or assertion errors. Third, the system-generated assertions might "look wrong" to the user.

Our behavior study, which is detailed in Wilson et al. (2003), provided two types of evidence that the rewards were indeed sufficient to convince the participants of the value of assertions. The strongest and most general is the fact that, when participants used assertions once, they used them again. (The mean was 18 assertions per participant.) Additional evidence is that, although participants did not enter assertions until almost 14 minutes (mean) into the first task, by the second task they began entering assertions much earlier.[5] In fact, 9 of the 16 users (56%) entered assertions within the first minute after beginning the second task. From this it seems clear that after users became familiar with assertions during the first task, they had learned to recognize their value by the second task. Further, all introduction to the assertions took place through the Surprise-Explain-Reward strategy itself: our experiment's tutorial never mentioned assertions or gave any insights into what they were or how to use them.

6. Fault Localization

Given the explicit, visualization-based support for WYSIWYT testing, an obvious opportunity is to leverage the users' testing information to help with fault localization once one of their tests reveals a failure. Our end-user software engineering work takes advantage of this opportunity through the use of slicing.

---

[5] There were two different spreadsheets, but the order they were given to the participants was varied. When we refer to the "first" or "second" task, we mean the first or second (respectively) spreadsheet in that particular participant's sequence.

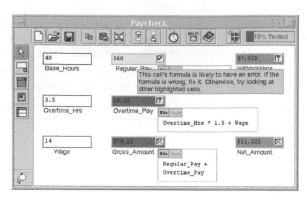

Figure 5.8. A Paycheck spreadsheet. The user is hovering the mouse over the Overtime_Pay cell to see the explanation of its dark red shading.

While incrementally developing a spreadsheet, a user can indicate his or her observation of a failure by marking a cell incorrect with an "X" instead of a checkmark. At this point, our fault localization techniques highlight in varying shades of red the cells that might have contributed to the failure, with the goal that the most likely-to-be faulty cells will be colored dark red. More specifically, each cell's interior is colored with one of six discrete fault likelihood colors so as to highlight the cells most likely to contain faults: "None" (no color), "Very Low," "Low," "Medium," "High," and "Very High" (very dark red). For example, in Figure 5.8, the fault likelihood of the Regular_Pay cell has been estimated as Very Low, the fault likelihoods of Withholdings and Net_Amount have been estimated as Medium, and the fault likelihoods of Overtime_Pay and Gross_Amount have been estimated as High.

6.1. THREE TECHNIQUES FOR ESTIMATING FAULT LIKELIHOOD

How should these colors be computed? Computing exact fault likelihood values for a cell, of course, is not possible. Instead, we must combine heuristics with deductions that can be drawn from analyzing the source code (formulas) and/or from the user's tests. We are currently experimenting with three different approaches to assisting end-user programmers with fault localization. All three techniques maintain the following three properties:

(1) Every cell that might have contributed to the computation of an incorrect value will be assigned some positive fault likelihood.
(2) The more incorrect calculations a cell contributes to, the greater the fault likelihood assigned to it.
(3) The more correct calculations a cell contributes to, the lower the fault likelihood assigned to it.

The first approach, like many other fault localization techniques, builds on previous research on slicing and dicing. [Tip (1995) provides a survey of that research.] In general, a program's backward slice is every portion of the program that affects a particular variable at a particular point. (Similarly, a forward slice is every portion of the program that the particular variable at that point affects.) In the spreadsheet paradigm, the concept of a backward (forward) slice simplifies to every cell whose value contributes to (is affected by) the cell in question. For example, in Figure 5.8 the backward slice of Gross_Amount is Regular_Pay and Overtime_Pay, plus the three cells used in the computation of those two. Since Gross_Amount is exhibiting a failure, its backward slice contains all the cells that could possibly contain the fault. A dice (Chen and Cheung, 1997) can reduce the number of cells being considered as having the fault by "subtracting out" of the slice the cells that contributed also to correct values.

In a manner reminiscent of program dicing, our first technique (Reichwein et al., 1999; Ruthruff et al., 2003), which we term the *Blocking Technique*, considers the dataflow relationships involving the X-marked cells that *reach C*. (An X-mark reaches C if there is a dataflow path from C to the X-marked cell that does not have any check-marks on the cells in the path. If any such checkmarks are present, they are said to *block* the X-mark from C along that path.) In this technique, the more X-marks that reach C, the greater the fault likelihood, supporting property (2) above. For example, in Figure 5.8, the checkmark in Regular_Pay blocks most of the effects of the X-marks downstream from affecting Regular_Pay's fault likelihood—but it does not completely block out the X-marks' effects because of property (1) above. Unlike previous algorithms, our algorithms are incremental, updating and reflecting fault likelihood after each user action (each formula edit, each placement of a checkmark or X-mark, etc.). The Blocking Technique is also different from previous algorithms in its use of reasoning about which marks are blocked from C by marks of the opposite type in C's forward slice.

Another way to reason about slices is via counts of successful/failed tests. Jones et al. (2002) developed Tarantula, which follows that type of strategy. Tarantula utilizes information from all passing and failing tests when highlighting possible locations for faults. It colors each statement to indicate the likelihood that it is faulty, determining colors via the ratio of failing to passing tests for tests that execute that statement. Like xSlice, Tarantula reports its results after running the entirety of a test suite and collecting information from all of the tests in the test suite. Our second technique, which we term the *Test Count Technique* (Fisher et al., 2002b; Ruthruff et al., 2003), follows the same general strategy but, as already mentioned above, our techniques incrementally update information about likely locations for faults as soon as the user applies tests to their spreadsheet.

Both the Blocking and Test Count techniques can be a bit too expensive to be practical for the highly responsive, incremental conventions of end-user programming environments. Under some circumstances, their time complexities approach $O(n^4)$ and $O(n^3)$, respectively, where n is the number of cells in the spreadsheet. [A complete discussion of complexities is given in (Ruthruff et al., 2003).] To address this issue, we devised a third technique that approximates the reasoning from both techniques at a lower cost, namely $O(n)$.

6.2. WHICH OF THE TECHNIQUES IS BEST?

We are currently conducting a variety of empirical studies to see which of the fault localization techniques just described is the most effective, given the testing end-user programmers actually do. Our empirical work on this question is still in early stages, so we are not ready to identify which is the "best" of the three techniques. But we can provide the following insights:

- Recall that these techniques are meant for *interactive, incremental* programming. Thus, feedback is needed before there is very much information available, such as after the very first X-mark the user places.
- Early experimental work suggests that the Blocking Technique outperforms the other two in ability to visually discriminate the faulty cells from the non-faulty ones at early stages (Ruthruff et al., 2003).
- In interactively judging the correctness of values, end-user programmers, being human, make mistakes. In a study we conducted (Prabhakararao et al., 2003), approximately 5% of the checkmarks end-users placed were incorrect.
- If a fault localization mechanism is not robust enough to tolerate mistakes, it can greatly interfere with the user's debugging success. In the study just mentioned, the 5% mistake rate seriously interfered with over half the participants' debugging sessions (using the Blocking Technique).
- In our empirical work, the Test Count Technique has been more robust than the other two techniques in tolerating a reasonably small mistake rate (Ruthruff et al., 2003). This is probably because the Test Count Technique is historical in nature. That is, it considers the entire history of test values, allowing the correct information to build up, essentially "outweighing" a small mistake rate. In contrast to this, the Blocking Technique emphasizes how the most recent test cases' set of judgments (checks and X-marks) interact.

In an experiment in which users were first familiarized with the presence of a fault localization mechanism, they tended to make use of it, but only after their own debugging sleuthing failed. When they did eventually turn to a fault localization mechanism, it was often quite helpful at leading them to the fault (Prabhakararao et al., 2003).

However, a puzzling problem we have observed in our empirical work is that, if users have not been made familiar with the presence of the fault localization mechanism, when they eventually encounter it they do not seem to trust it enough to make use of its assistance. This is entirely different from their response to assertions, which they seem to embrace wholeheartedly. We are currently working to learn the reasons for this marked difference in user attitude toward the two mechanisms.

7. Concluding Remarks

Our view is that giving end-user programmers ways to easily create their own programs is important, but is not enough. We believe that, like their counterparts in the world of professional programming, end-user programmers need support for other aspects of the software lifecycle. In this chapter, we have presented our approach to end-user software engineering, which integrates, in a fine-grained way, support for testing, assertions, and fault localization into the user's programming environment. As part of this work, we have also been working on how to motivate end-users to make use of the software engineering devices, and have gotten encouraging results via our Surprise-Explain-Reward strategy. Supporting software development activities beyond the programming stage—in a way that helps users make productive use of the devices but does not require them to invest in software engineering training—is the essence of our end-user software engineering vision.

Acknowledgments

This work was supported in part by NSF under ITR-0082265 and in part by the EU-SES Consortium via NSF's ITR-0325273. We would like to acknowledge the many students and collaborators who have contributed to the end-user software engineering methodologies and empirical studies described in this chapter: Miguel Arredondo-Castro, Laura Beckwith, Darren Brown, Joshua Cantrell, Mingming Cao, Nanyu Cao, Ledah Casburn, Frank Cort, Eugene Rogan Creswick, Christopher DuPuis, Mike Durham, Marc Fisher, Orion Granatir, Thomas Green, Dalai Jin, Daniel Keller, Andrew Ko, Vijay Krishna, John LeHoullier, Lixin Li, Martin Main, Omkar Pendse, Amit Phalgune, Shrinu Prabhakararao, James Reichwein, Bing Ren, T. J. Robertson, Karen Rothermel, Joseph Ruthruff, Justin Schonfeld, Prashant Shah, Andrei Sheretov, Jay Summet, Christine Wallace, and Aaron Wilson.

Appendix A: WYSIWYT Scenarios in Excel

The WYSIWYT methodology has been integrated into the research language Forms/3. Here are three scenarios illustrating how it might look if integrated into Excel.

A.1 SCENARIO 1: AN END-USER FIGURES OUT AND TESTS HER INCOME TAXES

An end-user has a printout of an income tax form from the U.S. Internal Revenue Service, such as in Figure 5.9, in front of her, and she wants to use Excel to figure out the answers. To do this, she has created the spreadsheet in Figure 5.10.

Although this spreadsheet is simple, there are several ways the user could end up reporting the wrong answer. Like many taxpayers, she may be struggling to gather all the required data, and may change her mind about the right data values to enter. If she has been taking shortcuts with the formulas, basing them on the conditions present in her first version of the data (such as not bothering to use a *max* operator in line 5 to prevent negatives), the formulas are probably not very general, and may cause problems if her data changes. For example, if she entered "line 4–line 3" as the formula for line 5, but later changes line 4–5500 because her parents tell her they did not claim her this year after all, then the formula for line 5 will not give the correct answer. Similar

Form **1040EZ**	Department of the Treasury - Internal Revenue Service **Income Tax Return for** **Single Filers With No Dependents** **1991**		

Name & Address

Use the IRS label (see page 10). If you don't have one, please print.

L
A
B
E
L
H
E
R
E

Print your name (first, initial, last)

Home address (number and street). (If you have a P.O. box, see page 11.)   Apt. no.

City, town or post office, state, and ZIP code. (If you have a foreign address, see page 11.)

Please see instructions on the back. Also, see the Form 1040EZ booklet.

Your social security number

Presidential Election Campaign   (see page 11)
Do you want $1 to go to this fund?

Yes No

Report your income

Attach Copy B of Form(s) W-2 here. Attach tax payment on top of Form(s) W-2.

Note: *You must check Yes or No.*

1 Total wages, salaries, and tips. This should be shown in Box 10 of your W-2 form(s). (Attach your W-2 form(s).)

2 Taxable interest income of $400 or less. If the total is more than $400, you cannot use Form 1040EZ.

3 Add line 1 and line 2. This is your **adjusted gross income**.

4 Can your parents (or someone else) claim you on their return?
☐ **Yes.** Enter amount from line E here.
☐ **No.** Enter 5,550.00. This is the total of your standard deduction and personal exemption.

5 Subtract line 4 from line 3. If line 4 is larger than line 3, enter 0. This is your **taxable income.**

Figure 5.9. A portion of a U.S. income tax form.

problems could arise if she discovers that she entered data from the wrong box of her W–2 form into line 1, and so on.

Even in this simple case, the WYSIWYT methodology can help. Figure 5.10 shows a mock-up of how it might be incorporated into Excel. All cells containing formulas (as opposed to data values) are initially red-bordered with checkboxes, as in Figure 5.11 (top). The first time the user sees a red border, she moves her mouse over it and the

1040EZ calculations:				
Presidential election?	yes			
1. Total wages	5132			
2. Taxable interest	297			
3. Adjusted gross	5429			
4. Parents?	1500		Line E	1500
5. Taxable income	3929			

Figure 5.10. The user's Excel spreadsheet to figure out the taxes. The first few cells are simply data values. Line 3's formula is "line 1 + line 2," line 4's formula is a reference to line E, and line 5's formula is "line 3–line 4."

1040EZ calculations:						
Presidential election?	yes					
1. Total wages	5132					
2. Taxable interest	297					
3. Adjusted gross	5429	[?]				
4. Parents?	1500	[?]		Line E		1500
5. Taxable income	3929	[?]				

1040EZ calculations:						
Presidential election?	yes					
1. Total wages	5132					
2. Taxable interest	297					
3. Adjusted gross	5429	☐				
4. Parents?	1500	☐		Line E		1500
5. Taxable income	3929	√				

1040EZ calculations:						
Presidential election?	yes					
1. Total wages	5132					
2. Taxable interest	297					
3. Adjusted gross	5429	☐				
4. Parents?	5500			Line E		1500
5. Taxable income	-71	[?]				

Figure 5.11. A mock-up of Excel if enhanced by the WYSIWYT technology. (Top): All cells containing formulas are initially red, meaning untested. (Middle): Whenever the user makes a decision that some data value is correct, she checks it off. The checkmark appears in the cell she explicitly validated, and all the borders of cells contributing to that correct value become more tested (closer to pure blue, shown as black in this picture). This example has such simple formulas, only the two colors red (light gray) and blue (black) are needed. (Bottom): The user changes the formula in line 4 to a constant. This change causes affected cells to be considered untested again.

tool tips inform her that "red borders mean untested and blue borders mean tested. You can check cells off when you approve of their values." The user checks off a value that she is sure is correct, and a checkmark ($\sqrt{}$) appears as in Figure 5.11 (middle). Further, the border of this explicitly approved cell, as well as of cells contributing to it, becomes blue. If she then changed some data, any affected checkmarks would be replaced with blanks or question marks ("?") as described earlier in this paper, because the current value has not been checked off. But suppose that instead of replacing a data value, the user makes the formula change in line 4 alluded to above, changing the previous formula to the constant 5500 instead of the former reference to line E. Since the change she made involved a formula (the one she just changed to a data value), the affected cells' borders revert to red and downstream $\sqrt{}$s disappear, indicating that these cells are now completely untested again. [See Figure 5.11 (bottom).] The maintenance of the "testedness" status of each cell throughout the editing process, as illustrated in Figure 5.11 (bottom), is an important benefit of the approach. Without this feature, the user may not remember that her previous testing became irrelevant with her formula change, and now needs to be redone.

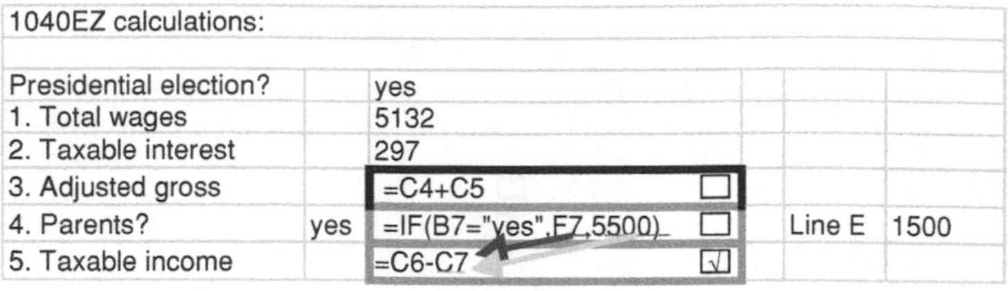

1040EZ calculations:						
Presidential election?		yes				
1. Total wages		5132				
2. Taxable interest		297				
3. Adjusted gross		=C4+C5	☐			
4. Parents?	yes	=IF(B7="yes",E7,5500)	☐		Line E	1500
5. Taxable income		=C6-C7	☑			

Figure 5.12. Some cells require more than one test value to become completely tested, as this formula view with purple (medium gray) cell borders and red (light gray) and blue (black) arrows between subexpressions shows.

A.2 SCENARIO 2: THE USER TESTS HER INCOME TAX SPREADSHEET
AS SHE MAKES IT MORE REUSABLE

The next year, the user may want to improve the spreadsheet so that she can use it year after year without having to redesign each formula in the context of the current year's data values. For example, she adds the yes/no box from the IRS form's line 4 to her spreadsheet's line 4 and uses the *if* operator in the formula for line 4. Because of this *if*, she will need to try at least two test cases for line 4's cell to be considered tested: one that exercises the "*yes*" case and one that exercises the "*no*" case.

Because of this, when the user checks off one data value as in Figure 5.12, the borders for lines 4 and 5 turn purple (50% blue and 50% red). To figure out how to make the purple cells turn blue, the user selects one of them and hits a "show details" key. The system then draws arrows pertaining to the subexpression relationships, with colors depicting which cases still need to be tested. The arrow from the last subexpression is red, telling the user that the "no" case still needs to be tried.

A.3 SCENARIO 3: A TEMPLATE DEVELOPER TESTS AN INCOME TAX
SPREADSHEET FOR SALE

It is well documented that many production spreadsheets contain bugs. To help address this problem, a developer with a full suite of income tax spreadsheet templates for sale could use the methodology to achieve organized test coverage of these income tax spreadsheets. This would not only be valuable when first developing the spreadsheets, but also in making sure that each formula change in subsequent years' revisions had been entered and tested.

References

Aho, A., Sethi, R. and Ullman, J. (1986). *Compilers, Principles, Techniques, and Tools*. Reading, MA: Addison-Wesley.

Ambler, A. and Burnett, M. (1990). Visual forms of iteration that preserve single assignment. *Journal of Visual Languages and Computing* 1(2), 159–181.

Beckwith, L., Burnett, M. and Cook, C. (2002). Reasoning about many-to-many requirement relationships in spreadsheets. In: *Proceedings of IEEE Symposium Human-Centric Computing*, Arlington VA, September, pp. 149–157.

Blackwell, A. (2002). First steps in programming: A rationale for attention investment models. In: *Proceedings of IEEE Human-Centric Computing Languages and Environments*, Arlington, VA, September 3–6, pp. 2–10.

Boehm, B., Abts, C., Brown, A., Chulani, S., Clark, B., Horowitz, E., Madachy, R., Reifer, J. and Steece, B. (2000). *Software Cost Estimation with COCOMO II*. Upper Saddle River, NJ: Prentice Hall PTR.

Brown, D., Burnett, M., Rothermel, G., Fujita, H. and Negoro, F. (2003). Generalizing WYSIWYT visual testing to screen transition languages. In: *Proceedings of IEEE Symposium Human-Centric Computing Languages and Environments*, Auckland, NZ, October 28–31, pp. 203–210.

Burnett, M., Atwood, J., Djang, R., Gottfried, H., Reichwein, J. and Yang, S. (2001a). Forms/3: A first-order visual language to explore the boundaries of the spreadsheet paradigm. *Journal of Functional Programming* 11(2), 155–206.

Burnett, M., Cook, C., Pendse, O., Rothermel, G., Summet, J. and Wallace, C. (2003). End-user software engineering with assertions in the spreadsheet paradigm. In: *Proceedings of International Conference Software Engineering*, Portland, OR, May 3–10, pp. 93–103.

Burnett, M., Ren, B., Ko, A., Cook, C. and Rothermel, G. (2001b). Visually testing recursive programs in spreadsheet languages. In: *Proceedings of IEEE Human-Centric Computing Languages and Environments*, Stresa, Italy, September 5–7, pp. 288–295.

Burnett, M., Sheretov, A., Ren, B. and Rothermel, G. (2002). Testing homogeneous spreadsheet grids with the 'what you see is what you test' methodology. *IEEE Transactions Software Engineering*, 576–594.

Carr, D. (2003). End-user programmers need improved development support. In: *Proceedings of CHI 2003 Workshop on Perspectives in End User Development*, April 16–18.

Carroll, J. and Mack, R. (1984). Learning to use a word processor by doing, by thinking, by knowing. In: J.C. Thomas and M.L. Schneider (eds.), *Human Factors in Computer Systems*. Norwood, NJ: Ablex, pp. 13–51.

Chen, T. and Cheung, Y. (1997). On program dicing. *Software Maintenance: Research and Practice* 9(1), 33–46.

Davis, J. (1996). Tools for spreadsheet auditing. International Journal of Human–Computer Studies 45, 429–442.

Duesterwald, E., Gupta, R. and Soffa, M.L., (1992). Rigorous data flow testing through output influences. In: *Proceedings of Second Irvine Software Symposium*, March, pp. 131–145.

Ferguson, R. and Korel, B. (1996). The chaining approach for software test generation. *ACM Transactions of Software Engineering and Methodology* 5(1), 63–86.

Fisher, M., Cao, M., Rothermel, G., Cook, C. and Burnett, M. (2002a). Automated test generation for spreadsheets. In: *Proceedings of International Conference of Software Engineering*, Orlando, FL, May, pp. 141–151.

Fisher, M., Jin, D., Rothermel, G. and Burnett, M. (2002b). Test reuse in the spreadsheet paradigm. In: *Proceedings of International Symposium Software Reliability Engineering*.

Frankl, P. and Weyuker, E. (1988). An applicable family of data flow criteria. *IEEE Transactions Software Engineering* 14(10), 1483–1498.

Green, T.R.G. and Petre, M. (1996). Usability analysis of visual programming environments: A 'cognitive dimensions' framework. *Journal of Visual Languages and Computing* 7(2), 131–174.

Heger, N., Cypher, A. and Smith, D. (1998). Cocoa at the visual programming challenge 1997. *Journal of Visual Languages and Computing* 9(2), 151–168.

Henderson, P. and Morris, J. (1976). A lazy evaluator. In: *Proceedings of ACM Symposium on Principles of Programming Languages*, Atlanta, GA, January 19–21, pp. 95–103.

Hughes, J. (1985). Lazy memo-functions, LNCS #201. In: J.-P. Jouannaud (ed.), *Functional Programming Languages and Computer Architecture*, Nancy, France, September 16–19, pp. 129–146.

Igarashi, T., Mackinlay, J., Chang, B.-W. and Zellweger, P. (1998). Fluid visualization of spreadsheet structures. In: *Proceedings of IEEE Symposium Visual Languages*, pp. 118–125.

Jones, J., Harrold, M. and Stasko, J. (2002). Visualization of test information to assist fault localization. In: *Proceedings of International Conference Software Engineering*, Orlando FL, May, pp. 467–477.

Karam, M. and Smedley, T. (2001). A testing methodology for a dataflow based visual programming language. In: *Proceedings of IEEE Symposium Human-Centric Computing Languages and Environments*, Stresa, Italy, September 5–7, pp. 280–287.

Korel, B. and Al-Yami, A. (1996). Assertion-oriented automated test data generation. In: *Proceedings International Conference Software Engineering*, Berlin Germany, March, pp. 71–80.

Krishna, V., Cook, C., Keller, D., Cantrell, J., Wallace, C., Burnett, M. and Rothermel, G. (2001). Incorporating incremental validation and impact analysis into spreadsheet maintenance: an empirical study. *Proceedings of International Conference Software Maintenance*, Florence, Italy, November, pp. 72–81.

Laski, J. and Korel, B. (1993). A data flow oriented program testing strategy. *IEEE Transactions Software Engineering* **9**(3), 347–354.

Lewis, C. (1990). NoPumpG: Creating interactive graphics with spreadsheet machinery. In: E.P. Glinert (ed.), *Visual Programming Environments: Paradigms and Systems*. Los Alamitos, CA: IEEE Computer Society Press, pp. 526–546.

Lieberman, H. (2001). *Your Wish Is My Command: Programming by Examp*. San Francisco, CA: Morgan Kaufmann.

Lieberman, H. and Fry, C. (1998), ZStep 95: A reversible, animated source code stepper. In: J. Stasko, J. Domingue, M. Brown and B. Price (eds.), *Software Visualization: Programming As a Multimedia Experience*. Cambridge, MA: MIT Press, pp. 277–292.

Lowenstein, G. (1994). The psychology of curiosity. *Psychological Bulletin* **116**(1), 75–98.

McDaniel, R. and Myers, B. (1999). Getting more out of programming-by-demonstration. In: *Proceedings of ACM Conference on Human Factors in Computing Systems*, Pittsburgh, PA, May 15–20, pp. 442–449.

Miller, R. and Myers, B. (2001). Outlier finding: Focusing user attention on possible errors. In: *Proceedings of User Interface Software and Technology*, Orlando, FL, November, pp. 81–90.

Myers, B. and Ko, A. (2003). Studying development and debugging to help create a better programming environment. In: *Proceedings of CHI 2003 Workshop on Perspectives in End User Development*, April, pp. 65–68.

Nardi, B. (1993). *A Small Matter of Programming: Perspectives on End-User Computing*. Cambridge, MA: MIT Press.

Pane, J., Myers, B. and Miller, L. (2002). Using HCI techniques to design a more usable programming system. In: *Proceedings. IEEE Human-Centric Computing Languages and Environments*, Arlington VA, September, pp. 198–206.

Panko, R. (1998). What we know about spreadsheet errors. *Journal of End User Computing*, Spring.

Paterno, F. and Mancini, C. (1999). Developing task models from informal scenarios. In: *Proceedings of ACM CHI'99 Late Breaking Results*, Pittsburgh, PA, May, pp. 228–220.

Prabhakararao, S., Cook, C., Ruthruff, J., Creswick, E., Main, M., Durham, M. and Burnett, M. (2003). Strategies and behaviors of end-user programmers with interactive fault localization. In: *Proceedings of IEEE Symposium Human-Centric Computing Languages and Environments*, Auckland, New Zealand, October 28–31, pp. 15–22.

Rapps, S. and Weyuker, E. (1985). Selected software test data using data flow information. *IEEE Transactions of Software Engineering* **11**(4), 367–375.

Raz, O., Koopman, P. and Shaw, M. (2002). Semantic anomaly detection in online data sources. In: *Proceedings of 24th International Conference on Software Engineering*, Orlando, FL, May 19–25, pp. 302–312.

Reichwein, J., Rothermel, G. and Burnett, M. (1999). Slicing spreadsheets: An integrated methodology for spreadsheet testing and debugging. In: *Proceedings of 2nd Conference Domain Specific Languages*, October, pp. 25–38.

Reimann, P. and Neubert, C. (2000). The role of self-explanation in learning to use a spreadsheet through examples. *Journal of Computer Assisted Learning* **16**, 316–325.

Repenning, A. and Ioannidou, A. (1997). Behavior processors: Layers between end-users and Java virtual machines. In: *1997 IEEE Symposium Visual Languages*, Capri, Italy, September, pp. 402–409.

Rosson, M. and Seals, C. (2001). Teachers as simulation programmers: Minimalist learning and reuse. In: *Proceedings of ACM Conference Human Factors in Computing Systems*, Seattle, WA, April, pp. 237–244.

Rothermel, G., Burnett, M., Li, L., DuPuis, C. and Sheretov, A. (2001). A methodology for testing spreadsheets. *ACM Transactions Software Engineering and Methodology* **10**(1), 110–147.

Rothermel, G., Li, L., DuPuis, C. and Burnett, M. (1998). What you see is what you test: A methodology for testing form-based visual programs. In: *Proceedings of International Conference Software Engineering*, Kyoto Japan, April, pp. 198–207.

Ruthruff, J., Creswick, E., Burnett, M., Cook, C., Prabhakararao, S., Fisher, M., II, and Main, M. (2003). End-user software visualizations for fault localization. In: *Proceedings of ACM Symposium Software Visualization*, San Diego, CA, June 11–13, pp. 123–132.

Sajanieme, J. (2000). Modeling spreadsheet audit: a rigorous approach to automatic visualization. *Journal of Visual Languages and Computing* **11**(1), 49–82.

Seals, C., Rosson, M., Carroll, J., Lewis, T. and Colson, L. (2002). Fun learning Stagecast Creator: An exercise in minimalism and collaboration. In: *Proceedings of IEEE Symposium Human-Centric Computing Languages and Environments*, Arlington VA, September, pp. 177–186.

Tip, F. (1995). A survey of program slicing techniques. *Journal of Programming Languages* **3**(3), 121–189.

Wagner, E. and Lieberman, H. (2003). An end-user tool for e-commerce debugging. In: *Proceedings of Intelligent User Interfaces*, Miami, Florida, January 12–15.

Wallace, C., Cook, C., Summet, J. and Burnett, M. (2002). Assertions in end-user software engineering: A think-aloud study (Tech Note). In: *Proceedings of IEEE Symposium Human-Centric Computing Languages and Environments*, Arlington, VA, September, pp. 63–65.

Wilcox, E., Atwood, J., Burnett, M., Cadiz, J. and Cook, C. (1997). Does continuous visual feedback aid debugging in direct-manipulation programming languages? In: *Proceedings of ACM Conference Human Factors in Computing Systems*, Atlanta, GA, March, pp. 258–265.

Wilson, A., Burnett, M., Beckwith, L., Granatir, O., Casburn, L., Cook, C., Durham, M. and Rothermel, G. (2003). Harnessing curiosity to increase correctness in end-user programming. In: *Proceedings of ACM Conference Human Factors in Computing Systems*, Ft. Lauderdale, FL, April 3–10, pp. 305–312.

Wulf, V. and Golombek, B. (2001). Exploration environments—concept and empirical evaluation. *Proceedings of GROUP*, 107–116.

Chapter 6

Component-Based Approaches to Tailorable Systems

MARKUS WON[1], OLIVER STIEMERLING[2], and VOLKER WULF[3]

[1]*International Institute for Socio-Informatics (IISI), Heerstr. 148, 53111 Bonn, won@iisi.de*
[2]*Ecambria Systems, Hospeltstr. 35a, 50825 Cologne, os@ecambria-systems.com*
[3]*University of Siegen, Hölderlinstr. 3, 57068 Siegen and Fraunhofer FIT, Scholoß Birlinghoven, 53754 Sankt Augustin, Germany, volker.wulf@uni-siegen.de*

Abstract. Flexibility is one of the most striking features of modern software. As the idea of integrating components is easily understood by programmers as well as end users, component architectures seem to be very promising to serve as a technological basis. In this chapter we give an overview of our work in the last years. A component model called FLEXIBEANS has been designed with the special notion to develop highly flexible and tailorable applications. The FREEVOLVE platform then serves as an environment in which compositions can be run and tailored. The second part of the chapter deals with the development and evaluation of different tailoring environments in which end users can compose their own applications or tailor existing ones. Users tests showed that besides a coherent technical basis and a manageable visual tailoring environment, there is a need for additional support techniques. We discuss how techniques to support users' individual and collective tailoring activities can be integrated into the user interface.

Key words. tailorability, platform, component architecture, user interface, collaborative tailoring, evalution.

1. Introduction

Software applied in organizations needs to be flexible; it has to cope with diversified and dynamic requirements. Software engineering approaches this challenge from the perspective of the software development process. Techniques and methods have been developed to make an evolutionary software engineering processes more efficient. Recently component-technology has gained considerable attention in this context (see e.g. Szyperski, 2002). However, software engineering tools and techniques focus on professional software developers. Beyond contributing to the appropriate requirements, users of software artifacts are traditionally not being considered as relevant actors in contributing to the flexibility of a software artifact.

Flexibility of software artifacts therefore was a major research issue in Human Computer Interaction from its very beginning. Since the individual abilities of specific users are diverse and develop constantly, suitability for individualization is an important principle for the design of the dialogue interface. In general, users were supposed to adapt the software artifact according to their abilities and requirements (Ackermann and Ulich, 1987; ISO, 9241). However, the scope of flexibility realized in early implementations was limited to simple parameterization of the dialogue interface. While

Henry Lieberman et al. (eds.), End User Development, 115–141.
© 2006 *Springer.*

this line of thoughts gave the users of software artifacts an active role, high levels of flexibility concerning the functionality of a system were originally not addressed.

Starting in the late 1980s, industrial demands, resulting from the wide spread of personal computers, lead to research efforts on flexible systems whose functionality or behavior can be modified by their users. Henderson and Kyng (1991) have worked out the concept of tailorability to name these activities. Tailoring is defined as the activity to modify a computer application within its context of use (Henderson and Kyng, 1991). Tailoring takes place after the original design and implementation phase of an application; it can start during or right after the installation of the application. Tailoring is usually carried out by individual users, local developers, helpdesk staff, or groups of users.

In the following, tailorable software artifacts, commercial products as well as research prototypes, have been developed. Regarding commercial products, spreadsheets and CAD systems were among the front riders. Buttons was one of the first highly tailorable research prototypes where users could change the dialogue interface and functionality on different levels of complexity (MacLean et al., 1990). Another system of tailoring functionality presents Mørch (1997).

With the emergence of networked application to support collective activities such as communication, cooperation, or knowledge exchange the need for tailorable software artifacts still increased (Bentley and Dourish, 1995; Schmidt, 1991; Wulf and Rohde, 1995). However, the distributed nature of these systems and the potential interrelation of individual activities posed new challenges to the design of tailorable applications (see Oberquelle, 1994; Stiemerling, 2000).

Empirical as well as design-oriented research has indicated different challenges in building tailorable systems (Mackay, 1990; MacLean et al., 1990; Nardi, 1993; Oppermann and Simm, 1994; Page et al., 1996; Wulf and Golombek, 2001a). As the following two issues had the highest priority from the user's point of view, we concentrated our research accordingly:

1. *Support for tailoring on different levels of complexity*: MacLean et al. (1990) have already pointed out to problems, which will arise if a considerable increase of the users' skills is required when trying to tailor a software artifact beyond simple parameterization (customization gulf). If users try to modify an application beyond parameterization, normally profound system knowledge and programming skills will be required. Therefore, tailorable applications should offer a gentle slope of increased complexity to stimulate learning. Different levels of tailoring complexity also tackles the problem of different skill levels among the users.

2. *Support for cooperative tailoring*: Empirical research indicates, that tailoring activities are typically carried out collectively (Mackay, 1990; Nardi, 1993; Wulf and Golombek, 2001a). System administrators, power users,[1] or gardeners are individuals who possess higher levels of technical skill or motivation, while users with less

---

[1] Very experienced users that are no it professionals (i.e. computer scientists) and do not have any programming experience are here referred to as power users.

technical skills or motivation may benefit by receiving direct support or just reusing tailored artifacts.

To some extent the discussion on component technologies in software engineering and the discussion on tailorable software artifacts have a similar motivation: the differentiation and dynamics of the context in which software artifacts are applied. However, software engineering directs its attention towards professional software developers during design time. The concept of tailorability directs its attention towards users during the actual use of the system (not necessarily during run-time, but certainly after the initial design of the system). Our work tries to apply component technology for the design of tailorable systems.

The term "component" is not used very consistently within the software engineering community. We refer conceptually to Szyperski's (2002) notion of components. He gives the following definition:

> A software component is a unit of composition with contractually specified interfaces and explicit context dependencies only. A software component can be deployed independently and is subject to composition by third parties (Szyperski, 2002, p. 41).

This idea of reducing (re-)design time by reusing strictly modularized code originates in the very beginning in the software engineering discourse (McIllroy, 1968). Szyperski (2002) also stresses the economic potentials of collective and distributed software engineering processes. Component technology allows to apply the same software module by many software developers in different artifacts. The developers who apply a component created by somebody else do not necessarily need to understand the implementation details. They may just access the services provided by the component via the interfaces. The visibility of the component's implementation can reach from black boxing (no visibility of the source code) to white boxing (full accessibility of the code) with different levels of gray (accessibility of parts of the code) in between.

Such an understanding of component technology has the potential to serve as foundation for the design of highly tailorable systems. Beyond parameterization and reprogramming, the composition of components provides a middle layer of tailoring complexity. This layer can be further differentiated by employing nested component structures, which provide partial insight into the implementation of the more complex components (similar in motivation to "gray-box" components). With regard to the support of cooperative tailoring activities, components and their composition can easily be extracted and shared with other users. Component technology, both in software engineering and in tailorable systems, needs to deal with the problem displaying the behavior of a component.

Applying components as the basis for tailorable software systems draws on the metaphor of constructing larger blocks of functionality from independent smaller pieces of software. Components can be sticked together according to their specific interfaces. We assume that users without programming experience can draw on their understanding of other forms of construction activities such as playing with Lego bricks or assembling physical artifacts such as cars (motor, wheels, car body, etc.).

While there are obvious similarities between software development and tailoring, there are also clear differences which need to be dealt with when applying component technology to the design of tailorable systems.[2] By definition tailoring is carried out after the initial design by users who are non-professional programmers. To allow for re-composition after design time, new concepts regarding the component model and tailoring platform have to be developed. Since users are the key actors, appropriate tailoring interfaces and an application-oriented decomposition of the software is required. Moreover, technical mechanisms to support the sharing of tailored artifacts among the users need to be developed.

In dealing with these issues, we will present results from research conducted at the University of Bonn and lately also at the University of Siegen. The design of tailorable groupware has been an important aspect of our work for almost a decade (e.g. Kahler, 2001a; Mørch et al., 2004; Stiemerling, 2000; Wulf, 1994, 2001).

In the next section, we will describe a component model which is specifically designed to support tailoring. Moreover, we describe the architecture of FREEVOLVE, a platform to tailor distributed applications. The third section deals with the design of graphical user interfaces which enable users to compose applications or change existing compositions. The second part of the chapter discusses additional features of the interface to support tailoring. Section 4 presents technical features to support the exchange of tailored artifacts among users. Finally, we discuss our work with regard to that of others and draw some conclusions from it.

2. Component Model and Tailoring Platform

As the technical foundation of our work, the FLEXIBEANS component model and the FREEVOLVE tailoring platform embody concepts and software developed by Stiemerling (1997, 2000), Won (1998) and Hinken (1999).[3] The current version of the FREEVOLVE platform is available under GPL as open-source (available at www.freevolve.de). Figure 6.1 gives a schematic overview of the platform:

Every application adhering to the FLEXIBEANS component model can be deployed on top of the FREEVOLVE platform. The basic application model supported by the FREEVOLVE-platform is the *client-server model*. Consequently the platform runs on one server and possibly several clients. The component definitions and their composition (CAT and DCAT, explained later on in this chapter) are initially stored on the FREEVOLVE server. They are instantiated and connected during start up on their respective target machines (client or server).

The platform provides an application programming interface (API) with a complete set of component-based tailoring operations that can be applied to the deployed and

---

[2] A very important issue here is which components are needed for one special application. Starting from one monolithic application tailorable parts have to be detected. This process of decomposition is described in Stevens and Quaisser in this volume.

[3] Before its release under GPL, the FREEVOLVE platform was called Evolve (e.g. Stiemerling et al., 1999 and Stiemerling, 2000, who provides a more profound discussion of the platform and the component model).

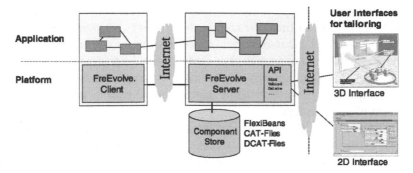

Figure 6.1. FREEVOLVE platform schematic overview.

already running application. The fact that via this API *different types of user interfaces* can be docked onto the same platform, thus offering the opportunity to critically compare and evaluate different concepts for representing component-based tailorability to end users (e.g. the 3D and 2D interfaces shown in Figure 6.1), is of particular importance for the work on end-user tailoring presented in this chapter.

While the FREEVOLVE platform through its API supports component-based tailoring operations on a generic, technical level, we will describe the component model and platform with end-user tailoring in mind, in order to pave the way for the work presented in the next chapters.

2.1. THE FLEXIBEANS COMPONENT MODEL

In the beginning, the JAVABEANS component model had been chosen as the basis for an exploratory investigation of the challenges and pitfalls of component-based tailorability (Stiemerling and Cremers, 1998). One result of these early experiments with a groupware search tool (see Won, 1998) was the insufficiency of the JAVABEANS model for full-fledged component-based tailorability. In the following, we will briefly describe the FLEXIBEANS model that was developed to solve the problems encountered (for a more formal investigation of appropriate component models for component-based tailorability the reader is referred to Stiemerling, 2000).

The atomic FLEXIBEANS components are implemented in Java, stored on the FREEVOLVE Server in binary format as Java class files, and packaged, if necessary, with other resources as JAR-files. At this end, one has to distinguish between the component and its instance. Every component can be instantiated in different compositions at the same time and each instance has its own state. Like in JAVABEANS the interaction between components is event-based in the way that messages are interchanged between components. So the state of an instance of a component can only change in case the instance possesses the control flow, or through interaction with a component which is in possession of the control flow. The composition of the components determines, which instances of components can interact with each other. Tailoring on the level of component composition happens through the connection of ports. To allow for tailorability at run-time, the atomic and abstract components and their ports have to be visualized at the user interface (see Section 3.1). A usable visualization for non-professional programmers though needs a more differentiated port model than JAVABEANS provides. Consequently, the JAVABEANS component model was extended in the following ways (also motivated by more technical reasons that are not relevant in the context of this chapter).

From the perspective of end user development, the most important extension is the concept of named ports. The JAVABEANS component model is solely based on typed event ports. Consequently, events of the same type (e.g. button click event) are always received on the same port. Incoming events have to be analyzed in the receiving component either by parsing the event's source or evaluating additional information, which is sent with the event. Such an approach makes it difficult for users to understand the different state transitions resulting from events of different sources (e.g. click events from two different buttons). Another strategy is to use dynamically generated adapter objects in order to distinguish between different event sources. Such an adapter will forward different events of the same type (e.g. different button click events) to different handling methods according to the event source. Both strategies hide a part of the real components' interaction, which is essential to be able to compose components appropriately. Therefore, the FLEXIBEANS component model allows for named ports in order to distinguish ports according to their types and their names. Named ports support an appropriate understanding of a component's use and semantics. Connections between components are only valid if the port's type and name match.[4]

The rather technical nature of these changes to the original JAVABEANS model demonstrates the importance of taking into account the cognitive properties of purely technical concepts when building systems whose working principles are supposed to be understood and eventually manipulated by end users.

2.2. THE DISTRIBUTED TAILORING PLATFORM FREEVOLVE

While the FLEXIBEANS model provides a way to implement components in a standardized fashion, the FREEVOLVE platform permits the deployment and run-time re-composition of distributed FLEXIBEANS-based applications. In regard to the re-composition of components during run time, a first challenge is the design of a language to describe the composition of the atomic components, which are black boxes for the end user. In traditional software engineering approaches, components are only visible during design time. After compilation, the explicit representation of the component structure is lost. Therefore, the CAT language has been developed to describe the composition of atomic components into complex structures. The syntax of the CAT file (Component

---

[4] Another extension is the introduction of a new interaction mechanism, the shared object interaction. Whereas the event-based communication is directed and unidirectional, shared objects allow for symmetric information exchange between two or more components (cf. Stiemerling, 2000).

Architecture for Tailoring) is described in Stiemerling (2000)[5]. A CAT file, or in the distributed setting a set of CAT files, describes the composition of an application out of atomic FLEXIBEANS components.

In order to support tailoring operations on different levels of complexity, the CAT language is designed to describe hierarchically nested component structures. In this fashion, a higher number of basic components can be composed into complex structures and stored as abstract components, which can be composed by the same mechanisms as atomic components. From the end-user's programming point of view this offers two advantages: (a) the necessary number of abstract components to build the final application is lower, and (b) their design can be more application-oriented. So, the necessary composition activities have a lower level of tailoring complexity than the composition activities on the atomic components level. The CAT language allows for arbitrary depth of nesting. Obviously, abstract components are white-box components. They can be explored and their content—that is a set of connected and parameterized components—can be changed.

For describing the composition of distributed component structures, CAT files representing structures on different machines can be connected via a *remote bind* file. The *remote bind* file (DCAT) describes the way fitting ports of two components being instantiated on different computers in the network are connected. To implement the interaction of distributed components via the Internet, the FREEVOLVE platform is based on Java RMI (Remote Method Invocation).

During start-up, the CAT files are evaluated on the server and relevant components (not their instances) are represented in the servers working memory. As soon as a user logs in and starts the client of the tailorable application, the client connects with the FREEVOLVE server, which then authenticates the users and sends the necessary components to the client. The client locally instantiates the atomic components and connects them according to the CAT file describing their composition. These instances are the base for the graphical representation of the components and their structure at the user interface (see below). When tailoring the application on the client side, the corresponding CAT file is updated and the system behavior is changed accordingly.

The CAT files for the client sides are stored centrally on the server, which allows different users to run the same client by applying the same CAT file. Therefore, changes on the client side are transmitted to the server, stored persistently, and propagated to those other active client machines, which use the same client. Since the propagation of tailoring activities to other users may lead to inconsistent system states, specific attention has to be paid to this problem when developing an application on the FREEVOLVE platform. A specific protocol has therefore been developed, which guarantees that in case of a breakdown, a completely consistent version of the application may be recovered (see Stiemerling, 2000). More details on the platform's object-oriented architecture and implementation are given by Hinken (1999) and Stiemerling et al. (1999).

---

[5] CAT draws on concepts already developed in port-based configuration languages such as DARWIN (see Magee et al., 1995) and OLAN (see Bellissard, 1996)

3. User Interface

Having presented the component model and the tailoring platform, the question arises how to design an appropriate user interface that enables users without programming skills to tailor applications by re-composing components.

The main challenges when designing an interface for tailorable software artifacts are according to our experience the following ones:

a) the options to tailor a software artifact need to be indicated consistently,
b) the actual state of a tailorable software artifact (composition of components) has to be represented intelligibly,
c) tailoring activities have to be carried out in a simple and efficient manner,
d) the effects of tailoring activities have to be easily perceivable for the user,
e) the tailoring environment should be fault tolerant in the sense that it indicates incorrect activities to the users and proposes advice.

We will first present three different approaches to visualize and manipulate the component structure of a tailorable software artifact (dealing with the challenges (b) and (c)). All these different tailoring environments dealt with the problem how to allow for "natural" tailoring as Pane and Myers (this volume) postulate. So our goal was to create a visual tailoring environment, where users are able to match between the application in run time and design time and to identify the aspects, which they want to tailor, easily. After that we will present additional features, which support users in finding options for tailoring, in checking the correctness of tailoring activities, and in evaluating the tailored artifact (dealing with the challenges (a), (d), and (e)).

The work on visualization of the tailoring interface was carried out by Won (1998, 2003), Hallenberger (2000), and Krüger (2003).[6] Additional features to support tailoring activities were developed by Engelskirchen (2000), Golombek (2000), Wulf (2001), Krings (2003), and Won (2003).[7]

3.1. VISUAL TAILORING ENVIRONMENTS

The characteristics of components made a graphical tailoring interface appear appropriate to changing the component structure. Within the graphical tailoring environment, the component structure of the software artifact was displayed as follows: instances of components were visualized as boxes, ports were indicated as connectors at the surface of these boxes, and the connection between two ports was represented by a line between these surface elements. Tailoring activities consisted of adding or deleting (instances of) components and rewiring their interaction. During the course of our work we have

---

[6] Stiemerling and Cremers (1998), Won (1998) and Wulf (2000) describe one of the 2D interface in detail. Stiemerling, Hallenberger and Cremers (2001) present details on a 3D interface.

[7] Wulf and Golombek (2001) describe the interface concept of direct activation which enables users to find tailoring options within a software artefact. Wulf (2000) and Wulf and Golombek (2001b) present research results concerning exploration environments which allow to test tailorable groupware. Won (2000) develops the concept of integrity control to indicate faulty or problematic compositions of components to the users.

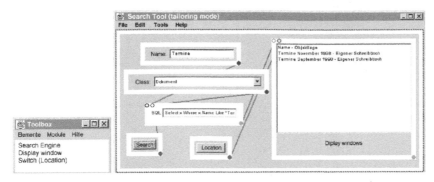

Figure 6.2. Two-dimensional graphical tailoring environment.

developed 2D and 3D versions of the visual tailoring environment. Note, that in the following we do not focus on the parameterization of single components, which we have realized in all three of the tailoring environments by selecting the component and choosing the parameter's value.

The first tailorable application we developed was a search tool for a groupware application. Later on we added different distributed groupware applications such as a chat tool and shared-to-do-lists. With regard to the search tool, the tailorable aspects were restricted to the client side, while the groupware application itself had a client server architecture. Figure 6.2 shows the 2D graphical environment to tailor the search tool.

A first workshop was held with employees of a German federal ministry. None of them had any experience in programming or system administration. Nevertheless, the users were able to compose different variations of the search tool window, which basically consisted in different graphical elements to specify search queries and different graphical elements to display the search results. To allow for these tailoring activities, the search tool consisted of six types of atomic components. Four of these component types were visible during use (inquiry elements, start button, display elements) while two just were while tailoring (the search engine and switches to direct search results towards specific graphical output elements). We made use of the categorizations of ports to represent them at the tailoring interface. The polarity of ports helps to distinguish between a component's input and output port: empty circles indicate input ports, filled circles indicate output ports. To support users in wiring the components appropriately, ports of the same type and name are given the same color, so users are hinted to fitting input and output ports by means of identical colors. Wired components are displayed by a connecting line in between their corresponding ports.

Abstract components are represented by a white frame around the atomic (or abstract) components they contain. If a power user has already designed several different abstract input and output components, other users can make first steps in constructing their personal search tool by combining two abstract components with each other.

The 2D approach presented so far has the advantage of enabling users to match directly between the runtime environment and the tailoring environment. When a user

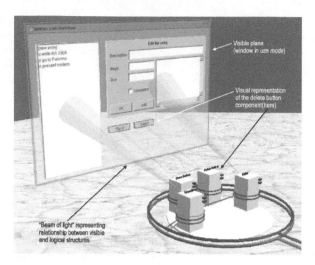

Figure 6.3. 3D graphical tailoring interface displaying a client's tailorable component structure.

changed into tailoring mode, the visible components of the interface stayed at the same place on the screen, while the invisible components, the ports and the connecting lines between them were added to the display. So the components which were invisible during runtime (search engine, switches for the results) had to be displayed additionally on the 2D screen. They were displayed at the same locations where they had been placed during the prior tailoring activities. Such a design of the tailoring environment had the consequences that locations, where non-visible components were placed during tailoring, could not be used by visible components during use.

Such a solution turned out to be viable if the tailoring problem deals with a high degree of components visible during use. In this case, it provides an intuitive transition from the use mode into the tailoring model. However, this approach does not make efficient use of the screen space as soon as bigger parts of the functionality "behind" the user interface can be tailored. Within the 2D approach it is also difficult to differentiate the scope of tailoring activities referring either to the client or to the server side. To overcome these problems, a 3D graphical tailoring interface, like presented in Figure 6.3 has been developed. The third display dimension is used (a) to decouple the presentation of the visible and the invisible components (b) to represent the location of the tailorable components (either on the client or the server).

The components are represented as three-dimensional boxes with the component's name on top of them that are disposed on a virtual plain. The ports are represented as rings around the components in order to facilitate connections from all directions. Like in the 2D case, the color indicates the type and name of a port. The polarity is expressed by the intensity of the color—an input port is represented by darker shading, an output port is indicated by lighter shading. Connections between components are represented by tube-like objects linking the corresponding rings.

Abstract components are represented like all other components by 3D boxes. However, the box's surface that encapsulates the containing components of lower hierarchical level gets increasingly more transparent as the user navigates closer to it until the visual barrier finally disappears completely while the rings representing the ports of the abstract component remain visible. The user can now navigate or manipulate the inner component structure. In our current implementation atomic components remain black boxes even if the user navigates into their neighborhood. A gray box strategy could allow navigating into an atomic component and inspecting those aspects of the code which can be modified.

The allocation of the components in the 3D space is presented to the user with the notion of a floor on which the different component boxes are standing (Figure 6.3). The distinction between client and server side is represented by a special arrangement that places the server (represented by its tailorable component structure) in the center while the different clients (represented by their tailorable component structure) are allocated in a semi-circle around the server.

In order to ease the transition from use into tailoring mode, we offered a reference between the visible components at the user interface and the invisible components "behind" the screen. If a user changes into the tailoring mode, the actual client's GUI window is projected into the 3D world on a semi-transparent plane. Beams of light connect specific elements of the GUI interface with those aspects of the client's component structure to which they refer. When the user starts tailoring and enters the 3D world, she is being positioned in front of the GUI projection. So she sees the GUI of her regular interface. However, the semi-transparent plane allows observing the component structure on the highest level of abstraction as well. Following the beams of light she can navigate through the plane into the 3D space and explore or change the component structure.

The results of an early "thinking-aloud" evaluation seem to indicate that the users are fascinated by the 3D world and to some extent able to navigate. We believe that the tool can be suitable to represent the distributed structure of a software architecture. However, we estimate that tailoring becomes more difficult as there is an abstraction barrier between the application seen in tailoring mode and the application during use. This barrier is caused by the changes of perspective the users have to cope with when switching between run time and design mode. Already with regard to the 2D tailoring environment, our investigations indicated that users had more problems to understand the functionality and the use of invisible components (more abstract to them) than of the visible ones.

Due to the experiences described above, our current approach has shifted back towards a 2D environment where the design mode can be seen as an enhanced view on the application during runtime. To overcome the problems of the original 2D environment, we try to represent the composition of components "behind the screen" by means of additional views. Two additional windows represent the composition of components and their interaction. We have divided this information into two windows since we assume that not all of the information that is needed to tailor a distributed application, needs

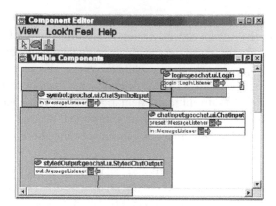

Figure 6.4. Visual components view.

to be permanently at hand. A synchronization feature supports the tailoring process by displaying information about the same aspects of the component structure at the same time in the three windows. For example, if in one window a component is highlighted it will be marked in the other windows, as well, or the user changes the composition in one view, the changes will immediately be displayed in all other views. In the following, we will describe the different views in more detail.

The first view is very similar to the original 2D tailoring environment shown above. As discussed above, if all components—especially the invisible ones and the ones on the server side—are shown in one single view, it may be confusing for less experienced users. Thus, in this view all invisible and server-sided components are hidden. For those users who tailor only the visible aspects of their own application, this view is sufficient. Like in the former 2D environment, size and position of all components are displayed exactly in the same way they appear during run time[8] (see Figure 6.4). Users are allowed to resize the visual components or relocate them interactively. Other tailoring operations (i.e. changing a parameter, adding or removing a component) are available via context menus. So, if a user marks a component and uses the right mouse button, he may directly change the parameters as well as add or remove components. Since all views are synchronized, tailoring activities can be continued by switching into one of the other views.

A second view (Figure 6.5) on the component structure that shows all the bindings between the components is given by the editor. Bindings can be added by drawing lines between the ports of the components or removed by selecting a connection and choosing the command "remove binding" in the context menu. Due to the fact, that most users will only be allowed to tailor the client-part of the application, this second view normally hides the composition on the server side, and thus, reduces complexity.

---

[8] The actual implementation shows just green rectangles instead of the actual screen display. This will be changed in a future version.

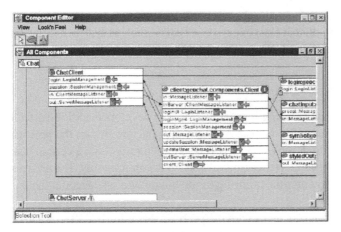

Figure 6.5. Component editor.

All components that reside on the client side are shown (visible and the invisible ones), which results in a more complex view than the first one. However, since both windows are synchronized, the components that are visible at the interface can be found easily and their relation to hidden components can be tracked.

If changes are executed on the server-side of the application, all users will be directly affected. The right to tailor on the server side therefore will typically be reserved to very experienced users or system administrators who are able to cope with the tailoring complexity of the complete application. For this group of users the components on the server side and their bindings may be displayed additionally.

The third view shows the whole hierarchical nested application in a very abstract view. All components are structured in a tree view which is a well-known representation pattern in file managers. As soon as a component is selected, its parameters and their actual values will be displayed. This third view (Figure 6.6) on the application shows the component structure of the whole application at once.

Figure 6.6. Component explorer.

So far we have carried out only a very preliminary evaluation study (see Krüger, 2003) revealing, that at least experienced users, such as system administrators, are able to benefit from this tailoring environment.

3.2. ADDITIONAL FEATURES

Beyond graphical tailoring interfaces, we have developed additional features that support users during tailoring. The first concept concentrates on the problem of finding a tailoring function. Mainly tailoring is done when users have a certain task to fulfill and the tool does not support this kind of work in the optimal way. The goal now is, not only to offer hooks to enter the tailoring mode but to take into account the current working context.

The second concept deals with the problem that tailoring often is avoided against the background of changing the current application in an unwanted way or even destroy it. So, we worked out the idea of checking the composition according to rules that are attached to atomic components. Those rules or constraints then describe how a component has to be used, how the parameters work together, and how this component has to be linked to others.

3.2.1. *Direct Activation*

An empirical study of users of a word processor indicated that finding the appropriate tailoring functions is a substantial barrier that either prevents tailoring at all or adds significantly to its costs (Wulf and Golombek, 2001a). Discussing our findings in the context of earlier work (see Mackay, 1990; Page et al., 1996), we identified two rather different occasions when users want to tailor an application (a) if a new version of the application is introduced (b) if the users' current task requires a modified functionality. The users need different patterns of support to find tailoring functions in both of these occasions. When tailoring a newly introduced version of an application, a survey of the given tailoring functions is an appropriate means to tackle the finding problem. The users get informed about the scope of the new version's tailorability. When the users' current task requires a modified functionality, a context specific representation of the tailoring functions' access points seems to be appropriate. In such a situation the user typically knows which aspects of the application she wants to modify, because the actual version of the function hinders her work.

In order to tackle the second case, we developed the concept *direct activation* that supports finding a tailoring function when it is required. Tailoring is needed when users perceive the state transition following a function's execution that does not lead to the intended effects. In this case, users are typically still aware of the function's access point at the interface. Therefore, the access point of the tailoring function should be designed related to the one of the function to be tailored. For instance in case of a toolbar, the access point towards its tailoring mode should be designed related to the toolbar, for example realize access via a specific button within the toolbar or via the context menu.

We defined the term "related" in two alternative ways. First, the visual representation of the access point of the tailoring function is placed in close proximity to the one of the tailorable function. Visual proximity of the access point can be realized as follows: In case certain parameters of the tailorable function have to be specified during the activation, visual proximity can be reached by displaying the access point of the tailoring functions next to the one for specifying the parameters (e.g. in the same window). If the tailorable function is executed without further specification from the menu or via an icon, the access point for the tailoring function could be placed next to the one of the tailorable function.

Second, the visual representation of the tailoring function's access point can be omitted under certain conditions, which seems to be acceptable if there is a consistent mode to activate the tailoring function. Mørch (1997) gives an example for a consistent mode to activate a tailoring function. In his system, a user can access different levels of tailoring functions by activating the tailorable function and pressing additionally either the "option," "shift," or "control" button. Restricted to specific functions, the Microsoft context menu gives another example of how to design a consistent mode to activate tailoring functions. Whenever the display of a screen object may be tailored, a specific mouse operation on this object allows accessing the tailoring function.

To evaluate the effectiveness of the concept *direct activation* in finding tailoring functions, we have implemented prototypes and carried out an evaluation study. The results of this study support our assumption that direct activation eases tailoring activities (see Wulf and Golombek, 2001a).

3.2.2. Checking the Integrity of Compositions

Beyond help for finding tailoring functions, we also developed concepts for supporting tailoring activities themselves. Empirical studies indicate that the fear to break an application is one of the major obstacles for tailoring activities (Mackay, 1990). We assumed that users would make errors when (re-)composing component structures. While these errors may threaten the functioning of the application, they are also opportunities for learning (see Frese et al., 1991). Although the differentiation of the ports helped already preventing certain misconnections among components, we additionally developed technical mechanisms that actively detect errors in the composition of components.

Such mechanisms for integrity check should control the validity of the composition, indicate the source of an error, give hints, or even correct the composition (see Won and Cremers, 2002). The rule-based integrity check presented here, consists of two different concepts: (a) constraints and actions and (b) analyzing the event flow. This sort of rule-based integrity checks are well known in data base management systems (Silberschatz et al., 2001). Rules are terms in first order logic that can be evaluated automatically. This technique may be used to add external conditions to the use of components. By restricting the use of a component, those constraints describe the "right use" of them. For example, if we have a set of GUI components, we can formulate a constraint like "all interface components have to have the same look and feel." If a user then tailors an application (i.e. adding a new component) this condition can be checked. Thus, by adding a constraint-based integrity check, that is stored externally in a XML-based format, we support tailoring. They may be changed over time according to the users' or organization's requirements.

Constraints are being enhanced by actions that either provide information to the user or correct certain errors. If a constraint is fulfilled (integrity error) an action that may indicate the error, give hints how to solve the problem, or even correct the error automatically, will be performed. Our goal here is not to compose applications automatically but to ease the learning and understanding of tailoring activities. All the system's interaction mentioned so far has been integrated into the user interface of the tailoring environment. As soon as an error is detected, the corresponding component will be marked and the user may get detailed information by clicking it.

A second technical mechanism is the check of event flow integrity. As we have seen before, the basic FLEXIBEANS component model allows for event-based component interaction. So, events are passed between independent components. In many cases, events that are created and passed to another component should be regarded as important information and therefore be "consumed." In order to implement the concept of event flow integrity, we classified the ports into essential and optional ones: essential ports have to be connected to other components whereas optional ports may not be used. For instance, the output component of the search tool that displays the found objects' names (see above) has two ports: one input port that is used to receive search result from the search engine and one output port that sends additional information (type, attributes) of selected search results to other components. To support users in building functional applications, the input part has been classified "essential," because it would be senseless to compose a search tool whose output window is not connected to any search engine. The output port can be classified as "optional," as one could use an output window without applying the additional information of the search results.

Such an integrity concept could also be described as constraints ("port x has to be bound"). However, in many cases this is not sufficient because events can be passed through a chain of components. In order to deal with such a flow of events, we have identified regular consumers. Checking an event flow, all essential event ports have to be connected to regular providers or consumers. For instance, we may compose a search tool by connecting a search engine to a filter component (that filters some of the search result) that then is connected to the output component. Here, the search engine has an essential output port. The filter component only passes events but is not a consumer, whereas the output component is a consumer of the search result and has an essential port that is finally connected.

Thus, we have to differentiate ports according to their function within a composition (producer, consumer, pass-though) and the need to be connected (essential, optional).

This information is described in external XML files and can be changed by system administrators. The integrity check is carried out by translating the composition into a Petri-net and then analyzing it (van der Aalst and Verbeek, 1997). In case the event flow analysis detects an error, the user is provided with corresponding information within his tailoring environment. Components and their ports are marked if they are essential and not connected correctly.

3.2.3. *Exploration Environments*

Beyond a technical support during composition, we also developed exploration environments to allow users to test their tailored artifacts. As a result of empirical investigations, Mackay (1990) and Oppermann and Simm (1994) hinted already to the importance of explorative activities. While research in HCI has already lead to different exploration mechanisms (e.g. undo function, freezing point, or experimental data), the distributed character of groupware poses new challenges. Users are often unable to understand the way groupware functions work because they cannot perceive the effects of the functions' execution at the other users' interface (e.g. the access rights granted to somebody else cannot be perceived by the owner). Only in case an application follows the WYSIWIS principle (What You See Is What I See) in a very strict manner (see Johansen, 1988), users can perceive the effects of a function's execution on the interface of the other users.

Therefore, we have developed the concept of exploration environments as an additional feature to support users in experimenting with tailorable groupware. An exploration environment allows simulating the execution of a tailorable groupware function by means of a specific system mode where the learner's own user interface, as well as the behavior of other users' interfaces, are simulated on the output device. If a function is executed in the exploration environment, the effects of its execution on the simulated user interfaces will be similar to the effects the "real" function's execution has on the "real" user interfaces. By executing a function in the exploration environment and switching between the simulation of his own and the other users' interfaces, a user can perceive how a newly tailored function works.

We have built specific exploration environments for three different tailorable groupware tools: an awareness service, a search tool for groupware, and a highly flexible access control for a shared workspace. To evaluate the effectiveness of exploration environments in tailorable groupware, we have carried out a field study and an experiment in a lab setting. The results of these studies indicate that exploration environments support tailoring activities in groupware (see Wulf, 2000; Wulf and Golombek, 2001b).

4. Cooperative Tailoring

Component-based software engineering is based on the assumption that software development can be organized best in a collective and distributed manner (Wulf, 1999). Component repositories together with monetary compensations for those who offer their source code for reuse are supposed to render software development more efficient (see Szyperski, 2002). Empirical studies on tailoring activities have revealed their collective nature (Pipek and Kahler, this volume). While monetary compensation did not play an important role, different patterns of cooperative activities have been found among users who differed in their commitment to and qualification for tailoring.

In our work, we deal with distinct types of social relationships: (a) on the level of the atomic components, the code is provided by professional developers to users and (b) on the level of the abstract components where users cooperate by providing each other with pre-integrated abstract components. Especially with regard to the second relationship, we focused on the design of shared workspaces to exchange tailored artifacts among users. Moreover, additional features had to be developed to document tailored artifacts for reuse by others.

Engelskirchen (2000) and Wulf (2001) have developed a shared workspace to exchange abstract components within a groupware application; Golombek (2000) and Kahler (2001b) have developed a shared repository to exchange tailored artifacts, such as document templates or button bars, among users of a word processor. Stevens (2002) has worked on metaphors which make visible and invisible component better understandable to users.[9]

Repositories in software engineering are expected to contain components to construct a wide variety of different applications. The proponents of component based software engineering assume that software developers direct themselves to the appropriate repository, browse it, and choose fitting components. Our experiences revealed the need for a more application- and user-oriented approach in designing repositories for the exchange of tailored artifacts. To allow for a seamless transition between use and tailoring activities, the shared repository needs to be integrated into the tailoring environment and should be activated directly with only those components that are relevant for a certain tailoring context being displayed.

Repositories to exchange tailored artifacts may be understood as shared workspaces, where compositions of components are exchanged. So, their basic functionality consists of functions to upload and download compositions of components. Additional features allow specifying the visibility of compositions and defining access rights for different subgroups of users. Moreover, a notification service informs users as soon as tailored artifacts are newly produced, modified or applied. Such a service contributes to the mutual awareness of distributed tailoring activities and may encourage the emergence of a tailoring culture (see Carter and Henderson, 1990). Since direct cooperation among the users should be supported as well, such a tailoring environment may provide a function to mail tailored artifacts directly to specific users or groups of users.

When applying the shared workspace in organizations, we found that users had problems in understanding abstract and atomic components created by others. To deal with this issue, we developed the following approaches to make atomic and abstract components more understandable to other (end) users. The solutions presented are the result of an evolutionary design process.

---

[9] Wulf (1999) gives an account of important results of the design and evaluation of the search tool repository. Kahler (2001b) presents results concerning the shared repository integrated into the word processor. Stevens and Wulf (2002) present work on the choice of metaphors to present components to users.

4.1. NAMING AND CLASSIFYING OF COMPONENTS

When offering atomic or abstract components we had to find meaningful names. Since users are typically confronted with a variety of different atomic and abstract components we list them at the interface. Due to limitations of screen space, the users first choice is based on a sparse visual presentation of the listed items where naming the components in a meaningful way has turned out to be of central importance. With regard to the atomic components, we have decomposed and named them according to a consistent metaphor (see Stevens and Quaisser, in this volume). This is a specific challenge for those components that are not represented at the user interface. Moreover, we added icons to the list presentation of the components that resemble the visual presentation of the components at the interface. Finding appropriate icons is again more difficult for those components that are not represented at the interface. With regard to abstract components, we can rely on naming only, since the selection of icons is too much of an extra work for the tailors.

In order to structure the list of components, a classification scheme is essential. For the classification of atomic components, we grouped them according to their ports, because we believe that this is indicative for the role they can play within the composition. The existence of ports can be a strong indicator of how the component interacts with other components and which task the component is able to fulfill. When classifying abstract components, the community of tailors needs to find appropriate conventions on how to compose and group these artifacts.

4.2. DESCRIBING COMPONENTS

Based on an earlier version of the 2D tailoring interface, a search tool for a groupware was introduced into a state government's representative body. As a result of collective tailoring activities over a period of several weeks, it turned out that users need additional support in distinguishing components beyond naming and classifying. Hence, we generated possibilities to textually describe atomic and abstract components. To describe atomic components, we created a hypertext-based help menu where help texts briefly explain the components' functionality and screen shots are added if necessary.

Descriptions for abstract components have to be created by the users themselves. Furthermore, we implemented an annotation window that consists of the following text fields: "name," "creator," "origin," "description," and "remarks." Since textual documentation of design rationales imposes extra burden, it is often omitted (see Grudin, 1996). So we tried to reduce the workload by providing automatic support in creating the descriptions where possible. For instance, the "creator" field is generated automatically by data taken from the user administration. The "origin" field contains a reference if an abstract component is created by modifying an existing one. This reference is created automatically, as well. The "description" field clarifies the functioning of an abstract component, whereas, the explanation of the original one is copied and put into italics to be modified in case the abstract component is created by modifying an existing one.

4.3. EXEMPLIFYING AND EXPERIMENTING WITH COMPONENT

Beyond textual descriptions, we allow users to experiment with components created by somebody else. In case of tailorable groupware, exploration environments have been applied (see Section 3.2) for this purpose. While exploration environments support experimenting with completely assembled functionality, we had to find new approaches to support experimenting with atomic or abstract components. Since they do not cover a whole functionality, these artifacts cannot be executed in the exploration environment by themselves which made us implement an option that allows the users to store the "missing parts" together with the corresponding atomic or compound components. Together with the components themselves, the "missing parts" should provide a characteristic example for the component's use when building functionality. Those examples than can be executed in the exploration environment.

5. Related Work

Our work on component-based tailorability has been drawn on previous results from the CSCW, software-engineering, and HCI community. However, up to our knowledge, it is rather unique in working out a component framework.

In the CSCW, tailorability is an important field of research and the changing software during use is a main aspect. In the following we will give a short overview on the works that influenced our approach. The Oval system (Malone et al., 1992) is one of the earliest approaches to design for tailorability. The main idea of Oval is that there are only four types of software modules (Objects, Views, Agents, and Links) that can be used to build groupware applications. While the composition of these modules provides a lot of the functionality, they are not sufficiently fine-grained to permit application building without system-level programming.

PROSPERO (Dourish, 1996) is a object-oriented framework that can be used to compose CSCW applications. It offers a number of technical abstractions of CSCW-functionality (e.g. converging and diverging streams of cooperative work) that developers can use as a basis to rapidly develop specific applications. PROSPERO addresses the concerns of developers of CSCW systems, it does not aim at tailoring by end users.

DCWPL (*Describing Collaborative Work Programming Language*; Cortes, 1999) is a framework that allows to separate computational and coordination issues when implementing groupware. Groupware applications consist of modules for computation and those for coordination. The computational modules are connected via coordinating modules implementing the multi-user aspects and are described in a DCWPL file. So, several language constructs may be used to describe session management, awareness support etc. As DCWPL files are interpreted at run time, tailoring is possible by changing the code. Like PROSPERO, DCWPL does not offer a tailoring environment directed to users without programming experience.

Repenning et al. (2000) built a simulation system in which cooperative agents can be programmed by end-users offering a visual programming language that allows changing the behavior of single agents. In a similar way we allow changing the behavior of a component by setting parameters. In Repenning et al. (2000) work, the interaction between the agents remains hidden and cannot be tailored, which differs from our approach, since we allow recomposing components via connecting ports. Another difference comes from the design of the tailoring language, as we implemented a tailoring language that can be applied to the recomposition of components in different fields of application. Just the set of components and the techniques for setting parameters are different for each field of application, whereas the programming language Visual AgenTalk needs to be redesigned for each field of application to ease understand.

In the TACTS framework, Teege (2000) has worked out the idea of feature-based composition to tailor groupware. Contrary to our approach, in his approach the interaction between components is not port-based, but the underlying architecture only provides for two basic communication styles: a broadcast to all components and a directed connection between two partners. In both cases the structure of the messages is not limited by the architecture. So all semantics have to be defined within the communicating partners. By adding a feature to a given software module, the functionality of an application can be changed during runtime.

The CoCoWare platform (Slagter et al., 2001) allows users to compose their own component-based groupware application. Each component itself is a small application, such as a session control or a conference manager. While their work is influenced by our approach and from a software-technical perspective closely related to it, the main difference bases on the granularity of the components: While their components represent whole applications, FLEXIBEANS are conceptualized to be more fine-grained. On the one hand this allows for more flexibility, on the other hand the tailoring becomes more complex.

In software engineering, there are many environments that allow modifying or composing components at design time. They generate applications that are monolithic after being compiled. For instance, this is the case with Visual Age for Java (IBM, 1998) or Visual Basic (Microsoft, 1996) that cannot be used to change an application during run time as may be the FREEVOLVE system.

The DARWIN system (Magee et al., 1995) is similar to the FREEVOLVE system on a conceptual level. It is based on a component model that provides for typed event-based interaction and hierarchical compositions. A difference can be seen in the granularity of the components. As in DARWIN each component has its own process and can be seen as a small independent application, DARWIN does not support the fine-grained tailorability demonstrated by the FREEVOLVE-Platform. DARWIN is a system that is intended to be used by administrators.

The Regis system (Magee et al., 1995) allows for distributed configuration management. Its 2D environment is similar to the first tailoring client of the FREEVOLVE system. In this way, it has the same problems concerning displaying all the information on one screen and dealing with the problem of invisible components, but as the underlying component model is based on the idea that a composition consists only of few components, these problems are less grave than in our works.

Many systems support the development process by graphical or visual programming environments for an overview see for example (Myers, 1990). Most of those environments try to visualize the whole program and all its facets, which is not our intention. We visualize only those parts of an applications that can be changed, such as the component structure. The functionality of a component can not be changed, therefore code is not be displayed.[10]

Some of those tools use multiple views to concentrate on distinct aspects of the application. For instance, in most programming environments, there is a code view and a GUI view. In the field of end-user tailorability, Morch and Mehandjiev (1999) use this technique: Their system ECHOES allows for tailoring applications that can be seen and changed in different representation views.

The HCI discussion has developed concepts that support learning the functionality of single user applications. These concepts are based on either structuring, describing, experimenting with or exemplifying the use of certain functions (e.g. Carroll, 1987; Carroll and Carrithers, 1984; Howes and Paynes, 1990; Paul, 1994; Yang, 1990). However, the concepts are developed under the assumption that programmers provide them to users. In our case, the learning situation is different as users have to learn about the tailored artifact provided by other users. Therefore, we had to rethink some of the concepts. With regard to exploration, we also had to extend the concepts to deal with the distributed character of these applications.

The functionality for sharing tailored artifacts among users is rather similar to shared workspaces in the CSCW discussion (Bentley et al., 1997). However, shared workspace functionality needed to be integrated both, with the groupware application and with the additional features for making the components intelligible.

6. Conclusion

We presented our work on how concepts of component-based tailorability can be made intelligible and manageable for end users. Due to the specific requirements of users, whose main interests are not focused on software development, in particular the user interfaces deviate from typical developer-oriented IDE in software engineering. In order to enable users to recompose applications, we had to develop specific tailoring environments. At this, we built and evaluated different types of 2D and 3D graphical interfaces. To provide additional support during tailoring activities, two types of rule-based integrity checks were developed. Exploration environments allow users to test their final compositions of groupware functionality. We worked out the concept of direct activation, to make users aware of tailoring functionality by means of a better dialogue structure of the interface. Finally, we developed shared repositories to allow users to exchange tailored artifacts. This feature is of special importance since the

---

[10] Users only can influence the functionality of a component by changing its parameters. So parameters and their current values can be displayed.

levels of qualification, interest, and dedication will be different among users involved in tailoring an application. So we need to support the emergence of a tailoring culture within the field of application (see Carter and Henderson, 1990).

While these results stem from long-term research activities that include the design and implementation of technological innovations as well as their evaluation in laboratory-settings and field studies, there are still many open issues. We do not yet know which applications are best suited for component-based approaches compared to other paradigms for decomposition, such as rule-based or agent-based ones. Our experiences so far seem to indicate, that applications or parts of them, whose control flow can be presented in a rather linear order, are well suited for component-based tailorability. Methods for finding appropriate decompositions of an application into atomic components are another issue for further investigation (see Stevens and Wulf, 2002; Stiemerling, 2000). Decomposition must be meaningful to users (see Stevens and Quaisser, in this issue). For different classes of applications, we need to find meaningful metaphors and approaches for decomposition. Another challenging issue is the development of appropriate tailoring platforms for peer2peer architectures and mobile systems (see Alda and Cremers, 2004).

Extending our approach, one can imagine to introduce additional levels of tailoring complexity by gray or even glass-boxing of atomic components. Thus, selected aspects of the code or even the whole code of an atomic component could become modifiable by certain users. With regard to the user interface for tailoring, one has to investigate whether a single interaction paradigm is sufficient for component-based tailorability or whether the interaction paradigm of the tailorable application needs to be taken into account for the design of the interface of the tailoring environment (see Nardi, 1993).

Supporting cooperative tailoring activities, we need to think of additional features that support users in selecting appropriate atomic or abstract components out of a larger set. Ye (2001) has developed a recommender system that supports software developers to share and reuse source code via a repository. We believe that similar functionalities will valuable for collaborative tailoring activities. Moreover, we will be able to learn from the open source movement and the discussion on social capital to design shared repositories in an appropriate manner (see Fischer et al., 2004; Huysman and Wulf, 2004).

Finally, we need to gain experiences on how to connect tailoring activities with processes of organizational development and change (see Wulf and Jarke, 2004). In order to improve flexibility and efficiency of business processes, the exploitation of tailorability needs to be integrated into the ongoing processes of organizational change. Therefore, we have developed the framework of Integrated Organization and Technology Development that connects tailorability with planned processes of organizational and technological development (see Wulf and Rohde, 1995). However, we need to investigate more on emergent change processes and the role of tailorability in technology appropriation (see Orlikowski and Hofman, 1997; Andriessen et al., 2003).

References

Ackermann, D. and Ulich, E. (1987). The chances of individualization in human-computer interaction and its consequences. In: M. Frese, E. Ulich and W. Dzida (eds.), *Psychological Issues of Human Computer Interaction in the Work Place*. Amsterdam: North Holland, pp. 131–146.

Alda, S. and Cremers, A.B. (2004). Strategies for component-based self-adaptability model in peer-to-peer architectures. In: *Proceedings of the 4th International Symposium on Component-based Software Engineering (CBSE7)*. LNCS. Edinburgh, Scotland (May), pp. 42–58.

Andriessen, J.H.E., Hettinga, M. and Wulf, V. (eds.) (2003). Special issue on evolving use of groupware. In: *Computer Supported Cooperative Work: The Journal of Collaborative Computing (JCSCW)*, Vol. 12, No. 4.

Bellissard, L., Atallah, S.B., Boyer, F., Reveill, M. (1996). Distributed application configuration. In: *Proceedings of 16th International Conference on Distributed Computing Systems (ICDCS)*, Hong Kong, IEEE Computer Society, 579–585.

Bentley, R., Appelt, W., Busbach, U., Hinrichs, E., Kerr, D., Sikkel, K., Trevor, J. and Woetzel, G. (1997). Basic support for cooperative work on the world wide web. In: *International Journal of Human Computer Studies* **46**, pp. 827–846.

Bentley, R. and Dourish, P. (1995). Medium versus mechanism. supporting collaboration through customisation. In: H. Marmolin, Y. Sundblad and K. Schmidt (eds.), *Proceedings of the Fourth European Conference on Computer Supported Cooperative Work—ECSCW '95*, Kluwer, pp. 133–148.

Carroll, J.M. (1987). Five gambits for the advisory interfaces dilemma. In: M. Frese, E. Ulich and W. Dzida (eds.), *Psychological Issues of Human Computer Interaction in the Work Place*, Amsterdam, pp. 257–274.

Carroll, J.M. and Carrithers, C. (1984). Training wheels in a user interface. In: *Communications of the ACM*, Vol. 27, S. 800–806.

Carter, K. and Henderson, A. (1990). Tailoring culture. In: R. Hellman, M. Ruohonen and P. Sorgard (eds.), *Proceedings of the 13th IRIS, Reports on Computer Science and Mathematics*, No. 107, Abo Akademi University, pp. 103–116.

Cortes, M. (2000). A coordination language for building collaborative applications. *Journal of Computer Supported Cooperative Work* (JCSCW), 9(1), 5–31.

Dourish, P. (1996). *Open Implementation and Flexibility in CSCW Toolkits*, Ph.D. Thesis. London: University College.

Engelskirchen, T. (2000). *Exploration Anpassbarer Groupware*, Master Thesis, Bonn: University of Bonn.

Fischer, G., Scharff, E. and Ye, Y. (2004). Fostering social creativity by increasing social capital. In: M. Huysman and V. Wulf (eds.), *Social Capital and Information Technology*, Cambridge, MA: MIT-Press.

Frese, M., Irmer, C. and Prümper, J. (1991). Das Konzept Fehlermanagement: Eine Strategie des Umgangs mit Handlungsfehlern in der Mensch-Computer Interaktion. In: C. Scarpelis (ed.), *Software für die Arbeit von morgen*, Berlin: Springer Verlag, pp. 241–252.

Golombek, B. (2000). *Implementierung und Evaluation der Konzepte "Explorative Ausführbarkeit" und "Direkte Aktivierbarkeit" für anpassbare Groupware*, Master Thesis, University of Bonn.

Grudin, J. (1996). Evaluating opportunities for design capture. In: T. Moran and J. Carroll (eds.), *Design Rationale: Concepts, Techniques, and use*, Lawrence Erlbaum Associates, Hillsdale, NJ, pp. 453–470.

Hallenberger, M. (2000). Programmierung einer interaktiven 3D-Schnittstelle am Beispiel einer Anpassungss chnittstelle für komponentenbasierte Anpassbarkeit, Diploma Thesis, Department of computer Science, University of Bonn, Germany.

Henderson, A. and Kyng, M. (1991). There's no place like home: Continuing design in use. In: J. Greenbaum and M. Kyng (eds.), *Design At Work—Cooperative Design of Computer Artefacts*, Hillsdale, New Jersey: Lawrence Erlbaum Associates, Publishers, pp. 219–240.

Hinken, R. (1999). *Verteilte Anpassbarkeit für Groupware—Eine Laufzeit und Anpassungsplattform*, Master Thesis, University of Bonn.

Howes, A. and Payne, S.J. (1990). Supporting exploratory learning. In: *Proceedings of INTERACT'90*, North-Holland, Amsterdam, pp. 881–885.

Huysman, M. and Wulf, V. (eds.) (2004). *Social Capital and Information Technology*. Cambridge MA: MIT Press.

IBM (1998). *Visual Age for Java*, Version 1.0.

ISO 9241. Ergonomic requirements for office work with visual display terminals (VDTs) Part 10: Dialogue Principles.

Johansen, R. (ed.) (1988). Current User Approaches to Groupware. In: *Groupware*, New York: Freepress, pp. 12–44.

Kahler, H. (2001a). *Supporting Collaborative Tailoring*, Ph.D. Thesis, Roskilde University, Denmark, Roskilde.

Kahler, H. (2001b). More than WORDSs: Collaborative tailoring of a word processor. *Journal on Universal Computer Science* (j.ucs) 7(9), 826–847.

Krings, M. (2003). *Erkennung semantischer Fehler in komponentenbasierten Architekturen*, Master Thesis, University of Bonn.

Krüger, M. (2003). *Semantische Integritätsprüfung für die Anpassung von Komponenten-Kompositionen*, Master Thesis, University of Bonn.

Mackay, W.E. (1990). *Users and Customizable Software: A Co-Adaptive Phenomenon*, Ph.D. Thesis, MIT, Boston (MA).

MacLean, A., Carter, K., Lövstrand, L. and Moran, T. (1990). User-tailorable systems: Pressing the issue with buttons. In: *Proceedings of the Conference on Computer Human Interaction (CHI '90)*, April 1–5, Seattle (Washington), ACM-Press, New York, pp. 175–182.

Magee, J., Dulay, N., Eisenbach, S. and Kramer, J. (1995). Specifying distributed software architectures. In: *Proceedings of 5th European Software Engineering Conference*, Barcelona.

Malone, T.W., Lai, K.-Y. and Fry, C. (1992). Experiments with oval: A radically tailorable tool for cooperative work. In: *Proceedings of CSCW*. Toronto, Canada, ACM Press, pp. 289–297.

McIlroy, D. (7th to 11th Oct. 1968). Mass-produced software components. In: P. Naur and B. Randell (eds.), *Software Engineering, Brussels*, 1969, Report of a Conference sponsored by the NATO Science Committee, Garmisch, Germany, pp. 138–155

Microsoft (1996). *Visual Basic*, Version 4.0.

Mørch, A. (1997). *Method and Tools for Tailoring of Object-oriented Applications: An Evolving Artifacts Approach*, PhD-Thesis, University of Oslo, Department of Computer Science, Research Report 241, Oslo.

Mørch, A.I. and Mehandjiev, N.D. (2003). Tailoring as collaboration: The mediating role of multiple representations and application units. *Journal on Computer Supported Cooperative Work (JCSCW)* 9(1), 75–100.

Mørch, A.I., Stevens, G., Won, M., Klann, M., Dittrich, Y. and Wulf, V. (2004). Component-based technologies for end user development. *Communications of the ACM* 47(9), 59–62.

Myers, B.A. (1990). Taxonomies of visual programming and program visualization. *Journal of Visual Languages and Computing* 1, 97–123.

Nardi, B.A. (1993). *A Small Matter of Programming—Perspectives on end-user computing*. Cambridge: MIT-Press.

Oberquelle, H. (1994). Situationsbedingte und benutzerorientierte Anpassbarkeit von Groupware. In: A. Hartmann, Th. Herrmann, M. Rohde, V. Wulf (eds.), *Menschengerechte Groupware*, Stuttgart, pp. 31–50.

Oppermann, R. and Simm, H. (1994). Adaptability: User-initiated individualization. In: R. Oppermann (ed.), *Adaptive User Support—Ergonomic Design of Manually and Automatically Adaptable Software*, LEA, Hillsdale, NJ.

Orlikowski, W.J. and Hofman, J. D. (1997). An improvisational model for change management: The case of groupware technologies. In: *Sloan Management Review* (Winter 1997), 11–21.

Page, S., Johnsgard, T., Albert, U. and Allen, C. (1996). User Customization of a Word Processor. In: *Proceedings of CHI '96*, (April 13–18), 340–346.

Paul, H. (1994). *Exploratives Agieren*. Frankfurt/M: Peter Lang, 1994.

Repenning, A., Ioannidou, A. and Zola, J. (2000), AgentSheets: End-user programmable simulations. *Journal of Artificial Societies and Social Simulation* 3(3).

Schmidt, K. (1991). Riding a tiger or computer supported cooperative work. In: L. Bannon, M. Robinson and K. Schmidt (eds.), *Proceedings ECSCW '91*, Kluwer, Dordrecht, pp. 1–16.

Silberschatz, A., Korth, H. and Sudarshan, S. (2001). *Database System Concepts*, Osborne: McGraw-Hill.

Stiemerling, O. (2000). *Component-based Tailorability*, Ph.D. Thesis, Department of Computer Science, University of Bonn, Bonn.

Stiemerling, O. and Cremers, A.B. (1998). Tailorable component architectures for CSCW-systems. In: A.M. Tyrell (ed.), *Proceedings of the 6th Euromicro Workshop on Parallel and Distributed Processing*, IEEE-Press 1998, pp. 302–308.

Stiemerling, O., Hinken, R. and Cremers, A.B. (1999). The evolve tailoring platform: Supporting the evolution of component-based groupware. In: *Proceedings of EDOC '99*, IEEE Press, Mannheim, September 27–30, pp. 106–115.

Stevens, G. (2002). *Komponentenbasierte Anpassbarkeit—FlexiBeans zur Realisierung einer erweiterten Zugriffskontrolle*, Master Thesis, University of Bonn.

Stevens, G. and Wulf, V. (2002). A new dimension in access control: Studying maintenance engineering across organizational boundaries. In: *Proceedings of ACM Conference on Computer Supported Cooperative Work (CSCW 2002)*, ACM-Press, New York, pp. 196–205.

Szyperski, C. (2002). *Component Software: Beyond Object Oriented Programming*, 2nd Edition, London: Addison Wesley.

Slagter, R., Biemans, M. and Ter Hofte, G.H. (2001). Evolution in use of groupware: Facilitating tailoring to the extreme. In: M. Borges, J. Haake and U. Hoppe (eds.), *Proceedings of the 7th International Workshop on Groupware (CRIWG 2001)*, 6–8 September 2001, Darmstadt, Germany.

Teege, G. (2000). *Users as Composers: Parts and Features as a Basis for Tailorability in CSCW Systems*, CSCW, Kluwer Academic Publishers, pp. 101–122.

van der Aalst, W.D.H. and Verbeek, H.M.W. (1997). A Petri-Net-based tool to analyze workflows. In: *Proceedings of Petri Nets in System Engineering (PNSE '97)*, Hamburg, Universität Hamburg, pp. 78–90.

Won, M. (1998). *Komponentenbasierte Anpassbarkeit—Anwendung auf ein Suchtool für Groupware*, Master Thesis, University of Bonn.

Won, M. (2002). Cremers, Armin B.: Supporting End-User Tailoring of Component-Based Software—Checking Integrity of Composition. In: *Proceedings of Colognet 2002 (Conjuction with LOPSTR 2002)*, Madrid, Spain, 19–20 September 2002, pp. 47–58.

Won, M. (2003). Supporting end-user development of component-based software by checking semantic integrity. In: *ASERC Workshop on Software Testing*, Febrauary 19, 2003, Banff, Canada.

Wulf, V. (1994). Volker Wulf: Anpaßbarkeit im Prozeß evolutionärer Systementwicklung. *GMD-Spiegel* 24(3/94), 41–46.

Wulf, V. (1999). "Let's see your Search-Tool!"—collaborative use of tailored artifacts in groupware. In: *Proceedings of GROUP '99*, ACM-Press, New York, 1999, pp. 50–60.

Wulf, V. (2000). Exploration environments: Supporting users to learn groupware functions. *Interacting with Computers* 13(2), 265–299.

Wulf, V. (2001). Zur anpassbaren Gestaltung von Groupware: Anforderungen, Konzepte, Implementierungen und Evaluationen, GMD Research Series, Nr. 10/2001, St. Augustin.

Wulf, V. and Golombek, B. (2001a). Direct activation: A concept to encourage tailoring activities. *Behavior and Information Technology* **20**(4), 249–263.

Wulf, V. and Golombek, B. (2001b). Exploration environments—concept and empirical evaluation. In: *Proceedings of GROUP 2001*, ACM-Press, New York, pp. 107–116.

Wulf, V. and Jarke, M. (2004). The economics of end user development. *Communications of the ACM* **47**(9), 41–42.

Wulf, V. and Rohde, M. (1995). Towards an integrated organization and technology development. In: *Proceedings of the Symposium on Designing Interactive Systems*, 23–25 August 1995, Ann Arbor (Michigan), ACM-Press, New York, pp. 55–64.

Yang, Y. (1990). Current approaches and new guidelines for undo-support design. In: *Proceedings of INTERACT'90*, North-Holland, Amsterdam, pp. 543–548.

Ye, Y. (2001). *Supporting Component-Based Software Development with Active Component Repository Systems*. Ph.D. Thesis, Department of Computer Science, University of Colorado at Boulder, Boulder 2001.

Chapter 7

Natural Development of Nomadic Interfaces Based on Conceptual Descriptions

SILVIA BERTI[1], FABIO PATERNÒ[2] and CARMEN SANTORO[3]
[1]*Dipartemento di Storia Moderna e Contemporanea, Università degli Studi di Roma La Sapienza, Rome, Italy, silvia.berti@isti.cnr.it*
[2]*ISTI–CNR Institute, Pisa, Italy, fabio.paterno@isti.cnr.it*
[3]*CNUCE–CNR Institute, Pisa, Italy, carmen.santoro@isti.cnr.it*

Abstract. Natural development aims to ease the development process of interactive software systems. This can be obtained through the use of familiar representations together with intelligent environments able to map them onto corresponding implementations of interactive systems. The main motivation for model-based approaches to user interface design has been to support development through the use of meaningful abstractions in order to avoid dealing with low-level details. Despite this potential benefit, their adoption has mainly been limited to professional designers. This paper shows how they should be extended in order to achieve natural development through environments that enable end-users to create or modify interactive applications still using conceptual models, but with continuous support that facilitates their development, analysis, and use. In particular, we discuss the application of the proposed criteria to the CTTE and TERESA environments, which support the design and development of multi-device interfaces.

1. Introduction

Two fundamental challenges for development environments in the coming years are end-user development (EUD) and interaction device heterogeneity. The former aims to allow people without any particular background in programming to develop their own applications. The increasing interactive capabilities of new devices have created the potential to overcome the traditional separation between end-users and software developers. Over the next few years, we will be moving from *easy-to-use* (which has still to be completely achieved) to *easy-to-develop interactive software systems*. EUD in general means the active participation of end-users in the software development process. From this perspective, tasks that have traditionally carried out by professional software developers are transferred to users, who need to be specifically supported in performing such activities. New environments able to seamlessly move between using and programming (or customising) software should be designed. The other challenge is raised by the ever-increasing introduction of new types of interactive devices, whose range varies from small devices such as interactive watches to very large flat displays. The availability of such platforms has forced designers to strive to make applications run on a wide spectrum of computing devices in order to enable users to seamlessly access information and services regardless of the device they are using and

Henry Lieberman et al. (eds.), End User Development, 143–159.

even when the system or the environment changes dynamically. Thus, there is a need for new development environments able to provide integrated solutions to these two main challenges.

One of the goals of EUD is to reach closeness of mapping: as Green and Petre put it (Green and Petre, 1996): "The closer the programming world is to the problem world, the easier the problem-solving ought to be. . . . Conventional textual languages have a long way to go before achieving that goal." Even graphical languages often fail to furnish immediately understandable representations for developers. The work in Myers' group aims to obtain natural programming (Pane and Myers, 1996), meaning programming through languages that work in the way people without any experience in this field would expect. We intend to take a more comprehensive view of the development cycle, thus not limited only to programming, but also including requirements, designing, modifying, tailoring, etc. Natural development implies that people should be able to work through familiar and immediately understandable representations that allow them to easily express and manipulate relevant concepts, and thereby create or modify interactive software artifacts. In contrast, since a software artifact needs to be precisely specified in order to be implemented, there will still be the need for environments supporting transformations from intuitive and familiar representations into more precise, but more difficult to develop, descriptions. In this paper, we discuss how to apply this paradigm to the CTTE and TERESA environments, which support the design and development of multiple interfaces adapted to the interaction resources of the various target platforms, starting with descriptions of the logical tasks to support.

In the next sections we first discuss related work, then we discuss some criteria for delivering natural development environments to informal programmers. In Section 4, we provide a general introduction to the different viewpoints that can be considered when dealing with interactive systems, while in Section 5 we focus on an authoring environment, TERESA, we developed for design of multi-device interfaces. An example of application using the TERESA approach is shown in Section 6, while some conclusions have been drawn in Section 7.

2. Related Work

Several years ago many people argued that programming is difficult because it requires the precise use of a textual language; the hope was that visual environments would have been inherently easier to use, based on the consideration that many people think and remember things in terms of pictures. In other words, they relate to the world in an inherently graphical way and use imagery as a primary component of creative thought. Visual programming methods like conventional flow charts and graphical programming languages have been widely studied in the last 20 years. On the one hand, reducing or removing entirely the necessity of translating visual ideas into textual representations can help to speed up and make easier the learning phase. On the other hand, end-users still have problems even when using visual environments. It seems that visual languages might be better for small tasks, but often breakdown for large tasks (Green and Petre, 1992). An example of adoption of the visual approach is the Unified

Modeling Language (UML) (OMG, 2001), which has become the de facto standard notation for software models. UML is a family of diagrammatic languages tailored to modeling all relevant aspects of a software system; and methods and pragmatics can define how these aspects can be consistently integrated. Visual modeling languages have been identified as promising candidates for defining models of the software systems to be produced. They inherently require abstractions and should deploy concepts, metaphors, and intuitive notations that allow professional software developers, domain experts, and users to communicate ideas and concepts. This requirement is of prominent importance if models are not only to be understood, but also used and even produced by end-users.

Generic languages are designed for general-purpose problems, whereas domain-specific programming languages are designed for a specific class of problems. In order to remain generic, the first type must accept a trade-off between the expressiveness of the constructs, their intuitiveness, and the need to suit a variety of needs. Languages of the second class focus on a specific type of problem. This facilitates narrowing the range of objectives and more properly defining the goals of the language. The consequence is that the language constructs are easier to learn because they are tailored to the task, while the user's background knowledge allows using high-level constructs and abstractions because some details are automatically dealt with. Such languages are able to quickly augment user productivity and some applications can be obtained through the use of a set of application-specific libraries that are able to enhance existing tools for EUD.

Natural programming has been defined as a "faithful method to represent nature or life, which works in the way the people expect" (Myers, 1998). In general, it is advisable that user interfaces are "natural" so that they are easier to learn and use, and will result in fewer errors. For example, (Nielsen, 1993) recommends that user interfaces should "speak the user's language"; this means that user interfaces should include a good mapping between the user's conceptual model of the information and the computer's interface for it. For this reason, it is important to enable users to speak their language for expressing their conceptual view in a natural way. A production-oriented programming style should be more natural; a possible approach is to use a well-known real-world system as a metaphor for the computational machine in order to make the programming procedure more concrete. Many previous research systems used metaphors, such as the "turtle" in Logo. However, the use of metaphors can lead to other intrinsic problems, for example the difficulty in finding an appropriate metaphoric model for a given programming environment. In addition, metaphors do not scale well; in fact, a metaphor that works well for a simple process in a simple program might fail as soon the process grows in size or complexity. Then, the use of appropriate metaphors, with their capabilities and limitations, differs widely depending on the users and their purposes. A useful method for natural programming is mixed-initiative dialogue, where both the user and the system can activate the interaction, which can result in a conversation about the program.

Another interesting direction in which end-user programming can be pursued is through the use of model-based approaches, which on the one hand are sometimes criticized due to problems in understanding/using them, but, on the other hand, are indisputably helpful in managing complexity, as they allow designers to focus on the most relevant concepts. In particular, since one of the basic usability principles is "focus on the users and their tasks," it becomes important to consider *task* models. Task models can be useful to provide an integrated description of system functionality and user interaction. Then, the development of the corresponding artifact able to support the identified features should be obtainable through environments that are able to suggest the most effective interaction and presentation techniques on the basis of a set of guidelines or design criteria. Various solutions have been proposed for this purpose. They vary according to a number of dimensions. For example, the automation level can be different: a completely automatic solution can provide meaningful results only when the application domain is rather narrow and consequently the space of the possible solutions regarding the mapping of tasks to interaction techniques is limited.

More general environments are based on the mixed initiative principle: the tool supporting the mapping provides suggestions that the designer can accept or modify. An example is the TERESA environment (Mori et al., 2004) that provides support for the design and development of multi-device interfaces, which can be accessed through different types of interaction devices. Other works have addressed similar issues but following different approaches, without considering EUD or model-based development. One example is a completely automatic solution, which is called transcoding, in which an application written in a language for a platform is automatically translated into an application coded in a language for another platform (see *IBM WebSphere Transcoding* for an example of HTML-to-WML transcoding). The main problem of such approaches is that they assume that the same tasks are provided on each platform, and tend to support them in the same manner without taking into account the specific features of the platform at hand, so providing poor results in terms of usability. Aura (De Sousa and Garlan, 2002) is a project whose goal is to provide an infrastructure that configures itself automatically for the mobile user. When a user moves to a different platform, Aura attempts to reconfigure the computing infrastructure so that the user can continue working on tasks started elsewhere. In this approach, tasks are considered as a cohesive collection of applications. Suppliers provide the abstract services, which are implemented by just wrapping existing applications and services to conform to Aura APIs. For instance, Emacs, Word, and NotePad can each be wrapped to become a supplier of text editing services. So, the different context is supported through a different application for the same goal (for example, text editing can be supported through MS Word or Emacs depending on the resources of the device at hand). TERESA provides a more flexible solution where the same application can have different interfaces depending on the interactive device available. This is obtained by exploiting the semantic information contained in the declarative descriptions of the tasks and the interface and using transformations that incorporate design criteria platform-dependent for generating multiple interfaces (one for each potential type of platform).

3. Criteria for Obtaining Natural Development Environments

In this section we discuss two important criteria that can be identified to obtain natural development environments based on the use of conceptual descriptions, providing concrete examples of their application.

3.1. INTEGRATING INFORMAL AND STRUCTURED REPRESENTATIONS

The use of informal techniques is typically associated with non-professional users, since it does not require any specific *a priori* knowledge. However, most end-user developers would benefit from a combined use of multiple representations and various levels of formality. Indeed, at the beginning of the design process many things are obscure and unclear, so it is hard to develop precise specifications from scratch. In addition, there is the problem of clearly understanding what user requirements are. Thus, it can be helpful to use the results of initial discussions to feed the more structured parts of the design process. In general, the main issue of EUD is how to use personal intuition, familiar metaphors and concepts to obtain or modify a software artifact, whose features need to be precisely defined in order to obtain consistent support for the desired functionality and behavior.

In this process we should address all the available multimedia possibilities. For example, support for vocal interaction is mature for the mass market. Its support for the Web is being standardized by W3C (Abbott, in press). The rationale for vocal interaction is that it makes practical operations quicker and more natural, and it also makes multimodal (graphic and vocal) interactions possible. Vocal interaction can be considered both for the resulting interactive application and for the supporting the development environment.

In CTTE (Mori et al., 2002), to support the initial modeling work we provide the possibility of loading an informal textual description of a scenario or a use case and interactively selecting the information of interest for the modeling work. To develop a task model from an informal textual description, designers first have to identify the different roles. Then, they can start to analyze the textual description of the scenario, trying to identify the main tasks that occur in the scenario and associate each task with a particular role. It is possible to specify the category of the task, in terms of performance allocation. In addition, a description of the task can be specified along with the logical objects used and handled. By reviewing the scenario description, the designer can identify the different tasks and then add them to the task list. Once designers have their list of activities to consider, they can start to create the hierarchical structure that describes the various levels of abstraction among tasks. The hierarchical structure obtained can then be further refined through the specification of the temporal relations among tasks and the tasks' attributes and objects. The use of these features is optional: designers can start to create the model directly using the graphical editor, but such features can facilitate the modeling work. U-Tel (Tam et al., 1998) provides a different type of support: through automatic analysis of scenario content, nouns are automatically associated with objects, and verbs with tasks. This approach provides some useful results, but it is too simple to be generalized and sometimes may fail (e.g., because a task might be defined by a verb followed by an object).

Another useful support can be derived from the consideration that people often spontaneously use sketches and rough designs even just to improve human-to-human communication. As a matter of fact, the result of brainstorming by either one single person or a group are often 'quick and dirty' pen/paper or whiteboard—based diagrams whose main objective is to effectively and rapidly fix/communicate ideas. Such techniques are effective because they allow people to concentrate on ideas instead of being distracted by low level details or getting stuck by some rigid symbolism. In addition, the possibility of developing through sketching can be highly appreciated especially if it is possible to capture the results of such process for further analysis. Such considerations foster application areas for intelligent whiteboard systems (Landay and Myers, 2001) or augmented reality techniques, as they are capable of exploiting such natural modes of interaction/communication. In fact, such informal techniques minimize the need for abstractions (which are mostly used with formal techniques) while specifying systems. Moreover, especially non-professional users feel particularly comfortable with them. Such systems are able to interpret sketches by recognizing graphical elements and converting them into a format that can be edited and analyzed by desktop tools. In addition, they should be able to recognize not only single elements, but also composite or complex groups/patterns regarding structure and navigation through an analysis of spatial relations between objects. Also, the possibility of specifying reusable custom graphical elements and extending the grammar through such composites should be envisaged and, in order to get a real "flavor" of the interactive system involved, the users should also be empowered with the ability to associate dynamic properties to such drawings. In this way, they can be enabled to intuitively outline not only the static layout of the user interface but also its dynamic behavior.

The use of such techniques paves the way for an iterative and progressive refinement process in which multiple levels of detail are progressively included by users (designers), who gradually adjust the design moving from inherently informal, imprecise, and ambiguous specifications to more rigorous and detailed designs. In this way, users are allowed to overcome the formal barriers that are traditionally associated with this process and smoothly bridge the cognitive gap from informal techniques to more structured methods and representations. We have designed a tool supporting the development task models using sketches. We have used technologies able to enrich a whiteboard in order to capture the sketches made by the user (such as the high-resolution ultrasonic position capture system provided by Mimio interactive technologies). The tool is able to capture the sketch from the whiteboards and convert it into vector SVG format. Then, we have developed a tool able to take such vectorial descriptions, analyze them and recognize the corresponding expressions in the CTT notation, which are then saved in an XML file (see Figure 7.1), and can be imported by the CTTE and TERESA tools for further editing.

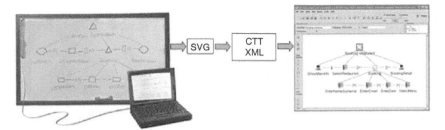

Figure 7.1. Example of use of sketches with CTTE.

Furthermore, in order to make some user commands and actions more natural, it is important that user interfaces support multiple modes of interaction, for example, enabling users to interact vocally or by means of an input device (such as a keypad, keyboard, mouse, stylus, etc.).

For many users it is easier and more natural to produce spoken commands than to remember the location of a function within menus and dialog boxes. Moreover, by using increasingly complex commands based on natural language enable rapid access to features that have traditionally been buried in sub-menus and dialogues. For examples, the command "Apply italic, 10 point, Arial" replaces multiple menu selections and mouse clicks. Programming in natural language might seem impossible but several studies found that when non-programmers are asked to write step-by-step informal natural language procedures, many different people use the same phrases to indicate standard programming tasks (Pane and Myers, 1996). Due to this fact, the vocal commands recognition is less complicated and focuses on a set of significant keywords and phrases. This technique has been adopted in a new version of the CTTE tool, where the users can define the task model by keyboard, mouse, and vocal commands. When they decide to use vocal interaction, the system produces a welcome message that helps to understand the information to provide; then an icon (e.g., a picture of a microphone) is visualized, allowing the user to turn off the input device. This feature is useful if the users need to have a different conversation with another person or machine, have to think about their next step, or gather material or information for the next step in order to reduce errors in speech recognition. Then, while the user vocally specifies the main tasks and associated properties, the system draws the related task model, using the symbols of the ConcurTaskTrees notation (Paternò, 1999). For example, if the user says: "At the beginning the user inserts name and password in order to access the system; then the system visualizes the personal page with information on areas of interest," the recognition system, by means of a specific grammar and vocabulary, analyses and interprets the vocal message. In this example the system identifies four tasks: three interaction tasks (*"Access the system"*, *"Insert name"*, and *"Insert password"*) and one application task (*"Visualise personal data"*) and also defines the main properties.

Additionally, the system defines the relations between the identified tasks by means of some keywords like temporal adverbs, prepositions, conjunctions, and so on. In

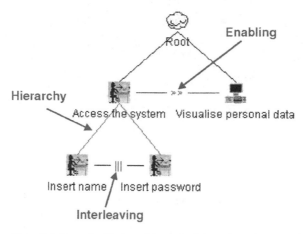

Figure 7.2. Example of task model generated through vocal commands.

our example three types of relations are automatically recognized (see Figure 7.2): the first one defines the hierarchy between the task "*Access the system*", (which is the parent), and "*Insert name*" and "*Insert password*"," (which are the children), since in the vocal command the user says the keyword "*in order to*". The second relation is between "*Insert name*" and "*Insert password,*" and it is an interleaving relation because the task can be performed in any order without any specific constraints (indeed the user says the keyword "*and*"). The last one is between "*Access the system*" and "*Visualize personal data*"," which is an enabling relation because the first task enables the second one as the user adopts the expression "*At the beginning task1, then task2.*"

During the conversation, if the recognition system does not understand some information or has some uncertainties, it asks the user to verify the properties settings or to explain it with further details. At any time, the user can close the vocal guided creation procedure and operate a fully customizable development process.

3.2. PROVIDING EFFECTIVE REPRESENTATIONS

Recent years have seen the widespread adoption of visual modeling techniques in the software design process. However, we are still far from visual representations that are easy to develop, analyze, and modify, especially when large case studies are considered. As soon as the visual model increases in complexity, designers have to interact with many graphical symbols connected in various ways and have difficulties in analyzing the specification and understanding the relations among the various parts. In addition, the ever-spreading introduction and adoption of disparate handheld interaction devices has further spurred designers to focus on the recurring problem of the lack of screen space for effectively visualizing large information structures on small screens while still maintaining awareness of the context.

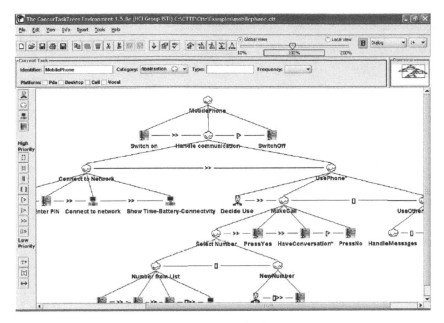

Figure 7.3. How CTTE provides focus+context representation.

In this regard, CTTE provides support through some representations that ease the analysis of a model. As shown in Figure 7.3, it provides a focus+context representation of the model (*focus* on details of immediate interest, plus *context* of the overall model), allowing the user to have a detailed view of a part of the model within the main window (because only a portion can be displayed when large models are considered), yet still providing a small overview pane (in the right-top part) that allows designers to orient themselves with regard to the location of the focus part in the overall model. The representation in the overview pane is limited to the overall hierarchical structure disregarding details like task names and icons (which represent how the tasks are allocated). The correspondence between the focus window and the context window is facilitated by the hierarchical structure of the model.

In addition, the application and extension of innovative interaction techniques, including those developed in the field of information visualization (Spence, 2001) (such as semantic zooming, fisheye, two-hand interactions, magic lens . . .), can noticeably improve the effectiveness of the environments aiming at providing different interactive representations depending on the abstraction level of interest, or the aspects that designers want to analyze or the type of issues that they want to address.

One of the most well-known approaches in this area is the *fisheye* view (Furnas, 1981). According to this work, it is possible to calculate the Degree Of Interest (DOI) of the various elements, which is a mathematical distance function used to magnify certain areas with a high level of interest while leaving out elements with a low DOI by means of using some de-emphasize techniques like filtering, zooming out, etc. An example of

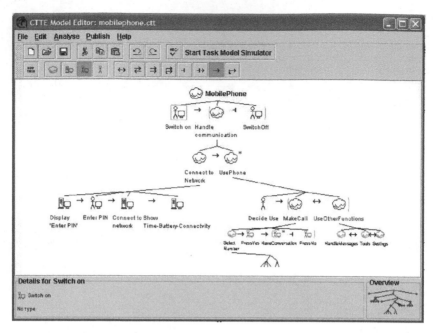

Figure 7.4. The fisheye-oriented representation of a task model in the new extension of CTTE.

a fish-eye oriented representation of a task model is given in Figure 7.4 which refers to a new extension of the CTTE tool (Paternò and Zini, 2004). The advantage of this approach is that it is able to dynamically highlight the areas of interest in the model by enlarging the elements that they contain. If we compare the representations in Figure 7.3 with that in Figure 7.4 (they refer to the same task model) we can notice that in Figure 7.4 there is a better management of the screen space since the most interesting elements (the focus in the representation in this figure is in the *Switch on* task) are more effectively highlighted. On the contrary, in Figure 7.3 all the tasks are equally represented, even the peripheral ones (the less interesting ones). The representation in Figure 7.4 applies both fisheye and semantic zoom representations. Fisheye is used to change the size of the representation for each task depending on its distance from the current focus (for example *Select Number* is smaller than *Switch on*). Semantic zoom is used to change representation for the most distant elements. In this case the task names and icons are not presented at all and only a representation of the corresponding tree structure is provided (an example is given by the subtasks of *Select Number* in Figure 7.4).

4. The Many Views on an Interactive System

It is important to consider the various viewpoints that are possible on an interactive system. Such viewpoints differ for the abstraction levels (to what extent the details are considered) and the focus (whether the task or the user interface is considered).

The model-based community has long discussed such possible viewpoints and in the CAMELEON project (http://giove.isti.cnr.it/cameleon.html) a study was conducted to better structure them and understand their relations through a reference framework. Such abstraction levels are:

- *Task and object model*, at this level, the logical activities that need to be performed in order to reach the users' goals are considered. Often they are represented hierarchically along with indications of the temporal relations among them and their associated attributes. The objects that have to be manipulated in order to perform tasks can be identified as well.
- *Abstract user interface*, in this case the focus shifts to the interaction objects supporting task performance. Only the main, modality-independent aspects are considered, thereby avoiding low-level details. An abstract user interface is defined in terms of presentations, identifying the set of user interface elements perceivable at the same time, and each presentation is composed of a number of interactors (Paternò and Leonardi, 1994), which are abstract interaction objects identified in terms of their semantics effects.
- *Concrete user interface*, at this point each abstract interactor is replaced with a concrete interaction object that depends on the type of platform and media available and has a number of attributes that define more concretely its appearance and behavior.
- *Final User interface*, at this level the concrete interface is translated into an interface defined by a specific software environment (e.g., XHTML, Java, . . .).

To better understand such abstraction levels we can consider an example of a task: making a hotel room reservation. It can be decomposed into selecting departure and arrival dates and other subtasks concerning required services/facilities. At the abstract user interface level we need to identify the interaction objects needed to support such tasks. For example, for specifying departure and arrival dates we need selection interaction objects. When we move on to the concrete user interface, we need to consider the specific interaction objects supported. So, in a desktop interface, selection can be supported by an object showing a calendar or by pull down menus allowing a controlled selection of month, day and year. The final user interface is the result of rendering such choices also considering the specific target environment of the device: it could involve attributes like the type and size of the font, the colors available, and decoration images.

Many transformations are possible among these four levels for each interaction platform considered: from higher level descriptions to more concrete ones or vice versa or between the same level of abstraction but for different types of platforms or even any combination of them. Consequently, a wide variety of situations can be addressed. More generally, the possibility of linking aspects related to user interface elements to more semantic aspects opens up the possibility of intelligent tools that can help in the design, evaluation, and run-time execution. In particular, they allow a development process starting with user oriented descriptions, which gradually transforms it into descriptions that adapt to various context of use.

5. Teresa: An Authoring Environment for Ubiquitous Interfaces

TERESA is a model-based environment supporting the design and development of nomadic applications (those that can be accessed through heterogeneous platforms and from different locations). The method underlying the TERESA tool is composed of a number of steps that allow designers to start with an envisioned overall task model of a nomadic application and then derive concrete and effective user interfaces for multiple devices through multiple levels of abstractions and related in-between transformations. The round trip engineering process supported by TERESA also allows maintaining links among elements at different abstraction levels, also helping users in understanding links between the various models. Further options are available within the tool, which implements the whole task/platform taxonomy (Paternò and Santoro, 2003) but provides at the same time different entry points to improve flexibility: for instance, when different devices referring to the same type of platform are considered, there is no need for a nomadic task model, since only one type of platform is involved. The tool is particularly geared towards generating Web interfaces but can be easily extended to other environments and, in order to improve interoperability with other tools, XML-based languages have been used within the tool to store user interface descriptions at various abstraction levels.

A feature particularly relevant with regard to EUD is the mixed initiative dialogue implemented within the tool, which supports different levels of automation (ranging from completely automatic solutions to highly interactive solutions where designers can tailor or even radically change the solutions proposed by the tool) suiting the various expertise levels of the target end-users. In fact, when designers are experts (or the application domain is either broad or has specific aspects) then more interactive environments are useful because they allow designers to directly make detailed design decisions. In other cases, e.g., when designers are not very skilled, the mixed-initiative interaction might provide more intelligent automatic support in order to take decisions on behalf of the user.

5.1. MAIN FUNCTIONALITIES

Figure 7.5 shows how our approach supports natural development. Thanks to the support of input captured through various modalities (sketches, vocal input, textual scenarios) that ease the specification of the tasks to carry out, the tool first identifies the logical activities to support. Such information is then processed through a number of steps that allow designers to derive user interfaces for multiple devices:

- *High-level task modeling of a multi-context application.* In this phase designers refine a single model that addresses the possible contexts of use and the roles involved and also all the objects that have to be manipulated to perform tasks and the relations among them. Such models are specified using ConcurTaskTrees. This specification allows designers to indicate the platforms suitable for each task.

Figure 7.5. The approach underlying TERESA.

- *Developing the system task model for the different platforms considered.* Here designers have just to filter the task model according to the target platform and, if necessary, further refine the task model, depending on the specific device considered, thus, obtaining the system task model for the platform considered.
- *From system task model to abstract user interface.* Here the tool supports a transformation to obtain an abstract description of the user interface composed of a set of abstract presentations that are identified through an analysis of the task relationships and structured by means of interactors composed of various operators. Both the task and the abstract user interface descriptions are obtained through a XML-based, platform-independent language.
- *User interface generation.* In this phase we have the generation of the user interface. This phase is completely platform-dependent and has to consider the specific properties of the target device. In order to support generation in new user interface languages only this transformation has to be modified.

6. An Example of Application

In this section we apply the approach pursued in TERESA to a digital agenda application, which presents the main features of creating and managing new appointments. As an example, we analyze the scenario of a user who wants to create a new appointment in his agenda.

First, the nomadic task model is created by the designer; the next step is to apply the filtering in order to obtain the appropriate task model for the specific platform (cellphone, desktop, PDA, vocal platform). The task model obtained can then be transformed into an abstract user interface. The TERESA tool supports various modalities for performing such a transformation, ranging from a completely automatic solution to a semiautomatic one, with various support levels. Once the abstract user interface has been obtained, the development process can evolve in different manners depending on the platform and the modality considered. Nevertheless, in every case the tool provides designers with the possibility of changing some parameters to customise concrete interfaces.

In order to illustrate this approach, the table below shows the presentations generated to support the same task (create a new appointment) on different devices. Some differences between the various application interfaces can be highlighted: for example, on the desktop system, due to the amount of screen space available, it is possible to set all the parameters concerning a new appointment within the same presentation, while, in the mobile system, the user has to navigate through two different presentations. In the case of a VoiceXML-enabled phone, the navigation is implemented by vocal dialogs.

Moreover, further differences can be identified as far as the various supported tasks are concerned. For instance, in the desktop system it is possible to insert a description of the appointment, while this task is not available in either the mobile or voice system, due to the specific interaction characteristics of those media which both discourage the users from providing verbose descriptions that are likely to increase the total interaction time requested.

Another interesting point is represented by the different ways in which objects are arranged within the different presentations on the various platforms. At the level of abstract user interface such compositions are expressed by abstract operators which mainly refer to well known layout arrangement techniques (like grouping, ordering, etc.) that can be rendered, at the concrete level, in different manners depending on the platform. For example, Table 7.1 shows the different implementations of the grouping operator on the cellphone and on the vocal platform. In the cellphone the grouped elements are graphically delimited within a certain region (see the fieldsets), whereas in the vocal interface sounds or brief pauses are used to identify the elements' group. In addition, also the navigation between the different pages can vary depending on the number of presentations that are provided; such number might be also dependent on the amount of elements that can be rendered in a single presentation. It is not by chance that, for instance, on handheld devices the pagination process splits up into different presentations a certain amount of information that, on device with larger screen can be rendered in a single presentation, so generating a bigger number of links on every presentation.

7. Conclusions

This paper provides a discussion of how model-based design should be extended in order to obtain natural development environments. After a brief discussion of the motivations

Table 7.1. Examples of different interfaces generated to support the same main task

Cellphone

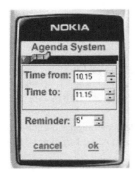 

Voice XML-Enabled Phone

System: " ... *(grouping sound)* Now you are ready to create a new appointment. Say a subject."

user: "meeting"

System: "Your subject is: *MEETING*. Say a place of appointment."

user: "CNR in Pisa"

System: "The place of appointment is: *CNR IN PISA*. Say the day of appointment"

user "12 December 2003"

System: "Your appointment is: *12 December 2003*. *(grouping sound)* Say the start time of appointment"

user "9 a.m."

System: "say the end time of appointment"

user "12 a.m."

System: "ok, the a ppointment will start at 9 and will finish at 12. *(Five seconds pause)* Say how many minutes before the appointment a reminder should be sounded."

user: "5"

System: "ok, the reminder will be sounded 5 minutes before the appointment."

If you would like to insert a new appointment say *OK* , or if would like to remove the appointment say *REMOVE* ....

for EUD based on conceptual representations, we set forth the criteria that should be pursued in order to obtain effective natural development environments. This can be achieved by extending model-based approaches to interface development. In order to make the discussion more concrete, specific environments for model-based design (CTTE and TERESA) have been considered and we have discussed their extension for supporting natural development of multi-device interfaces. The resulting interfaces implement usability criteria taking into account the limitations of the interaction resources in the various types of devices considered.

Acknowledgments

We gratefully acknowledge support from the European Commission through the EUD-Net Network of Excellence (http://giove.isti.cnr.it/eud.html).

References

Abbott, K.R. (in press). Voice Enabling Web Application: VoiceXML and Beyond.

Abrams, M., Phanouriou, C., Batongbacal, A., Williams, S. and Shuster, J. (1999). UIML: An Appliance-Independent XML User Interface Language. In *Proceedings of the 8th WWW conference.*

Cypher, A. (ed., 1993). Watch What I Do: Programming bydemonstration, co-edited by Halbert, D.C., Kurlander, D., Lieberman, H., Maulsby, D., Myers, B. and Alan, Turransky, The MIT Press Cambridge, Massachusetts.

Cooper, A. (1995). The Myth of Metaphor.

de Sousa, J. and Garlan, D. (2002). Aura: An Architectural Framework for User Mobility in Ubiquitous Computing Environments. IEEE-IFIP Conf. on Software Architecture, Montreal.

Eisenstein, J. and Puerta, A. (2000). Adaptation in Automated User-Interface Design. In: *Proceedings of Intelligent User Interfaces 9–12 January 2000*, New Orleans, LA: ACM Press, pp. 74–81.

Furnas, G. (1981). The FISHEYE view: A new look at structured files, technical Memorandum #81-11221-9, Bell Laboratories, Murray Hill, New Jersey 07974, USA, 12 October 1981.

Green, T.R.G., Petre, M., et al. (1991). Comprehensibility of Visual and Textual Programs: A Test of Superlativism Against the 'Match-Mismatch' Conjecture. Empirical Studies of Programming: Fourth Workshop. J. Koenemann-Belliveau, T. G. Moher and S. P. Robertson. New Brunswick, NJ, Ablex Publishing Corporation, 121–146.

Green, T.R.G. and Petre M. (1992). When Visual Programs are Harder to Read than Textual Programs. Human-Computer Interaction: Tasks and Organisation. In: G.C. van der Veer, M.J. Tauber, S. Bagnarola and M. Antavolits (eds.), *Proceedings of ECCE-6 (6th European Conference on Cognitive Ergonomics)*, Rome, CUD.

Green, T.R.G. and Petre, M. (1996). Usability analysis of visual programming environments: a 'cognitive dimensions' framework. *Journal of Visual Lang and Computing* 7(2), 131–174.

IBM WebSphere Transcoding Publisher, http://www.ibm.com/software/webservers/ transcoding/

Landay, J. and Myers, B. (2001). Sketching interfaces: Toward more human interface design. *IEEE Computer* 34(3), 56–64.

Lieberman, H. (2001). Your Wish is My Command: Programming by Example, Morgan Kaufmann.

Lieberman, H. and Liu, H. (2003). Feasibility Studies for Programming in Natural Language. In this book.

Mori, G., Paternò, F. and Santoro, C. (2002). CTTE: Support for Developing and Analysing Task Models for Interactive System Design, *IEEE Transactions in Software Engineering* 28(8), 797–813.

Mori, G., Paternò F. and Santoro C. (2004). Design and Development of Multi-Device User Interfaces through Multiple Logical Descriptions, *IEEE Transactions on Software Engineering* 30(8), 507–520.

Myers, B. (1998). Natural Programming: Project Overview and Proposal. Available at http://www-2.cs.cmu.edu/ ~NatProg/projectoverview.html

Myers, B., Hudson, S. and Pausch, R. (2000). Past, Present, Future of User Interface Tools. *Transactions on Computer–Human Interaction*, 7(1), 3–28.

Nielsen, J. (1993). Usability Engineering. Boston, Academic Press.

OMG. (2001). Unified Modeling Language Specification, Version 1.4, September 2001; available at http://www.omg.org/technology/documents/formal/uml.htm

Oppermann, R. (1995). Adaptive user support: Ergonomic design of manually and automatically adaptable software. Hillsdale, NJ: Erlbaum.

Pane, J. and Myers, B. (1996). Usability Issues in the Design of Novice Programming Systems TR# CMU-CS-96-132. Aug, 1996. http://www.cs.cmu.edu/~pane/cmu-cs-96-132.html

Paternò, F. (1999). Model-based Design and Evaluation of Interactive Applications, Springer Verlag, ISBN 1-85233-155-0.

Paternò, F. (2003). From Model-based to Natural Development. In: Proceedings HCI International 2003, Universal Access in HCI, Lawrence Erlbaum Associates, Publishers, pp. 592–596.

Paternò, F. and Leonardi, A. (1994). A Semantics-based Approach to the Design and Implementation of Interaction Objects. *Computer Graphics Forum* **13**(3), 195–204.

Paternò, F. and Santoro, C. (2003). A Unified Method for Designing Interactive Systems Adaptable to Mobile and Stationary Platforms. *Interacting with Computers* **15**(3), 347–364.

Paternò, F. and Zini, E. (2004). Applying Information Visualization Techniques to Visual Representations of Task Models, Proceedings TAMODIA 2004, Prague.

Puerta, A. and Eisenstein, J. (2002). XIML: A Common Representation for Interaction Data. In Proceedings IUI2002: Sixth International Conference on Intelligent User Interfaces, ACM.

Smith, D.C. and Cypher, A., et al. (1994). KidSim: Programming agents without a programming language. *Communications of the ACM* **37**(7), 54–67.

Spence, R. (2001). Information Visualization. Addison Wesley.

Tam, R.C.-M., Maulsby, D. and Puerta, A., (1998). U-TEL: A Tool for Eliciting User Task Models from Domain Experts. In Proceedings IUI'98, ACM Press, 1998.

Chapter 8

End User Development of Web Applications

JOCHEN RODE[1], MARY BETH ROSSON[2]
and MANUEL A. PÉREZ QUIÑONES[3]

[1] *Virginia Polytechnic Institute and State University, jochenrode@gmail.com*
[2] *Pennsylvania State University, mrosson@ist.psu.edu*
[3] *Virginia Polytechnic Institute and State University, perez@cs.vt.edu*

Abstract. This chapter investigates entry barriers and approaches for facilitating end-user web application development with the particular focus on shaping web programming technology and tools according to end-users' expectations and natural mental models. Our underlying assumption and motivation is that given the right tools and techniques even nonprogrammers may become successful web application developers. The main target audience for this research are "casual" webmasters without programming experience—a group likely to be interested in building web applications. As an important subset of web applications we focus on supporting the development of basic data collection, storage and retrieval applications such as online registrations forms, staff databases, or report tools.

First we analyze the factors contributing to the complexity of web application development through surveys and interviews of experienced programmers; then we explore the "natural mental models" of potential end-user web developers, and finally discuss our particular design solutions for lowering entry barriers, as embodied by a proof-of-concept development tool, called Click. Furthermore, we introduce and evaluate the concept of "Design-at-Runtime"—a new technique for facilitating and accelerating the development-test cycle when building web-based applications.

Key words. end user development, web applications

1. Introduction

Why would end users want to develop web applications? Why are they unable to do this with today's tools? Who are these end users? What are they like? To gain insight into these questions—and the topic of this chapter—contrast these scenarios:

Anna uses today's web tools	Anna uses tomorrow's web tools
As webmaster Anna manages a database for registering clients in her company's courses. Recently, she used a survey authoring tool to build a web-based system: clients now submit a registration form, which Anna receives by e-mail. She reads and re-enters the information she receives into a spreadsheet. If a course has seats she registers the person and emails a confirmation; if not, she contacts and coordinates with the client to re-schedule. Often Anna's boss asks for summary reports, which she creates by hand, a tedious process. Anna knows that these repetitive and time-consuming	A few weeks after her initial effort, Anna learns from a friend about a web development tool that has been targeted at nonprogrammers like her. She decides to give it a try, clicking on the "create new web application" link.
	The development environment guides her through the process of creating the screens for her registration application as well as the database behind the scenes. Designing the application becomes even enjoyable when Anna notices that the tool asks her the right questions at the right time and uses familiar language instead of the typical "techno-babble." At times it
	(continued)

Henry Lieberman et al. (eds.), End User Development, 161–182.
© 2006 *Springer.*

(*Continued*)

Anna uses today's web tools	Anna uses tomorrow's web tools
activities should be handled by the computer. But while she knows how to create websites using WYSIWIG editors she has no programming experience. She has heard of Javascript, so she enters "javascript registration database" into a web search engine. She is overwhelmed with results and quickly becomes discouraged because few of the pointers relate to her particular needs, and the information is highly technical.	even seems that the tool reads her mind. It allows her to quickly try out different options, entering her own test data and seeing what happens. Anna loses track of time, totally engaged by her design activity. Before the day is over she has fully automated the registration process. Anna has even managed to create a basic web-based report generator for her boss. She feels empowered and is proud of her achievement.

The contrast shown in these two scenarios sketches out the challenges and motivation underlying the work we report here. Our goal is to understand what end-user developers need, how they think, and what can be done, so that

a sophisticated user like Anna will not only be able to imagine that she should automate the tedious computing procedures in her life, but also have at her fingertips the support she needs to do it.

2. Related Work

The ubiquity of the World Wide Web and the resultant ease of publishing content to a huge audience has been an important element in the expanding skills and expectations of computer users. However, today, most web pages built by end users simply present information; creation of interactive web sites or web applications such online forms, surveys, and databases still requires considerable skill in programming and web technology. Our preliminary studies indicate that these limitations in users' web development activities are not due to lack of interest but rather to the difficulties inherent in interactive web development (Rode and Rosson 2003). Many end users can envision simple interactive applications that they might try to build if the right tools and techniques were available. If web development becomes possible for a wider audience, we may see a greater variety of useful applications, including applications not yet envisioned or as Deshpande and Hansen (2001) put it: "release the creative power of people." For organizations that cannot afford a professional programmer, end-user development (EUD) may help to streamline workflows, increase productivity and client satisfaction.

Tim Berners-Lee designed the web as a collaborative tool (Berners-Lee 1996). However, his early vision was one of document sharing, and recognition of the web's potential as a platform for dynamic collaboration has been an emergent phenomenon, with the result that much of the web's infrastructure is ill-suited for application development. Currently, development of a typical web application requires knowledge not only of traditional programming languages like Java, but also technologies and problems specific to the web, for example HTML, JavaScript, CSS, HTTP, and cross-platform, cross-browser compatibility issues. When compared to "traditional" end-user programming of single-user desktop applications, the sum of all these technological issues, the distributed nature of the web, and the highly volatile nature of requirements add the unique flavor to end-user development for the web (EUDWeb).

Our research mission is making web application development accessible to a broader audience. We are particularly interested in "informal web developers", people who have created a variety of web content, but who have not been trained in web programming languages or tools. We believe that these individuals are good candidates for end-user web programming—they have already shown themselves to be interested in web development but have not (yet) learned the languages and tools needed to add interactivity to their development efforts.

Two complementary domains of research and practice—*web engineering* and *end-user development*—have focused on methods and tools that could better support the web development needs of both programmers and nonprogrammers. Research in the domain of web engineering concentrates on making web professionals more productive and the websites that they produce more usable, reusable, modularized, scalable, and secure. In contrast, web-related research in end-user development centers on the idea of empowering nonprogrammer end users to autonomously create websites and web applications.

2.1. RESEARCH IN WEB ENGINEERING

The state-of-the-art in web engineering is the automatic generation of web applications based on high-level descriptions of data and application logic. Research ranges from a few full-scale processes like WebML (Ceri, Fraternali, Bongio 2000) to many light-weight code generators (e.g., Turau 2002). Typically, the developer can customize the layout of HTML pages after they have been generated using an external web editor, but these customizations are lost as soon as the code needs to be regenerated because of a needed change in the data or behavior. The lack of support for evolutionary development from start to finish is a major outstanding research problem.

Research on tailorability (e.g., MacLean et al. 1990; Stiemerling, Kahler, Wulf 1997) has focused on techniques that allow software to be customized by end users. The underlying assumption in this work is that customizable systems may address a large fraction of end users' needs. In a previous survey of webmasters (Rode and Rosson 2003), we found that approximately 40% of the web applications envisioned by respondents could in fact be satisfied by five customizable generic web applications: resource reservation, shopping cart and payment, message board, content management, and calendar.

The analysis of web developers' needs has received only little attention in the web engineering literature. A survey conducted by Vora (1998) is an exception. Vora queried web developers about the methods and tools that they use and the problems that they typically encounter. Some of the key problems that developers reported include ensuring web browser interoperability and usability, and standards compliance of WYSIWIG editors. In a similar vein, Fraternali (1999) proposes a taxonomy for web development tools that suggests some of the major dimensions of web development tasks. For example, he categorizes available web tools into Visual HTML Editors and Site Managers,

HTML-SQL integrators, Web-enabled form editors and database publishing wizards, and finally, Web application generators.

Newman et al. (2003) investigated the process of website development by interviewing 11 web development professionals. They found that these experts' design activities involve many informal stages and artifacts. Expert designers employ multiple site representations to highlight different aspects of their designs and use many different tools to accomplish their work. They concluded that there is a need for informal tools that help in the early stages of design and integrate well with the tools designers already use.

2.2. RESEARCH IN END-USER WEB DEVELOPMENT

Well before the development of the World Wide Web, end-user programming (EUP) of basic data management applications was a topic for academia and industry. Apple's HyperCard is an early example of a successful EUP tool. More recently, web development research projects such as WebFormulate (Ambler and Leopold 1998), FAR (Burnett, Chekka, Pandey 2001), DENIM (Newman et al. 2003), and WebSheets (Wolber, Su, Chiang 2002) have explored specific approaches to end-user programming of web applications. WebFormulate is an early tool for building web applications that is itself web-based and thus platform independent. FAR combines ideas from spreadsheets and rule-based programming with drag-and-drop web page layout to help end users develop online services. DENIM is a tool that can assist professional and nonprofessional web developers in the early stages of design with digital sketching of interactive prototypes. The WebSheets tool, although currently limited in power, is close to our holistic vision of end-user web development. It uses a mix of programming-by-example, query-by-example, and spreadsheet concepts to help nonprogrammers develop fully functional web applications.

2.3. COMMERCIAL WEB DEVELOPMENT TOOLS

The research community has devoted little effort to studying approaches and features found in commercially available web application development tools. There are a few notable exceptions including the aforementioned survey of web developers (Vora 1998) and the taxonomy of tools offered in (Fraternali 1999). Brief reviews of CodeCharge Studio, CodeJay, Microsoft Visual Studio, and Webmatrix from the perspective of productivity tools for programmers can be found in (Helman and Fertalj 2003).

3. A User-Centered Approach to Web Development Tools

Our review of existing tools and research literature indicates that there is great interest in supporting general web development needs, and that there is an emerging recognition that the tools used by professionals are not appropriate for less sophisticated users. However, very little work has been directed at understanding the requirements for web development *from an end users' perspective.* Thus we have adopted an approach that combines analytic investigations of features and solutions currently in use

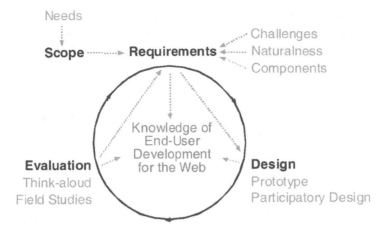

Figure 8.1. User-centered methods for building web development tools.

or under research with detailed empirical studies of end users' needs, preferences, and understanding of web development (Figure 8.1).

Although many tools for web development are already available, we do not yet know whether and how these tools meet the requirements of end users. For example, it is quite likely that professional development tools provide more functionality than is needed by nonprogrammers; we must understand what end users envision as web development projects, so that we can scope the supporting tools appropriately. At the same time, we must investigate how nonprogrammers think about the activities of web development, what concepts are more or less natural to them, what components or features they are able to comprehend.

Once we better understand the requirements for end-user web development tools, we can begin to explore techniques for meeting these requirements. This work takes place in two parallel streams, one aimed at developing and refining prototype tools, and the other at gathering detailed empirical evidence concerning the efficacy of the prototypes we build, along with comparative studies of other tools.

In the balance of the chapter we summarize our work on end-user web development. First we report a survey of sophisticated nonprogrammers (webmasters) that assessed their needs and preferences for web development; a complementary survey of programmer developers is also reported. We next describe our analysis of features present in existing web applications, as well as a usability analysis of commercial web development tools. We report two empirical studies of nonprogrammers that investigate how our target audience *naturally* thinks about typical web programming problems. We conclude with a brief description of our prototyping efforts in EUDWeb.

4. Needs Analysis for EUDWeb

Our first step toward defining a scope for our work in EUDWeb was to investigate the kinds of web applications our target population would like to build. Thus we conducted an online survey of webmasters at our university (Virginia Tech). We reasoned that while some webmasters may have been professionally trained in web development, in a university environment most are more casual developers, people who have not been trained as programmers but nonetheless have learned enough about web development to take responsibility for site development and maintenance. Typical examples are the webmasters for academic departments, research labs, or student organizations. Such individuals represent the population we wish to target: end users who are sophisticated enough to know what they might accomplish via web programming but unlikely to attempt it on their own.

Our analysis of the survey responses (67 replies) indicated that approximately one third of end users' needs could be addressed by a high-level development tool that offered basic data collection, storage and retrieval functionality. Another 40% of the requests could be satisfied through customization of five generic web applications (resource reservation, shopping cart and payment, message board, content management, calendar). Research on tailorability (e.g., MacLean et al. 1990) has shown that software can be designed for easy customization by end users. Diverse requests for more advanced applications comprised the remaining 25%. We were especially interested in the requests for applications involving basic data collection and management; such functionality seems quite reasonable to provide via an EUDWeb tool. Although this survey was a useful start, it was modest in size and restricted to one university computing population. Thus we are currently conducting a larger survey with the results expected for the first quarter of 2005 (excerpts of the results and a reference to the full results will be available at http://purl.vt.edu/people/jrode/publish/2005-05-webdevelopersurvey/).

5. Challenges Faced by Web Developers

As a second source of input to requirements development, we surveyed sophisticated developers regarding the challenges, tools, and processes within the domain of web application development. Our rationale was simple: issues that are troublesome for experienced developers may be insurmountable hurdles for novices.

We surveyed 31 experienced web developers and subsequently conducted in-depth interviews with 10 additional developers (still focusing on a university computing context). On average, the 31 respondents rated themselves just above the mid-point on a scale from "no knowledge in web application development" to "expert knowledge". Their self-reported years of experience in web application development were approximately equally distributed between "less than a year" and "more than 5 years." The 10 interview participants rated themselves in an average of 5.1 (SD = 1.3) on a scale from 1 (no knowledge) to 7 (expert knowledge). The average self-reported experience of the interview participants is somewhat higher than the mean experience of the survey participants which was only 4.3.

In both the survey and interviews we asked the developers to rate a list of potential web development problems and issues. Their responses are summarized in Figure 8.2. As the figure suggests, none of the concerns were considered to be particularly "severe";

	1	2	3	4	5	6	7
Ensuring security				4.4 ● ■ 4.8			
Browser compatibility			3.8 ●	■ 4.6			
Integrating different technologies			3.8 ● ■ 4.2				
Debugging			3.8 ●■ 4.0				
Cryptic error messages			■ 3.7				
Limitations of HTML for page layout			3.6 ●■ 3.7				
Ensuring usability			3.6 ●				
Designing & implementing the UI			3.6 ●				
Configuration of server software			3.4 ■ 3.4				
Different syntax for languages			■ 3.4				
Needs analysis			3.4 ●				
Authentication and authorization			3.4 ●				
Different Syntax embedded in each other			■ 3.3				
Database design and connectivity			3.1 ●				
Designing graphics & icons			3.0 ●				
Configuration of development environment		2.6 ■● 2.5					
Slow revision-test cycle			■ 2.5				

Figure 8.2. Ratings of problems in web application development (1 = not a problem at all; 7 = severe problem). The square markers are the mean ratings from the survey (value to right marker in italics; $N = 31$). The round markers are ratings from a pre-interview questionnaire (value to left of marker; $N = 10$). To facilitate comparison, the survey responses have been scaled from a 1–5 scale to a 1–7 scale.

most mean ratings were in the middle or lower half of the scale. This underscores the expected expertise of these respondents, who seem to be generally confident in their abilities to design and implement a range of web applications.

The top-rated issue in both the survey and interviews was ensuring security. Web applications are vulnerable against exploits on many different levels (e.g. operating system, web server software, database, dynamic scripting language, interactions of the aforementioned). Today it is very difficult to build even a "reasonably" secure application or to assess whether and when an application is secure. Web developers are not confident about these procedures and therefore are concerned.

The inconsistencies between different browsers, versions and platforms are another source of complaints of web developers. According to our respondents, compatibility problems are also a major reason for *avoiding* the development of advanced user interaction designs using Javascript, CSS2, or Flash. Such techniques are seen as ways to improve the user experience but very risky for applications that must run on a variety of different platforms. A similar concern was the complexity of web engineering technologies: while classical desktop applications typically use only one programming language (perhaps two when considering database interactions), most web applications combine five or more (HTML, Javascript, CSS, server-side language, SQL, and perhaps Flash, Java applets, Active X).

The resulting complexity leads to code that is hard to develop and maintain. Given these complexity and compatibility issues, it is not surprising that debugging was also acknowledged as an important concern.

The developers we surveyed were generally confident in their ability to solve web engineering problems, but even so acknowledged moderate concerns for the issues we probed. Several implications we drew from the survey were that EUDWeb tools should provide extensive support for security management; that cross-platform compatibility should be as transparent as possible; that the tools should automate integration of different web technologies; and that a debugger should be a basic service.

6. Cataloguing Key Components of Web Applications

In response to the needs analysis described earlier, we have chosen one particular genre of web applications as the focus of our research in EUDWeb: software that enables basic data collection and management. Once we had decided to concentrate on this specific class of applications, we needed a clear understanding of what components, concepts, and functionality would be needed to implement such software. We wanted to obtain a naturalistic sample of web components associated with this type of web application, so we gathered and analyzed the structure of database-centric websites that already existed at our university.

We used Google and its filtering capabilities (e.g., "filetype:asp site:vt.edu") to find applications in use at our institution. Using file extensions that indicate dynamic content (.asp, .aspx, .php, .php3, .cfm, .jsp, .pl, .cgi) we were able to find a large number of cases. We disregarded simple dynamic websites (scripting only used for navigation, header and footers, no database) and focused on those applications that were close to the needs expressed by the end-user survey respondents, ending up with a set of 61 example applications. These included databases for people, news items, publications, job offers, policies, conference sessions, plants, service providers and so on. We reviewed the applications that were publicly accessible and constructed a list of concepts and components found within these basic web applications. The essence of this analysis is shown in Table 8.1.

The components, concepts and functions that we derived can be viewed as high-level equivalents to low-level language constructs, predefined functions, objects and methods in classical text-based programming languages (e.g., for-loop, while-loop, if, print). Of course, commercial Web development tools already offer much of the high-level functionality listed in Table 8.1, but most of these tools are not aimed at nonprogrammers. We expect the list of elements to change and grow along with our knowledge about web applications and the progress of technology. We see this list as simply a start towards a functional requirements list for EUDWeb tools.

7. Analysis of State-of-the-Art Tools

Some of the most active work on EUDWeb is in commercial web development tools. Thus as yet another source of requirements, and to better ground our research in related

Table 8.1. Components, concepts and functionality of basic web applications.

Concept or function	Description
Session management	Maintaining state information when going from page to page, "fixing" HTTP's connectionless nature
Input validation	Validating user inputs for increased usability but also for increased security to preventing hacker attacks
Conditional output	e.g. only show "Hi John!" when John is logged in
Authentication and authorization	Restricting who can use the web application and which features can be used by whom
Database schema	The structure of the tables holding the data
Database lookup	e.g. resolving a user-ID to a full name
Overview-detail relationships	e.g. showing a list of employees on one web page and when clicking on the name, the details on another
Normalization & use of foreign keys	Addressing data redundancy issues
Uniqueness of data records	Being able to identify each record even though the data be the same
Calculating database statistics	e.g. showing the number of registrations in online registration database
Search	e.g. finding a person's e-mail in a staff database

work, we reviewed nine commercial web development tools. We analyzed each tool from the perspective of suitability for end-user development; looking across the nine tools we were able to compare and contrast alternative and best-of-breed approaches for many aspects of web application development (Rode et al. 2005).

7.1. OVERVIEW OF TOOLS ANALYSIS PROCESS

For our review we selected tools based on both their apparent market dominance and their potential sophistication. Although most web development tools have a particular focus regarding target development project and user group, we found that the majority of tools can be grouped into one of three categories: database-centric tools (we reviewed: FileMaker Pro 7), form-centric tools (we reviewed: Quask Form Artist), and website-centric tools (we reviewed: Microsoft Visual Web Developer 2005 Beta, YesSoftware CodeCharge Studio, H.E.I. Informations-systeme RADpage, Instantis SiteWand, Macromedia Dreamweaver 2004 MX, Macromedia Drumbeat 2000, Microsoft Front-Page 2003). To structure and constrain our review, we analyzed the commercial tools with a focus on how they approach the implementation of particular features that are common in web application development (Table 8.1). To make these features more concrete and to convey our assumptions about a likely end-users' goals and activities, we had constructed a reference scenario and persona. In the scenario, a nonprogrammer was attempting to build what we feel is a typical example of a data-driven website—an online employee database. We reviewed each tool for the approach and features needed to implement this scenario.

7.2. USABILITY FINDINGS

What does the ideal web application development tool look like? We believe that there cannot be only one such tool. Because developers have different needs and different skill sets, different developers will be best served by different tools. In general, our review suggests that while productivity tools for programmers like Microsoft Visual Web Developer have matured to provide significant support for web development, tools for nonprogrammer developers are still in their infancy.

Most of the end-user tools that we reviewed do not lack functionality but rather ease of use. For instance, even apparently simple problems such as implementing the intended look and feel become difficult when a novice has to use HTML-flow-based positioning instead of the more intuitive pixel-based positioning.

Although most tools offer wizards and other features to simplify particular aspects of development, none of the tools that we reviewed addresses the process of development as a whole, supporting end user developers at the same level of complexity from start to finish. Indeed, Fraternali's and Paolini's (2000) comment about web tools of five years ago seems to be still true today: ". . . a careful review of their features reveals that most solutions concentrate on implementation, paying little attention to the overall process of designing a Web application."

The otherwise comparatively novice-friendly Frontpage, for example, begins the creation of a new application by asking the developer to make a premature commitment to one of the following technologies: ASP, ASP.NET, FrontPage Server Extensions, or SharePoint Server. An excerpt from an online tutorial for FP illustrates the problem: ". . . You can also use the Form page Wizard and Database Interface Wizard with ASP or ASP.NET to edit, view, or search records from a Web page. The Form page Wizard works on a Web site running Windows SharePoint Services 2.0, yet the Database Interface Wizard does not." Such a selection is likely to confuse anyone but a seasoned web developer.

Currently, none of the tools that we reviewed would work without major problems for the informal web developer who wants to create more than a basic website. The tool that a user like Anna (from our introduction scenario) is looking for needs to provide multiple reference examples, well-guided but short wizards, an integrated zero-configuration web server for testing purposes, and good support during the deployment phase of the application. Also, as Anna becomes more familiar with the capabilities of the tool and her applications become more ambitious, the tool should help her learn by stepwise exposing the inner workings of the wizards and forms. Ideally, following the concept of the "gentle slope" (MacLean et al. 1990), the skills required to implement advanced features should only grow in proportion to the complexity of the desired functionality—"Make simple things easy, and hard things possible".

8. End Users' Understanding of Web Development

We can build better EUD tools if we know how end-user developers think. If a tool works in the way that a tool user expects and it feels "natural" from the beginning it is likely to be easy to learn and use. Alternatively, a tool can be designed to reshape the way that end-user developers think about a problem. In either way, it is beneficial to know the "mental model" of the end-user developer. In this context, "mental model" is meant to characterize the way that people visualize the inner workings of a web application, the cognitive representations they hold of the entities and workflows comprising a system. A person's mental model is shaped by his or her education and experience and will evolve as he or she continues to learn. The concept of "natural" or "naturalness" refers to the mental model that users hold before they start learning to use a tool or programming language.

What are the mental models of our target audience and how detailed are they? We report two studies in an attempt to this question. The studies adapt the methods of Pane, Ratanamahatana, and Myers (2001), who designed a "natural" programming language for children by first studying how children and adults use natural language to solve programming problems. In our variation of their method, we investigate how nonprogrammers naturally think about the behavior of web applications. The findings from this work have guided the design of our prototype EUDWeb tool, as will be discussed later.

8.1. EXPLORING END USERS' CONCEPTS AND LANGUAGE USE

Our first efforts at exploring end users' mental models [MMODELS-1] (Rode and Rosson 2003) were aimed at investigating the language, concepts, and the general level of problem-solving that end users employed when solving web programming problems.

8.1.1. *Participants and Study Procedures*

We recruited participants for a two-part paper and pencil study. Participants were asked to label screen elements and to specify the application behavior. We created a simple web application (member registration and management) for the study. Ten participants were sampled randomly from organizational webmasters who had reported in a previous survey that they had significant experience in web authoring but none or little in programming. Five were female, and five male. Pre- and post-study interviews revealed that one person had more programming experience than initially reported (use of Macromedia ColdFusion for a simple web application).

Participants were given a general introduction to the goals of the study, then asked to view and label all elements of three screenshots from the application (login, member list, add member). The labelling instructions included a sample labelled image (a room with objects), including nested items. This first phase of the study was intended to inform us about the language our audience uses to reference visible screen elements (left side of Figure 8.3).

Next, they were allowed to explore the application until they were comfortable with how it worked. After the familiarization phase, participants were given seven user tasks (login, paging, user-specific listing, add member, sort, search, delete) and asked to "teach" these behaviors to a "magical machine"; the machine was said to understand screenshots but not know which elements are static and which respond to users' actions. A paragraph of text within the written instructions explained this scenario to the participants. The seven tasks were illustrated by concise instructions that were designed to guide the user without biasing their response—for example,

4, The fields for first & last name, and email
Ore required fields. If one of those fields
is left blank the programming in the page
stops the information from being sent to the
Server when you hit "ok", the submit button. The
page then produces an error message telling you
which missing fields are required. Then clicking
"ok" in the error box allows you to function
again within the page. Once all required fields
are entered and you click "ok", the info is
sent to the server and the page is redirected
to a new one displaying some of your
entered information.

Figure 8.3. Annotated screenshot and a participant's description of the behavior of the "Add Member" dialog (MMODELS-1).

task 4 had the following description:

*Add a new member (just make up some data). Assume you do **not** have an e-mail address. Continue with "OK". Now enter an e-mail address. Continue with "OK". Describe how the web application behaves.*

The application was available for reference. Participants wrote responses using screenshots and blank paper (right side of Figure 8.3). We emphasized that they were free to choose how to communicate with the magical machine (using written words or sketches), but also that they should fully specify the application's behavior. We wanted to see what end users consider sufficient as a behavior specification.

8.1.2. *Study Findings*

Participants spent an average of about 90 minutes total on both parts of the study. The participants' annotated screenshots and written notes showed a general familiarity with "visible" elements of web applications (e.g., page, link, data table); however, they made little attempt to describe how "hidden" operations are accomplished. Given these users' background in web authoring, we were not surprised to find that they used terms common in WYSIWIG web editors to label screen elements. When describing the application's behavior, participants tended to combine procedural steps and declarative statements. They used declarative statements to specify constraints on behavior (e.g., "certain fields are required"). Procedural statements often conveyed a test and result (e.g., "If the password is incorrect, that field is cleared") or a page transaction (e.g., "Type the correct password into the field and Enter; this action opens the Members page"). With the exception of one participant, no one mentioned constructs such as variables and loops in the behavior specifications. Where looping constructs are required (e.g., authenticating a user), the participants specified one iteration, seeming to expect that it would apply (i.e., be repeated) as necessary.

We were particularly interested in how these users described web-specific data processing—e.g., client-server interaction, HTML generation, the web's stateless nature, and so on. Only three users included any description of what happens "behind the scenes" in a web application (e.g., mentioning interactions with a server). Even these participants made no effort to describe page transactions in detail (e.g., no one discussed how information is forwarded between pages). Most participants (7 of 10) referred to application data as a database; another talked about a file. This is consistent with their general use of a "technical" vocabulary. However, only one included communication between the application and database ("sends command to the database on the server telling it to query"). Though comfortable with the concept of a database, the others seem to see it as a placeholder for a background resource.

In a similar fashion, users often referred to a "member list" or a "member" as if these abstractions are simply available for use as needed; no one worried about how an application obtains or manages data. We thought that the search and sort tasks might evoke informal descriptions of algorithms, but most participants focused on a result (e.g., what the user sees next in a table) rather than on how a data listing was obtained. Six users seemed to assume that the "magical machine" manages user authentication; four offered as a detail that user data must be checked against a list or table of valid IDs.

8.2. MENTAL MODELS OF SPECIFIC WEB DEVELOPMENT TASKS

One problem with our study of concepts and language for web programming (MMODELS-1) was the generality of the problem-solving it required: we asked participants how web programming tasks would take place but did not direct their attention to specific constructs (e.g., iteration, input validation). Thus the results pointed to a few general (and rather predictable) tendencies in end users' mental models. We wanted to find out how end users would think about the specific components and features we had catalogued in our analysis of existing database-centric web applications (e.g., input validation, database lookups, overview-detail relationships). We carried out a second study [MMODELS-2] to explore these issues (Rode, Rosson, Pérez-Quiñones 2004). Our goal was to determine how end users *naturally think* about *typical concerns* in web application development.

We are concerned with naturalness in this sense: by studying the "stories" that nonprogrammer webmasters can generate about how a specific programming feature works, we hope to develop approaches for supporting this feature that will be intuitive to this user population.

We wanted to begin our investigation with programming concerns that are commonly addressed by web developers when creating a web application. Thus we selected a set of concerns that appeared frequently in an earlier analysis of 61 existing web applications (as discussed before). As experienced web developers, we also relied on our personal experiences to judge what programming concerns are most important in web development. Because many, if not most web applications work with databases, many of the programming issues are database-related.

8.2.1. *Participants and Study Procedures*

We recruited 13 participants (7 female, 4 male, and 2 who were later eliminated because they did not match our target audience) who, in a screening survey, identified themselves as having at least some knowledge of HTML and/or of a WYSIWIG web editor (≥ 2 out of 5) but very little or no programming background.

The screening survey did not question participants for their experience with databases. However, during the interview all but one participant indicated that they had at least some experience with databases (9 with Microsoft Access, 1 with FileMaker Pro). Although our sample size is too small to draw strong conclusions, this seems to indicate that casual web developers (our target audience) are very likely to have database experience. Assuming that this finding can be replicated in a more diverse sample, EUDWeb tools may be able to expose database concepts without overwhelming their users. Note though that our interviews suggest that the level of database understanding is novice to intermediate rather than expert.

The goal of this study was to better understand how webmasters who do not know how to program are able to imagine how a range of computational processes might take place "inside" an interactive web application. Probing naive expectations of this sort is a challenge, because the facilitator must provide enough information that a nonprogrammer can understand what aspect of the application is being called out for attention, but not so much that the inner workings of the application are revealed. So as to describe the application feature of interest in as concrete a fashion as possible, we presented and asked questions about nine scenarios (for full list of scenarios see Rode, Rosson, Pérez-Quiñones 2003), each describing one or more programming concerns related to a fictional web application—an online video library system.

Each scenario consisted of a mock-up of a screen shot, a short paragraph explaining what the mocked-up screen depicts, and a series of questions. As an example, Figure 8.4 shows the first of the nine scenarios. This particular scenario was designed to probe end users' mental models regarding session management (1a), database lookup (1b), and conditional output (1c). Some of the questions in the nine scenarios are targeted at the same concerns, but approach them from a different perspective. Most of the questions begin with the words: "What do you think the web site must do to . . . "; we hoped that

1) *After logging in* with your user-ID the web site always *shows your full name* and a logout button in the upper right corner.

a) What do you think the web site must do to keep track of the fact that you are logged in even though you go from page to page?

b) What do you think the web site must do to show your full name, although you only entered a short user-ID? Take the user-ID "jsmith" as an example and show step-by-step how the web site determines the name "John Smith".

c) Note that the library home page only displays your name when you are logged in. If you are not logged in, it shows a login box instead. How do you think this feature works behind the scene?

Figure 8.4. Scenario 1 of 9 as shown to each participant.

this probe would prompt the webmasters to direct their attention "inside" to the inner workings of the hypothetical application. Participants were asked to provide as many details as they could when answering the questions; the facilitator often prompted them for details if it seemed that the scenario had not been completely analyzed. Participants were also encouraged to use sketches to clarify their thoughts. The interviews took place in a one-on-one setting in a private atmosphere. Verbal responses were voice recorded for later analysis.

Not all users answered all questions. Sometimes a participant responded simply that "I have no idea" rather than attempting an explanation. In such cases we encouraged participants to give a "best guess", but occasionally we were forced to continue without an explanation. In general we were sensitive to participants' comfort level, and if an interviewee conveyed or said that they were feeling "stupid" we quickly moved on to another question.

We analysed the study in the following manner. First, we transcribed the recorded interview for each participant (focusing on analysis questions, and excluding unrelated remarks). If participants had made sketches we used those to understand and annotate their remarks. Second, in a separate document we listed the eleven web development concerns of interest, and inserted pieces of the transcribed interview under the aspects they referred to. Each remark was coded with a reference to the participant to enable later quantitative analysis. Often, we combined across answers from different scenarios or questions to give us a better understanding about a particular aspect of a webmaster's mental model. Finally, we summarized the results for each development concern by referring back to this document, and when necessary the transcribed interviews or even the original recordings.

8.2.2. *Study Findings*

In the balance of this section, we discuss what we have learned from our participants regarding their understanding of specific aspects of web application development and how these findings have influenced our thoughts about the design of future EUDWeb tools.

Session management. The majority of our participants assumed that session management is implicitly performed, and thus is not something that a developer would have to consciously consider. This suggests that an EUDWeb tool should automatically maintain the state of an application, perhaps even without exposing this fact to the developer. For novice web application developers this concept may introduce unnecessary complexity.

Input validation. The typical approach of defining an input mask using patterns or placeholders (as used by many existing tool, e.g. Microsoft Access) seems to be an appropriate abstraction for end users. Certainly, this result is unsurprising in light of the fact that ten participants had previous database experience and were familiar with this notion.

Conditional output. Although, the concept of "if-then" branching was frequently mentioned informally, the exact implementation (in particular when and where if-then rules would be applied) did not appear trivial to most participants. This suggests that while an EUD tool may use the notion of "if-then" at a high level of abstraction, it may need to automatically develop an implementation or guide the developer as to where to place these rules.

Authentication and authorization. Overall, the problems involved in permission management did not appear too taxing for our participants. However, the proposed implementations were rather variable and almost always incomplete, and were not powerful enough for a real-world application. We believe that our participants would not have many difficulties in *understanding* a good permission scheme, however may not be able to create a sufficiently powerful and secure one on their own. Therefore, an easy-to-use EUDWeb tool should offer permission management as a built-in feature and make it customizable by the developer.

Database schema. Overall, the table paradigm seems to be the prevalent mental model among our participants. This suggests that an EUDWeb tool may safely use the table metaphor for managing data. However, the management of more than one related data table may not be a trivial problem, as discussed further under the aspect of "Normalization and use of foreign keys."

Database lookup. Although the concept of database lookup (or select) did not seem difficult to the participants, the majority did not provide a detailed algorithm. This suggests that an EUDWeb tool should offer database lookup as predefined functionality that is customizable by the developer.

Overview-detail relationships. Overall, imagining how the linkage between overview page (list of all movies) and detail page (movie details) is implemented was quite a challenge for our participants. Almost all of the participants immediately stated that the information was "linked", "associated", "connected," or "referenced;" but the details of this linkage were quite unclear. This suggests that although an EUDWeb tool may be able to use words like "linking" to describe a relationship between two views, it will likely need to guide the developer as to what kind of information the link will carry (or abstract this detail completely).

Normalization and use of foreign keys. The results suggested that most of our participants would not design a normalized database representation but rather some redundant form of data storage such as that familiar from spreadsheet applications (which lack the concept of foreign key relationships). Therefore, if non-redundant data storage is required (of course, this may not be the case for small or ad hoc applications), an EUDWeb tool may have to make the developer aware of data redundancy problems and propose potential solutions and perhaps (semi-) automatically implement these solutions.

Uniqueness of data records. Our participants had no difficulties imagining the utility of a unique record identifier. However, as the results from the "Overview-detail relationships" aspect show, the correct use of this unique identifier often was unclear. Therefore, an EUDWeb tool may either automatically introduce a unique identifier as a data field or guide the developer towards defining one.

Calculating database statistics. Participants were asked to describe how the web application calculates the total number of checked-out movies. Most participants naturally selected the most likely implementation (application counts records on request). For the others, their prior knowledge of the workings of spreadsheet programs seemed to influence their mental models (self-updating counter). Overall, this question was not perceived as a stumbling block. We suggest that an EUDWeb tool should offer familiar predefined statistics such as column sums, averages etc. to aid the developer.

Search. The concept of searching appears to be well understood at a high-level of abstraction, including the possibility of multiple search parameters. However, the implementation of a search function was beyond the mental models of most of our participants. Therefore, EUD tools should offer a built-in query mechanism that lets developers specify parameters and connecting operators but does not expose the details of the implementation.

8.3. IMPLICATIONS FOR EUDWeb RESEARCH

From a methodological point of view we learned a number of lessons about studying webmasters' (or other end users') mental models. Extracting the participants' mental models was difficult and required a very involved interview. Participants frequently expressed that they simply did not know or had never thought about the implementation of a particular aspect. We are considering a refinement of the approach that has a more "graduated" set of scenarios and questions. For example, we might start out with a very straightforward question about database structure and follow that up with more explicit probes about how retrieval or filtering might be done. We are also considering the use of examples as a prop in the discussions: for example, when a nonprogrammer states that they have no idea how a process takes place, we might present them with two plausible alternatives (where one is "correct") and ask them to evaluate the differences.

We noted that in many cases participants had very sparse models of the programming functions we presented. Although a sort of "non-result", this observation is interesting in itself because it underscores the need for tools that provide transparent support of certain frequently-used functionality (e.g., session management, search). Note that participants often used appropriate language to refer to technical concepts even when they did not understand how they worked (e.g. key fields). Therefore, it seems plausible that casual web developers will be able to understand a toolkit that employs constructs like key fields or foreign-key relationships.

Based on our results so far, we would characterize a "prototypical" end-user web developer in the following way. He or she:

- Often uses technical terminology (e.g. fields, database) but without being specific and precise,
- Is capable of describing an application's visible and tangible behavior to a nearly complete level (if under-specification is pointed out to them),
- Naturally uses a mix of declarative language (e.g. constraints) and procedural language (e.g. if-then rules) to describe behavior, while being unclear about where and when these rules should be applied (lack of control flow),

- Does not care about, and often is unable to describe exactly how functionality is implemented "behind the scenes" (e.g. search, overview-detail relationships)
- Disregards intangible aspects of implementation technologies (e.g. session management, parameter passing, security checking),
- Understands the utility of advanced concepts (e.g. unique key fields, normalization) but is unlikely to implement them correctly without guidance,
- Thinks in terms of sets rather than in terms of iteration (e.g. show all records that contain "abc"),
- Imagines a spreadsheet table when reflecting on data storage and retrieval.

The type of mental models study we conducted can only determine what end users "naturally" think. In order to determine whether or not certain design solutions are easy to understand and easy to use we need to create and evaluate prototype tools—the focus of our current work.

9. Prototyping and Evaluating EUDWeb Tools

Prototyping is an integral part of our research on EUDWeb. First, it has helped to assess the feasibility of design ideas; second, prototypes serve as research instruments to support observational studies (e.g., end-user debugging behavior); and third, we are hoping to soon discover new requirements for EUDWeb through participatory design with the users of our prototype system in an ecologically valid manner. We have explored many different paths, including extensions to a popular web development tool (Macromedia Dreamweaver) to offer web application features more suitable to end users and implementing an online tool using Macromedia Flash (Rode and Rosson 2003). Although tools like Dreamweaver and FrontPage have substantial extension APIs, we found the inflexibility in controlling the users' workflow as the main hindrance to adopting this approach. Using Flash itself as a platform solves many layout and WYSIWYG issues but presents the problem that most users still want to produce HTML-based web sites. From many informal user studies we have learned that the web development tool that users envision is typically "Word for Web Apps", expressing a preference for a desktop-based tool that embraces the WIMP, drag-and-drop, and copy-and-paste metaphors, offers wizards, examples and template solutions, but yet lets the developer see and modify the code "behind the scenes." Our current approach uses an HTML/JavaScript/PHP-based online tool that is integrated with a database management system (MySQL). Figure 8.5 shows a screenshot from Click (Component-based Lightweight Internet-application Construction Kit), our most recent prototype (Rode et al. 2005). In the depicted scenario, the developer defines the behavior of a button component in a declarative way, that is, upon pressing the "Register" button the application would redirect the user to the web page "confirmationpage" if and only if the e-mail field is not left blank. Click distinguishes itself from other state-of-the-art EUDWeb tools in that it fully integrates the process of modelling the look and feel, component behavior, database connections, publishing and hosting, while working on a high level of abstraction appropriate for nonprogrammers.

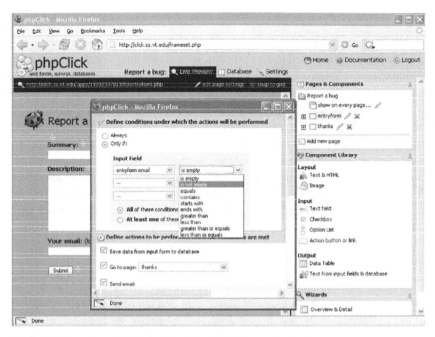

Figure 8.5. Screenshot of Click showing definition of a button's behavior.

Click implements what we call "design-at-runtime", applying Tanimoto's concept of liveness (Tanimoto 1990). This concept builds from the ideas of direct manipulation (Shneiderman 1983) and the "debugging into existence" behavior (Rosson and Carroll 1996) studied in professional programmers. At its core it is similar to the automatic recalculation aspect in spreadsheet programs. A critical piece of the concept is that the user is able to both develop and use the application without switching back and forth between programming and runtime modes. That is, the application is always usable to the fullest extent that it has been programmed, and when its boundaries are tested, the environment provides useful feedback suggesting next steps for the developer to take.

An important design goal for Click is to support evolutionary prototyping, to allow the developer to easily change virtually every aspect of the web application at any point in time For example, in the figure the user is updating the behavior of a submit button while in the midst of testing her application. This can be contrasted to most state-of-the-art tools that require significant "premature commitment", as Green (1989) might call it. For example, in many tools the database schema has to be fully defined before the application is implemented and is difficult to change after the fact.

Finally, Click provides several layers of programming support. While novices can customize existing applications or work with a predefined set of components and actions, more advanced developers can manually edit the underlying code which is based on HTML, PHP, and the event-driven PRADO framework (Xue 2005). Click strives to expose a "Gentle slope of complexity" as advocated by MacLean et al. (1990).

9.1. EVALUATION AND LESSONS LEARNED

Click has been released as an open source tool (http://phpclick.sourceforge.net) and may soon be formally released to the Virginia Tech computing community in an effort to elicit important requirements for EUDWeb through large-scale participatory design and as an instrument for field studies (see Figure 8.1). In the course of developing Click, we have also begun to carry out a series of usability evaluations, gathering feedback from representatives of our target audience. Although many usability issues are left to be resolved, Click already addresses many problems. For example, Click completely hides session management (all inputs entered on one web page are available at any later point in time), integrates the database management within the tool (as the developer creates a new input field on screen a matching database field is created), and allows the developer to design the layout in a true WYSIWYG fashion without having to revert to "tricks" like using HTML tables for alignment.

10. Summary and Conclusions

We have described the initial phases of a user-centered approach to understanding and supporting EUDWeb. From investigating end users' needs we have found that basic data collection, storage and retrieval applications such as surveys, registration systems, service forms, or database-driven websites are an important target for end-user development. These types of applications are also a *feasible* target considering that most web applications are simple—at least conceptually speaking. While currently the implementation of any non-trivial, secure, and cross-platform compatible web application requires expert knowledge, it does not have to be this way. Most of what makes web development difficult is not inherent complexity but rather an accumulation of many technical challenges. Concerning the main challenges in web application development, experienced web developers mentioned the issues of ensuring security, cross-platform compatibility, the problems related to integrating different web technologies such as Java, HTML, PHP, Javascript, CSS, SQL, and, the difficulties of debugging distributed applications.

Many web applications are quite similar on a conceptual level. By analysing existing applications we have compiled a list of frequently used components, functions, and concepts such as session management, search, and overview-detail relationships (Table 8.1). The web development process will become much easier and more accessible to nonprogrammers when tools integrate these concepts as building blocks on a high level of abstraction rather than requiring low level coding.

Much progress has been made by commercial web development tools. Most of the end-user tools that we reviewed do not lack functionality but rather ease-of-use. We also found that while many tools offer wizards and other features designed to facilitate specific aspects of end-user development, few (if any) take a holistic approach to web application development and integrate layout, styling, behavioral description, data modelling, publishing, and maintenance tasks. The "ideal" tool for end-user web developers would provide ease-of-use with the appropriate abstractions, absence of jargon, a library of examples and templates, wizards for complicated tasks and take a holistic approach by integrating all aspects of web development. Finally, such a tool would also support developers' growing needs and knowledge, offer power and flexibility by allowing the integration of user-defined and automatically-created code.

Understanding how end users naturally think may help us design tools that better match their expectations. In two studies we found, that end users frequently only have vague ideas of how web applications works behind the scenes, and that end users expect many aspects such as session management or search to work "out-of-the-box." However, the nonprogrammers we have observed, generally did not have problems to think on an abstract level about the concepts behind web application development and for example easily understood concepts like "if-then" branching although being unable to say where and how it would be implemented.

We have begun constructing and evaluating an EUDWeb tool prototype called Click that supports end user web application development from start (requirements elicitation through application prototyping) to finish (deployment and maintenance). We are confident that a tool like Click will soon make the "tomorrow" of the introduction scenario and end-user development for the web a reality.

Acknowledgements

We thank Julie Ballin and Brooke Toward for their roles in development and administration of a large-scale survey of web developers; Yogita Bhardwaj, and Jonathan Howarth for helping develop Click, our EUD prototype, and conducting a review of existing web tools; Betsy and Erv Blythe for supporting the idea of EUDWeb within Virginia Tech's IT department, and last but most definitely not least, B. Collier Jones, Jan Gibb, Kaye Kriz and Dr. Andrea Contreras for their valuable feedback and support throughout our research.

References

Ambler, A. and Leopold, J. (1998). Public Programming in a Web World. *IEEE Symposium on Visual Languages*, Nova Scotia, Canada: 100–107.

Berners-Lee, T. (1996). "WWW: past, present, and future." *IEEE Computer* **29**(10): 69–77.

Burnett, M., Chekka, S.K. and Pandey, R. (2001). FAR: An End user Language to Support Cottage E-Services. *HCC—2001 IEEE Symposia on Human-Centric Computing Languages and Environments*, Stresa, Italy: 195–202.

Ceri, S., Fraternali, P. and Bongio, A. (2000). "Web Modeling Language (WebML): A Modeling Language for Designing Web Sites." *Computer Networks* 33(1–6): 137–157.

Deshpande, Y. and Hansen, S. (2001). "Web Engineering: Creating a Discipline among Disciplines." *IEEE MultiMedia* **8**(2): 82–87.

Fraternali, P. (1999). "Tools and Approaches for Developing Data-Intensive Web Applications: A Survey." *ACM Computing Surveys* 31(3): 227–263.

Fraternali, P. and Paolini, P. (2000). "Model-Driven Development of WebApplications: The Autoweb System." *ACM Transactions on Information Systems* 28(4): 323–382.

Green, T.R.G. (1989). Cognitive dimensions of notations. In A. Sutcliffe & I. Macauley (eds.), *People and Computers IV*. Cambridge: Cambridge University Press.

Helman, T. and Fertalj, K. (2003). A Critique of Web Application Generators. *Information Technology Interfaces (ITI)*, June 16–19, 2003, Cavtat, Croatia.

MacLean, A., Carter, K., Lövstrand, L. and Moran, T. (1990). User-Tailorable Systems: Pressing Issues with Buttons. *ACM CHI 1990*: 175–182.

Newman, M., Lin, J., Hong, J.I. and Landay, J.A. (2003). "DENIM: An Informal Web Site Design Tool Inspired by Observations of Practice." *Human-Computer Interaction* **18**: 259–324.

Pane, J.F., Ratanamahatana, C.A. and Myers, B.A. (2001). "Studying the language and structure in non-programmers' solutions to programming problems." *International Journal of Human-Computer Studies* **54**(2): 237–264.

Rode, J. and Rosson, M.B. (2003). Programming at Runtime: Requirements & Paradigms for Non-programmer Web Application Development. *IEEE HCC 2003*. Auckland, New Zealand. Oct. 28–31.

Rode, J., Rosson, M.B. and Pérez-Quiñones, M.A. (2003). Participant Instructions. http://purl.vt.edu/people/jrode/publish/2003-09-interviews/instructions.pdf

Rode, J. Rosson, M.B. and Pérez-Quiñones, M.A. (2004). End users' Mental Models of Concepts Critical to Web Application Development. *IEEE HCC 2004*. Rome, Italy. Oct. 26–29.

Rode, J., Bhardwaj, Y., Rosson, M.B., Pérez Quiñones, M.A. and Howarth, J. (2005). Click: Component-based Lightweight Internet-application Construction Kit. http://phpclick.sourceforge.net

Rode. J., Howarth, J., Pérez Quiñones, M.A. and Rosson, M.B. (2005). An End-user Development Perspective on State-of-the-Art Web Development Tools. Virginia Tech Computer Science Tech Report #TR-05-03.

Rode, J., Bhardwaj, Y., Pérez-Quiñones, M.A., Rosson, M.B. and Howarth, J. (2005). As Easy as "Click": End-User Web Engineering. *International Conference on Web Engineering*. Sydney, Australia. July 27–29.

Rosson, M.B. and Carroll, J.M. (1996). "The reuse of uses in Smalltalk programming." *ACM TOCHI* **3**(3): 219–253.

Rosson, M. B., Ballin, J., Rode, J. and Toward, B. (2005). Designing for the Web revisited: A Survey of Casual and Experienced Web Developers. *International Conference on Web Engineering*. Sydney, Australia. July 27–29.

Shneiderman, B. (1983). "Direct Manipulation: A Step Beyond Programming Languages." *IEEE Computer* **16**: 57–60.

Stiemerling, O., Kahler, H. and Wulf, V. (1997). How to Make Software Softer—Designing Tailorable Applications. *Symposium on Designing Interactive Systems 1997*, 365–376.

Tanimoto, S. (1990). "VIVA: A Visual Language for Image Processing." *Journal of Visual Languages and Computing* **1**(2): 127–139.

Turau, V. (2002). A Framework for Automatic Generation of Web-based Data Entry Applications Based on XML. *17th Symposium on Applied Computing*, Madrid, Spain, ACM: 1121–1126.

Vora, P.R. (1998). Designing for the Web: A Survey. *ACM interactions* (May/June): 13–30.

Wolber, D., Su, Y. and Chiang, Y.T. (2002). Designing Dynamic Web Pages and Persistence in the WYSIWYG Interface. *IUI 2002*. Jan 13–16. San Francisco, CA, USA.

Xue, Q. (2005). PRADO: Component-based and event-driven Web programming framework for PHP 5. http://www.xisc.com/

Chapter 9

End-User Development: The Software Shaping Workshop Approach

MARIA FRANCESCA COSTABILE[1], DANIELA FOGLI[2], PIERO MUSSIO[3]
and ANTONIO PICCINNO[4]

[1]*Dipartimento di Informatica, Università di Bari, Bari, Italy, costabile@di.uniba.it*
[2]*Dipartimento di Elettronica per l'Automazione, Università di Brescia, Brescia, Italy, fogli@ing.unibs.it*
[3]*Dipartimento di Informatica e Comunicazione, Università di Milano, Milano, Italy, mussio@dico.unimi.it*
[4]*Dipartimento di Informatica, Università di Bari, Bari, Italy, piccinno@di.uniba.it*

Abstract. In the Information Society, end-users keep increasing very fast in number, as well as in their demand with respect to the activities they would like to perform with computer environments, without being obliged to become computer specialists. There is a great request to provide end-users with powerful and flexible environments, tailorable to the culture, skills, and needs of a very diverse end-user population. In this chapter, we discuss a framework for End-User Development and present our methodology for designing software environments that support the activities of a particular class of end-users, called domain-expert users, with the objective of making their work with the computer easier. Such environments are called Software Shaping Workshops, in analogy to artisan workshops: they provide users only with the necessary tools that allow them to accomplish their specific activities by properly shaping software artifacts without being lost in virtual space.

Key words. end-user development, domain expert, user diversity, gain, co-evolution, implicit information, tacit knowledge, user notation, HCI model.

1. Introduction

In the Information Society, new computer technologies have created the potential to overcome the traditional division between users and the individuals responsible for developing, operating, and maintaining systems. Organizational, business, and commercial technologies increasingly require information technologies to be placed directly in the hands of technicians, clerks, analysts, and managers (Brancheau and Brown, 1993). Cypher (1993) defines end-users as people who use a computer application as part of their daily life or daily work, but are not interested in computers per se. It is evident that several categories of end-users can be defined, for instance depending on whether the computer system is used for work, for personal use, for pleasure, for overcoming possible disabilities, etc. The end-user population is not uniform, but divided in non-mutually exclusive communities characterized by different goals, tasks, and activities. Even these communities cannot be considered uniform, because they include people with different cultural, educational, training, and employment background, who are

Henry Lieberman et al. (eds.), End User Development, 183–205.
© 2006 *Springer.*

novices or experts in the use of the computer, the very young and the elderly and those with different types of (dis)abilities. End-users operate in various interactive contexts and scenarios of use, they want to exploit computer systems to improve their work, but they often complain about the difficulties in the use of such systems.

Brancheau and Brown (1993) describe *end-user computing* as "... the adoption and use of information technology by people outside the information system department, to develop software applications in support of organizational tasks". The organization in which such people work requires them to perform end-user computing and to assume the responsibility of the results of this activity. In (Brancheau and Brown, 1993), the authors primarily analyze the needs of users who are experts in a specific discipline, but not in computer science. Our experience is focused on this kind of user, such as medical doctors, mechanical engineers, geologists, etc. This has motivated our definition of a particular class of end-users, that we call *domain-expert users* (or *d-experts* for short): they are experts in a specific domain, not necessarily experts in computer science, who use computer environments to perform their daily tasks. In the literature, other authors address the needs of *domain experts* (Borchers, 2001; Fischer et al., 2001). Such end-users have the responsibility for possible errors and mistakes, even those generated by wrong or inappropriate use of the software.

Indeed, one fundamental challenge for the next few years is to develop environments that allow people without a particular background in programming to develop and tailor their own applications, still maintaining the congruence within the different evolved instances of the system. Over the next few years, we will be moving from *easy-to-use* to *easy-to-develop-and-tailor* interactive software systems. We foresee the active participation of end-users in the software development process. In this perspective, tasks that are traditionally performed by professional software developers are transferred to the users, who need to be specifically supported in performing these tasks. Active user participation in the software development process can range from providing information about requirements, use cases and tasks, including participatory design (Schuler and Namioka, 1993), to end-user computing (Nardi, 1993). Companies producing software for the mass market are slowly moving in this direction; examples are the adaptive menus in MS Word^{TM} or some programming-by-example techniques in MS Excel^{TM}. However, we are still a long way from their systematic adoption.

In this chapter, we first analyze the activities domain-expert users usually perform or are willing to perform with computers. These people reason and communicate with each other through documents, expressed by notations, which represent abstract or concrete concepts, prescriptions, and results of activities. Often, dialects arise in a community, because the notation is used in different practical situations and environments. For example, mechanical drawings are organized according to rules, which are different in Europe and in the USA. D-experts often complain about the systems they use, they feel frustrated because of the difficulties they encounter interacting with them. Moreover, d-experts feel the need to perform various activities that may even lead to the creation or modification of software artifacts, in order to obtain a better support for their specific tasks, which are therefore considered End-User Development (EUD) activities. Indeed the definition provided by EUD-Net says that "EUD is a set of methods, techniques, and tools that allow users of software systems, who are acting as non-professional software developers, at some point to create or modify a software artifact" (EUD-net Thematic Network).

In this chapter we discuss a framework for EUD based on Software Shaping Workshops (SSWs), which are software environments that aim at supporting the activities of domain-expert users, with the objective of easing the way these users work with computers. In this framework, d-experts play two main roles: (1) performing their working tasks, and (2) participating in the development of the workshops, as representatives of the workshop users. As we explain in Section 5, in both roles d-experts perform EUD activities but are required neither to write codes, nor to know any programming language. D-experts interact with the system through visual languages, computerized versions of their traditional languages and tools. Thus, they can program with the feeling of manipulating the objects of interest in a way similar to what they do in the real world.

The chapter is organized as follows. Section 2 discusses the major reasons behind the difficulties in Human–Computer Interaction (HCI). Section 3 proposes a classification of EUD activities that domain-expert users need to perform. SSWs are then presented in Section 4: they aim at supporting users in their interaction with computers and in performing EUD activities. To provide an example of how d-experts work with SSWs, a case study in a medical domain is presented in Section 5. Section 6 reports a comparison with related works. Finally, Section 7 concludes the chapter.

2. Phenomena Affecting the Human–Computer Interaction Process

Several phenomena affecting the HCI process have emerged in the use of interactive systems. They have been observed, studied, and reported in the current literature, often separately and from different points of view, typically from the points of view of Usability Engineering, Software Engineering, and Information System Development. We present them from a unified, systemic point of view, framing them in the model of HCI which we have developed within the Pictorial Computing Laboratory (PCL) (Bottoni et al., 1999). Our aim is to understand their influence on the HCI process and to derive an approach for system design and development, which tries to overcome the hurdles these phenomena create and to exploit the possibilities they offer.

2.1. A MODEL OF THE HCI PROCESS

In this chapter, we capitalize on the model of the HCI process and on the theory of visual sentences developed by the PCL (Bottoni et al., 1999). In the PCL approach, HCI is modeled as a *syndetic* process (Barnard et al., 2000), i.e., a process in which systems of different nature (the cognitive human—the "mechanical" machine) cooperate to achieve a task. From this point of view, HCI is a process in which the user and the computer communicate by materializing and interpreting a sequence of messages at successive instants in time. If we only consider WIMP (Windows, Icons, Menus, Pointers) interaction (Dix et al., 1998), the messages exchanged are the whole images which appear on the screen display of a computer and include text, icons, graphs, and pictures. Two interpretations of each image on the screen and of each action arise in the interaction: one performed by the user performing the task, depending on his/her role in the task, as well as on his/her culture, experience and skills and the second internal to the system, associating the image with a computational meaning, as determined by the programs implemented in the system (Bottoni et al., 1999). From this point of view, the PCL model reflects a "computer semiotics" approach (Andersen, 2001), in that it "analyzes computer systems and their context of use under a specific perspective, namely as signs that users interpret to mean something" (Andersen, 1992). The HCI process is viewed as a sequence of cycles: the human detects the image on the screen, derives the message meaning, decides what to do next and manifests his/her intention by an activity performed by operating on the input devices of the system; the system perceives these operations as a stream of input events, interprets them with reference to the image on the screen, computes the response to human activity and materializes the results on the screen, so that they can be perceived and interpreted by the human. In theory, this cycle is repeated until the human decides that the process has to be stopped, either because the task has been achieved or has failed.

2.2. THE PHENOMENA

In our opinion, the major phenomena that affect the HCI process are: the communicational gap between designers and users (Majhew, 1992); the grain induced by tools (Dix et al., 1998); the co-evolution of system and users (Arondi et al., 2002; Bourguin et al., 2001; Carroll and Rosson, 1992; Nielsen, 1993); the availability of implicit information (Mussio, 2004) and tacit knowledge (Polanyi, 1967).

- *Communicational gap between designers and users.* The PCL model highlights the existence of two interpretations of each image on the screen and of each action performed to modify it. The first interpretation is performed by the user, the second by the system. The interpretation performed by the system reflects the designer understanding of the task considered, implemented in the programs that control the machine. Between designers and users there is a communicational gap due to their different cultural backgrounds. They adopt different approaches to abstraction, since, for instance, they may have different notions about the details that can be abridged. Moreover, users reason heuristically rather than algorithmically, using examples and analogies rather than deductive abstract tools, documenting activities, prescriptions, and results through their own developed notations, articulating their activities according to their traditional tools rather than computerized ones. On the whole, users and designers possess distinct types of knowledge and follow different approaches and reasoning strategies to modeling, performing, and documenting the tasks to be carried out in a given application domain. Interactive systems usually reflect the culture, skill, and articulatory abilities of the designers. Users often find hurdles in mapping features of the interactive system into their specific culture, skill, and articulatory abilities.
- *Grain.* Every tool is suited to specific strategies in performing a given task. Users are induced by the tool to follow strategies that are apparently easily executable,

but that may be non-optimal. This is called "grain" in (Dix et al., 1998), i.e., the tendency to push the users towards certain behaviors. Interactive systems tend to impose their grain on users' resolution strategies, a grain often not amenable to the users' reasoning and possibly even misleading for them.

- *User diversity.* As highlighted in the introduction, users do not belong to a uniform population, but constitute communities, characterized by different cultures, goals, and tasks. As a consequence, specialized user dialects grow in each user community, which develop particular abilities, knowledge, and notations. User diversity arises even within the same community, depending not only on user skill, culture, and knowledge, but also on specific abilities (physical and/or cognitive), tasks, and the context of the activity. If, during system design, this phenomenon is not taken into account, some users may be forced to adopt specific dialects related with the domain, but different from their own and possibly not fully understandable, thus making the interaction process difficult.

- *Co-evolution of systems and users.* It is well known that "using the system changes the users, and as they change they will use the system in new ways" (Nielsen, 1993). These new uses of the system make the working environment and organization evolve and force the designers to adapt the system to the evolved user, organization, and environment (Bourguin et al., 2001). This phenomenon is called co-evolution of system, environment, and users. Designers are traditionally in charge of managing the evolution of the system. This activity is made more difficult by the communicational gap.

- *Implicit information.* When adopting user defined notations, a relevant part of the information carried by the system is embedded in its visual organization and shape materialization. We call this part of the information carried by the system 'implicit information'. For example, in the documents of scientific communities, the use of bold characters and specific styles indicates the parts of the documents—paper title, abstract, section titles—which synthesize its meaning (Borchers, 2001). Strips of images, for example illustrating procedures or sequences of actions to be performed, are organized according to the reading habits of the expected reader: from left to right for Western readers, from right to left for Eastern ones. Furthermore, some icons, textual words, or images may be meaningful only to the experts in some discipline: for example, icons representing cells in a liver simulation may have a specific meaning only for hepatologists (Mussio et al., 1991), while a X-ray may be meaningful to physicians but not to other experts.

- *Tacit knowledge.* Implicit information is significant only to users who possess the knowledge to interpret it. Most of this knowledge is not explicit and codified but is tacit, namely it is knowledge that users possess and currently use to carry out tasks and to solve problems, but that they are unable to express in verbal terms and that they may even be unaware of. It is a common experience that in many application fields users exploit mainly their tacit knowledge, since they are often more able to do than to explain what they do. Tacit knowledge is related to the specific work domain and it is also exploited by users to interpret the messages from the software system. User notations let users exploit their tacit knowledge and allow the system constructed in these notations to incorporate it as a part of the implicit information.

2.3. SOME OBSERVATIONS CONCERNING THE USER

When the system imposes task execution strategies, which are alien to users, it becomes a *fence* that forces users to follow unfamiliar reasoning strategies and to adopt inefficient procedures. In order to design a system that meets users' needs and expectations, we must take into account the following observations:

1. The notations developed by the user communities from their working practice are not defined according to computer science formalisms, but they are concrete and situated in the specific context, in that they are based on icons, symbols, and words that resemble and schematize the tools and the entities which are to be used in the working environment. Such notations emerge from users' practical experience in their specific activity domain. They highlight the kind of information users consider important for achieving their tasks, even at the expense of obscuring other kinds and facilitate the problem solving strategies, adopted in the specific user community.
2. Software systems are in general designed without taking explicitly into account the problem of implicit information, user articulatory skills, and tacit knowledge. The systems produced can therefore be interpreted with high cognitive costs.
3. Implicit information and tacit knowledge need an externalizing process, which translates them into a form intelligible to a computer system. Implicit information must be conveyed by the layout and appearance of the systems, in order to be exploited by users in performing their work. The final aim is the creation of interactive software systems that the users may correctly perceive and work with.
4. A system acceptable to its users should have a gentle slope of complexity: this means it should avoid big steps in complexity and keep a reasonable trade-off between ease-of-use and functional complexity. Systems might offer users, for example, different levels of complexity in performing EUD activities, ranging from simply setting parameters to integrating existing components and extending the system by developing new components (EUD-Net Thematic Network; Myers et al., 2003; 1992). The system should then evolve with the users (co-evolution) (Arondi et al., 2002), thus offering them new functionalities only when needed.

Starting with these observations, we base our methodology for designing interactive software systems on three principles: (i) the language in which the interaction with systems is expressed must be based on notations traditionally adopted in the domain (this also supports the system designers in identifying the grain problems and in defining their solutions); (ii) systems must present only the tools necessary to perform the task at hand without overwhelming users with unnecessary tools and information; (iii) systems must provide a layout which simulates the traditional layout of the tools employed in the domain, such as mechanical machines or paper-based tools.

3. Domain-Expert Users' EUD Activities

In our work, we primarily address the needs of communities of experts in scientific and technological disciplines. These communities are characterized by different technical methods, languages, goals, tasks, ways of thinking, and documentation styles. The members of a community communicate with each other through documents, expressed in some notations, which represent (materialize) abstract or concrete concepts, prescriptions, and results of activities. Often dialects arise in a community, because the notation is applied in different practical situations and environments. For example, technical mechanical drawings are organized according to rules which are different in Europe and in the USA (ISO standard). Explicative annotations are written in different national languages. Often the whole document (drawing and text) is organized according to guidelines developed in each single company. The correct and complete understanding of a technical drawing depends on the recognition of the original standard, as well as on the understanding of the national (and also company developed) dialects.

Recognizing users as domain experts means recognizing the importance of their notations and dialects as reasoning and communication tools. This also suggests the development of tools customized to a single community. Supporting co-evolution requires in turn that the tools developed for a community should be tailored by its members to the newly emerging requirements (Mørch and Mehandjiev, 2000). Tailoring can be performed only after the system has been released and therefore when it is used in the working context. In fact, the contrast often emerging between the user working activity, which is situated, collaborative and changing, and the formal theories and models that underlie and constitute the software system can be overcome by allowing users themselves to adapt the system they are using.

The diversity of the users calls for the ability to represent the meaning of a concept with different materializations, e.g., text or image or sound and to associate to the same materialization a different meaning according, for example, to the context of interaction. For example, in the medical domain the same X-ray is interpreted in different ways by a radiologist and a pneumologist. These two d-experts are however collaborating to reach a common goal. Therefore, they use the same set of data (of a patient), which, however, is represented differently according to their specific skills. Often experts work in a team to perform a common task and the team might be composed of members of different sub-communities, each sub-community with different expertise. Members of a sub-community need an appropriate computer environment, suited to them to manage their own view of the activity to be performed.

In (Costabile et al., 2003b), some situations that show the real need for environments that allow d-experts to perform various types of EUD activities were described. They emerged from the work of the authors primarily with biologists and earth scientists. In the field of biology software for academic research, there are two types of software development: (1) large scale projects, developed in important bioinformatics centres; (2) local development by biologists who know some programming languages, for managing data, analyzing results, or testing scientific ideas. The second type of development can be considered EUD. Moreover, many biologists feel the need to modify the application they use to fit their needs better. Here is a list of real programming situations that occurred when working with molecular sequences, i.e., either DNA or protein sequences: *scripting*, i.e., search for a sequence pattern, then retrieve all the corresponding secondary structures in a database; *parsing*, i.e., search for the best match in a database similarity search report relative to each subsection; *formatting*, i.e., renumber one's sequence positions from −3000 to +500 instead of 0–3500; *variation*, i.e., search for patterns in a sequence, except repeated ones; *finer control on the computation*, i.e., control in what order multiple sequences are compared and aligned (sequences are called aligned when, after being compared, putative corresponding bases or amino-acid letters are put together); *simple operations*, i.e., search in a DNA sequence for some characters.

In the domain of earth science, some scientists and technicians analyze satellite images and produce documents such as thematic maps and reports, which include photographs, graphs, etc. and textual or numeric data related to the environmental phenomena of interest. Two sub-communities of d-experts are: (1) photo-interpreters who classify, interpret and annotate remote sensed data of glaciers; (2) service oriented clerks, who organize the interpreted images into documents to be delivered to different communities of clients. Photo-interpreters and clerks share environmental data archives, some models for their interpretation, some notations for their presentation, but they have to achieve different tasks, documented by different sub-notations and tools. Therefore, their notations can be considered two dialects of the Earth Scientist & Technologist general notation.

From these experiences, two classes of d-expert activities have been proposed (Costabile et al., 2003b):

- *Class 1* includes activities that allow users, by setting some parameters, to choose among alternative behaviors (or presentations or interaction mechanisms) already available in the application; in the literature such activities are usually called parameterization, customization or personalization.
- *Class 2* includes all activities that imply some programming in any programming paradigm, thus creating or modifying a software artifact. Since we want to be as close as possible to the user, we will usually consider novel programming paradigms, such as programming by demonstration, programming with examples, visual programming, and macro generation.

In Table 9.1 examples of activities of both classes are provided.

4. SOFTWARE SHAPING WORKSHOPS

In scientific and technological communities, such as mechanical engineers, geologists, and physicians, experts often work in a team to perform a common task. The team might be composed of members of different sub-communities, each sub-community with a different expertise. Such domain experts, when working with a software application, feel

Table 9.1. Examples of activities of classes and descriptions

Class	Activity name	Activity description
Class 1	Parameterization	This is intended as a specification of unanticipated constraints in data analysis. In this situation d-experts are required to associate specific computation parameters to specific parts of the data, or to use different models of computations available in the program.
	Annotation	This is the activity in which d-experts write comments next to the data and the result files in order to highlight their meaning.
Class 2	Modeling from data	The system supporting the d-expert derives some (formal) models by observing data, e.g. a kind of regular expression is inferred from selected parts of aligned sequences (Blackwell, 2000), or patterns of interactions are derived (Arondi et al., 2002).
	Programming by demonstration	D-experts show examples of property occurrences in the data and the system infers a (visual) function from them.
	Use of formula languages	This is available in spreadsheets and could be extended to other environments, such as Biok (Biology Interactive Object Kit) that is a programmable application for biologists (Letondal, 2001).
	Indirect interaction with application objects	As opposed to direct manipulation, traditional interaction style tools, e.g., command languages, can be provided to support user activities.
	Incremental programming	This is close to traditional programming, but limited to changing a small part of a program, such as a method in a class. It is easier than programming from scratch.
	Extended annotation	A new functionality is associated with the annotated data. This functionality can be defined by any technique previously described.

the need to perform various activities that may even lead to the creation or modification of software artifacts, in order to obtain better support for their specific tasks. These are considered EUD activities. The need for EUD is a consequence of the user diversity and evolution discussed in Section 2.

Our approach to the design of a software system devoted to a specific community of domain-expert users is to organize the system into various environments, each one for a specific sub-community. Such environments are organized in analogy with the artisan workshops, where the artisans find only the tools necessary to carry out their activities. In a similar way, d-experts using a virtual workshop find available only the tools required to develop their activities by properly shaping the software they use. These tools must be designed and must behave in such a way that they can be used by the d-expert in the current situation. For this reason, the software environments are called SSWs (Costabile et al., 2002). SSWs allow users to develop software artifacts without the burden of using a traditional programming language, using high level visual languages, tailored to their needs. Moreover, users have the feeling of simply manipulating the objects of interest in a way similar to what they do in the real world. Indeed, they are creating an electronic document through which they can perform some computation, without writing any textual program code.

An important activity in the professionals' work is the annotation of documents. In the SSW methodology, electronic annotation is a primitive operator, on which the communication among different d-experts and the production of new knowledge are based. A d-expert has the possibility of performing annotations of a piece of text, of a portion of an image or of the workshop in use to extend, make his/her current insights explicit regarding the considered problem, or even the features of the workshop. D-experts use annotation as a peer-to-peer communication tool when they exchange annotated documents to achieve a common task. By annotating the workshop they use, d-experts also use annotation as a tool to communicate with the design team in charge of the maintenance of the system.

D-experts play two main roles: (1) performing their working tasks, possibly informing the maintenance team of their usability problems; (2) participating in the development of the workshops. In the first role, at the time of use, d-experts can tailor the workshop to their current needs and context. For example, the annotation tools permit the definition of new widgets: as a reaction to the annotation activity performed by the d-expert, the workshop may transform the annotated document area into a new widget, to which a computational meaning is associated. This widget is added to the common knowledge base and is made accessible to other d-experts, each one accessing the data through his/her own workshop, enriched by the new widget that is adapted to the specific context. In the second role, at the design time, d-expert representatives participate directly in the development of the workshops for their daily work (*application workshops*). D-experts, even if they are non-professional software developers, are required to create or modify application workshops, i.e., software artifacts. To this end, different workshops (*system workshops*) are made available to them, which permit the customization of each application workshop to the d-expert community needs and requirements.

This approach leads to a workshop network that tries to bridge the communicational gap between designers and domain-expert users, since all cooperate in developing computer systems customized to the needs of the user communities without requiring them to become skilled programmers. Thus the workshop network permits domain-expert users to work cooperatively in different places and at different time to reach a common goal; in this sense it becomes a collaboratory, as defined by Wulf: "a center without walls, in which researchers [in our case professionals] can perform their research [work] without regard to physical location, interacting with colleagues, accessing instrumentation, sharing data and computational resources, and accessing information in digital libraries" (Wulf, 1989).

Two levels can be distinguished in the workshop network:

1. the top level, that we call the *design level*, involves a sub-network of system workshops, including the one used by the software engineers to lead the team in developing the other workshops and the system workshops which are used by the team of HCI and domain experts to generate and/or adapt other system workshops or application workshops;
2. the bottom level, that we call the *use level*, includes a network of application workshops, which are used by end-users to perform their tasks.

Each system workshop in the design level is exploited to incrementally translate concepts and tools expressed in computer-oriented languages into tools expressed in notations that resemble the traditional user notations and are therefore understandable and manageable by users. The network organization of the SSWs depends on the working organization of the user community to which the SSWs are dedicated.

To develop an SSW network, software engineers and d-experts have first to specify the pictorial and semantic aspects of the Interaction Visual Languages (IVLs) through which users interact with workshops. In our approach, we capitalize on the theory of visual sentences developed by the Pictorial Computing Laboratory (PCL) and on the model of WIMP interaction it entails (Bottoni et al., 1999). From this theory, we derive the formal tools to obtain the definition of IVLs. In the WIMP interaction, the messages exchanged between the user and the system are the entire images represented on the screen display, which include texts, pictures, icons, etc. and the user can manifest his/her intention by operating on the input devices of the system such as a keyboard or a mouse. Users understand the meaning of such messages because they recognize some subsets of pixels on the screen as functional or perceptual units, called characteristic structures (css) (Bottoni et al., 1999).

From the machine point of view, a cs is the manifestation of a computational process, that is the result of the computer interpretation of a portion of the program P specifying the interactive system. The computer interpretation creates an entity, that we call virtual entity (ve) and keeps it active. A ve is defined by specifying its behavior, for example through statecharts, from which P can be implemented. It is important, however, to specify the set CS of css, which can appear on the screen, as well as their relations to the states of P from which they are generated. A ve is therefore specified as ve$-<$P, CS, $<$INT, MAT$>>$, where INT (interpretation) is a function, mapping the current cs $\in$ CS of the ve to the state u of the program P, generating it and MAT (materialization), a function mapping u to cs. A simple example of ve is the "floppy disk" icon to save a file in the iconic toolbar of MS Word^{TM}. This ve has different materializations to indicate different states of the computational process: for example, once it is clicked by the user the disk shape is highlighted and the associated computational process saves the current version of the document in a disk file. Once the document is saved, the disk shape goes back to its usual materialization (not highlighted). However, ves extend the concept of widgets (as in the case of the previously mentioned disk icon) and virtual devices (Preece, 1994), which are more independent from the interface style and include interface components possibly defined by users at run time. The creation of virtual entities by users is an EUD activity and distinguishes our approach from traditional ones, such as Visual Basic scripted buttons in MS Word^{TM}. In Section 5, we will discuss the creation of a ve by a user in a medical domain.

The SSW approach is aimed at overcoming the communicational gap between designers and users by a "gentle slope" approach to the design complexity (Myers 2003; 1992). In fact, the team of designers performs their activity by: (a) developing several specialized system workshops tailored to the needs of each type of designer in the team (HCI specialists, software engineers, d-experts); and (b) using system workshops to develop application workshops through incremental prototypes (Carrara et al., 2002; Costabile et al., 2002). In summary, the design and implementation of application workshops is incremental and based on the contextual, progressive gain of insight into the user problems, which emerge from the activity of checking, revising, and updating the application workshops performed by each member of the design team.

The diversity of the users calls for the ability to represent the meaning of a concept with different materializations, in accordance with local cultures and the layouts used, sounds, colors, times and to associate a different meaning to the same materialization according, for example, to the context of interaction. The SSW methodology aims at developing application workshops which are tailored to the culture, skill, and articulatory abilities of specific user communities. To reach this goal, it becomes important to decouple the pictorial representation of data from their computational representation (Bottoni et al., 1999). In this way, the system is able to represent data according to the user needs, by taking into account user diversity. Several prototypes have been developed in this line, in medical and mechanical engineering (Mussio et al., 1992). XML technologies, which are based on the same concept of separating the materialization of a document from its content, are being extensively exploited.

To clarify the concepts on the SSW network, we refer to a prototype under study, designed to support different communities of physicians, namely radiologists and pneumologists, in the analysis of chest X-rays and in the generation of the diagnosis. Radiologists and pneumologists represent two sub-communities of the physicians community: they share patient-related data archives, some models for their interpretation, some notations for their presentation, but they have to perform different tasks, documented through different sub-notations and tools. Therefore, their notations can be considered two (visual) dialects of the physicians' general notation.

The SSW network for this prototype is presented in Figure 9.1. As we said, we distinguish two levels. At the top level, the design level includes the workshops used

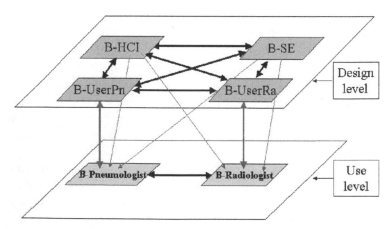

Figure 9.1. The network of Software Shaping Workshops involved in the co-evolutive use of B-Pneumologist and B-Radiologist.

by the members of the design team to develop the application workshops. The design level includes system workshops devoted to software engineers (*B-SE*), HCI experts (*B-HCI*), and d-experts (*B-UserPn, B-UserRa*), in our case, specialists in pneumology and radiology. The designers in the team collaborate in designing and updating, as required by co-evolution, the application workshops *B-Radiologist* and *B-Pneumologist*. In the design and updating phases, each member of the design team operates on the application workshop under development using his/her own system workshop tailored to his/her own culture, skills, and articulatory abilities. The application workshops are developed through a participatory design project which is carried out in an asynchronous and distributed way. At the use level, the pneumologist and radiologist, who are working in different wards or different hospitals and are involved in the study of the pulmonary diseases, can reach an agreed diagnosis using application workshops tailored to their culture, skills, and articulatory abilities, again in an asynchronous and distributed way.

In Section 5, we illustrate how EUD activities can be performed by working with *B-Radiologist* and *B-Pneumologist*. However, EUD activities can also be performed at design level: using *B-UserPn* and *B-UserRa* (see Figure 9.1), representatives of end-users may generate or adapt the application workshops *B-Radiologist* and *B-Pneumologist*. The development of *B-UserPn* and *B-UserRa* is in progress, so we focus here only on the EUD activity performed at the use level by interacting with two prototypes of *B-Radiologist* and *B-Pneumologist*. Such prototypes have been developed to speak with our domain experts, receive feedback from them about the functionalities the software system offers and understand their needs. In (Costabile et al., 2003a; Fogli et al., 2003), prototypes in the field of mechanical engineering illustrate how d-experts may perform EUD activity at the design time by interacting with software environments developed by following the SSW methodology.

5. SSWs for a Medical Domain

To concretize our view on SSWs, we introduce a scenario, drawn from an initial analysis of physicians collaborating to achieve a diagnosis (Costabile et al., 2002). In the scenario, a pneumologist and a radiologist incrementally gain insight into the case by successive interpretations and annotations of chest X-rays, performed in (possibly) different places and at (possibly) different times. They are supported by two interactive prototypes, *B-Radiologist* and *B-Pneumologist*, which share a knowledge repository. They achieve the diagnosis by updating the knowledge repository after each session of interpretation of the results reached so far and of annotation of their new findings. In particular, through the annotation activity, new software artifacts are created (e.g., a widget with a certain functionality): each new software artifact created in this way implements a virtual entity whose cs corresponds to the shape traced by the user on the X-ray and whose program P depends on the content of the annotation.

B-Radiologist and *B-Pneumologist* are application workshops that support the two physicians in recording and making the observational data available for reasoning and communication, as well as the paths of the activities physicians are performing and the progressively obtained results. To this end, they share the knowledge repository

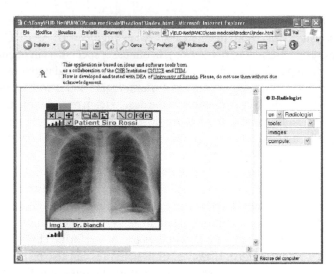

Figure 9.2. Web page with B-Radiologist workshop. The radiologist is analyzing a chest X-ray.

and also some tools for data annotation, archiving, and retrieving. However, they have to support physicians with different experience and cultural background, performing different tasks in the achievement of the diagnosis. Hence, each one is also equipped with tools specialized to the specific tasks to be performed by its own users and makes data and tools available by materializing them according to the specific culture, experience and situation of its current user.

Figure 9.2 displays a web page, as it appears to a radiologist—Dr. Bianchi, interacting with *B-Radiologist.* Due to space limitations, it is the only figure showing the complete web page, the remaining figures show only panes of our interest.

The screen is divided into two parts: the top presents the tools which interact with Internet Explorer^{TM}, the browser managing the process. The underlying part has a header at the top, presenting general information about the creators of the system. Below it, there is an *equipment area* on the right with a title identifying *B-Radiologist* as the workshop currently active and a *working area* on the left. In the equipment area, the radiologist has repositories of entities available to be worked (images and annotations) and equipment to work on the entities. Data and tools can be extracted and used or deployed in the working area and stored in the repositories. Tools are represented in the working area as icons and data as raster or vector images, materializing the css of interest. Each image represents an entity to be worked on and is associated to a handle, a toolbox and other identifiers. These four entities form a *bench.* The handle is a ve whose cs is a rectangle which identifies the bench. It is positioned on top of the toolbox and permits the bench selection and dislocation. The toolbox contains the tools required for the execution of the current task. The identifiers identify the physician performing the task, the patient to which the data refers and the image (set of data) referring to that patient.

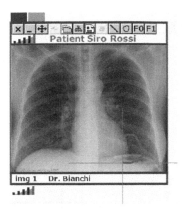

Figure 9.3. Using B-Radiologist, the radiologist circles a zone of pleural effusion.

In Figure 9.2, the radiologist is working on two benches, one associated to raster X-ray which underlies a bench associated to a transparent vector image, which is a support for annotation. Hence, two handles appear on top of the toolbox, while system generated identifiers identify Dr. Bianchi as the radiologist annotating the X-ray, Mr. Rossi as the patient and img1 as the considered image. Figure 9.2 resumes the state of the activity of interpretation of an X-ray after the radiologist (a) has obtained the data of his interest (an X-ray of the patient, whose surname is Rossi) and (b) has superimposed the annotation bench on the bench containing the X-ray.

In Figure 9.3, the radiologist (a) has recognized an area of interest denoting a pleural effusion; (b) has selected from the toolbox the tool for free-hand drawing of close curves, the tenth button from the left (whose cs is a close curve); and (c) *B-Radiologist* has reacted, presenting him with a cursor, whose cs is the cross. The radiologist is now circling the area of interest using a mouse to steer the cross, so identifying a cs. After closing the curve, the radiologist selects the eighth button ('a') in the top menu, firing the annotation activity; then he can type his classification of the cs 'Pleural effusion'. Figure 9.4 shows the radiologist storing these results by the selection of the 'add Note' button. As a reaction to this last user action, *B-Radiologist* (a) closes the annotation window; (b) adds to the framed area an icon of a pencil as an anchor to the annotation, and (c) transforms the framed area into a *widget*, by associating it to a pop-up menu. The menu title and items depend on the radiologist's classification of the css in the framed area. In other words, *B-Radiologist* creates an active widget whose characteristics depend on the contextual activity and which is added to the set of tools known to the system and then becomes available to the users. In particular, the pop-up menu associated with the widget allows the radiologist to choose between two activities related with pleural effusion areas: the density evaluation and the NMR analyses retrieval. After having obtained the results of the selected computations, the radiologist writes a new annotation suggesting a possible diagnosis to be shared with the pneumologist (potential pneumonia).

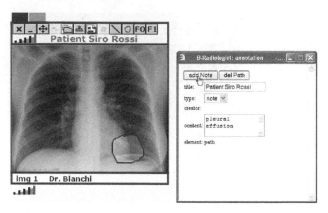

Figure 9.4. Using B-Radiologist, the radiologist annotates a zone of pleural effusion.

At the end of the annotation activity, *B-Radiologist* stores the annotation and other possible results from its activity in the knowledge repository shared with *B-Pneumologist*, permanently updating to the patient file, thus evolving *B-Radiologist*, *B-Pneumologist*, and the knowledge repository. In the current version, the radiologist sends an email message to the pneumologist whenever s/he wants to inform the other physician that the knowledge repository has been updated.

The workshops make two different types of tools available to their users: system predefined tools, which are always available and the tools created and associated to the data by the users, such as the annotation button. Their meaning depends on the medical context in which annotation is used. For example, in *B-Pneumologist*, a cs classified as 'pleural effusion' is not associated to the same menu as in *B-Radiologist*, but is associated to a multi-link to the records of available data on the patient, i.e., radiological interpretation, associated TACs, and hematic parameters. In *B-Pneumologist* the pencil associated to the area of interest outlined by the radiologist is associated to the tools for visualizing the data related to the patient and supporting their exploration in order to reach a final diagnosis. The linking to the new tools—the new computational meaning of the annotation—occurs at start-up time, i.e., when a physician accesses *B-Pneumologist* to initiate the interactive session. Therefore, when the pneumologist Dr. Neri selects the pencil, *B-Pneumologist* displays the text of the annotation performed by the radiologist and the multi-link (Figure 9.5). In Figure 9.5 the pneumologist selects 'Radiological interpretation' to query details on Dr. Bianchi's observations. He obtains the media and estimated error of the density of the pleural effusion. He can also add his diagnosis to the document recording the opinions increasingly annotated by Dr. Bianchi (Figure 9.6).

The SSW life cycle follows a star approach (Hix and Hartson, 1993), starting with the analysis of the users of the application workshops. The design process proceeds by developing incremental workshop prototypes at various levels in the hierarchy, going bottom-up as well as top-down. In the case study, user analysis started by examining how the radiologists classify, interpret, and annotate chest X-rays and how the pneumologists

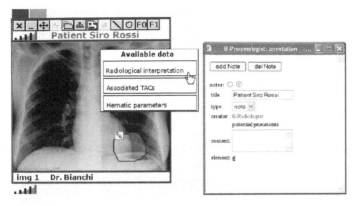

Figure 9.5. Working in B-Pneumologist the pneumologist accesses the radiological interpretation.

use the interpreted images, provide their diagnoses and record them using an annotation tool. On the basis of this analysis, the team of experts involved in the design felt the need to develop the two separate but consistent application workshops, each one dedicated to a specific sub-community. Moreover, the team of experts observed that not all situations can be foreseen in advance and that sometimes *B-Radiologist* and *B-Pneumologist* must both be consistently adapted to different new tasks and situations. This adaptation requires the knowledge of both dialects and activities, of the tasks to be executed and of the working organization and the awareness of the use of diagnostic documents outside the organization. Only senior physicians have such a global skill and knowledge and can assume this responsibility. Therefore, the team decided that a senior pneumologist and a senior radiologist should act as managers of the whole activity and be responsible for recognizing the tasks to be performed, identifying the dialect notations of interest, and consequently defining the system of consistent application workshops. The senior physicians achieve these goals using two system workshops, *B-UserRa* and *B-UserPn*,

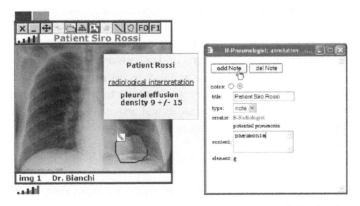

Figure 9.6. The pneumologist obtains the radiological interpretation and gives his diagnosis.

where they find usable tools for implementing and adapting both *B-Radiologist* and *B-Pneumologist* (see Figure 9.1). They can also collaborate with HCI experts and software engineers as required by the progressive results of the experiences.

6. Related Work

As designers, our challenge is to develop interactive software systems which (a) support their users in exploiting their "practical competence and professional artistry in achieving a task" (Schön, 1983) and (b) enable the practitioner to develop and extend the knowledge available to the profession (Schön, 1983). To achieve this goal, we adopt a 'semiotic computer' point of view (Andersen, 2001; 1992), recognizing the existence of two interpretations of each CS and the importance of notations developed by d-expert communities such as reasoning, communication, and documentation tools.

Another important issue in our design approach is the co-evolution of users and systems. Carroll and Rosson (1992) speak about co-evolution of users and tasks, while co-evolution of artifacts supporting HCI design in the different steps of the product lifecycle is discussed by (Brown et al., 1998). Co-evolution of users and systems, as proposed in this paper, stresses the importance of co-evolving the systems, as soon as users evolve the performance of their tasks. Co-evolution of users and systems is rooted in the usability engineering, in that it supports designers in collecting feedback on systems from the field of use, to improve the system usability (Nielsen, 1993). Tools designed to support co-evolution are suitable for observational evaluation in user-centered design approaches (Preece, 1994). Moreover, these evaluation tools integrated within the SSW networks allow system adaptation (Arondi et al., 2002), in the more general frame of co-evolution of users, organization, systems, and environment, as observed by Bourguin et al. (2001). This extends the view of Mackay, who postulates that the use of information technology is a co-adaptive phenomenon (Mackay, 1990). Co-evolution implies tailoring. SSWs are designed to permit tailoring, i.e. "further development of an application during use to adapt it to complex work situations" (Kahler et al., 2000) by end-users.

In our approach, d-experts play a role similar to the handymen in (MacLean et al., 1990). The handyman bridges between workers (people using a computer application) and computer professionals; s/he is able to work alongside users and communicate their needs to programmers. Similarly, d-experts bridge between workers and computer professionals, but are end-users themselves and not necessarily computer professionals. They must be provided with environments to be able to participate in SSWs development that are adapted to their culture, skills and articulatory abilities. In (Costabile et al., 2003a; Fogli et al., 2003) we describe an environment devoted to mechanical engineers who were the d-experts involved in the development of the application workshop devoted to assembly-line operators.

In (Mackay, 1991) and (Nardi, 1993) empirical studies are reported on activities performed by end-users and generally defined as tailoring activities. Mackay analyses how users of a UNIX software environment try to customize the system, intending as customization the possibility of modifying software to make persistent changes. She finds that many users do not customize their applications as much as they could. This also depends on the fact that it takes too much time and deviates from other activities. Nardi conducted empirical studies on users of spreadsheets and CAD software. She found out that these users actually perform activities of end user programming, thus generating new software artifacts; these users are even able to master the formal languages embedded in these applications when they have a real motivation for doing so.

SSWs are also in the area of research on *Gentle Slope Systems*, "which are systems where for each incremental increase in the level of customizability, the user only needs to learn an incremental amount" (Myers, 2003). In fact, the SSW methodology favors the construction of systems which are more acceptable to the users, since they are based on a knowledge (often tacit), languages, and notations belonging to the interested user community. Moreover, SSWs allow users to perform EUD activities, overcoming the problems currently affecting other types of EUD, such as the development of macros in spreadsheets or of scripts in active web pages, which usually require the learning of conventional programming (Myers, 2003).

Domain knowledge plays a key role in the approach to software system construction described by Fischer (1998), Fischer and Ostwald (2002), and Fischer et al. (2001). In these works, the authors propose designing systems as *seeds*, with a subsequent *evolutionary growth*, followed by a *reseeding* phase. SER (Seeding, Evolutionary growth, Reseeding) is thus a process model for the development and evolution of the so-called DODEs (Domain-Oriented Design Environments), which are "software systems that support design activities within particular domains and that are built specifically to evolve" (Fischer, 1998). Three intertwined levels of design activities and system development are envisaged: at the lower level, there is a multifaceted domain-independent architecture constituting the framework for building evolvable systems; at the middle level, the multifaceted architecture is instantiated for a particular domain in order to create a DODE; at the top level, there are individual artifacts in the domain, developed by exploiting the information contained in the DODE. The SER model describes the evolution of such environments at the three levels.

We have a domain-independent architecture as well, which can be instantiated according to the considered domain (Fogli et al., 2003). This architecture is implemented by exploiting open source code, such as XML-suite tools and ECMAscript language, so that a system SSW and the application SSWs generated from it have the same web-based structure. However, the construction of SSWs is always based on a formal specification of the Interaction Visual Languages through which the user interacts in order to guarantee a variety of properties [such as usability, determinism, viability, non-ambiguity (Preece, 1994)]. The architecture reflects the formal model proposed to specify the static and dynamics component of the systems. In the SSW framework there is a clear distinction between the design and the use level: the system workshops at the design level can be used by d-experts to create and/or update application workshops. Both system and application workshops can first represent seeds, which, according to the user interaction, can be evolved into new system and application workshops respectively, still remaining separate. This separation, which helps not to disorient the users during their task activities, is not so well established in the works with which we are comparing ours.

There is a separation between the design and use level in many commercial tools for authoring systems, such as, for example, Micromedia Flash or Toolbook. In these systems, the author mode and the user mode are present, but the author mode usually requires the use of a programming language (typically a scripting one). Therefore, these systems turn out to be less accessible and usable by experts in domains different from computer science. Moreover, both system and application workshops present the users with a familiar environment in which only the tools necessary to carry out the working task are available. On the other hand, also commercial tools allow the definition of libraries of personalized tools, but they may only be added to the tools already available in the developmental system.

7. Conclusions

Nowadays, new computer technologies force many users, who are not experts in computer science but are experts in their own domain of activity, to ask for software environments in which they can do some programming activity related to their tasks and adapt the environments to their emerging new needs. Therefore, in such a scenario, EUD becomes a challenging issue for future software systems. To study novel solutions to cope with this issue, we propose a unified view of the variety of phenomena affecting the HCI process, such as the communicational gap which often exists between designers and systems, the user diversity, the co-evolution of systems and users, the grain imposed by software tools, the implicit information, and tacit knowledge that influence users' behavior while interacting with software systems.

In the chapter we have analyzed these phenomena, by showing the hurdles they impose in user activities and the new interaction and communication possibilities they offer and have framed them in a systemic HCI model. Such a model underlies our approach to system design and development—the SSW methodology. Within the SSW methodology, EUD means that (1) d-experts may create other SSWs suitable to the considered domain by using simple facilities, such as a drag-and-drop; and (2) d-experts may create new tools within the workshop they are using, for example as a result of an annotation activity. The latter case has been analyzed in a medical domain: physicians use tailored environments (application workshops), which they can enrich by themselves with new tools through annotation activity. The results of the annotation are shared by the application workshops, so allowing physicians to create tools to be used also by their colleagues, possibly according to their own needs, background, expertise, and preferences. In both cases, users are required neither to write codes, nor to know any programming languages or paradigms. Users simply create programs by interacting with the system through visual languages resembling the activities they usually perform in their daily work. For the sake of brevity, the case study discussed in this paper shows only an example of the second type of EUD activity. More details about the first one are by Costabile et al., (2003a) and Fogli et al. (2003). The architecture we have implemented to develop SSWs is based on the W3C framework and the XML technology, thus permitting the construction of very "light" applications (Fogli et al., 2003).

Acknowledgments

The authors wish to thank the reviewers for their useful comments and Giuseppe Fresta for the stimulating discussions during the development of this work and for his contribution to the implementation of the prototypes presented in the paper. They also wish to thank Dr. Lynn Rudd for her help in correcting the English manuscript.

The support of EUD-Net Thematic Network (IST-2001-37470) is acknowledged.

References

Andersen, P.B. (1992). Computer semiotics. *Scandinavian Journal of Information Systems* **4**, 3–30.

Andersen, P.B. (2001). What semiotics can and cannot do for HCI. *Knowledge Based Systems* **14**, 419–424.

Arondi, S., Baroni, P., Fogli, D. and Mussio, P. (2002). Supporting co-evolution of users and systems by the recognition of Interaction Patterns. *Proceedings of the International Conference on Advanced Visual Interfaces (AVI 2002)*, Trento, Italy, New York: ACM Press, pp. 177–189.

Barnard, P., May, J., Duke, D. and Duce, D. (2000). Systems, Interactions, and Macrotheory. *ACM Trans. on Human-Computer Interaction* **7**(2), 222–262.

Blackwell, A. (2001). See what you need: Helping end users to build abstractions. *Journal of Visual Languages and Computing* **12**(5), 475–499.

Borchers, J. (2001). *A Pattern Approach to Interaction Design*, Chichester: John Wiley & Sons.

Bottoni, P., Costabile, M.F. and Mussio, P. (1999). Specification and dialogue control of visual interaction through visual rewriting systems. *ACM Trans. on Programming Languages and Systems (TOPLAS)* **21**(6), 1077–1136.

Bourguin, G., Derycke, A. and Tarby, J.C. (2001). Beyond the interface: Co-evolution inside interactive systems—A proposal founded on activity theory. *Proceedings of IHM-HCI 2001,* Lille, France, Berlin Heidelberg: Springer-Verlag, pp. 297–310.

Brancheau, J.C. and Brown, C.V. (1993). The Management of End-User Computing: Status and Directions. *ACM Computing Surveys* **25**(4), 437–482.

Brown, J., Graham, T.C.N. and Wright, T. (1998). The Vista environment for the coevolutionary design of user interfaces. *Proceedings of CHI 98,* Los Angeles, New York: ACM Press, 376–383.

Carrara, P., Fogli, D., Fresta, G. and Mussio, P. (2002). Toward overcoming culture, skill and situation hurdles in human-computer interaction. *International Journal Universal Access in the Information Society* **1**(4), 288–304.

Carroll, J.M. and Rosson, M.B. (1992). Deliberated evolution: Stalking the view matcher in design space. *Human-Computer Interaction* **6** (3 and 4), 281–318.

Costabile, M.F., Fogli, D., Fresta, G., Mussio, P. and Piccinno, A. (2002). Computer environments for improving end-user accessibility. *Proceedings of 7th ERCIM Workshop "User Interfaces For All"*, Paris, France, LNCS 2615, Berlin Heidelberg: Springer-Verlag, pp. 187–198.

Costabile, M. F., Fogli, D., Fresta, G, Mussio, P. and Piccinno, A. (2003a). Building environments for end-user development and tailoring. *Proceedings 2003 IEEE Symposia on Human Centric*

Computing Languages and Environments (HCC' 03), Aukland, New Zeland, Danvers: IEEE Computer Society, pp. 31–38.

Costabile, M.F., Fogli, D., Letondal, C., Mussio, P. and Piccinno, A. (2003b). Domain-expert users and their needs of software development, *Proceedings of UAHCI Conference*, Crete, London: Lawrence Erlbaum Associates, pp. 232–236.

Cypher, A. (1993). *Watch What I Do: Programming by Demonstration*. Cambridge: The MIT Press.

Dix, A., Finlay, J., Abowd, G. and Beale, R. (1998). *Human-Computer Interaction*, London: Prentice Hall.

EUD-Net Thematic Network, Network of Excellence on End-User Development, http://giove.cnuce. cnr.it/eud-net.htm.

Fischer, G., Grudin, J., McCall, R., Ostwald, J., Redmiles, D., Reeves, B. and Shipman, F. (2001). Seeding, evolutionary growth and reseeding: The incremental development of collaborative design environments. In: *Coordination Theory and Collaboration Technology*, Mahwah, NJ: Lawrence Erlbaum Associates, 447–472.

Fischer, G. and Ostwald, J. (2002). Seeding, evolutionary growth, and reseeding: Enriching participatory design with informed participation. *Proceedings of PDC'02*, Malmö, Sweden, New York: ACM Press, pp. 135–143.

Fischer, G. (1998). Seeding, evolutionary growth, and reseeding: Constructing, capturing, and evolving knowledge in domain-oriented design environments. *Automated Software Engineering* 5(4), 447–468.

Fogli, D., Piccinno A. and Salvi, D. (2003). What users see is what users need. *Proceedings of DMS 03*, Miami, USA, Skokie, USA: Knowledge Systems Institute, pp. 335–340.

Hix, D. and Hartson, H. R. (1993). *Developing User Interfaces: Ensuring Usability through Product & Process*. Chichester: John Wiley & Sons.

Kahler, H., Mørch, A., Stiemerling, O. and Wulf, V. (2000). Introduction to the special issue on tailorable systems and cooperative work. *Computer Supported Cooperative Work* 9, 1–4, Kluwer Academic Publishers.

ISO Standard: ISO 5456 Technical Drawing Projection Methods.

Letondal, C. (2001). Programmation et interaction, PhD thesis, Université de Paris XI, Orsay.

Mackay, W.E. (1990). Users and Customizable Software: A Co-Adaptive Phenomenon, Ph. D. Thesis, MIT.

Mackay, W.E. (1991). Triggers and barriers to customizing software. *Proceedings of ACM CHI'90*, New Orleans, USA. New York: ACM Press, pp. 153–160.

MacLean, A., Kathleen, C., Lövstrand, L. and Moran, T. (1990). User-tailorable systems: pressing the issues with buttons, *Proceedings of ACM CHI'90*, New Orleans, USA. New York: ACM Press, pp. 175–182.

Majhew, D.J. (1992). *Principles and Guideline in Software User Interface Design*, London: Prentice Hall.

Mørch, A. I. and Mehandjiev, N. D. (2000). Tailoring as collaboration: The mediating role of multiple representations and application units. *Computer Supported Cooperative Work* 9, 2000, 75–100.

Mussio, P. (2004). E-Documents as tools for the humanized management of community knowledge. In: H. Linger et al. (eds.), *Constructing the Infrastructure for the Knowledge Economy: Methods and Tools*; *Theory and Practice*. Dordrecht: Kluwer Academic, pp. 27–43.

Mussio P, Finadri M, Gentini P. and Colombo F. (1992). A bootstrap technique to visual interface design and development. *The Visual Computer* 8(2), 75–93.

Mussio, P., Pietrogrande, M. and Protti, M. (1991). Simulation of hepatological models: A study in visual interactive exploration of scientific problems. *Journal of Visual Languages and Computing* 2, 75–95.

Myers, B.A., Hudson, S. E. and Randy, P. (2003). Past, present, and future of user interface software tools. In Carroll (ed.), *Human-Computer Interaction in the New Millennium*, New York: Addison-Wesley, pp. 213–233.

Myers, B.A., Smith, D.C. and Horn, B. (1992). Report of the 'End-User Programming' Working Group. In: *Languages for Developing User Interfaces*. Boston, MA: Jones and Bartlett, pp. 343–366.

Nardi, B. (1993). *A small matter of programming: Perspectives on end user computing*. Cambridge: MIT Press.

Nielsen, J. (1993). *Usability Engineering*. San Diego: Academic Press.

Polanyi, M. (1967). *The Tacit Dimension*. London: Rouledge & Kegan Paul.

Preece, J. (1994). *Human-Computer Interaction*. Harlow: Addison-Wesley.

Schön, D. (1983). *The Reflective Practinioner—How Professionals Think in Action*. Jackson: Basic Books.

Schuler, D. and Namioka, A. (1993). *Preface—Participatory Design, Principles and Practice*, Lawrence Erlbaum Ass. N.J: Inc. Hillsday, vii.

Wulf, W.A. (1989). The National Collaboratory: A White Paper. Appendix A in Toward a National Collaboratory, *National Science Foundation invitational workshop* held at Rockfeller University, Washington D.C., p. 1.

Chapter 10

Participatory Programming: Developing Programmable Bioinformatics Tools for End-Users

CATHERINE LETONDAL[1]

[1]*Institute Pasteur, Paris, France, letondal@pasteur.fr*

Abstract. We describe participatory programming as a process that spans design, programming, use and tailoring of software. This process, that includes end-users at each stage, integrates participatory design and programmability. Programmability, as a property that relies on a reflective architecture, aims to let the end-users evolve the tools themselves according to their current, specific needs, and to let them control better the way results are computed. We present an environment that results from this approach, called *biok*, developed for researchers in biology, which is both domain-oriented and open to full programming.

1. Introduction

This chapter describes what we call "Participatory Programming," or how to integrate participatory design and programmability. We consider programming, not as a goal in itself, but rather as a potential feature, available if things go wrong in the context of use. We discuss how to better integrate the context of the user in the programming activity by both: (a) letting the user participate to the design of the tools and (b) providing access to programming via the user interface and from visible objects of interest, within a scaffolded software architecture. This approach applies to fields where users are both experts in their domain and able to develop basic programming skills to enhance their work.

Biology has seen a tremendous increase in the need for computing in recent years. Although biology labs may employ professional programmers and numerous ready-made tools are available, these are rarely sufficient to accommodate this fast moving domain. Individual biologists must cope with increasing quantities of data, new algorithms, and changing hypotheses. They have diverse, specialized computing needs which are strongly affected by their local work settings. This argues strongly for a better form of end-user development (EUD).

The problem is how best to provide access to programming for non-professional programmers. Can we determine, in advance, what kind of EUD is required or how the software might evolve? Must we limit EUD to specific well-defined features? Do end-users actually want to develop their own tools?

Our approach involves cooperative software development and co-evolution in two complementary ways: interviews and workshops with biologists to define their

Henry Lieberman et al. (eds.), End User Development, 207–242.
© 2006 *Springer.*

environments for data analysis, and software flexibility or *programmability*. This term refers to two main dimensions: (a) to let the end-users *evolve* these tools themselves according to their current specific needs; (b) to let the user better *control* the way results are computed.

In this chapter, we first describe some important characteristics of software development and evolution in biology, as well as situations where biologists who are not professional programmers may need to change the software they use. Next, we introduce our approach to help biologists better control their tools, the idea of *participatory programming*, and we provide a description of the participatory design process. We describe our prototype *biok* in Section 4, followed by a section that recounts uses of this prototype. The final section provides a discussion of our choices, where we address the general aspects of software flexibility and open systems with respect to EUD.

2. Problem Description

Having installed scientific software for 8 years at the Institut Pasteur and having taught biologists how to use these scientific tools, I have observed that, in the past decade, the development of computing tools for biology and genomics has increased at a fast pace to deal with huge genomic data and the need of algorithms to discover their meaning. Daily work has also changed for the standard biologist: using computer systems to perform their biological analyses is hardly possible without some basic programming (Tisdall, 2001). Indeed, although there are already many ready-to-use tools, including Web-based tools and software packages for the micro-computer this is not really sufficient, even for usual tasks.

In order to justify our objectives and our approach, we need to describe the context of this work. In the following sections, we describe the typical problems that have to be solved, the general idea of programming in scientific research and the more general issue of dealing with scientists as end-users. We have also performed several kinds of user studies that we describe below.

2.1. USE OF COMPUTING AT INSTITUT PASTEUR

We conducted a campus-wide survey in 1996, which consisted of 40 questions grouped in categories, regarding computing education, software and network use, access to technical documentation and types of technical problems encountered (Letondal, 1999b). Figure 10.1 shows the main groups that we identified through the analysis of the survey data (about 600 answers) plotted on two dimensions: level of programming autonomy and level of use of scientific computing:

- *Occasional users* were the largest group (36%) and had no direct use of scientific computer tools.
- *Non-Unix users* (15%) did not use the IT department training and technical support, they had their own PC and mostly ran statistical software.

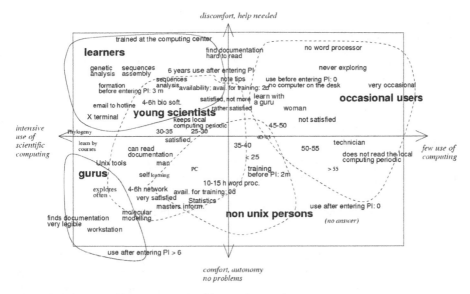

Figure 10.1. Campus-wide survey analysis of the use of computing.

- *Young scientists* (15%) were interested in bioinformatics, and were able to program or at least build Web sites. They could read software documentation and were able to teach themselves.
- *Learners* (15%) were more-established scientists who had recently taken a course to improve their know-how of scientific software. This training was often conducted by the IT department.
- *Gurus* (6%) were heavily involved in computing and programming scientific software. They often acted as local consultants or *gardeners* (Gantt and Nardi, 1992).

Both the computing skills and the available computer tools have changed greatly in the intervening years since this survey was taken. The Institut Pasteur has hired a significant number of bioinformaticians to act as local developers (Gantt and Nardi, 1992). In various laboratories, young scientists (Ph.Ds and post-doctoral fellows) are now more likely to have had formal training in computing and the number of convenient software packages for biologists has increased, particularly via the Internet.

2.2. TYPICAL PROBLEMS

In order to illustrate the need for EUD in the context of biology and bioinformatics, let us show some typical examples [see also (Costabile et al., 2003)]. Below is a list of real programming situation examples, drawn from interviews with biologists, news forum, or technical desk. These situations happened when working with molecular sequences, i.e., either DNA or protein sequences (a sequence is a molecule that is very often represented by a character string, composed of either DNA letters—A, C, T, and G—or amino-acid letters—20 letters).

- *Scripting.* Search for a sequence pattern, *then* retrieve all the corresponding secondary structures in a database.
- *Parsing.* Search for the best match in a database similarity search report *but relative to each sub-section.*
- *Formatting.* Renumber the positions of a sequence from -3000 to $+500$ instead of 0–3500.
- *Variation.* Search for patterns in a sequence, *except repeated ones.*
- *Finer control on the computation.* Control of the order in which multiple sequences are compared and aligned.
- *Simple operations.* Search in a DNA sequence for the characters other than A, C, T, and G.

As illustrated by these examples, unexpected problems may arise at any time. However, these scenarios involve rather simple programmatic manipulations, without any algorithmic difficulty or complex design. An important reason why programming is needed here is that the function, although easy to program, or even already implemented somewhere inside the program, has not been *explicitly* featured in the user interface of the tool.

2.3. PROGRAMMING IN SCIENTIFIC RESEARCH

Apart from these scenarios showing that everyday work leads to operations that involve some programming, there are fundamental reasons why scientific users, or at least a part of them, would need to program.

- *Sharing expertise.* Biologists, having accumulated a lot of knowledge through their academic and professional experience, in such a fast evolving area, are more able to know what kind of information is involved in solving scientific problems by a computational model. In her course on algorithmics for biologists (Letondal and Schuerer, 2002; Schuerer, 2003), Schuerer explains that sharing expertise requires some computing skills on the side of biologists, in order for them to be aware of the tacit hypotheses that are sometimes hidden in computer abstractions.
- *Programs as evolving artifacts.* A computer program *evolves*, not only for maintenance reasons, but also as a refutable and empirical theory (Morch, 1997): thus, being able to modify the underlying algorithm to adapt a method to emerging facts or ideas could be, if not easily feasible, *at least anticipated* (Letondal and Zdun, 2003).
- *Expression medium.* The field of bioinformatics and genomics is mostly composed of tasks that are defined by computer artifacts. In these fields the expression medium (DiSessa, 1999) for problem solving is encoded as strings, and problems are expressed as string operations (comparisons, counting, word search, etc).

3. Approach: Participatory Programming

What kind of solutions could help biologists to get their work done?

3.1. MORE TOOLS

One possibility is that biologists simply need more tools, with more parameters and more graphics. *This is maybe true*, but:

- Some features or needs, particularly in a fast evolving research field, where the researcher must be inventive, cannot be anticipated.
- Such software is complex: users must master many different tools, with specific syntax, behavior, constraints, and underlying assumptions; furthermore, these tools must be combined, with parsers and format converters to handle heterogeneous data.

3.2. A PROGRAMMER AT HAND

A second possibility could be for biologists to have a programmer at hand whenever they need to build or modify the programs. There are indeed many laboratories where one or more programmers are hired to perform programming tasks. This is, however, clearly not feasible for every biologist (for instance, the Institut Pasteur laboratories have about a dozen such local programmers, for more than 1500 biologists).

3.3. PROGRAMMING

A third possibility involves programming: biologists just have to learn some basic programming skills, since programming is the most general solution to deal with unforeseen computational needs. In fact, many biologists program, and even release software. Most of the programs for data analysis are in fact programmed by biologists. We see two clear types of development:

- large-scale projects such as (Stajich et al., 2002), developments in important bioinformatics centers such as the US National Center for Biotechnology Information (NCBI) or the European Bioinformatics Institute (EBI), or research in algorithmics by researchers in computer science;
- local developments by biologists who have learned some programming but who are not professional developers, either to deal with everyday tasks for managing data and analysis results, or to model and test scientific ideas.

The two lines often merge, since biologists also contribute to open-source projects and distribute the software they have programmed for their own research in public repositories.

However, as programming is also known to be difficult, not every biologist wants to become a programmer. Most of the time, this change implies a total switch from the bench to the computer.

3.4. PROGRAMMING WITH THE USER INTERFACE

An intermediate step is EUP (Eisenberg, 1997), which gives biologists access to programming with a familiar language, i.e., the language of the user interface. Programming by demonstration (PBD) (Cypher, 1993; Lieberman, 2000) lets the user program by using known functions of the tool: with some help from the system, the user can register procedures, automate repetitive tasks, or express specific models (styles and formats for word processors, patterns for visualization and discovery tools, etc). Visual programming languages, in contrast, offer a visual syntax for established programming concepts: programming with the user interface ideally means programming at the task level, which is more familiar to the end-user (Nardi, 1993).

Customization is related, but has a different goal: EUP provides tools or languages for *building* new artifacts, whereas customization enables to *change* the tool itself, usually from among a set of predefined choices or a composition of existing elements. Although these two different goals might be accomplished with similar techniques, this means that the level of the language is a base level in the case of EUP, whereas it is a meta-level in the case of customization.

3.5. PROGRAMMING IN THE USER INTERFACE

We introduce Programming *In* the User Interface as an approach that provides the end-user with a scaffolded access to general programming at use-time. We thus distinguish Programming *With* the User Interface from Programming *In* the User Interface. These approaches differ by essentially two aspects: (1) in our approach, programming is made available to the end-user, but the programming language is not necessarily the user interface language; and (2) in this approach, programming includes customization, i.e., modifying some parts of the software being used.

Related work also includes tailoring approaches which enable the user to change the software at use-time (Fischer and Ostwald, 2002; Henderson and Kyng, 1991; MacLean et al., 1990). Similar approaches also include programmable tools where the user can add functionalities to the tool by accessing to an embedded programming language and environment (Eisenberg, 1995; Morch, 1997; Smith and Ungar, 1995). Research such as (DiGiano, 1995; Wulf and Golombek, 2001) focusing on methods to encourage the user to tailor the software by lowering a technical, cognitive, or sociological barrier are very relevant as well.

Fischer's concept of Meta-Design (Fischer and Scharff, 2000) attempts to empower users by enabling them to act as designers at use-time. In this approach, software provides a domain-oriented language to the users and lets them re-design and adapt current features to their own need. As explained in (Fischer and Ostwald, 2002), user software artifacts can then re-seed the original design in a participatory way. Our approach is very similar: we first let users participate to the initial design by conducting workshops and various user studies. Then, we either take their programming artifacts as input to prototyping workshops or we put their modifications in *biok* back into the original tool. The main difference in our approach lies in the programming language that is provided to the user. We chose a standard programming language, that the user can re-use in other contexts, like Eisenberg (1995) who offers the concept of programmable applications in which users of a drawing tool can add features by programming in Scheme. Thus, our tool does not include an EUP language: we indeed observed that using a standard general-purpose programming language is not the main obstacle in the actual access to programming, in the context of bioinformatic analyses.

Some approaches offer the technical possibility for the user to change the application during use by having access to the underlying programming language. MacLean et al. (1990) describe how to build a whole application by combining, cloning, and editing small components (buttons), associated to simple individual actions. This seminal work has greatly inspired our work, where graphical programmable objects form the basis of an application, and are a technical extension of buttons to more general programmable graphical objects. In this regard, our technical environment is closer to Self (Smith et al., 1995) or Boxer (DiSessa, 1989) except that we needed to use an open environment and a scripting language featured with extensive graphical and network libraries. As in Morch (1997), graphical objects provide an architecture where a mapping is provided between application units and programming units in order for the user to easily locate programming chunks of interest. As in our approach, the user interface helps the user with access to programming, *only when needed*. Most of the time, the focus of the user is the analysis of his or her data. However, our approach is not only technical, it relies on a participative approach at design-time, which helps determine how to build such an environment.

The following sections discuss one of the main aspect of our approach, which is to provide full access to programming (Section 3.6), and explain how, by using contextual and participatory design methods, we address potential issues that could be raised by this access (Section 3.7). Section 4 describes *biok*, our prototype tool for participatory programming, which, according to this approach, is *both* an analysis tool and a programming environment. This leads to an environment that is both highly domain-oriented and highly generic and open to full programming.

3.6. THE PROBLEM OF PROGRAMMING

We decided to provide an access to a general programming language, as explained in the previous section, as discussed by Eisenberg (1995), and as opposed to EUP approaches. Let us discuss the choices we made:

- is programming really *too* difficult for end-users?
- is programming the *main* difficulty for end-users?
- is programming the problem at all?

Our thesis is that, focusing on the design of an end-user programming language and stressing programming difficulties, we do not progress toward a general solution regarding EUD in biology or similar fields.

3.6.1. *Difficulties of Programming*

Programming is indeed technically difficult and raises cognitive issues, but this is not the main reason for biologists not to program when they need it. Nardi (1993) has shown that having to write textual commands, one of the most "visible" and discriminating aspect of classical programming, is not really the main explanation for the technical barrier: for instance, users are able to enter formula in a spreadsheet, for example, or to copy and modify HTML pages. If the language is centered on the task to perform, the user will be able to learn and use it.

We have also been running an annual intensive 4-month course for research biologists to teach them various aspects of computing (Letondal and Schuerer, 2002). During this course, computer scientists and bioinformaticians from the IT department, as well as visiting professors, cover programming techniques, theoretical aspects (such as algorithm development, logic, problem modelling, and design methods), and technical applications (databases and Web technologies) that are relevant for biologists. According to our experience during this course, reducing the difficulty of programming to difficulties with algorithms is too simple. The first reason is that there is not much algorithmic complexity in their everyday programming. The second reason is that, whereas biology students had good aptitude for programming (they had to program in Scheme, Java, perl, or Python), and enough abstract reasoning for the required programming tasks, a significant part of them did not actually program after the course, even though they would need it. Why is that? This issue formed a basis for our reflection on both the technical and organizational contexts of the programming activity of biologists, that is illustrated by a case study described in Section 5.

Software engineering aspects is a more significant barrier. The occasional user faces more problems with programming-in-the-large than with syntax or abstraction. The tools that are actually used for bioinformatics analyses are often complex and large systems, rather than small software packages. Users cannot build such systems by themselves. Can they at least participate in those parts that depend on their expertise? Finally, biologists want to do biology, not computer science. Even if they can program, and could overcome specific technical problems, they prefer to spend their time on biology. Therefore, both the technical context (software being used) and the use context (data analyses) should be taken into account when designing programming tools for such users.

3.6.2. *What is Programming?*

We believe that seeking for the perfect programming language for end-users is both too simplistic and illusory. When I say to a colleague that "I am programming," he or she knows what I mean. This, however, does not lead to a definition of programming. There are indeed various and different definitions of programming: design of algorithms, automation, building of software, abstraction (Blackwell, 2002), delegation (Repenning, 1993) design of the static representation of a dynamic process (Lieberman and Fry, 1995), and problem definition (Nardi, 1993; Repenning, 1993). Thus, programming, being a polysemic term, that is not precisely defined, seems quite inappropriate for a specification to develop an end-user programming system (Letondal, 1999a,c). Even though programming claims to be a general solution and a general tool, it is also rather difficult to define programming *activity* without taking the sociological and professional context of this activity into account. A student learning programming to prepare for an exam and to enhance his or her reasoning capabilities is not pursuing the same objective as a software engineer building an application for a customer, and, more generally, one does not program the same way when programming for oneself than when programming for other people.

Furthermore, the definition of *what programming is* might benefit from the definition of *what programming is not*.

Figure 10.2 shows various concepts related to programming or non-programming opposed along three axes:

1. *the mode* (*x* axis): from batch, indirect and continuous to interactive, direct, and discontinuous,
2. *the underlying task* (*y* axis): from using to programming,
3. *the form of the expression* (*z* axis): from textual to graphical.

This diagram is inspired by the classification given in (Burnett et al., 1994), where visualization software is classified along three axes: mode, expression, and the compatibility of the system with legacy software. The expression (*z* axis) and mode (*x* axis) axes have been thoroughly studied, and it is not our purpose here to study them further. For instance, the expression (*z*) axis describes the difference between *programming in*

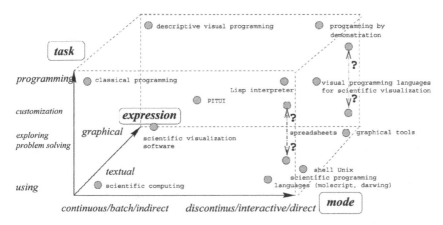

Figure 10.2. Dimensions to contrast programming and non-programming.

the C language and *programming in the Labview visual environment* (Labview, 1987). But it also describes the difference between reading a textual program result, such as searching for similarities in sequences databases, visualizing hits in a 3D graphical plot. The mode axis (x axis) describes the difference between programming with a compiler and programming within an interactive interpreter. This axis also describes the difference between using an interactive tool and running long batch analyses that read their input at the beginning of the computation and produce their output at the end (Burnett et al., 1994).

We can observe from this diagram that, even though we build it on dimensions that, taken separately, contrast programming to non-programming, clearly-identified programming activities often belong to the non-programming side of each: while programming is often opposed to interaction, learning to program with a Lisp interpreter is on the *interactive* end of the x axis; building a Petri Net or programming in Labview belong to the graphical end of the z axis, and writing a script to build a visual model of a molecule (Ploger and Lay, 1992) is on the *use* end of the y axis, since the goal is to understand and analyze a molecule, not to program. In fact, within these combined dimensions, programming activities fit within a continuum, which makes it difficult to rely only on a definition of programming to build an end-user programming environment.

In our diagram, we stress the importance of the *context of programming* as determined by the user's activity and goals: we use a task axis (y axis) instead of the compatibility axis from (Burnett et al., 1994), to describe the difference between *programming, building* a tool, and *using* it. This axis and the issues of why and when biologists need to program is the topic of the following section.

3.7. STUDYING THE CONTEXT OF PROGRAMMING

Having explained in the previous section why the *context* of programming should be taken into account more deeply than a definition of programming, we describe in this section the studies and participatory activities that have been organized to understand this context (Letondal and Mackay, 2004).

3.7.1. *Interviews*

Among a total of 65 interviews that were conducted in the context of various projects over the past 7 years, about 30 were dedicated to end-user programming. They were mainly intended to collect use scenarios, or to observe biologists using scientific software. Interviews were generally informal and open: we often just asked the biologists to act in front of us a scenario of a recent bioinformatic analysis. Some of the interviews have been videotaped or recorded, and annotated.

Several of these interviews enabled us to observe biologists programming, either by using standard programming environments and languages such as C or C++, or by, very often, scripting languages such as awk to parse large text files, perl to write simple Web applications, or Python to build scripts for analysing structural properties of proteins.

We also observed uses of visual programming environments such as HyperCard or even visual programming languages. Khoros (Rasure et al., 1990) for image analysis or Labview (Labview, 1987), for instance, are used in some laboratories, mostly due to their good libraries for driving hardware devices, and image or signal processing routines. We also observed various people using spreadsheets for performing simple sequence analyses.

During these interviews, we made several observations:

- *Re-use of knowledge*. Most of the time, biologists prefer using a technique or a language that they already know, rather than a language that is more appropriate for the task at hand, which is referred to as the assimilation bias by Carroll (1987). A researcher had learnt HyperCard to make games for his children, and used it in the laboratory for data analysis, even though nobody else knew it and thus was able to provide help. But the result was efficient and he almost never had to ask to the IT Center for help to find or install simple tools. Another researcher wrote small scripts in the only scripting language she knew: awk, although perl that is now often used and taught in biology would have been much more efficient. In summary, as long as the result is obtained, it does not matter how you get it. Similarly, a researcher tends to use a spreadsheet instead of learning to write simple scripts that would be more suitable to the task.
- *Opportunistic behavior*. Generally and as described by Mackay (1991b), biologist, even if they can program, will not do so, unless they feel that the result will be obtained really much faster by programming. If this is not the case, they prefer to switch to a non-programming methods, such as doing a repetitive task within a word processor or performing an experiment at the bench. There is no requirement nor any scientific reward for writing programs. They are only used as a means to an end, building hypotheses.
- *Simple programming problems*. During his or her everyday work, a biologist may encounter various situations where some programming is needed, such as simple formatting or scripting (for extracting gene names from the result of an analysis program and use them for a subsequent database search) and parsing, or simple operations, not provided in the user interface, such a searching for characters other than A, C, G, or T in a DNA sequence.
- *Need for modifying tools rather than building from scratch*. A frequent need for programming that we observed is to make a variant or add a function to an existing tool. Designing variants for standard published bench protocols is often needed in a biology laboratory. For instance, when constructing a primer for hybridisation,[1] it is often needed to adapt the number of washings according to the required length and composition of the primer, or to the product that is used. With software tools, this is however unfortunately seldom feasible, but it would be highly valuable since there are already many existing tools that perform helpful tasks, and biologists rarely want to build a tool from scratch.

---

[1] A primer is a short DNA sequence used to generate the complementary DNA of a given sequence.

- *Exploratory use of tools.* There is a plethora of tools, including new tools, for the everyday task of biologists, and these tools are often specialized for a specific type of data. This leads to a very interactive and exploratory use of computing tools (O'Day et al., 2001). For instance, an observed scenario started by the search of a protein pattern published in a recent paper. The user was looking for other proteins than those referred to in this paper and that also contained this motif. After an unsuccessful attempt—the results were too numerous for an interactive analysis—the researcher decided to use another program. This attempt failed again because his pattern was too short for the setting of this specific program. He then decided to extend it by adding another one, also belonging to the set of proteins mentioned in the paper. In the end, this enabled a final iterative analysis of each result. This is a brief summary that stands for many scenarios we have observed, often resulting in many failures due to a problem with the program, or with the format of the data.

This typical behavior might be both a barrier to and a reason for programming. It can be a barrier by preventing a user to think of a more efficient way to get a result [leading to an "active" user behavior as described by Carroll (1987)). However, at the same time, it can be a ground for programming since programming could help to rationalize, *a posteriori*, such an exploratory behavior. This, however, involves some kind of anticipation: for instance, it might be a good place for programming instruments such as history and macro recording.

3.7.2. Workshops

Biok has involved a series of video brainstorming and prototyping workshops over several years from 1996 to 2004. We drew prototyping themes from brainstorming sessions (Figure 10.3) and from use scenarios, which based on interviews and observation. Each workshop involved from 5 to 30 people, with participants from the Institut Pasteur or other biological research laboratories, as well as biology researchers who were students in our programming course.

Finding Potential Dimensions for Evolution

From the very beginning of the design process, it is important to consider the potential dimensions along which features may evolve. Interviews with users help inform

Figure 10.3. Prototyping a pattern-search and an annotation scenario.

concrete use scenarios, whereas brainstorming and future workshops create a design space within which design options can be explore. As Trigg (1992), Kjaer (1995), Stiemerling et al. (1997), or Kahler (1996) suggest participatory design helps identify which areas in a system are stable and which are suitable for variation. Stable parts require functionality to be available directly, without any programming, whereas variable parts must be subject to tailoring.

For example, the visual alignment tool in *biok* vertically displays corresponding letters in multiple related sequences (Figure 10.6, back window). Initial observations of biologists using this type of tool (Letondal, 2001b) revealed that they were rarely flexible enough: biologists preferred spreadsheets or text editors to manually adjust alignments, add styles and highlight specific parts. It became clear that this functionality was an area requiring explicit tailoring support.

Design of Meta-Techniques

Scenarios and workshops are important to effectively design meta-level features. Scenarios sometimes reveal programming areas as side issues. The goal is not to describe the programming activity per se, but rather to create an analogy between the task, how to perform it, and the relevant programming techniques. We identified several types of end-user programming scenarios:

- *Programming with examples.* One workshop participant suggested that the system learn new tags from examples (tags are visualization functions). Another proposed a system that infers regular expressions from a set of DNA sequences. These led to a design similar to SWYN (Blackwell, 2000).
- *Scripting.* One participant explained that text annotations, associated with data, can act as a "to do" list, which can be managed with small scripts associated with the data.
- *Command history.* A brainstorming session focusing on data versioning suggested the complementary idea of command history.

The *biok* tag editor design (Figure 10.6, front window) had to consider the following issues: Must programming be available in a special editor? Must it require a simplified programming interface? Should the user interface be interactive? Should it be accessible via graphical user interface menus?

We found prototyping workshops invaluable for addressing such issues: they help explore which interaction techniques best trigger programming actions and determine the level of complexity of a programming tool. For example, one group in an alignment sequence workshop built a pattern-search mock-up including syntax for constraints and errors (Figure 10.3).

One of the participatory design workshops was organized in the Winter of 2001 with five biologists to work on the *biok* prototype. Among the participants, four had followed a programming course, and programmed from time to time, but not in Tcl, except one who had programmed in Visual Tcl. Before the workshop, interviews had been conducted with discussions about the prototype, and participants were sent a small Tcl tutorial by e-mail. The aim of the workshop was to experiment the prototype and get familiar with it through a scenario (instructions were provided on a Web page). They had to play with graphical objects, and define a simple tag. The issues that would arise during this part would then be discussed and re-prototyped during a second part. The scenario had also spontaneously been "tested" by one of the participants who brought some feedback about it. Although the workshop was not directly aimed at properly testing the prototype, the participants behaved as if it was, and this actually brought some insights on the design of the prototype—briefly and among the most important ones:

- The participants were somewhat disturbed by a too large number of programming areas: formula box, shell, method editor, etc.
- They had trouble to understand, at a first sight, the various elements of the user interface and how they interact.
- They had the feeling that understanding the underlying model would help.

One of the tasks of the scenario was to define a tag. The only tool that the participants had for this was an enhanced text editor, only providing templates and interactive choosers for the graphical attributes. This tool proved completely unusable and participants got lost. The tool was indeed too programmer-centered, and difficult to use, and there was no unified view of the tag definition. This led to another workshop shortly after this one, and after a long brainstorming session, one participant built a paper-and-transparencies prototype. We created an A3-size storyboard mock-up and walked through the tag creation scenario with the biologists. The tag editor currently implemented in *biok* is a direct result of these workshops.

Participatory approaches are also helpful when designing language syntax (da Cunha and de Souza, 2003; Pane et al., 2001), or deciding on the *granularity* of code modification. As observed during the previously described workshop, the object-oriented architecture and the method definition task apparently did not disturb users that much. In a previous workshop that we started by displaying a video prototype showing the main features of *biok*, participants tended to adopt the words "object" and "method" that were used in the video. Interestingly, one of them used the term: "frame" all along the workshop in place of object, probably because objects in *biok* (and in the video prototype) are most often represented by graphical windows. In object-oriented programming terms, we found, however, that biologists are more likely to need new methods than new classes. Since defining new classes is a skilled modeling activity, we designed *biok* so that user modifications at the user level do not require sub-classing. User-edited methods are performed within the current method's class and are saved in directories that are loaded after the system. However, visualizing tags required the user to create new classes, which lead us to provide this as a mechanism in the user interface.

Setting a Design Context for Tailoring Situations

Our observations of biologists showed that most programming situations correspond with breakdowns: particular events cause users to reflect on their activities and trigger a switch to programming (Mackay, 1991a). Programming is not the focus of interest, but rather a means of fixing a problem. It is a distant, reflexive, and detached "mode," as described by Winograd (1995), Smith (1992), or Greenbaum (1993). While end-user programming tools may seek to blur the border between use and programming (Dittrich, 2003), it is important to take this disruptive aspect into account, by enabling programming *in context*. Developing and playing through scenarios are particularly useful for identifying breakdowns and visualizing how users would like to work around them.

3.7.3. *Participatory Design and Participatory Programming*

Participatory programming integrates participatory design and end-user programming. Participatory design is used for the design of an end-user programmable tool, yet biologists programming artifacts also participate in the making of tools. These artifacts are either produced by local developers, observed during interviews, or they can be produced by end-users using *biok*.

Henderson and Kyng (1991) and Fischer (2003) also discuss how to extend end-user participation in design to use-time. Our approach is very similar except that it includes programming participation and not only domain-level design artifact. Likewise, Stiemerling et al. (1997) or Kahler (1996) provide a detailed description illustrated with various examples of a participative development process for designing tailorable applications. Yet, in both cases, the tools that offer document search and access right management features, do not include programming.

4. Biok: Biological Interactive Object Kit

biok is a prototype of a programmable graphical application for biologists written in XOtcl (Neumann and Zdun, 2000) and the Tk graphical toolkit (Ousterhout, 1998). XOtcl is an object extension of Tcl, inspired by Otcl (Wetherall 1995), a dynamic object-oriented language. Tcl is not an end-user programming language: on the contrary, it is a general-purpose language, and moreover, it is not simple. Like (Wilkinson and Links, 2002), our experience teaching programming to biologists, show that languages such as Python are much easier to learn. However, we chose Tcl XOtcl for:

1. its incremental programming feature, i.e., the possibility to define or redefine methods for a class at any time, even when instances have been created, which is very convenient for enabling programming in the user interface,
2. its introspection tools that are generally available in Tcl software components and that are mandatory to get a reflective system;
3. its dynamic tools such as filters and mixins, that enabled us to build a debugging environment and some algorithmic flexibility features (Letondal and Zdun, 2003).

The purpose of *biok* is two-fold: to analyze biological data such as DNA, protein sequences or multiple alignments, and to support tailorability and extensions by the end-user through an integrated programming environment.

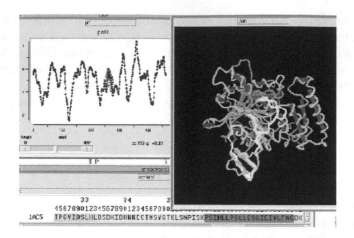

Figure 10.4. Analyzing biological data: a plot displays the hydrophobicity curve of a protein sequence, that is simultaneously displayed in a 3D viewer. Structural properties of the protein, namely transmembrane segments, are simultaneously highlighted in the two protein representations. The user, by selecting parts of the curve, can check to which hydrophobicity peaks these segments might correspond.

4.1. BIOLOGICAL DATA ANALYSES

The first purpose of biok is to provide an environment for biologists to analyze biological data. Currently, it includes a tool to compare and manually align several related sequences or display alignments that are computed by one of the numerous alignment programs available (Letondal, 2001a). A molecular 3D viewer is also provided (Tuffery et al., 2003; Figure 10.4). Thanks to this toolkit, biologists can compare similar objects in various representations, simultaneously highlighting specific features in the data: the alignment tool stresses common features among homologous sequences, whereas the 3D viewer shows their structural location, which provides useful hints regarding the potential function in the cell.

4.2. GRAPHICAL PROGRAMMABLE OBJECTS

The main unit for both using *and programming* in *biok* is what we call a "graphical object." Objects are indeed "visible" through a window having a name, or alias, that the user may use as a global Tcl variable (Figure 10.4 shows three such graphical objects). Graphical objects are programmable in several senses:

1. their "content" may be defined by a *formula*,
2. their *methods* may be edited, modified, and copied to define new methods,
3. their graphical components are accessible as *program objects*,
4. graphical attributes may be defined to implement *visualization functions*.

Graphical objects also have a command "shell," to either directly call the object's methods or to configure the Tk widget via a special "%w" command, as illustrated

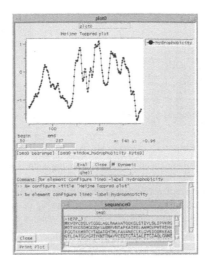

Figure 10.5. Graphical objects, formulas, and shell.

in Figure 10.5 where the plot's title and curve legend have been directly set up by Tk commands. Commands are stored in a class-specific editable history file as soon as they have been issued, so they can be instantaneously reused on another object of the same class.

4.3. DATAFLOW AND SPREADSHEET MODELS

Given the wide use of spreadsheets and the pervasiveness of its related dataflow computing paradigm, we have designed the content of graphical objects as being optionally defined by a formula involving one or more source objects. Figure 10.5 shows two graphical objects: one (front window) is a "Sequence" object, called "seq0," containing the letters representing the aminoacids of a protein. The other is a "Plot" object ("plot0"). Its formula returns two lists of floating point numbers: the first one represents the ticks of the x axis and the second the values of the curve, that displays the hydrophobicity peaks of the "seq0" object. Each time the sequence is modified, the curve is redisplayed, unless the "Dynamic" switch has been turned off. The "Plot" object is composed of a BLT graph, two sliders to select the displayed portion of the curve, and two fields showing the x and y values selected by the user.

4.4. PROGRAMMABLE VISUALIZATION FEATURES

One of the central tools of *biok* is a spreadsheet specialized in displaying and editing sequences alignments (Figure 10.6, back window). As in many other scientific research areas, visualization is critical in biology. Several graphical functions, or *tags*, are available in *biok*. A tag is a mechanism that highlights some parts of an object. For instance, segments of protein sequences showing a specific property, such as a high

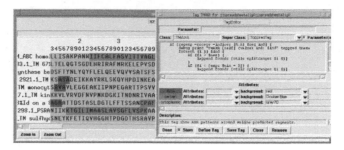

Figure 10.6. Tag editor (front) and alignment editor (back). In the tag editor, the top part displays a field to enter parameters for this tag, if needed. The part below contains a super-class chooser and an editor for the code to define tag values. The middle part is a tool to associate graphical attributes to tag values. The bottom part displays a short description of the tag. The positions associated with the various tag values are highlighted in the alignment editor. In this example, a tag showing transmembrane segments (in blue) is extended by a sub-tag highlighting small patterns around them (in red).

hydrophobicity, can be highlighted in the spreadsheet. Table 10.1 shows that a tag is composed of two relations:

1. between graphical attributes (such as colors, relief, or fonts) and predefined tag values,
2. between these values and positions in the annotated object.

New tags may also be defined with a dedicated editor (Figure 10.6, front window), where the user has to define a method to associate tag values to data positions in a script. This method is typically either a small script for simple tags, or an invocation to more complex methods that run analyses, notably from a Web Server (Letondal, 2001b).

biok comes with several predefined tags, which can be modified, or the user can create new ones with a set of super-classes of tags, that define e.g. row tags, column tags, cell tags, or sequence tags. For example, a tag class Toppred, named after a published algorithm for detecting transmembrane segments in a protein sequence (von Heijne, 1992), is available in *biok*. This tag was implemented by a biology student during her internship. We report a concrete case of a tag extension which highlights non-conventional patterns.

The spreadsheet tool, the tag editor and the 3D molecular visualization widget (Tuffery et al., 2003; Figure 10.4), have been the subject of numerous workshops. Among these workshops, the workshop dedicated to the design of the tag editor has been described previously.

Table 10.1. Tag relations

Graphical attributes	1.1.1 Tag values	1.1.2 Locations
Blue	Certain	36–55
dark green	Putative	137–157
Red	AXA	13–15

4.5. PROGRAMMING ENVIRONMENT

A method editor lets users redefine any method, save it, print it, search its code, and try it with different parameters (which just makes the editor a form to run the code), to set breakpoints, and to ask for trace.

User-created or re-defined methods and classes are saved in a user directory, on a per-class and per-method basis. This enables the user to go back to the system's version by removing unwanted methods files, and to manage the code outside of *biok*, with the system file commands and the preferred code editor. This double access and the fact that the result of user's programming work is not hidden in a mysterious format or database, where source code is stored as records organized in a way that the users are not able to understand, is very important to us.

biok features several navigational tools that enable the user to locate source code directly from the user interface, whenever needed during standard use of the tool:

1. methods browser and inspector available from any graphical objects: source code is available at the method level, on a per-object basis,
2. search tools for classes and methods that enable to search the name, body, or documentation,
3. a class browser.

The methods browser can be triggered from any graphical object, by a menu that only displays methods relevant to this object. In this menu, "Data analysis" methods are distinguished from methods dealing with "Graphical Display," the former being often more of interest to the biologists than the latter.

biok also has various debugging tools, that we were able to develop quite easily thanks to the dynamic introspection tools provided by the XOtcl language. Users can print keyed debug messages, put/remove breakpoints on method calls by simply clicking on a button in the method editor, and put breakpoints inside the code.

Figure 10.7 shows spy and trace tools. A button in the editor enables the user to trace method calls: this opens a "Methods stack" window displaying method calls with parameters and return values. In a way similar to direct activation (Wulf and Golombek, 2001), a concept to encourage tailoring, the user can spy the execution during a short period, and select specific methods from the list of those called (see "Spy" window in Figure 10.7). Thus, these tools are useful for both source code navigation and comprehension: combining browsers, spy or trace tools, and breakpoints is a good mean to find the location of a specific problem, or to understand the way the program works.

4.6. PROGRAMMING ERRORS

A frequent objection to our approach is that opening the source code to end-users might make programming errors or break the system. By providing programming and debugging tools, and by designing the environment for incremental changes, we sought a way to minimize the impact of errors, not to remove them.

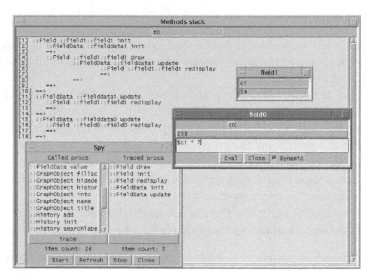

Figure 10.7. Spying and Tracing method calls. Object "c0" uses "c1" in its formula. The "Methods stacks" window displays methods called when a change occurs in "c1". The "Spy" window enables to start/stop spying and to select methods for being traced.

Breaking the system is indeed feasible at the user level, in the same way as with an open-source software that the user can download, install and modify locally. However, whenever the system incidentally breaks, there is a simple way to go back to a previous state: user source is saved as simple text files organized in easy to manage directories. If a new method breaks the class, for example, the user only has to remove its corresponding file from its class directory. There is no specific mechanism implemented yet in the prototype to organize source code management, for this can easily be implemented with standard versioning tools such as CVS.

We observed, though, that biologists are not really interested in challenging software robustness! On the contrary, as we observed during student projects, they are very cautious, and generally only focus on the part of the code they feel they have control over. According to Wulf and Golombek (2001) or Mackay (1991a), tailoring has even rather to be encouraged than prevented.

4.7. DESIGN RATIONALE SUMMARY

Our focus in *biok* is not on programming, but rather on the programming *context*. We provide, however, a full access to programming *as a key feature* of the tool. *biok* contextualizes the task of programming with respect to the biologist's scientific tasks and motivations. We stress:

1. *Focus.* The focus of the tool is on biology or bioinformatics tasks; coding software is possible, but not obligatory.

2. *Incremental programming.* Programming from scratch is difficult: whereas modifying an existing, working program, especially if it includes domain-centered examples, is motivating and helpful. The PITUI (Programming In The User Interface) approach enables incremental programming and progressive learning (Carroll, 1990).

3. *Integration of the graphical and coding levels.* An important aspect of a programmable application is to integrate code objects of interest and graphical representation of these objects (Wulf and Golombek, 2001). Integration should work both from the graphical object to the code object, and from the code to the graphical object. In (Eisenberg, 1995), some variables describe the user interface state, and some commands for modifying this state are available at the scripting level. The notion of graphical objects gets close to the extreme integration of graphical and coding elements that is provided in Boxer (DiSessa, 1989) or Self (Smith et al., 1995). Following the spreadsheet paradigm, and whenever possible, graphical objects of interest, such as sub-areas of objects, or tags, are available from the code.

4. *A good programming environment.* Motivation for the user to program, although existing, is probably discouraged by common standard environments (Lieberman and Fry, 1995).

5. Reports on the Uses of the Prototype

This section reports various uses of the prototype over the last years. It has three purposes: to show how the prototype can be used as a programming environment, either to tailor or to create simple functions; this also illustrates an aspect of the participatory programming process, where programming artifacts produced by end-users can be incorporated back into the tool to be shared with other users; to show that domain orientation is obviously important to sustain programming activity and to provide tailoring affordances; this shows, however, that this does not exclude encoding with a standard programming language; to illustrate the use of the prototype for design or re-design purposes.

5.1. METHODS OF THE EVALUATION STUDIES

Even though *biok* is not specifically aimed at students, it has mostly been used by them. The main reason for this is that it is a prototype and this is why I have preferred not to distribute it, for the moment. These students, however, were biologists with bioinformatics training, including a first exposure to programming (from a few hours to several weeks). An important part of bioinformatics work, and this is not only true in the Institut Pasteur, is performed by students, this makes them significant users of the tool. Moreover, none of these students were obliged to use the prototype. As a matter of fact, some of them did not, but used more standard programming tools such as a text editor and the Tcl interpreter instead. More established scientists indirectly used biok's although not alone, because it is not finished and stable enough, hence

Figure 10.8. Heijne algorithm.

they needed my help. They were interested by its incremental programming features particularly for visualization. For one of them, the possibility to superimpose several visualizations of patterns was interesting. Other scientists reported their need to use the prototype and urged me to finish it. For one of them, an alignment editor was a pivotal tool in bioinformatics, since it helps produce data that lead to a considerable quantity of other analysis tools. Added to this, she said that it was essential to be able to add functions, because it is impossible to have every function provided for in a single tool. Other scientists stressed the value of Web server tools integration (Letondal, 2000).

Student internships brought various types of information. None of projects that are described here can be considered as a proper user study with controlled setting. Our approach seeks to explore a complex problem space by conducting user studies and workshops, rather than to evaluate specific solutions. However, we did some user testing and since the prototype—that was still at development stage—has been used on a daily basis during the internships, the students' projects were an opportunity to informally observe how the environment and the task-centered tools could help.

Generally speaking, most of the students used a great deal the environment either for locating examples of code by using the navigation and search tools, for debugging their code and understanding interactions between objects, or just for modifying simple methods, for instance either by adding a parameter to a method that calculates the hydrophobicity of a protein, or by adding a default value to a parameter, or by adding a branch in a conditional, in a function that select the appropriate hydrophobicity scale for a given protein. The following sections provide a more detailed description of some specific projects using *biok*.

5.2. LEARNING TO PROGRAM

A first two months project (Spring, 2001) involved a student in biology having learnt some programming at the university, in a different language (Python). She first had a few days training in Tcl and *biok*, either from the documentation provided on a Web page, from Tcl books or with assistance from me. Then she had to implement a published algorithm (von Heijne, 1992) to predict transmembrane segments in proteins.

The algorithm consists in the computation of a weighted sum: $h_i^* w_i$ on a sliding window (Figure 10.8), with:

h_i = aminoacid hydrophobicity values

$w_i = i/S$ for $1 \leq i \leq n - q + 1$; $(n - q + 1)/S$ for $(n - q + 1) < i < (n + q + 1)$; $(2n + 2 - i)/S$ for $(n + q + 1) \leq i \leq 2n + 1$ with a normalization factor: $S = (1 + n)2 - q^2$ to get:

$$\sum_{i=1}^{2n+1} w_i = 1$$

At first, the student encountered a lot of problems in programming, since the course she had was too short and too difficult. At the beginning, she had no or very few understanding of computing or programming concepts such as functions, loops, parameter passing, etc. She was really discouraged.

The human environment helped a lot: several computer scientists of the team gave her advice, and she could at any time ask for information. We believe that *biok* helped her mainly by bringing a *real motivation*. We observed her positive reaction the first time she obtained a display of the curve she had to compute for the algorithm—a hydrophobicity curve (Figure 10.4). From this moment, she progressed much faster and explored spontaneously various alternatives, new computations, etc. She was also able to find out—with little help—how to add a graphical component to the plot object (field displaying the pointed location on the curve). Besides, she confirmed in interviews that programming with objects of interest makes a real change.

She also helped a lot to enhance *biok*. Convenient although very simple features, such as the "Print" button in the method editor or in the Plot object were added. She was always doing a cut-and-paste of single methods code into the emacs editor just to get a printed copy. The formula-level history also originated from seeing her copy-and-pasting the very same formula for the very same kind of objects.

However, she almost never used the debugging tools, although we did a quick demo. The reason for her not using the trace tool was probably that she had a dozen methods to program, where the order of method calls was always the same. The only tool that could have been helpful is the keyed print statement, to visualize variables' values, but this mechanism was too complex, compared to a simple print that one can interactively comment out. Furthermore, the breakpoint mechanism was not ready at the time of her internship.

We observed that implementing this type of algorithm (about 300 lines of code, divided in about 10 functions, with some simple embedded loops), is a current practice among bioinformaticians. Even though the program corresponding to the published algorithm is generally available from the authors, researchers might need to apply it to a variant set of data, or to take only a part of it for a similar problem. However, even though the code she has developed is now included in *biok*, and is the basis of the visualization tag, the implementation represented for her only exercise. Why are we reporting about this project? It is to show that that cognitive problems raised by programming decrease in a domain-oriented environment, *even if the programming language is a general-purpose language.*

5.3. ADDING NEW FEATURES IN AN EXISTING COMPONENT AND CONNECTING OBJECTS

Another bioinformatics student, who had learnt programming for a few months, spent 6 months (Spring, 2002) on a project where she had to refine a graphical object defined in *biok*, on top of a Tk widget for visualizing a molecule. She also had to link this object to the alignment editor, in order for features common to both representations to be simultaneously displayed by the mean of tags by using a simple protocol that is provided in *biok* to enable the user to synchronize selections (see Figure 10.4). This student was of course able to program, although as a beginner, for she had just learnt programming. The main benefit of this project for our approach was to provide a test-bench for our environment, that she used all the time. In particular, she used the debugging tools that proved quite useful to program interactions between graphical objects. She also used the method editor all the time, even though it is not a full featured editor, and although the use of another external editor such as emacs is possible in the environment. Several technical aspects we focused on in the design proved to be really useful for her: as a biologist, she especially liked the focus on the task. The incremental programming idea, and the direct connection between graphical objects and code enabled her to better control the appropriate parts of the program.

5.4. TAILORING A VISUALIZATION FUNCTION

We illustrate here a situation where a biologist came to me because he knew about the programming features of biok and he knew that it was the only mean to get his peptide features visualized in a reasonable time. This scientist wanted to search in a large set of protein sequences for a signal peptide recognized by non-conventional secretion enzymes. For this purpose, he had to check whether a short pattern, composed of three letters and corresponding to the following regular expression: $A.A$, also occurred in his sequences, either before the first predicted transmembrane segment, or after the last one. Defining a new tag for this purpose, required:

- to define a new tag in the tag editor as a sub-class of the Toppred tag (a menu to select a base-class is provided),
- to add about 20 lines of code to:

  - search for the positions of the first and last segment in a list of segments,
  - search for an occurrence of the $A.A$ pattern before the first position or after the last one,

- associate a color (red) to this new tag (Figure 10.6).

It is worth noting that such a specific problem could not have been anticipated in a general-purpose bioinformatic tool. This newly created tag, once saved, is then available to the user for the current and next sessions. It can be sent to a colleague as a separate and easy to locate file to be copied in his or her *biok* classes directory.

5.5. A PROTOTYPING TOOL FOR DESIGN

One convenient aspect of the sequences alignment editor is its flexibility and, thanks to its adequation to users domain and work practices, it also proved to be a quite powerful tool to explore design ideas.

Unexpectedly Using the Alignment Editor to Align Analyses

Figure 10.9 shows the visualization of three independent analyses of the same sequence. Although the possibility to compare analyses was not really anticipated, it could be quickly developed during the preparation of a workshop where visualization issues were addressed.

Exploring Algorithmic Problems

biok has been used in several occasions as an environment to explore new ideas regarding algorithmic issues. We report an attempt to open unexpected points of interactions within an algorithm. In this situation, we were again able to quickly prototype the idea, before re-implementing it in a more efficient programming language.

Demonstrating Ideas for Participatory Workshops

Although we have not directly used *biok* during workshops, as in Bodker and Gronbaek (1991), the tool has often been used before participatory workshops to demonstrate some ideas and open the design space.

6. Between End-User Programming and Open Systems: A Final Reflection

We have analyzed the programming practices among biologists and observed the context of programming, which often consists in adapting software to numerous specific and diverse situations. We wanted, as far as possible, to better deal with *unanticipated*

Figure 10.9. Comparing analyses: predator is a secondary structure analysis, showing helices and sheets. Toppred is a transmembrane segments predictor, another kind of secondary structure specific to membrane proteins, and zappo is a physico-chemical analysis, showing hydrophobic aminoacids, very often found in helices and transmembrane segments

software evolution (Letondal and Zdun, 2003) and adaptation, so it appeared important to consider general software flexibility issues. In (van Rossum, 1999) Rossum advocates for the access to programming for everybody through computing education, development of better programming tools and the building of a community of users. In this approach, access to programming not only enables end-users to build small programs or to customize their tools, but also to *modify* them. The approach also explicitly relies on the use of a general-purpose programming language, such as Python, that is easy for beginners to learn and yet is suited for building real-world professional applications. Thus it goes beyond end-user programming as described by Lieberman (2000). We agree with Rossum that, following the open-source movement, such a desirable development of end-user programming will change the nature of the software development process. In our approach, however, even though our objectives are very similar, we believe that more results from the EUD field should be taken into account to enhance access to programming. Powerful programming tools, such as enhanced Undo or program visualization tools are envisioned in (van Rossum, 1999). But these tools are still quite programmer-oriented and lack data visualization features or lack links to the domain-oriented concepts; this proved critical in the success of *biok* as a programming environment. Moreover, we believe that programmability requires powerful mechanisms such as introspection, that are lacking in Python, as well as powerful concepts such as meta-level interfaces, hence we will describe which general principles should be applied, related to software flexibility, as described by the Open Systems approach (Dourish, 1996; Kiczales et al., 1991). This section, by describing how these principles could be applied in EUD, is an attempt at bridging the gap between EUP, CP4E,[2] and Open Systems. We first report on the specific software flexibility issues we observed in our user studies. We then relate these problem to the work on reflective architectures and open system protocols. Finally, we describe how these principles have been applied in the *biok* architecture and how they could be adapted to end-user programming.

6.1. DIMENSIONS OF FLEXIBILITY

Object-oriented and component technology are generally acknowledged as an all purpose solution to achieve software flexibility, and this is why *biok* is based on object-oriented constructs. Yet, can we entirely rely on these technologies to address unanticipated software changes by the end-user? (Boyle, 1998; Chapman, 2000; Stajich et al., 2002) are examples of this approach in the field of bioinformatics, and at least for the latter ones, are extensively used even by novice programmers. However, we have observed during our user studies that this approach has some limitations, compared to the flexibility that biologists need, such as:

1. components should be modifiable (and they are often not),
2. components often do not easily adapt,

---

[2] CP4E: Computer Programming For Everybody

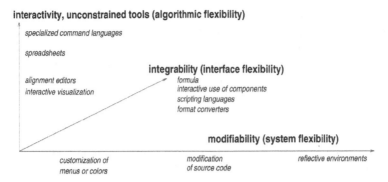

Figure 10.10. Dimensions of flexibility shows the important flexibility dimensions that emerged during the user studies.

3. the vast majority of tools are monolithic applications,
4. flexibility during the computation of a scientific result is often required.

In Figure 10.10 important flexibility . . . are shown.

1. Open systems or *system flexibility* addresses the possibilities to change the system, from simple customization to reflective systems.
2. Integrability or *interface flexibility* refers to the possibility to easily combine components. Bioinformatics is a fast evolving field: changes often occur at the component interface level. Typical solutions include dataflow systems (Bizzarro, 2000), wrappers, API (Stajich et al., 2002), and Web services (Wilkinson and Links, 2002). Along this dimension, explicit and interactive interface adaptation features by the end-user could be defined.
3. Interactivity or *algorithmic flexibility* describes systems that give a significant control on the computation to the user, from interactive visualization tools to domain-oriented programming languages such as Darwin (Gonnet et al., 2000). As observed by Repenning (1993), the whole field of HCI aims at building systems that provide control to the user at the appropriate moment. In this view, a programmable software enables the user to control the computation better. Typically, the user can provide hints to the heuristic of the algorithm. In a multiple alignment of several sequences, the user could control the order in which the sequences are compared. Interestingly, opening unforeseen points of control in a tool does not lead to more programming but to *more interaction*. At one end of this spectrum there are *unconstrained tools*, such as spreadsheets and word processors which according to (Nardi, 1994), lead to a level of flexibility necessary for visualizing scientific data. The more a system can be progressively adjusted with parameters in a rich dialog between the user and the tool, the more flexible and adaptable it (Burnett et al., 1994). One could even say that the most adjustable systems are these unconstrained tools we have just mentioned, i.e., systems whose "result" are entirely decided by the user. In bioinformatics, several tools already enable the user to interactively steer the computation, or even change

results. Several tools (Letondal, 2001b) allow the manual change of the output of algorithms that compute multiple alignments. However, changing the results can provoque mistakes. In (Letondal and Zdun, 2003), we describe an attempt to open new unexpected points of control in the algorithm: this mixed-initiative approach enhances the final result and prevents such mistakes.

6.2. REFLECTIVE AND OPEN ARCHITECTURES FOR UNANTICIPATED CHANGES

There are systems that anticipate their own modification: this starts from customizable systems, up to meta and reflective systems.

Nierstrasz and Tsichritzis (1995) identifies three main levels of software flexibility (three first levels of Figure 10.10):

1. *functional parameterization*, where the parameters may be values or functions, and where the system is composed of functions;
2. *software composition*, where the parameterized part includes the scripting to glue software components;
3. *programming*, where the user input is the program code, and the system is the programming language.

The third level is thus the most flexible, but too much freedom does not help the end-user, who needs scaffoldings. This is why a fourth level is needed: *reflexive architectures*, that both provides full programming and explicit structures for parameterization.

6.2.1. *Flexibility and Reflexivity*

Our goal is to achieve a general flexibility, similar to that in programming. In Figure 10.11, the fourth level shows that everything is "open" to the user, everything in the system becomes a parameter. Yet, as opposed to free programming (third level in Figure 10.11, here there is a scaffolding. This scaffolding is composed of an existing program, with components, structures, examples, as well as an environment to help use these objects. We put this approach in a coherent way related to free software and open systems, but this freedom does not prevent an inexperienced user to be involved.

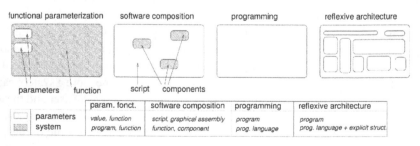

Figure 10.11. Software levels of flexibility: the blank part is the "free" part for user input, and the gray part the system.

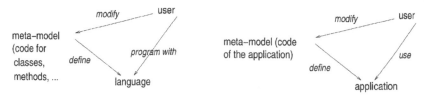

Figure 10.12. From meta-object protocol to meta-application protocol.

As demonstrated by Repenning (1993), one can consider that *the more a system makes its internal objects*—structure, functions, values, data structures—*explicit, the more flexible it is*. This principle is indeed made systematic in the reflective systems approach, which uses internal representation for standard computation and behavior (Maes, 1987). The principle that we have followed in *biok*, is both to provide a structured underlying architecture and framework to help the understanding of the code (see Section 6), and to provide dynamic navigation tools to help locate source code involved in a specific feature (Section 4.5 and Figure 10.11).

6.2.2. *Meta-Object Protocols*

Providing a reflective architecture requires a specific internal design, where internal components are available as an additional meta-level interface, potentially subject to modifications. The meta-object protocol (MOP) technology (Kiczales et al., 1991) gives a model of an explicit modification protocol for systems where changes of the system are anticipated. MOP was originally intended for object-oriented languages, to let the user change the way object, classes, inheritance, etc. behave. Figure 10.12 illustrates that this approach can be transposed to standard applications, as was done by Rao (1991) for a window system or by Dourish (1996) for a CSCW toolkit.

6.3. FLEXIBILITY FOR THE USER

A reflective architecture does not only require an additional interface. Giving a non-specialist that many possibilities to perform complex actions raises a usability issue. As explained by Morch (1997), or as modeled by da Cunha and de Souza (2003), the more the user interface offers programmability, the less usable the system is, since the user interface language departs from the user's task.

To avoid user confusion, a compromise must be found to deal with these different representations. How can we help the user understand which part of the source code corresponds to such and such user interface components? How can we articulate both languages by using an intermediate representation level? How can we structure the code in small enough components that correspond to the user's domain task units? In other words, internal architecture has to be handled and designed as an explicit, although additional, user interface. In Section 3.7, we explained that this design was greatly

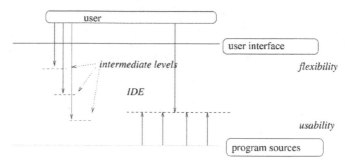

Figure 10.13. Adding intermediate programming levels and improving the programming environment usability: two complementary approaches.

influenced by the observations we made during interviews and the ideas that emerged in participatory workshops.

6.3.1. *Explicit Intermediate Meta-Level Interfaces*

In the context of EUP, several approaches exist to manage intermediate levels of access from the user interface to the code. Morch (1994) suggests a design where tailoring can occur at three levels: customization, integration, or extension. Extension can be performed through three kinds of interfaces: the standard user interface, design rationales, or source code. The design rationale fills the gap between the source code and the user interface. It is a pedagogical go-between which explains the behavior of the application units. For instance, a diagram can explain how the code deals with mouse movements in a drawing application.

More generally, our approach draws from the MAP model (Figure 10.13). Not only must this interface be explicit, it *must also belong to the user's working environment* so that the user does not have to switch from his or her work environment to an encoding environment.

In order to achieve this, we have built two kinds of intermediate interfaces that are directly accessible from the application: intermediate programming levels and a programming interface (Figure 10.13). Programming levels and intermediate meta-level user interfaces include:

1. a formula spreadsheet-like level,
2. a tag programming level to visualize biological functions,
3. a scripting level to facilitate program composition,
4. an object-oriented implementation level with a full-fledged integrated programming environment.

6.3.2. *Internal Framework: Explicit Elements of a Protocol*

In addition, we not only structure the software in order to make it "source-navigable", but also we borrow from the MOP approach the idea of having the source code follow a documented and explicit framework. In order to do this, we need well-known method names where the user can learn to go.[3] In *biok*, graphical objects define a set of protocols:

- *Graphical display.* Graphical objects define `draw` and `redisplay` methods for graphical components to be created, initialized and refreshed. If, for example, fields were missing in the tool for displaying curves, the user would just have to edit the `draw` method. This is what happened with a student who wanted to add the x and y fields in the initial tool (Figure 10.4).
- *Synchronized selections.* A simple protocol has been defined with another biology student as a set of three generic methods. These methods define which selections in objects should be synchronized (`interact`); what to do when a synchronization should occur (`propagate`); how to enforce selection in the target object (`highlight`).
- *Persistence.* Two methods deal with object contents (`value`) and persistence (`save`).

6.4. CONCLUDING CEMARKS ON FLEXIBILITY

In this section, we have tried to show that general software flexibility is desirable for educated end-users, as long as explicit tools are designed for it, and that this scaffolded flexibility is feasible through reflective mechanisms. We preferred to adopt a reflective architecture rather than a more explicit meta-descriptive system. The first reason is that the latter solution is more costly: we have chosen to reuse descriptive constructs (classes and methods) instead of rewriting a language, and to have them available and modifiable through introspection. Secondly, true reflective mechanisms ensure a causal connection between the running system and its source code (Macs, 1987). Finally, an explicit meta-descriptive system requires an additional abstraction level. Bentley and Dourish (1995) have demonstrated that computer abstractions, unlike mathematical ones, are often compromises, leaving potentially important aspects out of its scope. Hence, instead of being a positive tool to structure application, they become a barrier.

7. Conclusion

We built *biok* as an environment that enables biologists to conduct data analyses, combine them and visualize the results with graphical tools. In this environment, and according to their needs, biologists can locate and modify the code of methods, and create new ones. Through familiar entities such as programmable graphical objects corresponding to domain concepts, *biok* makes programming more accessible, but it still requires a basic knowledge of programming, as in (van Rossum, 1999) or (Eisenberg, 1995). Being embedded within a running application, the programming meta-level has

---

[3] Notice, however, that we are not looking for a framework-based approach. *biok* is not an abstract set of classes that first need to be instantiated. Yet, there is a documented framework within the running application. In *biok*, programming is possible, not required.

to rely on a well-designed internal architecture (Kiczales et al., 1991), where flexibility dimensions carefully correspond to the users needs. Participatory programming, a process that integrates participatory design and end-user programming, leads to enhanced flexibility in the right places (Kjaer 1995; Stiemerling et al., 1997; Trigg, 1992). Our work consists more in the exploration of the problem space: we wanted to investigate on the *context* of the programming tasks rather than programming itself, by addressing the following issues: *what* do users want or need to program? *when* do users want or need to program? The main outcome was that biologists preferred to program in the context of normal software use, or even that *they preferred not to program at all*. An important consequence is that a software with programming facilities should, through a careful design, both *maximize* the available programming features, and *minimize* the programming needs. This is why a better cooperation should take place in the building of software. Indeed, we discovered that problems arising when biologists need to program lie in the way common software is built rather than in the difficulty of the programming activity itself. This is why we shifted the problem focus from programming to flexibility, in order to take into account the fact that programming, in our context, is neither the goal nor the main difficulty for biology researchers.

Acknowledgments

My thanks to the many biologists, programmers and bioinformaticians who participate to the interviews and workshops. Special thanks to Volker Wulf, Wendy Mackay, Michel Beaudouin-Lafon, Katja Schuerer, Alexandre Dehne Garcia, Fabienne Dulin, Albane Le Roch, Alexis Gambis, Marie-France Sagot, Thierry Rose, Pierre Tuffery, Victoria Dominguez, Francois Huetz, Lionel Frangeul, Bertrand Neron, Pierre Dehoux and Stephane Bortzmeyer. Many thanks to Andrew Farr for his helpful assistance on the English.

References

Bentley, R. and Dourish, P. (1995). Medium versus mechanism: Supporting collaboration through customization. In: *Proceedings of ECSCW'95*, pp. 133–148.

Bizzaro, J.W. (2000). Distributing scientific applications with Gnu piper. Technical report, bioinformatics.org, http://bioinformatics.org/piper.

Blackwell, A.F. (2000). *Swyn:* a visual representation for regular expressions. In: *Your Wish is My Command: Giving Users the Power to Instruct their Software*. Morgan Kaufmann, pp. 245–270.

Blackwell, A.F. (2002). What is programming? In: *Proceedings of PPIG*, pp. 204–218.

Bodker, S. and Gronbaek, K. (1991). Design in action: From prototyping by demonstration to cooperative prototyping. In: *Design at Work: Cooperative Design of Computer Systems*. Hillsdale, New Jersey: Lawrence Erlbaum Associates, pp. 197–218.

Boyle, J. (1998). A visual environment for the manipulation and integration of java beans. *Bioinformatics* 14(8), 739–748.

Burnett, M.M., Hossli, R., Pulliam, T., VanVoorst, B. and Yang, X. (1994). Toward visual programming languages for steering in scientific visualization: A taxonomy. *IEEE Computational Science and Engineering*, 44–62.

Carroll, J.M. and Rosson, M.B. (1987). The paradox of the active user. In: J.M. Carroll (ed.), *Interfacing Thought: Cognitive Aspects of Human-Computer Interaction*. Cambridge, Mass: MIT Press, pp. 80–111.

Carroll, J.M., Singer, J.A., Bellamy, R.H.E. and Alpert, S.R. (1990). A view matcher for learning smalltalk. In: *Proceedings of ACM CHI'90 Conference on Human Factors in Computing Systems*, ACM Press, pp. 431–437.

Chapman, B. and Chang, J. (2000). Biopython: Python tools for computation biology. *ACM-SIGBIO Newsletter*.

Costabile, M.F., Fogli, D., Letondal, C., Mussio, P. and Piccino, A. (1993). Domain-expert users and their needs of software development. In: *Proceedings of the HCI 2003 End User Development Session*.

Cypher, A. (1993). *Watch What I Do. Programming by Demonstration*. MIT Press.

da Cunha, C.K.V. and de Souza, C.S. (2003). Toward a culture of end-user programming: understanding communication about extending applications. In: *Proceedings of the CHI'03 Workshop on End-User Development*, Apr. 2003.

DiGiano, C. and Eisenberg, M. (1995). Self-disclosing design tools: a gentle introduction to end-user programming. In: G. Olson and S. Schuon (eds.), In: *Proceedings of DIS '95 Symposium on Action Systems*, Ann Arbor, Michigan: ACM Press, pp. 189–197.

DiSessa, A. (1999). *Changing Minds: Computers, Learning, and Literacy*. MIT Press.

DiSessa, A. and Abelson, H., (1989). Boxer: a reconstructible computational medium. In: *Studying the Novice Programmer*, Lawrence Elbaum Associates, pp. 467–481.

Dittrich, Y., Lundberg, L. and Lindeberg, O. (2003). End user development by tailoring. Blurring the border between use and development. In: *Proceedings of the CHI'03 Workshop on End-User Development*, Apr. 2003.

Dourish, P. (1996). Open implementation and flexibility in CSCW toolkits. PhD Thesis, Dept of Computer Science, London: University College.

Eisenberg, M. (1995). Programmable applications: Interpreter meets interface. *ACM SIGCHI Bulletin* **27**(2), 68–93.

Eisenberg. M. (1997). End-user programming. In: *Handbook of Human Computer Interaction, Second, Completely Revised Edition*. North-Holland, pp. 1127–1146.

Fischer, G. (2003). Meta-design: Beyond user-centered and participatory design. In: C. Stephanidis (ed.), *Proceedings of HCI International 2003*, Crete, Greece, pp. 78–82.

Fischer, G. and Ostwald, J. (2002). Seeding, evolutionary growth, and reseeding: Enriching participatory design with informed participation. In: T. Binder, J. Gregory and I. Wagner (eds.), *Proceedings of the Participatory Design Conference (PDC'02)*. Sweden: Malmš University, pp. 135–143.

Fischer, G. and Scharff, E. (2000). Meta-design—design for designers. In: D. Boyarski and W. Kellogg, (eds), *Proceedings the 3rd International Conference on Designing Interactive Systems (DIS 2000)*. New York: ACM, pp. 396–405.

Gantt, M. and Nardi, B.A. (1992). Gardeners and gurus: patterns of cooperation among CAD users. In: *ACM conference on Human Factors in Computing Systems (Proceedings) (CHI '92)*, ACM Press, pp. 107–117.

Gonnet, H.H., Hallett, M.T., Korostensky, C. and Bernardin L. (2000). Darwin v. 2.0: an interpreted computer language for the biosciences. *Bioinformatics* **16**(2), 101–103.

Greenbaum, J. (1993). PD, a personal statement. *CACM* **36**(6), p. 47.

Henderson, A. and Kyng, M. (1991). There's no place like home: Continuing design in use. In: J. Greenbaum and M. Kyng (eds.), *Design at Work: Cooperative Design of Computer Systems*. Hillsdale, New Jersey: Lawrence Erlbaum Associates, Publishers, pp. 219–240.

Kahler, H. (1996). Developing groupware with evolution and participation. A case study. In: *Proceedings of the Participatory Design Conference 1996(PDC'96)*, Cambridge, MA, pp. 173–182.

Kiczales, G., des Rivieres, J. and Bobrow, D.G. (1991). *The Art of the Meta-Object Protocol.* Cambridge (MA), USA: MIT Press.

Kjaer, A. and Madsen, K.H. (1995). Participatory analysis of flexibility. *CACM* **38**(5), 53–60.

Labview: a demonstration. unpublished, 1987.

Letondal, C. (1999a). A practical and empirical approach for biologists who almost program. In: *CHI'99 Workshop on End-User Programming and Blended-User Programming*, May 1999. http://www.pasteur.fr/letondal/Papers/chi_pp.html.

Letondal, C. (1999b). Résultats de l'enquête sur l'utilisation de l'informatique à l'institut pasteur. Technical report, Institut Pasteur, Paris, Apr. 1999.

Letondal, C. (1999b). Une approche pragmatique de la programmation pour des biologistes qui programment presque. In: *Actes Onzième Conférence Francophone sur l'Interaction Homme Machine, IHM'99*, Montpellier (France), tome II, November 1999, pp. 5–8.

Letondal, C. (2000). A web interface generator for molecular biology programs in UNIX. *Bioinformatics* **17**(1), 73–82.

Letondal, C. (2001a). Programmation et interaction. PhD Thesis, Orsay: Université de Paris XI.

Letondal, C. (2001b). Software review: alignment edition, visualization and presentation. Technical report, Institut Pasteur, Paris, France, May 2001. http://bioweb.pasteur.fr/cgi-bin/seqanal/review-edital.pl.

Letondal, C. and Mackay W.E. (2004). Participatory programming and the scope of mutual responsibility: Balancing scientific, design and software commitment. In: *Proceedings of the Eighth Biennial Participatory Design Conference (PDC 2004)*, Toronto, Canada, July 2004.

Letondal, C. and Schuerer, K. (2002). Course in informatics for biology. Technical report, Institut Pasteur, Paris, 2002. http://www.pasteur.fr/formation/infobio.

Letondal, C. and Zdun, U. (2003). Anticipating scientific software evolution as a combined technological and design approach. In: *USE2003: Proceedings of the Second International Workshop on Unanticipated Software Evolution.* http://www.pasteur.fr/letondal/Papers/pc_ihm99.ps.gz.

Lieberman, H. (ed.). (2000). *Your Wish is My Command: Giving Users the Power to Instruct their Software.* Morgan Kaufmann.

Lieberman, H. and Fry, C. (1995). Bridging the gulf between code and behavior in programming. In: *Proceedings of ACM Conference on Human Factors in Computing Systems (Summary, Demonstrations) (CHI '95)*. ACM Press, pp. 480–486.

Mackay, W.E. (1991a). Triggers and barriers to customizing software. In: *Proceedings of ACM CHI'91 Conference on Human Factors in Computing Systems*. ACM Press, pp. 153–160.

Mackay, W.E. (1991b). Users and Customizable Software: A Co-Adaptive Phenomenon. PhD Thesis, Massachusetts Institute of Technology.

MacLean, A., Carter, K., Lovstrand, L. and Moran T. (1990). User-tailorable systems: Pressing the issues with buttons. In: *Proceedings of ACM CHI'90 Conference on Human Factors in Computing Systems*. ACM Press, pp. 175–182.

Maes, P. (1987). Concepts and experiments in computational reflection. In: *Proceedings of the OOPSLA'87: Conference on Object-Oriented Programming Systems, Languages and Applications*, Orlando, FL, pp. 147–155.

Morch, A. (1994). Designing for radical tailorability: Coupling artifact and rationale. *Knowledge-Based Systems*, **7**(4), 253–264.

Morch, A. (1997). Method and Tools for Tailoring of Object-oriented Applications: An Evolving Artifacts Approach. PhD Thesis, Department of Informatics, University of Oslo, April 1997.

Nardi, B.A. (1993). A small matter of programming: perspectives on end user computing. MIT Press, p. 162.

Nardi, B.A. and Johnson J.A. (1994). User preferences for task specific vs. generic application software. In: *ACM Conference on Human Factors in Computing Systems (Proceedings) (CHI '94)*. ACM Press, pp. 392–398.

Neumann, G. and Zdun, U. (2000). Xotcl, an object-oriented scripting language. In: *Proceedings of 7th Usenix Tcl/Tk Conference (Tcl2k)*, Austin, Texas, pp. 14–18.

Nierstrasz, O. and Tsichritzis, D. (eds). (1995). *Object-Oriented Software Composition*. Prentice Hall, p. 361.

O'Day, V.L., Adler, A., Kuchinsky, A. and Bouch, A. (2000). When worlds collide: Molecular biology as interdisciplinary collaboration. In: *Proceedings of ECSCW'01*, pp. 399–418.

Ousterhout, J.K. (1998). Scripting: Higher level programming for the 21st century. *IEEE Computer* **31**(3), 23–30.

Pane, J.F., Ratanamahatana, C.A. and Myers, B. (2001). Studying the language and structure in non-programmers' solutions to programming problems. *International Journal of Human-Computer Studies* **54**(2), 237–264.

Ploger, D. and Lay, E. (1992). The structure of programs and molecules. *Journal of Educational Computing Research* **8**(3), 347–364.

Rao, R. (1991). Implementational reflection in silica. In: *ECOOP '91 (LNCS 512)*, ACM Press, pp. 251–267.

Rasure, J., Argiro, D., Sauer, T. and Williams, C.S. (1990). A visual language and software development environment for image processing. *International Journal of Imaging Systems and Technology* **2**, 183–199.

Repenning, A. (1993). Agentsheets: A Tool for Building Domain-Oriented Dynamic, Visual Environments. PhD Thesis, University of Colorado at Boulder.

Schuerer, K. (2003). Course in informatics for biology: Introduction to Algorithmics. Technical report, Institut Pasteur, Paris, France.http://www.pasteur.fr/formation/infobio/algo/Introduction.pdf.

Smith, R.B. and Ungar D. (1995). Programming as an experience: The inspiration for Self. In: *Proceedings of ECOOP '95*, pp. 303–330.

Smith, R.B., Maloney, J. and Ungar, D. (1995). The Self-4.0 user interface: Manifesting a system-wide vision of concreteness, uniformity, and flexibility. In: *Proceedings of OOPSLA '95*, pp. 47–60.

Smith, R.B., Ungar, D. and Chang, B-W. (1992). The use-mention perspective on programming for the interface. In: *Languages for Developing User Interfaces*. Boston: Jones and Bartlett, Publishers, pp. 79–89.

Stajich, J.E., Block, D., Boulez, K., Brenner, S.E., Chervitz, S.A., Dagdigian, C., Fuellen, G., Gilbert J.G.R., Korf, I., Lapp, H., Lehvaslaiho H., Matsalla, C., Mungall, C.J., Osborne, B.I., Pocock, M.R., Schattner, P., Senger, M., Stein, L.D., Stupka, E., Wilkinson, M.D. and Birney, E. (2002). The bioperl toolkit: Perl modules for the life sciences. *Genome Research* **12**(10), 1611–1618.

Stiemerling, O., Kahler, H. and Wulf, V. (1997). How to make software softer—designing tailorable applications. In: *Proceedings of DIS'97 (Amsterdam)*, pp. 365–376.

Tisdall, J. Why biologists want to program computers. Technical report, O'Reilly, October 2001. http://www.oreilly.com/news/perlbio_1001.html.

Trigg, R.H. (1992). Participatory design meets the MOP: Informing the design of tailorable computer systems. In: G. Bjerknes, T. Bratteteig and K. Kautz (eds.), *Proceedings of the 15th IRIS (Information Systems Research seminar In Scandinavia)*, Larkollen, Norway, pp. 643–646.

Tuffery, P., Neron, B., Quang, M. and Letondal, C. i3DMol: Molecular visualization. Technical report, Institut Pasteur, Paris, France, 2003. http://www.pasteur.fr/letondal/biok/i3DMol.html.

van Rossum, G. (1999). Computer programming for everybody. Technical report, CNRI: Corporation for National Research Initiatives.

von Heijne, G. (1992). Membrane protein structure prediction. hydrophobicity analysis and the positive-inside rule. *Journal of Molecular Biology* **225**(2), 487–494.

Wang, L. and Pfeiffer, P. (2002). A qualitative analysis of the usability of Perl, Python, and Tcl. In: *Proceedings of The Tenth International Python Conference*.

Wetherall, D. and Lindblad, C.J. (1995). Extending Tcl for dynamic object-oriented programming. In: *Proceedings of the Tck/Tk Workshop 95*, Toronto, Ontario.

Wilkinson, M.D. and Links, M. (2002). Biomoby: An open-source biological web services proposal. *Briefings in Bioinformatics* **3**(4), 331–341.

Winograd, T. (1995). From programming environments to environments for designing. *CACM* **38**(6), 65–74.

Wulf, V. and Golombek, B. (2001). Direct activation: A concept to encourage tailoring activities. *Behaviour and Information Technology* **20**(4), 249–263.

Chapter 11

Challenges for End-User Development in Intelligent Environments

BORIS DE RUYTER and RICHARD VAN DE SLUIS
Philips Research, The Netherlands
boris.de.ruyter@philips.com, richard.vandesluis@philips.com

Abstract. Intelligent environments will be able to observe and sense the events that are happening around them. For these environments to become intelligent, however, they need to learn what appropriate and sensible behavior is in a given situation. The main challenge of ambient intelligent environments is not to *physically* integrate technology in the environment, but to *socially* integrate the system behavior into the fabric of everyday life. This means that an intelligent environment needs to be taught by its users how it should conduct and what position it should take. This paper will discuss two examples of end-user development in intelligent environments as a way to indicate the research challenges in this area.

Key words. (end-user development), ambient intelligence, home experience, content awareness.

1. Introduction

Many of today's devices already know what time and day it is, and what their location is. Besides this, in the near future, devices will be able to sense the things that are happening around them. This means that besides the *when* and the *where*, they will also figure out *who*'s around, and *what* they are doing. And when these devices become networked, they may be able to enrich this awareness of the user's context by gathering contextual cues and information from their neighboring peers. Being able to observe and sense is not enough for becoming an intelligent environment. The key question is *how* to behave in any particular situation. A system does not have a clue about the personality and the cultural background of an end-user. That means that in many cases it may only guess on what the appropriate system behavior would be in a given situation. It means that somehow, users need to teach the environment how to conduct and what position it should take.

Many researchers and futurologists envision a future of ambient intelligence, which refers to electronic environments that are sensitive and responsive to the presence of people (Aarts and Marzano, 2003; Dertouzos, 1999; Weiser, 1991). The idea is that the user is surrounded by a multitude of interconnected, embedded systems, which are integrated in the everyday environment and that can behave intelligently in order to improve the user's quality of life. However, the challenge is not only to physically integrate these systems in the environment, but also to integrate these intelligent systems into the social fabric of everyday life. This implies that having an understanding of everyday life, and of people's routines and rituals is of crucial importance in the creation

Henry Lieberman et al. (eds.), End User Development, 243–250.
© 2006 *Springer.*

of ambient intelligent systems. Since most of our work is targeted at the home domain, in earlier work, we have conducted extensive user studies to understand what "everyday life at home" actually means to people, and to find out how people would like to live in their "dream home." (Eggen et al., 2003). In this study, we explored people's home experiences and possible application and interaction concepts that can enhance this experience. This was done using a variety of techniques such as telling, drawing, writing, taking pictures, interviewing, and free association (Gaver et al., 1999). These techniques were employed to stimulate the families to express their personal home experience. An important conclusion from this study is that people, when they talk about home, they do not talk about appliances, devices, or home networks. People talk about home in terms of social activities and family rituals, such as having dinner together, bedtime storytelling or a birthday party.

In this study, people were also asked to think of their "dream home." They were asked to imagine that everything would be possible and that they should tell us what they would like. In general people would like the future home to take the role of an assistant. In many occasions it could give advise, create the right conditions, and support the family in their activities and with the things that have to be done. They described a home that would optimally facilitate them in their everyday routines and that could enhance the experience of their rituals.

When talking about their everyday life, people often refer to various recurring patterns of activities. In this respect, they clearly distinguish between routines and rituals. A ritual is something that people value, something that delivers a valuable experience, for instance, preparing a romantic dinner, having an extensive breakfast or smoking a delicate cigar. A routine, on the other hand, is related to certain tasks that people have to do. For instance, before going to bed one needs to lock the door, switch off the lights etc. Although it may be important that those things get done, people do not attach much value to the course of a routine. In summary, the experience of a ritual should be maintained or even enhanced, whereas the user experience of a routine may be minimized or even eliminated. It should be noted that the classification of activities into routines and rituals it a very subjective matter. Activities, like cooking or having dinner, can for some people have the meaning of cherished rituals, whereas others would consider them as necessary routines.

Through embedding some form of system intelligence into the environment, the user can be relieved from performing routine tasks. Moreover, the fact that a system is capable of taking over the routine tasks of the user brings the experience of freedom. Like with any form of automation it is very important that users are in control, that they have the option to define or modify a system's behavior. Beyond simple parameter specification we have investigated how end-user development can empower users to define or modify the behavior on an intelligent system or environment.

2. The Wake-Up Experience

In the user studies on the home experience, as referred to before, many people indicated that in their future home they expect to wake up in a more gentle way than they do nowadays. There is a broad area of sleep research that covers topics such as the different phases of sleep, sleep deprivation, dreaming, and the physiological effects of sleep (Chase and Weitzman, 1983; Ellman and Antrobus 1991; Thorpy and Yager, 1991). A great deal of work has been done in this area, with a special focus on sleeping and going to sleep. However, hardly any research has focused on the process of waking up and the subjective experience of awakening. Wensveen et al. (2000) have been exploring new ways to interact with an alarm clock. Their main research question was how a user can communicate his or her emotions to a product, and the alarm clock was used as an example product in this study.

We learnt from the family studies that people want the wake-up experience to be pleasant, in contrast to the current annoyance caused by a "beeping" alarm clock. This made us decide to focus part of our research on enhancing the wake-up experience. The main question is in what type of ambiences people would like to be awakened, and what an easy way is for people to "specify" such desired ambiences?

2.1. ANALYSIS

With an online questionnaire, additional data on user needs and requirements was gathered from 120 subjects spread all over the world. Target subjects were selected by the age, gender, and location in order to obtain a balanced group of different categories using a messenger program ICQ (www.icq.com). This program has a search engine, that provides the possibility to select a certain group of people by specified criteria.

Besides questions about the current wake-up process, people were also asked to describe their ideal "wake-up experience." 5776 requests were sent to ICQ users in 25 countries. 120 users replied with a filled-in questionnaire.

The results of the survey confirmed that most people are dissatisfied with their current wake-up experience. When asked to specify what their ideal wake-up experience should be like, respondents describe experiences that greatly differ from person to person. For instance, some people want to be awakened with the smell of coffee and the sound of singing birds in a forest. Others would prefer a piece of music or sunlight. In general, most people desire a soft and peaceful wake-up experience in the morning hours. Some people construct complete scenarios of how different pleasant stimuli should be generated gradually to wake them up in an ideal way. The following quote gives an example of such a scenario:

> The gradual and eventually rich strong aroma of coffee you get in cafes and the sound of birds chirping ever so slightly and gradually increasing in level. The lights will be very dark initially but the ceiling will illuminate to eventually produce a soft but bright light. The room temperature would regulate in concert with the temperature within the covers of the bed so that there is little temperature variance when first placing that foot on the floor ...

We formulated a set of requirements for a wake-up system based on this user input. For instance, it should be able to generate several stimuli simultaneously. It should also be easy to create a personal wake-up experience and to alter it every day. People should be able to set the intensity of the stimuli so that it would allow them to wake up in their own rhythm. Those specific requirements were used, in addition to the general design principles that were derived from the domain exploration, as basic input for the concept development phase.

2.2. DEVELOPMENT

The major question was how we could come up with an interaction concept that enables users to "specify" their desired wake-up experience in an easy way. It is generally known that people are not very good at programming. Many people have great difficulties in programming a videocassette recorder. This means that this "programming task" should be kept simple. It should ideally be a pleasant task, and it should stimulate people's creativity.

A workshop was held to generate many different concepts for creating one's desired wake-up experience. After weighing the concepts against criteria (such as feasibility, novelty, usability, and fun), one concept was selected to be developed further.

The selected concept is based on the analogy of making a painting. The idea is to use a pen-based pressure-sensitive display to let users "paint" their desired wake-up experience. This display could be positioned on the bedside table where it could act as any normal alarm clock, just showing the time. However, when the pen approaches the display, the clock changes into a painting canvas. Here, users can select a certain time interval, for instance from 7.00 to 7.30 a.m., for which they can start painting their desired wake-up experience. A timeline for the interval is shown at the bottom of the canvas. People can choose a color from a palette of predefined wake-up stimuli, such as sounds of nature, lighting, coffee, or music. The position of a stroke determines the time of "activation" of the stimulus, whereas the thickness of a stroke, controlled by the pressure on the pen, represents the intensity of the stimulus. At the moment of "painting" there is an immediate feedback on the type and intensity of the stimulus that is set (except for the coffee maker, for practical reasons). For instance, while making a green stroke, sounds from nature are played with the volume adjusted to the current stroke thickness.

In the morning at the adjusted time interval the system generates the created "wake-up experience" by controlling the devices in the networked environment (such as lighting, coffeemaker, music, and fan). Figure 11.1 shows an example of a "painted wake-up experience" starting at 6 a.m. lasting until 9 a.m. In this example the system would start to raise the room temperature (red), then activate soft lights (yellow) and soft sounds of nature (green). These stimuli will gradually increase in intensity. The coffee maker will be switched on after some time (brown) and somewhat later music will be played for a few minutes (blue).

3. Evaluation

The wake-up experience prototype was assessed by a small number of experts on its estimated level of user acceptance. Special attention was paid to usefulness, effort/benefit rate, and usability criteria. In general, the experts could understand and

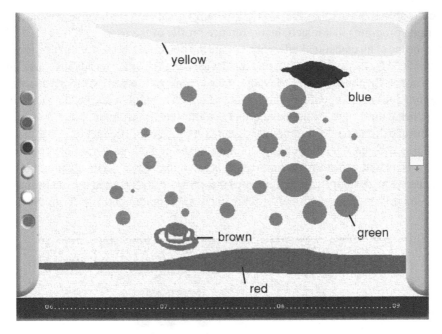

Figure 11.1. The wake-up experience prototype.

operate the system with little effort. A number of valuable suggestions were also made with respect to design improvements, extensions to the system (functions, and appliances), and alternative uses of the system. The most important suggestions for improvement of the design had to do with the icons, which were not clear enough, and with the timeline which should have a more detailed scale. Furthermore, it was stated that the pen should have a bigger contact area, and that there should be different pens in order to be able to make thin and thick strokes. The experts also suggested a number of extensions. For instance, it should be easily possible to "pre-experience" the programmed wake-up experience. Furthermore, it was suggested that the concept could be broadened for creating experiences for other parts of the day, for instance to create a party atmosphere, or a go-to-sleep experience.

4. A Context-Aware Remote Control

As discussed in the introduction, one important property of intelligent systems is their ability to be aware of the context in which they are being used. By adding some sensor and reasoning technology, a device can be made adaptive and exhibit adequate behavior for a given context.

As an example of a context-aware device, a universal remote control (based on the Philips PRONTO) with the ability to control different devices (such as TV, DVD, Audio set, etc.) is augmented with several context sensors. In addition to device control, the device is able to present an Electronic Program Guide (EPG) and give reminders for upcoming programs that match the preference profile of the user.

By means of an embedded inference engine the device can reason about the information obtained by the sensors. With this the device can (a) display an adaptive user interface to access the functionality relevant for the context of use and (b) modify the way of reminding the user of upcoming programs that match the preference profile of this user.

The behavioral rules of the device that use the sensor information are not fixed in the software of the device but are represented by means of production rules that can be processed by an inference engine running on the context-aware remote control. To provide users with the ability to modify these behavioral rules, adequate programming tools need to be developed. Today, users of the Philips PRONTO can use the ProntoEdit tool to modify the look-and-feel of their universal remote control (see Figure 11.2).

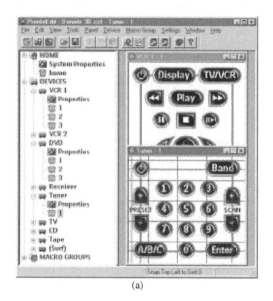

(a)

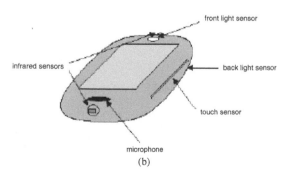

(b)

Figure 11.2. (a) The end-user tool for programming the look-and-feel of the Philips PRONTO. (b) The concept of a context-aware remote controlimplemented on the PRONTO.

To enable end users to modify the behavioral rules of context-aware devices, different programming metaphors need to be developed.

5. Conclusion

Technology trends can lead to future usage scenarios of consumer electronics that require users to interact more with system functionality than actually consuming Audio/Video content. The vision of Ambient Intelligence provides a framework in which embedded technology has to adapt to the needs of these users by being personalized, context-aware, adaptive, and anticipatory to the needs of users. However, by adding intelligence to interactive systems, we emphasize the importance of end-user development given the need for end-users to be in control. Two applications of Consumer Electronics that require end-user development are presented. These applications emphasize the need for suitable models of end-user development in the area of consumer electronics.

The following challenges for end-user programming can be formulated:

5.1. KEEP IT SIMPLE

Each small increase in complexity significantly reduces the number of potential users of the programming function. A solution should be found that allows users to adapt the system to their wishes in a straightforward way.

5.2. PROPER FEEDBACK

It is important that the user knows what he has programmed so far. The user should be able to easily "run" what is programmed on any moment in time. It would be even better if there were immediate feedback on what is currently being programmed.

5.3. MAKE IT FUN

The user programming method should invite the user to tailor his system or environment to his specific needs and wishes. The user should not have the feeling of being drowned in complexity. He should rather feel like a creative composer whose attention can be entirely focused on the desired composition itself rather than on the process.

References

Aarts, E. and Marzano, S. (2003). *The New Everyday—Views on Ambient Intelligence*. 010 Publishers, Rotterdam.
Chase, M.H. and Weitzman, E.D. (1983). *Sleep Disorders: Basic and Clinical Research*. New York: Spectrum.

Dertouzos, M. (1999). The oxygen project: The future of computing. *Science American* (August) 52–55.

Eggen, B., Hollemansu, G. and Van de Sluis, R. (2003). Exploring and Enhancing the Home Experience. *Cognition, Technology and Work* **5**(5), 44–54.

Ellman, S.J. and Antrobus, J. (1991). *The Mind in Sleep.* New York: Wiley.

Gaver, B., Dunne, T. and Pacenti, E. (1999). Cultural probes. *Interactions* (January to Feburary), 21–29.

Thorpy, J.J. and Yager, J. (1991). *The Encyclopaedia of Sleep and Sleep-Disorders. Facts on File*, New York.

Weiser, M. (1991). The computer for the twenty-first century. *Science American* **265**(3), 94–104.

Wensveen, S.A.G., Overbeeke, C.J., Djajadiningrat, J.P. (2000). Touch me, hit me and I know how you feel: A design approach to emotionally rich interaction. In: *Proceedings of DIS'00: Designing Interactive Systems.* New York: ACM, pp. 48–53.

Chapter 12

Fuzzy Rewriting[1]

Soft Program Semantics for Children

YASUNORI HARADA[1] and RICHARD POTTER[2]

[1]*NTT Communication Science Laboratories, hara@brl.ntt.co.jp*
[2]*Japan Science and Technology Agency, potter@osss.cs.tsukuba.ac.jp*

Abstract. Rewriting systems are popular in end-user programming because complex behavior can be described with few or no abstractions or variables. However, rewriting systems have been limited to manipulating non-rotatable objects on a grid, such as in Agentsheets or Stagecast Creator. Systems that allow free-form movement of objects must use other techniques, such as the sequential programming by demonstration in Squeak. Viscuit is a new rewriting system that introduces fuzzy rewriting, which allows freely positioned and rotated objects to interact using only rewriting rules. The result is a system that allows users to specify animations in a highly interactive way, without textual language or menu selections.

Key words. animation, rewriting system, visual programming language

1. Introduction

Animations are a major part of the Internet and are being created by more and more people. It typically requires programming-like activity, which can be frustrating to non-programmers who simply want to make their artistic creations move as desired. Simple techniques, like keyframe animation, can be tedious and produce static results. Rewriting systems allow one to create dynamic open-ended animations without programming. However, current systems are limited to animating objects on a fixed grid. Rotation is sometimes possible, but requires the user (or a professional) write a program. This puts many simple animations out of the reach of many end-users.

The main problem is that removing grids and allowing rotation gives each object a large number of possible positions and orientations. It is not practical to have a different rule for each orientation, so we propose a new rewriting mechanism, fuzzy rewriting,[2] that combines two techniques.

1. Fuzzy matching, which handles a range of relative distances and angles and
2. fuzzy generating, which infers a new (possibly unique) state that stays within the bounds of user intentions.

A similarity function for object relationships is defined. It is used during both matching and generating. The function should be designed according to end-users' cognition.

---

[1] This paper is a revised version of the paper from HCC 2003.
[2] We do not use the word "fuzzy" as a technical term.

Henry Lieberman et al. (eds.), End User Development, 251–267.

In this paper, however, we don't discuss the end-user aspect. Our function of similarity is defined artificially and has many parameters to widely change behavior. The fuzzy rewriting mechanism is implemented in a system called Viscuit, which allows freely positioned and rotated objects to interact using only rewriting rules.

This chapter is organized as follows. In the next section we compare our work with others. In Section 3, we describe the behavior of fuzzy rewriting. Viscuit is introduced in Section 4 and examples of its use are shown in Section 5. Section 6 shows precise computing for fuzzy rewriting.

2. Related Works

AgentsSheet (Repenning and Ambach, 1996) is an if-then rule-based visual language. It is suitable for simulation. In the condition part, several primitives, visual conditions, or non-visual conditions, can be used. The user can express object arrangements to express conditions in a functional programming manner. An object is located on a grid, so visual expressions are restricted. Kidsim (Cocoa, Stagecast Creator) (Cypher and Smith, 1995) is a rewriting visual language for objects on a grid. An object has several appearances, which can be used for expressing an object's direction, state, and so on. A rule rewrites arrangements of objects with its appearance. Flash and Director, by Macromedia, enable animation of objects that can be rotated, positioned, and scaled. Motion is directed by keyframes and is scripted exactly. An animation is tightly controlled by keyframes or algorithmically by scripting, so it is too difficult for our target end-users. BITPICT (Furnas, 1995) and Visulan (Yamamoto, 1996) are rewriting languages for bitmaps. They find bitmap patterns that are matched by a before-pattern of a rule and replace them with the after-patterns of the rules. Visulan has built-in patterns that express the mouse-button status. When the system knows the mouse-button status has changed, it changes the pattern into the corresponding built-in pattern. To write a program that interacts with a mouse, the user creates a normal rule that simply looks for the built-in pattern. BITPICT and Visulan use only bitmaps for data and programs. There is no hiding of information. Scott Kim defined this property as "visibility." His demonstration system, VIEWPOINT (Kim, 1988), combines a font editor, a word processor, and a keyboard layout manager. When a user types a key, the system copies a font pattern from the corresponding key on the keyboard layout into the cursor. Using this technique plus a few special rules, VIEWPOINT can function as a word processor with word wrap. ChemTrains (Bell and Lewis, 1993) is a graph-rewriting visual language. When the system finds a graph pattern matching the before-pattern of a rule, it replaces it with the after-pattern of the rule. It is a powerful language because of the high flexibility and expressiveness of the graph representation.

All the above systems except VIEWPOINT have two system modes: editing and running. Typically, using these systems involves writing programs, setting the initial state, running, and stopping. On the other hand, Vispatch (Harada et al., 1997) does not distinguish between these modes.

Vispatch is a graph rewriting visual language. Each rule has an event object in a before-pattern and zero or more event objects in an after-pattern. When a user clicks

Figure 12.1. Two objects of fuzzy rewriting.

on or drags on an object, rewriting is started. If an event object exists in the after-pattern of a fired rule, the system generates a new event that starts the next rewriting. Vispatch successfully achieves interactive rewriting. A rule in Vispatch is constructed as an object that can be rewritten by another Vispatch rule. This enables interactive reflection and makes a self-extensible graphics editor possible.

There has been much work on a motion generation. In (Arikan and Forsyth, 2002), for example, motion is generated from examples.

3. Fuzzy Rewriting

Fuzzy rewriting is a new rewriting mechanism. Let's look at some examples. Figure 12.1 is a simple rewriting rule. The horizontal arrow is a rule object that separates an object group into a before-pattern and an after-pattern. The left side of a rule object is a before-pattern (called the rule head), and the right side is an after-pattern (called the rule body). An explosion mark in a rule head expresses a mouse click event. The rule head in Figure 12.1 includes two objects, a boy and a girl, and one event. The rule body has the same two objects, only slightly rotated. This rule means that, when the boy is clicked, the boy and girl rotate.

Figure 12.2 shows three examples of rewriting with this rule. When the boy in the target-column is clicked, objects in the corresponding result-column replace objects in the corresponding target-column. In A, the arrangement of target-column objects is almost the same as rule-head objects, so the resulting arrangement is almost the same as the rule-body. In B, the boy is lower than the girl, so the boy in the result is also lower. In C, there is a deformation of arrangement, so the result is deformed.

Figure 12.3 shows two objects whose positions are swapped so that they are opposite from those in the rule in Figure 12.1. There are two possible results (Figure 12.3):[3] E preserves local constraints of the rule that keep rotation directions for each kind of object, so the boy rotates counter-clockwise and the girl clockwise. F preserves the global constraints of the rule that decides rotation direction based on a relative position (not its kind), so a left-hand-side object rotates clockwise and a right-hand-side object counter-clockwise.

Choosing the behavior raises difficult problems. The preferences of end-users and the attractiveness of the result are important. The system needs consistency.

---

[3] Of course, there is another possibility: The rules do not fire for different positions of objects like this. We can control this by changing the threshold for matching. This is discussed later.

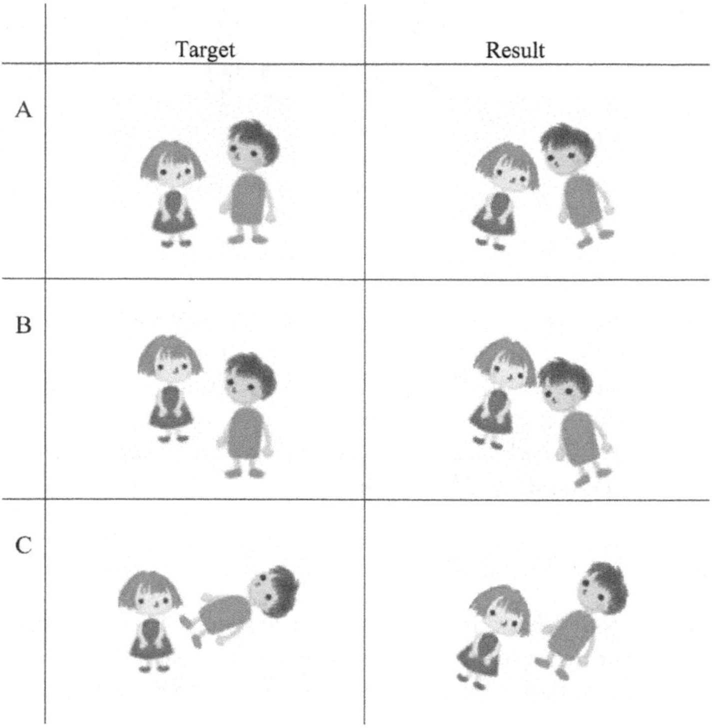

	Target	Result
A		
B		
C		

Figure 12.2. Executions of Figure 12.1.

	before	after
E		
F		

Figure 12.3. Possible results of Figure 12.1.

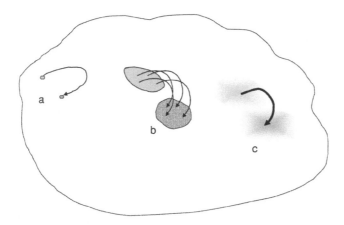

Figure 12.4. Several Rewritings.

We give priority to local constraints, because our experience is that this produces more attractive results. They are also the easiest to implement. Our system therefore works like E (not F).

Let's compare a traditional rewriting system and a fuzzy rewriting one. Figure 12.4 shows a data space to be rewritten and several rewritings on it, where a is a rewriting by a rule that has no variables, b is one by a rule that has variables, and c represents fuzzy rewriting. In a, a certain point (an input) is translated into another point (an output). In b, a certain area is translated into another certain area, and the correspondence between the input and the output area is defined by the rule. In c, like a, the rule has no variables. Points surrounding an input point are translated into other points surrounding an output point. Unlike b, input and output areas have no clear border.

4. Viscuit

Viscuit is a new visual language that rewrites objects using the fuzzy techniques described in the previous section. In this section, we discuss how programs are written and run with Viscuit.

Viscuit is composed of paper and objects. A user can place several objects with free position and rotation (but no scaling) on a piece of paper. Three objects have special use: A *rule object* has two sets of objects, the head set and body set. A rule head includes one *event mark* and a rule body includes zero or more *event marks*. An *event mark* indicates where a click event is expected (in rule heads) or will be generated (in rule bodies). A *pointer object* refers to another piece of paper.

When a user clicks on a piece of paper, the system traces pointer objects on the paper recursively, and collects all rules from the traversed paper. Using the position of a click and the arrangement of objects on the clicked paper, the system selects the rule and the most similar arrangement of target objects. After that the system rewrites objects according to the selected rule.

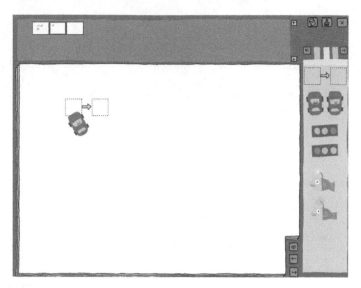

Figure 12.5. Create a rule.

Figures 12.5–12.8 show user views. There is an object palette in the right of Figure 12.5. To create a new object, a user drags the desired object from a palette and drops it into the target paper directly. A rule object captures its neighbor objects as rule's head or body. After preparing a rule, and setting up an object to rewrite, the user clicks the object to see the rewriting result. In Figure 12.6, the rule says when a car is clicked it moves forward, so this car (showing in the right part of the figure) moves forward by a user click.

When a rule fires, an event mark in a rule body generates a click event and enqueues it into the event queue, where it behaves like an actual user click. When there is no user interaction, the system dequeues a posted event and tries to rewrite. In Figure 12.7, the

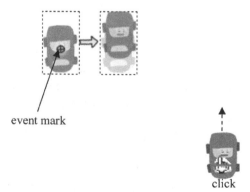

event mark

click

Figure 12.6. Execute a program.

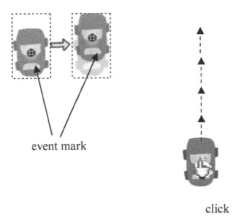

click

Figure 12.7. Continuous rewriting.

rule body has an event object. By clicking the target car, it moves upward continuously and disappears. A continuous rewriting behaves like a thread. Therefore, if there are several cars and they are each clicked by the user, then they move simultaneously.

Viscuit lets the user modify rules anytime. In Figure 12.8, the user rotates the car in the rule body while the target car moves straight. After modifying the rule, the target car turns. The user can drive the car by modifying rules.

5. Execution Examples

Figures 12.9 and 12.10 are two sets of rules that describe how a car should turn for a certain steering-wheel position. The difference between them is whether each rule includes a stand or not. In Figure 12.9, the car wants to move to the same absolute direction as the steering wheel. When the car heads upward and the steering wheel is turned toward the right, the car turns right because rule R is fired. Now that both the car and the steering wheel are pointing in the same direction, rule S will fire and the car will go straight (Figure 12.11, line A).

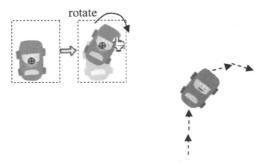

Figure 12.8. Rotating a car.

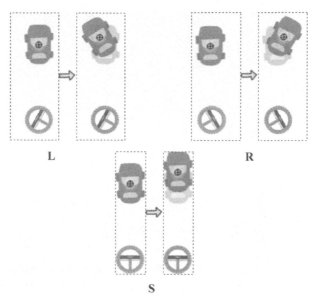

Figure 12.9. Rules for driving (A).

On the other hand, when the rules in Figure 12.10 are applied to the target in Figure 12.11, rule R in Figure 12.10 is always fired. So the car turns always (Figure 12.11, line B). If the steering wheel turns left, the car always turns left by rule L. If the steering wheel is straightened out, rule S would always fire and the car would always go straight.

The difference in these actions depends on the importance assigned to each relationship. In Figure 12.9, there is only one relationship, which is the relative angle between

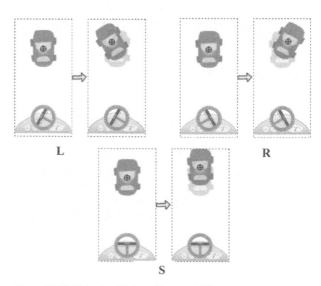

Figure 12.10. Rules for driving with a stand (B).

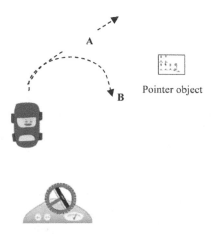

Figure 12.11. Execution of driving.

the steering-wheel heading and the car heading. The car direction therefore affects the rule selection every time. On the other hand, in Figure 12.10, the stand overlaps the steering wheel. Overlapped objects' relationships make higher similarity. Their relationships are assigned a higher importance than the car/steering-wheel relationship. Therefore, the rule is selected based on the relative angle between steering-wheel and stand.

Figure 12.12 shows a single rule that animates soccer players kicking a ball. Its meaning is that when a soccer ball gets near the soccer player's foot, the ball should be moved out and in front of the player's head. In Figure 12.13, for each click by a user or the system on the ball, the soccer player nearest the ball is selected, and the ball moves close to the foot of the next soccer player. In the resulting animation, the ball rotates clockwise like a soccer pass.

Figure 12.14 only has one soccer player, but still produces a continuous animation because after the rule fires, the ball is still close enough to the soccer players foot to make the rule fire again. When a user clicks, the ball bounces around the player's head. This is good because the system never gets in a state totally unlike any of the body patterns. Therefore, while the system is unpredictable at the fine-grain level, its overall behavior can be predicted from the rules.

Figure 12.12. Rule of soccer's pass.

Figure 12.13. Animation of soccer's passes.

Figure 12.14. Single play.

Figure 12.15. Rule of soccer play.

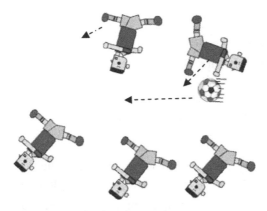

Figure 12.16. Animation of soccer play.

Figure 12.15 is a rule that shows a pass between two players. For each click on some player A, another player B is selected by object arrangement and the rule fires. This makes the ball move to B, and the system clicks B. Both A and B also move a small distance because they are shifted in the rule body pattern. The result is that players move about and seem to be passing the ball. Figure 12.16 shows a snapshot of the game in mid-play.

Figure 12.17 shows a swimming fish example. There are three rules: a fish turns down or up when a shell obstruct it and swims forward otherwise. Viscuit generates an animation makes the fish swim smoothly like A in the figure.

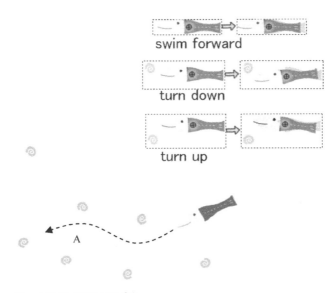

Figure 12.17. Swimming fish.

6. Matching and Generating Objects

In implementing Viscuit, our strategy is as follows:

1. Define a function rel2 that computes the arrangement similarity between a pair of objects and another pair of objects.
2. Use rel2 to define a function rel that computes the arrangement similarity between one group of objects and another group of objects.
3. Select the rule and its mapping between head objects and target objects that maximize the value of rel.
4. Fire the rule if normalized rel is higher than the threshold.
5. Remove and generate objects whose arrangement maximizes the value of rel.

We define an object as having four attributes: *kind*, *x*, *y*, and *direction*, where *kind* is the kind of object, *x* and *y* are real numbers that express a center position of the object, and *direction* is a real number between −180 and 180 that expresses the screen direction of the object.

The distance between the center of an object P and the center of an object Q is $|PQ|$, the relative direction from P to Q is rdir (P, Q), and the difference between the heading of P and the heading of Q is angle (P, Q) (see Figure 12.18).

The function rel2 (A, B, X, Y), which computes the similarity between relationship A and B and relationship X and Y is defined as

$$\text{rel2}\,(A, B, X, Y) = C_0\delta\,(|AB|, |XY|, W_0) + \xi C_1\delta\,(\text{rdir}\,(A, B), \text{rdir}\,(X, Y),$$
$$W_1) + \xi C_2\delta\,(\text{rdir}\,(A, B), \text{rdir}\,(X, Y), W_2)$$

where difference δ and weight ξ are

$$\delta\,(X, Y, Z) = e^{\frac{-(X-Y)^2}{W}}$$
$$\xi = 1 - e^{\frac{C_4}{(|AB|+|XY|+\varepsilon)^2}}$$

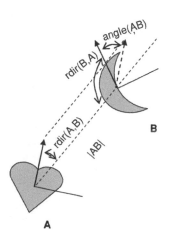 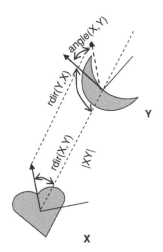

Figure 12.18. Similarity between two pairs.

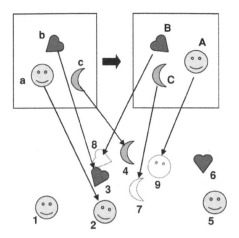

Figure 12.19. Matching and generating.

The $\delta(X, Y, W)$ becomes 1 if X and Y are the same, otherwise it is close to 0. ξ becomes 0 if A and B have the same position and X and Y have the same position, otherwise it is close to 1. Parameters C_j and W_i are constants for tuning the system behavior.

The first term of rel2 is a value showing how close distance $|AB|$ is to distance $|XY|$. The second term is one showing how close the relative direction rdir(A,B) is to the relative direction rdir(X,Y). The third term is one showing how close the relative direction rdir(B,A) is to the relative direction rdir(Y,X). rdir(A,B) is unstable if A and B are very close. Weight ξ is therefore multiplied in the second and third terms to stabilize rel2 behavior. The fourth term is a value showing how close angle(A,B) is to angle(X,Y).

Using rel2(A,B,X,Y), we define function rel, which computes the similarity between an object group A and another object group that is defined by mapping function map as

$$\text{rel}(A, \text{map}) = \sum_{i \in A, j \in A, i \neq j} w(i, j)\,\text{rel2}(i, j, \text{map}(i), \text{map}(j))$$

where $w(i, j)$ is a weight whose value changes according to whether object i and object j overlap or not. If they do, w has a higher value. This means overlapped objects get priority over other relationships.

Figure 12.19 shows an example of a fuzzy rewriting. There is a rule that includes head objects (a,b,c), body objects (A,B,C), and an event object on object a of the head. When a user clicks on object **2**, the system is activated. The system tries to match head objects and several objects on the target. Here, let some mapping mat be $2=\text{mat}(a)$, $3=\text{mat}(b)$ and $4=\text{mat}(c)$. The value of rel$(\{a, b, c\}, \text{mat})$, called the matching value of the rule, is computed by

$$\text{rel}(\{a, b, c\}, \text{mat}) = w(a, b)\,\text{rel2}(a, b, 2, 3) + w(b, c)\,\text{rel2}(b, c, 3, 4)$$
$$+ w(c, a)\,\text{rel2}(c, a, 4, 2)$$

The system looks for a mapping that maximizes the matching value of this rule. Let this matching value be the maximum matching value (MMV) of the rule and this mapping be the maximum mapping of the rule. For each available rule, the system selects one rule that has the maximum MMV. Whether the selected rule is fired or not depends on how similar the relationships are. MMV is normalized by percentage. A normalized MMV of 100% means the rule and the target have the same relationship exactly. If the normalized MMV of the selected rule is higher than the pre-defined threshold, the rule is fired.

After the rule is fired, objects corresponding to rule-head objects $\{2,3,4\}$ are deleted and other objects corresponding to rule body objects $\{7,8,9\}$ are generated. Let's denote the mapping gen corresponding to rule body objects and generated objects as $8=\mathrm{gen}(B)$, $9=\mathrm{gen}(A)$ and $7=\mathrm{gen}(C)$.

Arrangements of generated objects are computed by maximizing the following expression:

$$G\,(H,\,B,\,\mathrm{mat},\,\mathrm{gen}) = \sum_{i\in H, j\in B, i\neq j} [w\,(i,\,j)\,\mathrm{rel2}\,(i,\,j,\,\mathrm{mat}\,(i),\,\mathrm{gen}\,(j))]$$
$$+ \,\mathrm{rel}\,(B,\,\mathrm{gen})$$

This means the first term computes a value showing how similar the relationships of head-body objects are to those of deleted/generated objects. In this example, the first term is

$$w\,(a,\,A)\,\mathrm{rel2}\,(a,\,A,\,2,\,9)+w\,(b,\,B)\,\mathrm{rel2}\,(b,\,B,\,3,\,8)+w\,(c,\,C)\,\mathrm{rel2}\,(c,\,C,\,4,\,7)$$

The second term computes a value showing how similar the relationships of body objects are to those of generated objects. This is the reason for the swinging ball animation in Figure 12.13, there are opposite effects (a ball go upward or downward) from the first and second terms.

To simplify computing, if all attributes of a head object and a body are the same. The system doesn't touch it (i.e., doesn't delete and generate). A user interface support exists for this. When the user modifies a rule, a body object motion is snapped according to head objects location and angle.

7. Consideration

Viscuit inherits features of rewriting languages, so it has the basic mechanisms of computing. A sequence of click events has thread behavior, as already mentioned. Viscuit also has rule inheritance because object patterns can express inclusion relationships. For example, each rule in Figure 12.9 includes a rule in Figure 12.10. If we use these rule sets simultaneously, the rules of Figure 12.10 are used when the steering-wheel and stand overlap, and those of Figure 12.9 are used otherwise.

Figure 12.20 shows rewritings with several rules. In traditional rewriting, sometimes input areas of several rules with variables overlap like in d. In such a case, prioritizing the rules allows the system to control which rules should be fired. In this way, a complement

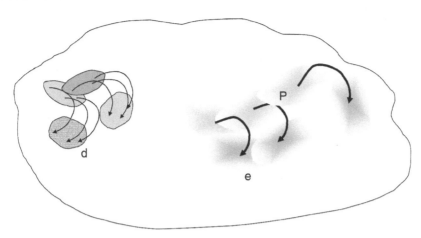

Figure 12.20. Rewriting with several rules.

of input areas can be expressed. On the other hand, in a fuzzy rewriting system, only fuzzy areas are expressed for each rule, so such a complement is difficult to express.

To express a complicated relationship by fuzzy rewriting, several rules (pairs of point) are given, like in **e**. These behave like a rule with variables (in Figure 12.4 b). This process is called Programming by Example (PBE). In a PBE system, if there are insufficient examples to generate rules (program), the system cannot proceed. However, in a fuzzy rewriting system, it is okay to do something, but the result becomes vague.

In Figure 12.10, although the steering-wheel direction is matched fuzzily, the generated car animation moves in only one of three discrete ways: straight, curving at a set radius to the right, or curving at a set radius to the left. On might ask how we could have the steering-wheel control the car's turn in fine increments. One area for future research is to consider how to merge rules when more than one has high similarity. This would allow linear approximations to be expressed, which would create smooth intermediate behaviors. This is an example of Figure 12.20 e.

The threshold of the fire ratio can be adjusted by the user. The user repeatedly issues an event but no rule fires, and the system automatically lowers the threshold until some rule will fire. On the other hand, if many rewritings occur whose ratio is much higher than the current threshold, then the threshold is automatically raised to avoid unwanted rewriting. An event generated by the system doesn't affect the threshold adjustment.

Viscuit can express a discrete computing like Stagecast. Figure 12.21 shows a logic circuit, an RS-flipflop, in the left-hand side and some of the rules in the right-hand side. For a two-input AND circuit, eight rules are needed. For example, if the inputs are 1–1 and the output is 0 then the output becomes 1 (rule A), and if the inputs are 1–1 and the output is 1 then do noting (rule B). Rule C and D are for pulse switches. When a user clicks a switch, a neighboring value changes from 1 to 0, waits a moment, and changes back to 1. To activate this simulation, a user must click each circuit. After that,

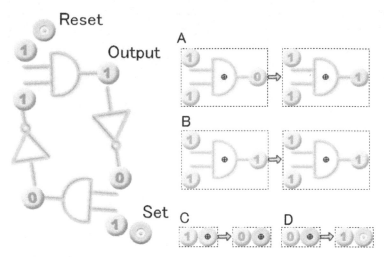

Figure 12.21. Logic circuit simulation.

the click mark in the body of each rule makes each circuit continue to update its state automatically.

An informal study of 40 children between age 6 and 10 was performed. The children were happy playing with the system for 30 minutes. In a post study interview, over 90% of the children said the system was interesting. They had no trouble creating rules, and experimented with them until they got the desired effect. However 25% of the children felt that Viscuit has user interface problems. We are improving the usability of the system based on this feedback. For example, Viscuit's technique for dragging objects allows both position and rotation to be changed with one mouse drag. Some children had trouble moving the objects without causing unintended rotation. This should be easy to fix by fine-tuning parameters that control such user interface behaviors.

8. Conclusion

We develop a new visual language, Viscuit, and its execution mechanism, fuzzy rewriting. Viscuit can treat an object as free-positioning and free-rotating. A rewriting rule is interpreted fuzzily, so a similar arrangement of objects can be rewritten as an appropriate arrangement. By continuous rewriting, Viscuit can express an animation whose local behavior is controlled by rules.

Demonstrations and the beta release of Viscuit can be found in http://www. viscuit.com.

Acknowledgment

We would like to thank Dr. Fusako Kusunoki and Miss Miyuki Kato of Tama Art University for their contribution to the visual design of Viscuit.

References

Arikan, O. and Forsyth, D.A. (2002). Interactive motion generation from examples. In: *Proceedings of the 29th Annual Conference on Computer Graphics and Interactive Techniques*, pp. 483–490.

Bell, B. and Lewis, C., ChemTrains: A Languages for Creating Behaving Pictures, VL' 93.

Cypher, A. and Smith D.C., KidSim: End User Programming of Simulations, CHI' 95.

Furnas, G.W., New Graphical Reasoning Models for Understanding Graphics Interfaces, CHI'95.

Harada, Y., Miyamoto, K., Onai V., VISPATCH: Graphical rule-based language controlled by user event, VL'97.

Kim, S. (1988). *Viewpoint: Toward a Computer for Visual Thinkers*. PhD thesis, Stanford University, 1988.

Repenning, A. and Ambach, J., Tactile Programming: A Unified Manipulation Paradigm Supporting Comprehension, Composition and Sharing, VL'96.

Yamamoto, K. (1996). 3D-Visulan: A 3D programming language for 3D applications. *Pacific Workshop on Distributed Multimedia Systems (DMS96)*, pp. 199–206.

Reference

Chapter 13

Breaking It Up: An Industrial Case Study of Component-Based Tailorable Software Design

GUNNAR STEVENS[1], GUNTER QUAISSER[2] and MARKUS KLANN[3]

[1] *Information Systems and New Media, University of Siegen, gunnar.stevens@uni-siegen.de*
[2] *Information Systems and New Media, University of Siegen, gunter.quaisser@uni-siegen.de*
[3] *Fraunhofer Institute for Applied Information Technology (FhG-FIT), markus.klann@fit.fraunhofer.de*

Abstract. Tailorability should enable users to fit computer systems to the application context. So tailoring options should be meaningful for end-users in their respective domains. This paper discusses how these design criteria can be realized within the technical framework of component-based tailorability. Component-based tailorability assumes that technical flexibility can be realized by allowing end-users to recompose components at runtime. To enable end-users to recompose components at runtime, the system has already appropriately broken down into modules at design time. Such a modularization of the software needs to meet two requirements: on the one hand it must provide sufficient flexibility with respect to the application context and on the other hand it must be understandable by the end-users. In an industrial case study we demonstrate how such a modularization can be established by applying ethnographic methods and choosing an appropriate design metaphor. The ethnographic study helps to capture tailoring needs of the application context. The design metaphor helps to break down software into components which are understandable by end-users. Subsequently, systematic interventions following an action research approach help to validate the design decisions.

Key words. component based software engineering, anticipation of change, tailorability, case study, ethnography

1. Introduction

There are different terms to describe systems that are changeable in the context of use. Such systems have been called *"tailorable,"* *"malleable,"* *"adaptable,"* and *"customizable."* From various angles explanations have been proposed to define what it means for a system to be tailorable.

From a technical perspective, a system can be called tailorable if during runtime end-users can modify specific aspects of its functionality in a persistent way. As stated by Stiemerling (2000) the tailorability of a system is then characterized by the design choices made for the following three elements:

- Representation of the tailorable system properties.
- Functionality to change this representation.
- Connection between the changes to this representation and the changes of the affected system properties.

Henry Lieberman et al. (eds.), End User Development, 269–294.

Going beyond this technical description of the meaning of tailorability, one has to consider the special characteristics of *tailoring* as being set in an application context: using Heideggerian[1] terminology, tailoring is carried out when a breakdown situation occurs while using a tool.[2] In such breakdown situations current system designs generally fall short in not supporting the transition from using a system to tailoring it. For example, Andersen (1999) criticized that "*(t)here is often too large a gap between the understanding developed during usage and the concepts needed for tailoring purposes, and users are often reluctant to accept this additional burden.*"[3]

Bentley and Dourish (1995) speak about the *customisation gulf* and observe that "*in traditional systems however, there is a gulf between the ability to customise aspects of process and functionality as opposed to interface and presentation.*"

In the literature one can find different requirements which tailorable systems need to fulfill. Here, we will only briefly describe two principles which are specifically relevant for the work presented here: (1) providing a gradual range of different levels of tailorability and (2) taking the application domain into account for system design.[4]

1.1. DIFFERENT LEVELS OF TAILORABILITY

Various authors have postulated, with slightly different motivations, a gradual range of tailoring techniques. For Gantt and Nardi (1992) the different tailoring levels are a way to support different kinds of users. The challenge of the system design is to provide tailoring levels that suit the competence of the users. Bentley and Dourish (1995) as well as Myers et al. (2001) demand a gentle slope of the required skills on one hand and the tailoring power of the tools on the other hand. Oberquelle (1994) provides a whole collection of tailoring techniques of different levels of complexity. Mørch (1997) presents a graduation of different tailoring levels. The purpose of these different levels is to overcome the distance between the presentation objects which are accessible for the user, and the underlying implementation. In his analysis Mørch (1997) distinguishes three different levels: *customisation, integration*, and *extension*. Mørch and Mehandjiev (2000) argue that a gradual range is a way to go easily from a user-, domain-, or task-oriented description to a system-oriented presentation.

---

[1] Cf. Winograd and Flores (1986) for a discussion of Heidegger in the context of designing computer artifacts.

[2] Breakdowns are specific to the situation of use. As Suchman (1987) demonstrated for help systems the situations cannot already be anticipated in the design phase. This situatedness of breakdowns is one of the reasons why it is so difficult to design the right tailoring options that should be provided by a system.

[3] Derived from this fact, Andersen (2002) postulates the visible computer as opposed to Donald Norman's vision of the invisible computer. In Andersen (1999), he has worked out the following principles for tailorable systems: (a) Experiences gained from using the system should be applicable for modifying and changing it. (b) The geometry of tailorable artifacts should be self-similar. (c) The Principle of Transparency: what goes on between two internal objects of the system is analogous to what goes on between the user and the interface objects. (d) The Principle of Tailorability: changing internal objects of the system is like changing the interface objects of the system.

[4] Regarding the customisation gulf, these principles are characterized by two interrelated problems.

> "*The first one is the level of customisation possible, and with most systems this lies above the functionality of the application, rather than within it. The second problem is the language of customisation, and traditional systems provide limited facilities to express customisation requirements using the skills users already have, requiring the learning of new languages to describe new system behaviours.*" (Bentley and Dourish, 1995).

1.2. THE ROLE OF THE APPLICATION DOMAIN IN DESIGNING TAILORING OPTIONS

Muller et al. (1997) classify tailoring in the context of participatory design. Tailorability is a way to integrate the user into the system design at a very late phase of the software lifecycle. The work of Mørch and Mehandjiev (2000) also is in line with this position. They regard the tailorability as a co-operation between developers and users which is obtained by the software system. Tailorable systems represent a special form of CSCW systems which are to be arranged in the "different time, different place"-corner of the Johansen matrix.[5] Especially Mørch deals with the idea of supporting this cooperation process through integration of design rationales into the artifacts.

Nardi (1993) postulates that end-user programming languages should include domain-specific elements.[6] Henderson and Kyng (1991) postulate systems where the users should have to use new mechanisms as little as possible to accomplish tailoring. Instead, they should accomplish modifications with familiar means.

In the following chapter, we will present the technical framework of component-based tailorability and our way to combine these general design concepts for building tailorable systems. Obviously, these concepts could be implemented in different ways. In particular, they leave open what aspects of the system should be tailorable. So we also discuss the issue of capturing the tailoring needs and their validation. As this is seldom examined in the literature,[7] we are going into these topics more deeply. In particular, we discuss these for building systems in dynamic environments. In the case study we will demonstrate how the general ideas can be applied. Section 2 ends with an introduction to the Tools & Materials (T&M) design approach. We need such an approach because our method of capturing the tailoring needs only gives hints as to what aspects should be tailorable but not how to design these aspects.

In Section 3, we describe a case study on building tailorable systems. The case study goes from the analysis of the application domain to finding a system architecture that is tailorable at the relevant point. We also explain how we evaluated our solution.

2. Concepts for Component-Based Tailorability

In the following we will introduce the framework of component-based tailorability on which the work presented in this paper is based (cf. Won et al., 2005). The core idea of component-based systems is to build systems by means of basic components that can be plugged together to form more complex components. Under a software-technical perspective the concept of component-based tailorability is a combination of this idea with the concept of dynamic software evolution. So users have the possibility to modify

---

[5] See Johansen (1988).

[6] The dual semiotic character of program text is also discussed by Dittrich (1997). On the one hand it is instructions for the computer; on the other it has a meaning for the programmer.

[7] Expections to this are the articles from Trigg (1992) and Kjaer and Madsen (1995). They illustrate how flexibility requirements were addressed in a development process by using participatory design techniques. But they do not show what this means for the system design and they do not present empirical data that allows the reader to check their statement.

the system by changing the component structures at run-time. Looking at component-based tailorability under this perspective one can distinguish three different levels of complexity:

Configuring a component. The configuration of an individual component is the easiest way to tailor a system, since this tailoring level offers the smallest complexity being limited to the so-called component slots only. Due to this restriction the tailoring action can be supported by providing special tailoring environments.[8] With the help of such special environments, it is much easier for the user to tailor these slots.

Changing the component composition. The changing of the composition allows for a more substantial adaptation. This level includes operations like inserting and deleting components, rewiring the components or building complex components. This level requires the user to understand not only the individual components but also their interactions.

Designing new components. This level increases the opportunities for tailoring since the user is not dependent on already existing components. However, when tailoring on this level the user has to understand the underlying programming language, the component model, and the implementation details.

The goal of component-based tailorability is to allow users to tailor a system to the domain context without designing new components. From a theoretical point of view this goal could be reached if the system was built up from basic components that simulate a programming language.[9] This way it is possible to simulate visual programming—as is exemplified by LabView—and tailoring activities could be performed by rewiring existing components. However, in this case the recomposition becomes an act of programming and it is not clear how writing a new component differs from restructuring the composition. To reduce the complexity in tailoring activities, the components have to be designed less generic and more application-specific. In this case the range of tailoring options is grounded in an adequately designed set of components. So the challenge in designing a system for component-based tailorability is to simultaneously fulfill the following requirements:

1. Find a decomposition that provides the needed flexibility.
2. Find a decomposition that is understandable to the end-user.

Since we want components to be meaningful in the application domain beyond pure (visual) programming, we have to restrict the flexibility of the software. In the best case we get a good fit between the restricted flexibility provided by the set of components and the one which is required by the domain context. Therefore, in

---

[8] For example, the JavaBean model allows the designer of a component to write also a bean customizer class for the component (cf. Hamilton, 1997).

[9] For example, one component represents a variable, another represents an IF-THEN ELSE structure or a loop structure.

designing a tailorable system one has to anticipate the tailoring needs of the application context.[10]

2.1. ANTICIPATING TAILORING NEEDS

Tailorability is no end in itself. In the traditional approach the primary goal of system design is to achieve a good fit between the systems functionality and requirements of the users without any need for tailoring. In order to achieve such a fit, one tries to capture the system requirements through a deep analysis of the application context. However, the dynamics of the environment and the situatedness of usage make it very difficult to exactly define the application context at design time. That is one of the reasons why tailorable systems are recurrently requested in the literature.

However, when designing tailorable systems one has to anticipate the tailoring needs. So actually there exists a design dilemma: The situatedness of the use and the dynamics of the environment make it necessary to build tailorable systems. However, at the same time these facts make it so difficult to provide the right dimensions of tailorability.

Although this dilemma cannot be fully solved, a requirements analysis can elicit those adjustments which seem to be most plausible in the future. Here we want to give some insights on capturing the tailoring needs. We follow the classification developed by Henderson and Kyng (1991). They find three different reasons of why systems do not fit to actual use situations: (a) diversity, (b) complexity, and (c) dynamics of the application domains.

As Henderson and Kyng make a retrospective analysis they give no hints on how these aspects can be analyzed prospectively. But this is necessary if the design should take such aspects into account.

In this section, we will mainly focus on the aspect of how to capture the dynamics of the application domain. We focus on this because this aspect is salient in our case study whereas the other aspects are of smaller importance. We had to anticipate those dynamics that were to be expected because of the transformation of work practices through the introduction of a collaboration support system and the resulting dynamics in the way the system was used. Whereas when designing tailorability for a well-established software product in a big yet stable market, probably the heterogeneity of customer wishes would be the more important factor. But in this aspect our case study did not yield sufficient results.

To capture and describe the dynamic processes during introduction and usage of IT systems one of the common points of reference is Gidden's theory of structurization. A prominent example is Orlikowski's investigation of appropriation and tailoring processes during the introduction of Lotus Notes (Orlikowski, 1992; Orlikowski and Hofman, 1997). Orlikowski distinguished three types of changes: anticipated, emergent, and opportunity-based changes. For Orlikowski anticipated changes are planned ahead

---

[10] It is always possible that in using the system tailoring wishes appear that cannot be granted by the existing composition. So a good decomposition should be easily extendable by new components. But this topic is outside the scope of this article.

of time and occur as intended. Emergent changes arise spontaneously out of local innovation. They are not originally anticipated or intended. The opportunity-based changes are not anticipated ahead of time but are introduced purposefully and intentionally during and in response of the change process (Orlikowski and Hofman, 1997).

The question, however, of how these dynamics can be dealt with in the design process and to what extent they can be anticipated at all is not solved by Orlikowski either. However, for design it is of crucial importance to what extent the dynamics can be discovered beforehand and used in a beneficial way. For this reason we propose here a slightly different typology for understanding transformation dynamics. It consists of the following three types:

1. deterministic transformation processes,
2. contingent transformation processes, and
3. inherently emergent transformation processes.

The transformation dynamics can then be understood as a superposition of these three types. The deterministic changes are those who can be fully anticipated. We call changes contingent when they stay in the confines of a predetermined frame of possibilities and thus at least these possibilities can be anticipated. In contrast, we will call dynamics inherently emergent if they arise through the appearance of new unforeseeable qualities and thus even the possibility of these dynamics cannot be anticipated.

Since the emergent dynamics are inaccessible to design, the design of tailorable systems has to identify the largest possible extent of those dynamics that are deterministic or contingent. The former can in principle be fully anticipated whereas at least the possibilities can be anticipated.

In the following we will expose the methodology that we have employed for identifying these dynamics. Our methodology is based on the assumption that empirical studies cannot only reveal the current practice but also the factors that contribute to the transformation of the practice. These factors can be intentional and actors can be consciously aware of them but partly they will also be latent in the sense that the actors are either not explicitly aware of them or that the actors hide them consciously for various reasons. Thus, these factors will have to be partly identified through analysis in the sense of an interpretative use of empirical findings.

These factors have to be identified first. Then, the deterministic and contingent parts of the transformational dynamics have to be evaluted. That way we can determine the resulting requirements for tailorability. For the precise identification of these dynamics ethnographical methods have to be used, in particular where actors are aware of them only latently (cf. Section 3.1).

The analysis of dynamics does not directly yield information on how to design the tailorability of the system. But it yields a reference that can be used to evaluate any design of tailorability. This reference identifies critical points in the design for which early feedback should be obtained from the different actors (cf. Section 3.2). Subsequently, a validation of the system should evaluate whether the identified dynamics can indeed be observed (cf. Section 3.3).

Whereas the analysis addresses the current practice with ethnographic methods, the use of the future system has to be evaluated as realistically as possible with the relevant users through participatory design techniques such as prototyping following an action research approach. The design and introduction of a system is always an intervention in the current work practice. Therefore, the designed artifact not only reflects the reality but also becomes a part of this reality. It has an independent meaning within the field of application from which emergent effects can potentially develop.

The simulation of future system's use has two purposes: One is to verify whether the forces identified in the preceding analysis are also relevant for the future system use, the other is to learn about emergent effects that only arise when using the system.

When simulating future use, the previously identified requirements for tailorability should again be evaluated explicitly. Here, the critical points have to be checked whether there are indeed contingencies that have to be taken into account for the tailorability of the system. Only if the practical test is explicitly in favor of flexibility or if the contingencies cannot be resolved in a consensual way or if it is clear that the result will not be stable, we can assume with certainty that at this point tailorability is required.

These dynamics can only be determined on a case-by-base basis. In our case study there were predominantly two factors that influenced the system design:

1. There was a discrepancy between the formally prescribed and the actual work practice. The introduction of the system will have an impact on this in a way that cannot be anticipated in advance (cf. Section 3.1.2).
2. There were irresolvable conflicts of interest among the different actors and organizations involved. These conflicts lead to fragile and only temporarily stable patterns of work practise. Due to this fragility the system should stay permanently tailorable at these points (cf. Section 3.1.3).

Before investigating these two factors in the context of our case study we will discuss them more generally.

The distinction between formally prescribed and actual work practice can be based on the work of Argyris and Schön's (1974) theory of action and their distinction between theory in use (what one actually does) and espoused theory (what one says). But we argue that beyond the cognitive level this concept must be extended to include the organizational level. On the organizational level one then has to differentiate between the image the organization holds of itself, e.g., by prescribing specific work processes, and its actual work practice. If there exists a discrepancy between these perspectives and this discrepancy is effected by the system to be designed, a certain degree of contingency results. This is due the fact that the new work practice will be established in a hardly predictable manner. If one takes just the formally prescribed perspective into account for the system design, it is rather likely that the actors will find pattern to work around the system. By contrary, if the system design takes only the actual work practice into account the system may become unacceptable for the organization's hierarchy. It also hinders the transformation of the working practice and some potentials of the technology get just poorly exploited. Consequently, system design should address both perspectives and offer possibilities for smooth transitions.

In order to be able to determine precisely the relation between formally prescribed and actual practice, the formal processes as well as the work practices must be investigated by means of ethnographic methods. On the basis of this data the domain logic of both the formally prescribed and actual practice needs to be reconstructed. An analysis can reveal why there is a discrepancy between "espoused theory" and "theory in use" and how their relationship may develop in the future. The analysis of these discrepancies defines a space of contingencies from which hints for the design of tailorability can be deduced.

The second factor relates to conflicting interests that have to be taken into account when designing a system. At first sight this aspect may appear as an instance of heterogeneous requirements as discussed by Henderson and Kyng (1991). However, these authors argue that within a heterogeneous group of users there will be different but yet stable use patterns of a given system. In our case, we deal with the question of how conflicting interests may lead to dynamic environments. In particular, the appropriation of collaboration systems will show dynamics that stem from users whose actions are influenced by tensions which result from different roles and interests. The permanent dynamics of system appropriation result in our case from human actors who have to find compromises in their work practise in order to satisfy conflicting interests. The resulting work practise may be stable for a certain period of time but can break up whenever any aspect of the environment changes.

On the perspective of design methodology, on needs to deal with both of the factors in a similar way. In particular, part of the discrepancy between formally prescribed and actual practice can be deduced from different interests that can be found in practice. Nonetheless, in the second case the empirical data will be analyzed from a somewhat different perspective. The goal is to determine the different interests within the field of application. On this basis one has to reason to what extent the actions of people can be deduced from the superposition of their interests. The actions are understood as establishing a temporarily stable equilibrium within the *net of forces* defined by the different interests. The definition of this *net of forces* allows assessing to what extent a stable compromise has evolved in the work practice. The analysis of the net allows in particular determining to what extent the future system challenges the existing practise and requires its renegotiation.

2.2. TOOLS & MATERIALS APPROACH

The last chapter discussed how to find requirements for a tailorable design. However, it does not give a constructive advice in the sense that it could guide the design of a set of components which is understandable for end users. We think that the concepts developed in the Tools & Materials (T&M) approach are a good starting point for this consideration.

The T&M approach was worked out in the nineties in the area of software engineering at the University of Hamburg (Budde and Züllighoven, 1990; Züllighoven, 1992; Züllighoven, 1998). The central concept of the Tools & Materials approach is to make use of the language of the application domain when designing computer systems.[11] The approach is strongly influenced by the idea of mutual learning between user and developer.[12] Züllighoven outlines the approach as follows:

> The central idea of the Tools & Materials approach is to take the objects and concepts of the application domain as the basis for the software model. This leads to a close correspondence between the application's specific structure of the concepts and the software architecture. The structural similarity has two decisive advantages: Users find the objects of their work and the concepts of their professional language represented in the computer system. Correspondingly, they can organize their work as they would normally do. Developers can relate software components and application concepts during changes on both the subject and the software level and thereby recognize mutual dependencies.
>
> *(Züllighoven, 1998).*[13]

The intended structural correspondence of the domain language and the software architecture makes the T&M approach interesting for component-based tailorability.[14] Finding meaningful concepts from the users' viewpoints is a challenge when designing tailorable systems.[15] By modeling the software, one has to rely on existing work tasks.

In the T&M approach a set of metaphors was developed which serves as an auxiliary means to analyze and categorize the work context. The most important metaphors are those of *tools, materials, automats,* and *work environment.* The metaphors guide the design process from a domain perspective "*at the critical interface between analysis and design*" (Züllighoven, 1998).[16]

3. Case Study

In Section 2 we formulated two requirements that tailorable systems should meet: they should provide the required level of flexibility and the provided flexibility should be understandable for the system's users. In the following we will discuss a case study in which we tried to satisfy these requirements. The discussion is divided into the following three parts: Section 3.1 establishes the context which defines the need for flexibility. Independent from this context the question of an appropriate tailorability can simply not be answered in any reasonable way. Against the background of this application context Section 3.2 then presents the research prototype. Section 3.3 finally explains how we validated the component-based system design.

---

[11] In German the approach is called "Werkzeug & Material" or abbreviated "WAM."

[12] See Floyd (1994) for the mutual learning and its importance for the field of software engineering. To this point, one also finds a relationship between the T&M approach and the view of the tailorability as a kind of cooperation between users and developers (Mørch and Mehandjiev, 2000).

[13] Originally quoted in German; translated by the authors.

[14] Regarding the value of using everyday expressions in program code compare (Dittrich, 1997).

[15] For the radical tailorability in the sense of Malone et al. (1995) the structural correspondence is so interesting because we think that this is a way of giving the user an intuitive entrance to the software architecture so that he or she can tailor the system to his or her needs more easily[0].

[16] Originally quoted in German; translated by the authors.

3.1. GATHERING THE TAILORING NEEDS

The field study deals with the cooperation between two engineering offices and a steel mill (Wulf et al., 1999). We have investigated the maintenance engineering processes of a major German steel mill in the Ruhr area over a period of three years. A goal was to improve the interorganizational cooperation between two engineering offices and the steel mill. The engineering offices are located 15 and 25 km from the steel mill. They do subcontractual work for the steel mill in the field of maintenance engineering, e.g., the construction and documentation of steel furnace components. A construction department inside the steel mill coordinates the planning, construction, and documentation processes and manages the contacts with external offices at the steel mill.

In order to meet the requirement for an appropriate design, the case study had in particular to analyze the relevant dynamics in this field of application. Such an analysis yields a system of reference against which to assess the flexibility that has to be provided for this application context. However, in order to avoid an unnecessary reduction of the design space, the analysis should not include concrete design implications. Instead, the internal logic of the work practice should be made understandable which determines the dynamics and thereby the requirements for adaptations.

One purpose of presenting our analysis is to allow for reflection and validation. However, there are yet two other reasons for presenting the results of the analysis. First, we want to illustrate the concepts developed in Section 2.1 by analyzing a concrete example. Second, we wanted to enable the reader to critically assess the conclusions we draw for our system architecture by providing a suitable description.

In the case study, we followed an action research framework called "Integrated Organization and Technology Development (OTD) (cf. Wulf and Rohde, 1995). The OTD process is characterized by a simultaneous development of the workplace, organizational, and technical systems, the management of (existing) conflicts by discursive means, and the participation of the organization members affected. The results presented in this paper come from a variety of different sources:

- Project workshops: During various workshops with members of the three organizations, organizational and technological interventions were discussed to improve the maintenance engineering process.
- Analysis of the work situation (semistructured interviews, workplace observations, and further questioning about special problem areas).
- Analysis of the available documents (the given documents and especially the drawings and system descriptions).
- System evaluation: The given archive systems were examined by means of a usability evaluation, especially with regard to task adequacy.

Especially in the early project phase discussions during the workshops with active participation of the involved people aimed at determining where problems occurred in their work practice. Subsequently, all participants of the workshop jointly thought about how the new possibilities of ICT could help with these problems. During the course of the project it turned out that external access to the steel mill's electronic archives became a crucial bottleneck. For this reason it was decided that external access to the drawings archive had to be facilitated. This can be seen as the conscious and planned part of transformation dynamics that was triggered by the project.

Further reflection about this decision revealed that it did not imply a specific requirement on how to design the system. At this moment a typical stage in such a transformation processes was reached since the involved actors seemed to assume that ICT should improve everything but actually should not change anything. In order to determine which solution was more applicable for this application context and to assess the contingencies connected to this transformation, a more thorough analysis of the cooperation practice between the steel mill and the external actors was conducted. In particular, the goal was to reconstruct the cooperative work practise for the access to the digital archive by collecting empirical data and interpreting it with respect to the planned transformation.

The analysis of the cooperation practice was conducted by the researchers using ethnographical methods. We did not feedback our empirical findings and interpretations into the organizations in a direct way. However, we used them to build mock ups and early prototypes. For this approach there were mainly three pragmatic reasons. Firstly, we cut short the interpretation of what was technically feasible based on our background knowledge as designers. Secondly, the actors simply did not have enough time to actively engage in browsing and interpreting the different types of material. Thirdly, at that time we did not want to explicitly engage the actors in openly discussing the underlying conflicts.

The interpretation by the researchers has to face a number of difficulties. For one, the (cooperative) practice is typically too engrained within the actors for them to be consciously aware of it. Furthermore, we decided that certain problems of the cooperative practice could not, being easily be talked about due to the micropolitics involved. Therefore, the work practice as described in interviews could not be used in an unreflected manner. The interviews needed to be triangulated with data from other sources, e.g., an analysis of documents in which the cooperative practice manifests itself (to the extent that these documents are available to the researchers).

Despite of all of these problems, external actors such as researchers, consultants or designers can play an important role in this requirements elicitation process. Since they are typically not involved in the cooperative practice and do not have to legitimize it, it is probably easier for them to identify the relevant social forces in the application context and to interpret them with respect to the contingencies of the subsequent use.

As stated in Section 2.1, one has to discover the discrepancies between the formally prescribed and actual work practice to identify the relevant forces influencing the dynamic transformation process. The other task was to discover the underlying (conflicting) interests of the different actors that may be affected by the system design. In the following we base our analysis on the material that we obtained following the methods described above.

3.1.1. *Process of Plant Maintenance: An Overview*

The Maintenance Engineering Department of the steel mill deals with repairing and improving the plant. Maintenance engineering is a distributed process in which different organizational units of the steel mill and of the external engineering offices are involved.

In general, the starting point for a maintenance order is the plant operator. When maintenance is necessary, the maintenance department of the plant operator asks the internal construction department for further processing. Depending on the type of order and the measures required, the transaction is handled internally or passed on to an external engineering office. An external order will be prepared and surveyed by the responsible contact person in the internal construction department. For this reason, the necessary drawings and documents are compiled from the archives and passed on to the engineering office for further processing.

After an external office finishes its engineering task, the internal construction department has to check it, include the modified and new drawings into the archives and initiate the production process of the required spare parts. While this is the general process scheme of maintenance engineering, various sorts of informal communication and self-organized variations of the process can be found.

In the early phases of the project the external engineering offices complained about insufficient task specification on the side of the steel mill and lacking electronic exchange of drawings between them and the steel mill. They suggested the opening of the electronic drawing archives at the steel mill to ease cooperation, whereas the attitude of the steel mill employees towards an external access to the archives was quite ambivalent. The attitude of the internal engineers could be described with the words: *The external service provider should be able to work independently but the steel mill has to keep the control.*

So we had to more closely investigate options for an external access to the archives.

3.1.2. *Work practice: Pattern of External Access*

With regard to the external engineers' access to the archives, we have to distinguish between the process prescribed by the steel mill's formal organization and the actual work practice. The division of labor prescribed by the formal organization of the steel mill may roughly be characterized as follows: The internal engineer in charge of handling a certain project finds all necessary drawings for the external service provider and passes them on to him. The external engineer works with the drawings, revises them when necessary, and later returns them to the steel mill. When the documentation of a project arrives in the mill, it undergoes a quality control carried out by the internal engineer.

In such an ideal case there is no need for an external access to the archives. In practice it often happens that additional drawings are requested continuously during the whole engineering process. The requests for the drawings are typically directed to the internal engineer responsible for the project. He normally checks the request, comments it, and passes it to the archives group. From the archives the drawings are picked up and later driven to the engineering offices.

However, it is often not easy to exactly specify the required drawings without having access to the archives. So the external engineers often drive to the mill and search the drawing archives together with an employee of the archives group or by themselves.

The internal engineers often try to limit their efforts to the absolutely necessary when passing over the documents. However, formally it is part of their task to decide whether a drawing should be handed over to an external engineering office. The dilemma for the internal construction department may be depicted as follows: If an external service provider contacts the archives directly, the internal construction department has less work. However, if problems arise, the internal department is responsible without being sufficiently involved. In certain cases they even lose control at the end of a project. Occasionally, the external office delivers the drawing directly to the archives without involving the construction department. In this case, they may not even become aware of the fact that something has been changed.

3.1.3. *Interorganizational Relationship: Between Competition and Cooperation*

More than 10 years ago, the steel mill had started to outsource an increasing amount of work in maintenance engineering. The outsourcing process has led to an increased uncertainty among the steel mill's maintenance engineers and has also changed the function of the internal construction department. Toward the external offices, it takes different roles which are partly conflicting. Especially the roles of the administrator of the orders, of the competing participant in the market, and of the security guard have to be mentioned here. In this sense, the internal construction department sees the external engineering offices not only as contractors but also as a competing actor. As the engineering offices work also for regional and global competing steel mills, in some cases they may even be seen as potential spies.

As competition is very fierce on the world market of steel, small technological innovations may lead to important competitive advantages. There is an unwritten rule that external service providers would not pass technological innovations from one client to another. However, the remaining risk increases if the external service providers could access the database in an unrestricted way. So there always exist identical as well as diverging interests between the internal and the external engineering organizations.

Based on these findings, the key requirement in this case study was to design flexible control mechanisms to access the drawings archive. We derived an extended model of access control resulting from these findings. These mechanisms allow restricting operations on shared data while they take place or even after they took place.[17] Based on this model we built a system which allows the external engineering offices to access the electronic drawings archives of the steel mill.

---

[17] For a further discussion of these models see Stevens (2002) and (Stevens and Wulf, 2002).

3.2. DESIGNING AN APPROPRIATE SET OF COMPONENTS

The analysis of the work context provides requirements for a tailorable design. However, it does not provide a design solution. We think that the T&M approach supplements our approach in capturing tailoring needs. The T&M approach guided the process of breaking a software up into components. Using the T&M approach the design of the software architecture is based on the concepts and the language of the domain. This can promote the understanding of the end-users. In our case, we applied the P.O.-box metaphor (see Section 3.2.2) which was developed in the context of the T&M approach. The resulting set of components was created by the designers. Afterwards, it was discussed with the end-users.[18]

3.2.1. *FREEVOLVE Platform*

The FREEVOLVE approach[19] defines a framework for the design of component-based tailorable systems.

Within the framework there are two types of components called FlexiBeans: atomic (also basic or implemented) and abstract components. Atomic components are written in Java and they are similar to JavaBeans. An implementation of a FlexiBean has to follow a number of coding conventions. These conventions are described by the FlexiBean model.

For its environment an atomic component consists of a set of parameters and a set of ports. The parameters are used to configure the component. By using the ports one can connect a component with other components. In the FlexiBean model there are two types of ports for the exchange of data between components: events (push-mechanism) and shared objects (pull-mechanism). Events allow components to notify state changes to other components. The idea behind the shared objects was to introduce something like shared variables into the FlexiBean Model (Stiemerling, 2000, p. 117)). The ports of the components are named and typed. They also have a polarity. The polarity of the port depending on either the service (events or shared object) is provided or requested by the component. When visualizing components in this paper (see Figure 13.1), we mark the event sources with a filled circle and the event-receiver with an empty circle. The provider of a shared object is marked with a filled square, the recipient of a shared object with an empty square. Only ports of the same type but with opposite polarity can be connected during runtime.

The atomic components form the basic modules for assembly. Once a component is defined, abstract components can be used to build compositions of higher levels of complexity. Hereby, an abstract component consists of a set of inner components and

---

[18] In the case study the decomposition was created by the designer and afterward, it was discussed with the end-users. We agree with the comments of Catherine Letondal that it could be interesting to ask the users to build lo-fi prototypes based on their own metaphors or transitive objects. A study of such prototypes can help to get a deeper understanding of the concept of domain-oriented system architectures.

[19] This section is a very brief introduction into FREEVOLVE. A more detailed introduction is given by the Ph.D. thesis of Stiemerling (2000) and Won et al. (2005).

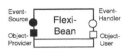

The circles and boxes are ports through which the components interact with each other. An instance of a component can be named individually to ease users' understanding.

Figure 13.1. Graphical representation of a FlexiBean.

their connections. Ports as parameters of inner components can be exported. For the environment an abstract component exists through its set of parameters and ports, so it looks just like an atomic component. This feature allows the building of hierarchical component structures.

The FREEVOLVE platform allows instantiation of new components, the (re)configuration of components and the (re)wiring of connections between the components at runtime.

3.2.2. *P.O.-box Metaphor*

In this section we will introduce the concept of the P.O.-box metaphor. Applying this metaphor we were able to model a system that allows an external access to the electronic drawings archive. The system design reflects the actual work practice in the relationship between the internal department and the external engineers.

Martina Wulf (1995) examined the meaning of P.O.-boxes in the area of cooperative work. She found out that P.O.-boxes are used in practice as a coordination medium. However, the meaning of the P.O.-box depends on its location and its use. She distinguishes public and private P.O.-boxes. An example of public P.O.-boxes are the generally accessible open mailboxes in a main hall of a newspaper editorial office described by (Stiemerling and Wulf, 2000). Their functionality is strongly related to the fact that the access to the box is visible to other people. Examples of private P.O.-boxes are boxes which are typically located on desktops. They are used to organize work. The designation of the P.O.-box transports the intended usage into the working context.[20] Finally, M. Wulf also differentiates between the input and the output type of a box.[21]

For our case, we enhanced the concept of the P.O.-box by the idea of sorters. Sorters have some similarities with e-mail filters. In the context of tailorability e-mail filters have been analyzed by Mackay (1990). Investigating the InfoLens system, she shows how users tailored the system in a not anticipated way by means of electronic P.O.-boxes and IF-THEN rules.[22] However, the system context is different from our case study.

---

[20] For example, if a sorter is called "Allow access?", it has a different meaning as if it is called "Deny access?", although the underlying composition is the same. See also De Souza and Barbosa (in this volume) and their concept of changes to lexical items.

[21] The distinction of an input and output type has the advantage that one can compose a system where only the input type of a P.O.-box is accessible. In this case P.O.-box works like a mailbox in which anyone can throw something in, but has no way to know its contents.

[22] By using the example of mail filters she shows that it is difficult to indicate general conditions when the filters should be applied but in the concrete situation there is no problem for the users to decide whether a filter should be used or not.

InfoLens deals with semistructured e-mail messages while we had to control the access
to shared resources.

3.2.3. *Applying the P.O.-box Metaphor*

The envisaged systems should on the one hand allow the external engineers to access
the internal drawings archive. But on the other hand, the internal department should
have control over this access. By using the FREEVOLVE framework the flexibility can
mainly be provided by the customization of individual components (level one) and by
rewiring the established component structure (level two).

The main challenge for the design process was to reify the abstract concept of accessing the drawings archive. This reification should be reflected in the system architecture
in a way that facilitates the end user to tailor the system. Based on the work of M.
Wulf the P.O.-box metaphor was taken as a starting point for the system design. The
P.O.-box metaphor helps us to tie in with the existing work practice where drawings are
requested and sent via e-mail.

In some sense the P.O.-box metaphor constitutes the identity of system design (c.f De
Souza and Barbosa, 2005). So, in the next step we must find components that provide
the flexibility for controlling the access on the one hand, but also follow the *identity*[23]
given by the P.O.-box metaphor on the other hand.

The system should work as follows: The external engineer initiates a search in
the electronic archives by writing an inquiry with the help of a special mail client.
Then, he sends it to a worker of the steel mill's internal construction department. The
workers of the internal department are equipped with a special mail client called ADOS-
X.[24] Depending upon the configuration of this program the inquiry will be answered
automatically or it will be put in a special P.O.-box. From this P.O.-box the answer to
the inquiry has to be triggered manually by the internal department.

Figure 13.2 shows a snapshot of the mail client for the internal department. The
inquiry looks basically like an e-mail. However, the users do not enter free text but fill
in a special search form. The appearance of the search form simulates the look and feel
of the input masks of the ADOS database's search tool which is used typically by the
engineers.

3.2.4. *System Architecture*

The design of the different components is guided mostly by the interaction of the
P.O-.boxes where inquiries are stored and by the sorters, which pass on the inquiries
automatically (see Table 13.1).

---

[23] Cf. De Souza and Barbosa (in this volume).

[24] The name of the electronic design archive is ADOS. X stands here for eXternal and/or eXtension. The mail
clients for the internal and external workers are mostly based on the same atomic components, but here we
concentrate on the internal department only.

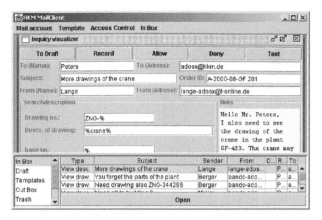

Figure 13.2. Interface of the realized prototype mail client for the internal engineer.

Table 13.1. Basic components of ADOS-X

Component	Description
Mail box	**Mailbox**: The mailbox is the residence for documents. Documents may be put in via the *in*-port or taken out via the *out*-port. If the state of the mailbox changes, an event is sent via the *trigger*-port. The *see*-port allows introspection via a *visualizer* component.
Sorter	**Sorter**: The sorter component has one entrance and two exits which can be linked to a mailbox. According to the setting of the sorter, a document is transported from the *in*-port to the *yes*-port or to the *no*-port. It is activated via the *trigger*-port.
Copy machine	**Copy machine**: The copy machine has one entrance and two exits which can be linked to mailboxes. The incoming message is transported from the *in*-port to the *original*-port. A copy is made and transported to the *copy*-port. The copy machine is activated via the *trigger*-entrance.
Visualizer	**Visualizer**: The visualizer allows viewing the content of a mailbox. It is activated via the *trigger*-port. The mailbox is connected via the *in*-port.[25]
ADOS	**ADOS**: The ADOS component provides the connection to the database. The mailbox containing the query is connected to the *in*-port. The component transmits the query to the database, receives the search results, and transfers them to the *out*-port. The component is activated via the *trigger*-port.
Receive automat / **Send automat**	**Receive- and Send automat**: These components are used to connect the mailbox with a mail server. The receive automat realizes a POP3 connection. One can configure the frequency at which the automat looks for new mail on the server. The send automat uses the SMTP protocol for communicating with the mail server. It is activated via the *trigger*-port.
Back	**Back**: The back (or retour) component is technically motivated. It is responsible for the swapping of the reverse receiver address and the sender address, so that inquiries can automatically be sent back to the sender. The transport of inquiries from the *in*- to the *out*-port by swapping the addresses at the same time will be trigged by an event through the *trigger* port.

---

[25] For the sake of simplicity, we left out some of the components which implement aspects of the visualization.

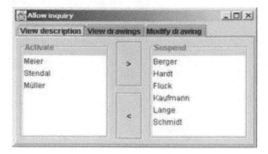

Figure 13.3. Interface for the configuration of a sorter component.

The P.O.-boxes are the places where inquiry mails reside. The flow through the P.O.-boxes can be realized by the sorters. By configuring the sorter one can decide which inquiries are to be answered automatically and which are not. The inquiries at the *in*-port are, depending on the configuration, passed on to the *yes*- and/or the *no*-Port. In a certain way this represents something like a traditional access control system. The access control strategy is expressed by the configuration of the sorter. In the current system version the configuration possibilities are limited to the most important criteria of the application field. The sorter is tailored by a special interface that is represented in Figure 13.3.

If a user wants to adjust a sorter, he or she first selects the persons to be granted access. The access is generally denied until it is explicitly permitted. Figure 13.3 shows how the access to read drawing descriptions can be granted (operation "view descriptions"). By clicking the "<"-button, a user can be moved to the list of those who have permission to view the describing attributes. Such a permission can be revoked by selecting a user and pushing the ">"-button.

The copy machine component was used to model access logging. The whole interaction with the inquiries and the user was realized by the (big) visualizer component. The link to the legacy system, ADOS, was hidden in the ADOS-component. The receive- and the send-automat provide a communication with a mail server. The back component was introduced primary for technical reasons.

Based on these atomic components we can now build a system that provides different access mechanisms. Figure 13.4 shows a default composition. We will describe the functionality of the default composition by showing different use scenarios that are provided by the composition.

First case: "access is manually authorized." ADOS-X can be configured in a way that any query of the external engineers needs to be authorized manually. For this purpose the "*Is this inquiry allowed to access ADOS?*"-sorter has to be tailored in a way that it moves the incoming documents to the "no"-exit. This means that all queries end up in the P.O.-box "*Inquiries not allowed.*" The internal engineer can now view these queries via the "*Not allowed*"-visualizer. The visualizer offers options for a manual

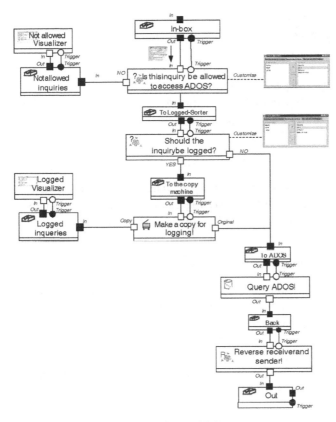

Figure 13.4. Default composition of an ADOS-X system.

treatment of the query such as forwarding it to ADOS, editing it, or sending it back to the external engineers. These options are not represented in Figure 13.4 but require a manual authorization of any attempt to access ADOS. As it corresponds to the actual practice, we have chosen ADOS-X as a standard configuration.

Second case: "access is allowed but electronically logged." The internal engineers can also configure the system to carry out all queries automatically but log them. In this case the *"Should the inquiry be logged?"*-Sorter must be configured in a way that it moves the queries to the *yes*-exit. Queries will take the way via the *"Copy-machine"*-component (*"Make a copy for logging!"*). This component copies the query and moves the copies via the *copy*-exit to the mailbox *"Logged inquiry."* A visualizer allows the internal engineers to check the queries later on. The original query is moved via the *original*-exit to the mailbox *"To ADOS."* Then the ADOS-component (*"Query ADOS!"*) processes the query and forwards the search results to the P.O.-box component *"Reverse receiver and sender!,"* prepares the inquiry for sending it back to the sender, and puts it in the *"Out"*-box. From this P.O.-box the research results could be sent back via e-mail to the external engineering office which posted the query.[26] As the queries of the external engineers are logged they are available for a subsequent check by the internal engineers.

Third case: "access is allowed." The deviation via the *"Copy-machine"*-component (*"Make a copy!"*) may be cut short by adjusting the *"Should the inquiry be logged?"*-sorter for documents accordingly. Via the *no*-exit, queries of certain engineers are now sent directly to the *"Query-ADOS!"*-component.

3.3. EVALUATING THE DESIGN FOR TAILORABILITY

The evaluation of the system has a twofold goal. First, we want to validate whether the system provides sufficient flexibility regarding the application context.[27] The second goal was to evaluate whether its tailorability is understandable by the end-users.

3.3.1. *Validation of the Tailoring Needs*

As mentioned in Section 2.1 the first goal is to validate the designed system against the identified dynamics. So one has to study the reactions of the different parties to the concrete system implementation and has to analyze what this means for the dynamics in the future. In particular, one has to check whether the system's use will generate more emergent needs for flexibility. We wanted to evaluate how the tailoring options were used in negotiation processes between the different actors. We were particularly interested in how the ambivalence between competition and cooperation would be reflected during system use.

Equipped with a paper mock-up that looks like the set of components presented in Figure 104, we evaluated our decomposition of the system with the construction department and external service provider. We explained the functionality of the different components and demonstrated various access modes by means of an example inquiry. While doing so, we ask the different actors to judge the technical options.

We specially asked the construction department to classify which documents are critical, not so critical or uncritical. We wanted to find out which access control strategy is suitable for the internal department. The internal engineers mentioned some criteria to characterize whether access to a document should be granted. They also stated that access to the meta-data is not problematic. Moreover, the external engineers should not be allowed to change the drawing archive without an explicit permission. That way they provided us with information to come up with a classification which can be used to define an access control strategy. The internal engineers emphasized that it will be

---

[26] In the composition you can see no receive automat or send automat, because the inbox and outbox of the composition should not directly be connected to a mail server. This is because the composition can be part of an enterprise solution, as mentioned in Stevens (2002).

[27] As Lindeberg and Dittrich (2003) rightly observe, there is not only one application context but design has to deal with different contexts. This is also true for the evaluation of the design. Correspondingly, one has to consider to what context an evaluation refers.

most important that the final control over the access remained with them. However, it did not become clear which access strategy they will exactly use in the future.

We also discussed the functionality of the paper mock-up with an engineer from an external service provider. During the discussion he stated that he is interested in getting drawings but additionally in the meta-data of the drawings. A direct reading access to the archive would be most important to simplify his work. However, he did not ask for write access rights because he feared to corrupt the database of the steel mill accidentally.

To evaluate the case of group-effective tailorability we presented the prototype in a live demonstration on a workshop in which different departments of the steel mill and the external engineering companies participated. The workshop was a kind of controlled intervention. We wanted to see how the different parties reacted towards the access strategies which were offered by the prototype. We demonstrated the functionality by writing fictitious inquiries and indicated how they would be handled by the prototype. We used the different scenarios mentioned in Section 3.2.4 to explain how to tailor the prototype by adjusting different sorters. In the following discussion the different interests became manifest with regard to the configuration of the access mechanisms. A representative of the external office criticized the options to manually authorize each access to a document. Such a policy would not correspond to the initially constituted agreements. An actor from the internal department defended this access mode by stating that control should remain with the internal department. The logged access history which is a mediating instance in some sense was not rejected by any of the parties. However, it was not taken up as a possible compromise solution either.

Following the assumption of a stable environment, the evaluation was a failure as it could not solve the contingencies. As a result of this, one can only make vague prognoses about the kind of access control strategy that will be used in practice. However, under the assumption of dynamic and heterogeneous environments one can find important hints within the evaluation. These hints relate to inherent issues of uncertainty inside the application domain. Following this interpretation, the evaluation validates the hypothesis that access control policies are critical issues within the field of application. Moreover, they seem to be negotiated in a concrete situation and cannot be predefined by the designers.

Since the research prototype was not introduced into practice, the question remains whether the system offered already sufficient flexibility or whether further access mechanisms would have to be implemented. The decision to stop the development of the prototype was due to the replacement of the existing electronic drawing archive by a solution from SAP. This change in the steel mill's IT strategy happened at the end of the project. The decision was taken at top management which was not involved in the project. For our design process it was an emergent change that could not be anticipated beforehand.

So, the critical reader might agree with our arguments in favor of flexible tools for access control. However, it is not proven that our solution is the best one. So we will discuss some other solutions theoretically.

As the case study is about access control, one may think that a traditional access control strategy would be a good solution. However, the analysis and the evaluation show that the internal department does not just want to grant or deny an access to an object. An important aspect of the given access control policy was the information of internal engineers about what was going on. Such an awareness is not supported by the traditional implementations of access control.

From the perspective of the internal engineering department one can argue that a solution which just allows for manual access control is sufficient (as long as the additional work resulting from the manual control is accepted by their organization). Although such a system makes the control work of the internal department more efficient, it would be suboptimal from the perspective of the external engineer. Indeed at this point one does not know whether any other control mechanisms would be accepted by the internal department. This question can only be answered in practice. However, if the system had just implemented a manual control mechanism, it doesn't support the practice to transform their control strategy.

While taking all factors of uncertainty into account, one can conclude that the given solution may be not optimal but a better solution than existing approaches to access control.

3.3.2. Evaluation of the Usability of the Set of Components

The second goal was to evaluate whether the set of components was understandable. Under a methodical perspective this evaluation is much easier since one does not need to anticipate future developments. Once it is clear what should become tailorable particular tailoring options can be evaluated by means of usability tests.

We carried out several tests within a small group of actors ($n = 5$) who represented different levels of qualification.[28] The goal of these tests was to check whether the meaning of the individual components was understandable to the users. Applying thinking aloud technique, we asked the participants to carry out some tasks. The duration of the test was an hour per subject. Although our test did not provide any statistical significance,[29] the analysis provided, as (Nielsen, 1993) shows, a good evaluation of the component's usability.

Although some of the test persons did not understand the technical details between shared objects and events, but nevertheless these test persons solved the tailoring tasks. The insights resulting from these tests indicate that the users are guided by every day's meanings of the component names and they interpret the components from the perspective of the tailoring task. For example, one of the test persons compared the mechanism of the copy machine component with the functions of an ordinary copy machine.

---

[28] The test persons were one computer science student, three students from other disciplines, and one person who called himself/herself a computer novice.

[29] Besides the missing of a big n that prevents representative results (n was only five test persons), the more principal problem was to prepare "representative" test exercises.

The summing up of the evaluation indicates that the users understand the components and the composition in general. For more details of the evaluation see (Stevens, 2002).

4. Conclusion

Tailoring activities are embedded in the use of a system. A central problem discussed in the literature is how to support a switch between use and tailoring. The state of the art identified a gap between domain-oriented user interface and a technically oriented system architecture. This gap is one of the obstacles that hinder a smooth transition. The state of the art suggests two approaches to design this switch: providing a range of tailoring options with a gentle slope of complexity and designing these tailoring options based on the application context.

When implementing these approaches, our experience indicates that a specific preparatory activity is required. This activity yields an analysis of the kind and scope of tailorability that has to be realized within the subsequent system. A domain-specific requirement analysis of tailoring needs is necessary to solve the trade-off tailorability and complexity which means that systems cannot be developed to be arbitrarily tailorable and of manageable complexity at the same time.

Since an analysis of tailoring needs is rarely discussed in the literature, we explicitly addressed the issues why tailorability is requested and how it can be taken into account in requirement analysis. Due to the set-up in our case study, we focussed on capturing the dynamic aspects of our application domain and on conclusions for system design. The resulting dynamic transformation processes can be analyzed as to their deterministic, contingent, and emergent facets. For the design of tailorable systems, understanding the contingent facets is particularly helpful (cf. Section 2.1).

In the case study the contingent dynamics were mostly due to contradictory social forces within the application domains. In the analysis we identified the discrepancy between formally prescribed and actual work practice and the different interests and roles of the actors. These forces produced a field of contingent usage. Ideally, there should be a close fit between the system flexibility and the dynamically changing requirements of use.

Even though these forces are likely to be different for other application domains, the case study yields as a general result that the design of tailorable systems requires a change of perspective in requirement analysis. Normally, the analysis examines the actual practice under the condition of completeness and consistency. However, such an approach is blind towards contradictions within the given practice. In order to assess the dynamics of an application domain, one must focus on the issues of conflict, diverging perspectives, and open questions. This is why the interests of the different actors and parties involved have to be investigated using ethnographical methods. The different interests form a field of forces from which the dynamics of the application area can be at least partially deduced.

Even though the research prototype was finally not put into practice and long-term studies could therefore not be conducted, the evaluation of the prototype suggests nonetheless that the dynamics identified during the analysis indeed lead to contingent usage requirements. The general goal of capturing and analyzing transformation dynamics in application domains and deducing consequences for the design and use of tailorable systems remains an open research challenge. It requires further empirical studies and a methodology that allows capturing such processes adequately. This case study only represents a first step in this direction.

Ethnographic studies are important since they help to find out what should be flexible and contextualize the process of designing for tailorability. To grasp the provided tailorability users need to understand the system architecture at a sufficient level. So, the tailorable parts of the system should be meaningful to end-users in their application domain. Knowing the world of the end-users helps designers to integrate the domain context into the system architecture.

A constructive method for building such meaningful components is the T&M approach developed in the context of the discourse on participatory design. The aim of the approach is to achieve a structural correspondence between the application domain and the system architecture.

We have shown how the T&M approach can be used to design component based tailorability in a case of access control. The validation of the system has demonstrated that the system was flexible at a point which was critical for the domain context. We also have shown that the flexibility goes beyond the standard access control mechanism. Further evaluations indicated that this modularization of the software can be understood by end-users.

However, it remains an open question if there is always a correspondence between the tailoring needs—coming up from the dynamics of the application domain—and a modularization that provides such flexibility in the terms of the user. In particular, this will be a problem if the abstract transformation dynamics cannot be reified by a metaphor that is known in the application context.

References

Andersen, P.B. (1999). Elastic interfaces. Maritime instrumentation as an example. In: *Proceedings of the CSAPC'99*, Valenciennes, France.

Andersen, P.B. (2002). The visible computer. http://www.cs.auc.dk/~pba/Preprints/NordiCHI.pdf (1.9.2003).

Argyris, M. and Schön, D. (1974). *Theory in Practice. Increasing Professional Effectiveness*. San Francisco: Jossey-Bass.

Bentley, R. and Dourish, P. (1995). Medium versus mechanism: Supporting collaboration through customisation. In: *Proceedings of ECSCW'95*, Stockholm, Sweden: Kluwer Academic Publishers.

Budde, R. and Züllighoven, H. (1990). Software-Werkzeuge in einer Programmierwerkstatt. In: *Berichte der GMD 182*.

De Souza, C.S. and Barbosa, S. (2005). A semiotic framing for end user development. In: H. Lieberman, F. Paternò and V. Wulf (eds.), *End User Development*, Dordrecht, Netherlands: Springer, pp. 395–420.

Dittrich, Y. (1997). *Computer Anwendungen und sprachlicher Kontext. Zu den Wechselwirkungen zwischen normaler und formaler Sprache bei Einsatz und Entwicklung von Software.* Frankfurt: Peter Lang.

Floyd, C. (1994). Software Engineering—und dann? *Informatik Spektrum* **17**, 29–37.

Gantt, M. and Nardi, B.A.C. (1992). Gardeners and gurus: Patterns of cooperation among CAD users. In: *Proceedings of CHI '92 Human factors in Computing Systems*, Monterey, CA: ACM Press.

Hamilton, G. (1997). Java Beans™ version 1.01. Technical Specification Sun, Microsystems, Palo Alto, Kalifornien, **24**.

Henderson, A. and Kyng, M. (1991). There's no place like home. Continuing design in use. *Design at Work.* Hillsdale: Lawrence Erlbaum Associates, pp. 219–240.

Johansen, R. (1988). Current user approaches to groupware. In: R. Johansen (ed.), *Groupware.* New York: Freepress, pp. 12–44.

Kjaer, A. and Madsen, K.H. (1995). Participatory analysis pf flexibility. *Communication of the ACM* **38**(5), 53–60.

Lindeberg, O. and Dittrich, Y. (2003). System design as artful integration of different contexts. In: *3rd Conference for the Promotion of Research in IT at New Universities and University of Colleges*, Sweden: Visby.

Mackay, W. (1990). *Users and Customizable Software: A Co-Adaptive Phenomenon.* Ph.D.-Thesis. Boston, MA: MIT.

Malone, T.W., Lai, K.Y. and Fry, C. (1995), Experiment with oval: A radically tailorable tool for cooperative work. ACM Transactions on Information Systems **13**(2), pp. 177–205.

Mørch, A. (1997). Three levels of end-user tailoring: Customization, integration and extension. *Computers and Design in Context.* Cambridge, MA: MIT Press, pp. 51–76.

Mørch, A. and Mehandjiev, N. (2000). Tailoring as collaboration: The mediating role of multiple representations and application units. *Journal of Computer Supported Cooperative Work (JCSCW)* **9**(1), 75–100.

Muller, M., J. Haslwanter, et al. (1997). Participatory practices in the software lifecycle. *Handbook of Human–Computer Interaction.* Amsterdam, Netherlands: Elsevier, pp. 255–313.

Myers, B., S. Hudson, et al. (2001). Past, present and future of user interface software tools. *HCI In the New Millennium.* ACM Press, Addison-Wesley, pp. 213–233.

Nardi, B.A. (1993). *A Small Matter of Programming—Perspectives on End User Computing.* Cambridge: MIT-Press.

Nielsen, J. (1993). *Usability Engineering.* New York: Academic Press.

Oberquelle, H. (1994). Situationsbedingte und benutzerorientierte Anpassbarkeit von Groupware. In: A. Hartmann, T. Herrmann, M. Rohde and V. Wulf (eds.), *Menschengerechte Groupware— Software-ergonomische Gestaltung und partizipative Umsetzung.* Stuttgart: Teubner, pp. 31–50.

Orlikowski, W.J. (1992). Learning from notes: Organizational issues in groupware implementation. In: *Proceedings of the 1992 ACM Conference on Computer-Supported Cooperative Work*, pp. 362–369.

Orlikowski, W.J. and Hofman, J.D. (1997). An improvisational model for change management: The case of groupware technologies. *Sloan Management Review*, **38**(2), 11–22.

Stevens, G. (2002). *Komponentenbasierte Anpassbarkeit—FlexiBean zur Realisierung einer erweiterten Zugriffskontrolle.* Diploma-Thesis. Institut für Informatik III. Bonn, Universität Bonn.

Stevens, G. and Wulf, V. (2002). A new dimension in access control: Studying maintenance engineering across organizational boundaries. In: *Proceedings of the 2002 ACM Conference on Computer Supported Cooperative Work*, New Orleans: ACM Press, pp. 196–205.

Stiemerling, O. (2000). *Component-based tailorability.* Ph.D.-Thesis, Mathematisch-Naturwissenschaftlichen Fakultät. Bonn: Universität Bonn.

Stiemerling, O. and Wulf, V. (2000). Beyond 'yes or no'—extending access control groupware with awareness and negotiation. *Group Decision and Negotiation* **9**, 221–235.

Suchman, L. (1987). *Plans and Situated Action*. Cambridge: Cambridge University Press.

Trigg, R. (1992). Participatory design meets the MOP: Accountability in the design of tailorable computer systems. In: *Proceedings of the 15th IRIS*, Larkollen, Norway.

Winograd, T. and Flores, F. (1986). *Understanding Computers and Cognition: A New Foundation for Design*. Norwood, NJ: Ablex.

Won, M., Stiemerling, O. and Wulf, V. (in this volume). Ccomponent-based approaches to tailorable systems. In: H. Lieberman, F. Paternò and V. Wulf (eds.), *End User Development*, Dordrecht, Netherlands: Springer, pp. 115–142.

Wulf, M. (1995). *Konzeption und Realisierung einer Umgebung rechnergestüzter Tätigkeiten in kooperativen Aarbeitsprozessen*. Diploma-Thesis. Fachbereich Informatik, Arbeitsbereich Softwaretechnik. Hamburg: Universität Hamburg.

Wulf, V., Krings, M., Stiemerling, O., Iacucci, G., Fuchs P.F., Hinrichs, J., Maidhof, M., Nett, B. and Peters, R. (1999). Improving inter-organizational processes with integrated organization and technology development. *JUCS* 5(6), 339–365.

Wulf, V. and Rohde, M. (1995). Towards an integrated organization and technology development. In: *Proceedings of the Symposium on Designing Interactive Systems*, Ann Arbor, Michigan, pp. 55–64.

Züllighoven, H. (1992). Umgang mit Software oder: Software als Werkzeug und Material. In: *Sichtweisen der Informatik*, Braunschweig, Vieweg, pp. 141–156.

Züllighoven, H. (ed.) (1998). *Das objektorientierte Konstruktionshandbuch nach dem Werkzeug—& Material-Ansatz*. Heidelberg: dpunkt.

Chapter 14

End-User Development as Adaptive Maintenance

Two Industrial Cases

YVONNE DITTRICH[1], OLLE LINDEBERG[2] and LARS LUNDBERG[3]

[1]*IT–University Copenhagen, Copenhagen, Denmark, ydi@itu.dk*
[2]*Department of Software Engineering and Computer Science, University of
Karlskrona/Ronneby, Ronneby, Sweden, Olle.Lindeberg@ipd.hk-r.se*
[3]*Blekinge Institute of Technology, Department of Software Engineering and
Computer Science, Ronneby, Sweden, Lars.Lundberg@bth.se*

Abstract. The change of change applications to suit the needs of users in different places and facilitate development over time has long been a major challenge for software maintenance experts. In this chapter we take up tailoring as a means of making software flexible. Starting with two case studies— one taking up tailoring for different users and the other addressing changes over time—the article discusses problems related to both the use and development of a tailorable application. Developing tailorable software presents new challenges: how do you create a user-friendly tailoring interface? How do you decide what should be tailorable, and how do you create a software architecture that permits this? How do you ensure that the tailorable system gives acceptable performance? Our experience shows that the borders between maintenance and use become blurred since tailorability can replace maintenance by professional software engineers by tailoring by advanced users. Using our experience of the two selected cases, we identify and discuss five important issues to consider when designing and implementing tailorable systems in industrial settings.

1. Introduction

Tailorability—the "light" version of End User Development allowing users to adjust and further develop a program during runtime—can be observed in many applications in use today. We all adjust the settings of our mail client, program the rules to sort mails into different folders or develop formats for our text processor. Though these applications have been around for quite a while there has been little research which addresses the software engineering of tailorable systems or the design in domains that require non-functional qualities for the software other than flexibility and tailorability. This chapter reports results from two industrial cases concerned with the development and maintenance of tailorable software:

1. The contract handler is an in-house-developed back-office system of a telecommunication provider administrating contracts and computing payments based on specific events. The types of contract as well as the events that are the subject of these contracts change over time as the business develops. The contract handler case addresses "design for change" rather than providing the possibility to adjust software to individual preferences.
2. The Billing Gateway (BGw) sorts and distributes call data records produced by phone calls to billing, statistics and fraud detection systems. It provides an

Henry Lieberman et al. (eds.), End User Development, 295–313.
© 2006 *Springer.*

interface for the tailoring of sorting algorithms to the network of which the specific implementation of the BGw is part, and for changing business requirements such as new fraud indicators.

Two features distinguish these two case studies from other research on tailorable systems. Research on tailorable systems to-date has focused mainly on the use and tailoring of commercial systems: it derives requirements and design implications from this or provides understanding of the social organization of and around tailoring activities. (see, e.g., Nardi, 1993; Trigg and Bødkers, 1994). Our research provides additional insights into the software development implications of designing for tailorability. We also consider the interaction between use, tailoring, maintenance and further development. Research addressing design issues almost exclusively uses laboratory prototypes. (e.g. Mørch, 2000, 2003). When real use contexts are addressed, researchers often act as developers. (e.g. Stevens, 2002; Stiemerling, 1997, 1998; Wulf, 1999; Wulf, 2000). Our findings partly confirm that the results of the existing research are also valid for commercially developed systems, but the cases add to the design issues the interaction between flexibility which facilitates tailoring and other software qualities such as performance and reliability.

The research on which the chapter is based relates to two different scientific discourses. The research around the contract and payment system focused not only on technical solutions but also on the software development practice and interaction between users and developers necessary to achieve a suitable solution. With respect to the research design, a specific version of action research was applied (Dittrich, 2002). In the Billing Gateway case, the research focused on performance issues and the deployment of parallel computing to improve performance. Mathematical abstraction, algorithms, technical solutions, and the evaluation of changes in the real-time behavior of the system are the means of argumentation in relation to this research discourse. The research methods and the involvement of researchers will be discussed in detail in the respective sections.

In this chapter we provide some answers to the question: "What are the most important issues when designing and implementing tailorable software in industrial settings?" In Section 3 we identify and discuss five such issues. These are then summarized in Section 4. Section 2 describes the two industrial cases that serve as the basis for our conclusion.

2. Experiences

This section reports on our experience of two different projects. Each of these is related to a sharp industrial application. In each of the projects we experimented with different solutions. Requirements from work and business contexts as well as from the technical context of the applications guided the evaluation of the respective prototypical solutions. In each case, a specific solution optimizes the deployment of available technology according to the situated requirements and constraints. These solutions raise a set of issues that will be discussed in the following section.

2.1. DESIGN FOR CHANGE

Our first case is related to a research project conducted in co-operation with a telecommunication provider—Vodafone Sweden—and a small software development company; the object was to re-develop a back office system. The program is not a standard application that has to be tailored to the needs of different customers. It is a special purpose business application developed by the in-house IT unit. Flexibility is introduced in order to accommodate changes in the business area.

The application under investigation is a system administrating specific payments. The system computes the payments based on contracts. They are triggered by events.[1] With the earlier application, only payments based on a certain event could be handled automatically. Business practice requires that payments are based on other events as well as new contract types.

The old system used for computing the payments had been in use for several years. It automated the then existing contract types and computed the respective payments. However, it was difficult to maintain, and after a while the users had to administrate some new contract types by hand and compute the respective payments manually as well. When even more radical changes in the business were discussed, it was decided to redevelop the system.

Even a new system accommodating the most recent developments would soon become outdated as the business continued to develop still further. Implementing a tailorable solution seemed a promising idea. With the help of prototypes we explored the possibility of programming a flexible solution based on a meta-modeling database system developed by the other project partner. The program that is currently in use in the company combines tailoring features with high maintainability so that even changes in the business area that go beyond the tailoring possibilities can be accommodated within an acceptable time frame. Based on this solution, we developed a new prototype using meta-object protocol to implement the tailoring features. Sections 2.2.2 and 2.2.3 present and discuss the latter two solutions. Section 2.2.1 presents our research approach. To be able to understand the designs, a conceptual model of the contract handler is presented first.

The system can be regarded as two loosely connected parts (Figure 14.1): the transaction handler and the contract handler. The transaction-handler-application handles the actual payments and also produces reports while its database stores data about the triggering events, payments and historical data about past payments. (1)[2] The data describing the triggering events is periodically imported from another system. (2) To compute the payments, the transaction handler calls a stored procedure in the contract handler's database. (3) The event is matched with the contracts; several hits may occur. Some of the contracts cancel others; some are paid out in parallel. We call the process of deciding which contracts to pay "prioritization." (4) The result is returned to the transaction handler. (5) Payment is made by sending a file to the economic system.

---

[1] To protect the business interest of our industrial partner, we cannot provide specific details about contracts.
[2] The numbers refer to Figure 14.1.

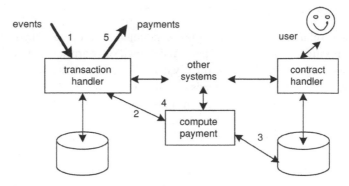

Figure 14.1. Overview over the contract handler.

To make the system adaptable to future changes a conceptual model that facilitates a meta-model-description of the system is needed. We first noted that a condition is meaningful in a contract only if the transaction handler can evaluate it when payment is due. This leads to the concept of event types; a payment is triggered by an event and all contract types belong to a particular event type. Each event type has a set of attributes associated with it that limits what a contract for such events can be based on. Contract types that are handled similarly are put together in one group. Secondly, we split up the computation of payments into two consecutive parts: first, find all matching contracts and thereafter select which to pay (prioritization).

2.1.1. *Research Methods*

To understand the kind of changes that might be required of the new contract handler, we reconstructed the history of the development and change of the software to be replaced by the application under development. At the same time, we started with participatory observation of the development project. We took part and taped meetings during the pre-study. During the implementation of the software one of us carried out a minor programming task in order to be closer to the now more intensive technical design and implementation. We contributed to the project by exploring possibilities for a flexible design together with project members: participatory design workshops with the users took place to understand, how a tailoring interface for the new application could look like. We organized two workshops with the software developers involved with the purpose of introducing meta-modeling techniques that in one way or another are necessary when designing for flexibility. Together, we implemented a set of prototypes thereby proving that an extremely flexible implementation of the application is possible when using a flexible database (Linderberg, 2002). Based on our experience of the design process, a meta-object protocol version of the contract handler was developed at the University. As the development project at the telecommunication provider was about to be concluded, no systematic or joint evaluation of the version was carried out.

Our involvement in the project can be seen as a specific interpretation of action research, one we call "co-operative method development" (Dittrich, 2002). Empirical observation of practice, workshops and implementation of methodological innovation build a learning cycle that allows for changes in software development practice and gives researchers feedback on the usefulness and applicability of the various methods.

2.1.2. *Flexibility Light*

The design of the finally implemented contract handler incorporates some meta-modeling features while at the same time using a normal relational database. The result was a flexible system which does not require any complex or non-standard software. Flexibility here means both tailorability and maintainability. Flexibility is primarily the result of five features of the design.

The most important design decision was to modularize the contract types internally as aggregations of objects handle single parameters and group these according to the kinds of parameters that defined them. In most cases, the program could handle all contracts belonging to the same contract type group in a uniform way and thereby simplify the program.

The second feature was to use the object-oriented capabilities of PowerBuilder, which was used to build the graphical user interface and the client part of the application. Powerbuilder is a 4th generation rapid development tool based on C++. The user interface is constructed with one window for each contract-group type. Different contract-group types have different sets of parameters but each parameter type occurs in several contract-group types. Some of the parameters are in themselves rather complicated objects, and the interfaces for them are also complicated. To simplify the system, each interface for a parameter was constructed as an object—an interface object. The interface for each contract-type group was built as a set of interface objects. Since the parameters are treated the same way in all contracts, this reduces the effort required to construct the interfaces and facilitates the addition of new ones. The interface objects also guarantee that the user interface handles parameters in a consistent way.

The third design decision was to use a non-normalized database. The contract types all have different parameters but they were nevertheless stored in the same database table which had fields for all parameters in all contracts. This produced a sparsely populated table which wasted disc space but allowed for unified access. It would have been unduly complicated to construct the interface objects otherwise.

As a fourth design feature, it was decided that part of the computation should be steered by a table indicating which contract type belongs to which contract type group. A new contract type that could be described as belonging to a contract type group would only require an additional line in the table. But even where a new contract type does not fit into one of the groups, it would only require a minimum of programming effort as the interface object and the database are already in place.

Last but not least, prioritization between different contracts triggered by the same event is controlled by a list describing which contract takes priority. In this way, the earlier hard-coded prioritization can be controlled in a more flexible way.

The design combines different implementation techniques which allow for flexibility. When regarding the specific situation with respect to use, operation and maintenance of the system, it was generally agreed that the design fitted well with the specific contexts of use and development required by the telecommunication provider. Above all, the design was found to be better suited to the situation at hand than a fictive fully-flexible system utilizing the above-mentioned flexible data base system. To our surprize, the "flexibility light" solution turned out to provide equal flexibility for anticipated changes though in some cases software engineers would have to do the adaptation. In cases where the system supported by the prototypes would have been preferable, the necessary changes would have entailed changes in other systems as well. In terms of usability, maintainability and reliability the "flexibility light" solution is clearly superior (Linderberg, 2001).

2.1.3. *Using Meta Object Protocol to Separate Tailoring Use in Software Architecture*

One of the reasons for the low maintainability and reliability of the more flexible solution was the interweaving of the meta-level that described the structure of the contracts and the base level to access the concrete data throughout the code, e.g. the metadata determining the structure of the contract type steered the layout on the screen. To explore whether it is possible to develop a better designed system from the point of view of maintenance, testing and debugging as well as flexibility, we implemented a prototype inspired by Kiczales' meta-object protocol (Kiczales, 1992). We also deployed the idea of designing the contracts as aggregations of building blocks, each modeling a specific parameter from the "flexibility light" solution.

The meta-object protocol is based on the idea of opening up the implementation of programming languages so that the developer is able to adjust the implementation to fit his or her needs. This idea has subsequently been generalized to systems other than compilers and programming languages (Kiczales, 1992). Any system that is constructed as a service to be used by client applications, e.g. operation systems or database servers can provide two interfaces: a base-level interface and a meta-level interface. The base-level interface gives access to the functionality of the underlying system and through the meta-level interface it is possible to alter special aspects of the underlying implementation of the system so that it suits the needs of the client application. The meta-level interface is called the "metaobject protocol" (MOP). The prototype uses this idea to separate tailoring and use in the software architecture. So it allows for a better structured design both in terms of tailoring features and base functionality.

For each value in the event data that can be used as a constraint in a contract, a class is defined that takes care of the functionality of the constraint as it displays it for viewing and editing, checks the consistency of the input data and stores and retrieves the specific values from the database. A contract is implemented as an aggregation of a number of such objects plus a set of objects handling mandatory contract specific data such as contract ID, creation date, validity dates, versioning information and so on. Each contract type is defined by a class that specifies what constraints an event must satisfy to trigger contracts belonging to this type.

New classes defining new contract types can be created in the meta-level interface. They are put together by selecting possible constraints from a menu. The meta-level also allows one to change existing contract type classes and define additional classes for implementing constraints. It is thus possible to adapt the new contract types to requirements which have not yet been anticipated. The meta level is implemented using a metaobject protocol: Through menu-driven selection the user assembles a new contract type. The class describing this contract type is written as Java code to a file. After translation, the class becomes part of the base level without even needing to restart the system.

The new contract type is available in the menu of the base level program. The base level program consists of a frame providing access to the contracts and to the existing contract types while designing a new contract. Although some of the Java reflection features are used, the base-level program is basically an ordinary Java program. Where errors or other problems occur, it is easy to test and debug. A system constructed in this way can be implemented with a traditional, sparsely populated database, or with a database system that allows one to change the data model during runtime.

The meta-object protocol design makes it possible to separate concerns. Business logic regarding the contracts and constraints is implemented in the building blocks and in the base level of the program. In some cases we may be dissatisfied with the resulting contract types, e.g. we may want a user interface that is specially constructed for this particular contract type. With the metaobject protocol design, this can easily be solved by using a hand-coded class instead of the automatically generated one—we are free to mix automatically generated classes and hand-coded classes. Also, special business logic can be incorporated in the program this way. The business logic guiding and constraining the assembly of contract types can be implemented in the meta level part of the program.

The main advantage of the metaobject protocol design is that it allows one to separate concerns. The base level of the program is a normal program in which some parts are automatically generated code. In the same way, the meta-level of the program is only concerned with the tailoring functionality. The functionality of the meta-level part can be tested independently. As the base program works as a normal program, it can be tested and debugged as usual. One could even develop specific test cases while creating a new contract type class. We used Java for implementing the prototype. The meta-object protocol solution is a viable option in conjunction with standard software and a standard database system.

As the flexibility light solution was already in operation when we finished the new prototype, we did not evaluate the meta-object prototype solution together with the telecom provider. However, we consider this solution does address some of the drawbacks identified during the evaluation of the early prototypes, and it is certainly more flexible than the "flexibility light" option implemented by the telecommunication provider.

2.1.4. *Tailoring, Software Evolution and Infrastructures*

The contract handler example shows that even relatively simple business applications must be flexible when supporting a developing business domain. It also shows that whatever kinds of changes can be anticipated, it is necessary to accommodate unanticipated developments. Use and tailoring might have to be interleaved with maintenance and further development by software engineers.

The decision as to what to implement as tailoring functionality and what to leave to maintenance by software engineers was in our case based on a well-established co-operation between the telecom provider's IT unit and the business units. A similar design would not have been acceptable if its development had been outsourced; this was confirmed during the evaluation of the project by the group manager of the IT unit responsible for the development.

A third factor that became obvious when evaluating the effort required to produce changes in the flexibility light version contra a fully-flexible system is that business systems in such data-intensive business domains are often part of an infrastructure of networked applications. Changes in business practice often entail changes in more than one program or in the interplay between different applications. Here "design for change" entails the sustainable development of heterogeneous infrastructures.

2.2. FLEXIBILITY IN LARGE TELECOMMUNICATIONS SYSTEMS

In telecommunications networks different kinds of devices producing and processing data of different formats must be integrated. For example, information about calls in a network is handled in call-data records (CDRs). The CDRs are generated by Network Elements such as telecom switches and can contain information about call duration, the origin of the telephone number, terminating telephone number, etc. The CDRs are sent to post processing systems (PPSs) to perform billing and fraud detection etc. Both the kind and format of data and the way it is distributed to the different post-processing systems can vary and it changes as the network develops. An additional difficulty in telecommunications networks is that the necessary computation must fulfill demanding real-time constraints and that massive amount of data must be handled.

The Ericsson Billing Gateway (BGw) is an example of such a performance demanding real-time telecommunications system, but it must also be customizable even after delivery. It functions as a mediation device connecting network elements with post processing systems such as billing systems, statistical analysis, and fraud detection.

Figure 14.2 shows the execution structure of the BGw. The structure consists of three major components: data collection, data processing, and data distribution. Each component is implemented as one (multithreaded) Unix process. All data processing including filtering and formatting is done by the processing process. The BGw can handle several different protocols and data formats and it can perform filtering, formatting and other forms of call data processing.

The data flow in the BGw is tailored using a graphical user interface. Icons are used to represent external systems. In Figure 14.3 files are retrieved from four Mobile

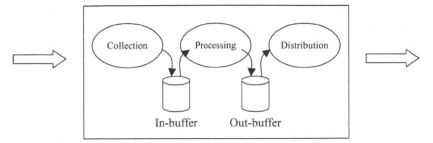

Figure 14.2. The execution structure of the BGw.

Switching Centers (MSCs) in two different versions. CDRs from the Paging System are formatted to conform to the older version ("ver 7 − > ver 6" n Figure 14.3), and all CDRs are checked to see if the calls are billable. Billable CDRs are sent to the billing system; others are saved for statistical purposes. CDRs from roaming calls are also separated from other CDRs. For more information about the BGw architecture see (Mejstad, 2002).

Complementing the flexible definition of the dataflow, the BGw contains an interface that allows the tailoring of the filters and formatters that sort and re-format the incoming call data records to the interfaces of the post processing systems.

2.2.1. *Methodology*

The main methodology used is experimentation and performance evaluations of different versions of the software. These performance evaluations were carried out by

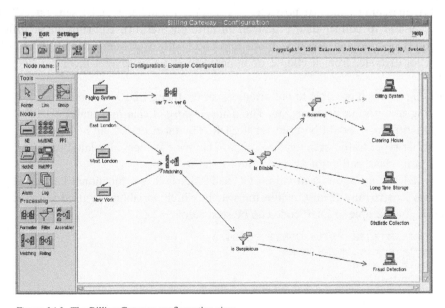

Figure 14.3. The Billing Gateway configuration view.

Ericsson using real-world configurations. We have also conducted interviews with the designers and end users of the software. The software is used in about 100 places all over the world; our contact has been primarily with users in Sweden, UK, and Italy. The software developers are located in Ronneby in the south of Sweden.

2.2.2. *Tailoring Filters and Formatters*

All data processed by the BGw must be defined in ASN.1, a standard for defining data types in telecommunication applications. The BGw builds up internal object structures of the data called Data Units. One of the Billing Gateway's strengths lies in the fact that the user can use a tailoring language—the "Data Unit Processing" (DUP) language—to operate on these internal structures.

Sorting and reformatting are tailored through the definition of filter, formatter, matching, and rating nodes in the user interface. This kind of node or component is represented in the user interface by an icon. Each node contains a script in the DUP language that is executed for every CDR passing through the BGw.

A filter node is used to filter out CDRs (e.g. IsBillable? in Figure 14.3). A filter node can, for example, filter out all roaming calls (a call made in a net other than the home net, e.g. when traveling in another country). The typical filter is rather simple and contains no more than around 10 lines of DUP code.

Sometimes it is necessary to convert a CDR from one format to another before sending it on to post processing systems (e.g. ver 7 − > ver 6 in Figure 14.3). The size in lines of code differs a great deal from one formatter to another. In its simplest form, it might only change a couple of fields whereas large formatters can contain several thousand lines of code.

CDR matching makes it possible to combine a number of CDRs in one CDR. It is possible to collect data produced in different network elements or at different points in time and combine these into one CDR. Matching nodes usually contain a lot of code, from a couple of hundred lines up to several thousand lines of code.

Rating makes it possible to put price tags or tariffs on CDRs. It can be divided into charging analysis and price setting. The main purpose of charging analysis is to define which tariff class should be used for a CDR. The tariff class may be determined by subscriber type, traffic activity, and so on. The price is then calculated based on the given tariff class, call duration, and time for start of charge.

The DUP language is a mixture of C and ASN.1. It is a functional language that borrows its structure from C while the way in which variables are used is based on ASN.1. An example of DUP code can be seen below:

```
CONST INTEGER add(a CONST INTEGER)
{declare result INTEGER;
result ::= 10;
result += a;
return result;}
```

Local variables can be declared at the beginning of a scope. A scope is enclosed by a "{' and a '}". A variable is declared with the keyword declare.

```
declare <variable name> <variable type>
```

The drag-and-drop interface for defining the dataflow and the DUP language to define the processing of data in the different nodes gives the BGw flexibility to suit a wide range of applications without the need for re-compilation since the functionality can be changed on-site by the customer.

Shortly after, development performance became an issue for the BGw. Slow processing of CDRs was one problem in the BGw. Our research on the performance of the BGw has identified severe multiprocessor scaling problems (Mejstad 2002). As a multi-threaded application, it is to be expected that performance will improve when a CPU is added. This was not, however, the case.

2.2.3. Performance Problems With the BGw

The implementation of the DUP language was identified as the major performance bottleneck and the main reason for poor scaling (Mejstad, 2002). The DUP language was implemented as an interpreted language suggesting that each interpretation results in a serious of function calls making heavy demands on the dynamic memory and thus the shared heap. This again results in threads being locked on mutexes as multiple threads try to allocate/de-allocate dynamic memory simultaneously. By replacing interpretation with compilation (see next sub-section), we were able to improve performance by a factor of two on a single-processor. The compiled version also scales better; this version was also four times faster than the interpreted version when a multiprocessor with eight processors was used.

The entire DUP implementation is accessed through three classes: DUPBuilder, DUPRouter, and DUPFormatter. A fourth class called DUProcessing is used by these classes.

The DUPBuilder uses an autmatically generated parser to build a syntax tree of the DUP-script. This means that a tree structure of C++ objects is created that represents the DUP source code. The DUPBuilder returns a DUProcessing object; this is the root node in the syntax tree.

2.2.4. Using Compilation Instead of Interpretation

The interpretation of the DUP-scripts introduced a great deal of overhead that reduced the performance of the BGw. The attempts to solve this problem by using parallel execution were only partly successful. In order to get to the root of the problem we wanted to remove the interpretation.

The obvious alternative to interpretation is compilation. Building a complete compiler is a major task so we decided to build a compiler that translates DUP scripts into C++ code and then use an ordinary C++ compiler to produce the binary code. The binary code is then included in the program with the aid of dynamic linking.

It turned out that the compiled version improved the average performance of the BGw by a factor of two when using a uni-processor. The compiled version also scaled much better than the version using the DUP interpreter; and the performance of the compiled version was eight times better than the version which used the interpreter on a multiprocessor with eight processors. In fact, the compiled version scales almost linearly with the number of processors.

2.2.5. *What is Development, What is Maintenance, What is Use?*

The BGw itself consists of 100,000–200,000 lines of C++ code. A typical BGw configuration contains 5000–50,000 lines of DUP code and there are more than 100 BGw configurations in the world today. This means that the total amount of DUP code is much larger than the size of the BGw itself. The DUP scripts are sometimes written by members of the use organization and sometimes by software engineers from the local Ericsson offices. The BGW is an example of an application where tailoring clearly becomes a matter of End-User Development as users not only write significant parts of the code but programming also changes the functionality of the system.

A great deal of effort has been put into making the architecture of the BGw itself as maintainable as possible, i.e. the cost of future changes should be kept at a minimum. However, since most of the BGw-related code is compiled close to the users and outside of the development organization in Sweden, the main cost of future changes will probably be related to changing and maintaining DUP scripts and not C++ code. This means that the most important aspect of minimizing the cost of maintenance is to make it easy to change DUP scripts. Since DUP scripts are one of the main ways in which the user interacts with a BGW, one can say that making it easier to change DUP scripts is almost the same as making the BGw more usable. This means that the borders between maintainability and usability are rather blurred as a large part of development work is carried out close to or by the users. This also puts forward new demands on tailoring and use interfaces. Testing, debugging, documentation, and version handling must be provided for. And it changes the role of the users. Some users might become local designers or even domain-specific software engineers.

3. Challenges, Problems, and Solutions

The two cases above show that tailorable software is an issue not only as a means of tailoring the user interface of a standard system but also in industrial development and deployment of software. It allows design decisions to be delayed until after the program is taken into use and to adapt software to changing business and user requirements. The two very different cases provide quite a spectrum of experiences. In this section we summarize the lessons learned so far as well as the challenges for software design and development.

3.1. USABILITY OF THE TAILORING INTERFACE

As normal interfaces, tailoring interfaces must be understandable from a user's perspective. They must represent the computational possibilities of the interface not only in a way that makes them accessible for the user but also helps him/her to understand how to combine them. As a result, the tailorable aspects of the software must be designed—even on the architecture level—to match a use perspective on the domain. The tailoring interface must also present the building blocks and the possible connections between them in a comprehensible way. Mørch's application units (Mørch, 2000, 2003) and Stiemerling et al.'s component-based approach (Stiemerling, 1997) are examples of such architecture concepts. Stevens and Wulf discuss this issue in connection with the designing of a component decomposition of a tailorable access control system (Stevens, 2002). This issue relates to a discussion of the relationship of the software architecture and the structure of the user interface, e.g. Züllighoven et al. (Züllighoven, 1998) developed an approach to the design of interactive systems that relates to the architectural design and the user interface using tools and materials to a common design metaphor. However, designing the contract handler in accordance with this approach would not automatically lead to an architectural design that facilitates tailorability.

Also, the contract handler presented the limited tailoring capabilities to the users in a form which was close to their own concepts. However, the users declared at an early stage that they did not want to make changes in the system themselves; they felt more comfortable letting the software engineers responsible for system maintenance do the tailoring. In the Billing Gateway, the data flow interface provides from the user's point of view a very intuitive interface. Also, the language for tailoring filters and formatters complies well with the technical education of its users. Nonetheless, end-users have shown some reluctance to tailor the application; in many cases tailoring was carried out by software engineers. The users felt insecure about the correctness of the results of the adaptation. This is discussed in greater detail in Section 3.4.

The above two cases show that the real challenge is to find ways to structure tailoring capabilities so that the program is easy to use and understand for the user at the same time as it provides tailoring capabilities that are powerful enough to provide the desired flexibility. In the two cases considered here, the end users felt (at least initially) that tailoring activities should be left to software engineers. However, we believe that the users' need for software engineering support will decrease as they become more used to the systems. More widespread and less powerful tailoring, e.g. adjusting the settings in mail programs and providing formulas in spreadsheet applications, shows that the support of software engineers is clearly not needed in such cases. For applications that are used by a large number of people with very different backgrounds, e.g. mail and spreadsheet programs, the trade-off between ease of use and powerful tailoring capabilities will be assessed differently from what we see in the two more specialized applications studied here. The systems considered here will be used by a relatively small number of people and it is thus reasonable to give higher priority to powerful tailoring, even if users initially require specialized training and/or support from software engineers.

One result of introducing powerful tailoring interfaces for certain specialized applications is that the users or a sub group of the users will become more of a domain-specific
developer. It also means that new versions of the applications will not always be the
result of re-engineering the software itself; they will, to an increasing extent, be done
by advanced tailoring. What was previously software development and maintenance
will thus become tailoring and use.

3.2. DECIDING WHAT SHOULD BE ADAPTABLE AND HOW TO DESIGN FOR IT

The requirements a software program should fulfill are difficult to determine in advance,
particularly in the case of adaptable software. In both our cases, the development organization had built similar software before. The contract handler was a re-development.
Experience with changing requirements was the main reason for looking into the design
of adaptable software. Ericsson has a long history in telecommunication; the decision to
make the Billing Gateway tailorable was made as the result of an increasing production
of different versions of the system for different customers.

Part of the design problem is the difficulty to anticipate changes for which to provide.
(Henderson, 1991; Stiemerling, 1997; Trigg, 1992) Understanding domain knowledge
and feedback from the user is important where flexibility is required.

However, in deciding what is fixed and how the adaptable parts should look, one also
implicitly determines the architecture of the whole system. In the case of the contract
handler design, the identification of fixed building blocks made it possible to implement
the contracts as assemblies of these blocks. In the case of the Billing Gateway, designing
filters and formatters as programmable manipulation of the dataflow also defined the
basic structure of the system and vice versa. Conversely, it is not until we have a basic
conceptual model of how the system is developed that we can understand what can be
made tailorable. An example of this is in the contract handler: only when contracts are
understood as sets of constraints to be matched by events, constraints can be defined as
building blocks for the drawing up of a contract. In both cases studied here, the design of
the stable and the adaptable aspects was dependent on each other. As with architectural
design, the design of the parts is only understandable in relation to the whole.

The evaluation of the flexibility light solution shows that the organization of the
software development also influences the design decision (Dittrich, 2002). In-house
development makes it possible for part of the regular adaptation to be left to software engineers. Outsourced development would have led to different design decisions.
Neither can users of off-the-shelf software rely on such co-operation with software developers. Here, users need to be supported with more comprehensive tailoring interfaces
for the necessary adaptations.

The challenge here is thus to find a good balance between which future adaptations of
a certain software should be made tailorable for the end user and which should be left to
software engineers who redesign and maintain the software itself. Leaving everything
(or at least a great deal) to the end user will cause problems since this will require
very advanced tailoring (which in turn may require help from software engineers); this

may in turn make testing and documentation difficult and thus generate problems with system reliability. On the other hand, leaving a great deal to the software engineer will significantly increase the time required for and cost of introducing new functionality. We believe that the trend goes toward functionality being made more tailorable; the two systems studied here are good examples. However, it is important to find a good balance between traditional software maintenance carried out by software engineers and tailoring done by the users.

There is yet no systematization of design for tailoring and EUD available. Here, perhaps a collection of high-level design patterns might slowly lead to a more systematic overview of different possibilities and their strengths and weaknesses. Our two cases indicate that the evaluation of solutions which have a good balance between tailoring and traditional software maintenance must take into account the way in which use and development are related. Moreover, the interplay between tailorability and non-functional requirements must be considered.

3.3. PERFORMANCE

Many design techniques to provide flexibility and tailorability of software reduce the performance of the program. In the Billing Gateway case in particular this has been a problem. However, this problem can often be taken care of by adopting a sound technical solution. In the BGW we first tried to improve performance by using multiprocessor technology. This approach only resulted in limited performance improvements. It turned out that the best way to handle the problem was to replace interpretation with compilation combined with dynamic linking, thus maintaining flexibility and tailorability and improving performance.

Experience with a very flexible and tailorable database system showed that initially performance was lower than in a traditional system by a factor of 10–20. The reason for this was that the system used one level of indirection, i.e. the system first had to look in a data base table for meta data before it could interpret any actual data values. This performance problem was removed by introducing some controlled redundancy, thereby reducing the slow down from a factor 10–20 to a factor of 2 (Diestelkamp, 2000).

These experiments show that the performance problems related to flexibility and tailorability can often be handled without too much trouble. Flexible and tailorable software can thus also be used in performance demanding real-time applications such as the Billing Gateway system.

3.4. SOFTWARE ENGINEERING EDUCATION AND TOOLS FOR END-USERS?

The Billing Gateway was designed to be adapted by the telecommunication providers themselves. Being technically trained people well-acquainted with the standards used for the description of the call data records, they should not have a problem with DUP language. However, the adaptations studied were mainly carried out by Ericsson personnel. The reason for this was that the end-users were afraid of implementing erroneous tailoring constructs with large financial losses for their organization as a result. The users of the contract handler had similar reasons for refusing to tailor the program. They did not want to be responsible for causing loss of money and reputation for the telecommunication provider by making mistakes when doing tailoring. The developers had access to test environments and tools used for ordinary software development and were able to check whether the change had the intended effect. Also, in the case of the contract handler, the users were reluctant to take responsibility for the tailoring. An interesting question is if better tools and training in testing and documenting would be of help to users. Other researchers have reported on similar needs for documenting and testing of tailoring constructs (Kahler, 2001; Stiemerling). Wulf (Wulf, 1999, 2000) proposes exploration environments that allow for safe trial and error. Burnett (Burnett) explores constraints-based testing and verification support for end-users. In the Meta-object version of the contract handler, the definition of contract types that do not make sense from a business point of view can be prohibited.

In our cases, analysis and design were also discussed in terms of tailoring. "If the system can handle any kind of contract, how do we decide on which kind of contracts we want to offer?" asked a manager from the business unit during a workshop when confronted with a mock-up showing a possible interface of a tailorable system. Involving and paying the IT unit that is run as an internal profit center provided enough effort to deliberate new contract types from a business point of view. Trigg and Bødker (1994) observed the development of an organizational infrastructure around the deployment of the tailoring features of a text editor in a government agency. The design of form letters used instead of individual ones prompted the establishment of a committee that included legal experts to help to review and decide on the form letters to be taken into use.

Other authors have observed the need to document tailoring constructs, keep different versions and share them (Henderson, 1991; Stiemerling, 1997). Such features are necessary even when tailoring the common artifact—as in the contract handler case—or the infrastructure of a business—as in the Billing Gateway. It seems that the user, when provided with the means to tailor the software must also be provided with the means and tools to deliberate, document, test, and re-use the tailoring constructs. Testing and documentation in particular must be provided for so that tailorability and EUD may be deployed more systematically in commercial contexts. Only experience will show the extent and kind of such "end-user software engineering" needed. We do, however, believe that users of tailorable systems will increasingly need better "software engineering" training and tools since they may become a kind of domain-specific software developer.

3.5. HOW DOES SOFTWARE DEVELOPMENT CHANGE IN CONNECTION WITH TAILORING?

Developing software that is adaptable to different ways of using or for a developing business area stimulates changes in software engineering. Designing a solution for a problem is no longer sufficient. One has to design spaces for adaptation to a set of diverse uses and anticipatable changes. In addition, one has to consciously defer part of the design to the user.

Tailorability allows the users to implement adaptations that would otherwise be subject to maintenance. For the Billing Gateway, the tailoring constructs can become a major part of the overall code developed. On one hand, maintenance effort is traded against tailoring effort for the users. (Henderson, 1991) and (Wulf, 1999) have already noted that tailorability rationalizes development as it prolongs the maintenance cycle. On the other hand, designing a tailorable system may be more complex, especially when performance is an important factor. Making a program tailorable will thus also shift the software engineering effort from the maintenance phase into the design phase and not solely from maintenance by professional software engineers into tailoring by advanced users.

Even if we can hope for less maintenance when designing, system tailorable maintenance will still be necessary when change requirements occur that cannot be accommodated by the adaptability the design provides. Tailorability will then produce a new set of problems. A new version of the system must allow users to keep the adaptations they have made to the old system. With the installation of a new version, not only the old data has to be translated, but also the tailoring constructs. More research is needed in this area.

The life cycle of software must accommodate the interleaving of development, use, tailoring, small maintenance tasks, and major re-development. This may entail more flexible ways of organizing software development and a less rigid division between the use and development of software. This will require increased communication between the software engineers and the advanced users. As early as in 1991 Trigg anticipated such a development (Trigg, 1992). Our research indicates that this is highly relevant when developing software that is part of an infrastructure for developing work and business practices (Dittrich, 2004).

4. Conclusion

Henderson and Kyng (Henderson, 1991) in their article "There's no place like home: Continuing design in use" take up three reasons for carrying out tailoring: "the situation of use changes," "it [is] difficult to anticipate [the use]" and when one is "creating a product which will be purchased by many people." In this chapter we have exemplified the first and last of these and we believe that tailoring has an essential role to play in industrial software development when it comes to solving these problems. As far as the problem of anticipating how the system will be used is concerned, tailoring is certainly a means of alleviating the problem.

Based on our experience of the two cases discussed here we have identified a number of important issues when designing and implementing tailorable systems in industrial settings:

The balance between providing a tailoring interface which is easy to use while still providing powerful tailoring possibilities. Our conclusion is that it makes sense to give higher priority to powerful tailoring in specialized applications such as the ones studied here as compared to more general applications, e.g. mail programs.

The balance between traditional software (re-)development and maintenance on the one hand and tailoring and use on the other. Our conclusion here is that the trend goes toward handling more and more of the need for future adaptability by tailoring.

The "conflict" between tailorability and flexibility on the one hand and performance on the other. Our conclusion here is that this problem can, in most cases, be solved by innovative technical solutions, and tailoring can thus also be used in performance demanding real-time applications.

There is a need for giving the end users better tools for testing, documentation and reuse/sharing of tailoring constructs as well as the necessary training to use them. This is particularly true for users of specialized tailorable applications such as the ones studied here. Some users may, in fact, become some kind of domain-specific software developers.

Software maintenance and (re-) development will to a growing extent be mixed and interlaced with tailoring. This will require increased communication between software engineers and advanced users.

Acknowledgments

We wish to thank the reviewers of previous versions of this chapter for their constructive criticism. And thanks to our research partners for their co-operation. For any errors, we accept full responsibility.

References

Burnett, M., Rothermel, G. and Cook, C. *An Integrated Software Engineering Approach for End-User Programmers*.This volume.

Diestelkamp, W. and Lundberg, L. (2000). Performance evaluation of a generic database system. *International Journal of Computers and Their Applications* 7(3), September, 122–129.

Dittrich, Y. (2002). Doing empirical research in software engineering—Finding a path between understanding, intervention and method development, In Y. Dittrich, C. Floyd, and R. Klischewski (eds.), *Social Thinking Software Practice*, Cambridge, USA: The MIT Press 2002.

Dittrich, Y. and Lindeberg, O. (2002). Designing for changing work and business practices. In: N. Patel (ed.), *Evolutionary and Adaptive Information Systems*. IDEA group publishing.

Dittrich, Y. and Lindeberg, O. (2004). How use-oriented development can take place. *Information and Software Technology* 46(9), July, pp. 603–617.

Henderson, A. and Kyng, M. (1991). There is no place like home: Continuing design in use. In J. Greenbaum and M. Kyng (eds.), *Design at Work*. Lawrence Erlbaum Associates, pp. 219–240.

Kahler, H. (2001). *Supporting Collaborative Tailoring*. Ph.D. thesis. Roskilde University. Datalogiske Skrifter, ISSN 0109–9779 No. 91, p. 232.

Kiczales, G. (1992). Towards a New Model of Abstraction in the Engineering of Software. In: *Proceedings of International Workshop on New Models for Software Architecture (IMSA): Reflection and Meta-Level Architecture.* Tama City, Tokyo, November.

Lindeberg, O. and Diestelkamp, W. (2001). How much Adaptability do you need? Evaluating Meta-modeling Techniques for Adaptable Special Purpose Systems. In: *Proceedings of the Fifth IASTED International Conference on Software Engineering and Applications, SEA.*

Lindeberg, O., Eriksson, J. and Dittrich, Y. (2002). Using metaobject protocol to implement tailoring; possibilities and problems. In: *The 6th World Conference on Integrated Design and Process Technology (IDPT '02)*, Pasadena, USA, 2002.

Mejstad, V., Tångby, K.-J. and Lundberg, L. (2002). Improving multiprocessor performance of a large telecommunication system by replacing interpretation with compilation. In *Proceedings of the 9th IEEE International Conference and Workshop on the Engineering of Computer-Based Systems,* April 2002, Lund Sweden, pp. 77–85.

Mørch, A.I. (2003). Tailoring as Collaboration: The Mediating Role of Multiple Representations and Application Units", In: N. Patel (ed.), *Adaptive Evolutionary Information Systems.* Idea group Inc.

Mørch, A.I. and Mehandjiev, N.D. (2000). Tailoring as collaboration: The mediating role of multiple representations and application units. In: *Computer Supported Work* 9(75–100), Kluwer Academic Publishers.

Nardi, B.A. (1993). *A Small Matter of Programming.* MIT Press, 1993.

Stevens, G. and Wulf, V. (2002). A new dimension in access control: studying maintenance engineering across organisational boundaries. *Proceedings of the CSCW 02, November 16–20,* New Orleans, Louisiana, USA.

Stiemerling, O. and Cremers, A.B. (1998). Tailorable component architectures for CSCW-systems. In: *Parallel and Distributed Processing,* 1998. PDP '98. *Proceedings of the Sixth Euromicro Workshop,* pp. 302–308, IEEE Computer Society.

Stiemerling, O., Kahler, H. and Wulf, V. (1997). How to make software softer– Designing tailorable applications. *Proceedings of the Designing Interactive Systems (DIS) 1997.*

Trigg, R. (1992). Participatory design meets the MOP: Accountability in the design of tailorable computer Systems. In: G. Bjerkness, G. Bratteteig, and K. Kauts (eds.), *Proceedings of the 15th IRIS,* Department of Informatics, University of Oslo, August.

Trigg, R. and Bødker, S. (1994). From implementation to design: Tailoring and the emergence of systematization in CSCW. *Proceedings of the CSCW '94,* ACM-Press, New York, 1994, pp. 45–55.

Truex, D.P., Baskerville, R. and Klein, H. (1999). Growing Systems in Emergent Organisations. *Communications of the ACM* 42, pp. 117–123.

Wulf, V. and Rohde, M. (1995). Towards an integrated organization and technology development. In: *Proceedings of the Symposium on Designing Interactive Systems,* 23–25 August, Ann Arbor (Michigan), ACM Press, New York, S. 55–64.

Wulf, V. "Let's see your Search Tool!" On the collaborative use of tailored artifacts. *Proceedings of the GROUP '99 conference,* ACM Press, New York, pp. 50–60.

Wulf, V. (2000). Exploration environments: Supporting users to learn groupware functions. *Interacting with Computers* 13(2), pp. 265–299.

Zuellighoven H. (1998). Das objektorientierte Konstruktionshandbuch nach dem Werkzeug & Material-Ansatz; dpunkt-Verlag Heidelberg.

Chapter 15

Supporting Collaborative Tailoring
Issues and Approaches

VOLKMAR PIPEK[1] and HELGE KAHLER[1]

[1] *IISI–International Institute for Socio-Informatics, Bonn, Germany,*
volkmar.pipek@iisi.de, helge.kahler@iisi.de

Abstract. In this chapter we depict collaborative aspects of tailoring software. We provide a categorization distinguishing between (at first) three levels of intensity of user ties regarding tools usage ("shared use," "shared context," and "shared tool") and discuss approaches to support collaborative tailoring in these scenarios. For the two levels with the most intense ties ("Shared Context" and "Shared Tool") we provide the relevant theoretical background as well as empirical evidence from our own fieldwork. Our taxonomy helps us to describe and address two important shortcomings of current tailoring environments. First, current considerations regarding tailorability usually address tailoring within one tool, while current work infrastructures (which we introduce as a forth scenario—"Shared Infrastructure"—in our taxonomy) require a thinking beyond one tool. Second, although studies on tailoring-in-practice and evolving use of organizational software show the importance of user-user-interaction in processes of technology configuration, this interaction was only treated as a side issue in the design of tailoring environments. Respecting the importance of that interaction, we suggest to stronger focus on opportunities to support those appropriation activities of users.

1. Introduction

More often than ever software is involved in the collaboration of computer users in offices. Thus, the way a software product is implemented, configured, and used influences the collaborative work of these users. In this chapter we describe approaches to support end-users in collaboratively finding and implementing tool configurations that are adequate for their form and intensity of collaboration. "Tailoring" has been defined by Henderson and Kyng (1991) as "changing stable aspects of an artefact" and distinguished from use as persistent manipulations that are not "being made to the subject matter of a tool" (e.g. a text), but "to the tool itself."[1] Traditionally, approaches to improve the "Tailorability" (Trigg et al., 1987; Henderson and Kyng, 1991) of software artefacts address the improvement of the necessary artefact flexibility (e.g. Malone et al., 1992; Stiemerling and Cremers, 2000; Wulf, 1999). But offering the necessary flexibility to make tools fit diverse and changing work contexts is only the first step of offering support. A deeper understanding of the role tailoring plays in the appropriation processes of individuals, groups and organizations has lead to new ideas to also support

---

[1] We use the terms "configuration" and "tailoring" synonymously, but with the former having a more technology-related notion, in contrast to the latter having a more socio-technical notion.

Henry Lieberman et al. (eds.), End User Development, 315–345.
© 2006 *Springer.*

tailoring *as an activity* within the tailored artefacts. Being aware of the organizational aspects of tailoring activities we explore opportunities to support these activities with additional functions.

Especially long-term studies of groupware systems (Karsten and Jones, 1998; Pipek and Wulf, 1999; Törpel et al., 2003) show that tailoring an application is only the technological condensation of an individual or social activity of designing a work setting for performing a certain task. In line with earlier experiences (Stallmann, 1981; Malone et al., 1988; Mackay, 1990) they show that tailoring activities often involve user-user interaction and collaboration. So, the "individual" decision how to tailor an artefact is to a certain extent always also social, since large parts of the knowledge used in the decision processes usually have been acquired through social interaction (e.g. knowledge on the capabilities of computers and tools, knowledge on the task the tool should serve in, etc.). So there is always a notion of cooperation in a tailoring activity, as it is in every activity of technology appropriation processes.

This general consideration of the sociality of tailoring processes has to be concretized to discuss possible opportunities for offering technical support for collaborative tailoring. To discuss existing approaches as well as new challenges, it is necessary to give some structure to support scenarios. In the next section, we develop four scenarios of collaborative tailoring that guide us through our discussions in this chapter. Focusing on technical support for particularly collaborative tailoring we will concentrate our discussion on those scenarios that show the biggest need for collaboration support. We close this chapter by describing new challenges for collaborative tailoring at modern workplaces and discuss extensions of tailoring interfaces to support the appropriation of groupware technologies in a broader sense.

2. The Collaborative Dimension of Tailoring Activities

What are the important aspects that motivate or even enforce cooperation in tailoring activities? Abstract perspectives on tailoring functionality have usually been dominated by distinguishing different tasks and complexity levels of tailoring interfaces (Henderson and Kyng, 1991; Mørch, 1997).

In the literature on tailorability collaborative aspects have been mentioned at several occasions since the early 1980ies. Already Stallman (1981) reports that users not only think of small changes and try them, but also pass them over to other users. Mackay (1990) researched how people actively shared their tailoring files with each other. Oberquelle (1994) proposes a classification of groupware tailoring distinguishing tailoring actors, who can be individuals or a group, from persons affected by a tailoring activity, who can again be individuals or a group (see Figure 15.1). This can also be used to classify collaborative tailoring. Different aspects and intensities of collaborative tailoring of a single-user software product and of groupware fit in the resulting four categories:

		Actors	
		Individuals	**Group**
Persons Affected	**Individuals**	Individualization	Individualization supported by group
	Group	Tailoring effective for group	Group tailoring

Figure 15.1. Classification of collaborative tailoring (Kahler, 2001b; following Oberquelle, 1994).

Individualization: individuals tailor for themselves and are the only ones affected by the tailoring activity—e.g. individual keyboard shortcuts or the window layout of an individual email client;

Tailoring effective for group: individuals can tailor for a whole group who then agree or are obliged to use the tailoring files—e.g. a system administrator or expert user provides a letterhead to be used by the group;

Individualization supported by group: a group can tailor synchronously or asynchronously for its members to use and change the tailoring file—e.g. several persons work on collection of macros that individuals can use;

Group tailoring: a group can tailor synchronously or asynchronously and its members agree or are obliged to use the tailoring files—e.g. several persons work on the introduction of semi-structured email templates valid for the whole group.

The strict borders between the four different categories mentioned blur when we try to apply them to practical examples (cf. Kahler, 2001b, p. 28). It is not easy to locate the different accountabilities in the process that lead to a tailoring activity and in the process of the tailoring activity itself. While it is usually clear who actually worked with the tailoring interface of an application, it is not clear whose assumptions, ideas and decisions influenced a new tool configuration.

The Oberquelle model focuses on the distinction of one or more actively designing user on the one hand (*the* tailoring activity), and the passive "target users" on the other. This distinction focuses too much on the tailoring activity itself, and it does not represent additional activities of counseling, discussing, evaluating, validating, idea creation, etc. that are also very relevant for collaboration success in tailoring activities.

We believe that, to understand and support collaboration in tailoring activities, it is necessary to distinguish ideas and approaches according to what actually motivates users to collaborate regarding the configuration of software tools. The classification we propose here aims at differentiating the field along the interests and technological ties that bind users together in the process of collaborative tailoring. These are, in our eyes, motivated by the organizational context of the users as well as by the architectural properties of the application to tailor. We believe that it is useful to distinguish four levels of ties that bind users together and motivate cooperation regarding the (re-)configuration of tools.

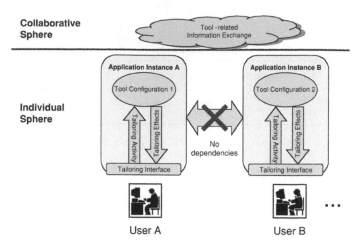

Figure 15.2. Collaboration in "Shared Use" scenarios.

2.1. TAILORING IN "SHARED USE" SCENARIOS

On the first level it is the tool usage itself that serves as a common denominator for cooperation. Users can be perceived as a "Community of Interest" regarding the usage of a tool. Tasks and activities may be related to acquiring knowledge about aspects of tailoring covering possible tool configurations as well as alternatives for tool replacement (cf. Stallman, 1981; Robertson, 1998; Kahler, 2001b). The common task of individualization of the tool is performed individually, but the existence and liveliness of user forums on single-user-applications (e.g. text processors) on the web indicate the social dimension of the task (see Figure 15.2).

Almost any office application can be considered as an example in this category. If we look a common modern text processor, we usually find support for several tasks in the document types and functions it offers (Text, Thesis, web page, circular letter, etc.) and for several use situations (e.g. language contexts). Configurations affect how these functions modify the document (e.g. the automated spell checking function) or how it is being presented to the user. Though software producers usually offer manuals and training support, existence and use of several newsgroups and web discussion fora for some text processors show that users are aware of other users and their expertise. The problems encountered when trying a new task are solved by discussing possible changes with other users (Mackay, 1990).

2.2. TAILORING IN "SHARED CONTEXT" SCENARIOS

The interdependencies between different users and their usage of tools increase dramatically if the users collaborate. Both, a shared task as well as a shared organizational context, add new dimensions even to configuring single-user tools. A standardization of tool configurations may lower costs of computer administration and ease tool-related

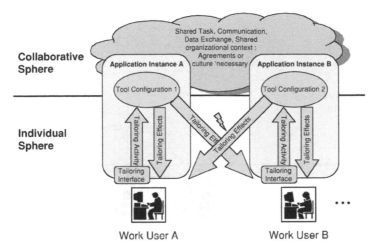

Figure 15.3. Collaboration in "Shared Context" scenarios.

communication among users in an organization. Collaborating on a common task may require an agreement on tool versions and technological standards (e.g. file formats to use) among the users involved (even beyond organizational borders). In general, tool configurations of one user may have effects on the work of other users as well. Social interaction regarding tool configurations in these settings is more focused and the shared context may support these interactions. Robertson (1998) described the occurrence of "tailoring cultures" in small design companies. So, these settings do both, they pose new requirements as well as offering new options for the technical support of tailoring. We call these settings "Shared Context" scenarios when we address technical support for collaborative tailoring (see also Figure 15.3).

If we again consider the use of a text processor in an organization, we find use patterns where configuration settings are being passed around because users are sufficiently familiar with each other's tasks and their similarities (Kahler, 2000). Tailoring can be delegated to other users that have similar tasks, and the results are used without necessarily having to understand how tailoring has been done. A shared task forces users to agree on some aspects, e.g. document formats and naming conventions for the documents produced. However, users are basically still free in deciding on the configuration of their own text processor instance. They have to perform the tailoring individually at their own workstation, even if it is only following tailoring instructions of other users.

2.3. TAILORING IN "SHARED TOOL" SCENARIOS

In settings where a groupware tool is used for collaboration, it results in even stronger interdependencies (e.g. Pipek and Wulf, 1999) of configuration decisions, and there are cases where for technical reasons there can be only one valid configuration (see below)

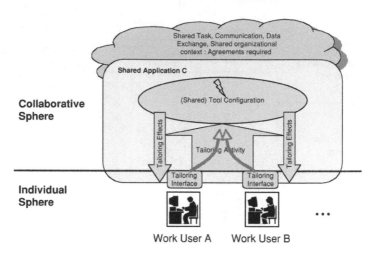

Figure 15.4. Collaboration in "Shared Tool" scenarios.

for a group of users. In these cases, after an agreement on the desired tool configuration is achieved, it is impossible or disadvantageous to deviate from the common ground found, and the decision of individuals to disagree may deny them tool usage at all. The ties between the users are even stronger, and call for a collaborative solution for the tailoring process itself. We will address this context of technical support for collaborative tailoring as a "Shared Tool" scenario (see Figure 15.4).

An example of a "Collaborative Tool" scenario is the configuration of access rights for the shared workspaces of a groupware. There can only be one set of access rights of a workspace, so the structure of the workspace and the visibility of documents it contains will be configured for all groupware users. In this case, users have to agree on the configurations appropriate for the necessities of collaboration as well as for the protection of privacy. We will later refer to another example with similar dynamics.

2.4. TAILORING IN "SHARED INFRASTRUCTURE" SCENARIOS

To catch the dynamics of modern workplaces it is necessary to extend the notion of the interdependencies described above also to tool "infrastructures" (Robertson, 1998; Dourish, 1999; Dourish and Edwards, 2000; Dittrich et al., 2002; Hansson et al., 2003), where similar situations occur when separate but tightly interwoven tools and technologies are being used (see Figure 15.5).

We can illustrate that with an example from our project practice: In an IT consultancy the decision to share contact information using the "LDAP" standard required an update of a Personal Information Management software. In this update, the designers of the tool have decided to change the default standard for address information exchange from the Electronic Business Card Standard "VCF 2.1" to version 3.0. Parts of the consultancy were involved in a research network where members shared contact information by

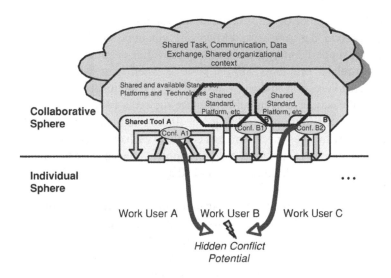

Figure 15.5. Collaboration in "Shared Infrastructure" scenarios.

storing ".vcf"-files in a shared directory, and suddenly the newest addresses from a central repository for Electronic Business Cards were not readable for some of the users. With the practices of sharing contact information via the LDAP protocol and of depositing VCF-files in a shared directory of a local network the users involved in both contexts introduced a hidden dependency into their work environment. In these "Shared Infrastructure" scenarios, dynamics similar to "Collaborative tool" settings can be encountered, but the dependencies are less obvious to users. These problems often occur because purchase of applications is a relatively uninformed decision where the applications' capabilities are more important than its dependencies, important future requirements are not anticipated and there is a lack of knowledge on the applications accountabilities (cf. Dourish, 1997).

We now want to discuss different options to support the settings of tailoring that we sketched here.

3. Support for Collaborative Tailoring in "Shared Use" Scenarios

"Shared Use" scenarios are those in which the users have the weakest ties; they may only share a common interest into a software artefact and its tailoring options. In contrast to "Shared Context" scenarios there may be no shared culture of usage or task congruency among the potential collaborators. There may be large variations of user interests regarding certain features of an application over space and time. A specific shared technological infrastructure can usually not be assumed beyond the basic Internet services (E-Mail, WWW, etc.). Consequently, there are only limited opportunities for a systematic support of collaboration in tailoring.

However, the emergence of tool-related discussion fora (partly initiated by the man-ufacturers themselves, e.g. Apple[2] and Microsoft[3]) on the web shows us that there is a solid baseline for support concepts in the idea of providing communication facilities for all kinds of tool-related problems. Similar positive experiences with newsgroups have also been reported in several studies (Mackay, 1990; Okamura et al., 1994). Addition-ally, a number of cases have been published that showed a combination of usual user support measures (providing opportunities for finding help and giving feedback) for software products with measures to connect clients to each other. But these approaches usually reflected more organizational or philosophical concepts. The technology sup-port did not go beyond the alternatives described above (Hansson et al., 2003; Dittrich et al., 2002).

Taking the need of communication about tools seriously, two aspects of the tailoring discussion should be highlighted. The first aspect is the need for tailoring objectifi-cations (Henderson and Kyng, 1991) as the entities that provide a meaningful closed subset of the possible manipulations of the software. It is also important to provide some kind of "tool ontology," names for these objectifications that may represent their meaning. Aside from using language, appropriate graphical representations of the applications and the tailoring interfaces are also helpful. As a second aspect, the provision of easy access to these virtual meeting places is also important. Today, this requirement is often covered by providing links to these web pages in the applications themselves.

4. Support for Collaborative Tailoring in "Shared Context" Scenarios

In this section we describe several aspects and approaches and one in-depth example for tailoring support in "Shared Context" scenarios. This is meant to clarify the qualitative difference of "Shared Context" scenarios as compared to "Shared Use" scenarios and how this new quality can be met by technical and organizational means.

4.1. ASPECTS AND APPROACHES FOR "SHARED CONTEXT" SCENARIOS

In "Shared Context" scenarios, of course all aspects described for "Shared Use" sce-narios also apply. But with the shared user context, be it an organization or a shared project, additional dynamics evolve. A culture of collaboration is established between separate users, a fact that brings new dependencies as well as new options (e.g. the delegation of tailoring activities to colleagues).

4.1.1. *Requesting and Sharing Ideas for Tailoring*

Mackay (1990) did one of the first larger studies on the role of collaboration in tailoring activities. The study was conducted at two research sites. At the first site, 18 people

---

[2] http://discussions.info.apple.com/
[3] http://www.microsoft.com/communities/default.mspx

using Information Lens (Malone et al., 1988) to tailor the management of their emails were observed over a period of three or more months. Depending on the job category (e.g. Manager, Secretary or Application Programmer) the different groups borrow and lend files with different intensity and have a different percentage (0–38%) of translators. Mackay concludes both cases by criticizing that staff members are often not rewarded for sharing tailoring files and requests that tailorable software should provide the ability to browse through others' useful ideas and that it should include better mechanisms for sharing customizations which then may serve to establish technical or procedural standard patterns.

Mackay (1991) studied the tailoring behavior of 51 users of a Unix software environment over a period of four months. Four main reasons that lead to tailoring have been identified: external events like job changes or office moves, social pressure like contact to colleagues who suggest changes, software changes like breakdowns or upgrades (the latter often retrofitting new software to behave like the old version), and internal factors like spare time or running across a previously unknown feature. The topmost barriers for the persons she asked were the individual factor *lack of time* (cited by 63% of the users) and the technological factor that the software was *too hard to modify* (33%).

4.1.2. *The Importance of Expert Users*

The role of a local expert was also highlighted by Gantt and Nardi (1992) who describe what they call patterns of cooperation among 24 CAD users. They distinguish between local developers who write macros, programs and scripts and help end users in tailoring on one hand, and on the other hand gardeners as a sub-group of local developers. Gantt and Nardi support the contention that the activities of local experts should be recognized and promoted since a local expert, and particularly a gardener, can save the organization's time and money by offering valuable resources, like macros and programs to the entire group. They admit, however, that it may be difficult to find a person with the right combination of technical and social skills.

Nardi and Miller (1991) present results from an in-depth-study where they conclude that spreadsheet co-development is the rule rather than the exception and that spreadsheets support the sharing of both programming and domain expertise. Considering the fact that more and more off-the-shelf software needs tailoring and offers mechanisms for it, the presented results encourage the tighter integration of using and tailoring.

4.1.3. *Tailoring Between Differentiation and Standardization of Tools*

Contrary to a criticism voiced often, tailoring must not necessarily lead to an abundance of confusing individual configurations but may also help good solutions to become standards. Trigg and Bødker (1994) found an emerging systematization of collaborative tailoring efforts in a government agency. In their study, tailoring showed aspects of what Fischer and Giaccardi (in this volume) called unself-conscious design, where situated knowledge is more important than an explicit description and where people solve their own problems rather than those of others as in a self-conscious culture of design. While it is often argued that tailoring leads to an unmanageable abundance of individualized solutions, several aspects imply that tailoring in this organization does rather have a standardizing effect. Standards of particular text blocks and of macros and button panels that reflect the work practice can be developed and widely used because the organization explicitly supports individual and collaborative tailoring and the distribution of tailored files. Wulf (1999) provides an example how the complexity of a tailorable search tool can be managed by organizational and technical means.

4.1.4. *Technical Support of Collaborative Tailoring*

Wasserschaff and Bentley (1997) describe how they supported collaboration through tailoring by enhancing the BSCW Shared Workspace system. They designed multi-user interfaces for the BSCW system, which allow users to take a certain view on the data in the shared workspace. These Tviews can be added to the shared workspace as objects in their own right, so others may take them individually, use them, and modify them in the same way as documents and folders.

In their Buttons system MacLean et al. (1990) explicitly supported the sending of tailored files via email. They propose that the two possibilities to make systems more tailorable for workers are to make the tailoring mechanisms accessible and to make tailoring a community effort. The notion of the importance of a community of people who tailor is supported by Carter and Henderson (1990). Based on their experiences with the Buttons system they claim that a Tailoring Culture is essential to the effective use of a tailorable technology.

The aforementioned examples stress that collaborative tailoring does not only occur among groupware users, but also in groups of users using the same software and thus being able to profit from the fact that this software is tailorable and that tailoring files may be exchangeable. Particularly the fact that more and more computers are connected to a local or wide area network creates the infrastructure to exchange tailoring files even of single user applications easily through the network. Therefore, the boundaries between collaborative tailoring of a single-user software product and a groupware become fuzzy (see also "Shared Infrastructure" scenario). We now look closer at one of our prototypes, which captures these dynamics.

4.2. COLLABORATIVE TAILORING OF A WORD PROCESSOR

Generic single user applications usually do not provide support to share tailoring files among its users. However, they are often tailored collaboratively. To support such collaborative aspects of tailoring single user applications, an extension to a common off-the-shelf software product that should allow the exchange of tailoring files was developed and resulted in a tool, which provided collaborative tailoring functionality as "Microsoft Word" extension (Kahler, 2001a).

4.2.1. *Setting*

To learn about users' habits and to inspire the design, we carried out a qualitative field study with users of Microsoft Word. 11 semi-structured interviews with users from four different fields were conducted (public administration, private company, research institute, and home users).

Depending on their field of application the interviewees reported about differences in the extent and the way tailoring is seen as a collaborative activity. We identified four typical use situations leading to design suggestions.

4.2.2. *From Use Situations to Design Suggestions*

While use situation IV ("Experience transfer among insulated home users") just deals with experience transfer, use situations I to III are based on an exchange of adaptations. In these use situations, this common use of adaptations is either technically non-supported (exchange of floppy disks) or supported by tools, which are realized apart from the word processor (intranet, LAN directory, groupware application). Both of these solutions seem to be problematic because they require the users to leave the application to acquire the adaptations. Therefore, it seems worthwhile considering to integrate the support for collaborative tailoring into the word processor's functionality.

To design such an integrated support, the following considerations seem to be of special importance. Depending on the state of a tailoring activity there are different groups of users involved in carrying them out (e.g., use situation II—Collaborative Tailoring and Organization-Wide Distribution). The extent to which adaptations are reasonably shared obviously corresponds to the tasks that are supported by them. Such a task can be specific to an individual (e.g., use situation IV—Experience Transfer Among Insulated Home Users), a group or a department (e.g., use situations II—Collaborative Tailoring and Organization-Wide Distribution -and III—Shared Document Templates and Notification of Users) or even a whole organization (use situation I—Central Repository for Standardized Forms).

Thus, support for collaborative tailoring should allow differentiating among various groups of users when sharing adaptations. There are obviously situations where mail support seems to be appropriate to exchange adaptations. E.g., in cases an experienced user builds an adaptation especially required by a user for the task at hand, a mail tool seems to be the appropriate technical support for distribution. On the other hand, in case adaptations by a specific user are not required instantly, a publicly accessible store allows selecting among these adaptations at the moment required by the task at hand (e.g., use situations I to III).

Finally there is a need to make users aware of the fact that somebody else has produced an adaptation with relevance to them. An integrated tool to support sharing of adaptations could provide additional awareness within the system.

Evaluating the use situations and summing up the results of the final discussion with the interviewees, the following main suggestions for the tool emerged. It turned out that this empirical evidence is in line with theoretical and empirical work described in the literature about tailorability:

Tight integration in the word processor application;

Mechanisms for sharing, sending and receiving tailoring files

A public store to provide a location to exchange tailoring files;

Mailing mechanisms for users to be able to send tailoring files directly to other single users and groups of users;

A private workspace for tailoring files, that may be copies of files from the public store or files received from others via the mailing mechanism;

An awareness service that notifies users about modifications of tailoring files.

Consequently, the respective features were provided in a prototype as an extension ("add-in") to Microsoft Word implemented in Microsoft Visual Basic for Applications.

Finally, a usability test of this add-in has been conducted by using the method *constructive interaction for testing collaborative systems—CITeCS* (Kahler, 2000).

4.2.3. *Discussion and Future Extensions*

The word processor case showed that even for single user applications collaborative aspects of tailoring are an issue. It also showed that, with relatively little effort, several important features for collaborative tailoring can be supported: the word processor was already tailorable on several levels (choosing from alternative behaviors, creating macros) and extensible by an add-in implemented in Basic; most organizations have their computers connected and already support some forms of shared workspaces. So the technology and infrastructure is mature enough to connect people who tailor single user applications individually in order to be able to introduce collaborative aspects. Moreover, the case showed how fuzzy the borders between use and tailoring are: The tailoring files most interesting to the word processor users were document templates, which are basically write-protected documents. However, as templates they were considered to be tailoring files, since they modified the functionality of the word processor in use, because the users could start the word processor by double-clicking a template and immediately were able to do their task of, say, writing a formal request.

Our results hint to the fact that a tool for sharing tailoring objects as described may increase the frequency of tailoring activities. We assume that such a tool may also serve as a medium that encourages groups to discuss group standards, e.g. for letter templates that then can be shared. The systematization of customizations (Trigg and Bødker, 1994) resulting from a collaborative tailoring process would then contribute to common norms and conventions needed for collaborative work (Wulf, 1997).

Suggestions for the use of such a tool cannot be restricted to technical design suggestions but must include organizational aspects as well. We are convinced that the establishment of a "gardener" (Nardi, 1993) or "translator" (Mackay, 1990), e.g. a local expert responsible for the coordination of tailoring activities, is a vital part of tailoring measures in organizations.

Right now it seems that adaptations are most usefully applied in the organizational context of their emergence supporting the tasks they are made for. The sharing tool in its current form is most helpful for small work groups with a rather similar work context.

Our hypothesis about the technical and organizational scalability of such a tool is that the model of public and private spaces and the distinction between creator and user of the artefacts need to be enhanced to more than two levels when the group size exceeds a certain limit. Like in shared workspaces for general purpose, a more sophisticated access control model is needed (Pankoke and Syri, 1997). Meta-information like annotations made by an adaptation's creator may help to compensate for part of a lacking context. If such a tool would allow distributing adaptations worldwide, e.g. via the World Wide Web (WWW), one could even think of supporting global teams or even establish widely accessible libraries for adaptations. Whether this is, however, reasonable in the light of the poverty of knowledge of organizational and task context is unclear. How context could possibly be provided and how large groups of participating contributors can be handled may be learned from experiences in distributed software development. This is particularly interesting when taking place without existence of a formal organization as in the case of the distributed development of Linux and its components. Anecdotal evidence shows that questions of ownership and membership play an equally important role here as they do in "ordinary" organizations and settings (Divitini et al., 2003).

However, in our experience it is clear, that collaborative tailoring does not scale easily. As always the question remains open how much administrative work the participating individuals are willing to contribute for the benefit of a group or organization and how much administrative effort is still reasonable to stay on the profitable side of collaborative tailoring. More refined tools to measure this and more refined categories to weigh the individual and group pains and gains against each other are needed.

An alternative to a tool presented above is the embedding of such a mechanism to exchange Microsoft Word related adaptations into a generic organizer of adaptations belonging to different applications. This organizer could combine mail mechanisms (or even be part of an email client) with the operating systems' functionality for access rights or shared workspaces and an enhanced explanation and commenting functionality.

5. Support for Collaborative Tailoring in "Shared Tool" Scenarios

We now describe different approaches for technological support of "Shared Tool" scenarios. Again, the main aspects discussed for tailoring support in "Shared Use" or "Shared Context" scenarios also apply here. But the necessity to agree on (parts of) a tool configuration increases the interdependencies among users again and requires a different kind of support. We discuss several approaches before we elaborate deeper on some aspects using one of our own concepts.

5.1. ASPECTS AND APPROACHES FOR "SHARED TOOL" SCENARIOS

We describe four approaches that cover also the collaborative dimension of tailoring a shared tool, in most of these cases a Groupware application. All of these approaches highlight different aspects of the role of collaboration in tailoring: While Oberquelle (1994) focuses on a process-oriented perspective on tailoring, Fischer (2002) marked important aspects of design-in-use. Wang and Haake (2000) tried to achieve high levels of flexibility for their tailoring environment. The final two approaches go beyond classical notions of tailoring activities: Mørch and Mehandijev (2000) focused on opportunities for a long-term in-use collaboration between designers and users, and Wulf et al. (2001) described an approach to defer the decision about how a groupware system should act until the occurrence of actual "use requests."

5.1.1. *Tailoring Groupware as a Collaborative Design Process*

Oberquelle (1994) investigated tailoring as a collaborative design process and proposed groupware support for several tasks within the tailoring process. He identified five tasks:

> *Discuss inadequacies:* A groupware system could provide an opportunity for "Meta-communication" to allow users to discuss inadequacies of the groupware system.
>
> *Conceptualize alternatives:* With the acknowledged requirement of "objectification" of tailoring alternatives given, this especially means to allow users to choose between or model a tailoring alternative.
>
> *Evaluate alternatives and decide:* All users should participate in the evaluation and the decision upon the tailoring task to process. The groupware system, with its messaging capabilities, could support this.
>
> *Implement the alternative chosen:* Finally, the tailoring alternative chosen should be implemented.
>
> *Notify affected users*: All users who are somehow affected by the tailoring alternative chosen should be notified that the change has been implemented now. Additionally, explanations of the "how" and "why" of tailoring can be given.

It is important to note that these task descriptions are not meant to be a model of consecutive, clearly distinguishable phases. Since tailoring processes can become quite complex regarding the functions modified in a tailoring activity, this would be an inappropriate restriction of the processes' flexibility. The ideas presented provide a first weak process model of collaborative tailoring activities.

5.1.2. *The "Meta-Design" Perspective*

The "Meta-Design"-philosophy is covered in an own chapter in this book (see there). We now only want to relate to some of its aspects (described in Fischer and Scharff, 2000) that we consider important for collaborative tailoring. The baseline of the argumentation is that most new technologies developed within the IT sector treat the user more as a consumer than as an active participant in a technological setting. Fischer and Scharff call for a notion of the user as an active (co-)designer of the technological settings he works with. Several perspectives on developing adequate design environments form the "Meta-design" philosophy. In a broader description of the idea and its context, Fischer (2002) called for designing technical infrastructure, organizational issues (learning environment and work organization) and a socio-technical environment for design-in-use at design time.

In this context, tailoring has the notion of a design-in-use activity where several designers (professional developers and users) are involved into designing the configuration of a tool. We point out some aspects and experiences that are relevant for particularly collaborative tailoring as an activity.

Fischer and Scharff stress the importance of *domain orientation* for design environments. They should reflect the entities that form the design problem as well as those relevant for describing possible solutions. In the design problem described, this is the domain of urban planning and mass transportation. The domain orientation does not only reflect in the concepts and abstractions used but also in their form: Tangible representations of the design problem result in more appropriate opportunities for articulations by participants.

In the example domain these tangible representations also play an important role for *collaborative representations*. Collaboratively developed representations are important for developing both, an individual understanding of the concepts and interests of others as well as a manifestation of the shared notions regarding the design problem.

In a related paper, Fischer and Ostwald (2002) described the combination of an *action space* with a *reflection space* as a basic useful architecture for collaborative design (e.g. in Urban Planning). In a way this can be associated with collaborative tools having a "use space" (the ordinary use interface) and a "tailoring space" (where there could be room for reflection).

The special facet of the "Meta-Design" idea to support *design communities* (instead of only individual designers) also is very relevant for collaborative tailoring. This aspect stresses that the design activity (or tailoring activity) also comprises secondary activities of learning, communicating and collaborating regarding issues important in the design process. These are also important to support. Finally, communities may provide a context of motivation and reward for participating in design activities ("good community citizenship").

While pointing out important directions to think about, many of the ideas have to be concretized to be able to guide the development of support for collaborative tailoring. Another important problem of the approach is that it mainly addresses "big," complex and separate design activities while tailoring activities are often much smaller and tightly interwoven with the work practice of the users.

5.1.3. The "Cooperative Hypermedia Approach"

Wang and Haake (2000) present CHIPS, a hypermedia-based CSCW toolkit with elaborated abstraction concepts (role models, process models, cooperation modes, etc.) in a three-level modelling scheme (meta-model, model and instance) that allows users to describe and tailor their cooperation scenarios. Generally based on an open hyperlink structure the system is extendable on any modelling level and thus should be able to support every cooperation scenario that may occur. In this respect it is similar to CSCW toolkits earlier proposed by Dourish (1996) or Malone et al. (1992).

Wang and Haake focus on the notion of tailoring as a collaborative activity. The main example they use to present the toolkit is the collaborative development of a work environment for a newly formed team. Their toolkit provides access rights systems and discourse representation facilities oriented at the method of issue-based information systems (IBIS, Rittel 1973; Conklin and Begemann 1988). The tailoring activity is incrementally described and performed within the hypermedia system as any other collaborative activity. In their example they use a weak process model with the steps idea creation, discussion of alternatives, decision-making and implementation that is similar to the ideas of Oberquelle (1994). The approach does not explicitly implement this process but the tools (especially the model and instance editors) are designed to facilitate that process.

In our eyes, the benefits of the approach are its openness, flexibility and extensibility. Although they do not provide an example from a real application field, it is credible that the architecture would cover a large set of collaboration scenarios and associated tailoring activities. The major drawback is that the cognitive costs for end users to apply the approach are very high (it requires understanding the modelling layers, the abstraction concepts and the tools). This might be acceptable in complex or model-oriented work environments (e.g. software engineering), but even then depending on the granularity of the modelled descriptions the work costs of keeping the models up to date might well outweigh the perceived benefits.

5.1.4. *Using "Multiple Representations" and "Application Units"*

Mørch and Mehandijev (2000) aim explicitly at supporting tailoring as a collaboration process between end users and professional software developers. They see this as a long-term cooperation to continuously improve software artefacts and develop concepts to support communication among the stakeholders involved in these settings (designers and end users).

They propose to provide *multiple representations* of the software artefact as well as the continuing design process and the design decisions taken so far. These representations can, for example, represent code, or more abstract perspectives like control flow diagram, design rationales or other documents produced in the context of earlier tailoring/design processes. To provide a better overview they should be grouped into *application units* that consist of representations of different abstraction levels that belong to one aspect of the software's functionality. These ideas have been successfully tested in two cases, and proved to produce a higher transparency within the process of continuous tailoring of an application. Mørch and Mehandijev formulate the finding of appropriate representations for users with different experience backgrounds and skill levels as an important open issue, a fact that also shows in their example cases, where representations still orient much at programming concepts.

5.1.5. *"Lazy Evaluation" of Tailoring Alternatives*

The approaches presented before cover tailoring activities that take place before the actual use situation occurs. As an important alternative, Wulf (1997; Wulf et al., 2001) described an approach of tailoring the access rights in a Groupware application *during* the actual use situation. Consciously delaying the specification of the access rights for every user or role in advance, the framework provides different ways of negotiating access to a document by means of communication channels between the requesting and the granting user. Contrary to the usual notion of tailoring as producing *persistent* changes, these changes are temporary and can be handled in very flexible ways. Implementation of these kinds of strategy complements the conservative notion of tailoring and may be especially important for settings where users with very heterogeneous interests share one tool, e.g. communities or virtual organizations (Stevens and Wulf, 2002).

5.2. COLLABORATIVE TAILORING AS "INTEGRATED DESIGN BY DISCOURSE"

From the approaches and concepts described above it already becomes obvious that in a "Shared tool" scenario, establishing an agreement about the appropriate configurations of tools becomes the main problem. In that way, the collaborative tailoring process resembles more a classical design process. In one of our own approaches (Pipek, 2003), we built a prototype of a collaborative tailoring environment that is based on the ideas described above. More specifically, it comprised dialogical environment that allows all users to articulate their needs and concerns, a weakly-structured design process that culminates in a decision procedure, and additional means to integrate the discourse and the technological alternatives under consideration.

The tailoring activity to support was the configuration of an "Awareness Service," an event notification service that aimed at providing users with contextual information relevant for their current work activities. It can be tailored by defining three rulesets: An individual "privacy" ruleset (for defining what events the other users are allowed to see), an individual "interest" ruleset (for defining what events from other users a user wants to see), and a "global" ruleset (that supersedes the other rulesets and defines visibility conventions for different groups of users on different organizational levels). The definition of that "group" ruleset is a classical representative of a "Shared Tool" scenario, and was the tailoring activity we wanted to support. The application field we designed the prototype for was a part of a German federal authority, whose evolving use of groupware we studied and supported over almost 4 years (see Pipek and Wulf, 1999 for details). Configuring the visibility of group members proved to be highly relevant for privacy as well as collaboration issues, and called for a participative approach.

The original prototype of the Awareness Service was implemented in the standard groupware system DEC LinkWorks, that offers similar services like Lotus Notes

(Shared Workspaces, messaging, workflow support, etc.) by Fuchs (1998). We extended the existing prototype to support collaborative tailoring as a design process (see Pipek, 2003 for implementation details). The basic idea was to support "meta-use" of the groupware features, to use these features to (re)design the groupware itself. We now reflect on some details.

5.2.1. *Tailoring as a Collaborative Design Process*

Besides a notion of the tasks and their order within this design process (we rely here on the descriptions by Oberquelle, 1994, see also above), it is important to consider the context the users are in when they want to tailor their application.

In general, tailoring does not belong to the primary work task of users. Users can only spend a very limited amount of time on the tailoring activities themselves as well as building up the knowledge necessary for a qualified participation. It is also important to note that collaborative tailoring can be a task where group-inherent conflicts may occur. It is necessary to not artificially restrict communications related to this task with a formal process or discourse model (see also Shipman and Marshall, 1999). Furthermore, tailoring as a design task occurs at different degrees of maturity of an organizations' groupware infrastructure. There can be no general assumption on the duration and perceived complexity of a tailoring activity.

5.2.2. *A Discourse Environment for Collaborative Tailoring*

Contrary to earlier approaches we did not focus on the configuration activity itself, but on the discourse process that would accompany it. The discourse then represents the tailoring activity as a design process that ends with a decision procedure.

We supported the design process itself by providing a decision procedure based on voting and my suggesting a duration for the tailoring activity. Of course, both aspects of the design process should be flexible. The question whether this flexibility should be managed by using shared process administration means, or by delegating this to a trusted facilitator was left open in our concept.

The participation of users was stimulated by not restricting access to the tailoring environment (i.e. every user could open a new "tailoring process" by suggesting a reconfiguration of a rule or ruleset, or just by articulating discontent with current conventions) and by a conflict detection mechanism that would notify users of ongoing tailoring activities that would affect them (e.g., because they earlier explicitly agreed on the convention rule that is now under revision, or, even stronger, because a suggested rule would conflict with their individual rulesets). A feature we called "discourse awareness" helped users tracing discussions they participated in (e.g., whenever someone comments on a tailoring alternative they proposed or answers to one of their statements, they get notified by email). We also addressed the problem of involving technologically less-skilled participants on different levels:

Location: The discourse environment could be found exactly where all other tool configurations of the groupware would be done.

Language: The "tailoring language" worked with the metaphors and entities that users already knew from using the groupware ("desk," "shelf," "file," documents, organizational entities, workflows, users, etc.). That initial rule language was revised to integrate concepts (mapped as predicates of the rule language) that were derived from ethnographic material collected earlier in the application field and that represented relations between groupware entities as the users considered them important (e.g., "user X was involved earlier in workflow Y for document Z"). In addition, we provided a natural language representation of the convention rules (following an approach described in Stiemerling et al. 1997). This relates to the idea of multiple representations (Mørch and Mehandijev, 2000) as well as to the necessity of domain-oriented languages (Fischer and Scharff, 2000).

Easy Articulation: Providing unrestricted means of communication within the design process is necessary to address and negotiate conflicts and other social issues. We additionally supported the free articulations within the discourse environment by providing means to integrate relevant aspects of the tailoring alternative under consideration into an articulation (by "quoting" technology, e.g., in our case natural language representations of the predicates of the conventions under consideration).

In general, we wanted to limit the complexity of the tools we provide for tailoring to minimize the learning efforts that would be necessary for a qualified participation. It should always be easy to join, leave and re-join the shared tailoring effort.

5.2.3. *Evaluation of the Prototype*

The design of the prototype was informed by about 25 interviews and workplace observations in the application field (e.g. the tailoring language). Due to re-organizations, at the time of the completion of our prototype our application field was not available anymore for a strong evaluation of our concepts in the work setting the prototype was designed for. We could evaluate the prototype only regarding the comprehensiveness of our concepts in a laboratory setting (using the "Heuristic Evaluation" method (Nielsen, 1993) although with persons familiar with the original field of application). Some observations are:

The representation of rules in natural language helps, although it does not significantly reduce the complexity of expressions necessary to achieve a desired result.

The discourse environment for comments can be used not only strictly related to the design process, but also for more general questions regarding the awareness feature. It can also contribute to a qualification of users.

The "Quoting" functionality is considered helpful, although it is still problematic to describe the actual problem with a (part of a) convention in words.

In general, the test users were able to orient themselves in the tailoring environment appropriately.

Stronger than the earlier approaches, our concept focussed on the necessity of end-user negotiation in collaborative tailoring processes. Of course, this concept and its implementation are just one other experiment in exploring possible solutions to support the continuous collaborative (re-) design of shared software artifacts. We will later describe a notion of opening the discussion of (collaborative) tailoring to support the appropriation of technologies in many different ways.

6. Collaborative Tailoring of and in "Shared Infrastructures"

We now move to areas of the discussion where we still find more challenges than solutions. In the preceding parts of this chapter we could draw from a rich variety of studies and concepts that have been published in CSCW research. However, the technological solutions that have been developed share one aspect: a typical tailoring activity is supposed to cover *one* tool or service. But this is not an appropriate perspective on current work environments, today the different services and technologies needed and used to establish computer-supported environments for cooperation can be almost arbitrarily distributed between operating system platforms, middleware applications, groupware applications and single-user-applications. With the emergence of more and more fragmented work environments (Virtual Communities, Virtual Organizations, Freelancer Networks, etc.), and the development of new technologies "beyond the Desktop" (Personal Digital Assistants, Mobile Phones, Wearable Computing, Ubiquitous Computing, etc.) the complexity of the technological *infrastructure* used for intra- and inter-organizational collaboration is likely to further increase (see illustrating cases e.g. in Robertson, 1998; Dittrich et al., 2002; Törpel et al., 2003). Regarding the scope of tailoring activities this means that there may be more than one tool or service to tailor to reach a desired state of the technological environment. But, as the example we used for "Shared Infrastructures" in the beginning of this chapter illustrates, there are also more and hidden dependencies between different artefacts. We are aware that part of the approaches that we described before can contribute to support for collaborative tailoring for part of the scenario we now look at. But first we should look at some special aspects of the "Shared Infrastructure" scenario.

6.1. THE NOTION OF "INNER" AND "OUTER" TAILORABILITY

Similar to the support concepts, also the general discussion of "tailorability" as a property of an artefact does not reflect the interdependencies with the (technological) context it is used in. It is useful to widen the perspective in the context of our discussion.

The considerations on tailoring described above assumed software artefacts (especially groupware tools) as the technologies to provide support for continuing design in use. In our setting we consider mixed reality environments that may provide a rich variety of hardware and software artefacts, input and output devices. We now try to frame our discussion on tailoring for this kind of settings.

From a user's perspective, all that matters for perceiving an IT artefact as helpful is whether or not the technology provides the use or functionality the user wanted. Maybe it is provided in a straightforward way, maybe the desired behavior of the technology can be achieved through tailoring it. If this is not possible, there may be another technology that serves the user better. This competition of technologies leads to use environments that contain different technologies or even technology fragments (in terms of only partial use of the functionality available). A new, complex image manipulation software product may be only used to remove the "red eyes" effect off a digital photograph. Maybe adding an annotation to it will be done using a presentation software product, and the resulting file will then be sent out to a relative with an email client—all this in spite of the fact that the image manipulation software initially used would have been able to support all three tasks described. Established technology usages may be only partially abandoned in favor of new technologies. The use of different fragmented technologies has been found in several organizational settings (Robertson, 1998; Dittrich et al., 2002; Törpel et al., 2003).

This use pattern lets us derive two kinds of tailorability. The "inner" tailorability addresses the flexibility and ease of manipulation of a tool or device itself to fit different use scenarios. This is the notion of tailorability that was part of most of the work described above. The use scenario with the image manipulation software requires something different that we refer to as "outer" tailorability: A technology has to be prepared for working together with other, even competing technologies to enable users to tailor their work environment by selecting and combining (partial) technologies. Technically technologies can achieve that by referring to a common, shared technological background that is—for desktop applications—usually provided by the operating system (e.g. providing a file system and a directory structure, or support for a software installation procedure), but also comprises standardized protocols (e.g. SQL, OLE), "common" hardware configurations (e.g. PCs being able to display graphics with a certain resolution) and a functionality composition and representation that shows the technology is aware of the fact that it may be used only partially or that it may be even replaced (Pipek and Wulf, 1999 show an example for a lack of that awareness). Even more, a technology may have to refer to "softer" standards like usability standards (e.g. interface items like checkboxes or drop-down menus) or established use patterns (e.g. copy-paste-functionality) to achieve "outer" tailorability. Additionally, concepts for the support for collaborative tailoring have to become also aware of "outer" tailorability issues.

6.2. INFRASTRUCTURE RECONSIDERED

Traditionally, tailoring activities have been seen connected with the organizational change in a work setting. But our notion of infrastructures and technology interdependencies indicates that the complexity of the technological environment may also require tailoring activities to just maintain current work practice in changing technological contexts. This "Retrofitting" has previously been observed in workplace settings on an individual level, e.g. when users tried to re-configure an application after an update to provide the "old" application behavior (Mackay, 1991). But this kind of "Maintenance Tailoring" (as we like to call it) is not always directed backwards (as the term "Retrofitting" implies), but also toward the future, e.g. if a user updates an application because collaborating partners have done so, just to maintain an existing practice of document exchange.

In this context, it is helpful to take into account another notion of "infrastructure," beyond just being a set of interconnected tools, technologies and devices. Star and Bowker (2002) describe infrastructure as something "in the background," that "runs underneath other structures," something that we rely on without paying much attention to it. But in the case of a breakdown it comes "into the foreground," we suddenly notice its importance, and the correction of the breakdown may become a comparatively urgent issue. Star and Bowker also stress that there has to be some stability and standardization to allow a perception of an infrastructure as supportive. Some of the approaches we described above relied on this requirement, and were able to support the tailoring of sets of heterogeneous tools, but only if the tools have been developed within a specific framework (e.g. Wang and Haake, 2000). However, cases from several virtual organizations showed there are also strong dynamics that work against standardization (Törpel et al., 2003; Karasti and Baker, 2004). For current developments in the field of distributed computing, like application service providing, web services and grid computing (Foster and Kesselmann, 1999), this observation should be taken into account.

For the field of collaborative tailoring, the hidden dependencies and the possible perceived urgency of detecting and correcting infrastructure breakdowns just to maintain the current work setting pose new challenges that can be illustrated by some questions:

> How do I know what part of my infrastructure did change and caused the breakdown? Who did the re-configuration that was responsible for that? How do I tell that it was someone else's tailoring activity, not an accident (e.g. power failure) that caused the breakdown? How can I react without negotiation in case the reconstitution of my infrastructure is urgent?
>
> How do I know who will be influenced by my tailoring activity? How do I negotiate about possible re-configurations of my tools/devices?

One possible way to answer these questions would be to use metadata on the applications and devices that reflect its capabilities regarding inner and outer tailorability. Once created, the resulting system of representations may be the foundation for new approaches to support collaborative tailoring.

6.3. POTENTIALS FOR SUPPORTING COLLABORATIVE TAILORING

One of the key features of the approaches for collaborative tailoring we described in the preceding sections is the use of representations of applications and tailoring objectifications as a basis for computer-supported communication, distribution, discussion and negotiation processes. It was possible to develop and describe concrete approaches because the scope of developing the tailoring support was within *one* application, and so it was within the scope of the development of the application itself. The developer of the application had complete control over the functionality and the possible tailoring activities. Now, looking at tailoring "beyond one tool," the scope of possible application-relevant (and use-relevant) tailoring activities goes beyond the scope of development of the application itself. This situation still carries aspects of the "Shared Context" and "Shared Tool" scenarios, but a "targeted" design of support for collaborative tailoring is not possible here. But we can discuss the issue along these general notion of application representations on the one hand and communication and collaboration facilities on the other.

There are obvious and simple ways to create representations of applications and tailoring objectifications using the screen capturing features of modern operating systems to produce screenshots. However, depending on the interface design these can be more or less useless to describe tailoring issues, and some aspects of an application can't be represented accordingly (e.g. its architecture or menu structure). The use of video and/or animation would illustrate problems better (Baecker, 2002), but the application itself may also provide more sophisticated representations of itself. It would be possible to draw on representations that have been made during application development (similar to those described by Mørch and Mehandijev 2000, or in the context of "design rationale" systems in Moran and Carroll, 1996). Dourish (1997) discussed the idea of providing "computational representations" of the behavior of application components for users at the interface as well as for other components to determine current activities of a component. Reaching the goal to enable every application (component) to exactly represent its "area of accountability" (e.g. a text processor is responsible for the spell check, but not for problems with the file system) would actually also help to manifest and visualize structure in "Shared Infrastructure" scenarios.

For communication and collaboration, levels of technology have to be used that are accessible for all the actors involved. As in the concepts developed by Kahler (2000), this is likely to be the traditional E-Mail infrastructure that can be found at almost every modern workplace. In another research approach we made first experiments with web-based forums to negotiate infrastructures (Pipek, subm.).

7. From Collaborative Tailoring to Appropriation Support

For the final part of our discussion we want to take a step back and look at the broader picture. Several long-term studies (Mackay, 1990; MacLean et al., 1990; Karsten and Jones, 1998; Pipek and Wulf, 1999; Törpel et al., 2003) pointed out that the technologies used in organizations are tailored again and again to match the changing user needs. Through the processes of familiarization, (re-) configuration and usage the technology is appropriated, that means it is being transformed and specialized from the more or less abstract notions of usage the technology designers once imagined to be possible with it, to the concrete interests, meanings and purposes of (a group of) users. In this process of appropriation, we see tailoring as the key activity, since every tailoring activity is in fact (at least partially) a re-discovery and re-invention of the practices that are possible with this technology. Exploring the collaborative dimensions of tailoring is—in our eyes—also a starting point for exploring the collaborative dimensions of technology appropriation, where the main point is to not only understand a technology and its affordances, but to also be able to develop and negotiate alternative scenarios in a group or organization. The provision of appropriate tailoring environments and technologies of flexibilization (e.g. component-based systems) is a technological prerequisite of appropriation processes, but we now turn from a perspective of more or less "targeted" tailoring activities to build an appropriate collaborative environment to "softer" tasks like getting new ideas for a better practice, learning about technological options and possible usages, and discussing and deciding on alternative scenarios (with implementation being only a secondary interest). Can't we do more in technology design to support group appropriation processes?

Robinson (1993) described the "common artefact" and the characteristics that afford its successful appropriation in order to inform the design of collaborative software. For supporting the appropriation of technology in groups and organizations, the concept of "double level language" is particularly valuable. It distinguishes between two mutually supportive modalities of communication: "implicit communication" in which the artefact (e.g. a distributed spreadsheet, "Flight progress strips" used by air traffic controllers, a key rack at a hotel reception) is a medium for communication (by transmitting the current state of work activities or work results), and "explicit communication" (e.g. speech, ad-hoc notes), in which the artefact is providing representations of work-related issues that can be referred to. This suggests an understanding in which a collaborative technology or tool is as well a medium for implicit communication as something that provides reference points for explicit work-related communication. But in addition to that, the discussions of collaborative tailoring above show that a collaborative technology can also provide the means for explicit communication, can prepare to be the subject of explicit communication (being a "work-related issue") and can support implicit communication regarding technology usage.

We pick up some aspects of the experiences discussed before to show that there is more to think about along this line of thought. We do that together with developing our notion of "appropriation activities." We try to distinguish three purposes of activities within appropriation processes, and discuss related issues and concepts from the experiences we described.

7.1. UNDERSTANDING TECHNOLOGIES

By understanding we mean the discovery and aggregation of knowledge on the basic principles and scopes of technologies ("This software is a text processor," "Before you can use software, you have to switch the computer on," "If you can't save your text on a floppy disk, it may be write-protected, it may be not formatted, your operating system is maybe occupied with doing something else, but it is not the word processor that is causing the trouble," etc.). This kind of knowledge is especially important for the case of breakdowns in the infrastructure. It is to some extent a prerequisite of technology usage, but it is also very general knowledge. Dourish (1997) pointed out one possible direction of technological improvements to support "understanding." He discussed the intransparency of current technological infrastructures and proposed to use behavioral descriptions of a technology (and its subparts) as a complement of current architectural descriptions. The general goal is to enable technologies to "understand" the behavior of other technologies to be able to orientate in a rich infrastructural setting. As a consequence they would also be able to deliver a more precise picture of their capabilities and limitations to the user.

Regarding collaborative aspects, we see this kind of knowledge being gained mostly through "legitimate peripheral participation" in communities of people who have and use this technology (cf. Wenger, 1998). Because of the weak shared interests of users, we consider this to be similar to the situation in "Shared Use" scenarios, and see similar (limited) opportunities for technological support.

7.2. LEARNING ABOUT A TECHNOLOGY

With learning we want to refer to the acquisition of knowledge necessary to use a technology according to the purposes that the technology designers embedded into it. It means to learn about the menu structure and other navigation instruments, and the functionality the technology offers. It also refers to learning about the means to modify and tailor the technology.

Currently, small tutorials, help systems and "application wizards" support users in learning about a software artefact together with non-computer-based means (books, courses, etc.). However, there could be even more and better representations of technologies using multimedia technology[4] and embedding it into the artefacts themselves. Another idea would be to offer more different representations of the artefact (e.g. behavioral descriptions). But, since learning as a "side effect" of collaborative tailoring has been mentioned before (Wulf and Golombek, 2001; Pipek, 2003), we again regard the direct support of tool-related communication as a key feature; and we could well imagine using concepts and experiences from the field of Computer-Supported Collaborative Learning to further improve current tailoring environments to better support appropriation.

Another important idea for a more active learning process was presented by Wulf and Golombek (2001). They addressed the problem that the consequences of tailoring activities are often not visible to the tailor. They suggested integrating "exploration

---

[4] It is interesting to observe that even in "Open Source {XE "Open Source"}" communities there are videos for explaining and training tool usage (for example for the Content Management System "Typo3": http://typo3.org/1407.0.html).

environments" into groupware tools that allow users to play with the tailoring interface of a tool without actually changing something in their organizational context. These exploration environments also presented the results of the exploratory tailoring activities from the perspective of the users affected by it. Again, we could well imagine additional benefit for appropriation processes if there would also be collaborative exploration environments where users share the experience of exploring the possible configurations of the technology they use.

7.3. SENSEMAKING OF TECHNOLOGIES

Maybe the most important step of appropriation happens when users start to answer the question: What can this technology do *for me (us)*? Usually this involves considering current abilities, tasks, technologies and their usages, but also the perceived value of the new technology at stake.

Several studies showed (Mackay, 1990; Pipek and Wulf, 1999) how a new technology "diffused" into an organization. In a department of a federal authority with approximately 25 staff members, the introduction of a groupware application took about 18 months from the first user working with it until the last computer was installed. Users discovered the value the new technology might have for them by observing other users in the same organizational context (Pipek and Wulf, 1999). Making usages of a technology better observable, maybe within the technology itself, could support this mechanism. Linton (2003) described a system for sharing expertise on using a word processor. He tried to record and associate the "use traces" (consecutive interface actions) of different users to give recommendations on tool usage. This could also be interesting for just visualizing the practice of other users. Complemented with additional communication facilities this might help a new user to assess the perceived value of a technology for other users in similar use scenarios. With the similar intent to allow users to "leave their traces" by enhancing their information spaces, Dourish (2003) described a system that allowed flexible end-user extension of document metadata ("properties") as well as attaching dynamic behavior through "active properties". Dittrich (1998) suggested to explicate the scenarios and assumptions that the designers had when developing the software in order to enable the users to understand what the intended use of the software was and what parts of these assumptions and scenarios apply to the current use situation the user is in. Similarly to Mørch and Mehandijev (2000) the idea relates to a designer-user dialogue for sensemaking, but can easily be expanded to support the user-user dialogue for sensemaking that we consider crucial to support technology appropriation in organizations.

Reconsidering the "exploration environments" (Wulf and Golombek, 2001) mentioned above, we could also imagine using these environments to demonstrate alternative use scenarios or technologies to a group of users. As a "test simulation" they can be especially valuable if it is possible to map aspects of the real existing work setting of the potential users.

7.4. BUILDING "COMMUNITIES OF TECHNOLOGY PRACTICE"

Concluding the discussion above, we want to develop a notion of technical support for "Communities of technology practice" (following the concept of "Community of practice" of Wenger (1998)). The ideas of understanding, learning and observing technology-in-use can be consolidated in a concept of "inhabited technology," where environments for collaborative tailoring are extended to give users a permanent presence within the technology, making the "tool" also a "place." It is still an open question, for which (levels of) technologies this is possible and appropriate (see discussion on "Shared Infrastructures" above).

Again, some of the approaches we described above focus on a perspective of supporting "user-user" communication, which we consider most important for appropriation support. Törpel et al. (2003) and Hansson et al. (2003) show example settings in which that communication emerged, and changed technology design and usage. The concepts and experiences developed for virtual communities, especially regarding communication and the visualization of users and issues, can be exploited to further enhance tailoring environments in that line of thought. Twidale and Nichols (1998) showed an example for this support regarding the definition of successful search queries for a library database system, although because of the lack of persistence (of communication partners as well as "tailoring objects") in that solution their system follows neither the notion of "tailoring" nor the notion of "community" we would like to establish here. But in their system design as well as their evaluation they also stress the importance of adequate representations (which are, in their case, visualizations of a query and the related search process of the database system) of the system's behavior not only for understanding, but also for communicating about a technology. Consequently, they also offer an embedded support for user-user communication.

That perspective above should be complemented by experiences and concepts published regarding the improvement of user-designer communication. Getting back on the ideas of Fischer and Scharff (2000) on the alternating phases of proliferation and consolidation (the "Seeding—Evolutionary Growth—Reseeding"—Model), a concept that Törpel et al. (2003) also encountered in practice, and of Mørch and Mehandijev (2000) on the need for a solid long-term collaboration between technology designers, tailors and users, it would be also feasible to incorporate the designers into this community. Hansson et al. (2003) showed an example of combining methods from Participatory Design and Agile Software Development in order to form a (non-virtual) "Community of Technology Practice" of software providers and users. This would also change the context of tool development, and complement the "technology push" of the designers with the "demand pull" of the users. This is common practice in many Open Source Projects, where users can request new features of software artefacts (e.g. the "requested features" on http://sourceforge.net/), and has also be reported in commercial contexts (Dittrich et al., 2002; Hansson et al., 2003). In that concept, the domains of traditional software development, tailoring and Participatory Design, could find a shared manifestation in technologies and technology development processes (see also Dittrich et al., 2002).

8. Conclusion

In this chapter we tried to capture the collaborative dimension of configuration activities, and explored opportunities for technological support of collaboration in tailoring activities. We distinguished four scenarios ("Shared Use," "Shared Context," "Shared Tool" and "Shared Infrastructure") with different intensities of ties between the potentially collaborating users, and described existing approaches as well as open research issues.

We pointed out, that especially "Shared Infrastructure" scenarios with their heterogeneous, intertwined and interdependent mixes of technologies, still pose a major challenge to research on tailorable systems. Tailoring activities "beyond one tool" have not been addressed in the current disussions on collaborative tailoring.

The general line of argumentation in the approaches was—in line with our own beliefs—that every technology should be aware of the fact that it is subject to communication and negotiation. The approaches tried to cover this requirement not only by offering the necessary granularity and flexibility to allow finely differentiated alternatives, but also by providing representations that are helpful in user-user communication and negotiation. Some also integrated communication facilities into tailoring interfaces.

In the final part of our discussion we addressed another shortcoming of the current discussions. While studies about tailoring always suggested a need of user-user-interaction in the context of tailoring, these activities have rarely found explicit support in technological approaches. Our taxonomy revealed the different necessities for interaction in the different scenarios, but we suggest to use the approaches we presented only as a starting point for a broader technological support of processes of technology appropriation. We suggested improving the safe explorability of technologies and the visualizations of technology usage. But we consider it most important to further improve the means of communicating and negotiating (especially user-user interaction, but also user-designer interaction) on the basis of these new ways to represent technology structures and use.

References

Baecker, R. (2002). Showing instead of telling. In: *ACM SIGDOC'02*. (Toronto, On, Canada, 2002), ACM Press, pp. 10–16.

Carter, K. and Henderson, A. (1990). Tailoring culture. In: *Reports on Computer Science and Mathematics no. 107. Proceedings of 13th IRIS*, Åbo Akademi University 1990, pp. 103–116.

Conklin, J. and Begemann, M.L. (1988). gIBIS: A hypertext tool for exploratory policy discussion. In: *Conference on Computer Supported Cooperative Work* (Portland, Oregon, USA, 1988), ACM, pp. 140–152.

Dittrich, Y. (1998). *How to make Sense of Software—Interpretability as an Issue for Design*, Department of Computer Science and Business Administration, University of Karlskrona/Ronneby, TR 98/19, Ronneby, Sweden, p. 9.

Dittrich, Y., Eriksen, S. and Hansson, C. (2002). PD in the wild; Evolving practices of design in use. In: *Participatory Design Conference* (Malmö, Sweden, 2002), CPSR, pp. 124–134.

Divitini, M., Jaccheri, L., Monteiro, E. and Trætteberg, H. (2003). Open source processes: No place for politics? *Proceedings of ICSE 2003 workshop on Open Source* (Portland, Oregon), pp. 39–44.

Dourish, P. (1996). *Open Implementation and Flexibility in CSCW Toolkits*. London, UK: University College London.

Dourish, P. (1997). Accounting for system behaviour: Representation, reflection and resourceful action. In: M. Kyng and L. Mathiassen (eds.), *Computers and Design in Context*. Cambridge: MIT Press, pp. 145–170.

Dourish, P. (2003). The appropriation of interactive technologies: Some lessons from placeless documents. *Computer Supported Cooperative Work (CSCW)—The Journal of Collaborative Computing* 12(4). pp. 465–490.

Dourish, P. (1999). Software infrastructures. In: M. Beaudouin-Lafon (ed.), *Computer Supported Co-operative Work*, Chichester, England: John Wiley & Sons, pp. 195–219.

Dourish, P. and Edwards, W.K. (2000). A tale of two toolkits: Relating infrastructure and use in flexible CSCW toolkits. In: *Computer-Supported Cooperative Work (CSCW)*, 9(1). pp. 33–51.

Fischer, G. (2002). *Beyond 'Couch Potatoes': From Consumers to Designers and Active Contributors*, Available at http://firstmonday.org/issues/issue7_12/fischer/, 2002. First Monday (Peer-Reviewed Journal on the Internet) 7(12).

Fischer, G. and Giaccardi, E. (in this volume). Meta-Design: A framework for the future of end user development.

Fischer, G. and Ostwald, J. (2002). Seeding, Evolutionary growth, and reseeding: Enriching participatory design with informed participation. In: *Participatory Design Conference* (Malmö, Sweden, 2002), CPSR, pp. 135–143.

Fischer, G. and Scharff, E. (2000). Meta-design: Design for designers. In: *International Conference on Designing Interactive Systems (DIS'00)*, (Brooklyn, New York, USA, 2000), ACM Press, pp. 396–405.

Foster, I. and Kesselmann, C. (eds.) (1999). The grid: Blueprint for a new computing infrastructure. Morgan Kaufmann Publ. Inc., San Francisco, CA, USA.

Fuchs, L. (1998). *Situationsorientierte Unterstützung von Gruppenwahrnehmung in CSCW-Systemen*, ("Situated Support for Group Awareness in CSCW—Systems"). PhD Thesis, FB Mathematik und Informatik, Uni-GHS Essen, Germany.

Gantt, M. and Nardi, B.A. (1992). Gardeners and Gurus: Patterns of Cooperation among CAD Users. In: *Proceedings of CHI '92*. pp. 107–117.

Hansson, C., Dittrich, Y. and Randall, D. (2003): "The development is driven by our users, not by ourselves"—including users in the development of off-the-shelf software. In: *26th Information Systems Research Seminar in Scandinavia (IRIS 26)*, (Haikko Manor, Finland, 2003), IRIS Association.

Henderson, A. and Kyng, M. (1991). There's no place like home: Continuing design in use. In: J. Greenbaum and M. Kyng (eds.), *Design at Work: Cooperative Design of Computer Systems*, Lawrence Erlbaum Ass., Hillsdale, NJ, pp. 219–240.

Kahler, H. (2000). Constructive interaction and collaborative work: Introducing a method for testing collaborative systems. In: *acm interactions* VII(3) (May/June 2000). pp. 27–34.

Kahler, H. (2001a). More than WORDs—collaborative tailoring of a word processor. In: *Journal of Universal Computer Science (j.ucs)* 7(9), pp. 826–847.

Kahler, H. (2001b). *Supporting Collaborative Tailoring*. Department of Communication, Journalism and Computer Science, Roskilde University, Roskilde.

Karasti, H. and Baker, K.S. (2004). Infrastructuring for the long-term: Ecological information management. In: *37th Hawaii International Conference on System Sciences (HICSS 2004)*, http://csdl.computer.org/comp/proceedings/hicss/2004/2056/01/205610020c.pdf. (9.3.2004).

Karsten, H. and Jones, M. (1998). The long and winding road: Collaborative IT and organisational change. *International Conference on Computer Supported Work (CSCW'98)* (Seattle, WA, USA, 1998), ACM Press, pp. 29–38.

Linton, F. (2003). OWL: A system for the automated sharing of expertise. In: M.S. Ackerman, V. Pipek, and V. Wulf (eds.), *Sharing Expertise: Beyond Knowledge Management*, MIT Press, Cambridge, MA, USA, pp. 383–401.

Mackay, W.E. (1990). Patterns of sharing customizable software. In: *Proceedings of CSCW '90*. pp. 209–221.

Mackay, W.E. (1991). Triggers and barriers to customizing software. In: *Proceedings of CHI '91*. pp. 153–160.

MacLean, A., Carter, K., Lövstrand, L. and Moran, T. (1990). User-tailorable systems: Pressing the issues with buttons. In: *Proceedings of CHI 90*. pp. 175–182.

Malone, T.W., Grant, K.R., Lai, K.-Y., Rao, R. and Rosenblitt, D. (1988). Semistructured messages are surprisingly useful for computer-supported coordination. In: *Proceedings of CSCW 88*. Morgan-Kaufmann Publishers. pp. 311–334.

Malone, T.W., Lai, K.-Y. and Fry, C. (1992). Experiments with Oval: A radically tailorable tool for cooperative work. In: *International Conference on CSCW (CSCW '92)* (Toronto, Canada, 1992), ACM Press, pp. 289–297.

Moran, T.P. and Carroll, J.M. (eds.) (1996). *Design Rationale: Concepts, Techniques and Use*. Mahwah, NJ, USA: Lawrence Erlbaum Assoc.

Mørch, A. (1997). Three levels of end-user tailoring: Customization, integration, and extension. In: M. Kyng and Mathiassen, L. (eds.), *Computers and Design in Context*, Cambridge, MA: MIT Press, pp. 51–76.

Mørch, A. and Mehandjiev, N. (2000). Tailoring as collaboration: Mediated by multiple representations and application units. *Computer Supported Cooperative Work: The Journal of Collaborative Computing*, Special issue on "Tailorable Systems and Cooperative Work" 9(1), 75–100.

Nardi, B.M. (1993). *A Small Matter of Programming*. Cambridge, MA: MIT Press.

Nardi, B.A. and Miller, J.R. (1991). Twinkling lights and nested loops: Distributed problem solving and spreadsheet development. *International Journal Man-Machine Studies* 34, pp. 161–184.

Nielsen, J. (1993). *Usability Engineering*. Boston, MA: Academic Press.

Oberquelle, H. (1994). Situationsbedingte und benutzerorientierte Anpaßbarkeit von Groupware. ("Situation-dependent and user-oriented Tailorablilty of Groupware"). In: A. Hartmann, T. Herrmann, M. Rohde, and V. Wulf (eds.), *Menschengerechte Groupware— Software-ergonomische Gestaltung und partizipative Umsetzung, Teubner*, Stuttgart, pp. 31–50.

Okamura, K., Fujimoto, M., Orlikowski, W.J. and Yates, J. (1994). Helping CSCW applications succeed: The role of mediators in the context of use. In: *International Conference on CSCW* (1994), ACM Press, pp. 55–65.

Pankoke, U. and Syri, A. (1997). Collaborative Workspaces for Time deferred Electronic Cooperation. In: *Proceedings of GROUP '97*. pp. 187–196.

Pipek, V. (2003). An Integrated Design Environment for Collaborative Tailoring. In: *ACIS International Conference on Software Engineering, Artificial Intelligence, Networking and Parallel/Distributed Computing (SNPD '03)* (Lübeck, Germany, 2003), ACIS, 430–438.

Pipek, V. (2005). Negotiating infrastructure: supporting the appropriation of collaborative software, International Reports on Socio-Informatics (IRSI), 2(1) IISI, Bonn, Germany, 44 p.

Pipek, V. and Wulf, V. (1999). A groupware's life. In: *European Conference on computer supported cooperative WORK (ECSCW '99)* (Copenhagen, Denmark, 1999), Kluwer, Dordrecht, Netherlands, pp. 199–218.

Rittel, H.W.J. (1973). On the planning crisis: Systems analysis of the first and the second generation. *Bedriftsokonomen* **8**. pp. 390–396.

Robertson, T. (1998). Shoppers and tailors: Participative practices in small Australian design companies. In: *Computer Supported Cooperative Work (CSCW)* 7(3–4), 205–221.

Robinson, M. (1993). Design for unanticipated use.... In: *European Conference on CSCW (ECSCW '93)* (Milan, Italy, 1993), Kluwer, Dordrecht, NL, pp. 187–202.

Shipman, F.M.I. and Marshall, C.C. (1999). Formality Considered Harmful: Experiences, Emerging Themes, and Directions on the Use of Formal Representations in Interactive Systems. *Journal on Computer Supported Cooperative Work*, **8**. pp. 333–352.

Stallman, R. (1981). EMACS: The Extensible, Customizable, Self-Documenting Display Editor. In: *Proceedings of the ACM SIGPLAN SIGOA* (1981), Mass. Institute of Technology, pp. 301–323.

Star, S.L. and Bowker, G.C. (2002). How to infrastructure. In: L.A. Lievrouw and S. Livingstone (eds.), *Handbook of New Media—Social Shaping and Consequences of ICTs*. London, UK: SAGE Pub. spp. 151–162.

Stevens, G. and Wulf, V. (2002). A new dimension in access control: Studying maintenance engineering across organizational boundaries. In: *International Conference on CSCW* (New Orleans, 2002), ACM Press, pp. 196–205.

Stiemerling, O. and Cremers, A.B. (2000). The EVOLVE project: Component-based tailorability for CSCW applications. *AI & Society* **14**, 120–141.

Stiemerling, O., Kahler, H. and Wulf, V. (1997). How to make software softer—designing tailorable applications. In: *DIS '97* (Amsterdam, 1997), ACM Press, pp. 365–376.

Törpel, B., Pipek, V. and Rittenbruch, M. (2003). Creating heterogeneity—Evolving use of groupware in a network of freelancers. *Special Issue of the International Journal on CSCW on "Evolving Use of Groupware"* **12**(4), pp. 381–409.

Trigg, R., Moran, T.P. and Halasz, F.G. (1987). Adaptability and tailorability in notecards. In: *INTERACT'87* (Stuttgart, Germany, 1987), pp. 723–728.

Trigg, R. and Bødker, S. (1994). From implementation to design: Tailoring and the emergence of systematization in CSCW. In: *Proceedings of CSCW '94*. pp. 45–54.

Twidale, M. and Nichols, D. (1998). Designing interfaces to support collaboration in information retrieval. *Interacting with Computers* **10**, pp. 177–193.

Wang, W. and Haake, J.M. (2000). Tailoring groupware: The cooperative hypermedia approach. *International Journal of Computer-Supported Cooperative Work* **9**(1), 2000.

Wasserschaff, M. and Bentley, R. (1997): Supporting cooperation through customisation: The tviews approach. In: *Computer Supported Cooperative Work: The Journal of Collaborative Computing (JCSCW)* **6**, pp. 305–325.

Wenger, E. (1998). *Communities of Practice—Learning, Meaning and Identity*. Cambridge University Press, Cambridge.

Wulf, V. (1997). *Konfliktmanagement bei Groupware* ("Conflict Management in Groupware applications"). Vieweg, Braunschweig.

Wulf, V. (1999). Evolving cooperation when introducing groupware-A self-organization perspective. In: *Cybernetics and Human Knowing* **6**(2), 55–75.

Wulf, V. (1999). "Let's see your Search-Tool!"—On the collaborative use of tailored artifacts. In: *Proceedings of GROUP '99*, New York: ACM-Press, pp. 50–60.

Wulf, V. and Golombek, B. (2001). Exploration environments: Concept and empirical evaluation. In: *International ACM SIGGROUP Conference on Supporting Group Work* (Boulder, Colorado, USA, 2001), ACM Press, pp. 107–116.

Wulf, V., Pipek, V. and Pfeifer, A. (2001). Resolving function-based conflicts in groupware systems. *AI & Society* **15**, 233–262.

Chapter 16

EUD as Integration of Components Off-The-Shelf: The Role of Software Professionals Knowledge Artifacts

STEFANIA BANDINI and CARLA SIMONE

Dipartimento di Informatica, Sistemistica e Comunicazione, Università degli Studi di Milano-Bicocca, via degli Arcimboldi, 8, 20126 Milano (Italy)

Abstract. An empirical case study highlights that software professionals develop and use specialized knowledge artifacts to improve the effectiveness of product design based on components-off-the-shelf integration. Computational counterparts of these artifacts improve the cooperative problem solving required by the design of applications fulfilling complex user requirements. Integration is likely to become a typical approach in EUD too, and tools supporting it are required. This chapter describes the outcomes of the case study. Lessons learned are discussed with regard to EUD, when it is interpreted as a creative discovery of components to be integrated.

Key words. Knowledge Artifact, Software Integration, Design as Discovery

1. Background and Motivations

In their contribution to this book, Pipek and Kahler (2004) aptly describe the combined effects of technological evolution and organizations needs for the design of techno-logical supports. This combination defines scenarios that raise new demands to the approaches proposed so far to empower end-user and make them able to tailor inno-vative applications. The authors explicitly recognize that in these scenarios there are more challenges than solutions: the aim of this chapter is to contribute to this aspect of EUD drawing inspiration from a study we conducted with professionals of a software company. We believe that the kind of support they required to improve their production process can suggest an interesting view on how to complement existing proposals for EUD in these emerging situations.

Innovative applications are often constructed as the integration of self-standing com-ponents supplied by different producers, the so called services or commercial-off-the-shelf (COTS) (Morisio et al. 2000, 2001). These modules, at different levels of ab-straction, are specialized to optimally solve problems requiring ad hoc competences in application domains or in specific infrastructural technologies. The trend to base software development on integration (e.g., the open source strategy) is not only the result of a rationalization process based on re-use but also a necessity. In fact, software companies may not want to acquire all the competences needed to guarantee the highest level of quality of all modules constituting the final solution. Our study confirms this trend: the company's professionals were mainly involved in integration activities.

Henry Lieberman et al. (eds.), End User Development, 347–369.
© 2006 *Springer.*

Integration requires modular approaches to software construction and tailorability. In EUD modularity has been achieved by means of component based approaches (Won et al., 2004) where components ideally belong to the same adaptable application. We refer to this situation as *composition*.[1] When the application is constructed as *integration* of self-standing components, the scenario is quite different. In fact, composition and integration, although conceptually similar, are pragmatically quite different. The former is more about the configuration at the *functional level* while the underlying *infrastructure* is in some way provided together with the components themselves. Instead, integration requires the joint selection of the functional components and of the infrastructure making them operational.

Accordingly, EUD can be viewed as composition or integration, and end-users as composer (Teege, 2000) or integrators. Although both views are possible and may coexist in the same reality, we focus our attention on the *role of integrator* since the current and expected trend in software production is likely to create this situation in an increasing way. In this view, integration requires a specialized support to improve EUD since both infrastructure and "glue" components have to be taken into account. The role of infrastructure in EUD is emphasized in (Pipek and Kahler, 2004) too: the authors mention the general "lack of knowledge on applications accountabilities", introduce the notion of "outer tailorability" and refer to "strong dynamics that work against standardization". All these aspects fit very well the concept of integration introduced above: our contribution builds on top of their arguments by considering what we have learnt in observing professionals playing as integrators.

When those professionals described their production process, they recognized that integration requires a stronger cooperation between technical and non-technical people (typically, involved in customer management and in company's strategy definition). In fact, both COTS and solutions integrating them have to be constantly maintained in front of the evolution of the COTS market. In addition, this dynamic situation stimulates customers to look for new opportunities to improve their technical supports. In this situation, professionals emphasized that integration exacerbates the role of the so called non-functional requirements (Chung et al., 1999) to obtain the quality of the final application from the end-user point of view. In fact, beside *functional requirements* that are focused on the desired set of functionalities and their correctness, *non-functional requirements* have to be considered to select the most appropriate solution among the possible compositions implementing the same set of functionalities. Non-functional requirements focus on the pragmatic aspects of the application and are more related to its context of use. Hence, professionals need to access information not only about the functionality incorporated in the various modules but also about those characteristics affecting the fulfillment of non-functional requirements. These characteristics—they claim—are seldom described in software documentation. On the contrary, they emerge from the combined experiences of different professionals cooperating in

---

[1] The terms *composition* and *integration* are defined here, irrespective of their possibly different connotations in the literature.

interdisciplinary production teams: experts in technical aspects, in application domains, in organizational contexts, in the risk evaluation of the envisioned solutions, in the overall costs of an experimented solution, and so on.

The final solution is the result of a cooperative effort combining diversified experiences: the latter are stratified in current and past design activities. Accordingly, professionals like to describe integration as an activity where explicit and tacit knowledge (Nonaka and Takeuchi, 1995) are jointly put at work. In fact, they perceive the management of explicit and, especially, tacit knowledge as a crucial success factor for their collaborative core activity.

If end-users have to play the role of integrators in EUD, it is worthwhile to look at professional integrators and see how they find solutions to manage the knowledge necessary to improve the quality of their products and the productivity of their collaborative design efforts. From this observation it is then possible to conceive tools that, complementing existing proposals, can more comprehensively support EUD. The following sections illustrate this point.

The chapter is organized as follows. The next sections describe our experience in the design of a tool supporting the production processes in a software integrator company. The outcomes of this experience are then reconsidered in the light of EUD in order to identify tools that may be used in combination with other tools supporting EUD from different perspectives.

2. Knowledge Artifacts Supporting Professional Design

We have been recently involved in a project sponsored by an American Telecommunications Company (Telcordia Technologies, Morristown, NJ) whose aim was the design of a technology supporting software integration, one of the company's core business (Bandini et al., 2002a,b). Telcordia is a quite big software company selling services and integrated solutions for Business-to-Business and Business-to-Consumer applications: its customer are companies of different size, typically engaged in on-line business. The company issued a call targeted to research institutions in order to involve in the project competences complementing the in-house ones.

The core issue was the productivity of the problem solving required by the design of software solutions in front of customer requests. The latter are of course all different from each other: however, the required problem solving is about recurrent design aspects and relies on the experience the involved professionals gained in previous integration efforts. The challenge was to identify a support that is actually usable and used by these professionals and at the same time powerful enough to manage the complexity of integration. It was immediately evident that in this context improving productivity means facilitating the stratification of experience and the fruition of the related knowledge without breaking the mechanisms actually put at work by the involved professionals when they interact and cooperate. A knowledge acquisition campaign was conducted to uncover these mechanisms and base the solution on them. In the following we focus on the aspects of this study that are related to EUD.

2.1. THE SETTING AND THE APPROACH

The integration process involves both technical and non-technical roles. Beside the obvious software competences owned by *software engineers*, integration requires additional knowledge: *business manages'* competences in technological products and customers needs in order to define the company's strategies, and *consultants'* competences to negotiate with customers the most suitable solutions for their specific needs. Moreover, software engineers are specialized in various technical domains: for example, web technology, communication technology, and so on.

In a situation of fragmented and specialized competencies that lead to fragmented and specialized professional languages, what makes cooperation possible? In the specific case, what makes sharing of experiences possible?

In order to answer these questions it was necessary to establish ways to grasp the current practices in a situation that was problematic from two perspectives: first, the geographical distance between the company and the research team, second a very strict policy protecting the information about company's customers and how they are approached by consultants. Both problems were solved by focusing on the cooperation among engineers and consultants on the one hand and on the other hand through the pivotal role of a company's member who had the possibility to regularly travel to Italy. Moreover, he owned a deep knowledge of the problem at hand since he was in charge of the coordination of the consultants' support. In this role, he was motivated and very active in involving engineers and consultants in the project, sometimes collecting them in virtual meetings when the topic was urgent or it was difficult to collect all of them in the same place. The visits of the research team at the company site were concentrated at the beginning of the project, to meet and interview about twenty people among engineers and consultants. This was mainly achieved in a week workshop during which experts were involved, in groups or individually, in unstructured interviews. Very soon the interactions concerned the demonstration and validation of various forms of prototypes: from mock-ups showing the conceptual schemes incorporating the knowledge put at work in the cooperation among them and with their costumers, up to first versions of their technological counterpart. In this phase, the above mentioned company's member played the role of mediator between the professionals and the research team, thus reducing the number of site visits. The process lasted about 8 months and ended with the computational artifacts described in Section 2.2.

The interviews highlighted that people playing different roles as mentioned above form an implicitly defined community of practice. The latter is identified by the common goal to make the company successful in the software competitive market, and by a community language that makes the community survive through the exchange of the experiences needed to achieve the above goal (Wenger, 1998).

The community language became the focus of our investigation. It borrows elements from all the specialized professional languages and is different from each of them. In fact, it captures the subset of concepts and relations that are useful to cooperate and, more important, at the level of detail that makes mutual understanding possible. Those concepts and relations with their level of specification constitute the elements of a pair of tacit knowledge artifacts that are cooperatively maintained and used by different professionals during integration processes. The elicitation of these artifacts was achieved by means of both narratives of recurrent scenarios of cooperation and discussions about the critical points they highlighted. In the interaction with the research team these artifacts were incrementally externalized (Nonaka and Takeuchi, 1995) and became the core of the technology supporting integration. Before describing them in more detail, it is interesting to notice that a similar situation was recognized in another project targeted to a completely different domain. The path to discover the pertinent knowledge artifacts was quite similar and led to an analogous technological solution (Bandini et al., 2003).

2.2. THE KNOWLEDGE ARTIFACTS

The design of software products based on the integration of COTS, requires the selection of a set of components that fulfill the functional and non-functional needs of specific customers. Since needs are usually conflicting, the aim is to define an application and an infrastructure that guarantee an acceptable quality degree.

2.2.1. *The Components Model*

The company's jargon recognizes two kinds of components the so called *Business Components* (BC) and *Middleware Service Components* (MSC).

A BC is the implementation of a business functionality: for example, a credit-card system component implements the business logic dealing with the payment process by credit card. It was recognized as a common practice that functionalities are associated with BCs by definition: hence, components implement well-known business concepts, and experts use that knowledge to assembly software systems. MSCs define the environment for BC, and therefore support their inter-operation. One relevant attribute of a MSC is its compliance with *standards*. An Enterprise Java Bean (EJB) container is an example of MSC that defines the services an EJB component can access and, in particular, the way it communicates with other EJB components.

Since a core value of the integration experience is the knowledge about how components can be safely combined, a set of basic relations express this knowledge in terms of links among them. A *collaboration by dependency* relation links BCs when it is *part of the experience* that a component requires other components to provide its functionality. For example if there is a BC supplying the billing functionality, it is common practice that a BC supplying the tax handler functionality must be included as well since the two functionalities are logically co-related. A similar relation holds among MSCs. *Compatibility by dependency* means that well-experienced compatibility relations are defined between MSCs. For example, web experts know very well that the Tomcat web server and the JBoss EJB container can be used together to develop web-based applications. Finally, two symmetric relations link BCs and MSCs: the *requires* relation expresses the need of a BC for services that can be supplied by one or more MSCs. The

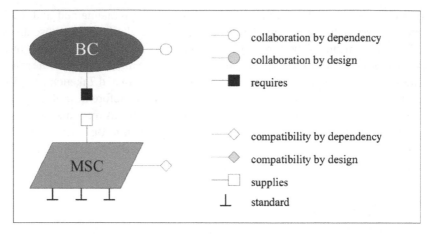

Figure 16.1. The component model.

supplies relation identifies the different services supplied by the MSCs and is the logical counterpart of the BCs *requires* relation.

In the above description, the crucial point is that the knowledge expressed by the various links is incorporated in the Component Model, and thus recognized as valuable, only if it is "part of the experience." In fact, relations do not express "official" knowledge that can be derived from components documentation (in the broad sense). They express facts that have been experienced: they can complete but also contradict the official information. In this respect, they incorporate the core knowledge characterizing the company's community of professionals.

Beside relations *by dependency*, professionals use two additional relations: *collaboration by design* and *compatibility by design*, that capture the stratification of experience in terms of integration of BCs and MSCs (respectively) in an open-ended set of software products that can be delivered to the costumers. Experienced architectures can be re-used as they are—or taken as—a starting point in the future negotiation with costumers.

The component model is summarized in Figure 16.1. It constitutes the knowledge artifact that professionals use to build the Component Repository (Comp-Rep). The latter is basically a labeled graph whose nodes are typed components carrying a name and a description of the related functionality/service, and whose arcs represent the above described relations. Before the introduction of the technology, the Component Model was used to document (in terms of experience of use) both single components or aggregations of them (full solutions or sub-assemblies). Small examples are given in Figure 16.2. Simplicity is the key success factor of the model: everybody can use it and, since it emerged from practice, everybody can understand the intended meaning of the documentation. Moreover, on the basis of their role, skill, and experience, professionals associate with symbols more detailed information, or at least are guided in the effort to look for it in other documentation supports that complement Comp-Rep. In any case, the latter is recognized as the primary reference artifact supporting co-design and sharing of experience among professionals. Software engineers are in charge to update the Comp-Rep since it mainly deals with technical aspects: updates may concern existing components or new ones, typically acquired in the market. In the latter case, the initial information is kept to the minimum and in any case considered as indicative, just to allow the component to be considered in future assemblies. Only the effective usage enriches its description, as discussed above. Consultants intervene to guarantee that all the solutions proposed to their customers have been appropriately stored and documented. In our study we analyzed in detail about 50 components that the company considered as a representative set. The company actually deals with some hundreds of them: hence, in order to efficiently manage the related information a computational support was needed.

The advantage of transforming Comp-Rep in a computational artifact is that it can be endowed with functionalities supporting the documentation and selection of components. Typically, it helps professionals in completing the selection in case of missing components linked to the selected ones in terms of *by dependency* relations. Moreover, the *requires* relation is used to identify all the MSCs that supply at least one of the services required by the BCs. When none of the available MSCs provides a required service, a *ghost-MSC* is introduced as a placeholder to complete the system architecture. The support identifies the characteristics that the actual MSC must have in order to fulfill the requirements: this information guides its acquisition in the market or its implementation. Relations *by design* are more problematic since they require human reasoning for their usage in the construction and validation of the target architecture. In fact, relations *by design* can express needs that previous solutions could not have considered. Anyway, the structure of the Comp-Rep helps professionals to identify the new solution and insert it as a piece of experienced design, i.e., as a new piece of core knowledge. In addition, the knowledge acquisition campaign highlighted patterns that are recurrently applied, and hence worth being specifically supported, to obtain consistent solutions. Basically, for any pairs of BCs related to *by design* relations, the patterns

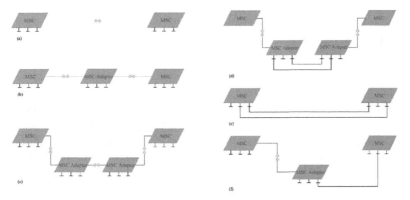

Figure 16.2. Possible configurations that satisfy the compatibility relationship between MSCs.

search the Comp-Rep for MSCs or combination of MSCs linked *by dependency* relations so that they form a path connecting the MSCs required by the initial BCs. Figure 16.2 proposes typical ways to "implement" a *by design* relation via different structures of MSCs linked by *compatibility by dependency* relations or by the compliance with the same standard (case d).

The identified patterns have been incorporated in a rule-based module that can be activated as an interactive support that is especially useful for new-comers, unexperienced professionals who are unaware of the common practice of the professionals' community. In fact, this practice emerges from, and can be experienced through, the dialogue supporting the selection of components.

This concludes the description of the computational knowledge artifact for what concerns the fulfillment of functional requirements.

2.2.2. *The Quality Tree*

A complete and consistent coverage of the functionalities that are necessary to address customer needs is not enough to provide them with an optimal solution. To this aim, non-functional requirements play an essential role either to evaluate a single solution or to compare alternative architectures satisfying the same set of functional requirements. The company's jargon puts all non-functional requirements under the umbrella of *quality*. The quality of the solution is the result of the combination of a variety of properties concerning the product and positioning it in the market. Accordingly, the jargon used to discuss quality is very rich: on the one hand, it contains elements coming from several professional languages; on the other hand, each quality aspect can be referred to at different levels of detail. In fact, professionals who are not experts in a domain typically speak of the related quality features using more generic terms than professional experts in that domain. To manage the quality problem the professionals constructed a second knowledge artifact: the *Quality Tree* that supports their discussions about the desired degree of quality of the target solution and about how to achieve it. Figure 16.3 shows a portion[2] of the Quality Tree that has been identified during the interaction with company's professionals.

The tree structure reflects the above mentioned richness in an adequate way: branches represent different quality features, while each hierarchical level corresponds to a specific degree of granularity for a particular quality feature. Thus, children of a particular feature node refine the quality metrics for that feature. The tree-structure shows the main distinction between *Marketing Quality Features* and *Technical Quality Features*. Each branch is extended to include and refine the pertinent quality values. For example, the marketing quality features have been refined adding three categories: *market position*, *investment risk*, and *cost*. Cost category has been further specified in *licensing*, *support*, *operation* (e.g., dedicated staff, etc.), and *configuration*. Through further refinements, professionals achieved a fine grain specification of the quality metrics. The tree

---

[2] IPR prevent us from giving more details about the actual Quality Tree structure.

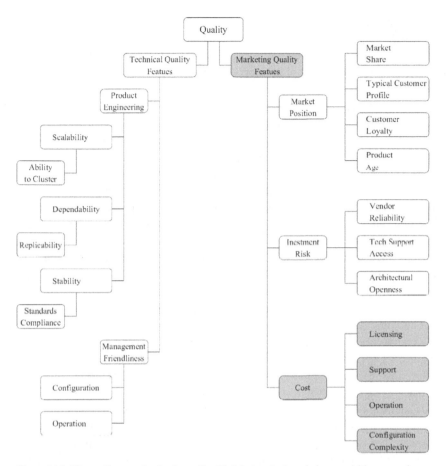

Figure 16.3. The quality tree that has been identified during the knowledge acquisition campaign.

structure naturally supports the extension of the Quality Tree both to add new features and to refine them. Hence the same structure was incorporated in the computational artifact.

The main role of the Quality Tree is to guide the characterization of components (BCs and MSCs) in terms of their quality features. To this aim, each element of the Comp-Rep has associated a Quality Tree whose values are defined, possibly in an incremental way, by an expert of the production team appointed to be responsible for it. Values are expressed in qualitative terms using a stratified set of linguistic conventions (ranges, terminology, etc.). Since the true meaning of non-functional requirements heavily depends on the specific architecture and on its context of use at the customer site, the *capability to correctly interpret the values* of the quality features is a competence that is owned by professionals irrespective of their specific expertise, and is a glue keeping the professionals community alive. In other terms, the unavoidable *under-specification* characterizing qualitative metrics does not prevent professionals from using the metrics in a very precise way for the aspects related to their domain of expertise. Moreover, they can still cooperate with other professionals by referring to the part of the metrics related to the different expertise of the latter at an appropriate level of precision. The coexistence of differently detailed interpretations is not a problem: rather, it is a mean to make cooperation smooth and effective.

The above considerations explain why experts assigning values to quality features play a very important role within the professionals' community. In fact, they master the knowledge concerning the deep pragmatic meaning of each feature. Moreover, they are able to use the professionals social network to balance possibly controversial opinions. For this reason these experts are the point of reference for any request of interpretation or motivation for the assigned values. The consciousness of the value of an adequate assessment of quality features pushes all professionals to assume a collaborative attitude towards the persons responsible for product characterization. Of course, the branch of the tree containing *Technical Quality features* is the main concern of software engineers while the branch containing *Marketing Quality features* is the main concern of consultants. But again, the two competences are blended to guarantee mutual consistency and understandability of the specific values. This practice of collaboration absorbs a considerable effort, typically at the end of the construction of a new technological solution, and characterizes the team of professionals as a community.

The computational artifact incorporating the Quality Tree contains functionalities to enhance its role in the definition of the most suitable product architecture. Beside the possibility to incrementally update and browse the Quality Trees, an additional functionality plays a more active role in component selection, again to help identifying (initial) solutions or supporting more un-experienced professionals. Comp-Rep users may select products based on their quality features by means of a "query-by-example" mechanism that reflects quality requirements for a given class of products. A query is a tree template that is isomorphic to the features tree defined above. Each node is associated with an expression defining a (possibly empty) constraint for the value of the corresponding node of the selected product quality tree. A typical constraint is a range. The goal of the query is to fetch a predefined (maximum) number of components (carrying with them the related components) whose trees satisfy the relational constraints or a relaxed version of them. This is achieved by first fetching a limited-size answer set; then its ranking is based on the number of required components (the fewer the better) and on three functions computed for each tree in the answer set: its distance from the query tree, a quality indicator, and a constraint violation index. Details of the ranking can be found in (Bandini et al., 2002b). In practice, professionals access a "wizard-like" interactive interface to input quality requirements that refer both to company's and customer needs. Users are confronted with simple, high level questions to establish the qualitative values, for example, the propensity to risk, software budget, and expected connectivity. Then the tool constructs the tree that represents the query, and submits it to the module responsible for product selection.

The Component Model, the Quality Tree and the tool incorporating them constitute a conceptual and technological framework characterizing the company and supporting the management of relevant parts of its core knowledge. This framework is currently in use with a "pragmatically" positive evaluation: the company wants to take the structure of the above knowledge artifacts as a standard, their software providers should comply with, in the documentation of their products. The framework is typically accessed by homogeneous groups of professionals to discuss topics under their responsibility: for example by consultants to prepare an offer. The incorporated language is used in conversations among different professionals who then access the framework to recover the details of the discussed topics.

3. Applying Professional Knowledge Artifacts in EUD

The experience described above shows characteristics that make it meaningful in the framework of EUD. Let us recall them briefly. First, software development is a knowledge-based activity where knowledge is about a rich set of software properties that are not only functional: non-functional ones are equally worth being managed and fulfilled. Second, collaboration among different professionals and the stratification of their experience are so relevant that it is natural for them to invest their energy in the definition of knowledge artifacts supporting both collaboration and stratification. These artifacts are unique to each given professionals community and reify their specific and tacit core knowledge. Third, tools based on these knowledge artifacts can be used effectively by professionals during their core activities, more than generic software engineering tools based on representations and visualizations that do not account for the company's culture.

The relevance of the above aspects for EUD relies on how much professional development and EUD share common problems. Obviously, we interpret EUD in the light of the considerations made in the introductory section, that is, interpreting development as the integration of off-the-shelf components.

The next section describes a scenario that illustrates how the artifacts can be put at work in a EUD situation. To this aim, let us suppose that the proposed framework is integrated with a component based one like FREEVOLVE (Won et al., 2004): we will discuss this integration in Section 3.3.

3.1. THE ARTIFACTS AND THE INVOLVED ROLES

Different roles interact with the artifacts supporting tailoring: typically, end-users, power users, technical professionals belonging to the organization, COTS providers. Users are not all alike. Their technical and non-technical competences are different as well as their attitude towards technology or their ability to play the role of teacher and promoter for less skilled or motivated colleagues. Several field studies reported in the literature have identified this role and called it "power users" (Won et al., 2004) or "gardeners" (Nardi, 1993). These individuals are likely to play the role of "experts" in the presented field study since power users or gardeners and experts show a similar behavior. They are involved in normal activities and their work to assist their colleagues and keep the artifacts updated is an additional effort they *informally* but highly *perspicuously* accept to perform for various motivations (social ties, personal visibility, professional maturity, etc). All the above mentioned roles influence the content of the tailoring artifacts in a more or less direct way as illustrated by the following scenario.

Technical professionals are in charge to look for COTS that providers make available in the market. This activity can be driven, top–down, by a strategy of the hosting organization, or, bottom-up, by specific end-users requests. In any case, they insert the "new" components in the Comp-Rep and fill in the Quality Tree for each of them using information contained in the documentation or directly obtained from the providers. This is an activity that implies a special care by the user. In fact, it requires translating standard documentations as produced by external suppliers, into the language incorporated in the above artifacts.

The new components are now part of the Comp-Rep together with the components that have already been used and validated in some applications. Moreover, the experience and knowledge owned by the technical professionals allow them to establish hypothetical links expressing the different compatibility relations constituting the underlying component model. Since they are dealing with COTS they can identify, again on the basis of their experience, "ghost" components (see Section 2.2.1) to mark that the use of some components requires ad hoc programming: this is again a valuable information for end-users in the evaluation of the most suitable solution fitting their needs. The presence of ghost components allows the Comp-Rep to stay coherent also in front of the lack of a uniform reference architecture against which component integration is defined. Moreover, ghost components can be incrementally substituted by actual ones when implemented solutions construct them, or when the technical staff wants to promote the adoption of specific components requiring them.

At this point, an end-user may want to tailor a specific aggregate of components constituting an application in use in order to add a new functionality. For sake of illustration let us consider a very simple case: the application is a word-processor and the desired functionality is about the management of bibliographical references. The user accesses the Comp-Rep, looks for a (compound) module implementing this functionality. Suppose that Comp-Rep proposes two possibilities: one component has limited functional capabilities but a fully supported auto-installation procedure; the second one is more flexible (e.g., it allows importing references, databases complying with different standards) but requires ad hoc configuration (e.g., in terms of APIs). These pieces of information are contained in the Comp-Rep and in the Quality Trees of the two components. A naive end-user realizes that the first solution is less flexible and has not yet been experienced. However, the auto-install feature makes it more appealing since, in principle, he does not need to look for help to perform its integration. When he completes it successfully, the tailoring support registers this fact so that who is in charge of the artifacts maintenance can store this information. The responsibility to update the tailoring artifacts can be assigned by adopting different policies depending on the kind of information to be stored: an automatic update is suitable when no human interpretation is required (as in the above case); an update performed by power users with an adequate level of expertise and experience is required when integration is of a limited complexity; finally, an update performed by the technical staff is necessary when integration requires more complex components or the development of glue ("ghost") components. In any case, on the one hand the policies are driven by the local culture and can be flexibly (re-)assigned (as in content management systems) depending on dynamic levels of mutual confidence among the various involved actors; on the other hand, the basic requirement to keep the highest level of trust in the stored information imposes that the role of the administrator (like in mailing lists) is assigned to the technical staff, at least in supervisory mode. We will come again to this point later on.

On the contrary, if the end-user is not happy with the simple solution, he decides to look at the second component to get the information related to its functional and non-functional aspects. If the solution has already been experienced with success, Comp-Rep already contains the required components: the user enters the FREEVOLVE-like part of the tailoring environment and is guided by its interface to establish the appropriate connections among them, possibly with the help of the end-users having performed a similar tailoring experience. In the opposite case, it is likely that power users are technically not enough empowered and gardeners, or more likely the technical staff, have to be involved to provide the ad hoc glue components. This is one of the main reasons why integration, more than composition, requires a strong collaboration among end-users, gardeners, and technical staff. When the tailoring effort is completed and the solution proved correct, the related information is introduced in Comp-Rep and in the affected Quality Trees, under the supervision of the technical staff, as discussed above: *collaboration by design* relations are complemented by *collaboration by dependency* relations involving glue components. The FREEVOLVE-like part of the tailoring environment has to be updated too by specifying the *interfaces* each involved component exposes to the other ones: in this way, they incorporate the experience of their current use and configuration, and can be taken into account in future applications. Details of these updates are discussed in Section 3.3.

The process continues with the usage of the tailored solution. Any experience contradicting what drove its selection and/or construction should generate an update of the two artifacts: typically, the malfunctioning of some integrated components or the change of non-functional aspects. For example, a provider associates to COTS an upgrade pricing policy. Sometimes, the provider directly proposes the upgrade to the user who might realize that the policy did change in terms of license, price, and the like. The same information can be uncovered by the technical staff, maybe later on. This is a relevant non-functional aspect that should be reported in the Quality Tree of these COTS. Failures, COTS upgrades, new needs, changes of the underlying technological infrastructure start new tailoring efforts that are based on the updated artifacts.

This scenario does not cover all the possible cases generated by a real and more complex tailoring: however, it gives an idea of how the artifacts can be used in an integrated way and of the functionality that the tailoring support should make available.

One might argue that maintaining the artifacts supporting tailoring is a too demanding activity for the target organization and for each individual involved role. The shortage of personnel, the increasing tailoring needs to improve domain specific applications of growing complexity, the recurrence of similar (although seldom identical) tailoring requests by the end-users, the different attitude of the latter toward tailoring efforts are all good motivations for a strategy decentralizing the adaptation of applications by means of an increasingly self-understandable tailoring technology. This strategy goes in the opposite direction with respect to managerial approaches, mainly induced by the availability of web technologies. These approaches implement a centralized adaptation that is standardized and offered as a black box: the end-users are trained on its new features and functionality. The management justifies the centralized approach in terms of efficiency, without considering its effectiveness: it often underestimates that the centralized strategy causes strained relations between users and technical staff. From the end-users point of view, the negative impacts of this strategy are frustration, lack of appropriation, alienation, lack of usability of the resulting technology: in fact, users are excluded from any learning process tailored to their needs. From the technical staff point of view, the tension is generated by what is perceived as a disorderly set of requests that can hardly be satisfied in an efficient and effective way.

3.2. DESIGN AS DISCOVERY

Many situations show that technology is used beyond its "anticipated" functionality: users "invent" a combination of technologically and socially based procedures to amplify the technological capability to cope with their needs. Consequently, the term "design for unanticipated use" has been proposed (Robinson, 1993) to stress how flexible the technology should be in order to cope with the above requirement. Composition, as interpreted in this chapter, shows a degree of flexibility that is circumscribed by the set of "anticipated" components constituting a potentially coherent application: the latter can be tailored through the appropriate selection of a subset of components. In this respect, composition gives a partial answer to "design for the unanticipated use" that in principle calls for an open-ended composition of basic functionalities made available by a dynamically identified set of components. This is exactly what integration is about: the available COTS are, by definition, open-ended and constructed by independent providers. Hence, their composition offers a wider range of possibilities but has to be managed with additional care.

In this radical view, *EUD* can be read as *End-User Discovery*. In front of an emergent need, the question (formulated in our software company's jargon) is: does the market provide BCs with the needed functionality? Which MSCs are needed and to what extent are they compatible with the installed technology at the BCs and MSCs levels? Do the new components possess a degree of quality that is compliant with the needs of their local context of use? Is the required effort commensurable with the available resources (time, knowledge, organizational and technological support)? As illustrated in the Section 2, these are the same questions professionals have to answer in front of a new customer request. Hence, professional development and EUD are not so far from each other: they at least share the same kind of involved knowledge.

Let us go deeper in this argumentation. End-users play different "professional" roles in the different stages of tailoring. In particular, they behave like "marketing people" when they have to figure out to what extent a solution fulfills their needs, by possibly adding and/or deleting or modifying existing functionalities. In this very preliminary stage of integration, the language incorporated in the identified Component Model allows them to deal with the problem at an adequate level of abstraction, that is, focusing on the possibility to find components fulfilling the desired functionality: the latter constitutes a (complete) set at the BCs and MSCs levels, and defines a solution that is acceptable in terms of non-functional requirements. Like professional marketing people, end-users are interested more in "what" the solution is about in terms of functionality, infrastructure, and quality than in "how" the solution is actually constructed. The latter is the focus on a different phase, when they play as "technical people" and have to connect properly the selected components. At this stage, the language has to express flexible information flows. Languages inspired by coordination models (Papadopolos and Arbab, 1998) can be the right choice since they propose different patterns to express connectivity on the basis of concepts like shared variables or tuples, ports, channels, streams, and message passing. For example, FREEVOLVE (Won et al., 2004) proposes a port-based visual language that helps end-users in establishing information flows among the selected components.

The proposed distinction between the "what" and the "how" is especially suitable since the identification of the optimal set of components (providing an equivalent functionality) can be based on features that have to be evaluated before the actual connections are defined. In fact, integration usually refers to components whose development is not in the hands of the end-users (or of the organization they belong to). License, upgrade, assistance policies and the actual related services can play an equally important role in selection as well as cost, easy installation and the like. The actual values of these features can be determined in a safe way through previous experience only: they can hardly be read in documentation. This is the added value of the language incorporated in the Quality Tree artifacts: they play a complementary and supportive role in selection as well as in communication among end-users.

In the long run, design as discovery promotes *creativity* in thinking about technology. The latter can be viewed as a tool to be defined, not as a constraint to comply with. Obviously, the initial experiences have to be positive in order to avoid frustration: the additional effort required by creativity has to be supported. Unlike professionals, end-users can refuse to perform any sort of development if they do not perceive that they can manage the task with tangible advantages. This support can be created in different ways, as described in the next sections.

3.3. THE TERRITORY OF DISCOVERY

As the kind of knowledge used in design as discovery is similar between end-users and professionals, the general approach and the conceptual framework characterizing the professionals knowledge artifacts presented in Section 2 can be considered in the EUD framework. In this view, knowledge artifacts like Comp-Rep and Quality Tree support EUD by providing end-users with tools to structure the territory where they move in an easier and more productive way.

The territory of (design as) discovery is likely to be populated by concepts describing functional and infrastructural components, by relations linking them, by quality features, and possibly by other objects that are uncovered on the way. This complexity can be managed if the set of tools ready at the hands of end-users allow for different and integrated views at different levels of abstraction (Mørch and Mehandjiev, 2000). Knowledge artifacts like Comp-Rep and Quality Tree give an example of how one of these views can be constructed and combined with views provided by other approaches. In order to illustrate this point, we consider again FREEVOLVE as a reference proposal, since it naturally complements the approach inspiring these artifacts. The two related component models are based on different relations: compatibility/dependency relations in the first case, data streams connection in the second one. In both cases, there is the possibility to build a hierarchy of increasingly complex aggregates of components that can be viewed as progressive refinements in aggregates of sub-components. These levels can support the flexible interplay of component roles as white, black, and gray components within the same hierarchy (Won et al., 2004). Suppose to have a framework including both hierarchies expressing composition in terms of the "what" and the "how" as illustrated in Section 3.2. The above flexibility is increased by allowing end-users to traverse both hierarchies at the same time in order to reason on the appropriated representation depending on their current "professional role." This simultaneous traversing accounts for the fact that end-users play the "marketing" and "technical" roles in an interleaved way. In fact, an end-user could browse or search the Comp-Rep and find a specific aggregation of components that implements the desired functionality and quality criteria, and requires an infrastructure that is feasible and compatible with the current technological environment of the user. In other words, Comp-Rep tells whether there is the possibility to realize an exchange of information among the selected components through the patterns shown in Figure 16.2, and gives an evaluation of the required effort. The patterns on the left side tell that no specific software is needed: at most local configuration is required. The ones on the right side show that glue software has to be constructed to make the components interoperate through standards: if the latter are connected by a link the solution requires a relatively small effort by experienced people to make this case fall again in the previous one. If the structure of the selected components does not correspond to any of the above patterns the desired aggregation either is not feasible or needs a programming effort requiring the competences of the technical staff.

Once the existence of a path connecting the selected components has been checked, the user needs to deal with the finer detail of how the components can be combined to define the actual streams of information flowing between them. To this aim, the more abstract *by dependency* and *by design* relations (of the "what" hierarchy) are complemented by more detailed information about the content of the interface of each component: what is imported or exported and the related data type and format. This finer grain information is typically incorporated in the technical description of each component to allow its integration in some architecture: in the worst case, it is embedded in a dedicated portion of the code. Of course, the identification of this information highly depends on the quality of the considered COTS and can be made easier by the recognition of recurrent connectivity patterns. Again, the construction of the hierarchy describing "how" components can be combined has to translate the technical information in a language understandable by the end-user.

The port-based language of FREEVOLVE nicely supports this need in the case of composition. In fact, its graphical interface allows the user to perceive the options to create the desired connections, to perform the tailoring in a simple and effective way, and finally to test the results of tailoring. Specifically, the visualization of the components and their named ports, together with the direction of the information flow and connection capabilities, suggest an approach that can be adapted to the case of integration, that is, to represent in terms of finer grained connectivity the information more abstractly contained in Comp-Rep. Moreover, the distinction between usage and tailoring mode nicely fits the distinction between BC and MSC components. In fact, the former are perceived through the application interface in use mode and become fully visible "through the projection of the interface in the tailoring space" when the user enters the tailoring mode: at this point, they are combined with the MSC components that are visible at this stage only. A naive user is likely to apply the above process to tailor the integration of BC components, and specifically the ones whose default (or proposed) fine grained architecture is not fully satisfactory. A more experienced end-user could play the same game at the MSCs level too.

To sum up, the conjectured integrated framework provides users with two different ways to move across levels of abstraction: the one that can be interpreted as *refinement* in sub-assemblies that are linked by the same kinds of relations (describing either the "what" or the "how"), and the one that allows users to *change perspective when moving across levels* (that is, alternatively considering the "what" and the related "how"). We are not claiming that the integration of the two hierarchies is straightforward: it requires additional functionalities to keep the two hierarchies mutually consistent and supportive for the end-users. However, we claim that this effort is worth being done in order to provide end-users with two perspectives that help them to manage the complexity of discovering what can be successfully integrated.

3.4. NEGOTIATION AND VISUALIZATION

The construction of a supportive framework based on the design as discovery requires additional considerations. First, the kind of knowledge incorporated in the Comp-Rep and Quality Tree artifacts is highly qualitative: the involved concepts and relations highly depend on the local culture and less on formalized technical aspects of the components. Although quite reasonable, the possibility to express whether a component is mandatory or simply complements a basic aggregation is not the only possible one. End-users can identify their favorite relations and how to express them. The point is that, as shown by the professional marketing people, appropriate artifacts incorporating the suitable relations can be profitably co-constructed and used by non-technical professionals too. This is an important point since end-users, although technically empowered, will still remain non-technical professionals. Co-construction requires negotiation of meaning (Boland and Takesi, 1995), concerning both the adopted concepts and the relations, and the descriptions of components classified according to them. This negotiation takes place, implicitly, as part of the normal interactions among different actors. However, power users are likely to play a basic role. In fact, when they support other end-users they are in the privileged position to collect their experiences and their points of view, and consequently to find the appropriate "underspecification" to (re)formulate descriptions that are understandable and usable for them. Moreover, they are the natural interlocutors of the technical staff when its members supervise the contents to guarantee their technical soundness. In fact, technical professionals should be aware that the descriptions must make sense to end-users and not to them. Hence, they have to accept a certain level of impreciseness they would probably not accept in discussing among them. However, this is exactly what happened in the reported case. "Experts" in charge of updating the artifacts belong to different professional roles, and are collectively responsible of the quality and usability of their content. Discussing meanings "in front of" a co-constructed artifact is perceived as an advantage since it makes the outcome of the negotiation permanent and re-usable at any moment (Sarini and Simone, 2002).

Second, the contents of the various artifacts have to be presented and accessed in the appropriate way: this is of course the second basic aspect of usability. Here tailorability recursively applies since end-users and the context in which they start integration are not all alike. The wizard like interface requested by professional marketing people (see Section 2.2.2) is suitable when users do not need to browse the Comp-Rep or the Quality Tree since they can formulate a satisfactory query-by-example to obtain the most suitable aggregate(s). Interfaces similar to the ones proposed, e.g., for FREEVOLVE (either 3D or 2D) could be offered to add information about the distributed structure of the target application. This aspect was, however, not emphasized by the professionals in the reported case since their focus was more on the interplay of functional and non-functional requirements in the selection of the suitable aggregation. They considered distribution more linked to "how" components are actually connected. To draw a conclusion from this experience, in the light of component based approaches like FREEVOLVE, we can say that the main visualization structure is the hierarchical component model with its relations among components. The Quality Tree associated to each component is usually navigated once a component or an aggregation is selected. The interesting aspect is that this special kind of "meta-data" is expressed in a hierarchical way too, allowing for different levels of detail that fit the needs of different professional roles. The effective visualization of graph structures is notably a difficult and challenging open problem (Pirolli et al., 2003), since the interface must support the visualization of a rich set of details associated to a node, without loosing the overall view of where the node is located in the broader structure. In hierarchical component models, the deeper the node is the more difficult it is to characterize its functionality and quality in a way that makes sense to the user. In fact, deep nodes usually correspond to general purpose components that can belong to several aggregates: their true meaning in the current search mainly depends on the path the user followed to reach them.

Negotiation of meanings and their visualization by interfaces usable both individually and cooperatively brings up the theme of collaboration in software development in general, and in EUD in particular.

3.5. COLLABORATIVE DISCOVERY

Discovery in unpredictable territory is a risky task that is usually performed by a team of people with different skills and experiences. Design as discovery in an open-ended market requires collaboration, much more than in other design situations. This was the basic motivation leading the professionals we have observed to become a community of practice "acting around" the two basic artifacts.

Collaboration cannot be taken for granted for all groups of end-users: some of them naturally behave as a community of practice, others take a more individualistic or competitive attitude. The challenge is to prove that in design as discovery, collaboration is a best practice which is worth to be supported and to show that a collaborative development and maintenance of useful tools is possible.

As for any kind of strategy to promote EUD, design by discovery asks end-users to assume a "professional" attitude to master the functionality and the quality of the final outcome. How this attitude is articulated and develops during EUD experiences depends on local culture, needs and practice. However, the promotion of the development of an end-user professional attitude cannot be based only on a technological training and support. In addition, it requires an educational effort to start or reinforce this process. Narratives have been recognized as a useful means to support education and sharing of experiences (Bruner, 1991). The case presented here can be used as an example of best practice. As already claimed, we are not suggesting a passive use of the same artifacts. Instead, the case can stimulate end-users to identify the relevant piece of knowledge that is useful to stratify and organize their own experience, and show how collaboration among end-users and software professionals is a basic means to make the collected knowledge effective. The advantage of using a professional case is that end-users become aware, in quite concrete terms, that software development (irrespective of how development is interpreted) is a hard job for professionals too, and that they have to take care of it (Ciborra, 1996) to become as successful as professionals are. On the positive side, they become aware that one key of this success is in their hands since it is based on the elicitation of the knowledge that is created by their experience and by their collaboration with other end-users and with software professionals.

Collaboration in design as discovery takes place inside groups of end-users and between them and software professionals. The first kind of collaboration is necessary when the target functionality involves many of them (as in the case of collaborative applications): in fact, all local needs and context of use have to be simultaneously taken into account.

The situations under which end-users may want to tailor their current technology can be different too: e.g., time pressure, critical functionality, overload, and so on. End-user collaboration can mitigate the impact of these differences through the sharing of their experiences and mutual assistance. To this aim, knowledge artifacts of the kind illustrated in the previous section complement other means of collaboration that have already been proposed for EUD (as reported by Pipek and Kahler, 2004), like face to face meetings, mail, newsgroup, etc. The artifacts proposed here make the contents of communication persistent since they support the stratification and sharing of experiences under the basic hypothesis that they capture the way in which the specific group of end-users speak about and solve problems related to (distributed) tailoring. In this way, tools supporting the construction of solutions which are more oriented to answer a single need (Kahler et al., 2000) can be profitably based on, or combined with, tools oriented to stratify and recover the knowledge and experience that this (collaborative) construction generates. The tools can be extended to incorporate functionalities to promote awareness (Dourish and Bellotti, 1992) of the changes of their contents. The literature proposes several approaches and technologies for awareness promotion (accounting to this rich literature is out of the scope of this paper). Irrespective of the differences among them, these technologies can be used to let the proposed artifacts notify different kinds of information: who performed the updates, which components were involved, who installed which aggregates, and so on. On the other hand, end-users can subscribe notification services and filter the information according to their interests. Awareness functionality contributes to making the tailoring tool an inhabited place, and hence stimulates its usage and collaborative maintenance. Moreover it can be combined with other functionalities supporting learning, understanding, making sense of the technology actually or potentially in use (Pipek and Kahler, 2004) to reward the maintenance effort.

The collaboration between end-users and (in-house) software professionals cannot be avoided in many EUD situations: for example, when the accumulated experience is not sufficient to construct new solutions, when the latter ask for the experimentation of new functional or infrastructure components, or when integration requires the ad hoc development of specialized software components (typically, wrappers, adapters, and so on). By the way, this interaction becomes mandatory in absence of any form of EUD since end-users fully depend on software professionals. As for any form of collaboration, a mutual learning process takes place (whose pace again depends on the attitude of the collaborating partners). Moreover, a common language is likely to be incrementally created to make the interaction possible (Mark et al., 1997). Knowledge artifacts incorporating the stratified contents of this mutually learning process empower end-users in their cooperation with professionals since they are stronger in discussing their needs and in understanding the more technical issues. In the opposite direction, it helps professionals to understand the end-users language that reifies their point of view, priorities, and needs.

To our knowledge, the research efforts towards EUD promotion and support do not explicitly consider most of the non-functional requirements constituting the Quality Tree artifact. The case reported here shows that all of them are a relevant part of the language used by the community of integrators and that the focus on functionality should not obscure their relevance for the success of the final solution. This is relevant for EUD too since in appropriation and re-use of experienced solutions infrastructure and quality are as relevant as functionality to put them at work. Moreover, distributed tailoring, by definition, has to do with the heterogeneity of the local contexts in terms of infrastructure and quality requirements.

But more importantly, the case shows that sharing and negotiating solutions is possible if it is supported by a common reference conceptual structure that incorporates the understanding of what the solution to be shared is about. As already mentioned, this understanding can involve views of the target solution from different perspectives, where the appropriate under-specification can play a relevant role to make communication and collaboration easier.

In addition, available solutions are "trusted" by who did not produce them if they have been experimented and assessed by reliable people. This kind of tacit knowledge, when supported and made as explicit as possible, is the key factor, the engine that makes the overall process work. It is not surprising that, being a knowledge work (Drucker, 1999), software design takes advantages of knowledge management approaches and technologies (see, e.g., Briand, 2002 and the series of Software Engineering and Knowledge Engineering conferences). The crucial point is the degree by which knowledge artifacts are being constructed starting from true experience, bearing in mind that the mechanisms by which the involved actors stratify knowledge and experience have not to be destroyed: these principles characterize the case reported in this chapter. Moreover, the case shows that it is possible to build a technological support of integration that also non-professionals can use to speak of functionality, quality, compatibility and so on, and to interact with software professionals when their knowledge and capabilities are required.

4. Concluding Remarks

EUD is a challenging goal that requires supporting users through several actions: education, motivation, and availability of tools to master the complexity of software development. EUD requires end-users taking a "professional" attitude toward this development if they want to avoid that the low quality of the final product thwarts their effort. Finally, EUD takes place in different contexts, asking end-users to act on the target software ranging from surface adaptation up to the design of its deep structure. Hence, EUD can be successful only in presence of different kinds of tools, possibly smoothly integrated, that end-users can use according to their needs, skill, and experience.

The paper suggests to identify a class of tools by considering software development as a knowledge work where technical support can be fruitfully integrated with tools allowing the stratification of experiences that end-users have gained in individual and cooperative efforts. The presented tools are examples and can be taken as a starting point to stimulate the identification of knowledge artifacts that serve the same purpose and reflect the end-users local culture and the way in which they act as a professional community.

According to the ongoing trend to avoid that users implement deep technical details, the proposed approach goes in the direction of supporting them in the creative identification of the most appropriate components to be integrated: in doing so, they focus their attention on the characterization of the context in which the final application operates and the quality features that make it successful. This approach, combined with other complementary proposals, allows them to interact with software professionals, when needed, in a more aware and profitable way. We have sketched a possible integration with tools supporting tailoring based on composition. Integration raises interesting challenges also to approaches based on End-Users Programming (Goodell et al., 1999) that, in the case of integration, should support the construction of glue components: environments supporting this kind of programming could be very useful at least when end-users have to implement recurrent patterns of connectivity. Last but not least, integration on a large scale, involving non-technical roles, is on the one hand an interesting market for COTS providers but, on the other hand, requires them to build and document components in the light of "outer tailorability": this effort would be a great contribution to EUD. The open source initiative could play a relevant role in this direction.

References

Bandini, S., De Paoli, F., Manzoni, S. and Mereghetti, P. (2002a). A Support System to COTS-based Software Development for Business Services. *Proceedings of the Fourteenth Conference on Software Engineering*, ACM Press, New York, NY, USA. pp. 307–314.

Bandini, S., Manzoni, S. and Mereghetti, P. (2002b). Business Service Components: a Knowledge Based Approach. *Proceedings of the 22nd SGAI. International Conference on Knowledge Based Systems and Applied Artificial Intelligence* (ES2002). Springer-Verlag, pp. 238–250.

Bandini, S., Colombo, E., Colombo, G., Sartori, F. and Simone C. (2003). The role of knowledge artifacts in innovation management: the case of a Chemical Compound CoP, M. Huysman, E. Wenger and V. Wulf (eds), *Communities and Technologies*, Kluwer Academic, pp. 327–345.

Boland, R.J. and Tenkasi, R.V. (1995). Perspective making and perspective taking in communities of knowing. *Organization Science* **4–6**, pp. 350–372.

Briand, L.C. (2002). On the may ways Software Engineering can benefit from Knowledge Engineering. *Proceedings of the 14th Conference on Software Engineering and Knowledge Engineering*, ACM Press, pp. 3–14.

Bruner, J. (1991). The Narrative Construction of Reality, Critical Inquiry 18. University of Chicago Press, Chicago, USA. pp. 1–21.

Chung, L., Nixon, B.A., Yu, E. and Mylopoulos, J. (1999). *Non-Functional Requirements in Software Engineering*, Kluwer Academic, Boston, USA.

Ciborra, C. (ed., 1996). *Groupware and Teamwork*, NY: John Wiley.

Dourish, P. and Bellotti, V. (1992). Awareness and coordination in shared workspaces. *Proceedings of the Conference on Computer Supported Cooperative Work (CSCW92')*, ACM Press, New York, USA. pp. 107–111.

Drucker, P. (1999). Knowledge-Worker Productivity: The Biggest Challenge. *California Management Review* **41–2**, 79–94.

Goodell, H., Kuhn, S., Maulsby D. and Traynor, C. (1999). End user programming/informal programming. *SIGCHI Bulleting* **31–64**, 17–21.

Kahler, H., Mørch, A., Stiemerling, O. and Wulf V. (eds., 2000). Tailorable systems and cooperative work. Computer Supported Cooperative Work: The Journal of Collaborative Computing (JCSCW) **9–1**, Kluwer Academic Publishers, Dordrecht.

Mark, G., Fuchs, L. and Sohlenkamp, M. (1997). Supporting groupware conventions through contextual awareness. *Proceedings of the European Conference on Computer Supported Cooperative Work (ECSCW97)*, Lancaster, England, Kluwer Academic Publishers, Dordrecht, pp. 253–268.

Mørch, A.I. and Mehandjiev, N.D. (2000). Tailoring as collaboration: the mediating role of multiple representations and applications units. Computer Supported Cooperative Work: The Journal of Collaborative Computing (JCSCW) **9–1**, Kluwer Academic Publishers, Dordrecht. 75–100.

Morisio, M., Seaman, C., Basili, V., Parra, A., Kraft, S. and Condon, S. (2002). COTS-based software development: Processes and open issues. *The Journal of Systems and Software* **61–3**, 189–199.

Morisio, M., Seaman, C., Parra, A., Basili, V., Condon, S. and Kraft, S. (2000). Investigating and Improving a COTS-Based Software Development Process. *Proceedings of the 22nd International Conference on Software Engineering (ICSE 2000)*, Elsevier, New York, USA. pp. 32–41.

Nardi, B.A. (1993). *A Small Matter of Programming*, MIT Press, Cambridge, MA.

Nonaka, I. and Takeuchi, H. (1995). *The Knowledge-Creating Company*. Oxford University Press, New York, USA.

Papadopolous, G. and Arbab, F. (1998). Coordination Models and Languages. *Advances in Computers* **46**, The Engineering of Large Systems, Academic Press.

Pipek, V. and Kahler, H. Supporting collaborative tailoring, in this volume.

Pirolli, P., Card, S. and van der Wege, M. (2003). The effects of information scent on visual search in the hyperbolic tree browser. *ACM Transactions on Computer Human Interaction* **10–1**, 20–53.

Robinson, M. (1993). Design for unanticipated use. *Proceedings of the European Conference on Computer Supported Cooperative Work (ECSCW'93)*, Milano, Italy, Kluwer Academic Publishers, Dordrecht, 187–202.

Sarini, M. and Simone, C. (2002). Recursive Articulation work in Ariadne: the alignment of meanings. *Proceedings of the Conference on Cooperative Systems Design (COOP2002)*. Saint-Raphael, France, IOS Press, 191–206.

Teege, G. (2000). Users as composers: parts and features as a basis for tailorability in CSCW systems. Computer Supported Cooperative Work: The Journal of Collaborative Computing (JCSCW) **9–1**, Kluwer Academic, pp. 101–122.

Wenger, E. (1998). *Community of Practice: Learning, Meaning and Identity*. Cambridge, MA: Cambridge University Press.

Won, M., Stiemerling, O. and Wulf, V. (2004). Component-based approaches to tailoring systems, in this volume.

Chapter 17

Organizational View of End-User Development

NIKOLAY MEHANDJIEV, ALISTAIR SUTCLIFFE
and DARREN LEE
School of Informatics, University of Manchester, U.K.
{N.Mehandjiev | Alistair.G.Sutcliffe}@manchester.ac.uk

Abstract. Assuming end-user development (EUD) is here to stay, we must begin to consider the economic, organizational and societal factors which would impact its adoption and use. Such studies have so far focused on the wider issues of IT adoption and users controlling information processing power (end-user computing), whilst EUD research has focused on the cognitive and technology aspects of programming by non-specialists. In this chapter we describe the start of a research programme addressing this gap. We present our findings from a pilot survey of researchers, practitioners and end-users conducted over several months in Spring/Summer 2003. The survey analysed two group discussions and 38 questionnaire returns to elicit organisational perceptions and views on End User Development, and to help formulate further research directions in the area, including an outline strategy for managing the integration of EUD.

Key words. organizational factors, EUD acceptance, survey of EUD perceptions

1. Introduction

End-user development (EUD) aims to enable non-software specialists to develop non-trivial software artefacts to support their work and improve the quality of their leisure time. It was estimated that by 2005 in the United States alone, there would be 55 million end-user developers as opposed to 2.75 million professional software developers (Boehm, 1995). Currently the most diffused EUD technology is the spreadsheet (United States Bureau of the Census, 1999).

We believe that the predicted number of end-user developers is an underestimate. As the complexity of information processing required of us in the office, on the Web and at home increases, we will have to interact with software in non-trivial ways, which will often cross the boundary from interaction to programming. And since there are not enough professionals to do the programming on our behalf, we will increasingly engage in programming activities in the context of our everyday work and leisure pursuits, regardless of our background and experience.

Assuming EUD is here to stay, we must begin to consider the changes it will bring to our society and organizations, or to take a less deterministic perspective ask what the requirements of society for this new technological artefact are. A body of work in end-user computing (Brancheau and Brown, 1993; Panko, 1988; Powell and Moore, 2002),

Henry Lieberman et al. (eds.), End User Development, 371–399.
© 2006 *Springer.*

for example, has looked at organizational implications of users controlling processing power such as desktop PCs and installing applications and databases.

EUD is, by contrast, focused on the activities of developing and modifying code by non-programmers, and has until now focused on enabling technical innovations and on the low-level cognitive and machine–centric interactions between system and user. Within this tradition, a growing body of research looks at the technological issues such as abstractions in language design (Fischer, 1994; Repenning, 1993), modes of interfaces (Burnett et al., 1995; Green and Petre, 1996), the AI approaches to the system inferring our programming intentions (Lieberman, 2001) and human factors of EUD (Nardi and Miller, 1991), while making often unsupported claims of revolutionary impacts on how we work and entertain ourselves throughout society. When research does look beyond the technology it does not go further than the dynamics of small groups with studies looking at the emergence of specialized team roles, such as Nardi's work on spreadsheets (Nardi, 1993). EUD research is rarely prescriptive; instead, it just reports findings without attempting to provide decision makers with the necessary knowledge of how to deal with problems and conflicts which are likely to emerge from the formalization of EUD.

We believe that the growing practical dimension of EUD calls for EUD researchers to step into the "macro world" of organizations and EUD economics, sharing findings with the end-user computing community and conducting focused investigation of the perceptions and implications of users developing code within social and organizational settings. Example questions to be investigated are: "How will EUD practices scale up to complex artefacts and work settings?" "How would EUD affect organizational strategy and profitability?" and "What are the impacts of EUD on human resources and corporate governance?"

Requirements found at this level will influence work at both organizational and technology levels, thus furthering EUD acceptance. Organizations should be helped to make the best of EUD by recognizing its occurrence and leveraging its benefits whilst hedging against its potential downsides. Before EUD can be sold to key organizational decision makers, we need to understand both what the problems with this technology are from an organizational perspective and how can they be managed.

In this chapter, we describe the start of a research programme addressing this area of investigation. We present our findings from a pilot survey of researchers, practitioners and end-users conducted over several months in Spring/Summer 2003. The survey analyzed two group discussions and 38 questionnaire returns to elicit organizational perceptions and views on EUD, and to help formulate further research directions in the area.

2. Data Collection

The data for this chapter was collected from a survey consisting of two group discussions at an industrial seminar held at the University of Manchester in April 2003, and a larger questionnaire survey conducted over several months in Spring/Summer of 2003.

2.1. SURVEY DESIGN

The survey was designed to capture a variety of attitudes, opinions, and experiences related to EUD. It combined a questionnaire and group discussions to balance the measurement and discovery aspects of the investigation.

2.1.1. *Aim and Objectives*

The overall aim of the survey is to gain an insight into the perceived costs and benefits to industry from the adoption of EUD techniques and tools, and thus to answer the research question: "What are the perceived costs and benefits of EUD?"

The survey *design objectives* were therefore specified as follows:

Objective 1: To identify perceived benefits of EUD to industry (Motivations).
Objective 2: To identify perceived costs of EUD to industry and understand the barriers preventing EUD from becoming a mainstream competitor to professional development (Disincentives).
Objective 3: To identify areas for future work.
Objective 4: To document interpretations of what EUD is as a concept and to measure the awareness of EUD as a label for the activities it describes.

2.1.2. *Questionnaire*

The primary instrument for the survey was a questionnaire consisting of three sections:

Section A contained questions aiming to gather some data about the respondent, their organizational role and their use and understanding of EUD technologies and tools, working toward Objective 4.

Section B contained 15 questions using a 5-point "Likert" scale to access attitudes toward uni-dimensional concepts of EUD. The questionnaire asked respondents to rate their agreement to a set of statements using a scale of *Agree Strongly, Agree, Indifferent, Disagree, Disagree Strongly*. The questions were designed to measure perceptions relevant to Objectives 1, 2, and 3 as cross-referenced in Appendix A.

Section C provided the opportunity for some open-ended responses and comments, unconstrained by the format in Sections A and B.

The questionnaire is reproduced in Appendix C.

2.1.3. *Group Discussions*

Group discussion sessions were structured in three stages. During Stage 1, participants were asked to answer the questionnaire, thus preparing their thoughts and ideas regarding the issues to be discussed. Group formation was the aim of Stage 2, which consisted of "round-the-table" introductions of each participant and their experiences with EUD technology and organizational structures. This stage also provided some input to Objective 4. The proper discussions took place during Stage 3, when each group was asked to discuss the following set of questions:

1. What are the business requirements for EUD? (Objectives 1 and 3)
2. How would you sell the benefits to your team or to the boardroom? (Objectives 1 and 2)
3. What are the management/social barriers to the uptake of new technologies and work practices related to EUD? (Objective 2)
4. What technical barriers do you see for practical EUD? (Objectives 2 and 3)
5. What technical innovations do you see impacting positively or negatively on EUD? (Objectives 1 and 2)
6. What contemporary organizational change factors do you see impacting positively or negatively on EUD? (Objectives 1 and 2)
7. Do you believe further concerted effort is needed in EUD? (Objective 3)

Each group had an appointed moderator whose main role was to steer discussions back on track and keep watch on the time available for discussing each point.

2.1.4. *Method*

The survey targeted individuals within industry, government organizations and universities. The academics were chosen for their work in the area of EUD; the other participants were selected for their practical experience in managing information technology within organizations, but they were not expected to be specialists in EUD. Invitations for the first workshop were sent to a large number of potential participants from the UK and Europe, using pre-existing lists of industrial contacts in the IT area. Questionnaires were distributed at this workshop and at a number of EUD-related events over the following months.

Following the Grounded Theory approach (Strauss and Corbin, 1998), the questions guiding the discussion; those from the questionnaire were treated as a set of generative questions which helped to guide the research but were not intended to confine its findings. The questionnaire, for example, included a section for open-ended comments and responses, and a semi-structured section to establish current EUD practices within an organization (see Section 2.1.2).

Aggregate information was collected regarding questionnaire responses as follows: The questionnaire responses were mapped on to a scale from 2 for "agree strongly," through 0 for "indifferent" to -2 for "disagree strongly." Distribution charts of answers and averages for each of the questions were then created as an indication of respondents' perceptions on a particular issue or statement. These are provided in Appendix B. To gain a broader understanding of the overall scope of perceptions, the questionnaire statements were divided into three groups according to the survey objective they were formulated to address, and a summary diagram was then created for each objective. We discuss these results in Section 2.3, but it is important to note that these results were also used to support results from analyzing and coding group discussions.

The group discussions were audio-recorded and transcribed at a later date. They were then analyzed following the *coding* process from the Grounded Theory approach (Strauss and Corbin, 1998), where the development of a theoretical framework was interwoven with open coding stages and integrative workshop sessions.

Table 17.1. Mapping between discussion topics and emergent themes.

Initial set of discussion topics	Emergent themes
Corporate Strategy	IT Strategy
Agility	Organisational demand for EUD
Market	
Control	Managerial controls
Success factors	Cost benefit of end-users
Learning burden	(who are doing delopment work)
End User Developer rewards	Worker Recognition and Responsibility
Testing and professional culture	EUD methodologies
	Professionalisation
The EUD technology	
Future technology needs and predictions	Tools to tasks match
Domain	

a) *Open coding.* During the initial stages of coding, discussion fragments were first grouped into an initial set of 11 discussion topics (see Table 17.1).

b) *Integrative sessions.* During these sessions the discussion topics were subjected to critical review by the authors, and re-arranged in eight emergent themes, using criticial analysis and integration with the quantitative aggregate information produced by analyzing the questionnaire responses, presented in Section 2.3.

The process of analysis resulted in eight emergent themes plus three core concepts of *risk*, *control*, and *motivation*, which served as a focus for a theoretical framework, and were used to guide the subsequent analysis of the data. Following the discussion, we created an influence model to guide the introduction of and support for EUD activities within an organization. The model is presented and discussed in Section 4.

2.2. PARTICIPANTS

Contributors to the group discussions had a good knowledge of information technology. In addition, they had either experience with end-user technologies as end-users, or knowledge of the implementation of EUD tools in organizations. There were 18 participants in the group discussions, of which 7 were from industrial companies, 4 were from government organizations, and 7 were academics involved in collaborative research with industrial companies.

The 38 questionnaire respondents included end users, consultants, auditors, regulatory authorities, and academic researchers, according to the following composition:

- − Government and regulators 5
- − Industrial and administrative 18, of which
  - − End-User Application Providers 2
  - − IT Implementers and Consultancies 4
  - − Industrial Research 1

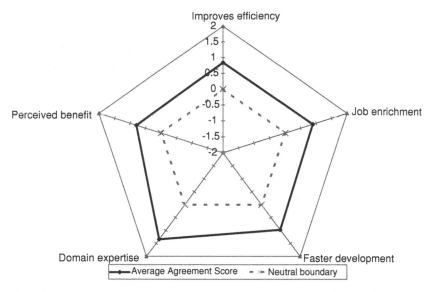

Figure 17.1. Perceptions of EUD benefits and motivator objective 2: perceived costs and barriers.

- Financial Services 6
- Administrators 5
- Academics 15

2.3. SURVEY RESULTS

2.3.1. *Questionnaire Results*

The results of the questionnaire analysis are summarized in Appendix A; they show, for example, that respondents were in slight disagreement with the statement "*Software development is the responsibility of software specialists*," resulting in an average score of −0.26; while the statement "*The domain expertise of end-users can create more effective software to support their activities*" resulted in a fairly strong agreement among respondents, with an average score of 1.34.

The table in Appendix A also contains cross-references between each question and the first three survey design objective(s) from Section 2.1.1. This cross-reference will now be used to review the contributions of the questionnaire responses to the survey objectives. In this we will use the average value of responses; detailed frequency charts of each question are provided in Appendix B. In each of the sections below, average responses for each group of questions are arranged in a radial graph, which has "strongly disagree" in its center (mapped to a value of −2). For an example see *Figure 17.1*. The "strongly agree" values (mapped to 2) are at the periphery of the chart. The dashed line halfway through the axis is the "neutral" point, so everything inside the dashed line indicates disagreement; answers in the outer sector of the chart indicate agreement with a particular statement in the survey.

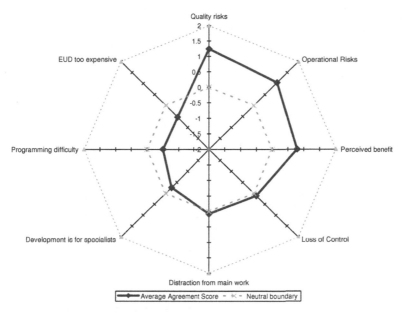

Figure 17.2. Perceptions of EUD costs and barriers.

Objective 1: EUD Benefits and Motivators

The responses indicate strong agreement with the five motivators for EUD acceptance we put forward as questionnaire statements. The strongest support was for the
role of domain expertise in producing more effective software with better fit to users'
tasks; see *Figure 17.1.*

Objective 2: Costs and Barriers

Responses to risk-related questions indicate strong agreement with the suggestion that
different risks associated with EUD are a major barrier to EUD acceptance. Interestingly, survey respondents on average disagreed with another set of suggested barriers,
including prohibitive EUD costs and difficulty of programming. A third set of suggested
barriers, such as loss of managerial control and distraction of main job function for end
users elicited neutral responses. See *Figure 17.2.*

Objective 3: Areas of Further Work

Responses to the three statements designed to test preferences for areas of further
work to be explored as a priority issue (*Figure 17.3*) indicated equal weight to all three
main directions suggested in the questionnaire. This can also be seen as a consequence
of the large number of respondees who are not research-oriented and would therefore
not have to think about future research directions within a "here-and-now"-focused
business environment.

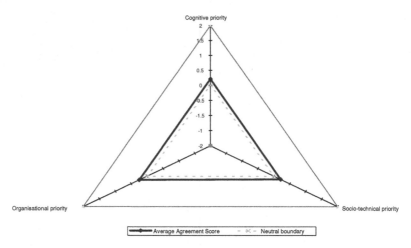

Figure 17.3. Perceptions regarding directions for further work.

2.3.2. *Discussion Results*

The method of analyzing discussion transcripts described in Section 2.1.4, which iterated between open coding and integrative workshops, resulted in the eventual emergence of eight themes out of the initial set of 11 discussion topics, following the mapping expressed in Table 17.1.

These eight themes were then positioned along the interactions between three core management concepts underpinning the themes: *Motivation* (for EUD), *Risk* (arising from EUD practices), and *Control* (of EUD practices). The resultant framework is discussed in detail in the next section.

3. Areas of Concern and Emergent Themes

The analysis of the results from the questionnaire and the emergent themes from the discussions allowed us to develop a framework of the main concerns of organizational decision makers toward the adoption of EUD of the three core concepts underpinning the main areas of concern in relation to EUD practices in organizations *Motivation* is rooted in the EUD benefits for both individuals and organizations. *Risk* refers to the potential of EUD to cause damage to operations and reputation. This could be through the changing of business processes which expose the firm to greater operational risk, poor implementation of models in spreadsheets, and the danger of untested code acting in unpredictable ways. At the social level any organizational change has a risk dimension to it; the introduction of new working practices and the changing of job descriptions and responsibilities can have a negative effect on organizations. Core competencies may be lost during such a change although the original idea might have been to enhance them. *Control* refers to the mechanisms used by the organization to allocate and audit the use of resources to best meet its goal, but it also includes political issues related to the power of individual managers. Indeed, EUD introduces new levels of autonomy

Figure 17.4. Emergent EUD themes.

into the work environment which may be perceived as a threat to the authority of some managers.

These three areas of concern underpin all eight themes emerging from the survey described in Section 2, to different degrees. *Figure 17.4* visualizes this by positioning the eight themes along the following three main axes of interaction: *Motivation and Risk.* Motivation for EUD and the EUD benefits balance the risks which can arise out of EUD practices. Four emergent themes can be seen as strongly relevant to this balance:

(a) *IT Strategy* determining the organization's attitudes toward IT-induced risks and benefits.
(b) *Organizational Demand for EUD* as a function of organizational perceptions of the balance between risks and benefits.
(c) *Cost benefit for end-users* doing development work, expressing the balance between risks and motivation at the level of individuals.
(d) *Tools to Tasks Match*, serving as a powerful factor for reducing learning costs and risks of failure for end-user development activities.

Control and Risk. Controls are introduced with the aim of reducing EUD risks, and the following emergent themes are relevant to this interaction:

(a) *IT Strategy* provides the general framework for organizational control of any IT activities, including EUD.
(b) *Managerial control* of EUD processes will consist of a set of measures designed to reduce risks by controlling EUD activities and practices.
(c) *EUD methodologies*, the EUD equivalent of SE methodologies, can be used to reduce those risks that relate to the actual development.
(d) *Professionalisation* describes organizational support for professional attitudes to EUD activities, a control which can alleviate risk to a significant degree.

Control and Motivation. In addition to controls seeking to reduce risks, there are some organizational controls which support EUD by increasing motivation as follows:

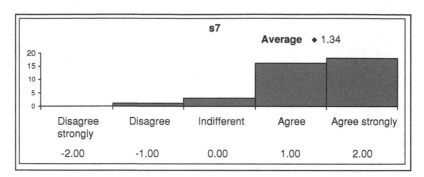

Figure 17.5. Histogram of responses to "The domain expertise of end users can create more effective software to support their activities" statement, with the average of 1.34 positioned above it.

(a) *Worker Recognition and Responsibility* focuses on the dual approach of increasing motivation by recognizing an individual's contribution whilst at the same time making clear the increased responsibilities brought about by EUD practices. This requires reward systems to recognize the contributions made by end-user developers to organizational effectiveness.
(b) *Professionalisation* of EUD relies on supporting individuals' motivation for a more professional approach to EUD.

It is worth noting that certain themes, such as IT Strategy, include elements of two interaction axes, and have therefore been mentioned more than once above. The more detailed discussion below, however, will include each emergent theme only once, under the first relevant interaction axis.

3.1. MOTIVATION AND RISK

The balance between motivation and risk will determine if decision makers within organizations think it is desirable to allow EUD to occur, and if individuals would be willing to engage in EUD activities. The four emergent themes grouped by this interaction are now reviewed in some detail.

3.1.1. *IT Strategy*

Discussion participants saw EUD as a useful mechanism to tailor information systems quickly in response to dynamic operating conditions. They believed that "EUD is good as it allows the operators of a business rather than programmers to themselves react to a changing situation."

Questionnaire responses mirror this by indicating a strong belief that EUD is perceived as increasing the capability and agility of the organizations at an affordable price. There was a strong agreement that the *Domain expertise* of end-users can create more effective software to support their activities (see histogram in *Figure 17.5*). A similar histogram pattern confirms agreement with the *Faster development* statement:

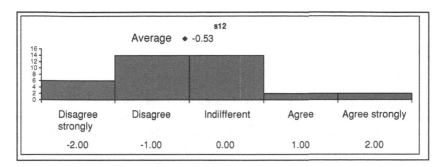

Figure 17.6. Histogram of responses to the statement "EUD is too expensive for organizations to implement," with the average disagreement of −0.53 positioned above it.

"EUD can speed up software development" (average of 0.97 out of 2). All histograms are included in Appendix B.

The costs of introducing EUD are perceived as being low enough to be worthwhile with an average score of −0.53 (mild disagreement) to the survey statement asserting that "*EUD is too expensive* for organizations to implement." The histogram of answers (*Figure 17.6*) is still with a single mode although with a less skewed pattern of answers compared to the previous case.

Interesting discussion points complemented and clarified the questionnaire opinions. Survey participants proposed that EUD should be used only as a "tactical weapon" due to the perception of its being cheap, and therefore potentially "dirty." This led to the idea that EUD artefacts should not be moved into the mainstream of an organization or be used in critical tasks without being audited by professional developers. Others thought that organizations would have "core business processes supported by software which must not be touched by end users because it would be too dangerous" and "other processes around the outside which the end user should be able to tailor." This was reinforced by the score of 1.05 agreeing with the *Operational Risks* statement: "EUD can be dangerous (e.g. data security)." The problem in deciding which process an end-user could tailor would depend on having a mechanism to identify core and peripheral processes; one suggestion was the idea of a *process risk map*. The risk map would be a "measurable business model" which allows an organization to asses the risk of altering critical processes; this model could be used to place the end-user developer in a "play-pen" of processes where it is safe to practice EUD, the underlying idea being that if the risks were quantifiable the consequences could be bounded. A play-pen approach should cover all organizational levels to avoid errors at the strategic level, such as developing a flawed spreadsheet model for a strategic decision. This could be as equally damaging as inadvertently affecting a core business process. For example Transalta lost $24 million due to a cut and paste error in one spreadsheet (Cullen, 2003).

Overall, the main conclusions related to the strategic value of EUD practices were focused on the added corporate value in terms of better support for agile working practices, but also on the need for appropriate auditing and control procedures related to the organizational diffusion of an EUD artefact. Indeed, issues of management control were quite pronounced at the discussions, and are covered in detail later on in this chapter.

3.1.2. Organizational Demand for EUD

Discussion transcripts confirmed the questionnaire responses that organizations are naturally interested in EUD because it promises agility and effective reaction to external market pressures as discussed in the previous section. However, the attitudes to EUD are shaped to a large extent by the culture of the organization, and by the presence or absence of quantified benefits. For example, the *Perceived benefit* questionnaire statement: "EUD success in organizations depends primarily on perceived benefits outweighing the perceived costs" elicited a positive agreement response with an average score of 0.79.

Business cases were identified as a very important driver for organizations exploring new technologies or practices such as EUD: "In today's economic environment, the benefits of EUD need to be quantified to stand a chance of selling it to the organization."

In terms of the market sector, "EUD is just part of a spectrum from COTS and ERP systems to reuse approaches." EUD tools such as Agentsheets will be in a competition with the following accepted practices:

a) Tailorable (but not by users) COTS systems such as ERP packages
b) Application Generators, and
c) Component Engineering.

Of these, tailorable COTS systems require a trade-off between ready-made functionality "out-of-the-box" and power of supporting complex business practices specific to the organization in question. Survey participants believed that the market had tended to favour ready-made functionality, which keeps organizations "straight-jacketed" into uniform systems and does not support business innovation. However, they hypothesized that "technology adoption goes with the business cycle," and that changing markets may require more agile organizations with tailored support for core business processes. This would ultimately benefit EUD acceptance.

3.1.3. Costs and Benefits to End-User Developers

Some costs for end-user developers should be taken into account when designing appropriate conditions for EUD. For example, learning curve costs tend to be quite high because of the rapid evolution of contemporary technologies, where "each new version of software creates a learning burden on the user." This is also compounded by the need for the EU Developer to "go back and change the underlying code" to make it work with the new technology.

These costs were not deemed unavoidable, for example the questionnaire statement on *Programming difficulty*: "Programming will always be too hard for the non-specialist" elicited a mild disagreement score of -0.5. Ways of reducing the costs were identified during the discussions; for example, one discussion participant stated that "the challenge of EUD systems is to make them so intuitive that the end-user does not realize that they are doing it," in other words we should aim to minimize the cognitive distance between the work task and the development task.

Reducing learning curve costs should be combined with increasing the benefits to end-user developers. Perceived benefits confirmed from questionnaire responses included EUD *Improves efficiency* statement: "Using EUD tools will make me more efficient in my main job task" (agreement of 0.84), and *Job enrichment* statement: "Using EUD tools could make my work more interesting" (agreement of 0.89).

Measures to further increase benefits were identified in the discussion, including the introduction of appropriate organizational processes and polices to recognize the extra work done. This is further discussed under the "Worker Recognition and Responsibility" theme below.

3.1.4. *Matching EUD Tasks to Appropriate EUD Tools*

The discussion outlined the importance of tuning EUD tools to the EUD tasks in hand. Many end users start their development activities on a very small scale addressing toy problems, and are surprised when their initial successes are not repeated when they have to deal with problems of realistic complexity.

If EUD tools are to "remove the cognitive effort so the focus is on the task," they have to use domain-specific languages, and it was felt that these "will come from the domains themselves, e.g. medicine, architecture, space physics already have well developed common languages for discussing the domain." The importance of domain expertise in producing good software was confirmed by the strong agreement (a score of 1.34) to the *Domain expertise* statement from the questionnaire: "The domain expertise of end users can create more effective software to support their activities."

Making EUD tools task- and domain-specific can help reduce their complexity and decrease the slope of their learning curve, thus redressing the balance between learning costs and effectiveness benefits, and creating a powerful source of motivation for using EUD.

3.2. CONTROL AND RISKS

Out of the four emergent themes relevant to the interaction between control and risks, this section will focus on the two specific to this axis of interaction; the rest are discussed in the other two sections.

3.2.1. *Management Control*

Naturally line management have a desire to maintain control over subordinate workers; EUD could impact this control dimension because the complexity of the artefacts may be difficult to audit and the hidden activities of workers may create a problem of software quality. There is a strong belief that "EUD creates a software quality issue," with questionnaire responses for this statement (labelled *Quality risks*) producing an average score of 1.26 with a large majority of answers indicating "agree" and no indifferent respondents (see Appendix B). This was supported by an average agreement score of 1.05 on the *Operational Risks* statement: "EUD can be dangerous (e.g. data security)." Questionnaire responses were also supported by the discussion, focusing on the need for "Good old-fashioned quality assurance."

To protect against the quality problems associated with EUD we need first to allocate the responsibility for the quality, and decide if it should be with the worker, with the user of an EUD artefact, with the local manager or with an external authority such as the IS department. Auditing was perceived as a viable approach to quality, as long as there is a clear point of responsibility for auditing EUD practices.

Different control policies were deemed necessary for different domains of EUD activities. For example "You would not want to prevent a user from filtering e-mail. So it is not just control, it is control of specific areas" and "Legislation and regulation could prevent the scope for EUD. Some domains are locked down so tightly for security and safety reasons that EUD will not happen."

An issue that emerged in relation to control is that EUD could create a power shift and affect ownership in the workplace by creating unnecessary barriers to information access. It is potentially the case that those who may have previously had informal access to information via conventional means may lose this access if information access is provided via an EUD application over which they have no control, compared to the end-user developer. The power generated by EUD practices was seen as requiring stronger levels of accountability and some clear auditing practices.

A nearly-neutral average of 0.11 on the loss of control statement: "EUD can undermine managerial authority" indicates that the sample of respondents were not sure about the relationship between EUD and management authority. During the discussions it emerged that this was because managers at present lack control of EUD practices, even those occurring within their immediate span of responsibility ("At present there is a lot of archaic development going on").

3.2.2. *EUD Methodology*

The strong concerns with the *quality risks* questionnaire statement discussed in the previous section were mirrored in a large number of discussion fragments about ways of ensuring quality and auditability of EUD activities. This included a re-visit of the idea of "incorporation of professional development methodologies," testing their suitability for structuring EUD activities and adapting them for the specific requirements of EUD. Participatory development may provide some of the initial ideas and instruments which can drive this adaptation. However, traditional software engineering methodologies may easily overwhelm any EUD effort with rigidity, process detail, and unnecessary structure.

New ways of constructing software were perceived to bring substantial changes to the way EUD will be conducted. The idea of delivering software not as a monolithic product but as a service composed and delivered at the point of need, for example, removes the need for software maintenance and replaces programming with procuring suitable services on a service marketplace. This software provision model, called Software-as-a-Service (Bennett et al., 2002) and presented at the Manchester workshop, can underpin a realistic EUD methodology in the future, but is clearly not applicable to the existing software environments supporting current-day EUD activities.

3.3. MOTIVATION AND CONTROL

The issues along this axis of interaction focus on the manner in which motivation may alleviate the need for top–down and procedural controls.

3.3.1. *Worker Recognition and Responsibility*

Survey respondees felt that using EUD tools could make their work more interesting and would make them more efficient in their main job task, with agreement averages of 0.89 to the *Job enrichment* statement, and 0.84 to the *improves efficiency* statement.

The discussion elaborated on the necessary reward mechanisms and models to reward EU developers for taking on the extra work associated with EUD. One discussion participant observed that "You get credit amongst your peers but not from elsewhere," whilst another stated that "EUD will require good reward models in organizations."

It was also felt that "Accountability of the role of end user is important. Freedom for EUD and accountability (for the artefacts produced) must come together." This duality of accountability and recognition for EUD was considered vital for acceptance by both management and workers.

3.3.2. *Professionalisation*

Survey respondents agreed strongly with the *Operational Risks* and *Quality Risks* statements (averages of 1.05 and 1.24). To counteract this perceived risk, the discussion focused on promoting professional approaches to EUD, including (a) customized Software Engineering methodologies (discussed in Section 3.2.2) and (b) promoting testing.

Indeed, testing practices and methods were perceived as an important sign of professionalism. A general lack of testing culture was perceived ("There is a lack of a culture of testing," "End users do not test."), because of the predominant paradigm of immediate results for short-term gain. One participant observed: "The pressure is to deliver the artefact, not on structure testing or load testing."

One way forward was to foster the transfer of testing practices from the users' professional domain to their software development activities. For example, marketing specialists and biologists use sophisticated testing approaches in their professional activities. The same culture of testing should be transferred to their programming activities as end-user developers, given the appropriate training and incentives.

Another way to stimulate the social acceptance of testing is to make the responsibility of the end user transparent. Highlighting the degree to which an EUD artefact has been tested is one technical approach to doing this (Burnett et al., 2002). For example, if a spreadsheet is full of red boxes then the others may not believe the figures. However, one participant observed that "Visible testedness will help make inroads into the acceptability of EUD, but there are probably problems with this idea moving away from the spreadsheet model." It was felt that technical solutions should be complemented by organizational procedures and rules to enforce testing of EUD artefacts at the level appropriate for each case.

4. Strategies for Managing the Integration of EUD

In this section we develop the implications of the survey to propose recommendations for management and EUD technology providers. We also draw on further sources, including a substantial EUD technology survey which has resulted in a comparative framework (Sutcliffe et al., 2003). As we have pointed out elsewhere (Sutcliffe et al., 2003), successful introduction of EUD depends on motivating end users to invest learning effort to use new tools and, conversely, on minimizing the costs of learning and operation. However, other barriers are more social in nature, as the survey reported in this chapter has demonstrated. Hence the future success of EUD will depend on improving the tools and integration of development activities into the end users' work tasks as well as on addressing managerial concerns of control and quality.

An overview influence diagram summarizing the issues involved in controlling the balance between motivation and risk is shown in *Figure 17.7*.

The centre of the figure outlines the core management process of (a) deciding to adopt EUD technology, (b) managing the change and planning the introduction of EUD, and (c) controlling EUD practices. Starting from the first stage in this process, Section 3 suggests we should look at four main ways to facilitate positive decisions regarding the adoption of EUD:

1. Improving EUD technology
2. Improving user motivation
3. Finding suitable applications
4. Positive assessment of risks.

The next two sub-sections will discuss the first two suggestions in detail.

4.1. EUD TECHNOLOGY

The current generation of EUD tools are still difficult to learn, although clearly, when motivated, users are prepared to invest in the necessary effort. The following three

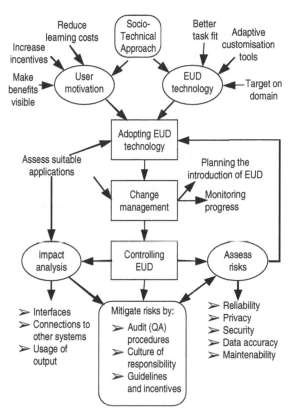

Figure 17.7. Summary of managerial issues in controlling the motivation and risk of EUD.

directions should be explored to improve the EUD technology and thus facilitate the adoption of EUD technology:

Adaptive customization tools include tools that are capable of intelligent adaptation or allow users to customize them (Oppermann, 1994). The former can reduce the users' effort but do so at the penalty of de-motivating errors when the system makes incorrect inferences (Sutcliffe et al., 2003). Adaptive systems should be restricted to areas where inference has a high probability of being accurate, and when there is doubt, mixed initiative dialogues are preferable.

User-customizable tools allow end-user developers to choose the level of programming sophistication they desire. However, customization imposes a learning burden on the user and increases the complexity of the user interface. One approach to mitigating the burden is to adopt a minimalist approach (Carroll, 1990) by revealing only essential customization functions first; then, as the user's confidence grows, the range of functions can be expanded.

EUD tools can also be tuned to achieve *better task fit*; for example, in control applications for home use the scope of programmability can be limited to the functions of the devices (e.g. lighting controls, thermostats), thus simplifying the learning burden. The *task fit* idea underpins supportive development environments where learning and creating are seamlessly integrated activities. Users should be encouraged to learn by experimentation while the system provides explanatory feedback to remedy mistakes. This requires ways of simulating effects so programs can be validated by inspection.

EUD support tools need to adopt the lessons from domain-oriented design environments (Fischer, 1994) and provide critics, templates, explanation facilities, and syntax directed editors to support design and learning in EUD.

The languages and techniques underpinning such tools should *target the user domain.* One example would be to use realistic metaphors based in the user domain, such as wiring together signal processing modules in LabView (National Instruments, 2004) to help the users understand programming actions and effects.

A natural development of this idea is to develop more natural lexicons and syntax to express instructions in a domain. Investigating sub-language theory from linguistics may provide a useful approach although there will be scope and expressability trade-offs, i.e. a language which applied EUD in a narrow domain, such a programming genomic analysis in bioinformatics, could be easy to learn for the domain experts but limited in application to a small number of such experts. More general EUD languages will solve the dilemma of being easy to learn while having sufficient power to address a wide range of problems.

One of the important lessons from our survey was the importance of the *socio-technical approach* to supporting EUD, including fostering supportive communities of developers, both end-user and expert who share problems and solutions. Tools will support EUD collaboration by allowing end-user developers to share designs, reusable code, examples, etc. (see the contribution of Pipek and Kahler in this volume).

On a cognitive level this is particularly important because learning to develop successfully requires not only mastering syntax of a language but also conceptual and abstract thinking about computation design. Education and sharing conceptual computation metaphors, data structures, models, and procedures are thus important user development tasks, and socio-technical design of the EUD support community ensures *better task fit* on the technical side and reduction of learning costs, as reviewed in detail in the next section.

4.2. USER MOTIVATION

To foster *user motivation*, user roles and incentives need to be designed with care. Some users will invest more effort in software/programming tools while others will have less motivation to do so. The socio-technical approach discussed above can help this through enabling supportive end-user communities, where end-user developer experts may emerge, called local experts (Mumford, 1981) or gardeners (Nardi, 1993). For discussion of the collective, cultural, and motivational aspects the reader is referred to

Carter and Henderson (1990). The following three policies should lead to increasing user motivation:

Make benefits visible by sharing examples of EUD success stories and demonstrations about how the technology can improve work efficiency. Note that this recommendation has implications for collaborative tools.

Increase incentives for individuals to engage in end-user development where appropriate, to share expertise and solutions. Plan diffusion of expertise within and across groups.

Reduce learning costs by ensuring end-users have time to learn new tools and attend training sessions. Costs of error can be dramatically reduced by providing a protective environment so end users can experiment and make mistakes safely while learning new tools.

4.3. CHANGE MANAGEMENT AND CONTROLLING EUD

One of the stronger indications from the survey was the concern about control of EUD. This revisits the debate from earlier generations of EUD languages (Martin, 1982, 1984). Controlling EUD practices relies on two core activities: *Impact Analysis* and *Assessing Risks*.

4.3.1. *Impact Analysis*

Impact analysis helps the management to strike the balance between (a) convenience and speed of development and (b) the need to maintain quality when developed systems might have lasted some time and have critical dependencies with other systems. It requires *assessment of suitability of applications* for EUD, depending on their *interfaces*, *connections to other systems* and *usage of their output*.

For example, stand-alone systems for personal use are considered suitable for EUD because they do not provide direct inputs to mission-critical systems. The key to managing potential exposure lies in careful assessment since EUD systems may have hidden indirect interfaces with other systems such as reports and data used by others for core decision-making.

Deciding whether to allow EUD for systems on a case by case basis can be laborious to implement so assessment of impact and risks may be conducted for types of systems rather than for individual applications.

4.3.2. *Assessing and Mitigating Risks*

The perceived dangers of applications created by end-users are poor software *reliability*, *maintainability*, *security*, *data accuracy*, and loss of *privacy*. All these factors constitute risks which need to be assessed and managed.

Risk assessment will depend on the duration and potential impact of system output, which are both results from the impact analysis activity.

Alternatively *risks can be mitigated* by one of the following approaches:

- Foster *culture of responsibility* so the onus of preventing reliability and accuracy exposures lies with the end users.
- Design and implement *audit (quality assessment) procedures* to check on EUD systems.
- Set *guidelines* for (a) data access and distribution of system output to safeguard privacy and confidentiality, and ensure compliance with data protection legislation; and (b) for best practice in development and project management of end-user activities.

The dilemma for management is that end-user activity is frequently motivated by agility and empowerment of users. Controls and standards militate against EUD which by its nature will tend to be less formal that traditional IS department procedures. EUD lends itself to agile methods, XP approaches, and prototyping style development rather than systematic engineering (Rational Corporation, 2002), and process maturity styles of management (Paulk et al., 1993).

The problem is how to draw the line between core corporate systems which need to be developed and managed by software professionals on one hand and "quick and dirty" development on the other. One model which traces its heritage to System Development (Jackson, 1982) is to maintain transaction processing and database updating systems under IS control while permitting reporting and information access functions to be controlled by end-users. However, this model needs to be extended to forecasting, planning and decision support system which end-users will want to develop themselves. The degree of audit and control of end-user DSS depends on the impact analysis of system output.

5. Conclusion

In this chapter we explore the social and contextual issues surrounding EUD and supporting technology. We report our findings from a questionnaire and two structured group discussions regarding perceptions of factors which may impede or support the introduction of EUD in organizations. We use the findings to develop a conceptual map of EUD issues with recommendations for the adoption and management of end-user activities. This map targets managers and technology developers, focusing attention on different ways to lower perceived costs and increase perceived benefits to motivate users and justify their investment in the effort of learning. In this respect, we see the following three main directions of future work in EUD.

Explore differences in the characteristics of EUD activities within different application domains. Our survey has highlighted that EUD in the home and personal entertainment domain would have different requirements, barriers, and motivating factors from EUD activities concerning business information systems. EUD of scientific applications such as bioinformatics would be different yet again. We need to create a map of such differences, and use this map to judge the suitability of different cognitive and organizational solutions, and thus guide the effort of technology developers in the area.

Address a number of tools and technology challenges. The cognitive fit between a particular EUD task and the supporting tool has been asserted as an important factor facilitating the acceptance of EUD in different contexts. Studies of different EUD tasks can help us identify appropriate development metaphors and features of design environments to optimize the trade-off between design power and need for abstract thinking by end-user developers.

Investigate social challenges to EUD acceptance. The survey has demonstrated the importance of carefully designing organizational rewards and responsibility systems to balance the costs and motivations for individuals capable of doing EUD. Organizations should also decide on the appropriate trade-off between control risks and the agility brought about by unconstrained EUD activities. Finally, we would like to explore the potential relationship between organizational learning and collaborative EUD activities and clarify benefits accruing from such a relationship.

APPENDIX A: Questionnaire Results and Relationship with Survey Objectives

Related to survey objective No					
1. Benefits and Motivators	2. Costs and Barriers	3. Further work areas	Question label	Statement	Agreement on scale (−2 to +2)
√			Domain expertise	The domain expertise of end-users can create more effective software to support their activities	1.34
√			Faster development	EUD could speed up software development.	0.97
√			Job enrichment	Using EUD tools could make my work more interesting.	0.89
√			Improves efficiency	Using EUD tools will make me more efficient in my main job task	0.84
√	√		Perceived benefit	EUD success in the organization depends primarily on the perceived benefits out-weighing the perceived costs	0.79
	√		Quality risks	EUD creates a software quality issue.	1.24
	√		Operational risks	EUD can be dangerous (e.g., Data security)	1.05
	√		Loss of control	EUD can undermine managerial authority	0.11
	√		Distraction from main work	Using EUD tools will consume time which I should be spending on my main job task	0.08

(Continued)

Related to survey objective No					
1. Benefits and Motivators	2. Costs and Barriers	3. Further work areas	Question label	Statement	Agreement on scale (−2 to +2)
	√		Development is for specialists	Software development is the responsibility of software specialists	−0.26
	√		Programming difficulty	Programming will always be too hard for the non-specialist.	−0.5
	√		EUD too expensive	EUD is too expensive for organizations to implement	−0.53
		√	Organizational priority	EUD work should focus on organizational issues first	0.24
		√	Cognitive priority	EUD work should focus on solving the cognitive issues first	0.21
		√	Socio-technical priority	EUD work should focus on socio-technical issues first	0.21

APPENDIX B: Histograms of Responses

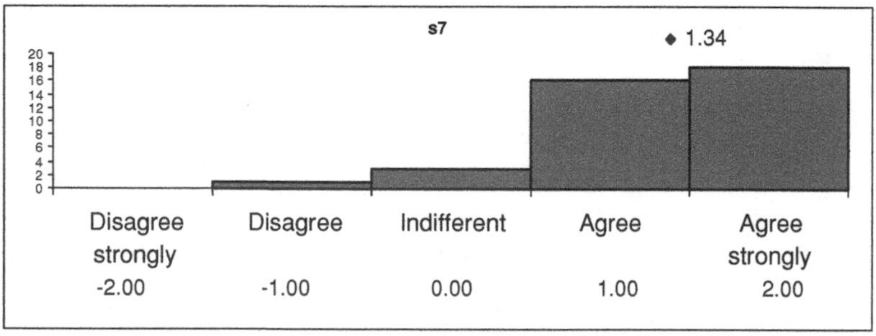

Figure 17.8. Answers to the "Domain expertise" question: 'The domain expertise of end-users can create more effective software to support their activities.'

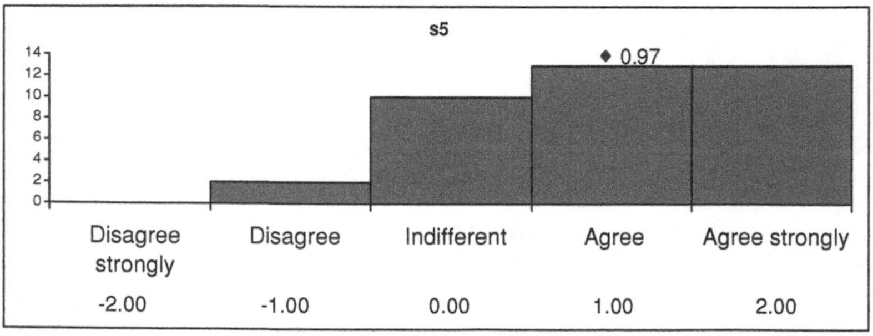

Figure 17.9. Answers to the "Faster development" question: 'EUD could speed up software development.'

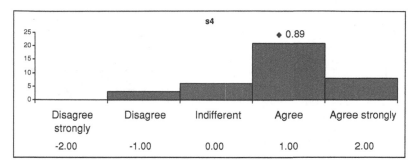

Figure 17.10. Answers to the "Job enrichment" question: 'Using EUD tools could make my work more interesting.'

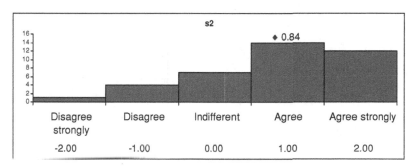

Figure 17.11. Answers to the "Improves efficiency" question: 'Using EUD tools will make me more efficient in my main job task.'

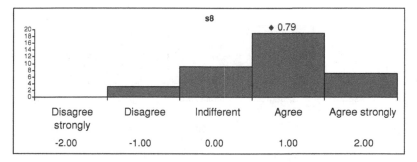

Figure 17.12. Answers to the "Perceived benefit" question: 'EUD success in the organisation depends primarily on the perceived benefits out-weighing the perceived costs.'

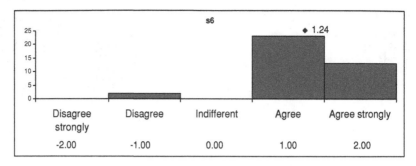

Figure 17.13. Answers to the "Quality risks" question: 'EUD creates a software quality issue.'

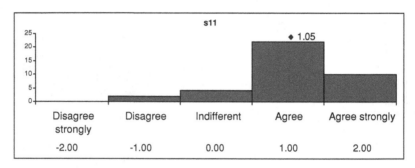

Figure 17.14. Answers to the "Operational Risks" question: 'EUD can be dangerous (e.g. Data security).'

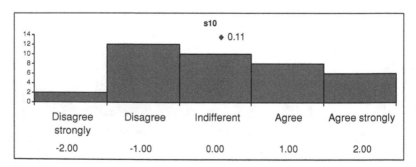

Figure 17.15. Answers to the "Loss of control" question: 'EUD can undermine managerial authority."

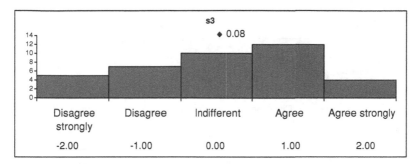

Figure 17.16. Answers to the "Distraction from main work" question: 'Using EUD tools will consume time which I should be spending on my main job task.'

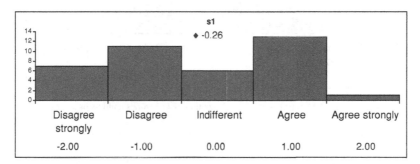

Figure 17.17. Answers to the "Development is for specialists" question: 'Software development is the responsibility of software specialists.'

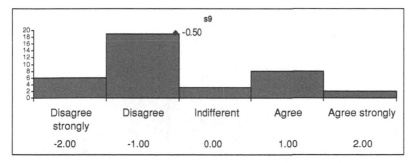

Figure 17.18. Answers to the "Programming difficulty" question: 'Programming will always be too hard for the non-specialist.'

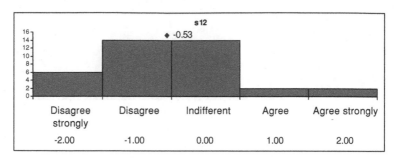

Figure 17.19. Answers to the "EUD too expensive" question: 'EUD is too expensive for organisations to implement.'

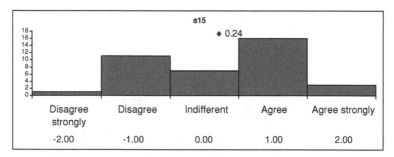

Figure 17.20. Answers to the "Organisational priority" question: 'EUD work should focus on organisational issues first.'

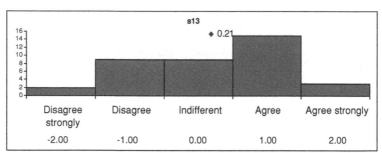

Figure 17.21. Answers to the "Cognitive priority" question: 'EUD work should focus on solving the cognitive issues first.'

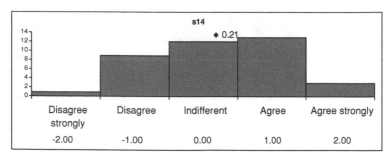

Figure 17.22. Answers to the "Socio-technical priority" question: 'EUD work should focus on socio-technical issues first.'

APPENDIX C: End User Development Perceptions Questionnaire

|PART A|
(Q1) Name: _____
(Q2) Organisation Size: _____
(Q3) How does your job relate to Information Technology? _____
_____

(E.g. are you an IS developer, Researcher, End-User....)

(Q4) Have you used End User Development technologies? Yes/No (please circle)

(Q5) If   yes   which?   _____
_____

(e.g. spreadsheets, macro programming....):

|PART B|
Please complete this section by rating your sentiments towards the statements. Place a mark in the box of the option which best describes opinion.

Statement	Agree strongly	Agree	Indifferent	Disagree	Disagree Strongly
(S1) Software development is the responsibility of software specialists.					
(S2) Using EUD tools will make me more efficient in my main job task.					
(S3)Using EUD tools will consume time which I should be spending on my main job task.					
(S4)Using EUD tools could make my work more interesting.					
(S5) EUD could speed up software development.					
(S6) EUD creates a software quality issue.					
(S7) The domain expertise of end-users can create more effective software to support their activities.					
(S8) EUD success in the organisation depends primarily on the perceived benefits out-weighing the perceived costs.					
(S9) Programming will always be too hard for the non-specialist.					
(S10)EUD can undermine managerial authority.					
(S11) EUD can be dangerous (e.g. Data security).					
(S12) EUD is too expensive for organisations to implement.					
(S13) EUD work should focus on solving the cognitive issues first.					
(S14) EUD work should focus on socio-technical issues first.					
(S15) EUD work should focus on organisational issues first.					

ORGANISATIONAL VIEW OF END-USER DEVELOPMENT

|PART C|
Please use this space for comments about either this questionnaire or on End-User
Development in general.

(QX)

Acknowledgments

This work was partially supported by the EU 5th Framework programme, Network of
Excellence EUD(End-User Development) Net. IST-2002-8.1.2.

References

Bennett, K.H., Gold, N.E., Munro, M., Xu, J., Layzell, P.J., Budgen, D., Brereton, O.P. and Mehandjiev, N. (2002). Prototype Implementations of an Architectural Model for Service-Based Flexible Software. In: Ralph, H. Sprague, Jr. (ed.), *Proceedings of 35th Hawaii International Conference on System Sciences (HICSS-35)*. CA: IEEE Computer Society, ISBN 0-7695-1435-9.

Boehm, B.W., Clark, B., Horowitz, E., Westland, C., Madachy, R. and Selby, R. (1995). In: J.D. Arthur S.M. Henry and J.C. Baltzer AG (eds.), *Cost models for future software life cycle processes: COCOMO 2.0, Annals of Software Engineering, Special Volume on Software Process and Product Measurement*. Amsterdam, The Netherlands: Science Publishers.

Brancheau, J.C. and Brown, C.V. (1993). The management of end user computing: Status and directions. *ACM Computing Surveys* 25(4), 437–482.

Burnett, M.M., Baker M.J., et al. (1995). Scaling up visual programming languages. *IEEE Computer,* 28(3), 45.

Burnett, M., Sheretov, A., Ren, B. and Rothermel, G. (2002). Testing homogeneous spreadsheet grids with the 'What You See Is What You Test' methodology. *IEEE Transactions on Software Engineering* 29(6), 576–594.

Carroll, J.M. (1990). *The Nurnberg Funnel: Designing Minimalist Instruction for Practical Computer Skill*. Cambridge, MA: MIT Press.

Carter, K. and Henderson, A. (1990). Tailoring culture. In: Reports on Computer Science and Mathematics no 107, Åbo Akademi university 1990, *Proceedings of 13th IRIS Conference*, pp. 103–116, Turku, Finland.

Cullen, D. (2003). Excel snafu costs firm $24m, published by *The Register*, available from http://www.theregister.co.uk/content/67/31298.html, last accessed 15 Nov 2003.

Fischer, G. (1994). Domain-oriented design environments. *Automated Software Engineering* 1(2), 177–203.

Green, T.R.G., and Petre, M. (1996). Usability analysis of visual programming environments: A cognitive dimensions framework. *Journal of Visual Languages and Computing* 7(2), 131–174.

Jackson, M. (1982). *System Development*. London: Prentice-Hall.

Lieberman, H. (Ed.). (2001). *Your Wish is my Command: Programming by Example*. San Francisco: Morgan Kaufmann.

Martin, J. (1982). *Application Development without Programmers*. London: Prentice Hall.

Martin, J. (1984). *An Information Systems Manifesto*. London: Prentice-Hall.

Mumford, E. (1981). Participative Systems Design: Structure and Method. *Systems, Objectives, Solutions* **1**(1), 5–19.

Nardi, B.A. (1993). *A Small Matter of Programming: Perspectives on End-User Computing*. Cambridge, MA: MIT Press.

Nardi, B.A. and Miller, J.R. (1991). Twinkling lights and nested loops: Distributed problem solving and spreadsheet development. *International Journal of Man-Machine Studies* **34**(2), 161–184.

National Instruments. (2004). LabVIEW—The Software that Powers Virtual Instrumentation, http://www.ni.com/labview/, last accessed on 4th May 2004.

Oppermann, R. (1994). *Adaptive User Support Ergonomic Design of Manually and Automatically Adaptable Software*. Hillsdale, New Jersey: Lawrence Erlbaum Associates.

Panko, R. (1988). *End User Computing: Management Applications and Technology*. Chichester: John Wiley & Sons.

Powell, A. and Moore, J.E. (2002). The focus of research in end user computing: Where have we come since the 1980ties? *Journal of End User Computing* **14**(1), 3–22.

Paulk, M.C., Curtis, B., Chrissis, M.B. and Weber, C.V. (1993). Capability Maturity Model for Software, Version 1.1. *IEEE Software* **10**(4), 18–27.

Repenning, A. (1993). *Agentsheets: A Tool for Building Domain Oriented Dynamic Visual Environments*. Technical Report, Dept of Computer Science, CU/CS/693/93. Boulder, CO: University of Colorado.

Rational Corporation. (2002). *The Rational Unified Process*, published 2002, now available. http://www.ibm.com/software/awdtools/rup/, last accessed 15 Nov 2003.

Strauss, A. and Corbin, J. (1998). *Basics of Qualitative Research: Techniques and Procedures for Developing Grounded Theory*, 2nd ed. Thousand Oaks, CA: Sage.

Sutcliffe, A., Lee, D. and Mehandjiev, N. (2003). Contributions, Costs and Prospects for End-user Development, *Human Computer Interaction—International Proceedings*. Mahwah NJ: Lawrence Erlbaum Associates.

United States Bureau of the Census. (1999). *Computer Use in the United States, October 1997*, Department of Commerce, Washington D.C, September 1999.

Chapter 18

A Semiotic Framing for End-User Development

CLARISSE SIECKENIUS DE SOUZA and SIMONE DINIZ
JUNQUEIRA BARBOSA
Departamento de Informática, PUC-Rio-Rua Marquês de São Vicente 225/410 RDC-Rio de Janeiro, RJ—Brasil, Clarisse@inf.puc-rio.br, Simone@inf.puc-rio.br

Abstract. One approach to designing usable and enjoyable computer applications is to say that designers need better methods and tools to understand users and their contexts, and to encode this understanding into closed computer systems. Another is to acknowledge that there will always be unattended user needs, and that the way to increase users' satisfaction is to help them modify systems in order to meet constantly changing requirements. Different techniques are proposed in one approach usually without reference to the other. We present an overarching perspective of human–computer interaction where both meet, and provide a semiotic characterization of designers' and users' activities that clarifies the tradeoffs involved in designing and choosing techniques in either approach. Central to this characterization is the role of intentions in what users mean to say and do when using computers. Our characterization is in line with a broader concept of usability, in which systems must support users' improvisation and creativity.

1. Meeting End-Users' Expectations

In spite of speedy technological evolution and voluminous knowledge generated by research and development in human–computer interaction (HCI), users of information technology (IT) products still have to live with a high dosage of frustration and confusion when trying to get systems to do what they want. Building usable and enjoyable systems remains a challenge for the IT industry, regardless of the excitement brought about by such things as miniature multi-function mobile devices, sophisticated virtual reality caves, or intelligent buildings and vehicles. The old challenge can be stated in very simple terms: how do we design technology that *meets the users' needs*?

Very large portions of contemporary work in HCI center around techniques and tools that can help designers enhance their understanding of users and use situations. Their aim is to minimize the mismatch between what users want to do with computer systems and how computer systems respond to their expectations. There is a variety of approaches for solving this problem, two of them lying at opposite ends. One seeks to increase a designer's ability to *capture* finer distinctions in the users' behavior and context, and to *encode* such improved distinctions into computer systems. The idea is to cover a maximum share of the users' world and to prepare the *system* to react appropriately as situations evolve. The other approach seeks to *empower users* with the ability to *tailor* computer systems to their specific needs, by customizing the systems'

Henry Lieberman et al. (eds.), End User Development, 401–426.

appearance and behavior, or by adding and assembling new functionality. The idea is to build applications that support a range of basic (re)design and (re)codification activities that enable the *user* to react creatively as situations evolve. End-user development (EUD) is a generalization of this approach.

An invariant strategy taken by adopters of both approaches has been an emphasis on producing *techniques* to solve perceived problems, rather than *accounts* of what these problems are at a more foundational level. As a consequence, telling why, when and how various techniques can or should be applied to improve the users' satisfaction has some times brought up more guesses than justifications. Useful answers to these questions require a deeper understanding not only of EUD and HCI problems, their nature and scope, but also of solutions and their implications, local and global. For example, among popular usability guidelines (Nielsen, 1993) we find explicit references to computer systems having to be flexible and efficient. However, we do not know when greater flexibility (achieved, say, through macro recording) becomes detrimental to other usability *musts* such as ease of use or robust error prevention. Likewise, we know that programming by demonstration (PbyD) can help users build small programs by means of relatively simple interactive patterns (Cypher, 1993; Lieberman, 2001). However, the reason why in spite of its power PbyD is not widely adopted in IT design or, when adopted, why it is not understood by most users is unclear to both researchers and developers.

In this chapter, we shift the focus of discussion from *techniques* to an integrated *account* of EUD as part of HCI. Unlike in other EUD approaches (for a brief overview see Fischer et al., 2004), in ours the development of applications "from scratch" does not constitute an immediate goal for EUD. We believe that this represents an advanced evolutionary stage in a "do-it-yourself computing" path, whose achievement depends on the applications' designers' ability to understand and respond to a number of relatively simpler EUD challenges. Our discussion centers mainly around two aspects of EUD that are of paramount importance for usable HCI products: *customizing* and *extending* applications. We use semiotic theory to substantiate our views, aiming at two main targets. First, we propose to show why the customization and extension of IT products should be taken as a fundamental usability requirement. We draw the reader's attention to the consequences of some constraints imposed by the irreducible gap that separates what users may *mean* from what computer systems can *understand*. Second, we propose a semiotic characterization of some of the practical issues that currently challenge EUD. By so doing, we expect to advance explanations about why EUD may still be difficult for most users, and to provide ingredients for the elaboration of enhanced technical solutions.

We start by retrieving some of the early connections between HCI and end-user programming, made by such researchers as Nardi (1993), Adler and Winograd (1992), and Fischer (1998). We then present a semiotic description of how *meaning* is expressed in signification systems and communication processes. In particular, we resort to the notion of *unlimited semiosis*, and show that what users and computer systems *mean* are fundamentally different things. Human meanings are indissociable from human intent—a highly contingent and changing factor in communication, with other humans or with computers. Computer meanings, however, are determined by semantic *rules* that systematically apply whenever certain predefined system states are achieved. This idea is akin to the one presented in Winograd and Flores (1986). Based on phenomenology and speech act theory, these two authors have set the basis for the *language-action perspective* in software design as to be practiced *by designers*. Our semiotic perspective allows us to go one step further and to inspect the very codification and interpretation of intent, when *users as designers* try to configure or program applications to do what they mean. We illustrate our characterization of EUD activities with examples drawn from different types of techniques, with special emphasis on the challenges and opportunities of PbyD (CACM, 2000; Lieberman, 2001), given their close connection with HCI. Finally, we discuss our integrative semiotic characterization of the user's activity, where interaction, customization, and extension are brought together. We show how it can help HCI and EUD designers frame design problems more clearly, and make more informed decisions about the tradeoffs between popular views of usability and user empowerment.

2. Usability Challenges and EUD

Adler and Winograd (1992) discuss *the usability challenge* proposing that usability should be viewed as a dialogue of change. In their own words, "the key criterion of a system's usability is the extent to which it supports the potential for people who work with it to understand it, to learn, and to make changes" (p. 7). They explicitly say that *usable* systems must allow users to cope with novelty, and that "design for usability must include [...] design for improvisation, and design for adaptation" (p. 7). Their view is echoed by Nardi (1993), for whom "users like computers because they get their work done" (p. 5). This may occasionally involve creating novel functions that serve some particular purpose, unanticipated by designers who produced the original system. From an end-user's point of view, the specific procedure required for creating new functions "is not important, so long as [this activity] is easy and relatively rapid" (p. 6). Nardi proposes that "human–computer communication is best facilitated by task-specific programming languages that tap users' task knowledge and related interests" (p. 10). This view brings interface and end-user programming *languages* together and makes designing them part of the *usability challenge*. The author remarks that different techniques such as PbyD or customization dialogues can help users tailor computer applications to their specific needs easily and rapidly.

Fischer (1998) says that "computational media have the unique potential to let people be designers or assist them to incrementally become designers. Unfortunately, most current computational environments do not allow users to act as contributors and designers" (p. 2). His view also points to Adler and Winograd's *usability challenge*, especially when he proposes that design should not produce technology that "restricts knowledgeable and skilled human professionals [...] to answering yes or no to questions generated by the system" (p. 2). The underlying message of Fisher's elaboration on his initial ideas—meta-design (Fischer et al., 2004; Fischer and Giaccardi, this volume), is that useful computer systems should be cast as environments for end-user design and end-user development.

An important usability question in this context is: how would users *express* their design? Before we propose possible answers to this question we should examine *what* users may wish to express.

3. A Semiotic Account of Meaning for Humans and Computers

One approach to finding how users would best express their design is to start with a more fundamental question: what do users *mean* to say when they interact with computer systems? This question underlines complex communicative aspects of HCI rarely tackled in cognitively inspired research on usability.

A semiotic account of communication, like the one proposed by Eco (1976) for example, identifies two important pillars that support human communicative exchanges. The first is that of *signification systems*, established by virtue of social and cultural conventions adopted by users of such systems. Signification systems determine codified associations between content and expression, like that between the topic of this paragraph—communication—and the words "communication" in English or "comunicação" in Portuguese. The second pillar is that of *communication processes*, through which sign producers explore the possibilities of established signification systems in order to achieve an open range of purposes. The important factor in communication, as defined by such semiotic theory, is that communicators are not constrained to expressing themselves exclusively by means of signs established by existing signification systems. They can, and most often do, invent novel ad hoc ways to communicate ideas originally. For example, people may use irony or humor to get their message across (two kinds of expression where the literal meaning of signs is usually a blatant lie with respect to what they systematically express in generic contexts). By so doing, they may improve certain aspects of their intent and meet their communicative goals with increased efficiency. People can also use puns or invent new terms and phrases to express the meanders of their imagination and expand the universe of communication. A contemporary token of this strategy is the term "*ear*con," which bears rich semiotic associations with the word "icon" and its pronunciation ("*eye*con"), made explicit in the definition of an earcon as "an auditory icon" (The Word Spy, 2004).

These characteristics draw our attention to an important factor in communication—*intent*. When communicating with others, we explore content-expression associations existing in our culture in order to cause certain effects on our listeners. Irony, humor, metaphor, invention, and all are expressive strategies that we may choose in order to maximize our efficiency in bringing about our intent or, as speech act theorists have put it, in doing things with words (Austin, 1962; Searle, 1969). Expression, content and intent are therefore three fundamental dimensions in human communication. Linguistic theories have usually aligned them to lexico-grammar, semantics, and pragmatics, respectively.

Nevertheless, the situation with computers is considerably different. Formal languages and automata theory (Hopcroft and Ullman, 1979), which provide the foundations for the design of computer languages, only refer to a lexico-grammatical component (usually split into vocabulary and syntax) and a semantic component. Ontologically, computers do not have any intent. A *system* can only get users to do things if *users* willingly assign intentionality to program-generated signs, which reproduced in strict accordance with the rules encoded in the formal signification systems that drive all computation. Thus, successful human–computer communication crucially depends on the effects that computer signs actually have on users (be it by design, or by chance). The reverse effect is even more critical in HCI, namely the effect that human-generated signs have on computer systems. Computers cannot *react* appropriately when humans step outside the limits of the signification systems encoded in programs, although humans may not even realize that they are doing it. For instance, if a user selects a table cell and commands a text editor to "paint it yellow" he may be amused (or perhaps annoyed) if the system replies that "a table cell cannot be painted," although when commanded to "change a table cell's fill color to yellow" the system immediately *paints it yellow*. Similar mysteries with systems that react as expected when told to "thicken a line" but fail to understand what the user means when told to "thicken a character" (although characters are literally thickened when users apply the command "bold") are encountered by users on a daily basis.

Semiotic theory can illuminate important facets of signs and their meaning, in human and computer contexts. First, in Peircean semiotics (Peirce, 1931–1958) a sign is *anything* that someone (or some mind) takes to be *meaningful*. So, for instance, a perceptible image in a system's interface may be a sign for one user, but not for the other. It *is* a sign for the user that takes the image to *mean* something (no matter what it means to the computer). Meaningless images are—by definition—not signs. Second, the structure of a sign includes three inter-related elements: a representation (the *representamen*), a referent (the *object*) and a meaning (the *interpretant*). However, the *interpretant* is itself another sign (which is another way to say that the meaning of a sign necessarily *means* other things). Thus, unlike views in which meaning is a static final entity (a mental state, a relational configuration between abstract and concrete worlds, a definable concept, or some other kind of delimited object), in this theory meaning is an infinite process that generates indefinitely many other meanings associated to each other by interpretive functions. This process is called unlimited semiosis (Eco, 1976). The shape and direction of associative chains, in shorter and longer time intervals, cannot be predicted in any strict sense. Although culture strongly motivates the occurrence of certain key signs in semiosis (which ultimately make communication possible), we should not expect culture to determine completely and uniquely the individual interpretations of signs. Quite contrarily, it is our individual ability to make free and creative sign associations in interpreting the world that allows us to capture innovative discourse produced by others, and to produce it ourselves.

Evidence of unlimited semiosis in HCI can be easily found. For instance, the meaning of such popular interface expression as "cancel" evolves as one gains experience with computers and applications. Regardless of the fact that "cancel" necessarily involves aspects of that which is being "canceled" (e.g., canceling a download process is different from canceling an installation process), the pragmatic effects of saying "cancel" in HCI cannot be fully defined. Although it is true, from a programming standpoint, that "canceling" may amount to a small and well-defined set of basic actions (e.g., halt current computation, restore previous system configuration, and the like), from a user's standpoint "canceling" may mean such different things as: "Oops! I made a mistake." or "Hmm, I do not know. . . better not do this."; or "Forget about it."; or "Stop."; or "This is not what I meant."; or whatever other paraphrase can be used to express the unlimited variety of *intent* that a user might be trying to achieve by saying "cancel." All of them become part of an evolving signification of what "cancel" *means* when interacting with computers.

Third, provisionally defined meanings play a critical role in fundamental sense-making activities that enable and support HCI. For example, let us examine the following interactive situation, which is analogous to many encountered outside the context of interacting with computers, and whose sequentially numbered stages concur to assigning meaning to what is really going on.

1. The user cannot open the file a:\file.pdf.
2. The user assumes that there is a general rule saying that pdf files can only be opened if some_viewer.exe is installed in the machine.
3. The user verifies that in fact some_viewer.exe is not installed in the machine and that, as expected, a:\ another_file.pdf and a:\ yet_another_file.pdf cannot be opened.
4. The user concludes that his not being able to open pdf files means that some_viewer.exe is not installed (or, in other words, that the absence of program some_viewer.exe explains his problem).
5. The user also concludes that if he installs some_viewer.exe in the machine, a:\file.pdf and the pdf files will then be normally opened.

So, in view of what this interactive breakdown means, the user proceeds to install `some_viewer.exe`. However, after having done this, the user sees that `a: \file.pdf` still cannot be opened. The user may equivocally conclude that (CACM, 2000) was wrong (which it was not, because pdf files do require `some_viewer.exe` in order to be viewed, or opened). Successful sense making in this case may only be achieved if the user produces further provisional meanings. For instance, the user may decide to test if drive a: is working properly. If `a:\file.txt` cannot be opened although the associated text editor for `txt` files is running properly in the machine, then the user has counter evidence for the equivocal conclusion that (CACM, 2000) was wrong, which may lead him to invoke another general rule that precedes the one in (Austin, 1962), namely that files in drive a: can only be opened if the hardware is working properly.

Notice that the computer meanings involved in this problem are fixed and algorithmically produced throughout the whole episode, regardless of the directions in which the user's semiosis evolves. "Open a:\file.pdf" *means*: access the file; and activate some_viewer.exe taking a:\file.pdf as input parameter. The role of HCI design is to provide the user with useful error message signs, so that the appropriate meanings are associated with the interactive events he experiences. In a typical Windows® environment, if some_viewer.exe is not installed in the machine, the system merely asks the user to indicate which application must be used to open the file (it does not tell the user that some_viewer.exe is not installed). However, if there is a hardware problem, the user gets a message with a more precise diagnosis of the problem: "a:\ is not accessible." Depending on how the user interprets the word "accessible" the appropriate meaning of not being able to open pdf files may be closer or farther away. The user's sense-making process is based on hypothetical reasoning, also known as *abduction*, that underlies all human interpretive processes in communication.

Because computer symbol processing rests on rule-based causal connections between symbols and physical machine behavior, computer *meanings* are not only ultimately predictable, but also essentially unchanging. As illustrated in the example above, in spite of all the learning process which leads users to stop and resume their interpretation of the same signs emitted by computers, the underlying meaning of such signs *for the computer* is ever the same. The rules that govern how symbols affect the machine's behavior define the semantic scope of all possible symbols that the machine can process. This is true even in the case of programs that can expand their initial semantic base by taking other programs as input. There must be rules defining how the meanings encoded in the input program are to interact with the ones of the host program and, consequently, what types of semantic expansions can be accommodated.

Given these differences between human semiosis and computer symbol processing, a semiotically-informed approach to usability carries the promise to help designers support the users' *semiosis* while engaged in computer-supported activities, and not strictly the users' tasks. Letting users customize and extend meanings encoded in computer languages enables systems to respond usefully to at least some portion of the evolving interpretations that users continually assign to their own activities, and subsequently incorporate to the way they express themselves about such activities.

4. Meeting the User's Intent Through EUD

Taking Adler and Winograd's approach to usability leads us to an integrated view of HCI and EUD. The *designers* of usable systems have to support the activities of users as designers; in Fischer's terms, they have to engage in *meta-design*. All design must be expressed through signification systems that not only allow users to express their intent to achieve task-related goals (like "format document"), but also to create, inspect, modify and elaborate on extensions that they may produce with various EUD techniques (like macro recording or PbyD). Thus, designers of usable computer systems have to (de Souza, 2004):

- synthesize a signification system to support HCI,
- communicate their design vision through this particular signification system,

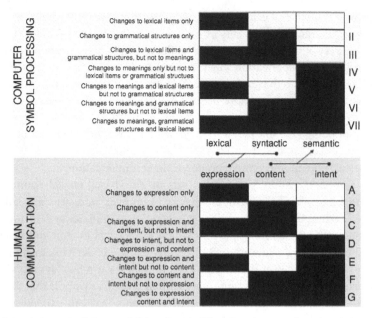

Figure 18.1. Semiotic manipulation possibilities of symbols and signs from a computer symbol-processing perspective and a human communication one.

- communicate the rules and principles according to which certain expressions are systematically associated to certain contents in order to achieve a specific range of intents,
- communicate if and how such principles and rules can be modified, and
- communicate how modified meanings can be effectively used in interaction with the application.

Users can only benefit from the qualities that such design adds to computer systems if they can:

- understand the designed signification system,
- formulate a satisfactory hypothesis of how meanings are encoded in this system,
- master its use for communicating intents to the system and achieving a variety of purposes with it,
- formulate a satisfactory hypothesis of which new meanings (or meaning modifications) can be encoded and how, and
- encode such meanings in the system and incorporate them to the possible varieties of interactive discourse with the application.

In Figure 18.1, we project the semiotic dimensions introduced in Section 3 onto two different tables. The upper table refers to the symbol-processing perspective that applies to computers. In it, manipulations of the lexical, syntactic, and semantic dimensions of the underlying signification system (i.e., the computer languages that users and/or programmers have access to) can be used to effect different symbolic transformations (numbered from I to VII). The lower table refers to the human communication perspective. In it, manipulations of the expression, content, and intent dimensions of the underlying signification system can be used to achieve different communicative goals (numbered from A to G). Computer and human semiotic dimensions involved in signification system manipulations projected in both tables are not in one-to-one correspondence with each other. Notice that the lexical and the syntactic dimension of computer languages refer to the expression dimension in human communications, whereas the content and intent dimensions in human communication collapse into a single symbol-processing dimension—semantics. As a consequence, it is not possible to establish clear-cut objective mappings between the two, saying for instance that changes in the users' expressive possibilities affect only the lexical dimensions of computer languages, or that changes in the semantics of computer languages refer only to changes of content in human communication. Because this is not the case, EUD involves very complex design decisions for professional developers.

However, Figure 18.1 shows that it is possible to identify two different subsets of manipulations in both tables. In the upper table, a dividing line can be drawn between the first three types of manipulations and the remaining four. Types I, II, and III are meaning-preserving manipulations of computer signification systems, because they do not affect the semantics of the application. The preservation of meaning thus becomes a convenient criterion to distinguish between customization and extension. Customization is an EUD activity that does not affect meanings encoded in computer program semantics. Extension is an EUD activity that does. This distinction is often fuzzy in EUD literature, possibly because proposals and discussions usually center around techniques rather than around the linguistic effects that they produce on the underlying models of applications. Notice that we are speaking strictly of computer symbol-processing dimensions, and not of human communicative goals. One of the benefits of distinguishing between customization and extension is that this can help us examine the pro's and con's of various techniques. For example, meaning-preserving EUD techniques have important consequences in terms of software architecture, modularization, program reuse, and the like. Systems developers can and perhaps should design applications in such a way that all types of customization affect only the interface component. If they do it, customized interfaces might be saved as interactive templates, interactive template libraries might be built, and so on. All such possibilities spring from the fact that one can safely distinguish between meaning-preserving and meaning-changing manipulations of computer signification systems.

Meaning-changing manipulations of type IV, V, VI, and VII, in their turn, affect the semantic base of an application. Some may be defined to affect only a pre-established subset of the system. For example, the scope of such manipulations may be limited to selected lexical, syntactic, and semantic items and rules. These usually represent type-controlled extensions to the base, like generalization and/or specialization of meanings (a popular form of EUD). Other manipulations, however, may be genuinely unrestricted, potentially affecting the whole range of items and rules in the computationally encoded signification system that users have access to. Such unrestricted types of manipulations can expand, retract, and modify—partially or completely—the original application. They may even enable the development of other applications altogether. Whereas compared to type-controlled extensions the power of users is undoubtfully greater, unrestricted manipulations of the underlying signification system make it difficult (if not impossible) to build "safety nets" for the users, like consistent error-prevention and error-recovery mechanisms, useful help systems, and sensible interactive design. Thus, they typically trade power for usability, since empowered users—in this case—cannot rely on the system to help it understand, correct, undo, or improve the way how their (re)programmed functionalities work.

In order to complete the semiotic characterization of such signification system manipulations, we finally define two useful concepts: that of application identity and that of sign impermeability. An application's *identity* refers to the designer's choice of what constitutes its core ontology. It comprises the minimal signification systems (and associated behavior) necessary for users to recognize, understand, and effectively use it as a legitimate computational tool.

The concept of *impermeability* is related to the encapsulation of signs. Users cannot get inside the atomic capsule of an *impermeable sign* and alter its meaning. Thus, the originally encoded meaning of impermeable signs is always preserved. Impermeable signs can be essential or accidental (in the Aristotelian sense). *Essential* impermeable signs can only be used in monotonic manipulations, those that do not destroy the basic meanings (identity) of the application. *Accidental* impermeable signs may not be changed either, but they may be subtracted from the application by means of an operation we call pruning (as in the case of add-ons or features which users may choose not to install, for instance). These concepts help us restrict EUD extensions to meaning-changing manipulations that preserve the original application's identity. This is a crucial requirement for usable EUD because it allows designers to predict the limits and contours of meaning manipulations, and to build the types of "safety nets" we have mentioned above.

In the remainder of this section, we give examples of how the semiotic characterization of signification system manipulations can be used to categorize design choices and probe the consequences they bring about.

4.1. TYPE I: CHANGES TO LEXICAL ITEMS ONLY (RENAMING AND ALIASING)

Type I changes correspond to renaming and aliasing operations that affect only the lexical component. Changing the label of a button or menu item and changing an icon in a toolbar button are examples of renaming (Figure 18.2). Renaming should be limited to lexical items that are not part of the application's identity. Otherwise, users might end up a situation where a "Save" menu item actually means "Exit", or vice-versa.

Aliasing may be illustrated by macro recording mechanisms, in which a new lexical item (name or graphical image) is designated to represent and activate a sequence of instructions (that have made available by the designer in the original system). In fact,

Original design   *after renaming manipulation*

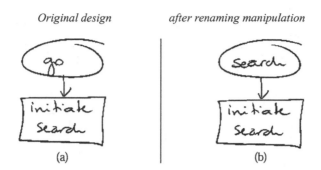

(a)   (b)

Figure 18.2. Illustration of renaming (type I manipulation).

in this kind of manipulation we are just giving different names to compositions of signs that exist in the original signification system (Figure 18.3). A significant source of interactive problems with aliasing achieved through macro recording is the scope of semantic variables associated to each individual instruction after and before aliasing. For instance, recording three interactive steps in a row—(1) save [current file] as . . . , (2) choose "HTML" code, and (3) confirm—under the name of "save as HTML" may end up in assigning the name and address of the file used when the macro was recorded to every file that the user wants to "save as HTML." This is because the original file name and address may have been encoded as a constant value in the resulting macro, instead of a variable whose value must be recalculated each time the recorded macro is run.

4.2. TYPE II: CHANGES TO GRAMMATICAL STRUCTURES ONLY

Type II manipulations involve making changes only to syntactic components, such as reordering: changing the layout sequence of user interface elements or the order in which operations are performed (Figure 18.4). Reordering can only be applied to components that do not involve mutual determination of signs across reordered components. The effect of changes is to allow for different sign combinations to express the same range of meanings as before, such as changing a command pattern from Action + Object to Object + Action. Visual programming techniques may be used in this case to enable and facilitate these kinds of manipulation.

original design   *after an aliasing manipulation*

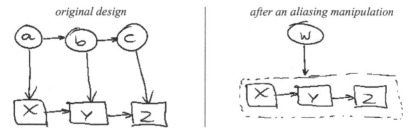

Figure 18.3. Illustration of aliasing (type I manipulation).

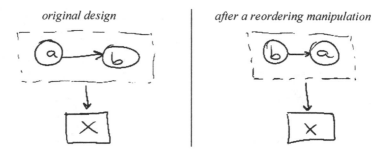

Figure 18.4. Illustration of reordering (type II manipulation).

For instance, in a text editor environment, the user might be able to switch the command pattern from (i) selecting the text to be searched and then activating the mechanism to (ii) activating the search mechanism first and then informing the desired search expression (Figure 18.5). The EUD mechanism for achieving this could use a workflow representation to let the users rearrange the individual task components at will.

In reordering tasks, there will usually be constraints to the kinds of valid manipulations, depending on pre- and post-conditions defined for each task component. Thus, in order to increase the usefulness of this kind of manipulation, designers may need to relate task components to plans associated to users' goals, and use plan recognition techniques to guide users in making sensible customizations.

4.3. TYPE III: CHANGES TO LEXICAL ITEMS AND GRAMMATICAL STRUCTURES, BUT NOT TO MEANINGS

The last kind of manipulation that affects only impermeable signs and preserves the application identity is "pruning." In a pruning operation, changes are made by removing non-essential (accidental) signs from the application. Such signs may be isolated items (such as "a→X" in Figure 18.6, a lexical component) or encapsulated sentences (such as "(b,c)→Y" in Figure 18.6, a syntactic component).

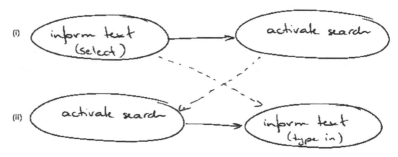

Figure 18.5. Workflow representation of tasks that may be reordered by end-users.

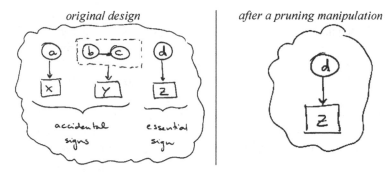

Figure 18.6. Illustration of pruning.

Pruning corresponds to the possibility of selecting non-essential components to be included in or excluded from the application. In other words, it is equivalent to turning on or off some of the system's features or modules, or choosing components during software installation. In most text editors, for instance, one of the main effects of uninstalling a feature such as a spell checker is to eliminate all interface signs corresponding to the uninstalled feature, such as menu items and graphical elements. This is a standard pruning operation.

Not only must pruning preserve the identity of the application, but also the impermeability of the pruned components. Thus, an important design decision in EUD is to select which of the impermeable signs can be pruned if the application's identity is to be preserved (or, put in another way, which signs constitute the application's identity). If internal sign structures (i.e., permeable signs) are changed, the operation is no longer called pruning. Instead, it is either a type-controlled or a type-free operation, as will be seen next.

4.4. TYPE IV: CHANGES TO MEANINGS ONLY BUT NOT TO LEXICAL ITEMS OR GRAMMATICAL STRUCTURES

This kind of manipulation involves using existing signs to *mean* something different from what they were designed to mean (Figure 18.7). To illustrate this kind of

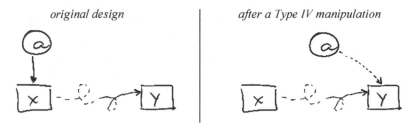

Figure 18.7. Illustration of type IV manipulations.

manipulation, suppose that a text editor user needs to print some documents. When no document is open and the user triggers the Print operation, the system would typically present an Open and Print dialog for him to select the file(s) to be printed. If all the files in a folder need to be printed, the user would need to select all the files individually (represented on the left-hand side of Figure 18.7 by a direct connection between "a" and "x" and an arbitrary path connecting "x" to the desired outcome "y"). An extension to this would be to have the system assign a useful interpretation to a "print folder" operation (represented on the right-hand side of Figure 18.7 by a direct connection between "a" and the desired outcome "y"). Applications that originally do not support multiple-file printing typically issue an error-handling or error-prevention message when the user combines the "print" and "folder" expressions. EUD and extensions may be achieved, however, if the error handling and preventing mechanisms are "relaxed." Inferencing mechanisms that enable systems to produce potential interpretations to existing sign combinations may lead to a gain in flexibility (Barbosa and de Souza, 2000; 2001).

Another example of extensions resulting from Type IV manipulations may involve a generalization of the existing drawing functionalities of a hypothetical application that can "fill shapes with background color," but has not been programmed to highlight text, for instance. If users combine "fill" and "shape" signs with "color" signs, the computer interpretation of the expression results in filling the shape's background with a specified color. However, if users combine "fill" and "text" signs with "color" signs, an error-preventing or error-handling message is issued. Just as in the preceding example, relaxing error prevention and handling along with increased inferencing power can enable the creation of new functionality—in this hypothetical text editor's case, the creation of a highlight text function expressed as "fill text background with color." These two examples illustrate the use of metonymies and metaphors in EUD, which we have discussed more extensively in previous publications (Barbosa and de Souza, 2000; 2001).

4.5. TYPE V: CHANGES TO MEANINGS AND LEXICAL ITEMS BUT NOT TO GRAMMATICAL STRUCTURES

This kind of manipulation is characterized by changes in the lexical and semantic dimensions. If in the Type IV example, above, the user gave a name (e.g., "highlight text") to the extension that fills text background with color, not only would the semantic base be extended, but also the vocabulary included in the lexical base of the original application. Other examples may be found with the use of formatting styles in contemporary text editors: users may introduce a new lexical item (the name of the new style) and associate some existing signs (formatting features) to it (Figure 18.8). The important distinguishing feature in this type of manipulation is that no further (syntactic) structure is associated to composite signs that are used to expand the semantic and lexical base of the application. Thus, the creation of "My Style" based on analogies with the "Body Text" style (see the right-hand side of (Figure 18.8) does not require

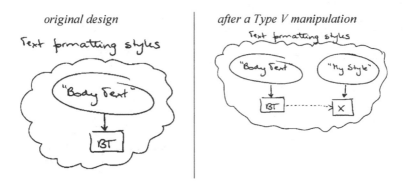

Figure 18.8. Illustration of type-controlled extension in which changes are made to lexical and semantic components (e.g., paragraph styles in MS Word).

the introduction of *new syntactic structures* in the signification system. Users can rely on existing expressive patterns that communicate style-formatting operations on text.

An interesting aspect of our semiotic characterization is to show that some features present in many commercial applications are actually related to EUD features that can be systematically applied to other parts of the application (and not be restricted to ad hoc instances of incidental design decisions).

Type V manipulations presents some special challenges for meta-design. If, for example, the creation of new functionality based on existing one is a *recursive* process—in other words, if it is possible to create a new component Z "based on" another *extended* component X—additional consistency-checking mechanisms must be included. One must be sure, for example, that if the user chooses to delete component X, the semantics associated to component Z is nevertheless preserved. Some significant breakdowns from a user's perspective may nevertheless follow from this possibility. For instance, if after recording the "save as HTML" macro mentioned when we explained Type I manipulations above the user reads or writes another macro—say "upload file to my website," which (1) executes the "save as HTML" macro, (2) executes "open FTP session with [my] IP address," (3) gets [file saved in HTML format], and (4) executes "close FTP session"—deleting "save as HTML" may ruin "upload file to my website," although this should not necessarily be the case.

4.6. TYPE VI: CHANGES TO MEANINGS AND GRAMMATICAL STRUCTURES BUT NOT TO LEXICAL ITEMS

Type VI manipulations are characterized by changes in the syntactic and semantic bases that are not accompanied by changes in the lexical base. They may involve reordering components or even eliminating components while shaping an application to the user's evolving needs and interpretations.

This kind of manipulation occurs when users are allowed to select default values for certain tasks, thus eliminating intermediate value-setting structures present in the

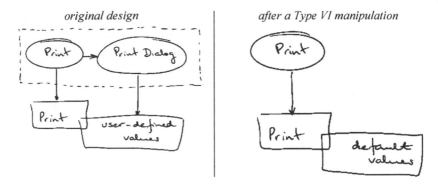

Figure 18.9. Illustration of type-controlled manipulation in which changes are made to syntactic and semantic components.

originally designed command. For instance, when triggering a print task, the system typically presents a print dialog asking users to select the target printer (this completes the *grammatical* specification of the "print document" command). If the user always prints files in a constant specific device, he might wish to define it as the default printer for that system (and thus shorten the grammatical specification of the "print document" command). This would be achieved by replacing the value-setting structures of the command with a constant (default) value. In this case, the next time the user issues a "print document" command, no value-setting elements need to be expressed and the document is printed in the default printer (Figure 18.9). The designer would, of course, need to provide straightforward means for users to change (or "undo") this configuration in the future, which is an important usability requirement associated to this extension strategy.

Notice that outside the scope of our semiotic framing, this type of EUD operation may be taken as an instance of customization, because it involves default parameter setting. However, as our framing helps to show, parameter-setting techniques can be used to achieve both customization and extension effects. The underlying computational complexity in each case, as well as the usability requirements associated to them, may be quite different in spite of the fact that the selected EUD *technique* is the same.

We also have a case of Type VI manipulations when we allow users to reorder task components and achieve different effects as a result. They differ from Type II manipulations, although visual programming techniques may be used to support the user's activities in both cases. Type VI reordering problems may occur if there is a partial ordering among the reordered components. In an image editor program, for instance, changing the order of the tasks from [Resize picture, Change to 256 colors] to [Change to 256 colors, Resize picture] may yield different and undesirable effects. Namely color schemes may affect image resolution in important ways and yield poor results, especially in the case of image magnification.

Useful Type VI manipulations may result from reordering other graphic editor commands. Taking Figure 18.10 as reference, suppose that in the original design (a) selecting

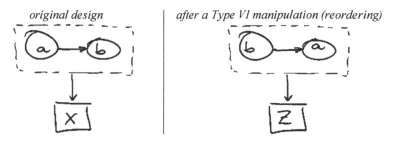

Figure 18.10. Illustration of a type-controlled manipulation of reordering.

a shape then (b) choosing a color value causes (x) the shape color to change to the chosen color value *and* the default color value to be restored. A Type VI manipulation may introduce an extension where (b) choosing a color value then (a) selecting a shape causes (z) the shape color to change to the chosen color value (but the default color value is not restored unless the user explicitly issues a restoring command). This extension is particularly convenient for repetitive tasks, usually handled with PbyD techniques which require heavy inferencing machinery.

4.7. TYPE VII: CHANGES TO MEANINGS, GRAMMATICAL STRUCTURES AND LEXICAL ITEMS

This last kind of manipulation can freely affect the *inside* of any sign capsule and thus it can potentially override the limits of the application's identity. Namely, they can go as far as reencoding original atomic meanings and reprogramming the application's *identity*. For example, a user of a text editor that supports searches for text with a given style (e.g., search text with font type Courier) may be annoyed by the fact that searches return one instance at a time, never letting him know the actual *scope* of replacing that style with another one. This user may decide to reprogram the "search style" function so as to have it present found items in the same way as a page sorter does in popular visual presentation applications—all pages containing text in the specified style are visualized side by side, which gives the user a better notion of how costly style changes may be. A convenient technique to achieve such reprogramming is to use components (Mørch et al., 2004; Won et al., this volume). Figure 18.11 shows an example of the effect of the reprogrammed search. The risk of such componental approach, as this example illustrates, is that, although the user's intention is only to *preview* pages in the way afforded by the component, a typical page sorter component allows for individual page *manipulation* (since they have been designed to support decisions about the order of page or slide presentations). So, when importing this component to a linear text editing environment, a user might end up (inadvertently or not) placing page 12 before page 9, and so on. The role of impermeable signs in this case is precisely to prevent such undesirable side effects (or at least prevent affording non-sensical interaction). Signs involved with linear text visualizations must not afford free page reordering (enabled in visualizations of presentation elements whose global coherence, unlike that

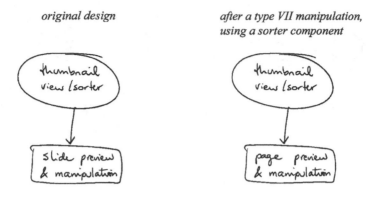

Figure 18.11. Illustration of full-fledged manipulation with a page sorter component.

of linear text, is not fully determined by ordering itself). In our view, EUD should adopt only a constrained version of Type VII manipulations—it should preserve the designed identity of the application. EUD within such limits requires that designers make careful decisions about how to control the types of modifications that will not destroy their original design vision.

Going back to Figure 18.1, where we proposed classifications and distinctions for manipulations of signification systems in both a symbol processing and a human communication perspective, we see that a dividing line can also be drawn with respect to the kinds of manipulations that help users make changes in the expression, content, and/or intent dimensions of the signification system underlying computer–human interaction. Manipulations of type A, B, and C can be said to correspond to intent-preserving changes. They amount to reencoding certain ways of achieving the same intent. Type A manipulations typically introduce synonyms in the signification system (different expressions that mean and achieve the same things). For instance, changing the label or name of inter-face signs is one such type of reencoding. Another is macro recording, when a new key chord can be assigned to express a series of sequential key chords that the user wishes to repeat frequently.

Type B and type C manipulations have *rhetorical* effects, since they change content to achieve the same range of intent (with or without changing the set of expressions defined in the system). Such rhetorical effects help humans achieve very fine goals in communication, but only because speaker and listener share the same pragmatic com-petence. However, because computer languages typically do not have an independent and enriched pragmatic component, even if such effects are attempted by users they do not systematically cause an appropriate response from a computer system. For instance, although a user may see that indenting a paragraph by "typing the paragraph, selecting it, and activating the indent function" is different from "creating an indented paragraph style, setting the style of the text about to be typed to this style, and then typing the paragraph," both have virtually the same immediate effect on the paragraph being typed (and all others that fall within the scope of the interactive commands that caused it). The effect on the system is not the same in each case. If the user creates an indented paragraph style, and gives it a name, the expression and the content base of the system are expanded. Even if the user does not realize it at that point in time, this expansion automatically enables a new range of intent (e.g., creating style sheets where "indented paragraph" can figure in the specifications of textual documents).

Type D manipulations handle the situation when a user wishes only to associate new intent to existing correspondences between expression and content of the signi-fication system he uses to communicate with a computer application. This amounts to *repurposing* the existing application, an interesting kind of modification that is not usually discussed in customization, extension, or end-user development activities. For instance, a table structure in HTML (marked by <table></table> tags) has been de-signed to support text representations in tabular form (with cells distributed across rows and columns). However, if a user discovers that table structures have certain inter-esting properties when a browser window is resized (i.e., they keep all text in the table within the user's view port, provided that certain table attributes like its width are set to the appropriate values) the *purpose* of the table structure may be extended. Instead of applying only to tabular forms of text, it may also come to be applied to text that must be kept within the user's view port across a variety of browser window sizes. Although it may not be considered EUD in the sense that the system has not been modified, it is certainly an expansion of the scope of system *usage*, especially in view of the user's unlimited semiosis process, where new meanings associated to view port control in text visualization become part of text formatting possibilities.

Type E manipulations introduce new intent marked by new expressions. However, these expressions do not signal a change of content. This effect is also *rhetorical* and very similar to type B and C manipulations; however there is an explicit change in the spectrum of intent. For instance, suppose that a user builds a macro in which he encodes the expression "Forget about this" as meaning the same as "close current window" (an element of the original signification system whose meaning is to abort all execution triggered by interaction expressed in the current window). For all practical purposes associated to the user semiosis, he may not distinguish between aborting execution and returning control to the next active function, so expressions associated to one and the other are *synonyms* (which only resembles what is computationally the case in special contexts where the aborted execution returns control to the previously activated application function and leaves no trace in the system state). If the user develops an *idiolect*, a personal way of using the signification system in communicating with the computer, where he uses the expression "Forget about this" to achieve the intent of communicating "None of these options is good," for instance, serious communicative problems may lie ahead. Although the user may be successful if the effect he wishes to achieve with his macro is, for example, to have a preview of file contents (in this case "Forget about this"—that is, closing the active window—is fine if the previewed material is useless), the same is not true if the macro is designed to import a spreadsheet into a text document. In the latter case, although "Forget about this" may sound fine if the user realizes that the wrong spreadsheet is about to be imported, "closing the active window" (i.e., aborting the spreadsheet editor activated by the import process) may have serious consequences on the integrity of the spreadsheet. This mismatch between what the users may *mean* and what computers may *interpret* is the cause of many problems both in HCI (where they take the guise of *usability* problems) and EUD (where they take the guise of *specification* problems).

Type F manipulations refer to the use of specific communicative strategies that very efficiently extend the spectrum of contents without necessarily expanding the set of basic items and structures that support linguistic expressions. They involve the use of *figurative speech*, in particular that of metaphors and metonymies. Studies in cognitive semantics (Lakoff and Johnson, 1980; Lakoff, 1987) have provided extensive evidence that human cognition is structured in terms of basic types of metaphors, and that these and other related tropes are powerful sources of new meanings and cognitive expansion (Eco, 1984; Jakobson and Halle, 1956; Turner and Fauconnier, 2000). A wide range of extensions can be achieved through the use of metaphors and metonymies (Barbosa and de Souza, 2001), provided that interface language interpreters be prepared to handle expressions like "delete the bold faces" (meaning a new procedure that searches all bold face words and turns this attribute off) or "create a document of documents" [defining a new (unnamed) concept and simultaneously creating an instance of it]. These expressions will most probably cause symbol processing to halt in regular interaction, although, as seen in Section 3, they belong to the vast majority of human verbal exchanges. The importance of metaphorical and metonymical expressions is that some applications are ready to process them during interaction (even as an ad hoc side effect of implementation strategies), but not ready to handle them when the user is specifying new functions or extensions to existing ones. For instance, Microsoft Word is apt to interpret the following commands as "change font face to bold":

(a): wor|d + Ctrl B $\Rightarrow$ **wor|d**
(b): word + Ctrl B $\Rightarrow$ **word**

The user's expression in (a) is metonymical, in that the word is not selected but the cursor ("|") being located within the word boundaries is interpreted as an equivalent of "take the object that contains this location"—a classical case of *contained for container* metonymy. The user's expression in (b) explicitly indicates the object of the formatting operation. Users should not be misled into thinking that all metonymical specifications will work as beautifully. For example, defining as new function "backup" as "saving a copy of the current file preserving its name and changing its extension to '.bkp'" is very likely to cause problems to users when working in different directories. In some operating systems, a file's *name* is a compound identifier that includes its name and address. So, if the user defined the function referring only to manipulations in the file's *name*, backup copies of files from different directories are likely to be all placed in one and the same directory. The metonymy "name for identifier" does not work.

Finally, type G manipulations require fine linguistic awareness, not to be encountered easily in typical end-user populations. Notice that users must be able to specify how certain innovative (or modified) expression/content associations are to be *systematically* related to the occurrence of certain kinds of intent. Compared to all other ways of introducing new meanings in an encoded system, this is by far the most powerful one, but also the one that requires a larger range of programming skills. From a human communication perspective, such manipulations can only be successful if the communicative abilities of both speaker and listener are considerably good, since they are innovating (or occasionally subverting) the established signification system by fully encoding expression-content-intent mappings just like culture (in natural settings) or full-fledged design (in artificial settings) can do. So, we can see that such skilled metalinguistic manipulations require semiotic expertise that is very unusual among end-users who do not have highly specialized professional training.

We conclude Section 4 by remarking that signification system manipulations are very different when analyzed from a computer language perspective and a human communication perspective. There is no one-to-one correspondence between what users *mean* to do and what computers *take* users' meanings to be. The absence of a pragmatic component that can handle intent—a fundamental dimension in human communication—may lie at the source of the greatest challenges for EUD. Moreover, as our analysis shows, this difference accounts for both usability problems and specification problems, typically dealt with in separation from one another by researchers interested in *techniques* that support better interaction or adaptations, extensions and development.

In the next section, we discuss the main implications of the semiotic characterization of signification system manipulations presented above.

5. Final Discussion

The need to bring HCI and EUD together has been recognized by Nardi (1993) and other researchers, especially those that propose the adoption of programming by demonstration (Cypher, 1993; Lieberman, 2001). Some of the main challenges and opportunities for PbyD in the current IT scenario have been discussed in recent years (CACM, 2000; Lieberman, 2001), restating the fact that PbyD is one of the few techniques that can nicely combine usability and specification issues. It addresses a major challenge that all EUD approaches must face: "Most computer end-users do not have the background, motivation, or time to use traditional programming approaches, nor do they typically have the means to hire professional programmers to create their programs" (Repenning and Perrone, 2001).

Most researchers doing PbyD have taken a technical perspective on HCI and EUD issues. For example, bye emphasizing that "it is important that there be a well-designed feedback mechanism so that users can understand and control what the system is doing and change the program later," Myers and McDaniel (2001) place the focus of research on designing appropriate EUD mechanisms. Seldom is the focus placed on inspecting the potential causes of the relatively timid success of PbyD in HCI at large. One exception is Smith, Cypher, and Tesler (2001), who raise important theoretical issues closely related to HCI and to computing. They draw on theoretical approaches to knowledge representation in order to drive their approach to the design of PbyD environments. However, they do not explicitly discuss the user's *intent*. As a result, their account falls short of capturing some points that ours clarifies precisely because our focus is placed on the semiotic dimensions of signification systems underlying both EUD and HCI. Among the most prominent ones we can list the fact that our approach can spell out the semiotic effects that existing techniques can achieve, as well as indicate some kinds of precautions that designers must take if final product usability is to be achieved. The most relevant distinctions and effects advanced by our approach are discussed in what follows.

5.1. DISTINGUISHING EUD FROM FULL-FLEDGED PROGRAMMING

Computer systems' designers *communicate* design to users through interface signs. These signs are organized in signification systems that can only be processed by computers if they conform to the basic symbol-processing model of Turing machines. However, such conformity brings up a crucial semiotic distinction between computer symbol-processing and human sense making—computers can only handle expressions that have fixed grounded meanings (encoded by systems' designers and developers at application development time).

Programming is achieved through various sub-systems and programs that must compute on grounded symbols. If users were allowed to make all sorts of meaning modifications, including modifications of how any processible symbol is grounded with respect to the application domain or the technology to which it refers, this would amount to *re-programming* the application (type VII manipulations). If, however, there were a subset of symbols whose grounding could not be changed (what we metaphorically call *impermeable* symbols), these would constrain the space of possible meaning modifications. Some of the impermeable symbols would be chosen to constitute the application's identity, whereas the remaining impermeable symbols would constitute encapsulated add-ons or features which can be subtracted from the application, but not internally modified (type III manipulations). Every application requires that users learn a new and unique signification system that is used in HCI. Therefore, the application's identity and the notion of impermeability are important to keep the user's semiosis sufficiently tied to the designer's vision, so that productive interpretations can be motivated, and unproductive ones discouraged. More extensive analyses of the role of identity-related signs on users' semiosis have been proposed by Brown and Duguid (1992), who talk about the role of motivated interpretations in design, and de Souza and co-authors (2001), who talk about the importance of establishing the core identity of end-user programming applications. We use the concept of *impermeability* to situate EUD in what has often been treated of a fuzzy continuum leading from mere user-system interaction to full-fledged programming by end-users (Myers, 1992). In our view, usable EUD must involve only manipulations on sign systems that are built on a culture of software *use* and interactive patterns (such as direct manipulation, for example). Because full-fledged programming (which is required for genuinely unconstrained end-user design activities involved in a "do it yourself computing") involves sign systems that are built upon a culture of software development and specification practices, end-users may have to deal with signs that are meaningless for them (i.e., they may even not be taken as signs at all). Hence the benefit of establishing semiotic boundaries for EUD. This allows designers to build "safety nets" like online help, powerful error-preventing and error-handling mechanisms, intelligent agents, and the like, based on application ontologies that can systematically refer to a culture of software *use* and not to knowledge derived from a culture of software *development* and *specification* practices.

5.2. DISTINGUISHING CUSTOMIZATION FROM EXTENSION

As we lay out the semiotic dimensions involved in sense-making and symbol-processing, some interesting distinctions become apparent. The most evident one is that between modifications that do and those that don't involve changes in meaning. In the context of human and social sciences this position is often disputed, in that for many theoreticians every alteration in expression is necessarily tied to an intended alteration in meaning at content and/or intent level (see papers in Silverman, 1998). However, in the HCI environment the situation is subtly different. Given that signification systems appearing in computer systems are engineered—they do not causally spring up from ongoing cultural process—users may intuit the arbitrary character of labeling a function "save" instead of "write," or in deciding that a line is deleted when you type "Ctrl+Y" instead of "Ctrl+K," or else that the appropriate syntax for a "grep" command in UNIX is "grep, [pattern], [file]" instead of "grep, [file], [pattern]." This realization grants a considerable degree of autonomy to expression with respect to content and intent.

From a symbol processing point of view, two different kinds of modifications can be made: meaning-preserving modifications (types I, II, and III) and meaning-changing ones (types IV through VII). Naturally, meaning-preserving manipulations of the original signification system keep the application's identity intact. This might be a convenient borderline between customization and extensions, another differentiation not too clearly established in some of the previous work about end-user development, including end-user programming, interface customization, and related topics (Myers, 1992; Nardi, 1993).

5.3. IDENTIFYING DIFFERENT SEMIOTIC DIMENSIONS IN EUD

A semiotic analysis also allows us to see that there are different dimensions involved in signification system manipulations when we take a symbol processing or a human communication perspective. One of the leading factors in such distinctions is the role played by intention. Whereas in a computer-centric semiotic characterization of signification systems intent and content are typically merged into computer language semantics, a human-centric characterization cannot disregard the fact that users know that there are (and consequently expect that there be) different ways to mean the same thing or to achieve the same intent. In social life, mastering such distinctions is the key to success in achieving goals that depend on communication. Attempts to map computer systems' and users' dimensions of semiotic competence onto each other reveal some important design challenges for building mechanisms to support EUD (as illustrated in the associations shown in Figure 18.1: lexical and syntactic with the expression dimension; content and intent with the semantic dimension). Typically what comes naturally to humans requires the addition of considerable reasoning power to basic symbol-processing in computation. Conversely, what is easily derivable from symbol-processing operations may be confusing or meaningless to users.

Another point that becomes explicit through the kind of analysis we propose is that certain interactive deviations that are usually taken as *mistakes* may in fact constitute rhetorical *manipulations* that the user really *means* to introduce in his experience with the application (type IV manipulations). Although these have virtually no computational effect, some relevant cognitive and/or communicative effects may be associated to them. As users develop their own idiolect to interact with applications they shape the signification system that will play a fundamental role in EUD tasks. Extensions where new expressions are designed (see the example involving the meaning of "Forget about this" when encoded as meaning the same as "close active window") are prime instances of the decisive role played by the user's interactive idiolect in enhancing the usability of computer applications.

5.4. ORGANIZING THE PROBLEM SPACE FOR INTEGRATED HCI AND EUD DESIGN

Finally, by looking at the results of a comparative semiotic analysis of encoded sign systems manipulations, the designer of interfaces for EUD applications may become more aware of the challenges and possibilities of various EUD techniques. Combined with the distinction between customization and extension, EUD and full-fledged programming, this kind of awareness represents a powerful resource for framing EUD design problems more consistently and, consequently, for searching and selecting improved problem-solving strategies.

Our proposed analysis can help us organize the design space. We do not claim that ours is the only possible organization, nor that it is the best. However, it certainly represents one step in the direction of more systematic research about EUD, springing from theories rather than techniques. Many of our perceptions and interpretations require further studies. The advantage of being backed by theories is that some global relations between phenomena can be more easily traced. This may help designers and researchers take a more holistic perspective on EUD and aim at advancing the field in a more concerted way.

Moreover, this perspective redresses the usability challenge posed by Adler and Winograd more than a decade ago. It shows that supporting users' improvisation and creativity (i.e., good HCI design) *requires* EUD. It also shows how different ontologies (from computer languages and human communication languages) may be brought together and constrain each other, when supporting users as they adapt and extend applications to meet their individual goals and expectations.

Acknowledgments

The authors would like to thank the Brazilian Council for Scientific and Technological Development (CNPq) for ongoing support to their research.

References

Adler, P. and Winograd, T. (1992). *Usability: Turning Technologies into Tools*. New York, NY: Oxford University Press.

Austin, J.L. (1962). *How to do Things With Words*. Cambridge, MA: Harvard University Press.

Barbosa, S.D.J. and de Souza, C.S. (2000). Extending software through metaphors and metonymies. *Knowledge-Based Systems*, **14**, 15–27.

Brown, J.S. and Duguid, P. (1992). Enacting design for the workplace. In: P.S. Adler and T. Winograd (Eds.), *Usability: Turning Technologies into Tools*, New York, NY: Oxford University Press, pp. 164–197.

CACM. (2000). Programming by example. *Communications of the ACM*, **43**(3), 72–114.

Cypher, A. (ed.). (1993). *Watch What I Do: Programming by Demonstration*. Cambridge, MA: The MIT Press.

de Souza, C.S., Barbosa, S.D.J. and da Silva, S.R.P. (2001). Semiotic engineering principles for evaluating end-user programming environments. *Interacting with Computers*, **13**(4), 467–495.

de Souza, C.S. (2004). *The Semiotic Engineering of Human–Computer Interaction*. Cambridge, MA: The MIT Press.

Eco, U. (1976). *A Theory of Semiotics*. Bloomington IN: Indiana University Press.

Eco, U. (1984). *Semiotics and the Philosophy of Language*. Bloomington, IN: Indiana University Press.

Fischer, G. (1998). Beyond 'couch potatoes': from consumers to designers. In: *Proceedings of the 5th Asia Pacific Computer—Human Interaction Conference. IEEE Computer Society*, pp. 2–9.

Fischer, G., Giaccardi, E., Ye, Y.; Sutcliffe, A.G. and Mehandjiev, N. (2004). Meta-design: a manifesto for end-user development. *Communications of the ACM*, **47**(9), 33–37.

Hopcroft, J.E. and Ullman, J.D. (1979). *Introduction to Automata Theory, Languages, and Computation. Reading*. MA: Addison-Wesley.

Jakobson, R. and Halle, M. (1956) *Fundamentals of Language*. The Hague: Mouton.

Lakoff, G. and Johnson, M. (1980). *Metaphors We Live By*. Chicago: The University of Chicago Press.

Lakoff, G. (1987). *Women, Fire, and Dangerous Things*. Chicago: The University of Chicago Press.

Lieberman, H. (ed.). (2001). *Your Wish is My Command: Programming by Example*. San Francisco, CA: Morgan Kaufmann Publishers.

Mørch, A.I., Stevens, G., Won, M., Klann, M., Dittrich, Y. and Wulf, V. (2004). Component-based technologies for end-user development. *Communications of the ACM*, **47**(9), 59–62.

Myers, B.A. (ed.). (1992). *Languages for Developing User Interfaces*. Boston: Jones and Bartlett Publishers, Inc.

Myers, B.A. and McDaniel, R. (2001). Sometimes you need a little intelligence, sometimes you need a lot. In: Henry Lieberman (ed.), *Your Wish is My Command: Programming by Example*. San Francisco, CA: Morgan Kaufmann Publishers, pp. 45–60.

Nardi, B. (1993). *A Small Matter of Programming*. Cambridge, MA: The MIT Press.

Nielsen, J. (1993). *Usability Engineering*. Boston: Academic Press.

Peirce, C.S. (1931). *Collected Papers*. Cambridge, MA: Harvard University Press (excerpted in Buchler, Justus, ed., Philosophical Writings of Peirce, New York: Dover, 1958).

Repenning, A. and Perrone, C. (2001). Programming by analogous examples." In: Henry Lieberman (ed.), *Your Wish is My Command: Programming by Example*. San Francisco, CA: Morgan Kaufmann Publishers, pp. 351–369.

Searle, J.R. (1969). *Speech Acts*. Cambridge: Cambridge University Press.

Silverman, H.J. (1998). *Cultural Semiosis—Tracing the Signifier*. London: Routledge.

Smith, D.C., Cypher, A. and Tesler, L. (2001). Novice programming comes of age. In: Henry Lieberman (ed.), *Your Wish is My Command: Programming by Example*. San Francisco, CA: Morgan Kaufmann Publishers, pp. 7–19.

The Word Spy (2004). A web site by Paul McFedries. http://www.wordspy.com/words/earcon.asp/. Last visited in October.

Turner, M. and Fauconnier, G. (2000). Metaphor, metonymy, and binding. In: Barcelona, A. (ed.), *Metonymy and Metaphor at the Crossroads*. Berlin: Mouton de Gruyter, pp. 133–145.

Winograd, T. and Flores, F. (1986). *Understanding Computers and Cognition: New Foundations for Design*. Reading, MA: Addison Wesley.

Chapter 19

Meta-design: A Framework for the Future of End-User Development

GERHARD FISCHER AND ELISA GIACCARDI
Center for Lifelong Learning & Design (L3D), Department of Computer Science and Institute of Cognitive Science, University of Colorado, Campus Box 430, Boulder, CO 80309-0430, USA, gerhard@colorado.edu, elisa.giaccardi@colorado.edu

Abstract. In a world that is not predictable, improvisation, evolution, and innovation are more than a luxury: they are a necessity. The challenge of design is not a matter of getting rid of the emergent, but rather of including it and making it an opportunity for more creative and more adequate solutions to problems.

Meta-design is an emerging conceptual framework aimed at defining and creating social and technical infrastructures in which new forms of collaborative design can take place. It extends the traditional notion of system design beyond the original development of a system to include a co-adaptive process between users and a system, in which the users become co-developers or co-designers. It is grounded in the basic assumption that future uses and problems cannot be completely anticipated at design time, when a system is developed. Users, at use time, will discover mismatches between their needs and the support that an existing system can provide for them. These mismatches will lead to breakdowns that serve as potential sources of new insights, new knowledge, and new understanding.

This chapter is structured in four parts: conceptual framework, environments, applications, and findings and challenges. Along the structure of the chapter, we discuss and explore the following essential components of meta-design, providing requirements, guidelines, and models for the future of end-user development: (1) the relationship of meta-design to other design methodologies; (2) the *Seeding, Evolutionary Growth, Reseeding Model*, a process model for large evolving design artifacts; (3) the characteristics of *unself-conscious cultures of design*, their strengths and their weaknesses, and the necessity for owners of problems to be empowered to engage in end-user development; (4) the possibilities created by meta-design to bring *co-creation* alive; and (5) the need for an integrated design space that brings together a *technical infrastructure* that is evolvable, for the design of *learning environments and work organizations* that allow end-users to become active contributors, and for the design of *relational settings* in which users can relate, find motivations and rewards, and accumulate social capital.

Key words. co-creation, design for change, design space, design time, domain-oriented design environments, Envisionment and Discovery Collaboratory, interactive art, open systems, SER model, social capital, underdesign, unself-conscious cultures of design, use time, value-feelings.

1. Introduction

Considering end-user development and meta-design as a challenge, one has to move beyond the binary choice of low-level, domain-unspecific interactive programming environments and over-specialized application systems defined by the two end-points on a spectrum:

Henry Lieberman et al. (eds.), End User Development, 427–457.
© 2006 *Springer.*

- Turing tar pit: "Beware of the Turing Tar Pit, in which everything is possible, but nothing of interest is easy." (Alan Perlis)
- The inverse of the Turing tar pit: "Beware of over-specialized systems, where operations are easy, but little of interest is possible."

The Turing tar pit argument provides a supporting argument as to why interactive programming environments, such as Lisp, Logo, Smalltalk, Squeak, Agentsheets, and many others (Lieberman, 2001) are not ideal for supporting meta-design. These tools provide the ultimate level of openness and flexibility (e.g., Squeak is an open source implementation of Smalltalk written entirely in itself). As general-purpose programming languages, they are capable of representing any problem that computers can be used to solve, and as open systems they let users change any aspect of the system if necessary. Although these systems are useful as computational substrates, they by themselves are insufficient for meta-design. The essential problem with these systems is that they provide the incorrect level of representation for most problems (Shaw, 1989). Expressing a problem and designing a solution in these systems requires creating a mapping from the context of the problem to the core constructs provided by the programming language and its supporting library. On the other side of the spectrum, *domain-specific but closed systems* [e.g., SimCity 4 (Electronic-Arts, 2004)] provide extensive support for certain problem contexts, but the ability to extend these environments is fundamentally limited.

Based on our research over the last two decades at the Center for Lifelong Learning and Design at the University of Colorado, Boulder, we will first provide some arguments for the desirability and need of meta-design. We will then develop a conceptual framework for meta-design and illustrate the approach with prototype developments mostly drawn from our own work. The description of meta-design approaches in several application areas (with a focus on interactive art) shows the potential and applicability of the concept. We will conclude with a section of findings and challenges for future developments. Figure 19.1 illustrates how different themes of the chapter are interrelated and how they contribute to the unifying theme of meta-design.

2. The Rationale for Meta-Design

In a world that is not predictable, improvisation, evolution, and innovation are more than luxuries: they are necessities. The challenge of design is not a matter of getting rid of the emergent, but rather of including it and making it an opportunity for more creative and more adequate solutions to problems. Meta-design is a conceptual framework defining and creating social and technical infrastructures in which new forms of collaborative design can take place. For most of the design domains that we have studied over many years (e.g., urban design, software design, design of learning environments, and interactive art) the knowledge to understand, frame, and solve problems is not given, but is constructed and evolved during the problem-solving process.

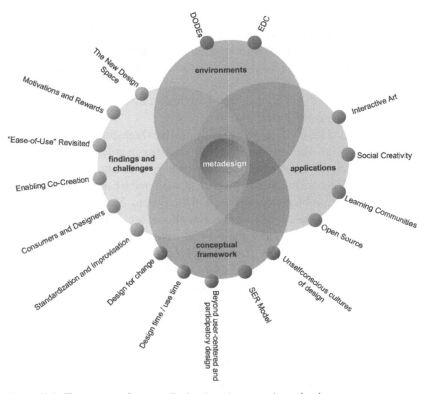

Figure 19.1. The structure of our contribution: how themes are interrelated.

Meta-design addresses the following three necessities for socio-technical environments (Fischer and Scharff, 2000):

1. They must be flexible and evolve because they cannot be completely designed prior to use.
2. They must evolve to some extent at the hands of the users.
3. They must be designed for evolution.

The goal of making systems modifiable and evolvable by users does not imply transferring the responsibility of good system design to the user. Domain experts (who see software development as a means to an end) will design tools and create contents of a different quality than professional software designers (for whom software is both a means and an ends). Domain experts are not concerned with the tool per se, but in doing their work. However, if the tool created by the developer does not satisfy the needs or the tastes of the user (who knows best), then the user should be able to adapt the system without always requiring the assistance of the developer.

Meta-design extends the traditional notion of system design beyond the original development of a system to include a co-adaptive process between users and system, in which the users become *co-developers* (Mackay, 1990). Users learn to operate a system and adapt to its functionality, and systems are modified to adapt to the practices of its users. Meta-design supports the dialog evolving between the participants in the process of co-adaptivity—that is, the software artifact and the human subject—so that both move beyond their original states. In this way, meta-design sustains the interactive feedback of information amongst technological and human systems and their components, a practice early recognized and adopted by those artists that utilized technology in the production of art (Shanken, 2002).

An example that we have studied extensively involves high-functionality applications (HFAs) (Fischer, 2001). These systems already contain too much unused functionality (at least in the abstract)—so why would it be necessary to create even more functionality? Even though HFAs are large and complex, it is often the case that the functionality required for a specific problem does not exist in the system. Meta-design approaches to HFAs (Eisenberg and Fischer, 1994) are necessary because (1) the information and functionality represented in the system can never be complete because the world changes and new requirements emerge and (2) skilled domain professionals change their work practices over time. Their understanding and use of a system will be very different after a month compared to after several years. If systems cannot be modified to support new practices, users will be locked into old patterns of use, and they will abandon a system in favor of one that better supports the way they want to work.

3. A Conceptual Framework for Meta-Design

Extending the traditional notion of system design beyond the original development of a system, *meta-design* (Fischer and Scharff, 2000; Giaccardi, 2003) includes a process in which users become *co-designers* not only at design time, but throughout the whole existence of the system. A necessary, although not sufficient condition for meta-design is that software systems include advanced features permitting users to create complex customizations and extensions. Rather than presenting users with closed systems, meta-design provides them with opportunities, tools, and social reward structures to extend the system to fit their needs. Meta-design shares some important objectives with user-centered and participatory design, but it *transcends* these objectives in several important dimensions, and it has changed the processes by which systems and content are designed. Meta-design has shifted some *control* from designers to users and empowered users to create and contribute their own visions and objectives. Meta-design is a useful perspective for projects for which "designing the design process" is a first-class activity [this perspective of meta-design is not restricted to end-user development, but can be applied to the work of professional software engineers as well (Floyd et al., 1992)]. This means that creating the technical and social conditions for broad participation in design activities is as important as creating the artifact itself (Wright et al., 2002) because "a piece of software does not guarantee you autonomy. What it is, what it is mixed with, how it is used are all variables in the algorithms of power and invention that course through software and what it connects to" (Fuller, 2003) (Table 19.1).

Table 19.1. Traditional design versus meta-design

Traditional design	Meta-design
Guidelines and rules	Exceptions and negotiations
Representation	Construction
Content	Context
Object	Process
Perspective	Immersion
Certainty	Contingency
Planning	Emergence
Top-down	Bottom-up
Complete system	Seeding
Autonomous creation	Co-creation
Autonomous mind	Distributed mind
Specific solutions	Solutions spaces
Design-as-instrumental	Design-as-adaptive
Accountability, know-what (rational decisioning)	Affective model, know-how (embodied interactionism)

Compared to traditional design approaches, meta-design puts the emphasis on different objectives [see Giaccardi, (2003); some of these shifts overlap with those emerging in the esthetics of interactive art (Ascott, 2003)]. A number of these objectives are further elaborated and discussed in the following sections.

3.1. DESIGN FOR CHANGE

Meta-design has to do not only with *situatedness* in order to fit new needs at use time and account for changing tasks, it has to do also with the *embeddedness* of computer artifacts in our daily life and practices (Ehn and Malmborg, 1999). This represents a challenge to the idea of user participation and empowerment, as well as tailorability, because it becomes necessary to look not only to professional work practices, but also to a private life more and more blurred with professional life within "mixed reality environments" (Pipek and Kahler, 2004). To argue that design for change (in buildings, in systems, and in socio-technical environments) (Dittrich and Lindeberg, 2003) is nearly universal does not help much in understanding how the process works, nor in conjuring how it might go better. Our idea of design must be reframed. Meta-design contributes to the invention and design of cultures in which humans can express themselves and engage in personally meaningful activities. The conceptual frameworks that we have developed around meta-design explore some fundamental challenges associated with design for change:

1. How we can support skilled domain workers who are neither novices nor naive users, but who are interested in their work and who see the computer as a means rather than as an end?
2. How we can create co-adaptive environments, in which users change because they learn, and in which systems change because users become co-developers and active contributors?

3. How we can deal with the active participation and empowerment of a subject, the profile of which tends to blur and dissolve beyond the limits of definite and independent professional domains, practices, and technologies?

3.2. DESIGN TIME AND USE TIME

In all design processes, two basic stages can be differentiated: design time and use time (see Figure 19.2). At *design time*, system developers (with or without user involvement) create environments and tools. In conventional design approaches, they create complete systems for the world-as-imagined. At *use time*, users use the system but their needs, objectives, and situational contexts can only be anticipated at design time, thus, the system often requires modification to fit the user's needs. To accommodate unexpected issues at use time, systems need to be underdesigned at design time, while directly experiencing their own world. *Underdesign* (Brand, 1995) in this context does not mean less work and fewer demands for the design team, but it is fundamentally different from creating complete systems. The primary challenge of underdesign is in developing not solutions, but environments that allow the "owners of problems" (Fischer, 1994b) to create the solutions themselves at use time. This can be done by providing a context and a background against which situated cases, coming up later, can be interpreted (Fischer, 1994a). Underdesign is a defining activity for meta-design aimed at creating design spaces for others.

However, as indicated in Figure 19.3, we do not assume that being a consumer or a designer is a binary choice for the user: it is rather a continuum ranging from passive consumer, to well-informed consumer (Fischer, 2002), to end-user, to power users (Nardi, 1993), to domain designer (Fischer, 1994a) all the way to meta-designer [a similar role distribution or division of labor for domain-oriented design environments is defined in Figure 19.5]. It is also the case that the same person is and wants

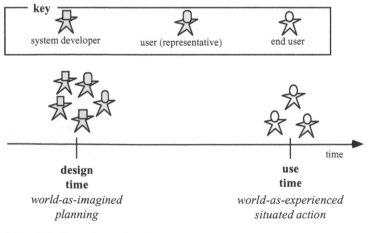

Figure 19.2. Design time and use time.

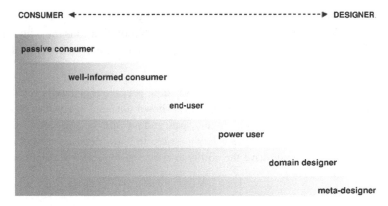

Figure 19.3. Beyond binary choices—the consumer/designer spectrum.

to be a consumer in some situations and in others a designer; therefore *"consumer/designer" is not an attribute of a person, but a role assumed in a specific context.*

A critical challenge addressed by our research is to support a *migration path* (Burton et al., 1984) between the different roles mentioned in Figure 19.3: consumers, power users, and designers are nurtured and educated, not born, and people must be supported to assume these roles.

3.3. BEYOND USER-CENTERED DESIGN AND PARTICIPATORY DESIGN

User-centered design approaches (Norman and Draper, 1986) (whether done *for* users, *by* users, or *with* users) have focused primarily on activities and processes taking place at design time in the systems' original development, and have given little emphasis and provided few mechanisms to support systems as *living* entities that can be evolved by their users. In user-centered design, designers generate solutions that place users mainly in reactive roles.

Participatory design approaches (Schuler and Namioka, 1993) seek to involve users more deeply in the process as co-designers by empowering them to propose and generate design alternatives themselves. Participatory design supports diverse ways of thinking, planning, and acting by making work, technologies, and social institutions more responsive to human needs. It requires the social inclusion and active participation of the users. Participatory design has focused on system development at design time by bringing developers and users together to envision the contexts of use. But despite the best efforts at design time, systems need to be evolvable to fit new needs, account for changing tasks, deal with subjects and contexts that increasingly blur professional and private life, couple with the socio-technical environment in which they are embedded, and incorporate new technologies (Henderson and Kyng, 1991).

Different from these approaches, meta-design creates *open systems* that can be modified by their users and evolve at use time, supporting more complex interactions (rather than linear or iterative processes). Open systems allow significant modifications when the need arises. The evolution that takes place through modifications must be supported as a "first-class design activity." The call for open, evolvable systems was eloquently advocated by Nardi (1993):

> We have only scratched the surface of what would be possible if end users could freely program their own applications.... As has been shown time and again, no matter how much designers and programmers try to anticipate and provide for what users will need, the effort always falls short because it is impossible to know in advance what may be needed.... End users should have the ability to create customizations, extensions, and applications...(p. 3).

3.4. THE SEEDING, EVOLUTIONARY GROWTH, AND RESEEDING PROCESS MODEL

The seeding, evolutionary growth, and reseeding (SER) model (Fischer and Ostwald, 2002) is a process model for large evolving systems and information repositories based on the postulate that systems that evolve over a sustained time span must continually alternate between periods of activity and unplanned evolutions and periods of deliberate (re)structuring and enhancement. The SER model encourages designers to conceptualize their activity as meta-design, thereby supporting users as designers in their own right, rather than restricting them to being passive consumers. Figure 19.4 provides an illustration of the SER model.

We have explored the feasibility and usefulness of the SER model in the development of complex socio-technical systems. The evolutions of these systems share common elements, all of which relate to sustained knowledge use and construction in support of informed participation.

3.4.1. *Seeding*

System design methodologies of the past were focused on the objective of building complex information systems as "complete" artifacts through *the large efforts of a*

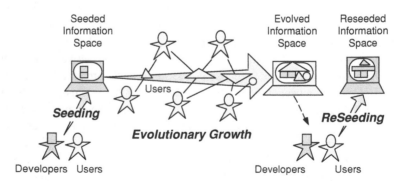

Figure 19.4. The seeding, evolutionary growth, and reseeding process model.

small number of people. Conversely, instead of attempting to build complete and closed systems, the SER model advocates building seeds that can be evolved over time through *the small contributions of a large number of people.*

A *seed* is an initial collection of domain knowledge that is designed to evolve at use time. It is created by environment developers and future users to be as complete as possible. However, no information repository can be truly complete due to the *situated and tacit nature of knowledge* as well as the constant changes occurring in the environment in which the system is embedded (Suchman, 1987; Winograd and Flores, 1986). No absolute requirements exist for the completeness, correctness, or specificity of the information in the seed, but the shortcomings and breakdowns often provoke users to add new information to the seed.

3.4.2. *Evolutionary Growth*

The evolutionary growth phase is one of decentralized evolution as the seed is used and extended to do work or explore a problem. In this phase, developers are not directly involved because the focus is on problem framing and problem solving. Instead, the participants have a direct stake in the problem at hand and are designing solutions to problems.

During the evolutionary growth phase, the information repository plays two roles simultaneously: (1) it provides resources for work (information that has been accumulated from prior use) and (2) it accumulates the products of work, as each project contributes new information to the seed. During the evolutionary growth phase, users focus on solving a specific problem and creating problem-specific information rather than on creating reusable information. As a result, the information added during this phase may not be well integrated with the rest of the information in the seed.

3.4.3. *Reseeding*

Reseeding is a deliberate and centralized effort to organize, formalize, and generalize information and artifacts created during the evolutionary growth phase (Shipman and McCall, 1994). The goal of reseeding is to create an information repository in which useful information can be found, reused, and extended. As in the seeding phase, developers are needed to perform substantial system and information space modifications, but users must also participate because only they can judge what information is useful and what structures will serve their work practices.

Reseeding is necessary when evolutionary growth no longer proceeds smoothly. It is an opportunity to assess the information created in the context of specific projects and activities, and to decide what should be incorporated into a new seed to support the next cycle of evolutionary growth and reseeding. For example, *open source software systems* (Raymond and Young, 2001) often evolve for some time by adding patches, but eventually a new major version must be created that incorporates the patches in a coherent fashion.

3.5. TOWARD AN UNSELF-CONSCIOUS CULTURE OF DESIGN

Being ill-defined (Rittel, 1984), design problems cannot be delegated (e.g., from users to professionals) because they are not understood well enough to be described in sufficient detail. Partial solutions need to "talk back" (Schön, 1983) to the owners of the problems who have the necessary knowledge to incrementally refine them. Alexander (1964) has introduced the distinction between an unself-conscious culture of design and a self-conscious culture of design. In an *unself-conscious* culture of design, the failure or inadequacy of the form leads directly to an action to change or improve it. This closeness of contact between designer and product allows constant rearrangement of unsatisfactory details. By putting owners of problems in charge, the positive elements of an unself-conscious culture of design can be exploited in meta-design approaches by creating media that support people in working on their tasks, rather than requiring them to focus their intellectual resources on the medium itself (Table 19.2).

Informed participation (Brown and Duguid, 2000), for instance, is a form of collaborative design in which participants from all walks of life (not just skilled computer professionals) transcend beyond the information given to incrementally acquire ownership in problems and to contribute actively to their solutions. It addresses the challenges associated with open-ended and multidisciplinary design problems. These problems, involving a combination of social and technological issues, *do not have "right" answers*, and the knowledge to understand and resolve them changes rapidly. To successfully cope with informed participation requires social changes as well as new interactive systems that provide the opportunity and resources for social debate and discussion rather than merely delivering predigested information to users.

Table 19.2. Comparing self-conscious and unself-conscious cultures of design

	Self-conscious	Unself-conscious
Definition	An explicit, externalized description of a design exists (theoretical knowledge)	Process of slow adaptation and error reduction (situated knowledge)
Original association	Professionally dominated design, design for others	Primitive societies, handmade things, design for self
Primary goal	Solve problems of others	Solve own problems
Examples	Designed cities: Brasilia, Canberra; Microsoft Windows	Naturally grown cities: London, Paris; Linux
Strengths	Activities can be delegated; division of labor becomes possible	Many small improvements; artifacts well suited to their function; copes with ill-defined problems
Weaknesses	Many artifacts are ill-suited to the job expected of them	No general theories exist or can be studied (because the activity is not externalized)
Requirements	Externalized descriptions must exist	Owners of problems must be involved because they have relevant, unarticulated knowledge
Evaluation criteria	High production value; efficient process; robust; reliable	Personally meaningful; pleasant and engaging experience; self-expression
Relation with context	Context required for the framing of the problem	Both problem framing and solving take place within the bigger context

4. Environments Supporting Meta-Design

The objectives and the impact of meta-design transcend the development of new computational environments and address mindsets, control, motivations, and the willingness to collaborate with others. Even the most sophisticated computational environments will not be sufficient to achieve these objectives, but they are necessary to allow owners of problems to act as informed participants in personally meaningful tasks. Meta-design will benefit from all of the following developments (many of them discussed in other chapters of this book):

- to offer task-specific languages that take advantage of existing user knowledge among domain professionals (National-Research-Council, 2003) and to hide low-level computational details as much as possible from users (see Figure 19.5);
- to provide programming environments such as Squeak, Agentsheets, and others (Lieberman, 2001) that make the functionality of the system transparent and accessible so that the computational drudgery required of the user can be substantially reduced;
- to exploit the power of collaboration (Arias et al., 2000; Nardi and Zarmer, 1993); and
- to support customization, reuse, and redesign effectively (Morch, 1997; Ye and Fischer, 2002).

In this section, we briefly describe two of our developments (*domain-oriented design environments* and the Envisionment and Discovery Collaboratory) that were inspired by meta-design and in return contributed to our understanding of meta-design.

4.1. DOMAIN-ORIENTED DESIGN ENVIRONMENTS

Domain-oriented design environments (Fischer, 1994a) support meta-design by advancing human–computer interaction to *human problem–domain interaction*. Because systems are modeled at a conceptual level with which users are familiar, the interaction

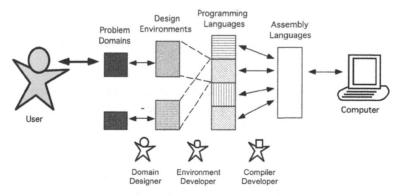

Figure 19.5. A layered architecture supporting human problem–domain interaction.

mechanisms take advantage of existing user knowledge and make the functionality of the system transparent and accessible. Thus, the computational drudgery required of users can be substantially reduced.

Figure 19.5 illustrates a layered architecture in support of *human problem–domain interaction*. This architecture allows domain designers to engage in end-user development by describing their problems with the concepts of a design environment rather than with low-level computer abstractions (Girgensohn, 1992).

4.2. THE ENVISIONMENT AND DISCOVERY COLLABORATORY

The *Envisionment and Discovery Collaboratory* (Arias et al., 2000) is a second-generation design environment focused on the support of *collaborative design* by integrating physical and computational components to encourage and facilitate informed participation by all users in the design process.

The Envisionment and Discovery Collaboratory represents an explicit attempt to create an *open system* (following the process of the SER model) to address some of the shortcomings of closed systems. Closed systems (in which the essentialfunctionality is anticipated and designed at design time; see Figure 19.2) are inadequate to cope with the tacit nature of knowledge and the situatedness of real-world problems. In our research, we have carefully analyzed why simulation environments such as SimCity (Electronic-Arts, 2004) are not used for real planning and working environments. Sim-City supports some superficial kinds of modifications (such as changing the appearance of buildings in the city), but most functional aspects of the simulation environment have been determined at the original design time. For example, the only way to reduce crime in a simulated city is to add more police stations. It is impossible to explore other solutions, such as increasing social services. Because the functionality of the system was fixed when the system was created, exploring concepts that were not conceived by the system designers is difficult. Due to SimCity's closed nature, it may be a good tool for passive education or entertainment, but it is inadequate for actual city planning tasks, as our empirical investigations have demonstrated (Arias et al., 2000). One vision that drives the Envisionment and Discovery Collaboratory is to create an end-user extensible version of SimCity.

The Envisionment and Discovery Collaboratory supports users to create *externalizations* (Bruner, 1996) that have the following essential roles to support informed participation:

- They assist in translating vague mental conceptualizations of ideas into more concrete representations. They require the expression of ideas in an explicit form, and in this process may reveal ideas and assumptions that previously were only tacit (Polanyi, 1966).
- They provide a means for users to interact with, react to, negotiate around, and build upon ideas. Such a "conversation with the materials" of the design problem (Schön, 1983) is a crucial mode of design that can inspire new and creative ideas.

- They focus discussions upon relevant aspects of the framing and understanding the problem being studied, thereby providing a concrete grounding and a common language among users.

5. Application of Meta-Design Approaches

Different domains express a meta-design approach, applying related concepts and methodologies. Some of these applications, when conceptualized as meta-design, suggest new insights (e.g., interactive art), others rather represent a concrete assessment of our conceptual framework (e.g., learning communities). We illustrate here how the application of meta-design approaches have transformed existing design approaches in different domains, including interactive art, information repositories, design environments, and classrooms as design studios.

5.1. INTERACTIVE ART

Interactive art, conceptualized as meta-design, focuses on *collaboration and co-creation*. The original design (representing a *seed* in our framework) establishes a context in which users can create and manipulate at the level of code, behavior, and/or content, and perform meaningful activities. Interactive art is based on the premise that computational media, as discrete structures, allow people to operate at the sources of the creative process, and that this creativity can be shared and no longer limited to the realm of professional artists. Therefore, interactive art puts the *tools* rather than the object of design in the hands of users. It creates interactive systems that do not define content and processes, but rather the *conditions for the process of interaction*. These objectives correspond to cultural shifts in the emerging esthetics of interactive art (Ascott, 2003).

Interactive artworks have an "experiential" or esthetic dimension that justifies their status as art, rather than as information design. According to Manovich (2001), these dimensions include a particular configuration of space, time, and surface articulated in the work; a particular sequence of user's activities over time to interact with the work; and a particular formal, material, and phenomenological user experience. But most of all, when conceptualized as meta-design, they include the *indeterminacy of the event of creation* (Giaccardi, 2001a), given by the empowerment of users' creative capabilities in an open and collaborative environment. Through interactivity, users do not simply send and receive a mono-directional flow of information, but act as performers of a mutual exchange between themselves and the computer, or between themselves and other users. Interactive art is concerned with setting up and seeding the place of this exchange, and sees interaction itself as the real *object* of creative production.

The esthetics of co-creation developed in interactive art comes up with an approach to design that shares with meta-design concerns about interaction, participation, and collaboration as means for an expansion of human creativity. Interactive art shows us how different kinds and different layers of interactivity and connectivity (Giaccardi,

1999) can affect the socio-technical flexibility of the system. Hence, we are shown its capability to increase the scope and complexity of the space of creation (which can correspond to the space of problem framing/problem solving from a non-artistic perspective).

5.1.1. *Electronic Café*

Artistic practices based on the interactive and participatory use of networked technologies adopted meta-design as a term for an alternative design approach and art vision since the beginning of the 1980s. One of the earliest practices of meta-design in the field of interactive art was the Electronic Café project, designed by Kit Gallowey and Sherrie Rabinowitz in 1984 (http://www.ecafe.com/; see Figure 19.6). This project integrates social and technological systems by setting up computational environments and a wide range of interactions that enable people to control the context of their cultural and artistic production as autonomous, electronic communities (Youngblood, 1984).

The Electronic Café was a pervasive telecommunications system characterized as an accessible, flexible, end-user modifiable (in terms of files, archives, and environment), and visual components-based system. By incorporating fully interactive word processing, handwriting, drawing, animation and slow-scan video, and providing the ability to combine these elements, the Electronic Café provided a structure that allowed its users the greatest possible freedom (at that time) to design and control their own information environments.

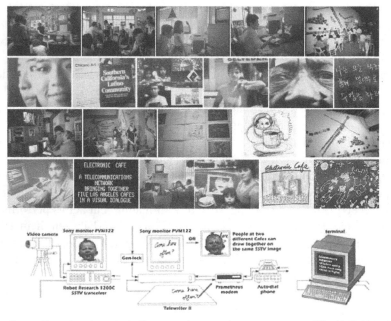

Figure 19.6. The Electronic Café Project. © 1995/2002 Kit Galloway *and* Sherrie Rabinowitz.

With their work, the artists highlighted design requirements and guidelines that characterize a consistent path of research and experimentations in the field of interactive art. In particular, the *visual component* of environments was important to determine the transcendence of barriers of literacy and language. Also important was users' exposure to the esthetic sensibility of the involved artists in a *direct, experiential manner*; that is to say, by being in the world in the same way. According to Rabinowitz: "It's a kind of spontaneous encounter that can't be engineered or marketed" (Youngblood, 1984).

5.1.2. *A-Volve*

As new technological possibilities arise, so do interactive art advances, enhancing the layers of interaction and collaboration. New computational development not only allows users to create content, fostering evolution by elaborations, completions, and additions, they also allow the modification of the behavior of an interactive system or the change of the interactive system itself. In the first case, the user can modify the behavior of the system at use time through interaction with the system. In *A-Volve* (http://www.iamas.ac.jp/~christa/; see Figure 19.7), for example, users interact in real time with virtual creatures in the space of a water-filled glass pool. These virtual creatures are products of evolutionary rules and are influenced by human creation and decision. Users can design any kind of shape and profile with their fingers on a touch screen and automatically the designed creature will be "alive," able to swim in the real water of the pool and to react to users' hand movements in the water. In A-Volve, algorithms are the seed, and they ensure the "animal-like" behavior of the creatures, but none of the creatures is pre-calculated. They are all born exclusively in real time and evolve through *different layers of interaction* (creation, human–creature interaction, creature–creature interaction, and human–human interaction) (Sommerer and Mignonneau, 1997a,b).

5.1.3. *SITO*

Current projects of interactive art, especially when networked, allow the modification or the development from scratch of the interactive system and its features. In these projects, the source is often developed by a community of artists, and can be adjusted

Figure 19.7. "A-Volve"—Design and Interaction. ©1994/1995, Christa Sommerer and Laurent Mignonneau interactive computer installation supported by ICC-NTT Japan and NCSA, USA.

Figure 19.8. One layer of interaction in SITO/Gridcosm.

and improved at different levels and different times according to the "talk back" deriving from the continuing and direct experience of the creative environment and the
resulting changing needs. For example, in SITO, which is a virtual community of *"ar-
ticipants"* (artists-participants), interaction and evolution occur both at the level of the
development of the source and at the level of the creation, elaboration, and completion
of collective artworks (in the section called Synergy). SITO (http://www.sito.org; see
Figure 19.8) is active for 24 hours and is open to anyone. Most of SITO's collaborative
art projects (such as Gridcosm) start from seed images by different artists and involve
the serial manipulation or the creation of several "generations" of images, variously
interlinked.

The focus is on shaping a *"collaborative synchronicity"* (a concept close to the idea
of a work practice in the business field) in which users interact and communicate both
by expressing opinions about the community and their projects and by discussing the
on-going collaborative process (concepts, technical aspects, interaction rules, image
creation and esthetical issues, and suggestions for further developments) (Verle, 1999).
This allows the system and the supporting scripts to be modified by the power users
(Nardi, 1993) of the community on the basis of *continuous feedback and suggestions*
(Table 19.3).

5.2. SOCIAL CREATIVITY

Complex design problems require more knowledge than any single person can possess,
and the knowledge relevant to a problem is often distributed among all users, each
of whom has a different perspective and background knowledge, thus providing the
foundation for *social creativity* (Arias et al., 2000). Bringing together different points
of view and trying to create a shared understanding among all users can lead to new
insights, new ideas, and new artifacts. Social creativity can be supported by innovative

Table 19.3. Comparing three interactive art projects from a meta-design perspective

	The Electronic Café (1984)	A-Volve (1997)	SITO synergy (since 1993)
Design contributions of the users	Participation in system development and content generation (these two activities occur at different times)	Participation in content generation and algorithm instantiation (these two activities overlap)	Participation in content generation and manipulation; support of script development and modification; definition and negotiation of interaction rules (all these activities are continuous)
Capabilities of the users	Creation, storage and retrieval of texts, images and videos (both individual and collective)	Generation and modification of artificial life creatures, their behavior and evolution	Creation, elaboration, and completion of collective images
Empirical analysis	Users and artists collaborate both at design time and use time: seeding (data bank)	Users and artists collaborate both at design time and use time: seeding, evolutionary growth (artificial creatures)	Users/artists collaborate both at design time and use time: seeding, evolutionary growth, reseeding (images and interaction schemes)
Selection criteria	Early attempt; direct "encounter" between people and artists through the system	Interactive installation open to an "ordinary" audience; different layers of interaction and collaboration (creation, human–creature interaction, creature–creature interaction, and human–human interaction); *embeddedness*	Online community of art lovers; different layers of interaction and collaboration (content, rules, source); *situatedness*

computer systems that allow all users to contribute to framing and solving these problems collaboratively. By giving all users a voice and empowering them to contribute, meta-design approaches are a prerequisite to bring social creativity alive.

Project complexity forces large and heterogeneous groups to work together on projects over long periods of time. The large and growing discrepancy between the amount of such relevant knowledge and the amount any one designer can remember imposes a limit on progress in design. For socio-technical systems to effectively support collaborative design, they must adequately address not only the problem situations, but also the collaborative activity surrounding the problem. By addressing real-world problems that are inherently ill-structured and ill-defined, systems must cope with problem contexts that change over time.

Providing *closed systems*, in which the essential functionality is fixed when the system is designed, is inadequate for coping with dynamic problem contexts. Providing *open systems* is an essential part of supporting collaborative design. By creating the opportunities to shape the systems, the owners of the problems can be involved in the formulation and evolution of those problems through the system. The challenge for these open systems is to provide opportunities for extension and modification that are appropriate for the people who need to make changes. The Envisionment and Discovery Collaboratory (see Section 4.2), for example, supports social creativity by empowering users to act as designers.

5.3. LEARNING COMMUNITIES

One of the most impoverished paradigms of education is a setting in which "a single, all-knowing teacher tells or shows presumably unknowing learners something they presumably know nothing about" (Bruner, 1996). Courses-as-seeds (dePaula et al., 2001) is an educational model that explores meta-design in the context of university courses by creating a culture of informed participation (Brown et al., 1994). It explores how to supplement community-based learning theories (Rogoff et al., 1998) with innovative collaborative technologies. Participants shift among the roles of learner, designer, and active contributor. The predominant mode of learning is peer-to-peer (P2P), and the teacher acts as a "guide on the side" (a meta-designer) rather than as a "sage on the stage."

Courses are conceptualized as *seeds* [see Section 3.4 and (dePaula et al., 2001)], rather than as finished products, and students are viewed as informed participants who play active roles in defining the problems they investigate. The output of each course contributes to an evolving information space that is collaboratively designed by all course participants, past and present.

As in all meta-design activities, the meta-designer (i.e., the teacher) gives up some control; there is little room for micro-managed curricula and precise schedules. The courses-as-seeds model requires a mindset in which plans conceived at the beginning of the course do not determine the direction of learning but instead provide a resource for interpreting unanticipated situations that arise during the course (Suchman, 1987). Examples of courses-as-seeds can be found at http://www.cs.colorado.edu/~gerhard/courses/.

5.4. OPEN SOURCE

Open source development (Fischer et al., 2003; Raymond and Young, 2001; Scharff, 2002) is not *directly* applicable to end-user development because the users/domain designers in open source communities are highly sophisticated programmers. But there are many lessons to be learned in open source developments for meta-design, and the meta-design framework can in turn contribute to a better understanding of open source development by analyzing it as a *success model* for organizing large-scale distributed cooperative work (Resnick, 1994).

In open source development, a community of software developers collaboratively constructs systems to help solve problems of shared interest and for mutual benefit. The ability to change source code is an enabling condition for collaborative construction of software by changing software from a fixed entity that is produced and controlled by a closed group of designers to an open effort that allows a community to design collaboratively on the basis of their personal desires and following the framework provided by the SER process model (Fischer and Ostwald, 2002). Open source invites passive consumers to become active contributors (Fischer, 2002).

Open source development (Raymond and Young, 2001; Resnick, 1994; Scacchi, 2002, 2004) is an example of unself-conscious design because (1) the developers are the owners of problems, (2) they create software systems primarily for their specific needs, and (3) the software is personally meaningful and important. *Sharing and collaborating* is common in open source communities. People reuse the whole system developed by others by adapting the system to their own needs.

Using open source as a success model for collaborative design (Scharff, 2002), we have identified the following principles relevant to meta-design (Fischer et al., 2003):

1. *Making changes must seem possible:* Users should not be intimidated and should not have the impression that they are incapable of making changes; the more users become convinced that changes are not as difficult as they think they are, the more they may be willing to participate.
2. *Changes must be technically feasible:* If a system is closed, then users cannot make any changes; as a necessary prerequisite, there needs to be possibilities for extension.
3. *Benefits must be perceived:* Contributors have to believe that what they get in return justifies the investment they make. The benefits perceived may vary and can include: professional benefits (helping for one's own work), social benefits (increased status in a community, possibilities for jobs), and personal benefits (engaging in fun activities).
4. *Open source environments must support tasks that people engage in:* The best open source system will not succeed if it is focused on activities that people do rarely or consider of marginal value.
5. *Low barriers must exist to sharing changes*: If sharing is awkward, it creates an unnecessary burden that participants are unwilling to overcome. Evolutionary growth is greatly accelerated in systems in which participants can share changes and keep track of multiple versions easily.

6. Findings and Challenges for The Future

This section provides some findings and challenges that can be seen as open questions for the future of end-user development: the tension between standardization and improvisation, and between being a consumer and/or a designer; ways of enabling co-creative processes and supporting meaningful activities as an issue of motivation and finally of technology appropriation; and the new design space defined by meta-design and its shifts from traditional design.

6.1. STANDARDIZATION AND IMPROVISATION

Meta-design creates an inherent tension between standardization and improvisation. The SAP Info (July 2003, p. 33) argues to reduce the number of customer modifications for the following reasons: "every customer modification implies costs because it has to be maintained by the customer. Each time a support package is imported there is a risk that the customer modification my have to be adjusted or re-implemented. To reduce the costs of such on-going maintenance of customer-specific changes, one of the key targets during an upgrade should be to return to the SAP standard wherever this is possible." Finding the right balance between standardization (which can suppress innovation and creativity) and improvisation (which can lead to a Babel of different and incompatible versions) has been noted as a challenge in open source environments in which forking has often led developers in different directions. The reseeding phase of the SER models tries to address this problem.

6.2. CONSUMERS AND DESIGNERS

Cultures are substantially defined by their media and their tools for thinking, working, learning, and collaborating. A great amount of new media is designed to see humans only as consumers (Fischer, 2002). The importance of meta-design rests on the fundamental belief that humans (not all of them, not at all times, and not in all contexts) want to be and act as designers in personally meaningful activities. Meta-design encourages users to be actively engaged in generating creative extensions to the artifacts given to them and has the potential to break down the strict counterproductive barriers between consumers and designers (Brown and Duguid, 2000).

Many computer users and designers today are domain professionals, competent practitioners, and discretionary users, and should not be considered as naïve users or "dummies." They worry about tasks, they are motivated to contribute and to create good products, they care about personal growth, and they want to have convivial tools that make them independent of *"high-tech scribes"* (whose role is defined by the fact that the world of computing is still too much separated into a population of elite scribes who can act as designers and a much larger population of intellectually disenfranchised computer phobes who are *forced* into consumer roles). The experience of having participated in the framing and solving of a problem or in the creation of an artifact makes a difference to those who are affected by the solution and therefore consider it personally meaningful and important.

A fundamental challenge for the next generation of computational media and new technologies is not to deliver predigested information to individuals, but to provide the opportunity and resources for social debate, discussion, and collaborative design. In many design activities, learning cannot be restricted to finding knowledge that is "out there." For most design problems (ranging from urban design to graphics design and software design, which we have studied over many years), the knowledge to understand, frame, and solve problems does not exist; rather, it is constructed and evolved during the process of solving these problems, exploiting the power of *"breakdowns"* (Fischer, 1994c; Schön, 1983). From this perspective, *access* to existing information and knowledge (often seen as the major advance of new media) is a very limiting concept (Arias et al., 1999; Brown et al., 1994).

By arguing for the desirability of humans to be designers, we want to state explicitly that there is nothing wrong with being a consumer and that we can learn and enjoy many things in a consumer role (e.g., listening to a lecture, watching a tennis match, attending a concert, and admiring a piece of art). As argued in Section 3.2, "consumer/designer" is not an attribute of a person, but a role assumed in a specific context. Good designers, for instance, should be well-informed consumers (e.g., they should exploit reuse as a powerful design strategy by "consuming" existing information and using the contributions of the "giants" who preceded them).

Meta-design creates the enabling conditions "to engage the talent pool of the whole world" (Raymond and Young, 2001). Design engagement, from participation in planning to participation in continuous change (from do-it-yourself to adaptable environments), gives all the people access to the tools, resources, and power that have been jealously guarded prerogatives of the professional. The idea of a possible "design by all" always produces strong reactions in the field of professional designers, who perceive meta-design and end-user development as a challenge to their design expertise. The goal of making systems modifiable by users does not imply transferring the responsibility of good system design to the user. In general, "normal" users do not build tools of the quality that a professional designer would because users are not concerned with the tool per se, but in doing their work. Even so, professionalism is a particular kind of specialization, and specialization is the technique of production-line technology. As we develop new technologies, we need also to develop new roles and new images of ourselves.

Designers have to give up some control. Content creation in large information repositories must be *distributed*. This distribution can be supported by meta-design, as evidenced by digital libraries (Wright et al., 2002), the worldwide web, open source software (Scharff, 2002), and interactive art (Giaccardi, 2003). Designers must engage in co-creative and evolutionary processes that enable people to design for themselves. To do so, meta-designers seed both the technical infrastructure and the social environment in which the system is embedded. Their goal of creating the technical and social conditions for collaborative design activities becomes as important as creating the artifact itself, and it requires attitude and capabilities. Meta-designers need to be good *systems integrators* (Kit Galloway, personal communication), able to actively interface a multiplicity of tools, services, and organizations, as well as good *facilitators*, capable of establishing collaborative relationships and using their own creativity to set the socio-technical environment in which other people can, in turn, be creative.

6.3. ENABLING CO-CREATION

In a world that is not predictable, and where solutions are neither given nor confined in one single mind, meta-design allows exploration of the collaborative dimension of human creativity. This produces a novel approach in the design of both interactive systems and their socio-technical environment that aims to include the emergent as an opportunity for evolution and innovation. Meta-design deals with *co-creation* (Giaccardi, 2003). It enables and activates collaborative processes that allow the emergence of creative activities in open and evolvable environments.

The possibility for the user to transform from viewer to co-creator, or from consumer to co-designer requires (National-Research-Council, 2003) an expansion of the creative process in art and in design, respectively. Interactive art—and its networked practices in particular—explores the expansion of human creativity in terms of an expansion of the inter-subjective dimension, and deals primarily, although not exclusively, with feelings and emotions rather than with rational decision making.

A cross-case analysis of networked practices of interactive art shows that co-creation is perceived by users as an inter-subjective experience engendered by collaborative activities, which does not show necessarily any explicit goal. Main motivational paths to co-creation are emotionally driven and based on the perception of the environment as open and unpredictable. Computationally, such an environment enables co-creation by allowing two main techniques (Giaccardi, 2003):

- *Emotional seeding* is based mainly on an exploitation of non-verbal communication. It takes place thanks to the visual embodiment of the emotional tone and activities of participants within the interactive system. The embodiment (Dourish, 2001) of participants in the computational environment, as engendered by emotional seeding, ensures that time, space, and physicality are experienced in relational, rather than merely informational, terms.
- *Agency patterning* is the setting of specific spatial-temporal parameters aimed to let dynamic agencies emerge from the system. It defines size, resolution, and level of the agency that is performing a global activity.

The attention paid by interactive art to the design of *relational settings and affective bodies* (i.e., to the conditions and dynamics for mutual interaction) produces an understanding of the spatial-temporal parameters of an interactive system in terms of inter-subjective proximity and individuals' intentionality. That is, interactive art deals in terms of how "closely" people interact with each other, and how their intentions determine and recognize chains of actions and meaningful events, over time.

6.4. "EASE-OF-USE" REVISITED

"Ease-of-use" along with the "burden of learning something" are often used as arguments for why people will not engage in design. Building systems that support users to act as designers and not just as consumers is often less successful than the meta-designers have hoped for. A student in one of our courses reacted to our attempts to establish a meta-design culture as follows: "Humans want things as easy as possible for them. The reason why we are a consumer society is because that's what we want to be."

The end-user modifiability and end-user programming features themselves add even considerably more functionality to already very complex environments (such as high functionality applications and large software reuse libraries)—and our empirical analyses clearly show that not too many users of such systems are willing to engage in this additional learning effort. Beyond just defining them, extensions need to be integrated (stored, made retrievable, and sustained) in the work environment. The answer to this challenging situation may be in the development of social structures around these systems such as *collaborative work practices* (Nardi, 1993; National-Research-Council, 2003).

Without the willingness to learn something, users remain trapped with "overspecialized systems where operations are easy, but little of interest is possible" (see Section 1). Based on our work with user communities (Arias et al., 2000), it is obvious that serious working and learning do not have to be unpleasant—they can be empowering, engaging, and fun. Many times the problem is not that *programming is difficult, but that it is boring* (e.g., in cases where domain designers are forced to think and articulate themselves at the level of human–computer interaction rather than human problem–domain interaction; see Figure 19.5). Highly creative owners of problems struggle and learn tools that are useful to them, rather than believing in the alternative of "ease-of-use," which limits them to pre-programmed features (National-Research-Council, 2003).

Meta-design can tackle this learning problem in two different ways by paying attention to the following equation:

utility = value/effort,

Meaning that people will decide on the worthiness of doing something (utility) by relating the (perceived) value of an activity to the (perceived) effort of doing it. In many design activities, the question to be asked is: "Who puts in the effort?" Often an important trade-off exists: *more effort at design time results in smaller effort at use time.* From a meta-design perspective, to create the structures that will empower users at use time and greatly reduce their endeavor, major efforts at design time are needed. However, *value consideration at design time* can induce an organization to put in the effort in order to establish a culture of "design in use" and produce "better" systems that: (1) more people will buy (*economic incentive*) or (2) more people will use (*social capital*).

At the same time, *value consideration at use time* is greatly influenced by allowing people to engage in personally meaningful tasks, and it can induce them to serious working and learning. People are willing to spend considerable effort on things that are important to them, so the value dimension for truly personal meaningful activities is more important than the effort dimension. For example, learning to drive an automobile is not an easy task, but almost all people learn it because they associate a high personal value with it.

6.5. MOTIVATION AND REWARDS

The creation of new environments and the emergence of new social mindsets and expectations lead to succeeding waves of new technologies. P2P computing, open source, and extreme programming (XP), for instance, could be considered in software design as new developments mostly originating with user communities (i.e., P2P and open source) that reflect a shift of human motives and express the human desire to be in control of human destiny (Raymond and Young, 2001). For an example in existing technology, we could consider the Internet, and describe the following *socio-technical upward spiral* (Giaccardi, 2003): (1) exploitation of computational malleability and modifiability (e.g., the worldwide web); (2) shared design activities and reinterpretation for democratic purposes (e.g., online communities); or (3) the emergence of new social mindsets and expectations as a result of new environments.

What makes people, over time, become active contributors and designers and share their knowledge requires therefore a new "design culture," involving a mindset change and principles of social capital accumulation. But before new social mindsets and expectations emerge, users' active participation comes as a function of simple motivational mechanisms and activities considered personally meaningful. One focus of meta-design is the design of the socio-technical environment in which the interactive system is embedded, and in which users are recognized and rewarded for their contributions and can accumulate social capital. *Social capital* is based on specific benefits that flow from the trust, reciprocity, information, and cooperation associated with social networks (Fischer et al., 2003; Florida, 2002; Putnam, 2000). However, an *analysis* of co-creation, and a survey (Giaccardi, 2003) of the way in which some theories and practices of meta-design address the issue of motivation in relation to the new social relationships produced by emergent artificiality and increasing interconnectivity contribute to question the values plane associated with the design of socio-technical environments. Beside the consideration and evaluation of the specific benefits that can be associated with social networks, the "lasting value" of social capital can be conceptualized as a form of human creativity, and fundamentally based on inter-subjective relationships, feelings, and emotions. We assign importance through *value-feelings* that make us experience emotion only in regard to that which matters (Thompson, 1999). *Emotions*, as value-feelings, generate the world of our values, and enable us to "see" a situation that addresses us immediately, *here and now*, before deliberating rationally about it (Donaldson, 1991).

Meta-design enhances spontaneous and autonomous ways of relating and interacting, and in doing so it liberates processes of construction of reality that enable substantial participation and flexibility in the transformation of our environment. From this perspective, meta-design can be seen as *socio-technical know-how* (Giaccardi, 2003) embodied in the evolving practices of fluid and interdependent communities, rather than driven exclusively by explicit motivations and benefits. This orientation toward a co-creative framework matches those trends in socio-technical systems design, which— assuming a technological modifiability both at design and use time—call for attention to the relationships and interconnections occurring between the micro and macro levels of the socio-technical environment (Callon and Latour, 1981; Mumford, 1987). It also matches the need for "non-targeted" design in a "shared infrastructure" scenario, where technologies (and we would add human and social systems, i.e., organizations) are heterogeneous, intertwined, and interdependent (Pipek and Kahler, 2004).

6.6. THE NEW DESIGN SPACE OF META-DESIGN

Meta-design encompasses three levels of design, meant as a new "design space." These three levels of design can be summarized as: (1) *designing design*; (2) *designing together*; and (3) *designing the "in-between."* Such levels of design refer to the field of meanings that the term meta-design has developed in the course of its various uses. They correspond, quite evidently, to the anticipatory, participatory, and socio-technical issues raised by meta-design, and highlighted in this chapter. We can think of the design space of meta-design as *a threefold design space* (Giaccardi, 2003) aimed at integrating the design of (1) a technical infrastructure that is evolvable, (2) a learning environment and work organization that allows users to become active contributors, and (3) a socio-technical system in which users can relate and find motivations and rewards.

The *first level of meta-design* (*designing design*) refers to the concept of *higher-order design*, and the possibility of a malleability and modifiability of structures and processes, as provided by computational media. It can be seen as the ground for a design approach that focuses on general structures and processes, rather than on fixed objects and contents. Methodologically, this first level entails methods and techniques for designing at a meta-level (e.g., *underdesign*). It can be seen as the field where meta-designers play an important role in establishing the conditions that will allow users, in turn, to become designers. This first level of meta-design concerns the impossible task of fully anticipating at design time users' needs and tasks, situations and behaviors. The possibility of transforming and modifying components, contents, and even contexts by interacting with the system and adjusting it allows the user to respond to the deficit between what can be foreseen at design time and what emerges at use time. This non-anticipatory feature of meta-design is realized through principles of *end-user modifiability and programming* (Girgensohn, 1992; Lieberman, 2001) and *seeding mechanisms* (Fischer and Ostwald, 2002). It provokes a creative and unplanned opportunism, which focuses on situated processes and emergent conditions, rather than on the anticipatory aspects of decision making.

The *second level of meta-design* (*designing together*) is concerned with the way in which designers and users can *collaborate* on the design activity, both at design time and at use time. Methodologically, this second level provides participatory methods and techniques for letting users be involved in the initial setting stage at design time, and it relies on *critiquing methods and techniques* (Fischer et al., 1998) for enabling users to learn and become in turn designers at use time. It can be seen as the level at which designers and users play a fluid role in the collaborative design activity at different times and different planes of social interaction (i.e., from individual to communitarian).

This second fold can be framed as a response to issues concerning the participation of the users in the design process due to the impossibility of completely anticipating users' needs and tasks at design time. Compared to traditional participatory approaches to design, meta-design represents an advance on the methodological level by supporting structural changes and co-evolutionary processes and transforming participation into a *participative status* (Dourish, 2001) of the user coupling with the system rather than as a way of increasing the probability a design will be used as intended.

The *third level of meta-design* (*designing the "in-between"*) concerns the design of *relational settings and affective bodies*. It aims to support existing social networks, and to shape new ones. Both existing and novel social networks, though, are not simply determined by technology. Rather, they are a system of relationships that people experience and negotiate in relation to technology itself. From this perspective, technology is seen as "a trigger for structural change" or an intervention into the active relationship between people and their organizational structures that can alter roles and patterns of interaction (Dourish, 2001). Within an interactive system conceived as a relational system, co-evolution takes place through reciprocal and recursive interactions (Maturana, 1997), whereas co-creation is triggered by the senses, emotions, and interactions of the users "embedded" and active within the computational environment (Giaccardi, 2003) and therefore capable of affecting and being affected ("affective bodies").

Methodologically, the third level of meta-design defines how co-evolutionary processes and co-creative behaviors can be sustained and empowered on the basis of the way in which people relate (both with the technical system and among themselves) within a computational environment. This level can be seen as a response to socio-technical issues. The design of the socio-technical system is neither only a matter of designing and adjusting technological artifacts in harmony with the people that will use that system, nor only a matter of understanding how to accumulate social capital. It is also a matter of methods and techniques to allow those sensing, emotioning, and "affective" activities (e.g., *emotional seeding and agency patterning*) that can sustain a condition of "inhabited technology" (Giaccardi, 2001b; Pipek and Kahler, 2004).

These three levels of meta-design are interdependent. They provide a structural openness given by computational malleability (first level of meta-design) corresponding to and integrated with an interactive openness (Stalder, 1997) given by collaborative (second level) and embodied (third level) relationships and activities. They can also be considered dimensions of meta-design, encompassing at different levels the cognitive (self-conscious versus unself-conscious design), social (social creativity), computational (systems and environments), and methodological aspects relevant to meta-design, finally meant not only as a collaborative design activity, but also as a possible cultural strategy of technology appropriation according to which the "tool" is also a "place" (Giaccardi, 2001b; Pipek and Kahler, 2004). Table 19.4 provides on overview of the different relationships.

Table 19.4. Overview of the design space for meta-design

Levels	Description of the level	Problem	Dimensions	Methods and techniques
First level	Designing design: meta-designers play an important role in establishing the conditions that will allow users to become designers	Anticipation. Users' needs and tasks cannot be fully anticipated at design time (they are ill-defined and change over time)	Epistemological/ computational	End-user development and seeding: users transform, modify, and adjust systems to achieve greater fit between what can be foreseen at design time and what emerges at use time
Second level	Designing together: designers and users collaborate in the design activity, both at design time and at use time, and at different levels of social aggregation (as an individual, group, and/or community)	Participation. Users need to be engaged in the problem framing/problem-solving process both at design time and use time	Social/cognitive	Participatory design: users are involved in the initial setting stage at design time, while critiquing and other support techniques empower users to learn and become designers at use time
Third level	Designing the in-between: defines how co-evolutionary processes and co-creative behaviors can be sustained	Socio-technical. Social and technical dimensions need to be integrated not only in order to be optimized and efficient, but to let new interactions and relationships emerge	Cognitive/social	Emotional seeding and agency patterning: methods and techniques to allow sensing, emotioning, and "affective" activities among users

7. Conclusions

Meta-design is not only a technical problem, it also requires new cultures and new mindsets. If the most important role of digital media in the future is to provide people with a powerful medium to express themselves and engage in personally meaningful activities, the medium should support them to work on the task, rather than require them to focus their intellectual resources on the medium itself. In this sense, computers are empowering artifacts: they are not only powerful tools, but also powerful *meta-tools* that can be used to create problem-specific tools. This empowerment, though, cannot be fully utilized until owners of problems are enabled "to retool." By putting the computational technology directly into the hands of owners of problems, meta-design is an important step to unleash the ultimate power of computer technology.

Meta-design is a conceptual framework informing a specific socio-technical methodology for end-user development, which includes design techniques (e.g., underdesign), process models (e.g., the SER model), and motivational mechanisms for communication, collaboration, and social capital accumulation (e.g., emotional seeding and reward structures). We have evaluated our approach in different settings, with different task domains, and with different users. Meta-design is a promising approach to overcome the limitations of closed systems and to support applications of informed participation and social creativity. However, it creates many fundamental challenges in the technical domain as well as in the social domain, including: (1) the tension between standardization and improvisation, (2) the additional efforts to integrate the work into the shared environment, (3) the willingness of users to engage in additional learning to become designers, (4) effective ways of supporting meaningful activities and enabling co-creation, (5) the need for social capital and technology appropriation, and (6) the need for a new, integrated design space that brings together the design of both technical and social conditions.

Meta-design allows a sort of creative and unplanned opportunism (Wood, 2000), and it addresses one of the fundamental challenges of a knowledge society (Florida, 2002): to invent and design a culture in which all participants in a collaborative design process can express themselves and engage in personally meaningful activities. End-user development requires a change in mindsets and cultures—people who *want to be active contributors and designers, not just consumers*. If we achieve this culture and mindset change and we provide people with the right computational environments, then we will have a chance to make one of the most challenging and exciting research topics a reality!

Acknowledgments

The authors thank the members of the Center for LifeLong Learning and Design at the University of Colorado, who have made major contributions to the conceptual framework described in this chapter. Anders Morch provided us with important feedback on earlier version of this chapter. The research was supported by (1) the National Science Foundation, Grants (a) REC-0106976 "Social Creativity and Meta-Design in Lifelong Learning Communities," and (b) CCR-0204277 "A Social-Technical Approach to the Evolutionary Construction of Reusable Software Component Repositories"; (2) SRA Key Technology Laboratory, Inc., Tokyo, Japan; (3) the Coleman Institute, Boulder, CO; and (4) Fondazione Eni Enrico Mattei, Grant "Ideas for the Future," for the aspects related to interactive art.

References

Alexander, C. 1964, *The Synthesis of Form*. Cambridge, MA: Harvard University Press.
Arias, E.G., Eden, H., Fischer, G., Gorman, A. and Scharff, E. (1999). Beyond access: Informed participation and empowerment. In: *Proceedings of the Computer Supported Collaborative Learning (CSCL '99) Conference*, Stanford, pp. 20–32.
Arias, E.G., Eden, H., Fischer, G., Gorman, A. and Scharff, E. (2000). Transcending the individual human mind—creating shared understanding through collaborative design. *ACM Transactions on Computer–Human Interaction* 7(1), 84–113.

Ascott, R. (2003). *Telematic embrace: Visionary theories of art, technology, and consciousness*. In: E.A. Shanken (ed.), Berkeley: University of California Press.

Brand, S. (1995). *How Buildings Learn: What Happens After They're Built*. New York: Penguin Books.

Brown, J.S. and Duguid, P. (2000). *The Social Life of Information*. Boston, MA: Harvard Business School Press.

Brown, J.S., Duguid, P. and Haviland, S. (1994). Toward informed participation: Six scenarios in search of democracy in the information age. *The Aspen Institute Quarterly* 6(4), 49–73.

Bruner, J. (1996). *The Culture of Education*. Cambridge, MA: Harvard University Press.

Burton, R.R., Brown, J.S. and Fischer, G. (1984). Analysis of skiing as a success model of instruction: Manipulating the learning environment to enhance skill acquisition. In: B. Rogoff and J. Lave (eds.), *Everyday Cognition: Its Development in Social Context*. Cambridge, MA: Harvard University Press, pp. 139–150.

Callon, M. and Latour, B. (1981). Unscrewing the big leviathan: How actors macro-structure reality and how sociologists help them to do so. In: K. Knorr-Cetina and A. Cicourel (eds.), *Advances in Social Theory and Methodology: Toward an Integration of Micro- and Macro-Sociologies*. Boston, London, and Henley: Routledge and Kegan Paul, pp. 277–303.

dePaula, R., Fischer, G. and Ostwald, J. (2001). Courses as seeds: Expectations and realities. In: *Proceedings of the Second European Conference on Computer-Supported Collaborative Learning(Euro-CSCL' 2001)*, Maastricht, Netherlands, pp. 494–501.

Dittrich, Y. and Lindeberg, O. (2003). Designing for changing work and business practices. In: N. Patel (ed.), *Adaptive Evolutionary Information Systems*. Hershey, PA: Idea group Inc, pp. 152–171.

Donaldson, M. (1991). *Human Minds: An Exploration*. London: Penguin Books.

Dourish, P. (2001). *Where the Action Is—The Foundations of Embodied Interaction*. Cambridge, MA: The MIT Press.

Ehn, P. and Malmborg, L. (1999). Everything that rises must converge. http://www.nordic-interactive.org/nimres2/html/malmborg_ehn.html.

Eisenberg, M. and Fischer, G. (1994). Programmable design environments: integrating end-user programming with domain-oriented assistance. In: *Human Factors in Computing Systems, CHI'94 (Boston, MA)*, ACM, New York, pp. 431–437.

Electronic-Arts (2004). SimCity 4. http://simcity.ea.com/.

Fischer, G. (1994a). Domain-oriented design environments. *Automated Software Engineering* 1(2), 177–203.

Fischer, G. (1994b). Putting the owners of problems in charge with domain-oriented design environments. In: D. Gilmore, R. Winder and F. Detienne (eds.), *User-Centered Requirements for Software Engineering Environments*. Heidelberg: Springer Verlag, pp. 297–306.

Fischer, G. (1994c). Turning breakdowns into opportunities for creativity. *Knowledge-Based Systems, Special Issue on Creativity and Cognition* 7(4), 221–232.

Fischer, G. (2001). User modeling in human–computer interaction. *User Modeling and User-Adapted Interaction (UMUAI)* 11(1), 65–86.

Fischer, G. (2002). Beyond 'couch potatoes': From consumers to designers and active contributors, in firstmonday (Peer-Reviewed Journal on the Internet). http://firstmonday.org/issues/issue7_12/fischer/.

Fischer, G., Nakakoji, K., Ostwald, J., Stahl, G. and Sumner, T. (1998). Embedding critics in design environments. In: M.T. Maybury and W. Wahlster (eds.), *Readings in Intelligent User Interfaces*. San Francisco: Morgan Kaufmann, pp. 537–559.

Fischer, G. and Ostwald, J. (2002). Seeding, evolutionary growth, and reseeding: enriching participatory design with informed participation. In: T. Binder, J. Gregory and I. Wagner (eds.), *Proceedings of the Participatory Design Conference (PDC'2002)*, CPSR, Malmö University, Sweden, pp. 135–143.

Fischer, G. and Scharff, E. (2000). Meta-design—design for designers. In: *3rd International Conference on Designing Interactive Systems (DIS 2000)*, New York, pp. 396–405.

Fischer, G., Scharff, E. and Ye, Y. (2004). Fostering social creativity by increasing social capital. In: M. Huysman and V. Wulf (eds.), *Social Capital and Information Technology*. Cambridge, MA: MIT Press, pp. 355–399.

Florida, R. (2002). *The Rise of the Creative Class and How It's Transforming Work, Leisure, Community and Everyday Life*. New York, NY: Basic Books.

Floyd, C., Züllighoven, H. and Budde, R., Keil-Slawik, R. (eds.) (1992). *Software Development and Reality Construction*. Berlin, Heidelberg: Springer.

Fuller, M. (2003). Grid unlocked. http://9.waag.org/Info/grid_en.html.

Giaccardi, E. (1999). Interactive strategies of network art relationships and agency. In: *CADE '99: Third Conference on Computers in Art* and *Design Education*, Teesside, Middlesbrough.

Giaccardi, E. (2001a). Interconnectivity and relational embodiment in art and design. In: *Proceedings of ISEA2000—Révélation: 10th International Symposium on Electronic Art*, Paris, France.

Giaccardi, E. (2001b). Transcultural vision and epistemological shift: from aesthetics to high tech society. In: G. Marchianò and R. Milani (eds.), *Frontiers of Transculturality in Contemporary Aesthetics*, Trauben, Torino, pp. 507–519.

Giaccardi, E. (2003). *Principles of Metadesign: Processes and Levels of Co-Creation in the New Design Space*. Ph.D. Dissertation. CAiiA-STAR, School of Computing, Plymouth, UK.

Girgensohn, A. (1992). *End-User Modifiability in Knowledge-Based Design Environments*. Ph.D. Dissertation. University of Colorado at Boulder.

Henderson, A. and Kyng, M. (1991). There's no place like home: Continuing design in use. In: J. Greenbaum and M. Kyng (eds.), *Design at Work: Cooperative Design of Computer Systems*. Hillsdale, NJ: Lawrence Erlbaum Associates, Inc., pp. 219–240.

Lieberman, H. (ed.) (2001). *Your Wish is My Command: Programming by Example*. San Francisco: Morgan Kaufmann.

Mackay, W.E. (1990). *Users and Customizable Software: A Co-Adaptive Phenomenon*. Sloan School of Management Dissertation. Massachusetts Institute of Technology.

Manovich, L. (2001). *The Language of New Media*. Cambridge, MA: MIT Press.

Maturana, H.R. (1997). Metadesign. http://www.hum.auc.dk/~rasand/Artikler/metadesign.htm.

Morch, A. (1997). Three levels of end-user tailoring: customization, integration, and extension. In: M. Kyng and L. Mathiassen (eds.), *Computers and Design in Context*. Cambridge, MA: MIT Press, pp. 51–76.

Mumford, E. (1987). Sociotechnical systems design: Evolving theory and practice. In: G. Bjerknes, P. Ehn and M. Kyng (eds.), *Computers and Democracy*. Brookfield, VT: Avebury, pp. 59–77.

Nardi, B.A. (1993). *A Small Matter of Programming*. Cambridge, MA: The MIT Press.

Nardi, B.A. and Zarmer, C. (1993). Beyond models and metaphors: Visual formalisms in user interface design. *Journal of Visual Languages and Computing* 4(1), 5–33.

National-Research-Council (2003). *Beyond Productivity: Information Technology, Innovation, and Creativity*. Washington, DC: National Academy Press.

Norman, D.A. and Draper, S.W. (eds.) (1986). *User-Centered System Design, New Perspectives on Human–Computer Interaction*. Hillsdale, NJ: Lawrence Erlbaum Associates, Inc.

Pipek, V. and Kahler, H. (2004). Supporting collaborative tailoring: Issues and approaches. In: V. Wulf (ed.), *End User Development—Empowering People to Flexibly Employ Advanced Information and Communication Technology*. Dordrecht, The Netherlands: Kluwer Academic Publishers.

Polanyi, M. (1966). *The Tacit Dimension*. Garden City, NY: Doubleday.

Putnam, R. (2000). *Bowling Alone: The Collapse and Revival of American Community*. New York, NY: Simon and Schuster.

Raymond, E.S. and Young, B. (2001). *The Cathedral and the Bazaar: Musings on Linux and Open Source by an Accidental Revolutionary*. Sebastopol, CA: O'Reilly and Associates.

Resnick, M. (1994). *Turtles, Termites, and Traffic Jams*. Cambridge, MA: The MIT Press.

Rittel, H. (1984). Second-generation design methods. In: N. Cross (ed.), *Developments in Design Methodology*. New York: John Wiley and Sons, pp. 317–327.

Rogoff, B., Matsuov, E. and White, C. (1998). Models of teaching and learning: Participation in a community of learners. In: D.R. Olsen and N. Torrance (eds.), *The Handbook of Education and Human Development—New Models of Learning, Teaching and Schooling*. Oxford: Blackwell, pp. 388–414.

Scacchi, W. (2002). Understanding the requirements for developing open source software systems. *IEEE Proceedings—Software* **149**(1), 24–39.

Scacchi, W. (2004). Socio-technical design. In: W.S. Bainbrigde (ed.), *The Encyclopedia of Human–Computer Interaction*. Berkshire Publishing Group, pp. 656–659.

Scharff, E. (2002). *Open Source Software, a Conceptual Framework for Collaborative Artifact and Knowledge Construction*. Ph.D. Dissertation. University of Colorado at Boulder.

Schön, D.A. (1983). *The Reflective Practitioner: How Professionals Think in Action*. New York: Basic Books.

Schuler, D. and Namioka, A. (eds.) (1993). *Participatory Design: Principles and Practices*. Hillsdale, NJ: Lawrence Erlbaum Associates.

Shanken, E.A. (2002). Art in the information age: Technology and conceptual art. *Leonardo* **35**(4), 433–488.

Shaw, M. (1989). Maybe your next programming language shouldn't be a programming language. In: C. Science and T. Board (eds.), *Scaling Up: A Research Agenda for Software Engineering*. Washington, DC: National Academy Press, pp. 75–82.

Shipman, F. and McCall, R. (1994). Supporting knowledge-base evolution with incremental formalization. In: *Human Factors in Computing Systems, INTERCHI'94 Conference Proceedings*, ACM, New York, pp. 285–291.

Sommerer, C. and Mignonneau, L. (1997a). Interacting with artificial life: A-Volve. *Complexity Journal* **2**(6), 13–21.

Sommerer, C. and Mignonneau, L. (1997b). A-Volve—an evolutionary artificial life environment. In: V.C. Langton and K. Shimohara (eds.), *Artificial Life*. Boston: MIT Press, pp. 167–175.

Stalder, F. (1997). *Actor-Network-Theory and Communication Networks: Toward Convergence*. Ph.D. Dissertation. Faculty of Information Studies, University of Toronto, http://felix.openflows.org/html/Network_Theory.html.

Suchman, L.A. (1987). *Plans and Situated Actions*. Cambridge, UK: Cambridge University Press.

Thompson, E. (1999). Human consciousness: From intersubjectivity to interbeing (A proposal to the Fetzer Institute). http://www.consciousness.arizona.edu/pcs/pcsfetz1.html.

Verle, L. (1999). *Novas Imagens Para Um Novo Meio: Um Estudo de Caso do Website de Arte Interativa SITO*. M.A. Dissertation. Pontificia Universidade Catolica do Rio Grande do Sul, Brasil.

Winograd, T. and Flores, F. (1986). *Understanding Computers and Cognition: A New Foundation for Design*. Norwood, NJ: Ablex Publishing Corporation.

Wood, J. (2000). Towards an ethics of flow: Design as an anticipatory system. *International Journal of Computing Anticipatory Systems*. Liège, Belgium: Centre for Hyperincursive Anticipation in Ordered Systems, pp. 87–102.

Wright, M., Marlino, M. and Sumner, T. (2002). Meta-design of a community digital library, D-Lib magazine, Volume 8, Number 5. http://www.dlib.org/dlib/may02/wright/05wright.html.

Ye, Y. and Fischer, G. (2002). Supporting reuse by delivering task-relevant and personalized information. In: *Proceedings of 2002 International Conference on Software Engineering (ICSE'02)*, Orlando, FL, pp. 513–523.

Youngblood, G. (1984). Virtual space. The electronic environments of mobile image, ars electronica symposium. http://kultur.aec.at/20Jahre/.

Chapter 20

Feasibility Studies for Programming
in Natural Language

HENRY LIEBERMAN and HUGO LIU
Media Laboratory, Massachusetts Institute of Technology, {lieber, hugo}@media.mit.edu

Abstract. We think it is time to take another look at an old dream—that one could program a computer by speaking to it in natural language. Programming in natural language might seem impossible, because it would appear to require complete natural language understanding and dealing with the vagueness of human descriptions of programs. But we think that several developments might now make programming in natural language feasible. First, improved broad coverage natural language parsers and semantic extraction techniques permit partial understanding. Second, mixed-initiative dialogues can be used for meaning disambiguation. And finally, where direct understanding techniques fail, we hope to fall back on Programming by Example, and other techniques for specifying the program in a more fail-soft manner. To assess the feasibility of this project, as a first step, we are studying how non-programming users describe programs in unconstrained natural language. We are exploring how to design dialogs that help the user make precise their intentions for the program, while constraining them as little as possible.

Key words. natural language programming, natural language processing, parsing, part-of-speech tagging, computer science education, programming languages, scripting languages, computer games.

1. Introduction

We want to make computers easier to use and enable people who are not professional computer scientists to be able to teach new behavior to their computers. The Holy Grail of easy-to-use interfaces for programming would be a natural language interface—just *tell* the computer what you want! Computer science has assumed this is impossible because it would be presumed to be "AI Complete"—require full natural language understanding.

But our goal is not to enable the user to use completely unconstrained natural language for any possible programming task. Instead, what we might hope to achieve is to attain enough partial understanding to enable using natural language as a communication medium for the user and the computer to cooperatively arrive at a program, obviating the need for the user to learn a formal computer programming language. Initially, we will work with typed textual input, but ultimately we would hope for a spoken language interface, once speech recognizers are up to the task. We are now evaluating commercially available speech recognizers, and are developing new techniques for correction of speech recognition errors based on Common Sense knowledge (Stocky et al., 2004).

We believe that several developments might now make natural language programming possible where it was not feasible in the past.

Henry Lieberman et al. (eds.), End User Development, 459–473.
© 2006 *Springer.*

- *Improved language technology.* While complete natural language understanding still remains out of reach, we think that there is a chance that recent improvements in robust broad-coverage parsing (Collins, 2003) (MontyLingua), semantically informed syntactic parsing and chunking, and the successful deployment of natural language command-and-control systems (Liu, 2003) might enable enough partial understanding to get a practical system off the ground.
- *Mixed-initiative dialogue.* We do not expect that a user would simply "read the code aloud." Instead, we believe that the user and the system should *have a conversation* about the program. The system should try as hard as it can to interpret what the user chooses to say about the program, and then ask the user about what it doesn't understand, to supply missing information, and to correct misconceptions.
- *Programming by Example.* We will adopt a *show and tell* methodology, which combines natural language descriptions with concrete example-based demonstrations. Sometimes it is easier to demonstrate what you want then to describe it in words. The user can tell the system "here is what I want," and the system can verify its understanding with "Is this what you mean?" This will make the system more *fail-soft* in the case where the language cannot be directly understood, and, in the case of extreme breakdown of the more sophisticated techniques, we will simply allow the user to type in code.

2. Feasibility Study

We were inspired by the Natural Programming Project of Pane and Myers at Carnegie-Mellon University (Pane et al., 2001). Pane and Myers (2004) conducted studies asking non-programming fifth-grade users to write descriptions of a Pac-Mac game (in another study, college students were given a spreadsheet programming task). The participants also drew sketches of the game so they could make deictic references.

Pane and Myers then analyzed the descriptions to discover what underlying abstract programming models were implied by the users' natural language descriptions. They then used this analysis in the design of the HANDS programming language. HANDS uses a direct-manipulation, demonstrational interface. While still a formal programming language, it hopefully embodies a programming model that is closer to users' "natural" understanding of the programming process before they are "corrupted" by being taught a conventional programming language. They learned several important principles, such as that users rarely referred to loops explicitly, and preferred event-driven paradigms.

Our aim is more ambitious. We wish to directly support the computer understanding of these natural language descriptions, so that one could do "programming by talking" in the way that these users were perhaps naively expecting when they wrote the descriptions.

As part of the feasibility study, we are transcribing many of the natural language descriptions and seeing how well they will be handled by our parsing technology (Liu, online). Can we figure out where the nouns and verbs are? When is the user talking about a variable, loop, or conditional?

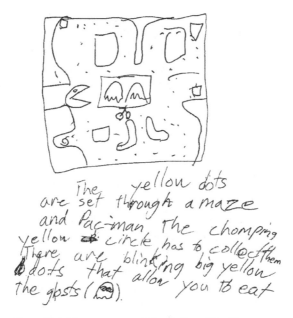

Figure 20.1. Non-programmer's description of Pac-Man.

One of our guiding principles will be to abandon the programming language dogma of having a single representation for each programming construct. Instead, we will try to collect as many verbal representations of each programming construct as we can, and see if we can permit the system to accept *all* of them.

3. Designing Dialogue Management for Natural Language Programming

The paradigm for the user interaction should reproduce the situation of the user talking to a more knowledgeable programmer, who knows all the implementation techniques. The goal for the user is to communicate their intent.

We have been inspired by some of the dialogue management philosophy of Collagen (Rich et al., 2001). Collagen uses a discourse model to support a user and an on-screen agent cooperatively working on a task. Either the user or the system can take initiative at any point, and the system keeps track of such dialogue management issues as which goals are being worked on and which are pending.

We envision a possible dialogue as follows, inspired by the Pac-Man example above,

User: We are going to program a game, Pac-Man.
System: OK. I know a few things about how to make games. We need to decide what the playing field looks like, design some characters for the game, how the users are going to control the characters, and how the scoring system is going to work. OK?

U: Sure. The yellow dots are set through a maze, and Pac-Man, the chomping yellow circle, has to collect them (see the user's sketch in Figure 20.1).

S: OK, let me see if I have got this straight. You want the playing field to be a grid of squares, each containing a yellow dot, right? (System displays a grid of squares with yellow dots). To make it a maze, we need to have some walls. Can you draw some walls for me?

(1).   U: (User draws in walls, selecting color, texture, etc.)

S: Pac-Man is the name of a character in the game, represented as a yellow circle, is that right? How is this? (System displays a yellow circle in one of the grid squares).

(2).   U: Oh, the dots should be red. (Things do not have to be done "in order." You can refer to something previously said.)

S: OK. What does it mean for Pac-Man to "collect" a dot?

U: Whenever Pac-Man is on a square with a dot, he eats it. That means that the dot is gone and the player gets another point. (The system introduces a variable to count the number of dots eaten by Pac-Man).

S: OK, now I do not understand what "eats" means. Can you explain it?

U: When you draw Pac-Man, you alternate between a picture of Pac-Man with his mouth open and a picture of Pac-Man with his mouth closed.

S: Can you draw me what Pac-Man looks like when he has his mouth open? Mouth closed?

(3).   U: (Draws.) There are blinking big yellow dots that allow you to eat the ghosts (draws picture of ghost).

S: (Continues dialogue about dots and ghosts ....)

Below, we give some analysis of the above-presented dialog. From (1), the system must recognize that a "game" is the top-level programming goal. To conduct the rest of the dialog, we assume the system has some script- or frame-based knowledge about the major programming subgoals in programming a game. It should leverage this understanding to dually know what to expect from the user, and to act as a tutor to guide the user.

As (3) demonstrates, users will attempt to convey a lot of information all at once. It is the job of the language understanding system to identify major intended *actions* (e.g., "set through"), each of which are associated with a thematic *agent* role (e.g., "the yellow dots"), and a thematic *patient* role (e.g., "a maze"). The system will also try to correlate these filled role slots with its repertoire of programming tricks. For example, in (3), "yellow dots" might be visual primitives, and "a maze" might invoke a script about how to construct such a structure on the screen and in code. In (4), the dialog management system reconfirms its interpretation to the user, giving the user the opportunity to catch any glitches in understanding.

In (5), the system demonstrates how it might mix natural language input with input from other modalities as required. Certainly we have not reached the point where good graphic design can be dictated in natural language! Having completed the maze layout subgoal, the system planning agency steps through some other undigested information gleaned from (3). In (6), it makes some inference that Pac-Man is a character in this game based on its script knowledge of a game.

Again in (9), the user presents the system with a lot of new information to process. The system places the to-be-digested information on a stack and patiently steps through to understand each piece. In (10), the system does not know what "eats" should do, so it asks the user to explain that in further detail. And so on.

While we may not be able to ultimately achieve all of the language understanding implied in the example dialogue above, and we may have to further constrain the dialogue, the above example does illustrate some important strategies, including iterative deepening of the program's understanding (Lieberman and Liu, 2002).

4. Designing Natural Language Understanding for Programming

Constructing a natural language understanding system for programming must be distinguished from the far more difficult task of open domain story understanding. Luckily, natural language understanding for programming is easier than open domain story understanding because the discourse in the programming domain is variously constrained by the task model and the domain model. This section attempts to flesh out the benefits and challenges which are unique to a language understanding system for programming.

4.1. CONSTRAINTS FROM AN UNDERLYING SEMANTIC MODEL

The language of discourse in natural language programming is first and foremost, constrained by the underlying semantic model of the program being constructed. Consider, for instance, the following passage from a fifth-grader non-programmer's description of the Pacman game:

> *Pacman eats a big blink dot and then the ghosts turn blue or red and pacman is able to eat them. Also his score advances by 50 points.*

In the previous section, we argued that through mixed-initiative dialogue, we can begin to progressively disambiguate a programmatic description like the one shown above, into an underlying semantic model of a *game*. Establishing that "Pacman" is the main character in the game helps us to parse the description. We can, for example, recognize that the utterances "Pac man" and "pacman" probably both *refer* to the character "Pacman" in the game, because both are lexicographically similar to "Pacman," but there is also the confirming evidence that both "Pac man" and "pacman" take the action "to eat," which is an action typically taken by an agent or character. Having *resolved* the meanings of "Pac man" and "pacman" into the character "Pacman," we can now resolve "his" to "Pacman" because "his" refers to a single agent, and "Pacman" is the only plausible referent in the description. We can now infer that "eat" refers to an ability of the agent "Pacman," and "score" is a member variable associated with "Pacman," and that the score has the ability to advance, and so on and so forth.

In summary, the underlying semantic model of a program provides us with *unambiguous referents* that a language understanding system can parse text into. All levels of a language processing system, including speech recognition, semantic grouping, part-of-speech tagging, syntactic parsing, and semantic interpretation, benefit from this phenomena of *reference*. Although the natural language input is ideally unconstrained, the semantic model we are mapping into is well-constrained. Language resolution also has a nice cascading effect, which is, the more resolutions you make, the more you are able to make (by leveraging existing "*islands of certainty*"). Resolving "Pac man" and "pacman" in turn allows us to resolve "his" and these in turn allow us to resolve "eat" and "score." Of course, in our proposed mixed-initiative model, we can always prompt the user for confirmation of any ambiguities which cannot be resolved.

In the above example, we discuss how objects and actions get resolved, but what about programmatic controls? Are these easy to recognize and resolve? By studying the "programming by talking" styles of many users, we expect to be able to identify a manageable set of salient keywords, phrases, and structures which indicate programmatic controls like conditionals and loops. Although, it would come as no surprise if "programming by talking" maps somewhat indirectly rather than directly onto programming control structures. For example, in the usability studies of Pane and Myers, it is uncommon to find explicit language to describe loops directly. Instead, there is evidence for natural language descriptions mapping into *implicit loop operations* in the form of Lisp-style list processing functions like "map," "filter," and "reduce." For example, the utterance, "*Pacman tries to eat all the big blinking dots*" does not seem like a programmatic control, but it actually expresses several loops implicitly (and quite elegantly, as we might add). We can paraphrase the utterance in pseudo-code as follows:

```
map(Pacman.eat,
    filter(lambda dot:
        dot.big AND dot.blinking,
        dots))
```

We are aided in the generation of this pseudo-code interpretation by knowledge of the preferences/constraints of the underlying semantic model, i.e., something that Pacman can do is eat ($x.y$ () relation), a dot is something which can be eaten ($x(y)$ relation), and dots can be big and blinking ($x.y$ relations).

Thus far, we have generally outlined a strategy for mapping a programmatic description into a code model by progressive stages of semantic resolution, but we have not been rigorous about presenting a framework for semantic interpretation. Now, we will propose to leverage the following ontological framework given by Liu (2003), which enumerates ways of resolving English into code:

- function $x.y$()
- ability $x.y$()
- param $x(y)$

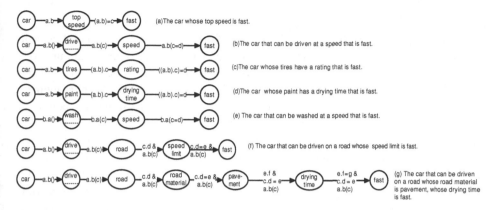

Figure 20.2. An underlying semantic model of English is used to generate interpretations of "fast car." From (Liu, 2003).

- property $x.y$
- isA $x:y$ (subtype)
- value $x = y$
- assoc x-related-to-y

In (Liu, 2003), it is proposed that natural language phrases can be understood in terms of compositions using the above ontology. An "interpretation" of a phrase is thus defined as one possible mapping from the surface language to some path in the network semantic model (Figure 20.2).

In our task of mapping surface natural language to programmatic code, we could view the problem in a way analogous to (Liu, 2003), i.e., an underlying semantic model of programming can be used to generate possible interpretations of inputted natural language, followed by the use of contextual cues, further semantic constraints, and dialog with the user to disambiguate from all possible interpretations to one or two likely interpretations.

Our approach to generating and selecting interpretive mappings from programmatic description to code is also supported by the natural language understanding literature, where there is precedent for exploiting semantic constraints for meaning disambiguation. BCL Spoken Language User Interface Toolkit (Liu, Alam and Hartomo, 2002), developed by BCL Technologies R&D, used Chomsky's Projection Principle and Parameters Model for command and control. In the principle and parameters model, surface features of natural language are seen as projections from the lexicon. The insight of this approach is that by explicitly parameterizing the possible behaviors of each lexical item, we can more easily perform language processing. We expect to be able to apply the principle and parameters model to our task, because the variables and structures present in computer programs can be seen as forming a naturally parameterized lexicon. An approach for using domain constraints to make natural language interaction reliable is also outlined in Yates (2003).

4.2. EVOLVABLE

The approach we have described thus far is fairly standard for natural language command-and-control systems. However, in our programming domain, the underlying semantic system is not static. Underlying objects can be created, used, and destroyed all within the breath of one sentence. This introduces the need for our language understanding system to be dynamic enough to *evolve* itself in real-time. The condition of the underlying semantic system including the state of objects and variables must be kept up-to-date and this model must be maximally exploited by all the modules of the language system for disambiguation. This is a challenge that is relatively uncommon to most language processing systems, in which the behavior of lexicons and grammars are usually defined or trained *a priori* and are not very amenable to change at run-time. Anyone who has endeavored to build a natural language programming system will likely have discovered that it is not simply the case that an off-the-shelf natural language processing packaging can be used.

To most optimally exploit the information given by the underlying semantic model, the natural language processing system will need to be intimately integrated with and informed by feedback from this evolving model. For example, consider the following fifth-grader non-programmer's description.

Pacman gets eaten if a ghost lands in the same space.

Without information from the underlying semantic model, some pretrained part-of-speech taggers will interpret "lands" as a noun, causing a cascade of misinterpretations, such as interpreting "ghost lands" as a new object. However, our underlying semantic model may know that "ghost" is a character in the game. If this knowledge is trickled back to the part-of-speech tagger, that tagger can have enough smarts to prefer the interpretation of "lands" as a verb untaken by the agent "ghost." This example illustrates that natural language processing must be intimately informed by the underlying semantic model, and ideally, the whole natural language programming system will be built end-to-end.

4.3. FLEXIBLE

Whereas traditional styles of language understanding consider every utterance to be relevant and therefore must be understood, we take the approach that in a "programming by talking" paradigm, some utterances are more salient than others. That is to say, we should take a selective parsing approach which resembles *information extraction*–style understanding. One criticism to this approach might be that it loses out on valuable information garnered from the user. However, we would argued that it is not necessary to fully understand every utterance in one pass because we are proposing a natural language dialog management system to further refine the information dictated by the user, giving the user more opportunities to fill in the gaps.

Such a strategy also pays off in its natural tolerance for user's disfluencies; thus, adding robustness to the understanding mechanism. In working with user's emails in a natural language meeting command-and-control task, Liu et al. found that user disfluencies such as bad grammar, poor word choice, and run-on sentences deeply impacted the performance of traditional syntactic parsers based on fixed grammars. Liu et al. found better performance in a more flexible collocational semantic grammar, which spotted for certain words and phrases, while ignoring many less-important words which did not greatly affect semantic interpretation. The import of such an approach to our problem domain will be much greater robustness and a greater ability to handle unconstrained natural language.

4.4. ADAPTIVE

In working with any particular user in a programming task, it is desirable to recognize and exploit the specific discourse style of that user in order to increase the performance of the language understanding system. In our analysis of the natural language programming user studies performed by Pane and Myers (2004), we note that some users give a multi-tiered description of the program, starting with the most abstract description and iteratively becoming more concrete, while others proceed linearly and concretely in describing objects and functions. Consider for example, how the following two fifth-grader non-programmers begin their descriptions of Pacman quite differently:

The object of the game is to eat all the yellow dots. If you['re] corn[er]ed and there is a blinking dot eat that and the ghosts will turn a color and when you eat them you get 200 points. When you eat all the dots you win the game.

To tell the computer how to move the Pacman I would push letters, and arrows. If I push the letter A[,] pacman moves up. When I push Q it moves down. To make it go left and right I use the arrows.

Whereas the first non-programmer begins with a breadth-first description of the game, starting from the highest-level goals of the game, the second non-programmer begins with the behavioral specifics of user control, and never really explicates the overarching goals of game anywhere in the whole description. Understanding the descriptive style of the user allows us to improve the quality of the parsing and dialogue. If the user is accustomed to top–down multi-tiered descriptions like non-programmer #1, the system can assume that the first few utterances in a description will expose many of the globally salient objects in the semantic model that will later be referred to. For example, from the utterance, "*The object of the game is to eat all the yellow dots,*" we can assume that "yellow dots" are salient globally, and that "eat" is an action central to the game. If, however, the user is accustomed to giving details straight away like non-programmer #2, the system can perhaps be more proactive to ask the user for clarifications and context for what the program is about, e.g., asking the user, "Are you programming a game?"

There are also many other dimensions along with user style can vary, such as *inter alia*, example-driven scenario giving versus if-then-else explication, describing positive behavior of a system versus negative behavior, and giving first-person character description (e.g., "*You like to eat dots*") versus third-person declarative description (e.g., *"There is a Pacman who eats dots"*) versus first-person user description (e.g., *"You press the left arrow key to move Pacman."*). A natural language programming system should characterize and recognize many of these styles and style-dimensions, and to use this knowledge to inform both an adaptive case-based parsing strategy, and an adaptive case-based dialogue strategy.

4.5. CAN NOVICES' DESCRIPTIONS OF PROGRAMS BE FULLY OPERATIONALIZED?

In addition to concerns about natural language understanding *per se*, there is also the concern that novice descriptions of programs are vague, ambiguous, erroneous, and otherwise not fully precise in the way the programming language code would be. Our analysis of the CMU data shows that, indeed, this is often the case. But that does not render the cause of natural language programming hopeless. The imprecision manifests itself in different forms, each of which has important consequences for the dialog design.

4.6. INTENTIONAL DESCRIPTIONS

Above, we discussed some of the linguistic problems surrounding determining the referents of natural language expressions such as "it" or "him." These issues consist of figuring out ways to map expressions either to known objects in the program or to recognize when new objects are being introduced or created. In addition there is the problem of determining when objects are referred to by descriptive phrases rather than direct references.

We often saw descriptions such as "the player being chased," where in a conventional program, one might see a direct reference to a program variable. We need to be able to distinguish between intentional descriptions used to reference objects that the system knows about "at compile time," e.g., "When the ghosts chase a player, the player being chased has to run away" (two different ways of referring to a particular player), and those that imply a "run time" search, e.g., "Find a player who is being chased and turn him green."

Further, people use different levels of specificity to refer to an object. "Pac-Man" (by name), "the yellow circle" (by appearance), "the player" (by role) can be interchangeable in the discourse, but may have vastly different effects when the program is re-executed in a different context. In Programming by Example (Lieberman, 2001) this is referred to as the "data description problem," and is also a central problem here. The best way to deal with that problem is to give the user sufficient feedback when future examples are executed, so that the user will see the consequences of a learned description. New examples can be executed step-by-step, and the system can feed back its description, so that users understand the relation between descriptions and selected objects, and change them if they are incorrect. Systems like Lieberman, Nardi and Wright's Grammex (Lieberman et al., 2001) provide ways of incrementally generalizing and specializing descriptions or sub-descriptions so that a desired result is achieved. To some extent, however, the user needs to learn that the exact way in which an object is described will have consequences for the learning system. Even at best, it is not possible to be as sloppy about descriptive phrases as we typically are in interpersonal discourse. This is a crucial part of what it means to learn to "think like a programmer."

4.7. ASSUMING CONTEXT

Natural language descriptions of programs tend to make a lot of assumptions about context that are not explicitly represented in the text. In programming languages, such context is represented by the scope of declarations and placement of statements. In natural language discourse, speakers assume that the listener can figure out what the context is, either by such cues as recently mentioned objects and actions, or by filling in necessary background knowledge. In doing natural language programming in the context of a programming by example system, we have the advantage of having a runtime context available which can help us discern what the user is talking about.

You should put the name and the score and move everyone below the new score down one.

Nowhere in this phrase does it include the implied context, "When one of the players has achieved a new total, and the scoreboard is displayed." However, if the user is programming interactively with concrete examples, the most likely time for the user to make such a statement is just *when* such a new score has occurred. It is the responsibility of the programming environment to figure out that what is important about the current situation is the posting of a new score. In Wolber and Myers (2001) discuss the problem of demonstrating *when* to do something as well as *how* to do it, under the rubric of Stimulus-Response Programming by Example.

Again, in the case of failure to recognize the context for a statement, the strategy is to initiate a dialogue with the user explicitly about in what context the statement is to be taken.

4.8. OUT-OF-ORDER SEQUENCES AND ADVICE

As noted by Pane and Myers (2004), users tend not to think linearly, and provide instructions that are not properly ordered, which is why they adopted an event driven style for HANDS. Sometimes, this is a matter of making assumptions about the temporal context in which commands will be executed.

Packman gets eaten if a ghost lands in the same space as Packman.
If Packman gets a power pill, then he gets points by landing in the same space as a ghost.

Taken literally as code, these statements are in the wrong order—the condition of eating the power pill should be checked *before* deciding what action to take when Pac-Man and the ghost arrive at the same spot. But the user is adopting the quite reasonable strategy of telling us what the *usual* or most common case is first, and only then informing us about the rare exceptions. The system needs to be able to untangle such cases.

Other natural language statements provide *advice*. Advice is not directly executable, but may affect what gets executed at future points in the interaction. Advice may incrementally supply parameters or modifiers to other commands. Advice may affect the level of generality of object descriptions. This is an important style of interaction that is not well supported by current programming methodologies (Lieberman, 2001).

> *The object of the game is to eat as many dots as you can without getting eaten by the ghosts.*

Some utterances are not actually code themselves, but directives to *make edits* to the program.

> *When monsters are red... [they] run ... to the other side of the screen. Same goes for Pac-Man.*

Here, "same goes" means "write the same code for Pac-Man as you did for the red monsters." This suggests that users are assuming a capability for high level program manipulation, that can, for example, insert statements into already-written code or generate code from design patterns. The best-known project for providing such capabilities directly to a programmer is The Programmer's Apprentice (Rich, 1990).

4.9. MISSING OR CONFLICTING CASES

Because order constraints are more relaxed in a natural language style interaction, it is often more difficult to determine if all cases have been covered. Of course, even in conventional programming, nothing prevents writing underconstrained or overconstrained programs. Some software engineering test methodologies for end users do attempt to infer case coverage in some situations (Ruthruff), and we envision similar techniques might be applied in our domain.

In an event driven style as advocated by Pane and Myers it is also possible for handlers of different events to conflict. Graphical- and example-based feedback helps avoid, and catch cases of, underconstrained and overconstrained situations. We also like the critique-based interaction found by McDaniel (2001), where directions "stop this" (for overconstrained situations) and "do something" (for underconstrained situations) correct the system's responses.

4.10. CHANGE OF PERSPECTIVE

Users do not always describe things from a consistent viewpoint. They may switch, unannounced, between local and global viewpoints, between subjective and objective viewpoints, between the viewpoints of various actors in the program. For example, a user might say *"When you hit a wall... "* (*you* meaning a screen representation of a game character), and *"When you score a point... "* (*you* meaning the human user), in the same program without warning. Again, this is a form of missing context which

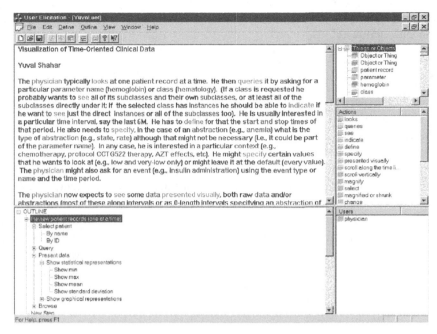

Figure 20.3. Tam et al's U-Tel lets users annotate text describing a program.

the reader is expected to supply. People do recognize the inherent ambiguity of such references, so they are often willing to supply clarification if necessary.

5. Annotation Interfaces

Another, less radical, possibility for a natural language programming interface is to let the user *annotate* a natural language description. The idea would be for the user to type or speech-transcribe a natural language description of the program, and then manually select pieces of the text that correspond to meaningful entities in the program. This reduces the burden on the system of reliably parsing the text. Such an approach was taken by Tam et al., (1998) in U-Tel (see Figure 20.3), which has an underlying model-based interface methodology. In the illustration, the full text appears in the upper left, and highlighted words for "steps," "actions," and "objects" are collected in the other panes.

U-Tel, however, did not construct a complete program; rather it functioned mainly as a knowledge elicitation aid, and required further action by a programmer conversant in the Mobi-D model-based formalism.

The annotation approach is attractive in many circumstances, particularly where a natural language description of a procedure already exists, perhaps for the purpose of communicating the procedure to other people. We believe the approach could be extended to support full procedural programming. Other attractive features of this approach are that it is less sensitive to order, and does not require the system to understand everything the user says. Even in natural language programming, users "comment" their code!

6. Note

Portions of this paper were written by dictation into the speech recognition program IBM ViaVoice, by the first author when he was recovering from hand injuries sustained in a bicycle accident.

Current speech interfaces are not good enough to perform unaided transcription; all require a mixed-initiative critique and correction interface to display recognition hypotheses and allow rapid correction. The author thus experienced many issues similar to those that will arise in natural language programming; among them: inherent ambiguity (no speech program can distinguish between *too* and *two* by audio alone), underspecification and misunderstanding of natural language directives. Although today's speech interfaces leave a lot to be desired, we were struck by how successfully the interaction is able to make up for deficiencies in the underlying recognition; this gives us hope for the approach. We apologize for any errors that remain in the paper as a result of the transcription.

7. Conclusion

Programming directly in natural language, without the need for a formal programming language, has long been a dream of computer science. Even COBOL, one of the very early programming languages, and for a long time, the dominant business programming language, was designed to look as close as possible to natural language to enhance readability. Since then, very few have explored the possibility that natural language programming could be made to work.

In this paper, we have proposed an approach based on advances in natural language parsing technology, mixed-initiative dialog, and programming by example. To assess the feasibility of such an approach we have analyzed dialogs taken from experiments where non-programmer users were asked to describe tasks, and it seems that many of the important features of these dialogs can be handled by this approach. We look forward to the day when computers will do what we say, if only we ask them nicely.

Acknowledgments

We would like to thank John Pane and Brad Myers for sharing with us the data for their Natural Programming experiments.

References

Alam, H., Rahman, A., Tjahjadi, T., H. Cheng, H., Llido, P., Kumar, A., Hartono, R., Tarnikova, Y. and Wilcox, C. (2002). Development of spoken language user interfaces: A tool kit approach. In:

T. Caelli, A. Amin, R. Duin, M. Kamel and D. Ridder (eds.), *Lecture Notes in Computer Science LNCS 2396*, 339–347.

Collins, M. (2003). Head-driven statistical models for natural language parsing. *Computational Linguistics* **29**(4), MIT Press, Cambridge, MA, USA.

Lieberman, H., Nardi, B. and Wright, D. (2001). Training agents to recognize text by example. In: H. Lieberman (ed.), *Your Wish is My Command: Programming by Example*, Morgan Kaufmann, San Francisco, CA, USA.

Lieberman, H. (2001). Interfaces that give and take advice, in human–computer interaction for the new millenium, John Carroll (ed.), ACM Press/Addison-Wesley, Reading, MA, USA, pp. 475–485.

Lieberman, H. and Liu, H. (2002). Adaptive linking between text and photos using common sense reasoning. In: De Bra, Brusilovsky, Conejo (eds.), *Adaptive Hypermedia and Adaptive Web*, 2nd International Conference, AH 2002, Malaga, Spain, May 29–31, Proceedings. Lecture Notes in Computer Science 2347 Springer 2002, ISBN 3-540-43737-1, pp. 2–11.

Liu, H., Alam, H. and Hartono, R. Meeting Runner: An Automatic Email-Based Meeting Scheduler. BCL Technologies—US. Dept of Commerce ATP Contract Technical Report. Available at: http://www.media.mit.edu/~hugo/publications/

Liu, H. (2003). Unpacking meaning from words: A context-centered approach to computational lexicon design. In: Blackburn et al. (eds.), Modeling and Using Context, 4th International and Interdisciplinary Conference, CONTEXT 2003, Stanford, CA, USA, June 23–25, 2003, Proceedings. Lecture Notes in Computer Science 2680 Springer 2003, ISBN 3-540-40380-9, pp. 218–232.

Liu, H. (2003). MontyLingua: An End-to-End Understander for English. At: http://web.media.mit.edu/~hugo/montylingua.

McDaniel, R. (2001). Demonstrating the Hidden Features That Make an Application Work, in Your Wish is My Command, H. Lieberman (ed.), Morgan Kaufmann, San Francisco, CA, USA.

Pane, J.F., Ratanamahatana, C.A. and Myers, B.A. (2001). Studying the language and structure in non-programmers' solutions to programming problems. *International Journal of Human-Computer Studies*, **54**(2), 237–264. http://web.cs.cmu.edu/~pane/IJHCS.html.

Pane, J.F. and Myers B.A. (2004). More Natural Programming Languages and Environments, in End-User Development, Kluwer, Dordrecht, Netherlands.

Rich, C., Sidner, C.L. and Lesh, N.B. (2001). COLLAGEN: Applying collaborative discourse theory to human–computer interaction. *Artificial Intelligence*, **22**(4), Winter, 15–25.

Rich, C.H. and Waters, R.C. (1990). *The Programmer's Apprentice*. Reading, MA, USA: Addison-Wesley.

Ruthruff, J.R., Prabhakararao, S., Reichwein, J., Cook, C., Creswick, E. and Burnett, M. (in appear). Interactive Visual Fault Localization Support for End-User Programmers, *Journal of Visual Languages and Computing*.

Stocky, T., Faaborg, A., Espinosa, J., Lieberman, H. A Commonsense Approch to Predictive Text Entry, ACM Conference on Computer-Human Interaction (CHI-04), Vienna, Austria, April 2004.

Tam, R.C., Maulsby, D. and Puerta, A.R. U-TEL: A Tool for Eliciting User Task Models from Domain Experts. IUI98: International Conference on Intelligent User Interfaces, San Francisco, January 1998, pp. 77–80.

Wolber, D. and Myers, B. (2001). Stimulus-Response PBD: Demontrating "When" as Well as "What", In: H. Lieberman (ed.), *Your Wish is My Command*, Morgan Kaufmann, San Francisco, CA, USA.

Yates, A., Etzioni O. and Weld, D. (2003). A Reliable Natural Language Interface to Household Appliances, Conference on Intelligent User Interfaces, Miami, Florida. *Association for Computing Machinery*, New York, NY, USA.

Chapter 21

Future Perspectives in End-User Development

MARKUS KLANN[1], FABIO PATERNÒ[2] and VOLKER WULF[3]
[1] *Fraunhofer FIT, Schloß Birlinghoven, 53754 Sankt Augustin, Germany, markus.klann@fit.fraunhofer.de*
[2] *ISTI—CNR, Via G. Moruzzi 1, 56124 Pisa, Italy, fabio.paterno@isti.cnr.it*
[3] *University of Siegen, Hölderlinstr. 3, 57068 Siegen and Fraunhofer FIT, Schloß Birlinghoven, 53754 Sankt Augustin, Germany, volker.wulf@uni-siegen.de*

Abstract. The research field of end-user development has evolved, during recent years, to a certain degree of internal structure, problem awareness and consistency. Both academia and industry have begun to consider it an important field for research and development. In order to let EUD research contribute to the Information Societies, research and development must continue in a consolidated and well-balanced way. This chapter provides an overview of major challenges, motivates why these challenges should be addressed with considerable effort to bring about an Information Society with empowered end-users, and finally discusses how these challenges should be translated into a concrete research and development agenda for the short- and mid-term future.

Key words. tailorability, end user programming, flexibility, usability

1. Introduction

This concluding chapter presents the most important aspects for future EUD research and development, and tries to identify the principle lines along which EUD should or will most likely unfold. Being a relatively young field, EUD is yet rather diversified in terms of terminology, approaches and subject areas considered. Recently, a number of activities started within academia and industry to gain a better understanding of this field, consolidate the terminology and identify the most urging research questions.

In the center of EUD are the users who change IT-systems to better meet their requirements. As such, EUD defines a specific perspective on the practical application level of IT-systems, rather than a specific set of technological or methodological questions concerning such systems. EUD has its roots in various disciplines and fields of research, including HCI, cognitive science, requirements engineering, software engineering, artificial intelligence, CSCW, user communities, information systems, and the psychology of programming. EUD can be considered a focus in the application domain, bringing together the various more specific or technical research done in these fields into one approach of high practical relevance. Increased networking between key players in research and industry is thus a prerequisite for developing interdisciplinary solutions and marketable products.

The environments IT-systems are operating in are increasingly characterized by change and diversity. As an example, networked mobile devices and computerized

Henry Lieberman et al. (eds.), End User Development, 475–486.
© 2006 *Springer.*

artifacts will enable computing anywhere and anytime in rapidly changing and diverse contexts of use. Also, IT-systems are used by heterogeneous groups of people, having diversified requirements that depend on the users' level of expertise, current task and other factors. Systems should adapt to these changing contexts and requirements. It is the goal of EUD to empower users to carry out and control these adaptations themselves.

Flexibility at this level, necessitating highly adaptable systems as well as users willing and capable of these adaptations, would allow for what may be EUDs central goal: a co-evolution of users and IT-systems through mutual adaptation to share a common context.

In the following we will look at a number of aspects that are important for EUDs future development. In particular we will discuss the needs of users and the software industry, areas of application, important technical requirements, appropriate methods, and design criteria. Finally, we will present a roadmap for EUDs development until 2020, pointing at some of the probable milestones and discussing how the unfolding Information Society relates to this process.

2. How to Carry on With EUD

A major goal of research on EUD is to provide techniques to make IT-systems cope with changes. Quite generally, this means making them easier to develop, including setting up the initial design before use, as well as modifying them during use. In order to adapt IT-systems to their needs, individuals have to invest time and attention that they would normally focus on the task at hand, and being responsible for their operations they run the risk of committing errors. Accordingly, research on EUD has to provide the means for end-users to understand the consequences of their EUD operations, carry them out as safely as possible, and exercise an appropriate level of control. Also, end-users must be motivated to pay the (cognitive) cost of performing EUD operations. To this end, EUD research has to find ways of keeping these costs at a minimum, to make operations intuitive, to provide assistance and to make the benefits transparent and assessable. Possibly, incentive systems could be used to encourage people in carrying out EUD activities. Another issue to be resolved is that EUD beyond a certain level of complexity will require people to acquire voluntarily additional skills beforehand. Finally, doing EUD in collaboration with other people will involve new communication and work processes, as well as privacy issues, for which research will have to provide solutions.

What seems to be clear is that good environments for end-user development (EUD) will differ from tools conventionally used in software engineering because of the different needs of end-users and organizations running EUD-systems. Within organizations, for example, there is particular need for support of collaborative EUD activities. Nonetheless, it is of course a promising approach to investigate what methods and tools from professional software engineering can be adapted to the needs of end-user developers.

Before starting with specific research topics, let's take a look at three more general requirements EUD research should comply to.

1. Research should be driven by sound theoretical assumptions about user needs. These assumptions can be identified and refined by a variety of methods: situated (ethnographical) analysis, prototype-led development of future scenarios, task analysis, cognitive modelling, and both successful and failing case studies.
2. There is a strong consensus for the need of a sound empirical base. These may be conducted to determine people's EUD behavior (e.g. their motivation), to investigate the long-term changes of IT-systems and the contexts of use, to validate methodology, tools and representational formats, and to study the impact of EUD on conventional software engineering processes.
3. EUD research must find good solutions for a number of trade-offs created by empowering end-users to carry out substantial adaptations of IT-systems at a complexity-level no higher than needed for the task at hand. These trade-offs exist between expressiveness, freedom, and being general-purpose on the one hand and usability, learnability, control, and being domain-specific on the other.

In the following, we shall present a number of areas that are important for current and future EUD research.

2.1. APPLICATION DOMAINS FOR EUD

A survey questionnaire filled out by several parties from both academia and industry indicated that office, home, and research are considered the most promising application domains for EUD (Costabile and Piccinno, 2003). Other application domains, not listed in the questionnaire, were also pointed out: education (indicated by most people), decision analysis, and the medical domain. We will take a brief look at some of these application domains.

In their homes people are likely to interact with more and more electronic devices that will become interconnected and much more flexible in the near future. This will create a mass-market where people will want to adapt systems to their specific context and requirements and where they will value personalized, adaptive, and anticipatory system behavior. Such contextually embedded or "social devices" are obviously a hot spot for EUD research. Particularly interesting is the question of how to deal with adapting shared resources through collaborative EUD techniques such as negotiation and conflict resolution.

Another interesting application domain is industrial design in manufacturing enterprises, usually supported by CAD systems, with evident potential for improving financial and quality aspects of their development process. Designers as end-users, who have deep knowledge of their specific environment and who are not professional developers, must be supplied with visual development tools to adapt their design systems to their needs.

In the scientific domain there is a lot of interest in EUD. For example in biology, experience acquired at the Pasteur Institute in Paris during several years indicates that in the field of biology applications there are many local developments in order to deal with daily tasks, such as managing data, analyzing results, or testing scientific ideas (cf. Letondal, in this volume). Moreover, it is worth mentioning that many biologists have no or very limited programming skills, and yet feel the need of modifying the application they use to better fit their needs.

Enterprise Resource Planning (ERP) is an important sector in the software industry. Again, leading companies in the market have recently realized the importance of end-user concepts that allow various types of users of large ERP systems to modify the software in order to obtain systems more suitable for their actual needs (cf. Beringer, 2004). Over the past years, we have seen a significant change in the expectation of business applications. Traditional ERP applications gravitated very much around one single functional area and the dominant user scenarios were data entry, reporting, and ERP workflow. This simplified user model is not sufficient for modern business solutions like Customer Relationship Management, Human Capital Management, Knowledge Management, and Supplier Relationship Management. In these systems, the user is an active knowledge worker who needs communication tools, analytics, content management, and ad-hoc collaborative workflow and the capability of tailoring the system to his own needs. At the same time, the total cost of ownership (TCO) of ERP software becomes the main competitive argument. TCO can only be reduced by dramatically simplifying the customization process and by enabling business experts and end-users to modify the software themselves without the need of hiring IT consultants or IT-administrators (cf. Beringer, 2004; Wulf and Jarke, 2004). Already today, Enterprise Portals offer the personalization or creation of custom-made web pages and reports. Last but not least, companies such as SAP see a shift into a service-based architecture of business applications that may result in a new application development paradigm in which traditional coding is replaced by orchestration of existing enterprise services. Service composition including generation of user-interfaces may become an activity of business experts using simplified development environments with pre-packaged semantics. Considering these changes in the user model of ERP software, such companies see an increasing relevance of EUD-functionality in their products.

Another application domain is the one related to systems supporting data intensive businesses like telecommunication, e-government or banking. Computer applications become integrated in infrastructures connecting different work practices within and across organizational borders. The flexibility of such infrastructures is of strategic importance when developing new services. Often the need to redevelop part of the computer support to accommodate business or organizational development prohibits the entire development. Thus, tailorable systems and domain specific EUD provide a competitive advantage.

2.2. ARCHITECTURES AND GENERAL EUD FUNCTIONALITY

The recurrent theme of EUD is that end-users should be empowered to make substantial adaptations to IT-systems easily. The answer to the apparent contradiction is that there should be means of adaptation that are comparable in complexity to the problem at hand. This means that end-users will generally not program in a conventional programming language but will use higher-level means of adaptation that can do the job but are otherwise as simple as possible. The thing to observe here is that ultimately the modified system must be executed regardless of the means by which adaptations were carried out. Hence, allowing for adaptations from an ideally gentle slope of adaptation complexity to consistently and safely change a system's run-time behavior requires an appropriately specialized system architecture. For EUD to become a widespread success such architectures must become generally available in the form of frameworks to substantially facilitate the development of EUD-enabled systems.

There are a number of additional requirements that EUD architectures must provide for others than the adaptations as such. One is that EUD-systems must remain maintainable and interoperable in the face of run-time changes. Another is that EUD-systems should allow for reflexivity and inspection to make users understand the current system status and enable them to assess the consequences of their adaptation activities. Finally, knowledge on the relation between adaptation operations and system properties should be used as much as possible to analyze adaptation operations and restrict those that are insecure or otherwise undesirable.

One promising approach is to add a model-layer to the architecture of IT-systems allowing for relatively easy modifications of the underlying system. A similar approach is not to build-in the system behavior into the actual architecture and implementation, but to separate it into a sort of meta-description, which the system interprets during run-time.

Component-based EUD systems are another promising approach, allowing for a gentle slope of complexity by way of successive decomposition of components in case the overall component structure has been properly designed (cf. Won et al., in this volume). One challenge here is to find "patterns of decomposition" that facilitate finding appropriate component structures when designing new applications (cf. Stevens et al., in this volume). Another challenge is to combine general component interfaces, which may not be very intuitive to end-users, with domain-specific components, which users know how to handle within their domain of expertise.

The architectural challenge for EUD-enabled systems becomes particularly apparent in the vision of ubiquitous computing. Here, an array of distributed and interconnected devices is supposed to create and provide in an ad-hoc way a consistent, personalized, and context-sensitive service to its users. The context of use can be considered as the combination of the user (with his background, interests, tasks, . . .), the surrounding environment, and the devices at hand. While adaptivity and self-configuration can certainly carry a long way, user-driven adaptability remains crucial so that users can fine-tune the system to their work practices, business goals, etc. These adaptation activities will also enhance the users' competence and support their understanding of the system. An example in this direction is the TERESA environment (Mori et al., 2003) that provides support for the design and development of nomadic applications, which can be accessed through different types of interaction platforms.

2.3. USER INTERFACES

As EUD wants to empower end-users to perform substantial modifications to IT-systems, while at the same time not hampering them in their every-day work, extending user-interfaces with EUD-functionality is as important as it is difficult. Users must be able to understand and assess the existing systems and to specify and test their own EUD operations. In order to enable end-users to go from the running system to a change-able representation and back again, EUD-environments must support both reverse and forward engineering processes. Also, representational formats must be devised that are especially suitable for end-users, keeping them from making errors typical of conventional programming languages. Research is necessary on creating and evaluating domain-specific and graphical (2D and 3D) formats. Interfaces should proactively assist the user to explore and understand the systems and to create and annotate new EUD artifacts. To this end, various interesting approaches exist, like "interactive microworlds," zoomable multi-scale interfaces, tangible user-interfaces (TUIs), augmented reality (AR), etc. Another requirement is that EUD functionality has to be presented as unobtrusively as possible and only when needed, so as to deviate as little of the users' attention as possible from their primary task.

Generally speaking, interfaces and representational formats play an important role in mediating communication processes between different actors, like software professionals and end-users during initial system design as well as between groups of end-users during cooperative EUD activities.

2.4. COOPERATIVE ACTIVITIES AND ORGANIZATIONAL SETTINGS

Cooperation is an essential part of EUD. Future research will have to investigate effective means for communities of end-users to communicate about their adaptation problems, negotiate solutions, and share both their EUD expertise and reusable EUD artifacts. Cooperation on EUD activities is largely a social phenomenon and research will have to understand how an appropriate EUD culture can be fostered by incentive mechanisms, trust building, and community awareness.

As with any cooperation the organizational context must be taken into account when developing and deploying EUD systems. They must be properly embedded into their organizational environment to be interoperable with existing IT-systems, and thus to fully exploit the benefit of widespread EUD activities within the organization and to motivate end-users to actually carry out such activities. Conversely, EUD will have an impact on organizational structure and processes, allowing faster and more precise adaptations of IT-systems to support, for example, the setting up of project-specific team structures and collaborative processes. Research is needed to determine how organizations must change to exploit the full potential of EUD for becoming more flexible and powerful.

One of the difficulties associated with EUD-software used within organizations is that administration and support of the software has to deal with a system that is continuously changing through its users' adaptations. For such changing EUD-systems new ways of professional IT-services must be developed that go beyond the "If you change it, we won't support it!" mind-set while still being manageable for the service providers. One first step is to restrict the number of potentially hazardous end-user adaptations by defining and enforcing certain desired system properties, such as consistency.

2.5. THE ROLE OF ADAPTIVITY

As noted above, interfaces should provide users only with such an amount of EUD-functionality that is appropriate to their current context. In particular, for normal use requiring no adaptations, interfaces should rather hide EUD-functionality and may just offer a specific access point, for instance via the context menu. Moreover, systems may proactively assist their users by adapting themselves automatically if sufficient information is available, or at least generate suggestions for partial solutions for the users to choose from. In order to do this, research is needed on how systems can build up a knowledge base by monitoring their environment (e.g. user, task, place, time, etc.) and on how this context-awareness can be turned into adaptive system behavior (cf. Dey and Sohn, 2003). One promising approach is to investigate how an EUD-system might build-up a history of its own use and of the EUD operations it has been subjected to and to generate suggestions for future EUD operations in similar situations.

2.6. QUALITY ASSURANCE

Giving end-users the means to substantially alter IT-systems goes with the risk of having them produce erroneous adaptations. While it is possible to reduce this risk by properly designing the means for EUD operations, errors cannot be ruled out altogether. But it is possible to assist the end-users in detecting and correcting errors, by continuously monitoring and checking different system properties like coherence, consistency, and correctness, alerting the user in case an error has been detected and possibly making suggestions on how to correct it (cf. Burnett et al., in this volume; Won, 2003). To reduce the damage caused by errors, EUD-systems should provide some sort of "simulation environment" where users can test their modifications without risk (cf. Wulf, 2000). Moreover, systems should provide an undo-mechanism, so that users can easily and confidently reverse their operations. Finally, a more social mechanism of making the reliability of already existing EUD artifacts assessable to the users is to annotate the artifacts with information about their creator(s) and about their history of use (e.g. uses, malfunctions, and ratings) (cf. Costabile et al., 2002; Wulf, 1999). Research on these topics is needed to provide what might be called "quality assurance" for EUD.

2.7. INDUSTRIAL PERSPECTIVES

Understandably, industry players interested in EUD are looking for practical applicability and fast deployment, while not being enthusiastic about major changes to their development processes. As explained above, this can be done by integrating EUD with existing development practices. Nonetheless, finding the right processes and organizational structure for EUD development, and making appropriate changes will still be necessary. To this end, results from EUD research must be validated in real-world projects within the industry and the acquired experience must effectively be disseminated in adequate communities within industry and research. An example of a promising area for EUD applications of industrial interest is that of services for mobile devices. In the near future many people will access interactive software services through their mobile phones or PDAs. It will become important that such services will be modifiable and adaptable. Users should be enabled to carry out certain of these adaptations even by means of their mobile devices overcoming the limits of the limited input and output interfaces.

One specific field of industrial interest is to use results from EUD to foster the understanding of existing IT-systems and support the integration of new applications by generating comprehensible representations at an appropriate level of complexity.

Generally speaking, the industry will have to find out how the promising potential of EUD translates into concrete market opportunities for profitable products and services. This concerns the costs of providing EUD systems, and, for example, whether there is a market for selling software components that can be used and adapted in such EUD systems. Competition between various component vendors may cause interoperability issues, when, for example, one vendor will add proprietary extensions to his components to defend or extend his market share. This has not been uncommon in the software industry and as it constitutes a serious threat to a widespread success of EUD, industrial standardization efforts are crucial.

3. An EUD-Roadmap to an Information Society With Empowered End-Users

In order to outline a roadmap for research in EUD, as illustrated in Figure 21.1, we suggest here to focus on three intertwined lines of research: software architectures, interfaces, and support for collaboration.

Starting with the current state of EUD, we discuss what research activities could reasonably be carried out until about 2007, what status would then be reached, and how research could continue until 2012. As for the predictions for 2012 and 2020, they are obviously rather general in nature and do not yet include concrete recommendations for research activities. Rather, they deal with the impact of EUD on the Information Society, state possible applications and societal aspects and make guesses on what EUD goals might be achieved at the corresponding time.

With regard to software architectures a number of different approaches exist in research (e.g. agent-based, component-based, and rule-based). However, empirical knowledge on suitability in real-world settings is still insufficient. A major challenge is to refine existing approaches and to develop new architectures permitting both systems and users to evolve. The combination with conventional architectures and the adaptation

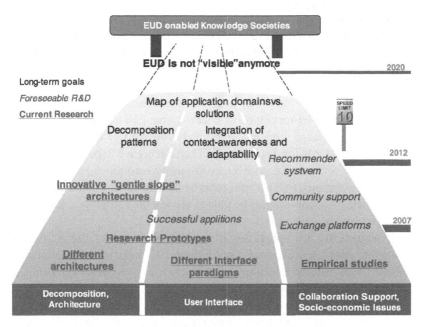

Figure 21.1. The future of end-user development.

of the respective development processes have to be investigated. Moreover, one has to look into the suitability of different EUD-architectures to support run-time changes with a gentle slope of complexity. Case studies need to show the suitability of these frameworks for different application domains.

With regard to interfaces, research has been carried out on various interface techniques, for example, Augmented Reality and Tangible User Interfaces. One of the main goals of current research in user interfaces is to obtain natural interaction, where users can interact with their applications in a way similar to how they communicate with other humans. This paradigm can be successfully applied to EUD. Natural development (Berti et al., 2004) implies that people should be able to work through familiar and immediately understandable representations that allow them to easily express relevant concepts, and thereby create or modify applications. On the other hand, since a software artifact needs to be precisely specified in order to be implemented, there will still be the need for environments supporting transformations from intuitive and familiar representations into precise—but more difficult to develop—-escriptions. Examples of informal input for more structured representations are sketches on board (Landay and Myers, 2001). For example, non-programmer users feel comfortable with sketch-based systems that allow them to concentrate on concepts by exploiting natural interactions, instead of being distracted by cumbersome low-level details required by rigid symbolisms. Such systems are generally able to recognize graphical elements and convert them into formats that can be edited and analyzed by other software tools.

New UI-techniques, for example, combining adaptability and adaptive context-sensitive system behavior (Klann et al., 2003), need to be developed. Moreover, interfaces need to be developed that make EUD-functionality available with a gentle slope of complexity.

Collaborative aspects have been taken up in research as a key element of EUD (e.g. gardening-metaphor). However, empirical knowledge on collaborative EUD is still insufficient and implementations of collaborative EUD-functionality are only in their beginnings. Therefore, concepts for collaborative EUD have to be developed. Conventions and standards for describing EUD artifacts have to be worked out to make them exchangeable, for example, with regard to quality, recommendations, and purpose. Based on such conventions, EUD-artifacts can be described and placed into repositories for sharing. Software agents should be able to recommend suitable artifacts available from such repositories.

Looking toward 2012, we believe that architectural frameworks, decomposition techniques, patterns, interfaces, and tools for collaboration support can exist in a consolidated and integrated manner. End-users will be supported by tools for exploring, testing, and assessing while carrying out EUD activities. Cases of best practices will have been documented to explain EUD as an activity that is embedded in social networks. Concepts to acquire EUD-skills will be integrated into educational curricula. EUD will become an important aspect of applications in most domains: education, scientific research (e.g. bioinformatics), business (CAD, ERP, GIS), and domestic domains.

Toward 2020, substantial adaptability has become a property of all newly developed software systems. Adaptable software-systems have penetrated into all domains, for example, business, leisure, home, culture. Most people have skills in EUD. EUD has become an important activity for most jobs and for the majority of people. A high level of adaptivity in all devices is a big part of what is called "Ambient Intelligence." EUD has gained central importance in the application of information technology and the use of EUD techniques has become a common practice for users of all ages and professional background. EUD has become an integral aspect of their cultural practices and appropriation of IT.

4. Conclusion

EUD can be seen as an important contribution to create a user-friendly Information Society, where people will be able to easily access information specific to their current context and to their cognitive and physiological abilities or disabilities. People will have access to adapt IT-systems to their individual requirements, and if all actors will be involved the design of IT-systems will find a higher common acceptance. Providing end-users with effective development environments is therefore one strategic goal for the European Information Society.

On the economic side, EUD has the potential to enhance productivity and to create a competitive advantage by empowering employees to quickly and continuously adapt IT-systems to their specific business requirements.

As Figure 21.1 shows, the road to achieving an EUD enabled Information Society is still long, even if prototypes, mainly research ones, have already appeared. Particularly challenging areas that will be addressed in the near future are novel interface techniques for EUD, integration of context-awareness and adaptability, effective sharing of EUD artifacts through repositories with recommendation support, and decomposition guidelines for flexible component-based systems. Quite generally there is further need for theoretical research on the foundations of EUD as well as applied research to gain experience in and develop methods for EUDs various application domains.

The ultimate goal is to provide end-users with non-intrusive, "invisible" support for their developments and thus empower them to use their domain specific know-how to shape the IT tools to better support them in their daily practices. As such, EUD will become an integrative part of our cultural practices and should be considered part of a comprehensive computer literacy.

Acknowledgments

Our understanding of the research field of EUD and the problems associated with its industrial uptake, as expressed in this chapter, was substantially deepened by the valuable discussions we had within the context of the EUD-Net project. At several events organized by EUD-Net a number of participants from outside the project made further important contributions to this discussion. We thank everybody from academia and industry who shared their approaches and experiences with us.

References

Arondi, S., Baroni, P. et al. (2002). Supporting co-evolution of users and systems by the recognition of Interaction Patterns. *AVI 2002*, Trento, Italy.

Beringer, J. (2004). Reducing expertise tension, in communications of the ACM. **47**(9), 39–40.

Berti, S., Paternò, F. and Santoro C. (2004). Natural development of ubiquitous interfaces. *Communications of the ACM* (September), 63–64, ACM Press.

Boehm, B.W., Abts, C. et al. (2000). *Software Cost Estimation with COCOMO II*. Upper Saddle River, NJ: Prentice Hall PTR.

Burnett, M., Rothermel, G. and Cook, C. (in this volume). An Integrated Software Engineering Approach for End-User Programmers.

Cockburn, A. (2002). Agile Software Development, Addison Wesley.

Costabile, M.F., Fogli, D. et al. (2002). Computer environments for improving end-user accessibility. *ERCIM Workshop "User Interfaces For All"*, Paris.

Costabile, M.F., Fogli, D. et al. (2003). Building environments for end-user development and tailoring. *IEEE Symposia on Human Centric Computing Languages and Environmnets*, Aukland.

Costabile, M.F. and Piccinno A. (2003). *Analysis of EUD Survey Questionnaire*, D4.2, EUD-Net.

Dey, A.K. and Sohn, T. (2003). Supporting end user programming of context-aware applications. *Workshop on End-User Development at CHI 2003*, Fort Lauderdale, Florida.

Henderson, A. and Henderson, K.M. (1991). There's No Place Like Home. *Continuing Design in Use. Design at Work*, Lawrence Erlbaum Assoc., 219–240.

Klann, M., Eisenhauer, M. et al. (2003). Shared initiative: Cross-fertilisation between system adaptivity and adaptability. *UAHCII 2003*, Crete.

Landay, J. and Myers, B. (2001). Sketching interfaces: Toward more human interface design. *IEEE Computer* **34**(3), 56–64.

Lehman, M. (1980). Programs, Life Cycles, and Laws of Software Evolution. *IEEE 68*.

Letondal, C. (2001). Programmation et interaction, Phd-thesis, Orsay, Université de Paris XI.

Letondal, C. (in this volume). Participatory Programming: Developping Programmable Bioinformatics Tools for End-Users in context.

Liebermann, H. (2001). *Your Wish is My Command: Programming by Example*. Morgan Kaufmann, San Francisco.

Majhew, D.J. (1992). *Principles and Guideline in Software User Interface Design*, Prentice Hall.

Mehandjiev, N. and Bottaci, L. (1995). End user development with visual programming and object orientation. *1st International Workshop on End User Development at CaiSE'95*, Juvaskyla, Finland.

Mehandjiev, N. and Bottaci, L. (1996). User-enhanceability for organizational information systems through visual programming. *Advanced Information Systems Engineering: 8th International Conference*, CAiSE'96, Springer-Verlag.

Mørch, A.I. and Mehandjiev, N.D. (2000). Tailoring as collaboration: The mediating role of multiple representations and application units. *Computer Supported Cooperative Work* **9**(1), 75–100.

Mori, G., Paternò, F. and Santoro, C. (2003). Tool support for designing nomadic applications. In: *Proceedings ACM IUI'03*, Miami, pp. 141–148, ACM Press.

Oppermann, R. and Simm, H. (1994). Adaptability: User-initiated individualization. *Adaptive User Support—Ergonomic Design of Manually and Automatically Adaptable Software*. R. Oppermann. Hillsdale, New Jersey, Lawrence Erlbaum Ass.

Orlikowski, W.J. and Hofman, J.D. (Pipek 1997). An improvisational model for change man-agement: The case of groupware technologies. *Sloan Management Review*, pp. 11–21.

Paternò, F. (1999). *Model-Based Design and Evaluation of Interactive Applications*, Springer Verlag.

Repenning, A., Ioannidou, A. et al. (2000). AgentSheets: End-user programmable simulations. *Journal of Artificial Societies and Social Simulation* **3**(3).

Stevens, G., Quaißer, G. and Klann M. (in this volume). Breaking it Up—An Industrial Case Study of Component-based Tailorable Software Design.

Sutcliffe, A., Lee, D. et al. (2003). Contributions, costs and prospects for end-user development. *HCI International 2003*, Crete, Greece, Lawrence Erlbaum Associates.

Won, M. (2003). Supporting end-user development of component-based software by checking semantic integrity. *ASERC Workshop on Software Testing*, Banff, Canada.

Won, M., Stiemerling, O. and Wulf, V. (in this volume). Component-based Approaches to Tailorable Systems.

Wulf, V. (1999). "Let's see your Search-Tool!"—Collaborative Use of Tailored Artifacts in Groupware. In: *Proceedings of GROUP '99*, ACM-Press, New York, 1999, pp. 50–60.

Wulf, V. (2000). Exploration environments: Supporting users to learn groupware functions. *Interacting with Computers* **13**(2), 265–299.

Wulf, V. and Jarke, M. (2004). The economics of end user development. *Communications of the ACM* **47**(9), 41–42.

Index